# Microsoft® Excel® 2010

## ILLUSTRATED

**Complete**

D0781416

# Microsoft® Excel® 2010

## ILLUSTRATED

**Complete**

Elizabeth Eisner Reding • Lynn Wermers

COURSE TECHNOLOGY
CENGAGE Learning

Australia • Brazil • Japan • Korea • Mexico • Singapore • Spain • United Kingdom • United States

**COURSE TECHNOLOGY**
**CENGAGE Learning™**

**Microsoft® Excel® 2010—Illustrated Complete**

**Elizabeth Eisner Reding, Lynn Wermers**

Vice President, Publisher: Nicole Jones Pinard

Executive Editor: Marjorie Hunt

Associate Acquisitions Editor: Brandi Shailer

Senior Product Manager: Christina Kling Garrett

Associate Product Manager: Michelle Camisa

Editorial Assistant: Kim Klasner

Director of Marketing: Cheryl Costantini

Senior Marketing Manager: Ryan DeGrote

Marketing Coordinator: Kristen Panciocco

Contributing Authors: Barbara Clemens, Carol Cram

Developmental Editors: Barbara Clemens, Jeanne Herring, Pamela Conrad

Content Project Manager: Danielle Chouhan

Copy Editor: Mark Goodin

Proofreader: Vicki Zimmer

Indexer: BIM Indexing and Proofreading Services

QA Manuscript Reviewers: John Frietas, Serge Palladino, Jeff Schwartz, Danielle Shaw, Marianne Snow, Susan Whalen

Print Buyer: Fola Orekoya

Cover Designer: GEX Publishing Services

Cover Artist: Mark Hunt

Composition: GEX Publishing Services

© 2011 Course Technology, Cengage Learning

ALL RIGHTS RESERVED. No part of this work covered by the copyright herein may be reproduced, transmitted, stored or used in any form or by any means graphic, electronic, or mechanical, including but not limited to photocopying, recording, scanning, digitizing, taping, Web distribution, information networks, or information storage and retrieval systems, except as permitted under Section 107 or 108 of the 1976 United States Copyright Act, without the prior written permission of the publisher.

For product information and technology assistance, contact us at
**Cengage Learning Customer & Sales Support, 1-800-354-9706**
For permission to use material from this text or product, submit all
requests online at **www.cengage.com/permissions**
Further permissions questions can be emailed to
**permissionrequest@cengage.com**

Trademarks:

Some of the product names and company names used in this book have been used for identification purposes only and may be trademarks or registered trademarks of their respective manufacturers and sellers.

Microsoft and the Office logo are either registered trademarks or trademarks of Microsoft Corporation in the United States and/or other countries. Course Technology, Cengage Learning is an independent entity from Microsoft Corporation, and not affiliated with Microsoft in any manner.

The Microsoft Office Specialist Exams, the Exam Objectives, logos, the Microsoft Office Specialist Program, the Microsoft Technology Associate Certification Paths and the VAC Program are the sole property of Microsoft Corporation.

Library of Congress Control Number: 2010933988

ISBN-13: 978-0-538-74713-4
ISBN-10: 0-538-74713-7

**Course Technology**
20 Channel Center Street
Boston, MA 02210
USA

Cengage Learning is a leading provider of customized learning solutions with office locations around the globe, including Singapore, the United Kingdom, Australia, Mexico, Brazil, and Japan. Locate your local office at: **international.cengage.com/region**

Cengage Learning products are represented in Canada by Nelson Education, Ltd.

To learn more about Course Technology, visit **www.cengage.com/coursetechnology**

To learn more about Cengage Learning, visit **www.cengage.com**

Purchase any of our products at your local college store or at our preferred online store **www.cengagebrain.com**

Printed in the United States of America
2 3 4 5 6 7 8 9 18 17 16 15 14 13 12 11

# Brief Contents

# Contents

## Office 2010

# Preface

Welcome to *Microsoft Excel 2010—Illustrated Complete*. If this is your first experience with the Illustrated series, you'll see that this book has a unique design: each skill is presented on two facing pages, with steps on the left and screens on the right. The layout makes it easy to learn a skill without having to read a lot of text and flip pages to see an illustration.

This book is an ideal learning tool for a wide range of learners—the "rookies" will find the clean design easy to follow and focused with only essential information presented, and the "hotshots" will appreciate being able to move quickly through the lessons to find the information they need without reading a lot of text. The design also makes this a great reference after the course is over! See the illustration on the right to learn more about the pedagogical and design elements of a typical lesson.

## What's New In This Edition

- **Fully Updated.** Highlights the new features of Microsoft Excel 2010 including creating and adding sparklines to a worksheet, using Paste Preview, the new Backstage view, screen clipping, inserting an equation into a worksheet, using slicer to filter a PivotTable and customizing the Ribbon. A new appendix covers cloud computing concepts and using Microsoft Office Web Apps. Examples and exercises are updated throughout.

- **Maps to SAM 2010.** This book is designed to work with SAM (Skills Assessment Manager) 2010. **SAM Assessment** contains performance-based, hands-on SAM exams for each unit of this book, and **SAM Training** provides hands-on training for skills covered in the book. Some exercises are available in **SAM Projects**, which is auto-grading software that provides both students and instructors with immediate, detailed feedback (SAM sold separately.) See page xii for more information on SAM.

Each two-page spread focuses on a single skill.

Introduction briefly explains why the lesson skill is important.

A case scenario motivates the the steps and puts learning in context.

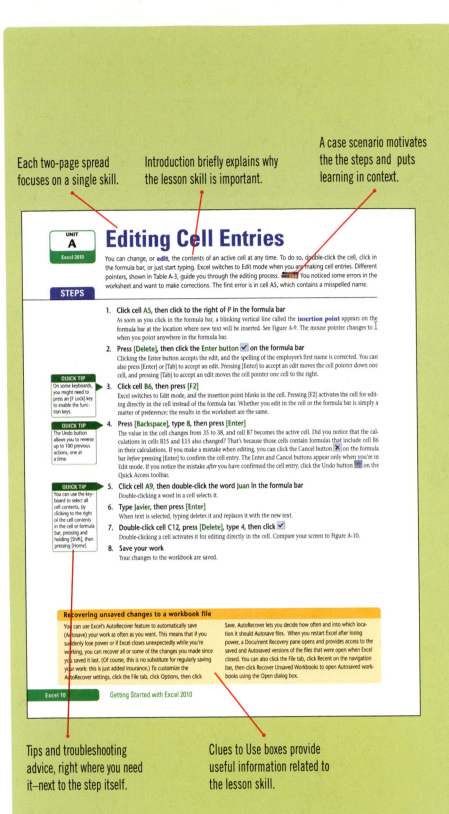

Tips and troubleshooting advice, right where you need it—next to the step itself.

Clues to Use boxes provide useful information related to the lesson skill.

Large screen shots keep students on track as they complete steps.

Brightly colored tabs indicate which section of the book you are in.

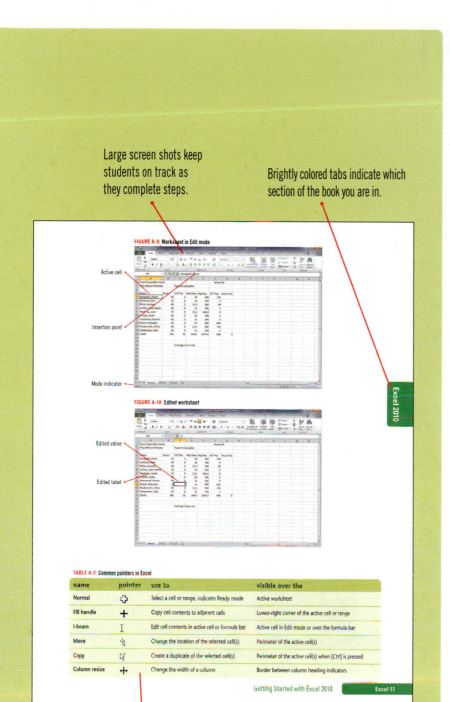

Tables provide helpful summaries of key terms, buttons, or keyboard shortcuts.

## Assignments

The lessons use Quest Specialty Travel, a fictional adventure travel company, as the case study. The assignments on the light yellow pages at the end of each unit increase in difficulty. Assignments include:

- **Concepts Review** consist of multiple choice, matching, and screen identification questions.

- **Skills Reviews** are hands-on, step-by-step exercises that review the skills covered in each lesson in the unit.

- **Independent Challenges** are case projects requiring critical thinking and application of the unit skills. The Independent Challenges increase in difficulty, with the first one in each unit being the easiest. Independent Challenges 2 and 3 become increasingly open-ended, requiring more independent problem solving.

- **SAM Projects** is live-in-the-application autograding software that provides immediate and detailed feedback reports to students and instructors. Some exercises in this book are available in SAM Projects. (Purchase of a SAM Projects pincode is required.)

- **Real Life Independent Challenges** are practical exercises in which students create documents to help them with their every day lives.

- **Advanced Challenge Exercises** set within the Independent Challenges provide optional steps for more advanced students.

- **Visual Workshops** are practical, self-graded capstone projects that require independent problem solving.

# About SAM

SAM is the premier proficiency-based assessment and training environment for Microsoft Office. Web-based software along with an inviting user interface provide maximum teaching and learning flexibility. SAM builds students' skills and confidence with a variety of real-life simulations, and SAM Projects' assignments prepare students for today's workplace.

The SAM system includes Assessment, Training, and Projects, featuring page references and remediation for this book as well as Course Technology's Microsoft Office textbooks. With SAM, instructors can enjoy the flexibility of creating assignments based on content from their favorite Microsoft Office books or based on specific course objectives. Instructors appreciate the scheduling and reporting options that have made SAM the market-leading online testing and training software for over a decade. Over 2,000 performance-based questions and matching Training simulations, as well as tens of thousands of objective-based questions from many Course Technology texts, provide instructors with a variety of choices across multiple applications from the introductory level through the comprehensive level. The inclusion of hands-on Projects guarantee that student knowledge will skyrocket from the practice of solving real-world situations using Microsoft Office software.

## SAM Assessment

- Content for these hands-on, performance-based tasks includes Word, Excel, Access, PowerPoint, Internet Explorer, Outlook, and Windows. Includes tens of thousands of objective-based questions from many Course Technology texts.

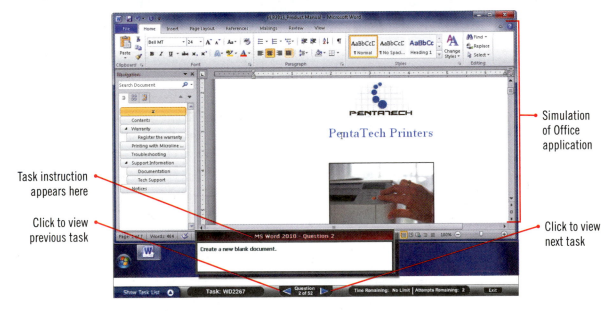

Task instruction appears here

Click to view previous task

Simulation of Office application

Click to view next task

## SAM Training

- Observe mode allows the student to watch and listen to a task as it is being completed.
- Practice mode allows the student to follow guided arrows and hear audio prompts to help visual learners know how to complete a task.
- Apply mode allows the student to prove what they've learned by completing a task using helpful instructions.

## SAM Projects

- Live-in-the-application assignments in Word, Excel, Access and PowerPoint that help students be sure they know how to effectively communicate, solve a problem or make a decision.
- Students receive detailed feedback on their project within minutes.
- Additionally, teaches proper file management techniques.
- Ensures that academic integrity is not compromised, with unique anti-cheating detection encrypted into the data files.

# Instructor Resources

The Instructor Resources CD is Course Technology's way of putting the resources and information needed to teach and learn effectively into your hands. With an integrated array of teaching and learning tools that offer you and your students a broad range of technology-based instructional options, we believe this CD represents the highest quality and most cutting edge resources available to instructors today. The resources available with this book are:

- **Instructor's Manual**—Available as an electronic file, the Instructor's Manual includes detailed lecture topics with teaching tips for each unit.

- **Sample Syllabus**—Prepare and customize your course easily using this sample course outline.

- **PowerPoint Presentations**—Each unit has a corresponding PowerPoint presentation that you can use in lecture, distribute to your students, or customize to suit your course.

- **Figure Files**—The figures in the text are provided on the Instructor Resources CD to help you illustrate key topics or concepts. You can create traditional overhead transparencies by printing the figure files. Or you can create electronic slide shows by using the figures in a presentation program such as PowerPoint.

- **Solutions to Exercises**—Solutions to Exercises contains every file students are asked to create or modify in the lessons and end-of-unit material. Also provided in this section, there is a document outlining the solutions for the end-of-unit Concepts Review, Skills Review, and Independent Challenges. An Annotated Solution File and Grading Rubric accompany each file and can be used together for quick and easy grading.

- **Data Files for Students**—To complete most of the units in this book, your students will need Data Files. You can post the Data Files on a file server for students to copy. The Data Files are available on the Instructor Resources CD-ROM, the Review Pack, and can also be downloaded from cengagebrain.com. For more information on how to download the Data Files, see the inside back cover.

Instruct students to use the Data Files List included on the Review Pack and the Instructor Resources CD. This list gives instructions on copying and organizing files.

- **ExamView**—ExamView is a powerful testing software package that allows you to create and administer printed, computer (LAN-based), and Internet exams. ExamView includes hundreds of questions that correspond to the topics covered in this text, enabling students to generate detailed study guides that include page references for further review. The computer-based and Internet testing components allow students to take exams at their computers, and also saves you time by grading each exam automatically.

## Content for Online Learning.

Course Technology has partnered with the leading distance learning solution providers and class-management platforms today. To access this material, visit www.cengage.com/webtutor and search for your title. Instructor resources include the following: additional case projects, sample syllabi, PowerPoint presentations, and more. For additional information, please contact your sales representative. For students to access this material, they must have purchased a WebTutor PIN-code specific to this title and your campus platform. The resources for students might include (based on instructor preferences): topic reviews, review questions, practice tests, and more.

# Acknowledgements

## Instructor Advisory Board

We thank our Instructor Advisory Board who gave us their opinions and guided our decisions as we updated our texts for Microsoft Office 2010. They are as follows:

**Terri Helfand**, Chaffey Community College

**Barbara Comfort**, J. Sargeant Reynolds Community College

**Brenda Nielsen**, Mesa Community College

**Sharon Cotman**, Thomas Nelson Community College

**Marian Meyer**, Central New Mexico Community College

**Audrey Styer**, Morton College

**Richard Alexander**, Heald College

**Xiaodong Qiao**, Heald College

## Student Advisory Board

We also thank our Student Advisory Board members, who shared their experiences using the book and offered suggestions to make it better: **Latasha Jefferson**, Thomas Nelson Community College, **Gary Williams**, Thomas Nelson Community College, **Stephanie Miller**, J. Sargeant Reynolds Community College, **Sarah Styer**, Morton Community College, **Missy Marino**, Chaffey College

## Author Acknowledgements

**Elizabeth Eisner Reding**  Creating a book of this magnitude is a team effort. I would like to thank my husband, Michael, as well as Christina Kling Garrett, the project manager, and my development editor, Jeanne Herring, for her suggestions and corrections. I would also like to thank the production and editorial staff for all their hard work that made this project a reality.

**Lynn Wermers**  Thanks to Barbara Clemens for her insightful contributions, invaluable feedback, great humor, and patience. Thanks also to Christina Kling Garrett for her encouragement and support in guiding and managing this project.

# Read This Before You Begin

## Frequently Asked Questions

### What are Data Files?

A Data File is a partially completed Excel workbook or another type of file that you use to complete the steps in the units and exercises to create the final document that you submit to your instructor. Each unit opener page lists the Data Files that you need for that unit.

### Where are the Data Files?

Your instructor will provide the Data Files to you or direct you to a location on a network drive from which you can download them. For information on how to download the Data Files from cengagebrain.com, see the inside back cover.

### What software was used to write and test this book?

This book was written and tested using a typical installation of Microsoft Office 2010 Professional Plus on a computer with a typical installation of Microsoft Windows 7 Ultimate.

The browser used for any Web-dependent steps is Internet Explorer 8.

### Do I need to be connected to the Internet to complete the steps and exercises in this book?

Some of the exercises in this book require that your computer be connected to the Internet. If you are not connected to the Internet, see your instructor for information on how to complete the exercises.

### What do I do if my screen is different from the figures shown in this book?

This book was written and tested on computers with monitors set at a resolution of 1024 × 768. If your screen shows more or less information than the figures in the book, your monitor is probably set at a higher or lower resolution. If you don't see something on your screen, you might have to scroll down or up to see the object identified in the figures.

The Ribbon—the blue area at the top of the screen—in Microsoft Office 2010 adapts to different resolutions. If your monitor is set at a lower resolution than 1024 × 768, you might not see all of the buttons shown in the figures. The groups of buttons will always appear, but the entire group might be condensed into a single button that you need to click to access the buttons described in the instructions.

**COURSECASTS** **Learning on the Go. Always Available...Always Relevant.**

Our fast-paced world is driven by technology. You know because you are an active participant—always on the go, always keeping up with technological trends, and always learning new ways to embrace technology to power your life. Let CourseCasts, hosted by Ken Baldauf of Florida State University, be your guide into weekly updates in this ever-changing space. These timely, relevant podcasts are produced weekly and are available for download at http://coursecasts.course.com or directly from iTunes (search by CourseCasts). CourseCasts are a perfect solution to getting students (and even instructors) to learn on the go!

## What is the Microsoft® Office Specialist Program?

The Microsoft Office Specialist Program enables candidates to show that they have something exceptional to offer—proven expertise in certain Microsoft programs. Recognized by businesses and schools around the world, over 4 million certifications have been obtained in over 100 different countries. The Microsoft Office Specialist Program is the only Microsoft-approved certification program of its kind.

## What is the Microsoft Office Specialist Certification?

The Microsoft Office Specialist certification validates through the use of exams that you have obtained specific skill sets within the applicable Microsoft Office programs and other Microsoft programs included in the Microsoft Office Specialist Program. The candidate can choose which exam(s) they want to take according to which skills they want to validate.

The available Microsoft Office Specialist Program exams include*:

- Using Windows Vista®
- Using Microsoft® Office Word 2007
- Using Microsoft® Office Word 2007 – Expert
- Using Microsoft® Office Excel® 2007
- Using Microsoft® Office Excel® 2007 – Expert
- Using Microsoft® Office PowerPoint® 2007
- Using Microsoft® Office Access® 2007
- Using Microsoft® Office Outlook® 2007
- Using Microsoft SharePoint® 2007

The Microsoft Office Specialist Program 2010 exams will include*:

- Microsoft Word 2010
- Microsoft Word 2010 Expert
- Microsoft Excel® 2010
- Microsoft Excel® 2010 Expert
- Microsoft PowerPoint® 2010
- Microsoft Access® 2010
- Microsoft Outlook® 2010
- Microsoft SharePoint® 2010

## What does the Microsoft Office Specialist Approved Courseware logo represent?

The logo indicates that this courseware has been approved by Microsoft to cover the course objectives that will be included in the relevant exam. It also means that after utilizing this courseware, you may be better prepared to pass the exams required to become a certified Microsoft Office Specialist.

## For more information:

To learn more about Microsoft Office Specialist exams, visit www.microsoft.com/learning/msbc

To learn about other Microsoft approved courseware from Course Technology, visit www.cengage.com/coursetechnology

* The availability of Microsoft Office Specialist certification exams varies by Microsoft program, program version and language. Visit www.microsoft.com/learning for exam availability.

Microsoft, Access, Excel, the Office Logo, Outlook, PowerPoint, SharePoint, and Windows Vista are either registered trademarks or trademarks of Microsoft Corporation in the United States and/or other countries. The Microsoft Office Specialist logo and the Microsoft Office Specialist Approved Courseware logo are used under license from Microsoft Corporation.

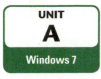

# Getting Started with Windows 7

**Files You Will Need:**

No files needed.

The Windows 7 operating system lets you use your computer. Windows 7 shares many features with other Windows programs, so once you learn how to work with Windows 7, you will find it easier to use the programs that run on your computer. In this unit, you learn to start Windows 7 and work with windows and other screen objects. You work with icons that represent programs and files, and you move and resize windows. As you use your computer, you will often have more than one window on your screen, so it's important that you learn how to manage them. As you complete this unit, you create a simple drawing in a program called Paint to help you learn how to use buttons, menus, and dialog boxes. After finding assistance in the Windows 7 Help and Support system, you end your Windows 7 session. As a new Oceania tour manager for Quest Specialty Travel (QST), you need to develop basic Windows skills to keep track of tour bookings.

**OBJECTIVES**

Start Windows 7

Learn the Windows 7 desktop

Point and click

Start a Windows 7 program

Work with windows

Work with multiple windows

Use command buttons, menus, and dialog boxes

Get help

Exit Windows 7

# Starting Windows 7

Windows 7 is an **operating system**, which is a program that lets you run your computer. A **program** is a set of instructions written for a computer. When you turn on your computer, the Windows 7 operating system starts automatically. If your computer did not have an operating system, you wouldn't see anything on the screen when you turn it on. For each user, the operating system can reserve a special area called a **user account** where each user can keep his or her own files. If your computer is set up for more than one user, you might need to **log in**, or select your user account name when the computer starts. If you are the only user on your computer, you won't have to select an account. You might also need to enter a **password**, a special sequence of numbers and letters each user can create. A password allows you to enter and use the files in your user account area. Users cannot see each others' account areas without their passwords, so passwords help keep your computer information secure. After you log in, you see a welcome message, and then the Windows 7 desktop. You will learn about the desktop in the next lesson.  Your supervisor, Evelyn Swazey, asks you to start learning about the Windows 7 operating system.

## STEPS

1. **Push your computer's power button, which might look like ⊙ or [⏻], then if the monitor is not turned on, press its power button to turn it on**

   On a desktop computer, the power button is probably on the front panel. On a laptop computer it's most likely at the top of the keys on your keyboard. After a few moments, a Starting Windows message appears. Then you might see a screen that lets you choose a user account, as shown in Figure A-1.

   > **TROUBLE**
   > If you do not see a screen that lets you choose a user account, go to Step 3.

2. **Click a user name if necessary**

   The name you click represents your user account that lets you use the computer. The user account may have your name assigned to it, or it might have a general name, like Student, or Lab User. A password screen may appear. If necessary, ask your instructor or technical support person which user account and password you should use.

   > **TROUBLE**
   > If you clicked the wrong user in Step 2, change to the correct user by clicking the Switch user button on the password screen.

3. **Type your password if necessary, using uppercase and lowercase letters as necessary, as shown in Figure A-2**

   Passwords are **case sensitive**, which means that if you type any letter using capital letters when lowercase letters are needed, Windows will not allow you to access your account. For example, if your password is "book", typing "Book" or "BOOK" will not let you enter your account. As you type your password, its characters appear as a series of dots on the screen. This makes it more difficult for anyone watching you to see your password, giving you additional security.

   > **TROUBLE**
   > If you type your password incorrectly, you see "The user name or password is incorrect." Click OK to try again. To help you remember, Windows shows the Password Hint that you entered when you created your password.

4. **Click the Go button ⊙**

   You see a welcome message, and then the Windows 7 desktop, shown in Figure A-3.

**FIGURE A-1:** Selecting a user name

Name and picture represent each user's account on this computer

You might have a different version of Windows 7

Ease of access button shows accessibility options

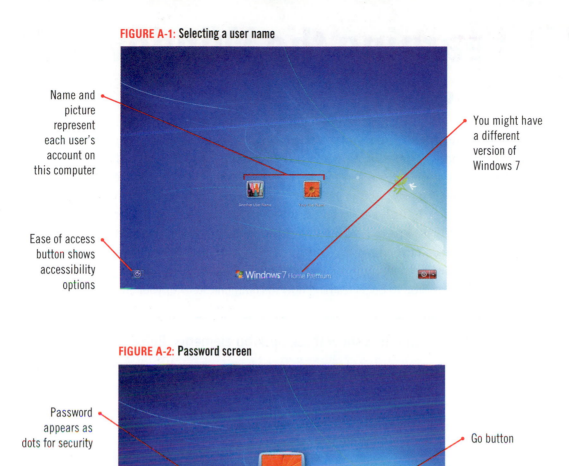

**FIGURE A-2:** Password screen

Password appears as dots for security

Go button

**FIGURE A-3:** Windows 7 desktop

# Learning the Windows 7 Desktop

After Windows 7 starts up, you see the Windows 7 desktop. The **desktop** consists of a shaded or picture background with small graphics called icons. **Icons** are small images that represent items such as the Recycle Bin on your computer. You can rearrange, add, and delete desktop icons. Like an actual desktop, the Windows 7 desktop acts as your work area. You can use the desktop to manage the files and folders on your computer. A **file** is a collection of stored information, such as a letter, video, or program. A **folder** is a container that helps you organize your files, just like a cardboard folder on your desk. If you're using a new installation of Windows, the desktop might show only a Recycle Bin icon in the upper-left corner and the **taskbar**, the horizontal bar at the bottom of your screen.  Evelyn asks you to explore the Windows 7 desktop to begin learning how to communicate with your computer.

**DETAILS**

### Windows 7 computers show these desktop elements. Refer to Figure A-4.

- **Start button**

  The **Start button** is your launching point when you want to communicate with your computer. You can use the Start button to start programs, to open windows that show you the contents of your computer, and to end your Windows session and turn off your computer.

**QUICK TIP**

If your taskbar is a different color than the one in Figure A-4, your computer might have different settings. This won't affect your work in this chapter.

- **Taskbar**

  The **taskbar** is the horizontal bar at the bottom of the desktop. The taskbar contains the Start button as well as other buttons representing programs, folders, and files. You can use these buttons to immediately open programs or view files and programs that are on your computer.

- **Notification area**

  The **notification area** at the right side of the taskbar contains icons that represent informational messages and programs you might find useful. It also contains information about the current date and time. Some programs automatically place icons here so they are easily available to you. The notification area also displays pop-up messages when something on your computer needs your attention.

- **Recycle Bin**

  Like the wastepaper basket in your office, the **Recycle Bin** is where you place the files and folders that you don't need anymore and want to delete. All objects you place in the Recycle Bin stay there until you empty it. If you put an object there by mistake, you can easily retrieve it, as long as you haven't emptied the bin.

- **Desktop background**

  The **desktop background** is the shaded area behind your desktop objects. You can change the desktop background to show different colors or even pictures.

### You might see the following on your desktop:

- **Icons and shortcuts**

  On the desktop background, you can place icons called **shortcuts**, which you can double-click to access programs, files, folders, and devices that you use frequently. That way, they are immediately available to you.

- **Gadgets**

  **Gadgets** are optional programs that present helpful or entertaining information on your desktop. They include items such as clocks, current news headlines, calendars, picture albums, and weather reports. Some gadgets come with Windows 7 and you can easily place them on your desktop. You can download additional gadgets from the Internet. Figure A-5 shows a desktop that has a desktop background picture and shortcuts to programs, folders, and devices, as well as four gadgets.

**FIGURE A-4:** Windows 7 desktop after a new Windows installation

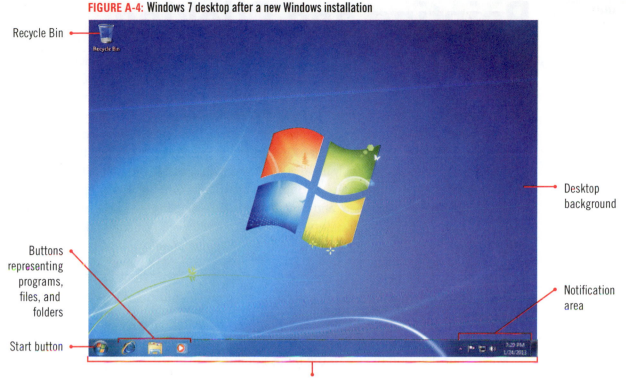

Recycle Bin

Buttons representing programs, files, and folders

Start button

Desktop background

Notification area

Taskbar

**FIGURE A-5:** Windows 7 desktop with shortcuts, gadgets, and a picture background

Shortcuts to devices

Shortcuts to folders

Shortcuts to programs

Taskbar icons

Gadgets for time, weather, currency rates, and news headlines

Desktop background picture

### What if my desktop looks different from these figures?

If you are using a computer that has been used by others, a different version of Windows 7, or a computer in a school lab, your desktop might be a different color, it might have a different design on it, or it might have different shortcuts and gadgets. Your Recycle Bin might be in a different desktop location. Don't be concerned with these differences. They will not interfere with your work in these units.

# Pointing and Clicking

After you start Windows 7 and see the desktop, you can communicate with Windows using a pointing device. A **pointing device** controls the movement of the mouse pointer on your computer screen. The **mouse pointer** is a small arrow or other symbol that moves on the screen. The mouse pointer's shape changes depending on where you point and on the options available to you when you point. Your pointing device could be a mouse, trackball, touchpad, pointing stick, on-screen touch pointer, or a tablet. Figure A-6 shows some common pointing devices. A pointing device might be attached to your computer with a wire, connect wirelessly using an electronic signal, or it might be built into your computer. There are five basic **pointing device actions** you use to communicate with your computer: pointing, clicking, double-clicking, dragging, and right-clicking. Table A-1 describes each action. 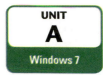 As you prepare to work on your tour schedule, you communicate with your computer using the basic pointing device actions.

## STEPS

1. **Locate the mouse pointer on the desktop, then move your pointing device left, right, up, and down**

   The mouse pointer moves in the same direction as your pointing device.

2. **Move your pointing device so the mouse pointer is over the Recycle Bin**

   You are pointing to the Recycle Bin. The pointer shape is the **Select pointer** ⌕. The Recycle Bin icon becomes **highlighted,** looking as though it is framed in a box with a lighter color background and a border.

   > **QUICK TIP**
   > Use the tip of the pointer when pointing to an object.

3. **While pointing to the Recycle Bin, press and quickly release the left mouse button once, then move the pointer away from the Recycle Bin**

   Click a desktop icon once to **select** it, and then the interior of the border around it changes color. When you select an icon, you signal Windows 7 that you want to perform an action. You can also use pointing to identify screen items.

4. **Point to (but do not click) the Internet Explorer button 🅮 on the taskbar**

   The button border appears and an informational message called a **ScreenTip** identifies the program the button represents.

5. **Move the mouse pointer over the time and date in the notification area in the lower-right corner of the screen, read the ScreenTip, then click once**

   A pop-up window appears, containing a calendar and a clock displaying the current date and time.

   > **TROUBLE**
   > You need to double-click quickly, with a fast click-click, without moving the mouse. If a window didn't open, try again with a faster click-click.

6. **Place the tip of the mouse pointer over the Recycle Bin, then quickly click twice**

   You **double-clicked** the Recycle Bin. A window opens, showing the contents of the Recycle Bin, shown in Figure A-7. The area near the top of the screen is the **Address bar**, which shows the name of the item you have opened. If your Recycle Bin contains any discarded items, they appear in the white area below the Address bar. You can use single clicking to close a window.

7. **Place the tip of the mouse pointer over the Close button 🗙 in the upper-right corner of the Recycle Bin window, notice the Close ScreenTip, then click once**

   The Recycle Bin window closes. You can use dragging to move icons on the desktop.

   > **QUICK TIP**
   > You'll use dragging in other Windows 7 programs to move folders, files, and other objects to new locations.

8. **Point to the Recycle Bin icon, press and hold down the left mouse button, move the pointing device (or drag your finger over the touchpad) so the object moves right about an inch, as shown in Figure A-8, then release the mouse button**

   You dragged the Recycle Bin icon to a new location.

9. **Repeat Step 8 to drag the Recycle Bin back to its original location**

**FIGURE A-6:** Pointing devices

Mouse

Trackball

Touchpad

Pointing stick

**FIGURE A-7:** Recycle Bin window

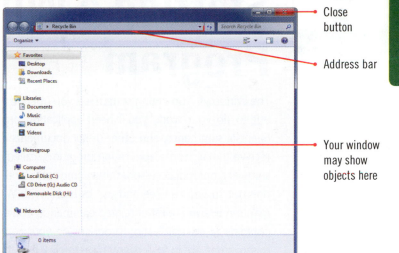

Close button

Address bar

Your window may show objects here

**FIGURE A-8:** Dragging the Recycle Bin icon

Releasing mouse button moves object to this location

**TABLE A-1:** Five pointing device actions

| action | how to | use for |
|--------|--------|---------|
| Pointing | Move the pointing device to position the tip of the pointer over an object, option, or item | Highlighting objects or options, or displaying informational boxes called ScreenTips |
| Clicking | Quickly press and release the left mouse button once | Selecting objects or commands, opening menus or items on the taskbar |
| Double-clicking | Quickly press and release the left mouse button twice | Opening programs, folders, or files represented by desktop icons |
| Dragging | Point to an object, press and hold down the left mouse button, move the object to a new location, then release the mouse button | Moving objects, such as icons on the desktop |
| Right-clicking | Point to an object, then press and release the right mouse button | Displaying a shortcut menu containing options specific to the object |

## Using right-clicking

For some actions, you click items using the right mouse button, known as right-clicking. You can **right-click** almost any icon on your desktop to open a shortcut menu. A **shortcut menu** lists common commands for an object. A **command** is an instruction to perform a task, such as emptying the Recycle Bin. The shortcut menu commands depend on the object you right-click. Figure A-9 shows the shortcut menu that appears if you right-click the Recycle Bin. Then you click (with the left mouse button) a shortcut menu command to issue that command.

**FIGURE A-9:** Right-click to show shortcut menu

# Starting a Windows 7 Program

The Windows 7 operating system lets you operate your computer and see the programs and files it contains. But to do your work, you'll need application programs. **Application programs** let you create letters, financial summaries, and other useful documents as well as view Web pages on the Internet and send and receive e-mail. Some application programs, called **accessories**, come with Windows 7. (See Table A-2 for some examples of accessories that come with Windows 7.) To use an application program, you must start (or open) it so you can see and use its tools. With Windows 7 you start application programs using the Start menu. A **menu** is a list of related commands. You use the Start menu to open the All Programs menu, which contains all the application programs on your computer. You can see some programs on the All Programs menu; some are in folders you have to click first. To start a program, you click its name on the All Programs menu. Evelyn asks you to explore the Paint accessory program for creating brochure graphics.

## STEPS

1.  **Click the Start button** on the taskbar in the lower-left corner of screen

    The Start menu opens, showing frequently used programs on the left side. The gray area on the right contains links to folders and other locations you are likely to use frequently. It also lets you get help and shut down your computer. See Figure A-10. Not all the programs available on your computer are shown.

2.  **Point to All Programs**

    This menu shows programs installed on your computer. Your program list will differ, depending on what you (or your lab) have installed on your machine. Some program names are immediately available, and others are inside folders.

3.  **Click the Accessories folder**

    A list of Windows accessory programs appears, as shown in Figure A-11. The program names are indented to the right from the Accessories folder, meaning that they are inside that folder.

4.  **Move the pointer over Paint and click once**

    The Paint program window opens on your screen, as shown in Figure A-12. When Windows opens an application program, it starts the program from your computer's hard disk, where it's permanently stored. Then it places the program in your computer's memory so you can use it.

5.  **If your Paint window fills the screen completely, click the Restore Down button in the upper-right corner of the window**

    If your Paint window doesn't look like Figure A-12, point to the lower-right corner of the window until the pointer becomes ⬉, then drag until it matches the figure.

### Searching for programs and files using the Start menu

If you need to find a program, folder, or file on your computer quickly, the Search programs and files box on the Start menu can help. Click the Start button, then type the name of the item you want to find in the Search programs and files box. As you type, Windows 7 lists all programs, documents, e-mail messages, and files that contain the text you typed in a box above the Search box. The items appear as links, which means you only have to click the hand pointer on the item you want, and Windows 7 opens it.

**FIGURE A-10:** Start menu

**FIGURE A-11:** Accessories folder on All Programs menu

Start menu (your menu may differ)

Start button

Frequently used programs

Links to folders, files, settings, and features you are likely to use often

Accessories folder

Accessory programs in folder

Search programs and files box

**FIGURE A-12:** Paint program window

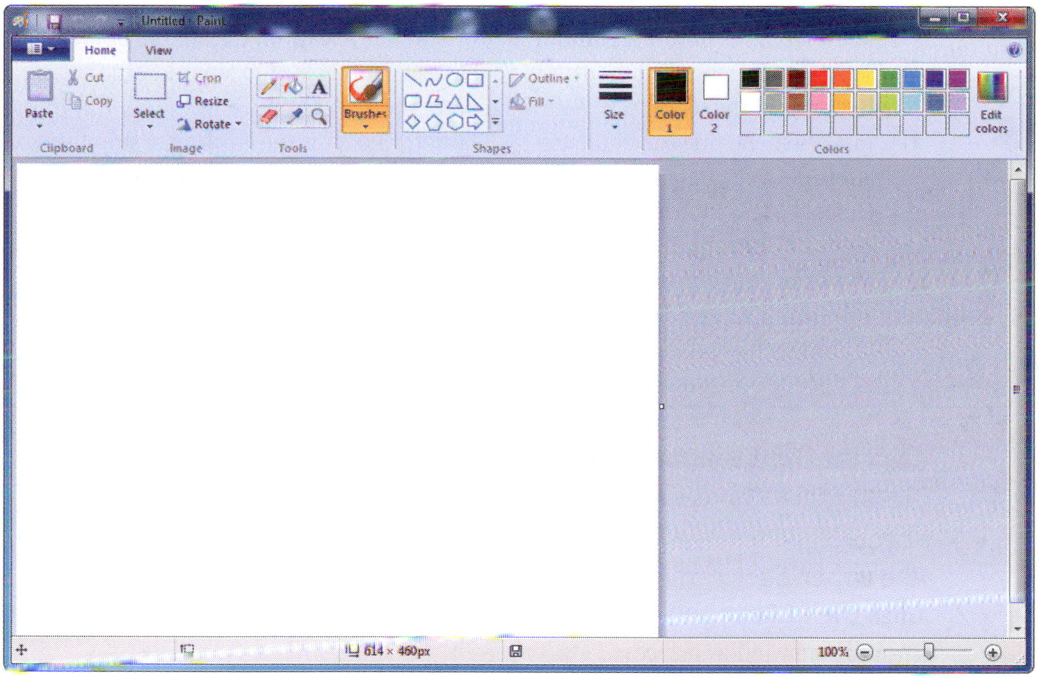

**TABLE A-2:** Some Windows 7 Accessory programs

| accessory program name | use to |
|---|---|
| Math Input Panel | Interpret math expressions handwritten on a tablet and create a formula suitable for printing or inserting in another program |
| Notepad | Create text files with basic text formatting |
| Paint | Create and edit drawings using lines, shapes, and colors |
| Snipping Tool | Capture an image of any screen area that you can save to use in a document |
| Sticky Notes | Create short text notes that you can use to set reminders or create to-do lists for yourself |
| Windows Explorer | View and organize the files and folders on your computer |
| WordPad | Type letters or other text documents with formatting |

# Working with Windows

When you start an application program, its **program window** opens, showing you the tools you need to use the program. A new, blank file also opens. In the Paint program, you create a drawing that you can save as a file and print. All windows in the Windows 7 operating system have similar window elements. Once you can use a window in one program, you can then work with windows in many other programs.  As you develop your tour marketing plans, you work with the open Paint window using Windows 7 elements.

**DETAILS**

### Many windows have the following common elements. Refer to Figure A-13:

- At the top of every open window, you see a **title bar**, a transparent or solid-colored strip that contains the name of the program and document you opened. This document has not been saved, so it has the temporary name "Untitled." On the right side of the title bar, you see three icons.

  The **Minimize button** temporarily hides the window, making it a button on the taskbar. The program is still running, but its window is hidden until you click its taskbar button to display it again. The **Maximize button** enlarges the window to fill the entire computer screen. If a window is already maximized, the Maximize button changes to the **Restore Down button**. Restoring a window reduces it to the last nonmaximized size. The **Close button** closes the program. To use it later, you need to start it again.

- Many windows have a **scroll bar** on the right side and/or on the bottom of the window. You click the scroll bar elements to show parts of your document that are hidden below the bottom edge or off to the right side of the screen. See Table A-3 to learn the parts of a scroll bar.

- Just below the title bar, at the top of the Paint window, is the **Ribbon**, a strip that contains tabs. **Tabs** are pages that contain buttons that you click to perform actions. The Paint window has two tabs, the Home tab and the View tab. Tabs are divided into **groups** of command buttons. The Home tab has five groups: Clipboard, Image, Tools, Shapes, and Colors. Some programs have **menus**, words you click to show lists of commands, and **toolbars**, containing program buttons.

- The **Quick Access toolbar**, in the upper-left corner of the window, lets you quickly perform common actions such as saving a file.

**QUICK TIP**

If your Ribbon looks different from Figure A-13, your window is a little narrower. A narrow window collapses some buttons so you can only see group names. In that case, you might need to click a group name to see buttons.

**STEPS**

1. **Click the Paint window Minimize button**

   The program is now represented only by its button on the taskbar. See Figure A-14. The taskbar button for the Paint program now has a gradient background with blue and white shading. Taskbar buttons for closed programs have a solid blue background.

2. **Click the taskbar button representing the Paint program**

   The program window reappears.

3. **Drag the Paint scroll box down, notice the lower edge of the Paint canvas that appears, then click the Paint Up scroll arrow until you see the top edge of the canvas**

   In the Ribbon, the Home tab is in front of the View tab.

4. **Point to the View tab with the tip of the mouse pointer, then click the View tab once**

   The View tab moves in front of the Home tab and shows commands for viewing your drawings. The View tab has three groups: Zoom, Show or hide, and Display.

5. **Click the Home tab**

6. **Click the Paint window Maximize button**

   The window fills the screen and the Maximize button becomes the Restore Down button.

7. **Click the Paint window's Restore Down button**

   The Paint window returns to its previous size on the screen.

**TROUBLE**

If your screen resolution is set higher than 1024 × 768, you might not see a scroll box. You can continue with the lesson.

**QUICK TIP**

To quickly restore down the selected window, press and hold down the key and then press the down arrow key.

**FIGURE A-13:** Paint program window elements

Quick Access toolbar

Paint program button

Ribbon

Tabs

Window control buttons

Title bar

Scroll bar

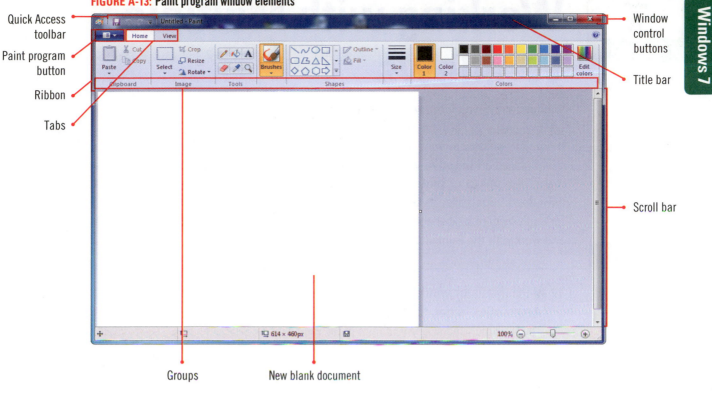

Groups

New blank document

**FIGURE A-14:** Taskbar showing Paint program button

Paint program button with gradient background indicates program is open

**TABLE A-3:** Parts of a scroll bar

| name | looks like | use for |
|------|-----------|---------|
| Scroll box | (Size may vary) | Drag to scroll quickly through a long document |
| Scroll arrows | | Click to scroll up or down in small amounts |
| Shaded area | (Above and below scroll box) | Click to move up or down by one screen |

### Using the Quick Access toolbar

On the left side of the title bar, the Quick Access toolbar lets you perform common tasks with just one click. The Save button saves the changes you have made to a document. The Undo button lets you reverse (undo) the last action you performed. The Redo button reinstates the change you just undid. Use the Customize Quick Access Toolbar button to add other frequently used buttons to the toolbar, move the toolbar below the Ribbon, or hide the Ribbon.

# Working with Multiple Windows

Windows 7 lets you work with more than one program at a time. If you open two or more programs, a window opens for each one. You can work with each open program window, going back and forth between them. The window in front is called the **active window**. Any other open window behind the active window is called an **inactive window**. For ease in working with multiple windows, you can move, arrange, make them smaller or larger, minimize, or restore them so they're not in the way. To resize a window, drag a window's edge, called its **border**. You can also use the taskbar to switch between windows. See Table A-4 for a summary of taskbar actions.  Keeping the Paint program open, you open the WordPad program and work with the Paint and WordPad program windows.

## STEPS

1. **With the Paint window open, click the Start button ⊛, point to All Programs, click the Accessories folder, then click WordPad**

   The WordPad window opens in front of the Paint window. See Figure A-15. The WordPad window is in front, indicating that it is the active window. The Paint window is the inactive window. On the taskbar, the gradient backgrounds on the WordPad and Paint program buttons on the taskbar tell you that both programs are open. You want to move the WordPad window out of the way so you can see both windows at once.

   > **QUICK TIP**
   > To click an inactive window to make it active, click its title bar, window edge, or a blank area. To move a window, you must drag its title bar.

2. **Point to a blank part of the WordPad window title bar, then drag the WordPad window so you can see more of the Paint window**

3. **Click once on the Paint window's title bar**

   The Paint window is now the active window and appears in front of the WordPad window. You can make any window active by clicking it. You can use the taskbar to do the same thing. You can also move among open program windows by pressing and holding down the [Alt] key on your keyboard and pressing the [Tab] key. A small window opens in the middle of the screen, showing miniature versions of each open program window. Each time you press [Tab], you select the next open program window. When you release [Tab] and [Alt], the selected program window becomes active.

   > **QUICK TIP**
   > To instantly minimize all inactive windows, point to the active window's title bar, and quickly "shake" the window back and forth. This feature is called Aero Shake.

4. **On the taskbar, click the WordPad window button 🖼**

   The WordPad window is now active. When you open multiple windows on the desktop, you may need to resize windows so they don't get in the way of other open windows. You can use dragging to resize a window.

   > **TROUBLE**
   > Point to any edge of a window until you see the ⬌ or ⬍ pointer and drag to make it larger or smaller in one direction only.

5. **Point to the lower-right corner of the WordPad window until the pointer becomes ⬂, then drag up and to the left about an inch to make the window smaller**

   Windows 7 has a special feature that lets you automatically resize a window so it fills half the screen.

6. **Point to the WordPad window title bar, drag the window to the left side of the screen until the mouse pointer reaches the screen edge and the left half of the screen turns a transparent blue color, then release the mouse button**

   The WordPad window "snaps" to fill the left side of the screen.

7. **Point to the Paint window title bar, then drag the window to the right side of the screen until it snaps to fill the right half of the screen**

   The Paint window fills the right side of the screen. The Snap feature makes it easy to arrange windows side by side to view the contents of both at the same time.

8. **Click the WordPad window Close button ⬛ then click the Maximize button ⬜ in the Paint window's title bar**

   The WordPad program closes, so you can no longer use its tools unless you open it again. The Paint program window remains open and fills the screen.

**FIGURE A-15:** WordPad window in front of Paint window

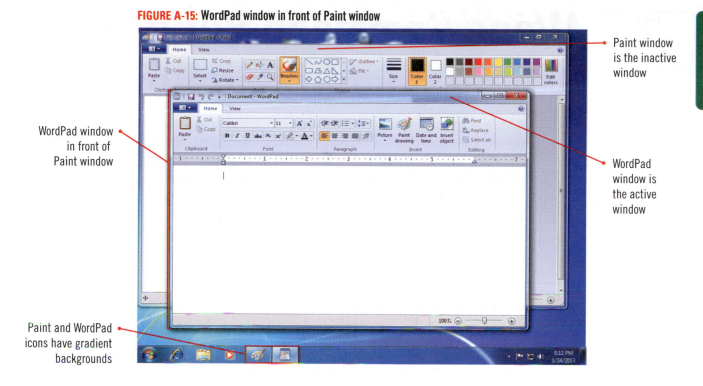

Paint window is the inactive window

WordPad window in front of Paint window

WordPad window is the active window

Paint and WordPad icons have gradient backgrounds

**TABLE A-4:** Using the Windows taskbar

| to | do this |
|---|---|
| Add buttons to taskbar | Drag a program name from the Start menu over the taskbar, until a ScreenTip reads Pin to Taskbar |
| Change order of taskbar buttons | Drag any icon to a new taskbar location |
| See a list of recent documents opened in a taskbar program | Right-click taskbar program button |
| Close a document using the taskbar | Point to taskbar button, point to document name in jump list, then click Close button |
| Minimize all open windows | Click Show desktop button to the right of taskbar date and time |
| Redisplay all minimized windows | Click Show desktop button to the right of taskbar date and time |
| Make all windows transparent (Aero only) | Point to Show desktop button to the right of taskbar date and time |
| See preview of documents in taskbar (Aero only) | Point to taskbar button for open program |

### Switching windows with Windows Aero

**Windows Aero** is a set of special effects for Windows 7. If your windows have transparent "glass" backgrounds like those shown in the figures in this book, your Aero feature is turned on. Your windows show subtle animations when you minimize, maximize, and move windows. When you arrange windows using Aero, your windows can appear in a three-dimensional stack that you can quickly view without having to click the taskbar. To achieve this effect, called **Aero Flip 3D**, press and hold [Ctrl][⊞], then press [Tab]. Press [Tab]

repeatedly to move through the stack, then press [Enter] to enlarge the document in the front of the stack. In addition, when you point to a taskbar button, Aero shows you small previews of the document, photo, or video—a feature called **Aero Peek**. Aero is turned on automatically when you start Windows, if you have an appropriate video card and enough computer memory to run Aero. If it is not on, to turn on the Aero feature, right-click the desktop, left-click Personalize, then select one of the Aero Themes.

# Using Command Buttons, Menus, and Dialog Boxes

When you work in an open program window, you communicate with the program using command buttons, menus, and dialog boxes. **Command buttons** let you issue instructions to modify program objects. Command buttons are sometimes organized on a Ribbon into tabs, and then into groups like those in the Paint window. Some command buttons have text on them, and others only have icons that represent what they do. Other command buttons reveal **menus**, lists of commands you can choose. And some command buttons open up a **dialog box**, a window with controls that lets you tell Windows what you want. Table A-5 lists the common types of controls you find in dialog boxes.  You use command buttons, menus, and dialog boxes to communicate with the Paint program.

## STEPS

1. In the Shapes group on the Home tab, click the Rectangle button ☐

**QUICK TIP**
If you need to move the oval, use the keyboard arrow keys to move it left, right, up, or down.

2. In the Colors group, click the Gold button ▨, move the pointer over the white drawing area, called the **canvas**, then drag to draw a rectangle a similar size to the one in Figure A-16

3. In the Shapes group, click the Oval button ⬭, click the Green color button ▨ in the Colors group, then drag a small oval above the rectangle, using Figure A-16 as a guide

**TROUBLE**
Don't be concerned if your object isn't exactly like the one in the figure.

4. Click the Fill with color icon ▨ in the Tools group, click the Light turquoise color button in the Colors group, click ▨ inside the oval, click the Purple color button, then click inside the rectangle, and compare your drawing to Figure A-16

5. In the Image group, click the Select list arrow, then click Select all, as shown in Figure A-17
   The Select menu has several menu commands. The Select all command selects the entire drawing, as indicated by the dotted line surrounding the white drawing area.

6. In the Image group, click the Rotate or flip button, then click Rotate right 90°

7. Click the Paint menu button ▨ just below the title bar, then click Print
   The Print dialog box opens, as shown in Figure A-18. This dialog box lets you choose a printer, specify which part of your document or drawing you want to print, and choose how many copies you want to print. The **default**, or automatically selected, number of copies is 1, which is what you want.

**TROUBLE**
If you prefer not to print your document, click Cancel.

8. Click Print
   The drawing prints on your printer. You decide to close the program without saving your drawing.

9. Click ▨, click Exit, then click Don't Save

**TABLE A-5: Common dialog box controls**

| element | example | description |
|---|---|---|
| Text box | 132 | A box in which you type text or numbers |
| Spin box | 1 | A box with up and down arrows; click arrows or type to increase or decrease value |
| Option button | ○ | A small circle you click to select the option |
| Check box | ☑ | Turns an option on when checked or off when unchecked |
| List box | Select Printer / Add Printer / Dell Laser Printer 3000cn PCL6 / Fax | A box that lets you select an option from a list of options |
| Command button | Save | A button that completes or cancels the selected settings |

**FIGURE A-16:** Rectangle and oval shapes with fill

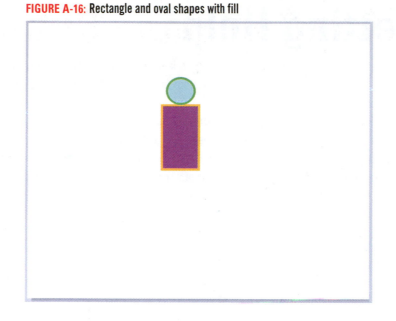

**FIGURE A-17:** Select list arrow

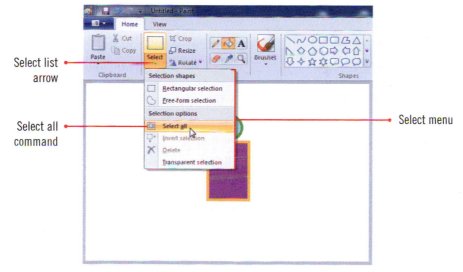

Select list arrow

Select all command

Select menu

**FIGURE A-18:** Print dialog box

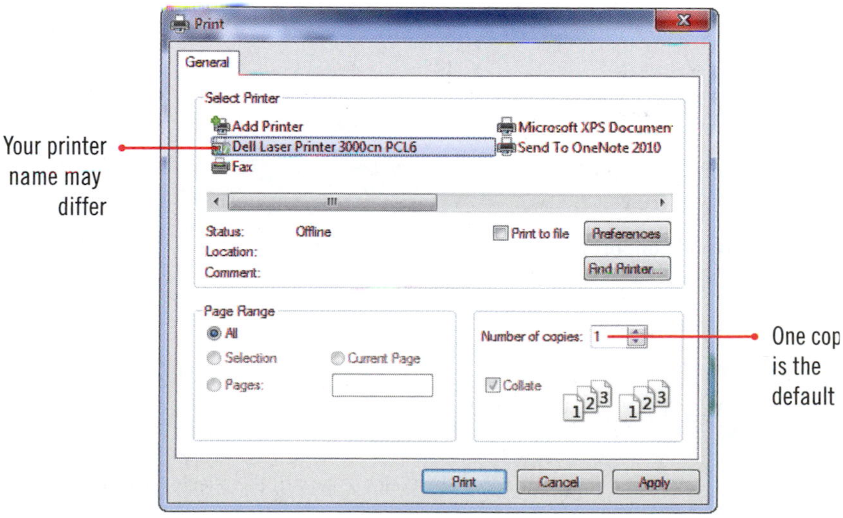

Your printer name may differ

One copy is the default

# Getting Help

As you use Windows 7, you might feel ready to learn more about it, or you might have a problem and need some advice. You can open the Windows 7 Help and Support to find information you need. You can browse Help and Support topics by clicking a category, such as "Learn about Windows Basics." Within this category, you see more specific categories. Each category has topics in blue or purple text called **links** that you can click to learn more. You can also search Help and Support by typing one or more descriptive words called **keywords**, such as "taskbar," to ask Windows to find topics related to your keywords. The Help toolbar contains icons that give you more Help options. Table A-6 describes the Help toolbar icons. You use Windows 7 help to learn more about Windows and the WordPad accessory.

## STEPS

> **TROUBLE**
> If your computer is not connected to the Internet, you will see an alert at the top of the Help window. You can continue with the steps in this lesson.

1. **Click the Start button** 🏁, **then on the right side of the Start menu, click Help and Support**

   The Windows Help and Support window opens, as shown in Figure A-19. A search box appears near the top of the window. Three topics appear as blue or purple text, meaning that they are links. Below them, you see descriptive text and a link to a Web site that contains more information about Windows.

2. **Under Not sure where to start?, position the hand pointer** 👆 **over Learn about Windows Basics, then click once**

   Several categories of Windows Basics topics appear, with links under each one.

3. **Under Desktop fundamentals, click The desktop (overview)**

   Help and Support information about the desktop appears, divided into several categories. Some of the text appears as a blue or purple link.

> **QUICK TIP**
> If you are using a mouse with a scroll wheel, you can use the scroll wheel to scroll up and down. If you are using a touchpad, the right side of your touchpad might let you scroll.

4. **Drag the scroll box down to view the information, then drag the scroll box back to the top of the scroll bar**

   You decide to learn more about the taskbar.

5. **Under The desktop (overview), click the blue or purple text The taskbar (overview), then scroll down and read the information about the taskbar**

> **QUICK TIP**
> Search text is not case sensitive. Typing wordpad, Wordpad, or WordPad finds the same results.

6. **Click in the Search Help text box, type wordpad, then click the Search Help button** 🔍

   A list of links related to the WordPad accessory program appears. See Figure A-20.

7. **Click Using WordPad, scroll down if necessary, then click Create, open, and save documents**

8. **Scroll down and view the information, clicking any other links that interest you**

9. **Click the Close button** ❌ **in the upper-right corner of the Windows Help and Support window**

   The Windows Help and Support window closes.

---

**TABLE A-6:** Help toolbar icons

| help toolbar icon | name | action |
|---|---|---|
| 🏠 | Help and Support home | Displays the Help and Support Home page |
| 🖨 | Print | Prints the currently-displayed help topic |
| 📘 | Browse Help | Displays a list of Help topics organized by subject |
| 👥 Ask | Ask | Describes other ways to get help |
| Options ▾ | Options | Lets you print, browse, search, set Help text size, and adjust settings |

**FIGURE A-19:** Windows Help and Support window

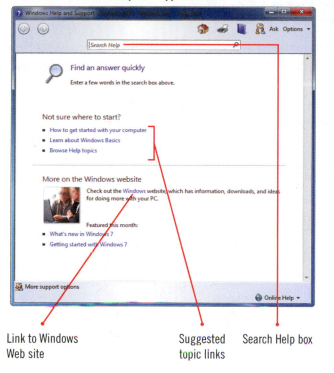

**FIGURE A-20:** Results of a search on WordPad

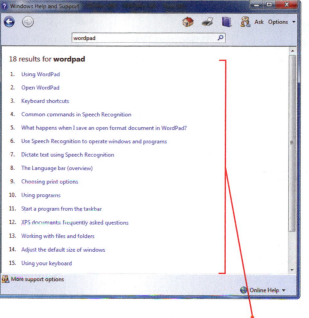

Link to Windows
Web site

Suggested
topic links

Search Help box

Suggested topic links
(your links may differ)

### Finding other ways to get help

As you use Windows 7, you might want more help than you can find by clicking links or searching. You will find many other methods in the Windows Help and Support Home window. Click the Windows website link to locate blogs (Web logs, which are personal commentaries), downloads, Windows 7 video tours, and other current Windows 7 resources. Click the Ask button in the Help and Support window toolbar to learn about **Windows Remote Assistance**, which lets you connect with another computer, perhaps that of a trusted friend or instructor, so they can operate your computer using an Internet connection. The same window lets you open Microsoft Answers. **Microsoft Answers** is a website the lets you search **forums** (electronic gathering places where anyone can add questions and answers on computer issues), Microsoft help files, and even on-screen video demonstrations about selected topics.

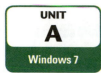

## UNIT A
Windows 7

# Exiting Windows 7

When you finish working on your computer, save and close any open files, close any open programs, close any open windows, and exit (or **shut down**) Windows 7. Table A-7 shows several options for ending your Windows 7 sessions. Whichever option you choose, it's important to shut down your computer in an orderly way. If you turn off or unplug the computer while Windows 7 is running, you could lose data or damage Windows 7 and your computer. If you are working in a computer lab, follow your instructor's directions and your lab's policies for ending your Windows 7 session. You have examined the basic ways you can use Windows 7, so you are ready to end your Windows 7 session.

## STEPS

1. **Click the Start button 🏁 on the taskbar**

   The lower-right corner of the Start menu lets you shut down your computer. It also displays a menu with other options for ending a Windows 7 session.

<table>
<tr><td>

**TROUBLE**

If a previous user has customized your computer, your button and menu commands might be in different locations. For example, the Power button may show "Restart," and "Shut down" may appear on the menu.

</td></tr>
</table>

2. **Point to the Power button list arrow ▶, as shown in Figure A-21**

   The Power button menu lists other shutdown options.

3. **If you are working in a computer lab, follow the instructions provided by your instructor or technical support person for ending your Windows 7 session. If you are working on your own computer, click Shut down or the option you prefer for ending your Windows 7 session**

4. **After you shut down your computer, you may also need to turn off your monitor and other hardware devices, such as a printer, to conserve energy**

---

**Installing updates when you exit Windows**

Sometimes, after you shut down your machine, you might find that your machine does not shut down immediately. Instead, Windows might install software updates. If your power button shows this yellow icon 🔶, that means that Windows will install updates on your next shutdown. If you see a window indicating that updates are being installed, do not unplug or press the power switch to turn off your machine. Allow the updates to install completely. After the updates are installed, your computer will shut down, as you originally requested.

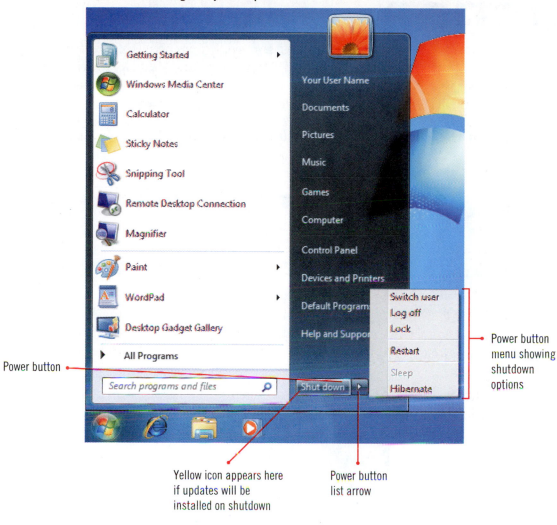

**FIGURE A-21:** Shutting down your computer

Power button

Power button menu showing shutdown options

Yellow icon appears here if updates will be installed on shutdown

Power button list arrow

**TABLE A-7:** Options for ending a Windows 7 session

| option | description | click |
|---|---|---|
| Shut down | Completely turns off your computer | Start button, Shut down |
| Switch user | Locks your user account and displays the Welcome screen so another user can log on | Start button, Power button list arrow, Switch user |
| Log off | Closes all windows, programs, and documents, then displays the Log in screen | Start button, Power button list arrow, Log off |
| Lock | Locks computer so only current user (or administrator) can use it | Start button, Power button list arrow, Lock |
| Restart | Shuts down your computer, then restarts it | Start button, Power button list arrow, Restart |
| Sleep | Puts computer in a low-power state while preserving your session in the computer's memory | Start button, Power button list arrow, Sleep |
| Hibernate | Turns off computer drives and screens but saves image of your work; when you turn machine on, it starts where you left off | Start button, Power button list arrow, Hibernate |

# Practice

For current SAM information, including versions and content details, visit SAM Central (http://samcentral.course. com). If you have a SAM user profile, you may have access to hands-on instruction, practice, and assessment of the skills covered in this unit. Since various versions of SAM are supported throughout the life of this text, check with your instructor for the correct instructions and URL/Web site for accessing assignments.

## Concepts Review

**Label the elements of the Windows 7 window shown in Figure A-22.**

**FIGURE A-22**

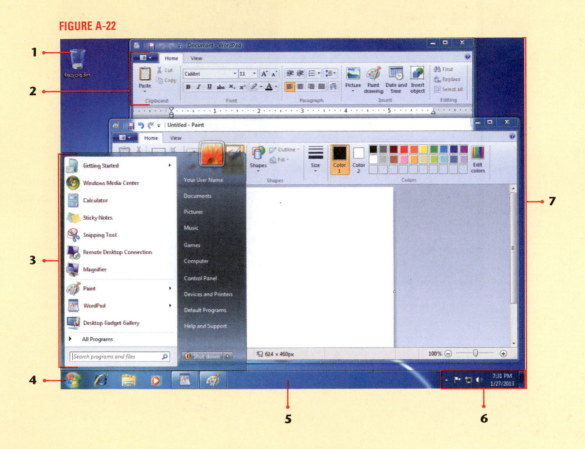

**Match each term with the statement that best describes it.**

8. **Accessory**
9. **Keyword**
10. **Trackball**
11. **Active window**
12. **Password**
13. **Operating system**
14. **Taskbar**

a. A sequence of numbers and letters users create to keep information secure
b. The window in front of other windows
c. Horizontal strip at bottom of screen that contains buttons
d. A pointing device
e. Application program that comes with Windows 7
f. Descriptive word you use to search Windows Help and Support
g. A program necessary to run your computer

**Select the best answer from the list of choices.**

15. **What part of a window shows the name of the program you opened?**
   a. Title bar
   b. Scroll bar
   c. Ribbon
   d. Quick Access toolbar

16. **You use the Maximize button to:**

   a. Restore a window to a previous size.

   b. Expand a window to fill the entire screen.

   c. Temporarily hide a window.

   d. Scroll down a window.

17. **Which of the following is not an accessory program?**

   a. Snipping Tool

   b. Paint

   c. WordPad

   d. Windows 7

18. **Which button do you click to reduce an open window to a button on the taskbar?**

   a. Maximize button

   b. Restore Down button

   c. Minimize button

   d. Close button

19. **Right-clicking is an action that:**

   a. Starts a program.

   b. Requires a password.

   c. Displays a shortcut menu.

   d. Opens the taskbar.

20. **The Windows 7 feature that shows windows with transparent "glass" backgrounds is:**

   a. Paint.

   b. Aero.

   c. Taskbar.

   d. Sticky Notes.

21. **Windows 7 is a(n):**

   a. Accessory program.

   b. Application program.

   c. Operating system.

   d. Gadget.

## Skills Review

1. **Start Windows 7.**

   a. If your computer and monitor are not running, press your computer's and your monitor's power buttons.

   b. If necessary, click the user name that represents your user account.

   c. Enter a password if necessary, using correct uppercase and lowercase letters.

2. **Learn the Windows 7 desktop.**

   a. Examine the Windows 7 desktop to identify the Start button, the taskbar, the notification area, the Recycle Bin, the desktop background, desktop icons, and gadgets, if any.

3. **Point and click.**

   a. On the Windows desktop, select the Recycle Bin.

   b. Open the Start menu, then close it.

   c. Open the clock and calendar on the right side of the taskbar.

   d. Click the desktop to close the calendar.

   e. Open the Recycle Bin window, then close it.

4. **Start a Windows 7 program.**

   a. Use the Start button to open the Start menu.

   b. Open the All Programs menu.

   c. On the All Programs menu, open the Accessories folder.

   d. Open the WordPad accessory.

5. **Work with Windows.**

   a. Minimize the WordPad window.

   b. Redisplay it using a taskbar button.

   c. In the WordPad window, click the WordPad button in the Ribbon, then click the About WordPad command. (*Hint*: The WordPad button is next to the Home tab.)

   d. Close the About WordPad window.

   e. Maximize the WordPad window, then restore it down.

   f. Display the View tab in the WordPad window.

6. **Work with multiple windows.**

   a. Leaving WordPad open, open Paint.

   b. Make the WordPad window the active window.

   c. Make the Paint window the active window.

   d. Minimize the Paint window.

   e. Drag the WordPad window so it automatically fills the left side of the screen.

   f. Redisplay the Paint window.

   g. Drag the Paint window so it automatically fills the right side of the screen.

   h. Close the WordPad window, maximize the Paint window, then restore down the Paint window.

7. **Use command buttons, menus, and dialog boxes.**

   a. In the Paint window, draw a red triangle, similar to Figure A-23.

   b. Use the Fill with color button to fill the triangle with a gold color.

   c. Draw a green rectangle just below the triangle.

   d. Use the Fill with color button to fill the green triangle with a light turquoise color.

   e. Fill the drawing background with purple and compare your drawing with Figure A-23.

   f. Use the Select list arrow and menu to select the entire drawing, then use the Rotate or flip command to rotate the drawing left 90°.

   g. Close the Paint program without saving the drawing.

**FIGURE A-23**

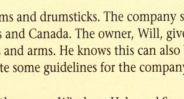

8. **Get help.**

   a. Open the Windows Help and Support window.

   b. Open the "How to get started with your computer" topic.

   c. Open the "First week tasks" topic, click a link called "Create a user account", then read the topic information.

   d. In the Search Help text box, search for help about user accounts.

   e. Find the link that describes what a user account is and click it.

   f. Read the topic, then close the Windows Help and Support window.

9. **Exit Windows 7.**

   a. Shut down your computer using the Shut down command or the command for your work or school setting.

   b. Turn off your monitor.

# Independent Challenge 1

You work for Will's Percussion, an Oregon manufacturer of drums and drumsticks. The company ships percussion instruments and supplies to music stores and musicians in the United States and Canada. The owner, Will, gives seminars at drummer conventions on how to avoid repetitive stress injuries to the hands and arms. He knows this can also be a big problem for computer users as well, so he asks you to research the topic and write some guidelines for the company's employees.

   a. Start your computer, log on to Windows 7 if necessary, then open Windows Help and Support.

   b. Click the Learn about Windows Basics link.

   c. In the Learn about your computer section, read the topic about using your mouse.

   d. At the bottom of the topic, read the Tips for using your mouse safely.

   e. Using pencil and paper, write a short memo to Will listing, in your own words, the most important tips for avoiding soreness or injury when using a mouse. Close the Windows Help and Support window, then exit Windows.

# Independent Challenge 2

You are the new manager for Katharine Anne's Designs, a business that supplies floral arrangements to New York businesses. The company maintains four delivery vans that supply flowers to various locations. Katharine asks you to investigate how the Windows 7 Calculator accessory can help her company be a responsible energy consumer.

## Independent Challenge 2 (continued)

a. Start your computer, log on to Windows 7 if necessary, then open the Windows 7 accessory called Calculator.

b. Drag the Calculator window to place it in the lower-left corner of the desktop just above the taskbar.

**FIGURE A-24**

c. Minimize the Calculator window, then redisplay it.

d. Click to enter the number 87 on the Calculator.

e. Click the division sign (/) button.

f. Click the number 2.

g. Click the equals sign button (=), and write the result shown in the Calculator window on a piece of paper. See Figure A-24.

h. Click the Help menu in the Calculator window, then click View Help. In the Using Calculator window, determine the three ways of entering calculations in the Calculator. Write the three methods on your handwritten list.

i. Close the Help window.

### Advanced Challenge Exercise

- Open the View menu on the Calculator window, and click Date calculation.
- Click the list arrow under Select the date calculation you want, then click Calculate the difference between two dates.
- Write how Katharine's business might use this to calculate the length of time it takes a customer to pay an invoice.
- Click the View menu, point to Worksheets, then click Fuel economy (mpg).
- Click in the Distance (miles) text box and enter 100; click in the Fuel used (gallons) text box and type 5, then use the Calculate button to calculate the mileage.
- Write a short paragraph on how Katharine can use this feature to help calculate her van mileage.
- Click the View menu and return to the Basic view.
- Try to click the Calculator window's Maximize button. Note the result and add this fact to your document.

j. Close the Calculator, then exit Windows.

## Independent Challenge 3

You are the office manager for Peter's Pet Shipping, a service business in Vancouver, BC that specializes in air shipping of cats and dogs to Canada and the northern United States. It's important to know the temperature in the destination city, so that the animals won't be in danger from extreme temperatures when they are unloaded from the aircraft. Peter has asked you to find a way to easily monitor temperatures in destination cities. You decide to use a Windows gadget so you can see current temperatures in Celsius on your desktop.

To complete this Independent Challenge, you need an Internet connection. You also need permission to add gadgets to the Windows Desktop. If you are working in a computer lab, check with your instructor or technical support person.

a. Start your computer, log on to Windows 7 if necessary, then click the Start button, open the All Programs menu, then click Desktop Gadget Gallery.

b. Double-click the Weather gadget, then close the Gallery window.

c. Move the pointer over the Weather gadget on the desktop, then notice the small buttons that appear on its right side.

d. Click the Larger size button (the middle button).

e. Click the Options button (the third button down) to open the weather options window.

f. In the Select current location text box, type Juneau, Alaska, then click the Search button.

g. Verify that the window shows the current location as "Juneau, Alaska."

h. Click the Celsius option button, then click OK.

i. To close the gadget, point to the gadget, then click the Close button (the top button).

j. Write Peter a memo outlining how you can use the Windows Weather gadget to help keep pets safe, then exit Windows.

# Real Life Independent Challenge

As a professional photographer, you often evaluate pictures. You decide to explore a Windows Desktop gadget that will let you display a slide show on your desktop using photos you choose.

To complete this Independent Challenge, you need an Internet connection. You also need permission to add gadgets to the Windows Desktop. If you are working in a computer lab, check with your instructor or technical support person.

a. Start your computer, log on to Windows 7 if necessary, click the Start button, open the All Programs menu, then click Desktop Gadget Gallery.

b. Double-click the Slide Show gadget, then close the Gallery window.

c. Move the pointer over the Slide Show gadget on the desktop, then notice the small buttons that appear on its right side.

d. Click the Larger size button (the second button down).

e. Click the Options button (the third button down) to open the Slide Show options window.

f. Click the Folder list arrow and click the My Pictures folder. If you do not have pictures on your computer, click the Sample Pictures folder.

g. Click the Show each picture list arrow and select a duration.

h. Click the Transition between pictures list arrow and select a transition.

i. If you want the pictures to be in random order, click the Shuffle pictures check box.

j. Click OK.

## Advanced Challenge Exercise

- Place the mouse pointer over the Slide Show window, then right-click.
- Point to Opacity and left-click an opacity level, then move the mouse pointer over the desktop. Adjust the opacity to the level you prefer.
- Drag the gadget to the desktop location you choose.

k. View your slide show, click the Slide Show window's Close button, then exit Windows.

# Visual Workshop

As owner of Icons Plus, an icon design business, you decide to customize your desktop and resize your Help window to better suit your needs as you work with Paint. Organize your screen as shown in Figure A-25. Note the position of the Recycle Bin, the location of the Paint window, and the size and location of the Help and Support window. Write a paragraph summarizing how you used clicking and dragging to make your screen look like Figure A-25. Then exit Windows.

**FIGURE A-25**

# Understanding File Management

**Files You Will Need:**

No files needed.

To work with the folders and files on your computer, you need to understand how your computer stores them. You should also know how to organize them so you can always find the information you need. These skills are called **file management** skills. When you create a document and save it as a file, it is important that you save the file in a place where you can find it later. To keep your computer files organized, you will need to copy, move, and rename them. When you have files you don't need any more, it's a good idea to move or delete them so your computer has only current files.  Your supervisor, Evelyn Swazey, asks you to learn how to manage your computer files so you can begin creating and organizing documents for the upcoming Oceania tours.

**OBJECTIVES**

Understand folders and files

Create and save a file

Explore the files and folders on your computer

Change file and folder views

Open, edit, and save files

Copy files

Move and rename files

Search for files, folders, and programs

Delete and restore files

# Understanding Folders and Files

As you work with your computer programs, you create and save files, such as letters, drawings, or budgets. When you save files, you usually save them inside folders, which are storage areas on your computer. You use folders to group related files, as with paper folders in a file cabinet. The files and folders on your computer are organized in a **file hierarchy**, a system that arranges files and folders in different levels, like the branches of a tree. Figure B-1 shows a sample file hierarchy. Evelyn asks you to look at some important facts about files and folders to help you store your Oceania tour files.

**DETAILS**

## Use the following guidelines as you organize files using your computer's file hierarchy:

- ### Use folders and subfolders to organize files
  As you work with your computer, you can add folders to your hierarchy and rename them to help you organize your work. You should give folders unique names that help you easily identify them. You can also create **subfolders**, which are folders that are inside of other folders. Windows comes with several existing folders, such as My Documents, My Music, and My Pictures, that you can use as a starting point.

**QUICK TIP**
You can also start Windows Explorer by clicking the Windows Explorer button on the taskbar.

- ### View files in windows
  You view your computer contents by opening a **window**, like the one in Figure B-2. A window is divided into sections. The **Navigation pane** on the left side of the window shows the folder structure on your computer. When you click a folder in the Navigation pane, you see its contents in the **File list** on the right side. The **Details pane** at the bottom of the window provides information about selected files in the File list. A window actually opens in an accessory program called **Windows Explorer**, although the program name does not appear on the window. You can open this program from the Start menu, or just double-click a folder to open its window and view its contents.

- ### Understand file addresses
  A window also contains an **Address bar**, an area just below the title bar that shows the location, or address, of the files that appear in the File list. An **address** is a sequence of folder names separated by the ▶ symbol that describes a file's location in the file hierarchy. An address shows the folder with the highest hierarchy level on the left and steps through each hierarchy level toward the right, sometimes called a **path**. For example, the My Documents folder might contain a subfolder named Notes. In this case, the Address bar would show My Documents ▶ Notes. Each location between the ▶ symbols represents a level in the file hierarchy.

**QUICK TIP**
Remember that you single-click a folder or subfolder in the Address bar to show its contents. But in the File list, you double-click a subfolder to open it.

- ### Navigate upward and downward using the Address bar and File list
  You can use the Address bar and the File list to move up or down in the hierarchy one or more levels at a time. To **navigate upward** in your computer's hierarchy, you can click a folder or subfolder name in the Address bar. For example, in Figure B-2, you would move up in the hierarchy by clicking once on Users in the Address bar. Then the File list would show the subfolders and files inside the Users folder. To **navigate downward** in the hierarchy, double-click a subfolder in the File list. The path in the Address bar then shows the path to that subfolder.

- ### Navigate upward and downward using the Navigation pane
  You can also use the Navigation pane to navigate among folders. Move the mouse pointer over the Navigation pane, then click the small triangles or to the left of a folder name to show ▷ or hide ◢ the folder's contents under the folder name. Subfolders appear indented under the folders that contain them, showing that they are inside that folder. Figure B-2 shows a folder named Users in the Navigation pane. The subfolders Katharine, Public, and Your User Name are inside the Users folder.

**FIGURE B-1:** Sample folder and file hierarchy

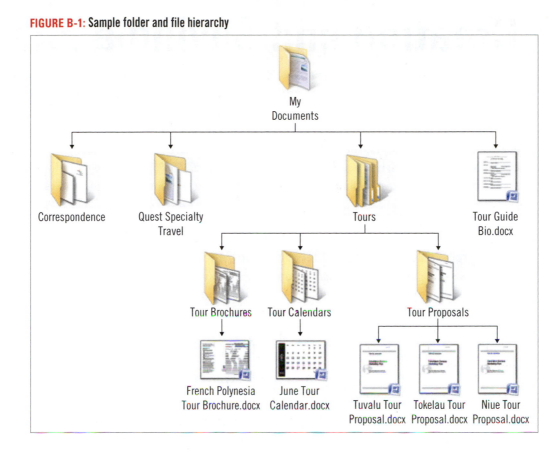

**FIGURE B-2:** Windows Explorer window

Address shows path to Your User Name folder in file hierarchy

Click Users to move up one level in hierarchy

Double-click any folder to move one level down in hierarchy

Navigation pane

Users folder

Subfolders inside the Your User Name folder

File list shows contents of selected Your User Name folder

Details pane

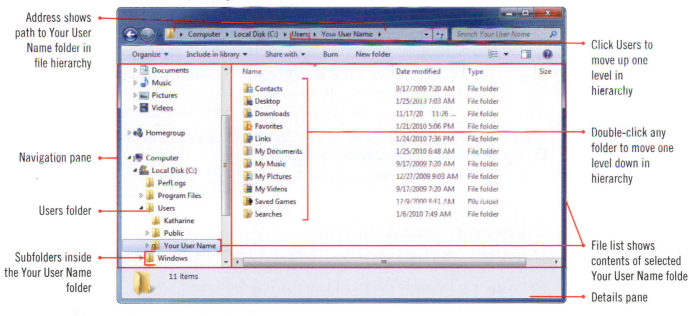

## Plan your file organization

As you manage your files, you should plan how you want to organize them. First, identify the types of files you work with, such as images, music, and reports. Think about the content, such as personal, business, clients, or projects. Then think of a folder organization that will help you find them later. For example, use subfolders in the My Pictures folder to separate family photos from business photos or to group them by year. In the My Documents folder, you might group personal files in one subfolder and business files in another subfolder. Then create additional subfolders to further separate sets of files. You can always move files among folders and rename folders. You should periodically reevaluate your folder structure to make sure that it continues to meet your needs.

Understanding File Management

# Creating and Saving a File

After you start a program and create a new file, the file exists only in your computer's **random access memory (RAM)**, which is a temporary storage location. RAM only contains information when your computer is on. When you turn off your computer, it automatically clears the contents of RAM. So you need to save a new file onto a storage device that permanently stores the file so that you can open, change, and use it later. One important storage device is your computer's hard disk built into your computer. Another popular option is a **USB flash drive**, a small, portable storage device.  Evelyn asks you to use the WordPad accessory program to create a short summary of an Oceania tour planning meeting and save it.

## STEPS

1. **Start Windows if necessary, click the Start button** 🪟 **on the taskbar, point to All Programs, click Accessories, then click WordPad**

   The WordPad program opens. Near the top of the screen you see the Ribbon containing command buttons, similar to those you used in Paint in Unit A. The Home tab appears in front. A new, blank document appears in the document window. The blinking insertion point shows you where the next character you type will appear.

2. **Type Meeting Notes, October 11, then press [Enter]**

   WordPad inserts a new blank line and places the insertion point at the beginning of the next line.

   > **TROUBLE**
   > If you make a typing mistake, press [Backspace] to delete the character to the left of the insertion point.

3. **Type The 2013 tour will visit:, press [Enter], type Australia, press [Enter], type Micronesia, press [Enter], type New Zealand, press [Enter], then type your name; see Figure B-3**

4. **Click the WordPad button** 📄▾ **on the upper-left side of the window below the title bar, then click Save on the WordPad menu**

   The first time you save a file using the Save button, the Save As dialog box opens. Use this dialog box to name the document file and choose a storage location for it. The Save As dialog box has many of the same elements as a Windows Explorer window, including an Address bar, a Navigation pane, and a File list. Below the Address bar, the **toolbar** contains command buttons you can click to perform actions. In the Address bar, you can see that WordPad chose the Documents library (which includes the My Documents folder) as the storage location.

   > **TROUBLE**
   > If you don't have a USB flash drive, save the document in the My Documents folder instead.

5. **Plug your USB flash drive into a USB port** 🔌 **on your computer, if necessary**

   On a laptop computer, the USB port is on the left or right side of your computer. On a desktop computer, the USB port is on the front panel (you may need to open a small door to see it), or on the back panel.

6. **In the Navigation pane scroll bar, click the Down scroll arrow** 🔽 **as needed to see Computer and any storage devices listed under it**

   Under Computer, you see the storage locations available on your computer, such as Local Disk (C:) (your hard drive) and Removable Disk (H:) (your USB drive name and letter might differ). These storage locations act like folders because you can open them and store files in them.

   > **TROUBLE**
   > If your Save As dialog box or title bar does not show the .rtf file extension, open any Windows Explorer window, click Organize in the toolbar, click Folder and search options, click the View tab, then under Files and Folders, click to remove the check mark from Hide extensions for known file types.

7. **Click the name for your USB flash drive**

   The files and folders on your USB drive, if any, appear in the File list. The Address bar shows the location where the file will be saved, which is now Computer > Removable Disk (H:) (or the name of your drive). You need to give your document a meaningful name so you can find it later.

8. **Click in the Filename text box to select the default name Document, type Oceania Meeting, compare your screen to Figure B-4, then click Save**

   The document is saved as a file on your USB flash drive. The filename Oceania Meeting.rtf appears in the title bar at the top of the window. The ".rtf" at the end of the filename is the file extension. A **file extension** is a three- or four-letter sequence, preceded by a period, that identifies the file as a particular type of document, in this case Rich Text Format, to your computer. The WordPad program creates files using the RTF format. Windows adds the .rtf file extension automatically after you click Save.

9. **Click the Close button** ❎ **on the WordPad window**

   The WordPad program closes. Your meeting minutes are now saved on your USB flash drive.

Understanding File Management

**FIGURE B-3:** Saving a document

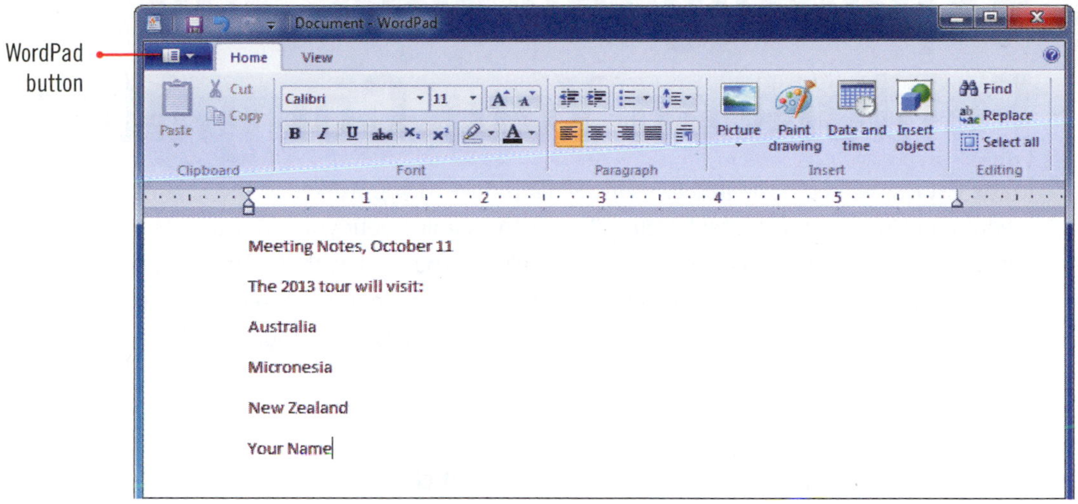

WordPad
button

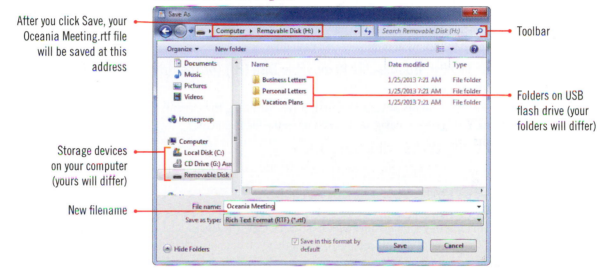

**FIGURE B-4:** Save As dialog box

After you click Save, your
Oceania Meeting.rtf file
will be saved at this
address

Toolbar

Folders on USB
flash drive (your
folders will differ)

Storage devices
on your computer
(yours will differ)

New filename

## Using Windows 7 libraries

The Navigation pane contains not only files and folders, but also Libraries. A **library** gathers files and folders from different locations on your computer and displays them in one location. For example, you might have pictures in several different folders on your storage devices. You can add these folder locations to your Pictures library. Then when you want to see all your pictures, you open your Pictures library, instead of several different folders. The picture files stay in their original locations, but their names appear in the Pictures library. A library is not a folder that stores files, but rather a way of viewing similar types of documents that you have stored in multiple locations on your computer. Figure B-5 shows the four libraries that come with Windows 7: Documents, Music, Pictures, and Videos. To help you distinguish between library locations and actual folder locations, library names differ from actual folder names. For example, the My Documents folder is on your hard drive, but the library name is Documents. To add a location to a library, click the blue locations link (at the top of the File list) in the library you want to add to, click the Add button, navigate to the folder location you want to add,

then click Include folder. If you delete a file or folder from a library, you delete them from their source locations. If you delete a library, you do not delete the files in it. The Documents Library that comes with Windows already has the My Documents folder listed as a save location. So if you save a document to the Documents library, it is automatically saved to your My Documents folder.

**FIGURE B-5:** Libraries

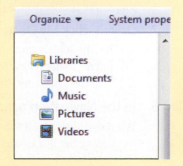

# Exploring the Files and Folders on Your Computer

In the last lesson, you navigated to your USB flash drive as you worked in the Save As dialog box. But even if you're not saving a document, you will want to examine your computer and its existing folder and file structure. That way, you'll know where to save files as you work with Windows application programs. In a Windows Explorer window, you can navigate through your computer contents using the File list, the Address bar, and the Navigation pane.  As you prepare for the Oceania tours, you look at the files and folders on your computer.

## STEPS

**TROUBLE**
If you don't see the colored bar, click the More Options list arrow ▤ ▾ on the menu bar, then click Tiles.

1. **Click the Start button ⊕ on the taskbar, then click Computer**

   Your computer's storage devices appear in a window, as shown in Figure B-6, including hard drives; devices with removable storage, such as CD and DVD drives or USB flash drives; and portable devices such as personal digital assistants (PDAs). Table B-1 lists examples of different drive types. A colored bar shows you how much space has been taken up on your hard drive. You decide to move down a level in your computer's hierarchy and see what is on your USB flash drive.

**TROUBLE**
If you do not have a USB flash drive, click the Documents library in the Navigation pane instead.

2. **In the File list, double-click Removable Disk (H:) (or the drive name and letter for your USB flash drive)**

   You see the contents of your USB flash drive, including the Oceania Meeting.rtf file you saved in the last lesson. You decide to navigate one level up in the file hierarchy.

3. **In the Address bar, click Computer**

   You return to the Computer window showing your storage devices. You decide to look at the contents of your hard drive.

4. **In the Navigation pane, click Local Disk (C:)**

   The contents of your hard drive appear in the File list. The Users folder contains a subfolder for each user who has a user account on this computer. Recall that you double-click items in the File list to open them. In the Address bar and in the Navigation pane, you only need to single-click.

5. **In the File list, double-click the Users folder**

   You see folders for each user registered on your computer. You might see a folder with your user account name on it. Each user's folder contains that person's documents. User folder names are the log-in names that were entered when your computer was set up. When a user logs in, the computer allows that user access to the folder with the same user name. If you are using a computer with more than one user, you might not have permission to view other users' folders. There is also a Public folder that any user can open.

**QUICK TIP**
Click the Back button, to the left of the Address bar, to return to the window you last viewed. In the Address bar, click ▸ to the right of a folder name to see a list of the subfolders. If the folder is open, its name appears in bold.

6. **Double-click the folder with your user name on it**

   Depending on how your computer is set up, this folder might be labeled with your name; however, if you are using a computer in a lab or a public location, your folder might be called Student or Computer User or something similar. You see a list of folders, such as My Documents, My Music, and others. See Figure B-7.

7. **Double-click My Documents**

   You see the folders and documents you can open and work with. In the Address bar, the path to the My Documents folder is Computer ▸ Local Disk (C:) ▸ Users ▸ Your User Name ▸ My Documents. You decide to return to the Computer window.

8. **In the Navigation pane, click Computer**

   You moved up three levels in your hierarchy. You can also move one level up at a time in your file hierarchy by pressing the [Backspace] key on your keyboard. You once again see your computer's storage devices.

Understanding File Management

**FIGURE B-6:** Computer window showing storage devices

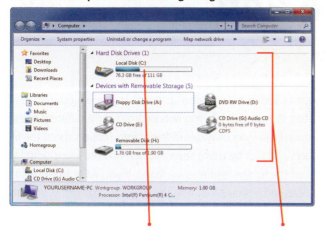

Colored bar indicates
the hard drive is about
one-third full

Your computer's
storage devices
might differ

**FIGURE B-7:** Your User Name folder

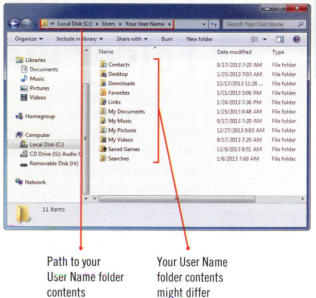

Path to your
User Name folder
contents

Your User Name
folder contents
might differ

**TABLE B-1:** Drive names and icons

| drive type | drive icon | drive name |
|---|---|---|
| hard drive | | C: |
| CD drive | | Next available drive letter, such as D: |
| DVD drive | | Next available drive letter, such as E: |
| USB flash drive | | Next available drive letter, such as F, G:, or H: |

## Sharing information with homegroups and libraries

Windows 7 lets you create a **homegroup**, a named set of computers
that can share information. If your computer is in a homegroup with
other Windows 7 computers, you can share libraries and printers
with those computers. Click Start, then click Control Panel. Under
Network and Internet, click Choose homegroup and sharing options.
Click to place a check mark next to the libraries and printers you
want to share, then click Save changes. To share libraries that you
have created on your computer with others in your homegroup,
click Start, click your user name, then in the Navigation pane, click
the library you want to share, click Share with on the toolbar, then
click the sharing option you want, as shown in Figure B-8.

**FIGURE B-8:** Sharing a library

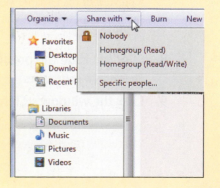

Understanding File Management

# Changing File and Folder Views

As you view your folders and files, you might want to see as many items as possible in a window. At other times, you might want to see details about each item. Windows 7 lets you choose from eight different **views**, which are appearance choices for your folder contents. Each view provides different information about the files and folders in different ways. You can list your folders and files by using several different-sized icons or in lists. You can also **sort** them to change the order in which the folders and files are listed. If you want to see what a file looks like, but don't want to open the file, you can see a preview of it in the window. ▨ As you plan the Oceania tour, you review picture files in various views.

## STEPS

**1. In the Navigation pane, under Libraries, click Pictures, then in the File list, double-click the Sample Pictures folder**

You opened the Sample Pictures folder, which is inside your Pictures library.

**2. In the toolbar, click the More options list arrow next to the Change your view icon ▥▾**

The list of available views appears in a shortcut menu. See Figure B-9.

**QUICK TIP**

You can also click the Change your view button ▤▾ (not its list arrow) repeatedly to cycle through five of the eight views.

**3. Click Large Icons**

In this view, the pictures appear as large-sized icons in the File list, as shown in Figure B-10. For image files, this view is very helpful. You can click any view name or you can drag a slider control to move through each of the available views.

**4. Click the Change your view More options list arrow ▥▾ again, point to the slider ▨ , then drag it so it's next to Details**

As you drag, Live Preview shows you how each view looks in your folder. In Details view, you can see filenames, the date that files were created or modified, and other information. In Details view, you can also control the order in which the folders and files appear. In the Name column heading, you see a small triangle
| Name ⏶ |. This indicates that the sample pictures are in alphabetical order (A, B, C,...).

**QUICK TIP**

Click a column heading a second time to reverse the order.

**5. Click the Name column heading**

The items now appear in descending (Z, Y, X,...) order. The icon in the column header changes to
| Name ⏷ |.

**6. Click the Show the preview pane button ▤ in the toolbar**

The Preview pane opens on the right side of the screen. The **Preview pane** is an area on the right side of a window that shows you what a selected file looks like without opening it. It is especially useful for document files so you can see the first few paragraphs of a large document.

**QUICK TIP**

The Navigation pane also contains Favorites, which are links to folders you use frequently. To add a folder to your Favorites list, open the folder in the File list. Right-click the Favorites link in the Navigation pane, then left-click Add current location to Favorites.

**▶ 7. Click the name of your USB flash drive in the Navigation pane, then click the Oceania Meeting.rtf filename in the File list**

A preview of the Oceania Meeting file you created earlier in this unit appears in the Preview pane. The Word-Pad file is not open, but you can still see its contents. The Details pane gives you information about the selected file. See Figure B-11.

**8. Click the Hide the preview pane button ▢**

The Preview pane closes.

**9. Click the window's Close button ▣**

**FIGURE B-9:** More options shortcut menu showing views

Slider

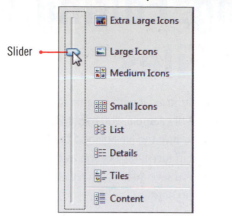

**FIGURE B-10:** Sample pictures library as large icons

Your pictures
might differ

**FIGURE B-11:** Preview of selected Oceania Meeting.rtf file

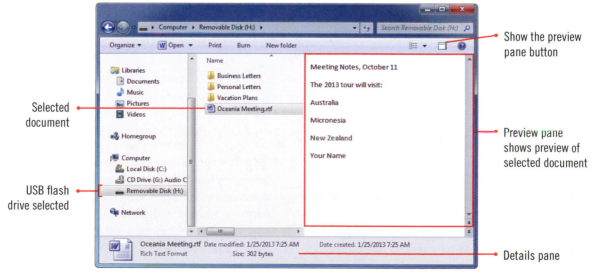

Show the preview
pane button

Selected
document

Preview pane
shows preview of
selected document

USB flash
drive selected

Details pane

Understanding File Management

# Opening, Editing, and Saving Files

Once you have created a file and saved it with a name in a folder on a storage device, you can easily open it and **edit** (make changes to) it. For example, you might want to add or delete text to a document, or change the color in a drawing. Then you save the file again so that it contains your latest changes. Usually you save a file with the same filename and in the same location as the original, which replaces the existing file with the latest, updated version. When you save a file you have changed, you use the Save command.  Evelyn asks you to complete the meeting notes.

STEPS

1.  **Click the Start button 🏁 on the taskbar, point to All Programs, click the Accessories folder, then click WordPad**

    If you use WordPad frequently, it's name might appear on the left side of the Start menu. If it does, you can click it there to open it.

2.  **Click the WordPad button ▣▾, then click Open**

    The Open dialog box opens. It has the same sections as the Save As dialog box and the Windows Explorer windows you used earlier in this unit. You decide to navigate to the location where you saved your Oceania Meeting.rtf file so you can open it.

    > **TROUBLE**
    > If you are not using a USB flash drive, click an appropriate storage location in the Navigation pane.

3.  **Scroll down in the Navigation pane if necessary until you see Computer, then click Removable Disk (H:) (or the drive name and letter for your USB flash drive)**

    The contents of your USB flash drive appear in the File list, as shown in Figure B-12.

    > **QUICK TIP**
    > You can also double-click the filename in the File list to open the file.

4.  **Click Oceania Meeting.rtf in the File list, then click Open**

    The document you created earlier opens.

5.  **Click to the right of the "d" in New Zealand, press [Enter], then type Evelyn Swazey closed the meeting.**

    The edited document includes the text you just typed. See Figure B-13.

    > **QUICK TIP**
    > Instead of using the WordPad menu and Save command to save a document, you can also click the Save button. 🖫 in the Quick Access toolbar at the top of the WordPad window.

6.  **Click the WordPad button ▣▾, then click Save, as shown in Figure B-14**

    WordPad saves the document with your most recent changes, using the filename and location you specified when you saved it for the first time. When you save an existing file, the Save As dialog box does not open.

7.  **Click ▣▾, then click Exit**

## Comparing Save and Save As

The WordPad menu has two save command options—Save and Save As. When you first save a file, the Save As dialog box opens (whether you choose Save or Save As). Here you can select the drive and folder where you want to save the file and enter its filename. If you edit a previously saved file, you can save the file to the same location with the same filename using the Save command. The Save command updates the stored file using the same location and filename without opening the Save As dialog box. In some situations, you might want to save another copy of the existing document using a different filename or in a different storage location. To do this, open the document, use the Save As command, and then navigate to a different location, and/or edit the name of the file.

**FIGURE B-12:** Navigating in the Open dialog box

The folders on your drive will differ

**FIGURE B-13:** Edited document

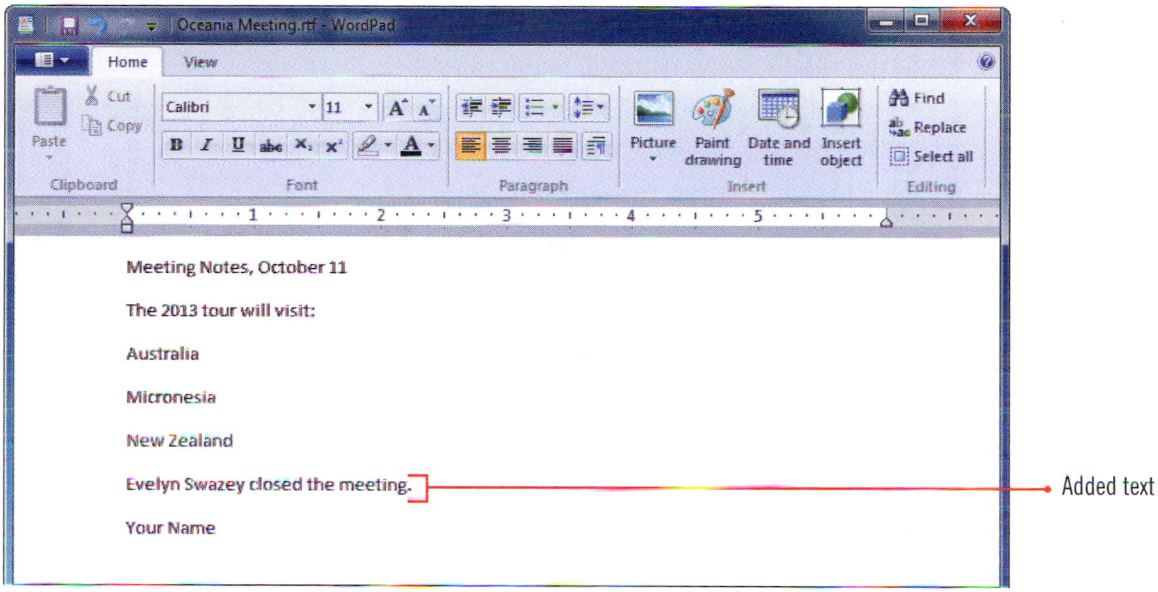

Meeting Notes, October 11

The 2013 tour will visit:

Australia

Micronesia

New Zealand

Evelyn Swazey closed the meeting.          Added text

Your Name

**FIGURE B-14:** Saving a revised document

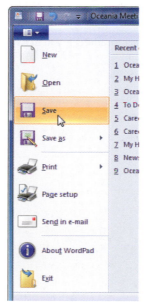

Understanding File Management

# Copying Files

As you have learned, saving a file in a location on your hard drive stores it so you can open it later. But sometimes you will want to make a copy of a file. For example, you might want to put a copy on a USB flash drive so you can open the file on another machine or share a file with a friend or colleague. Or you might want to create a copy as a **backup**, or replacement, in case something happens to your original file. You copy files and folders using the Copy command and then place the copy in another location using the Paste command. You cannot have two copies of a file with the same name in the same folder. If you attempt to do this, Windows 7 will ask you if you want to replace the first one then gives you a chance to give the second copy a different name.  Evelyn asks you to create a backup copy of the meeting notes document you created and paste it in a new folder you create on your USB flash drive.

## STEPS

1.  **Click the Start button 🪟 on the taskbar, then click Computer**

2.  **In the File list, double-click Removable Disk (H:) (or the drive name and letter for your USB flash drive)**
    First you create the new folder Evelyn needs.

3.  **In the toolbar, click the New folder button**
    A new folder appears in the File list, with its name, New folder, selected. Because the folder name is selected, any text you type replaces the selected text as the folder name.

4.  **Type Meeting Notes, then press [Enter]**
    You named the new folder Meeting Notes. Next, you copy your original Oceania Meeting.rtf file.

**QUICK TIP**

You can also copy a file by right-clicking the file in the File list and then clicking Copy. To use the keyboard, press and hold [Ctrl] and press [C], then release both keys.

5.  **In the File list, click the Oceania Meeting.rtf document you saved earlier, click the Organize button on the toolbar, then click Copy, as shown in Figure B-15**
    When you use the Copy command, Windows 7 places a duplicate copy of the file in an area of your computer's random access memory called the **clipboard**, ready to paste, or place, in a new location. Copying and pasting a file leaves the file in its original location. The copied file remains on the clipboard until you copy something else or end your Windows 7 session.

6.  **In the File list, double-click the Meeting Notes folder**
    The folder opens.

**QUICK TIP**

To paste using the keyboard, press and hold [Ctrl] and press [V], then release both keys.

7.  **Click the Organize button on the toolbar, then click Paste**
    A copy of your Oceania Meeting.rtf file is pasted into your new Meeting Notes folder. See Figure B-16. You now have two copies of the Oceania Meeting.rtf file: one on your USB flash drive in the main folder, and a copy of the file in a folder called Meeting Notes on your USB flash drive. The file remains on the clipboard so you can paste it again to other locations if you like.

**FIGURE B-15:** Copying a file

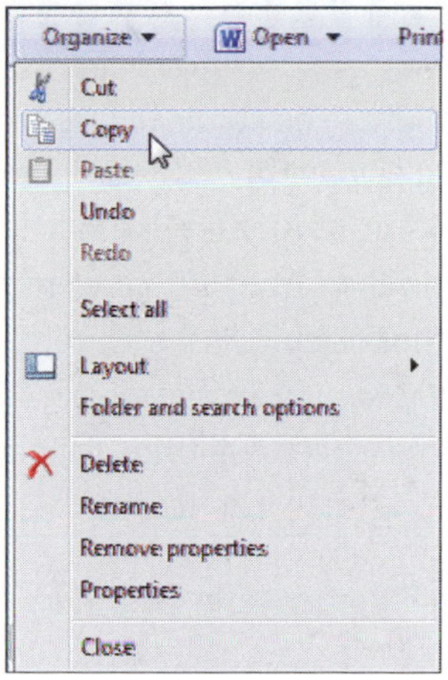

**FIGURE B-16:** Duplicate file pasted into Meeting Notes folder

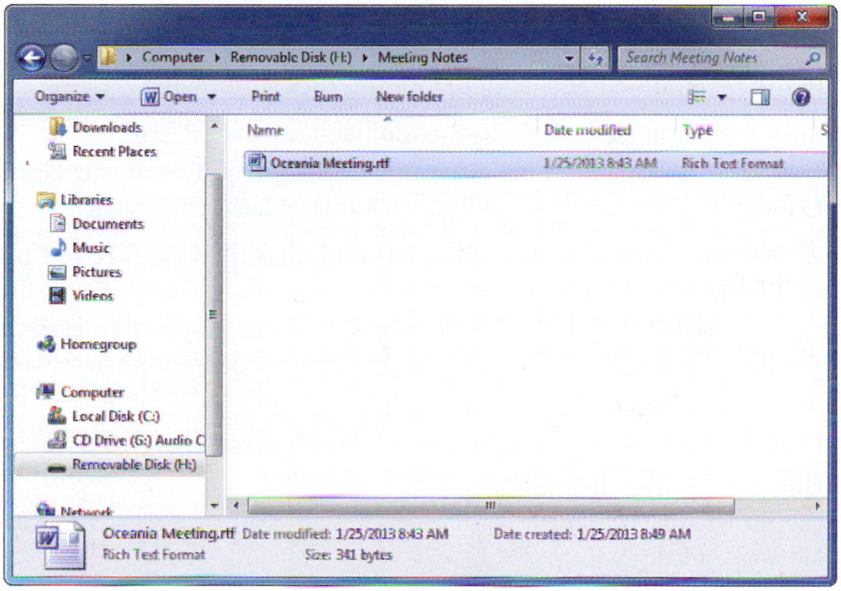

## Copying files using Send to

You can also copy and paste a file to an external storage device using the Send to command. In a window, right-click the file you want to copy, point to Send to, then in the shortcut menu, click the name of the device where you want to send a copy of the file. This leaves the original file on your hard drive and creates a copy on the external device, all with just one command. See Table B-2 for a short summary of other shortcut menu commands.

**TABLE B-2:** Selected Send to menu commands

| menu option | use to | menu option | use to |
|---|---|---|---|
| Compressed (zipped) folder | Create a new compressed (smaller) file with a .zip file extension | Documents | Copy the file to the Documents library |
| Desktop (create shortcut) | Create a shortcut (link) for the file on the desktop | DVD RW Drive (D:) | Copy the file to your computer's DVD drive |
| Mail recipient | Create an e-mail with the file attached to it (only if you have an e-mail program on your computer) | Removable Disk (H:) | Copy the file to your removable disk (H:) |

# Moving and Renaming Files

As you work with files, you might need to move files or folders to another location. You can move one or more files or folders. You might move them to a different folder on the same drive or a different drive. When you **move** a file, the file is transferred to the new location and no longer exists in its original location. You can move a file using the Cut and Paste commands. After you create a file, you might find that the original name you gave the file isn't clear anymore, so you can rename it to make it more descriptive or accurate.  You decide to move your original Oceania Meeting.rtf document to your Documents library. After you move it, you decide to edit the filename so it better describes the file contents.

## STEPS

**QUICK TIP**

You can also cut a file by right-clicking the file in the File list and then clicking Cut. To use the keyboard, press and hold [Ctrl] and press [X], then release both keys.

**QUICK TIP**

You can also paste a file by right-clicking an empty area in the File list and then clicking Paste. To use the keyboard, press and hold [Ctrl] and press [V], then release both keys.

1. **In the Address bar, click Removable Disk (H:) (or the drive name and letter for your USB flash drive)**

2. **Click the Oceania Meeting.rtf document to select it**

3. **Click the Organize button on the toolbar, then click Cut**

   The icon representing the cut file becomes lighter in color, indicating you have cut it, as shown in Figure B-17. You navigate to your Documents library, in preparation for pasting the cut document there.

4. **In the Navigation Pane, under Libraries, click Documents**

5. **Click the Organize button on the toolbar, then click Paste**

   The Oceania Meeting.rtf document appears in your Documents library. See Figure B-18. The filename could be clearer, to help you remember that it contains notes from your meeting.

6. **With the Oceania Meeting.rtf file selected, click the Organize button on the toolbar, then click Rename**

   The filename is highlighted. In a window, the file extension cannot change because it identifies the file to WordPad. If you delete the file extension, the file cannot be opened. You could type a new name to replace the old one, but you decide to add the word "Notes" to the end of the filename instead.

7. **Click the I after the "g" in "Meeting", press [Spacebar], then type Notes, as shown in Figure B-19, then press [Enter]**

   You changed the name of the document copy in the Documents library. The filename now reads Oceania Meeting Notes.rtf.

8. **Close the window**

**FIGURE B-17:** Cutting a file

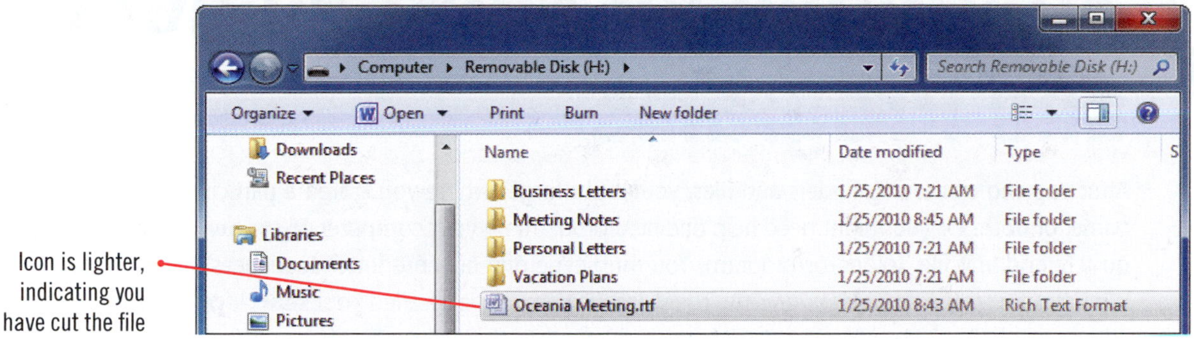

Icon is lighter, indicating you have cut the file

| Name | Date modified | Type |
|------|---------------|------|
| Business Letters | 1/25/2010 7:21 AM | File folder |
| Meeting Notes | 1/25/2010 8:45 AM | File folder |
| Personal Letters | 1/25/2010 7:21 AM | File folder |
| Vacation Plans | 1/25/2010 7:21 AM | File folder |
| Oceania Meeting.rtf | 1/25/2010 8:43 AM | Rich Text Format |

**FIGURE B-18:** Pasted file in Documents library

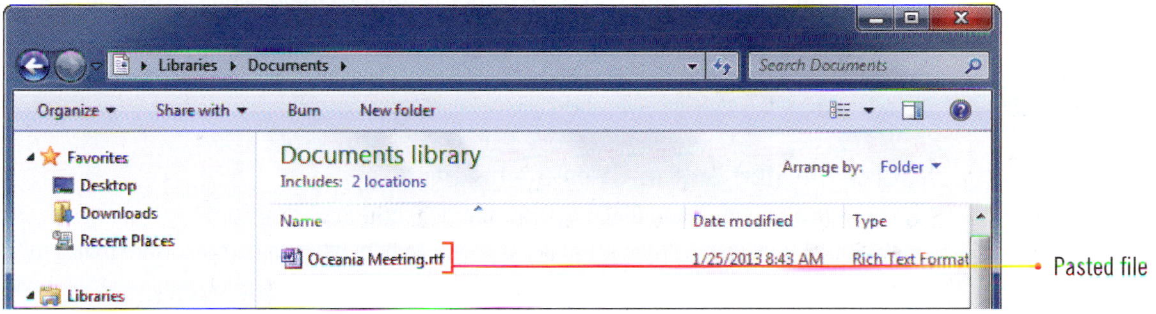

Documents library
Includes: 2 locations

| Name | Date modified | Type |
|------|---------------|------|
| Oceania Meeting.rtf | 1/25/2013 8:43 AM | Rich Text Format |

Pasted file

**FIGURE B-19:** Renaming a file

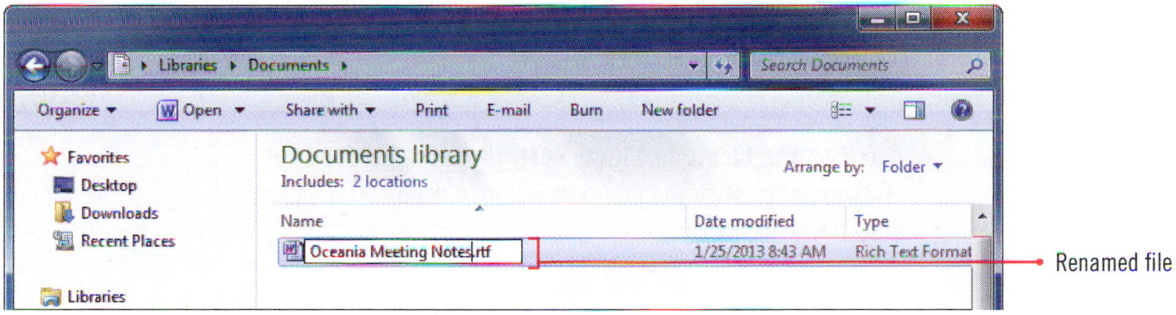

Documents library
Includes: 2 locations

| Name | Date modified | Type |
|------|---------------|------|
| Oceania Meeting Notes.rtf | 1/25/2013 8:43 AM | Rich Text Format |

Renamed file

## Using drag and drop to copy or move files to new locations

You can also use the mouse to copy a file and place the copy in a new location. **Drag and drop** is a technique in which you use your pointing device to drag a file or folder into a different folder and then drop it, or let go of the mouse button, to place it in that folder. Using drag and drop does not copy your file to the clipboard. If you drag and drop a file to a folder on another drive, Windows *copies* the file. See Figure B-20. However, if you drag and drop a file to a folder on the same drive, Windows 7 *moves* the file into that folder instead. If you want to move a file to another drive, hold down [Shift] while you drag and drop. If you want to copy a file to another folder on the same drive, hold down [Ctrl] while you drag and drop.

**FIGURE B-20:** Copying a file using drag and drop

# Searching for Files, Folders, and Programs

After copying or moving folders and files, you might forget where you stored a particular folder or file, its name, or both. Or you might need help finding a program on your computer. **Windows Search** helps you quickly find any file, folder, or program. You must type one or more letter sequences or words that help Windows 7 identify the item you want. The search text you type is called your **search criteria**. Your search criteria can be a filename, part of a filename, or any other characters you choose. Windows 7 will find files with that information in its name or with that information inside the file. For example, if you type "word," Windows 7 will find the program Microsoft Word, any documents with "word" in its title, or any document with "word" inside the file. To search your entire computer, including its attached drives, you can use the Search box on the Start menu. To search within a particular folder, you can use the Search box in a Windows Explorer window.  You want to locate the copy of the Oceania Meeting Notes.rtf document so you can print it for a colleague.

## STEPS

1. **Click the Start button 🏁 on the taskbar**

    The Search programs and files box at the bottom of the Start menu already contains the insertion point, ready for you to type search criteria. You begin your search by typing a part of a word that is in the filename.

2. **Type me**

    Even before you finish typing the word "meeting", the Start menu lists all programs, files, and Control Panel items that have the letters "me" in their title or somewhere inside the file or the file properties. See Figure B-21. Your search results will differ, depending on the programs and files on your computer. **File properties** are details that Windows stores about a file. Windows arranges the search results into categories.

3. **Type e**

    The search results narrow to only the files that contain "mee". The search results become more specific every time you add more text to your criteria finding the two versions of your meeting notes file. See Figure B-22.

4. **Point to the Oceania Meeting.rtf filename under Files**

    The ScreenTip shows the file location. This Oceania Meeting.rtf file is on the USB flash drive. The filenames are links to the document. You only need to single-click a file to open it.

5. **Under Documents, click Oceania Meeting Notes.rtf**

    The file opens in WordPad.

6. **Click the Close button ✖ in the program window's title bar**

    You can search in a folder or on a drive using the search box in any Windows Explorer window.

7. **Click 🏁, click Computer, in the Navigation pane click Removable Disk (H:) (or the drive name and letter for your USB flash drive)**

8. **Click the Search Removable Disk (H:) text box, to the right of the Address bar**

9. **Type mee to list all files and folders on your USB flash drive that contain "mee"**

    The search criterion, mee, is highlighted in the filenames. The results include the folder called Meeting Notes and the file named Oceania Meeting.rtf. Because you navigated to your USB flash drive, Windows only lists the document version that is on that drive. See Figure B-23.

10. **Double-click Oceania Meeting.rtf in the File list to open the document file in WordPad, view the file, close WordPad, then close the Windows Explorer window**

**QUICK TIP**

Search text is not case sensitive. Typing lowercase "mee", you will still find items that start with "Mee" or "mee".

**TROUBLE**

Your file might open in another program on your computer that reads RTF files. You can continue with the lesson.

**TROUBLE**

If you do not have a USB flash drive, click another storage location in the Navigation pane.

**FIGURE B-21:** Searching on criterion "me"

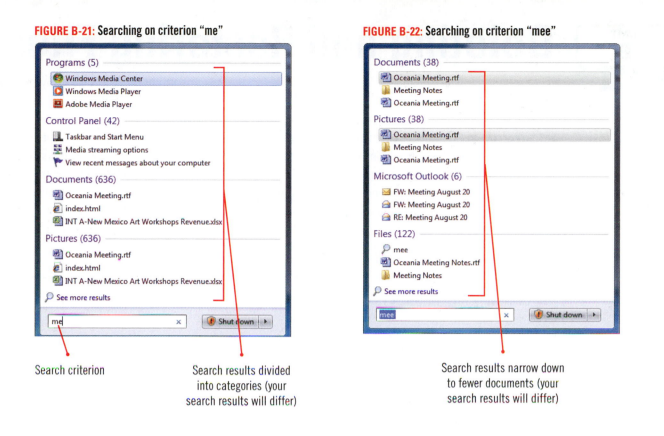

Search criterion

Search results divided
into categories (your
search results will differ)

**FIGURE B-22:** Searching on criterion "mee"

Search results narrow down
to fewer documents (your
search results will differ)

**FIGURE B-23:** Searching using the Search Computer text box in folder window

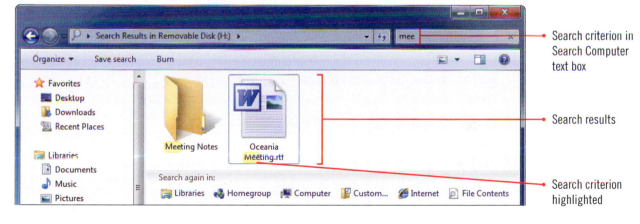

Search criterion in
Search Computer
text box

Search results

Search criterion
highlighted

## Performing more advanced searches

To locate all files that have the same file extension (such as .rtf), type the file extension as your search criterion. If you want to locate files created by a certain person, use the first name, last name, or first and last name as your search criteria. If you want to locate files created on a certain date, type the date (for example, 7/9/2012) as your search criterion. If you remember the title in a document, type the title as your search criterion. If you have created e-mail contacts in your Contacts folder, you can type the person's name to find his or her e-mail address.

# Deleting and Restoring Files

If you no longer need a folder or file, you can delete (or remove) it from the storage device. By regularly deleting files and folders you no longer need and emptying the Recycle Bin, you free up valuable storage space on your computer. This also keeps your computer uncluttered. Windows 7 places folders and files you delete from your hard drive in the Recycle Bin. If you delete a folder, Windows 7 removes the folder as well as all files and subfolders stored in it. If you later discover that you need a deleted file or folder, you can restore it to its original location, but only if you have not yet emptied the Recycle Bin. Emptying the Recycle Bin permanently removes the deleted folders and files from your computer. However, files and folders you delete from a removable drive, such as a USB flash drive, do not go to the Recycle Bin. They are immediately and permanently deleted and cannot be restored. 🎨 You delete the meeting notes copy saved in the Documents library and then restore it.

## STEPS

1. **Click the Start button 🏁 on the taskbar, then click Documents**
   Your Documents library opens.

2. **Click Oceania Meeting Notes.rtf to select it, click the Organize button on the toolbar, then click Delete**
   The Delete File dialog box opens so you can confirm the deletion, as shown in Figure B-24.

3. **Click Yes**
   You deleted the file from the Documents library. Windows moved it into the Recycle Bin.

**QUICK TIP**
If the Recycle Bin icon does not contain crumpled paper, then it is empty.

4. **Click the Minimize button 🔲 on the window's title bar and examine the Recycle Bin icon**
   The Recycle Bin icon appears to contain crumpled paper. This tells you that the Recycle Bin contains deleted folders and files.

5. **Double-click the Recycle Bin icon on the desktop**
   The Recycle Bin window opens and displays any previously deleted folders and files, including the Oceania Meeting Notes.rtf file.

6. **Click the Oceania Meeting Notes.rtf file to select it, then click the Restore this item button on the Recycle Bin toolbar, as shown in Figure B-25**
   The file returns to its original location and no longer appears in the Recycle Bin window.

**QUICK TIP**
To delete a file completely in one action, click the file to select it, press and hold [Shift], then press [Delete]. A message will ask if you want to permanently delete the file. If you click Yes, Windows deletes the file without sending it to the Recycle Bin. Use caution, however, because you cannot restore the file.

7. **In the Navigation pane, click the Documents library**
   The Documents library window contains the restored file. You decide to permanently delete this file.

8. **Click the Oceania Meeting Notes.rtf file, press the [Delete] key on your keyboard, then click Yes in the Delete File dialog box**
   The Oceania Meeting Notes.rtf file moves from the Documents library to the Recycle Bin. You decide to permanently delete all documents in the Recycle Bin.
   NOTE: If you are using a computer that belongs to someone else, or that is in a computer lab, make sure you have permission to empty the Recycle Bin before proceeding with the next step.

9. **Minimize the window, double-click the Recycle Bin, click the Empty the Recycle Bin button on the toolbar, click Yes in the dialog box, then close all open windows**

**FIGURE B-24:** Delete File dialog box

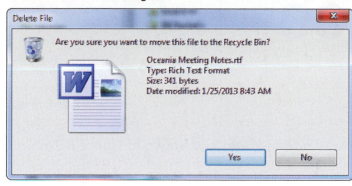

**FIGURE B-25:** Restoring a file from the Recycle Bin

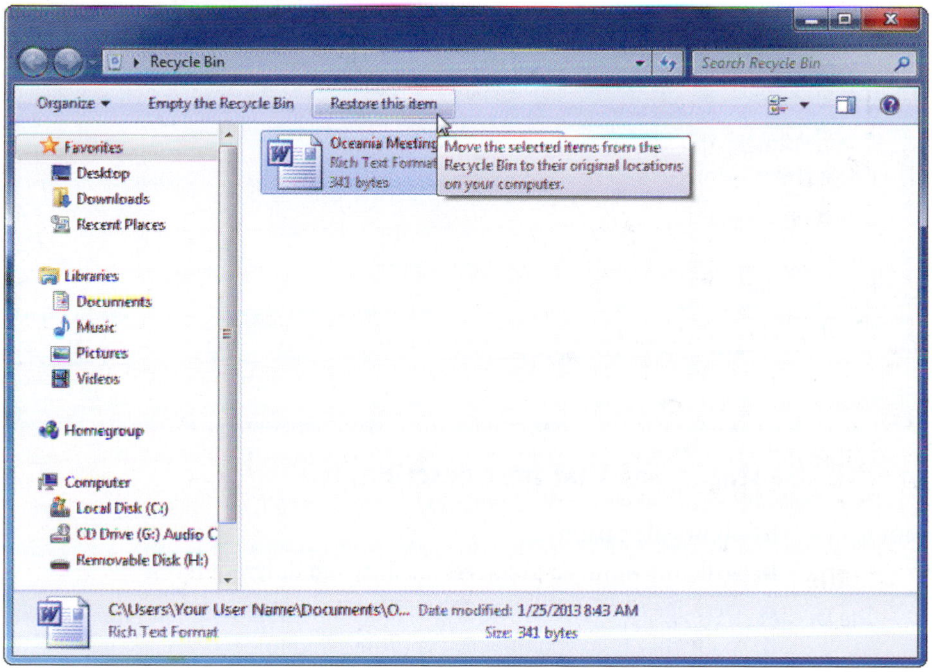

## Selecting more than one file

You might want to select a group of files or folders in order to cut, copy, or delete them all at once. To select a group of items that are next to each other in a window, click the first item in the group, press and hold [Shift], then click the last item in the group. Both items you click and all the items between them become selected. To select files that are not next to each other, click the first file, press and hold [Ctrl], then click the other items you want to select as a group. Then you can copy, cut, or delete the group of files or folders you selected.

# Practice

**SAM**

For current SAM information, including versions and content details, visit SAM Central (http://samcentral.course.com). If you have a SAM user profile, you may have access to hands-on instruction, practice, and assessment of the skills covered in this unit. Since various versions of SAM are supported throughout the life of this text, check with your instructor for the correct instructions and URL/Web site for accessing assignments.

## Concepts Review

**Label the elements of the Windows 7 window shown in Figure B-26.**

**FIGURE B-26**

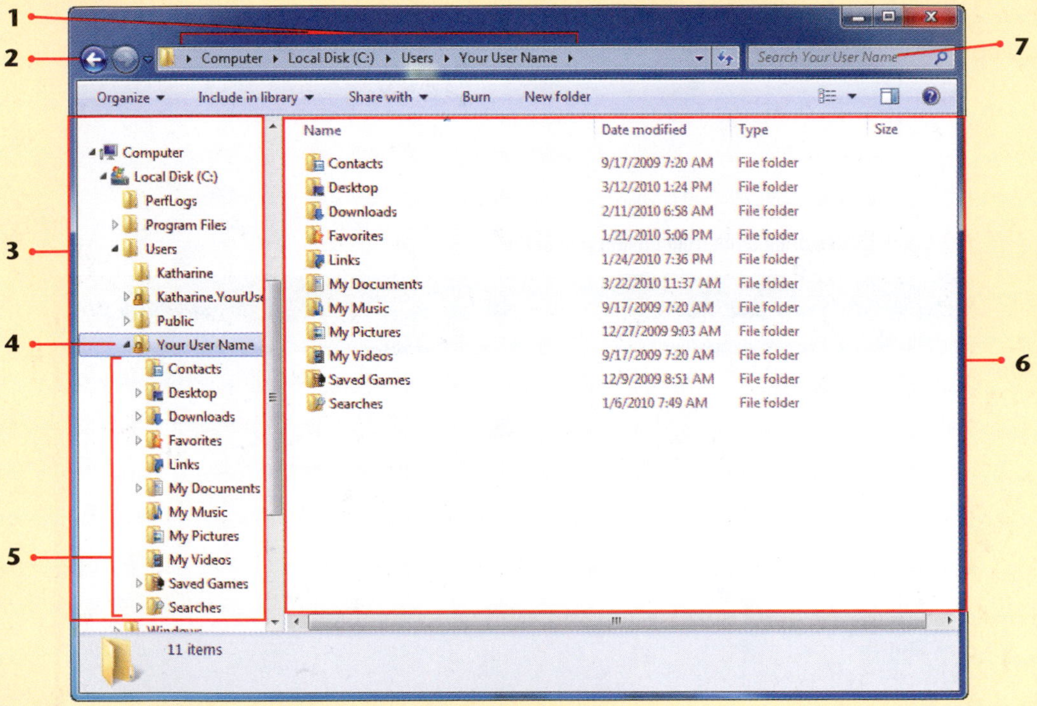

**Match each term with the statement that best describes it.**

| | | |
|---|---|---|
| 8. File management | a. | Shows file's path |
| 9. File extension | b. | Structure of files and folders organized in different levels |
| 10. Address bar | c. | Describes a file's location in the file hierarchy |
| 11. Path | d. | Skills that help you organize your files and folders |
| 12. Library | e. | Contains buttons in a Windows Explorer window |
| 13. Toolbar | f. | A three- or four-letter sequence, preceded by a period, that identifies the type of file |
| 14. File hierarchy | g. | Gathers files and folders from different computer locations |

**Select the best answer from the list of choices.**

15. **The way your files appear in the Details window is determined by the:**
   a. Path.
   b. View.
   c. Subfolder.
   d. Criterion.

16. **When you move a file:**
   a. It remains in its original location.
   b. It is no longer in its original location.
   c. It is copied to another location.
   d. It is no longer in your file hierarchy.

17. **The text you type in the Search programs and files box on the Start menu is called:**
   a. Search criteria.
   b. RAM.
   c. Sorting.
   d. Clipboard.

18. **Which of the following is not a window section?**
a. Address bar
c. Navigation pane
b. File list
d. Clipboard

19. **Which part of a window lets you see a file's contents without opening the file?**
a. File list
c. Navigation pane
b. Preview pane
d. Address bar

20. **In a file hierarchy, a folder inside another folder is called a:**
a. Subfolder.
c. Clipboard.
b. Internal hard disk.
d. Path.

21. **After you delete a file from your hard disk, it is automatically placed in the:**
a. USB flash drive.
c. Recycle bin.
b. Clipboard.
d. Search box.

22. **When you copy a file, it is automatically placed on the:**
a. Preview pane.
c. Hierarchy.
b. My Documents folder.
d. Clipboard.

# Skills Review

1. **Understand folders and files.**
   a. Assume that you sell books as a home business. How would you organize your folders and files using a file hierarchy? How would you use folders and subfolders? Draw a diagram and write a short paragraph explaining your answer.

2. **Create and save a file.**
   a. Connect your USB flash drive to a USB port on your computer, then open WordPad from the All Programs menu.
   b. Type **Marketing Plan: Oceania Tours** as the title, then start a new line.
   c. Type your name, then press [Enter] twice.
   d. Create the following list:
      **Brochures**
      **Direct e-mail**
      **Web ads**
      **Travel conventions**
   e. Save the WordPad file with the filename **Oceania Marketing Plan.rtf** on your USB flash drive.
   f. View the filename in the WordPad title bar, then close WordPad.

3. **Explore the files and folders on your computer.**
   a. Open a Windows Explorer window that shows the contents of your computer.
   b. Use the File list to navigate to your USB flash drive. (If you do not have a USB flash drive, navigate to your Documents library using the Navigation pane.)
   c. Use the Address bar to navigate to Computer again.
   d. Use the Navigation pane to navigate to your hard drive.
   e. Use the File list to open the Users folder, and then open the folder that represents your user name.
   f. Open the My Documents folder. (*Hint*: The path is Local Disk (C:) ▸ Users ▸ [Your User Name] ▸ My Documents.)
   g. Use the Navigation pane to navigate back to your computer contents.

4. **Change file and folder views.**
   a. Navigate to your USB flash drive using the method of your choice.
   b. View its contents as large icons.
   c. Use the View slider to view the drive contents in all the other seven views.
   d. Use the Change your view button to cycle through the five available views.
   e. Open the Preview pane, then click a file and view its preview. Repeat with two more files.
   f. Close the Preview pane.

5. **Open, edit, and save files.**

   **a.** Open WordPad.

   **b.** Use the Open dialog box to open the Oceania Marketing Plan.rtf document you created.

   **c.** After the text "Travel conventions," add a line with the text **Canadian magazines**.

   **d.** Save the document and close WordPad.

6. **Copy files.**

   **a.** In the Windows Explorer window, navigate to your USB flash drive if necessary.

   **b.** Copy the Oceania Marketing Plan.rtf document.

   **c.** Create a new folder named **Marketing** on your USB flash drive, then open the folder. (If you don't have a USB flash drive, create the folder in your Documents library.)

   **d.** Paste the document copy in the new folder.

7. **Move and rename files.**

   **a.** Navigate to your USB flash drive.

   **b.** Select the original Oceania Marketing Plan.rtf document, then cut it.

   **c.** Navigate to your Documents library and paste the file there.

   **d.** Rename the file **Oceania Marketing Plan - Backup.rtf**.

8. **Search for files, folders, and programs.**

   **a.** Use the Search programs and files box on the Start menu to enter the search criterion **ma**.

   **b.** Change your search criterion so it reads **mar**.

   **c.** Open the backup copy of your Oceania Marketing Plan document from the Start menu, then close WordPad.

   **d.** In Windows Explorer, navigate to your Documents library, then use the criterion **mar** in the Search Documents box.

   **e.** Open the backup copy of the Oceania Marketing Plan document from the File list, then close WordPad.

9. **Delete and restore files.**

   **a.** Navigate to your Documents library if necessary.

   **b.** Delete the Oceania Marketing Plan - Backup.rtf file.

   **c.** Open the Recycle Bin, and restore the document to its original location, navigate to your Documents library, then move the Oceania Marketing Plan - Backup file to your USB flash drive.

# Independent Challenge 1

To meet the needs of pet owners in your town, you have opened a pet-sitting business named PetCare. Customers hire you to care for their pets in their own homes when the pet owners go on vacation. To promote your new business, you want to develop a newspaper ad and a flyer.

   **a.** Connect your USB flash drive to your computer, if necessary.

   **b.** Create a new folder named **PetCare** on your USB flash drive.

   **c.** In the PetCare folder, create two subfolders named **Advertising** and **Flyers**.

   **d.** Use WordPad to create a short ad for your local newspaper that describes your business:

   • Use the name of the business as the title for your document.

   • Write a short paragraph about the business. Include a fictitious location, street address, and phone number.

   • After the paragraph, type your name.

   **e.** Save the WordPad document with the filename **Newspaper Ad** in the Advertising folder, then close the document and exit WordPad.

   **f.** Open a Windows Explorer window, and navigate to the Advertising folder.

   **g.** View the contents in at least three different views, then choose the view option that you prefer.

   **h.** Copy the Newspaper Ad.rtf file, and paste a copy in the Flyers folder.

   **i.** Rename the copy **Newspaper Ad Backup.rtf**.

   **j.** Close the folder.

# Independent Challenge 2

As a freelance editor for several national publishers, you depend on your computer to meet critical deadlines. Whenever you encounter a computer problem, you contact a computer consultant who helps you resolve the problem. This consultant asked you to document, or keep records of, your computer's current settings.

a. Connect your USB flash drive to your computer, if necessary.

b. Open the Computer window so that you can view information on your drives and other installed hardware.

c. View the window contents using three different views, then choose the one you prefer.

d. Open WordPad and create a document with the title **My Hardware Documentation** and your name on separate lines.

e. List the names of the hard drive (or drives), devices with removable storage, and any other hardware devices, installed on the computer you are using. Also include the total size and amount of free space on your hard drive(s) and removable storage drive(s). (*Hint*: If you need to check the Computer window for this information, use the taskbar button for the Computer window to view your drives, then use the WordPad taskbar button to return to WordPad.)

### Advanced Challenge Exercise

■ Navigate your computer's file hierarchy, and determine its various levels.

■ On paper, draw a diagram showing your file hierarchy, starting with Computer at the top, and going down at least four levels if available.

f. Save the WordPad document with the filename **My Hardware Documentation** on your USB flash drive.

g. Preview your document, print your WordPad document, then close WordPad.

# Independent Challenge 3

You are an attorney at Lopez, Rickland, and Willgor, a large law firm. You participate in your firm's community outreach program by speaking at career days in area high schools. You teach students about career opportunities available in the field of law. You want to create a folder structure on your USB flash drive to store the files for each session.

a. Connect your USB flash drive to your computer, then open the window for your USB flash drive.

b. Create a folder named **Career Days**.

c. In the Career Days folder, create a subfolder named **Mather High**.

### Advanced Challenge Exercise

■ In the Mather High folder, create subfolders named **Class Outline** and **Visual Aids**.

■ Rename the Visual Aids folder **Class Handouts**.

■ Create a new folder named **Interactive Presentations** in the Class Handouts subfolder.

d. Close the Mather High window.

e. Use WordPad to create a document with the title **Career Areas** and your name on separate lines, and the following list of items:
**Current Opportunities:**
**Attorney**
**Corrections Officer**
**Forensic Scientist**
**Paralegal**
**Judge**

f. Save the WordPad document with the filename **Careers Listing.rtf** in the Mather High folder. (*Hint:* After you switch to your USB flash drive in the Save As dialog box, open the Career Days folder, then open the Mather High folder before saving the file.)

g. Close WordPad.

## Independent Challenge 3 (continued)

**h.** Open WordPad and the Careers Listing document again, then add **Court Reporter** to the bottom of the list, then save the file and close WordPad.

**i.** Using pencil and paper, draw a diagram of your new folder structure.

**j.** Use the Start menu to search your computer using the search criterion **car**. Locate the Careers Listing.rtf document in the list, and use the link to open the file.

**k.** Close the file.

## Real Life Independent Challenge

Think of a hobby or volunteer activity that you do now, or one that you would like to do. You will use your computer to help you manage your plans or ideas for this activity.

**a.** Using paper and a pencil, sketch a folder structure using at least two subfolders that you could create on your USB flash drive to contain your documents for this activity.

**b.** Connect your USB flash drive to your computer, then open the window for your USB flash drive.

**c.** Create the folder structure for your activity, using your sketch as a reference.

**d.** Think of at least three tasks that you can do to further your work in your chosen activity.

**e.** Open WordPad and create a document with the title **Next Steps** at the top of the page and your name on the next line.

**f.** List the three tasks, then save the file in one of the folders you created on your USB flash drive, using the title **To Do.rtf**.

**g.** Close WordPad, then open a Windows Explorer window for the folder where you stored the document.

**h.** Create a copy of the file, give the copy a new name, then place a copy of the document in your Documents library.

**i.** Delete the document copy from your Documents library.

**j.** Open the Recycle Bin window, and restore the document to the Documents library.

## Visual Workshop

You are a technical support specialist at Emergency Services. The company supplies medical staff members to hospital emergency rooms in Los Angeles. You need to respond to your company's employee questions quickly and thoroughly. You decide that it is time to evaluate and reorganize the folder structure on your computer. That way, you'll be able to respond more quickly to staff requests. Create the folder structure shown in Figure B-27 on your USB flash drive. As you work, use WordPad to prepare a simple outline of the steps you follow to create the folder structure. Add your name to the document, and store it in an appropriate location.

**FIGURE B-27**

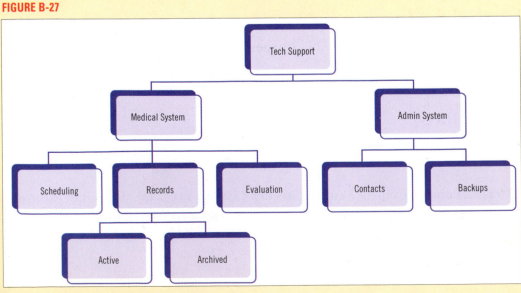

# Getting Started with Microsoft Office 2010

**Files You Will Need:**

OFFICE A-1.xlsx

Microsoft Office 2010 is a group of software programs designed to help you create documents, collaborate with coworkers, and track and analyze information. Each program is designed so you can work quickly and efficiently to create professional-looking results. You use different Office programs to accomplish specific tasks, such as writing a letter or producing a sales presentation, yet all the programs have a similar look and feel. Once you become familiar with one program, you'll find it easy to transfer your knowledge to the others. This unit introduces you to the most frequently used programs in Office, as well as common features they all share.

**OBJECTIVES**

Understand the Office 2010 suite

Start and exit an Office program

View the Office 2010 user interface

Create and save a file

Open a file and save it with a new name

View and print your work

Get Help and close a file

# Understanding the Office 2010 Suite

Microsoft Office 2010 features an intuitive, context-sensitive user interface, so you can get up to speed faster and use advanced features with greater ease. The programs in Office are bundled together in a group called a **suite** (although you can also purchase them separately). The Office suite is available in several configurations, but all include Word, Excel, and PowerPoint. Other configurations include Access, Outlook, Publisher, and other programs.  Each program in Office is best suited for completing specific types of tasks, though there is some overlap in capabilities.

### The Office programs covered in this book include:

- **Microsoft Word 2010**

  When you need to create any kind of text-based document, such as a memo, newsletter, or multipage report, Word is the program to use. You can easily make your documents look great by inserting eye-catching graphics and using formatting tools such as themes, which are available in most Office programs. **Themes** are predesigned combinations of color and formatting attributes you can apply to a document. The Word document shown in Figure A-1 was formatted with the Solstice theme.

- **Microsoft Excel 2010**

  Excel is the perfect solution when you need to work with numeric values and make calculations. It puts the power of formulas, functions, charts, and other analytical tools into the hands of every user, so you can analyze sales projections, calculate loan payments, and present your findings in style. The Excel worksheet shown in Figure A-1 tracks personal expenses. Because Excel automatically recalculates results whenever a value changes, the information is always up to date. A chart illustrates how the monthly expenses are broken down.

- **Microsoft PowerPoint 2010**

  Using PowerPoint, it's easy to create powerful presentations complete with graphics, transitions, and even a soundtrack. Using professionally designed themes and clip art, you can quickly and easily create dynamic slide shows such as the one shown in Figure A-1.

- **Microsoft Access 2010**

  Access helps you keep track of large amounts of quantitative data, such as product inventories or employee records. The form shown in Figure A-1 was created for a grocery store inventory database. Employees use the form to enter data about each item. Using Access enables employees to quickly find specific information such as price and quantity without hunting through store shelves and stockrooms.

### Microsoft Office has benefits beyond the power of each program, including:

- **Common user interface: Improving business processes**

  Because the Office suite programs have a similar **interface**, or look and feel, your experience using one program's tools makes it easy to learn those in the other programs. In addition, Office documents are **compatible** with one another, meaning that you can easily incorporate, or **integrate**, an Excel chart into a PowerPoint slide, or an Access table into a Word document.

- **Collaboration: Simplifying how people work together**

  Office recognizes the way people do business today, and supports the emphasis on communication and knowledge sharing within companies and across the globe. All Office programs include the capability to incorporate feedback—called **online collaboration**—across the Internet or a company network.

**FIGURE A-1:** Microsoft Office 2010 documents

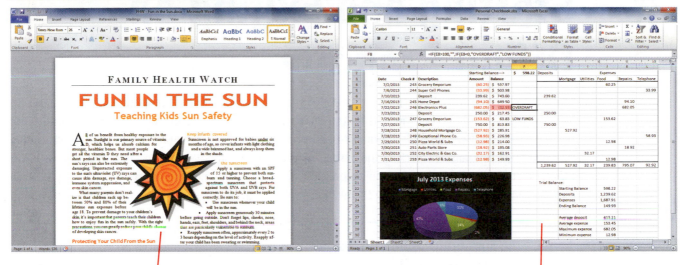

Newsletter created in Word

Checkbook register created in Excel

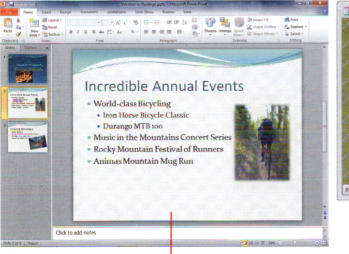

Tourism presentation created in PowerPoint

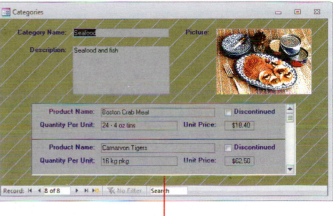

Store inventory form created in Access

## Deciding which program to use

Every Office program includes tools that go far beyond what you might expect. For example, although Excel is primarily designed for making calculations, you can use it to create a database. So when you're planning a project, how do you decide which Office program to use? The general rule of thumb is to use the program best suited for your intended task, and make use of supporting tools in the program if you need them. Word is best for creating text-based documents, Excel is best for making mathematical calculations, PowerPoint is best for preparing presentations, and Access is best for managing quantitative data. Although the capabilities of Office are so vast that you *could* create an inventory in Excel or a budget in Word, you'll find greater flexibility and efficiency by using the program designed for the task. And remember, you can always create a file in one program, and then insert it in a document in another program when you need to, such as including sales projections (Excel) in a memo (Word).

# Starting and Exiting an Office Program

The first step in using an Office program is to open, or **launch**, it on your computer. The easiest ways to launch a program are to click the Start button on the Windows taskbar or to double-click an icon on your desktop. You can have multiple programs open on your computer simultaneously, and you can move between open programs by clicking the desired program or document button on the taskbar or by using the [Alt][Tab] keyboard shortcut combination.  When working, you'll often want to open multiple programs in Office and switch among them as you work. Begin by launching a few Office programs now.

## STEPS

**QUICK TIP**
You can also launch a program by double-clicking a desktop icon or clicking the program name on the Start menu.

1. **Click the Start button ⊕ on the taskbar**

   The Start menu opens. If the taskbar is hidden, you can display it by pointing to the bottom of the screen. Depending on your taskbar property settings, the taskbar may be displayed at all times, or only when you point to that area of the screen. For more information, or to change your taskbar properties, consult your instructor or technical support person.

2. **Click All Programs, scroll down if necessary in the All Programs menu, click Microsoft Office as shown in Figure A-2, then click Microsoft Word 2010**

   Word 2010 starts, and the program window opens on your screen.

**QUICK TIP**
It is not necessary to close one program before opening another.

3. **Click ⊕ on the taskbar, click All Programs, click Microsoft Office, then click Microsoft Excel 2010**

   Excel 2010 starts, and the program window opens, as shown in Figure A-3. Word is no longer visible, but it remains open. The taskbar displays a button for each open program and document. Because this Excel document is **active**, or in front and available, the Excel button on the taskbar appears slightly lighter.

**QUICK TIP**
As you work in Windows, your computer adapts to your activities. You may notice that after clicking the Start button, the name of the program you want to open appears in the Start menu above All Programs; if so, you can click it to start the program.

4. **Point to the Word program button 🄦 on the taskbar, then click 🄦**

   The Word program window is now in front. When the Aero feature is turned on in Windows 7, pointing to a program button on the taskbar displays a thumbnail version of each open window in that program above the program button. Clicking a program button on the taskbar activates that program and the most recently active document. Clicking a thumbnail of a document activates that document.

5. **Click ⊕ on the taskbar, click All Programs, click Microsoft Office, then click Microsoft PowerPoint 2010**

   PowerPoint 2010 starts and becomes the active program.

6. **Click the Excel program button 🄴 on the taskbar**

   Excel is now the active program.

**TROUBLE**
If you don't have Access installed on your computer, proceed to the next lesson.

7. **Click ⊕ on the taskbar, click All Programs, click Microsoft Office, then click Microsoft Access 2010**

   Access 2010 starts and becomes the active program. Now all four Office programs are open at the same time.

8. **Click Exit on the navigation bar in the Access program window, as shown in Figure A-4**

   Access closes, leaving Excel active and Word and PowerPoint open.

---

### Using shortcut keys to move between Office programs

As an alternative to the Windows taskbar, you can use a keyboard shortcut to move among open Office programs. The [Alt][Tab] keyboard combination lets you either switch quickly to the next open program or file or choose one from a gallery. To switch immediately to the next open program or file, press [Alt][Tab]. To choose from all open programs and files, press and hold [Alt], then press and release [Tab] without releasing [Alt]. A gallery opens on screen, displaying the filename and a thumbnail image of each open program and file, as well as of the desktop. Each time you press [Tab] while holding [Alt], the selection cycles to the next open file or location. Release [Alt] when the program, file, or location you want to activate is selected.

**FIGURE A-2:** Start menu

**FIGURE A-3:** Excel program window and Windows taskbar

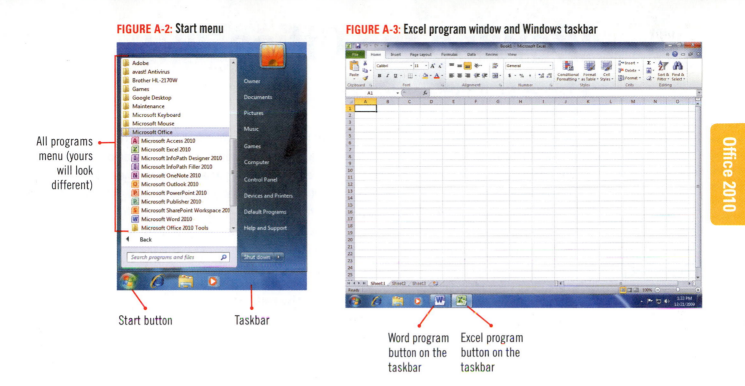

All programs menu (yours will look different)

Start button

Taskbar

Word program button on the taskbar

Excel program button on the taskbar

**FIGURE A-4:** Access program window

File tab

Navigation bar

Exit command

## Windows Live and Microsoft Office Web Apps

All Office programs include the capability to incorporate feedback—called online collaboration—across the Internet or a company network. Using **cloud computing** (work done in a virtual environment), you can take advantage of Web programs called Microsoft Office Web Apps, which are simplified versions of the programs found in the Microsoft Office 2010 suite. Because these programs are online, they take up no computer disk space and are accessed using

Windows Live SkyDrive, a free service from Microsoft. Using Windows Live SkyDrive, you and your colleagues can create and store documents in a "cloud" and make the documents available to whomever you grant access. To use Windows Live SkyDrive, you need a free Windows Live ID, which you obtain at the Windows Live Web site. You can find more information in the "Working with Windows Live and Office Web Apps" appendix.

# Viewing the Office 2010 User Interface

One of the benefits of using Office is that the programs have much in common, making them easy to learn and making it simple to move from one to another. Individual Office programs have always shared many features, but the innovations in the Office 2010 user interface mean even greater similarity among them all. That means you can also use your knowledge of one program to get up to speed in another. A **user interface** is a collective term for all the ways you interact with a software program. The user interface in Office 2010 provides intuitive ways to choose commands, work with files, and navigate in the program window.  Familiarize yourself with some of the common interface elements in Office by examining the PowerPoint program window.

## STEPS

**QUICK TIP**

In addition to the standard tabs on the Ribbon, **contextual tabs** open when needed to complete a specific task; they appear in an accent color and close when no longer needed. To minimize the display of the buttons and commands on tabs, click the Minimize the Ribbon button on the right end of the Ribbon.

1. **Click the PowerPoint program button on the taskbar**

   PowerPoint becomes the active program. Refer to Figure A-5 to identify common elements of the Office user interface. The **document window** occupies most of the screen. In PowerPoint, a blank slide appears in the document window, so you can build your slide show. At the top of every Office program window is a **title bar** that displays the document name and program name. Below the title bar is the **Ribbon**, which displays commands you're likely to need for the current task. Commands are organized onto **tabs**. The tab names appear at the top of the Ribbon, and the active tab appears in front. The Ribbon in every Office program includes tabs specific to the program, but all Office programs include a File tab and Home tab on the left end of the Ribbon.

2. **Click the File tab**

   The File tab opens, displaying **Backstage view**. The navigation bar on the left side of Backstage view contains commands to perform actions common to most Office programs, such as opening a file, saving a file, and closing the current program. Just above the File tab is the **Quick Access toolbar**, which also includes buttons for common Office commands.

3. **Click the File tab again to close Backstage view and return to the document window, then click the Design tab on the Ribbon**

   To display a different tab, you click the tab on the Ribbon. Each tab contains related commands arranged into **groups** to make features easy to find. On the Design tab, the Themes group displays available design themes in a **gallery**, or visual collection of choices you can browse. Many groups contain a **dialog box launcher**, an icon you can click to open a dialog box or task pane from which to choose related commands.

**QUICK TIP**

Live Preview is available in many galleries and menus throughout Office.

4. **Move the mouse pointer over the Angles theme in the Themes group as shown in Figure A-6, but do not click the mouse button**

   The Angles theme is temporarily applied to the slide in the document window. However, because you did not click the theme, you did not permanently change the slide. With the **Live Preview** feature, you can point to a choice, see the results right in the document, and then decide if you want to make the change.

**QUICK TIP**

If you accidentally click a theme, click the Undo button on the Quick Access toolbar.

5. **Move away from the Ribbon and towards the slide**

   If you had clicked the Angles theme, it would be applied to this slide. Instead, the slide remains unchanged.

**QUICK TIP**

You can also use the Zoom button in the Zoom group on the View tab to enlarge or reduce a document's appearance.

6. **Point to the Zoom slider on the status bar, then drag to the right until the Zoom level reads 166%**

   The slide display is enlarged. Zoom tools are located on the status bar. You can drag the slider or click the Zoom In or Zoom Out buttons to zoom in or out on an area of interest. **Zooming in**, or choosing a higher percentage, makes a document appear bigger on screen, but less of it fits on the screen at once; **zooming out**, or choosing a lower percentage, lets you see more of the document but at a reduced size.

7. **Drag on the status bar to the left until the Zoom level reads 73%**

**FIGURE A-5:** PowerPoint program window

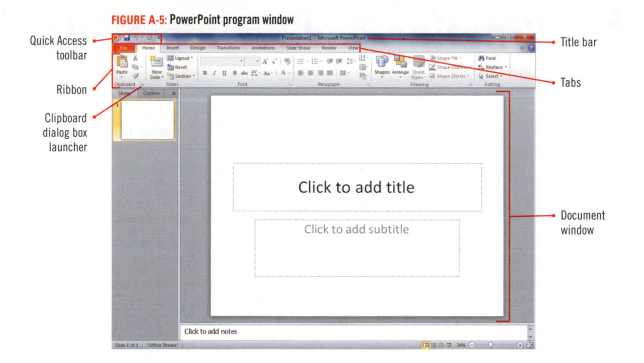

Quick Access toolbar

Ribbon

Clipboard dialog box launcher

Title bar

Tabs

Document window

**FIGURE A-6:** Viewing a theme with Live Preview

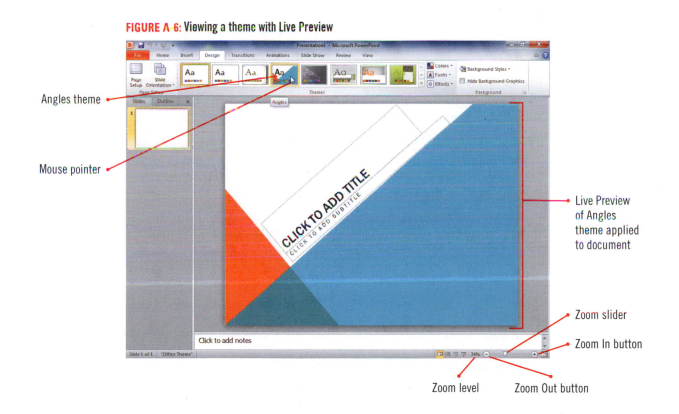

Angles theme

Mouse pointer

Live Preview of Angles theme applied to document

Zoom slider

Zoom In button

Zoom level

Zoom Out button

## Using Backstage view

**Backstage view** in each Microsoft Office program offers "one stop shopping" for many commonly performed tasks, such as opening and saving a file, printing and previewing a document, defining document properties, sharing information, and exiting a program.

Backstage view opens when you click the File tab in any Office program, and while features such as the Ribbon, Mini toolbar, and Live Preview all help you work *in* your documents, the File tab and Backstage view help you work *with* your documents.

# Creating and Saving a File

When working in a program, one of the first things you need to do is to create and save a file. A **file** is a stored collection of data. Saving a file enables you to work on a project now, then put it away and work on it again later. In some Office programs, including Word, Excel, and PowerPoint, a new file is automatically created when you start the program, so all you have to do is enter some data and save it. In Access, you must expressly create a file before you enter any data. You should give your files meaningful names and save them in an appropriate location so that they're easy to find. 🖌️ Use Word to familiarize yourself with the process of creating and saving a document. First you'll type some notes about a possible location for a corporate meeting, then you'll save the information for later use.

## STEPS

1. **Click the Word program button 🗒️ on the taskbar**

2. **Type Locations for Corporate Meeting, then press [Enter] twice**

   The text appears in the document window, and the **insertion point** blinks on a new blank line. The insertion point indicates where the next typed text will appear.

3. **Type Las Vegas, NV, press [Enter], type Orlando, FL, press [Enter], type Boston, MA, press [Enter] twice, then type your name**

   Compare your document to Figure A-7.

   **QUICK TIP**

   A filename can be up to 255 characters, including a file extension, and can include upper- or lowercase characters and spaces, but not ?, ", /, \, <, >, *, |, or :.

4. **Click the Save button 💾 on the Quick Access toolbar**

   Because this is the first time you are saving this document, the Save As dialog box opens, as shown in Figure A-8. The Save As dialog box includes options for assigning a filename and storage location. Once you save a file for the first time, clicking 💾 saves any changes to the file *without* opening the Save As dialog box, because no additional information is needed. The Address bar in the Save As dialog box displays the default location for saving the file, but you can change it to any location. The File name field contains a suggested name for the document based on text in the file, but you can enter a different name.

5. **Type OF A-Potential Corporate Meeting Locations**

   The text you type replaces the highlighted text. (The "OF A-" in the filename indicates that the file is created in Office Unit A. You will see similar designations throughout this book when files are named. For example, a file named in Excel Unit B would begin with "EX B-" .)

   **QUICK TIP**

   Saving a file to the Desktop creates a desktop icon that you can double-click to both launch a program and open a document.

6. ▶ **In the Save As dialog box, use the Address bar or Navigation Pane to navigate to the drive and folder where you store your Data Files**

   Many students store files on a flash drive, but you can also store files on your computer, a network drive, or any storage device indicated by your instructor or technical support person.

7. **Click Save**

   The Save As dialog box closes, the new file is saved to the location you specified, then the name of the document appears in the title bar, as shown in Figure A-9. (You may or may not see the file extension ".docx" after the filename.) See Table A-1 for a description of the different types of files you create in Office, and the file extensions associated with each.

   **QUICK TIP**

   To create a new blank file when a file is open, click the File tab, click New on the navigation bar, then click Create near the bottom of the document preview pane.

**TABLE A-1:** Common filenames and default file extensions

| file created in | is called a | and has the default extension |
| --- | --- | --- |
| Word | document | .docx |
| Excel | workbook | .xlsx |
| PowerPoint | presentation | .pptx |
| Access | database | .accdb |

**FIGURE A-7:** Document created in Word

Save button

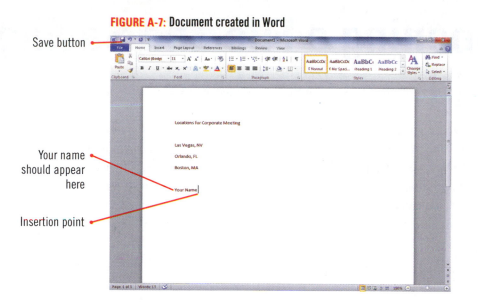

Your name
should appear
here

Insertion point

**FIGURE A-8:** Save As dialog box

Navigation
Pane; your
links and
folders
may differ

File name field;
your computer
may not display
file extensions

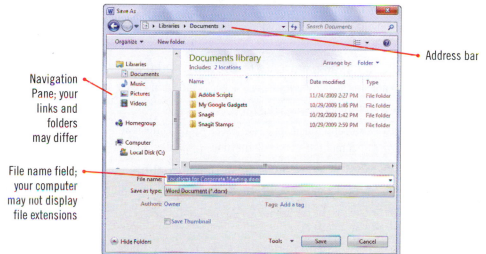

Address bar

**FIGURE A-9:** Saved and named Word document

Filename
appears in
title bar

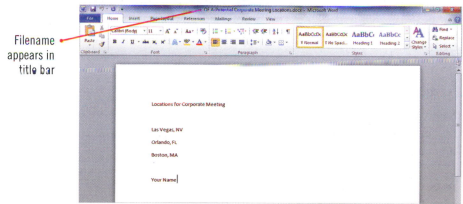

## Using the Office Clipboard

You can use the Office Clipboard to cut and copy items from one Office program and paste them into others. The Office Clipboard can store a maximum of 24 items. To access it, open the Office Clipboard task pane by clicking the dialog box launcher in the Clipboard group on the Home tab. Each time you copy a selection, it is saved in the Office Clipboard. Each entry in the Office Clipboard includes an icon that tells you the program it was created in. To paste an entry, click in the document where you want it to appear, then click the item in the Office Clipboard. To delete an item from the Office Clipboard, right-click the item, then click Delete.

# Opening a File and Saving It with a New Name

In many cases as you work in Office, you start with a blank document, but often you need to use an existing file. It might be a file you or a coworker created earlier as a work in progress, or it could be a complete document that you want to use as the basis for another. For example, you might want to create a budget for this year using the budget you created last year; you could type in all the categories and information from scratch, or you could open last year's budget, save it with a new name, and just make changes to update it for the current year. By opening the existing file and saving it with the Save As command, you create a duplicate that you can modify to your heart's content, while the original file remains intact. Use Excel to open an existing workbook file, and save it with a new name so the original remains unchanged.

## STEPS

**QUICK TIP**

Click Recent on the navigation bar to display a list of recent workbooks; click a file in the list to open it.

1. **Click the Excel program button** ⊞ **on the taskbar, click the File tab, then click Open on the navigation bar**

   The Open dialog box opens, where you can navigate to any drive or folder accessible to your computer to locate a file.

2. **In the Open dialog box, navigate to the drive and folder where you store your Data Files**

   The files available in the current folder are listed, as shown in Figure A-10. This folder contains one file.

**TROUBLE**

Click Enable Editing on the Protected View bar near the top of your document window if prompted.

3. **Click OFFICE A-1.xlsx, then click Open**

   The dialog box closes, and the file opens in Excel. An Excel file is an electronic spreadsheet, so it looks different from a Word document or a PowerPoint slide.

4. **Click the File tab, then click Save As on the navigation bar**

   The Save As dialog box opens, and the current filename is highlighted in the File name text box. Using the Save As command enables you to create a copy of the current, existing file with a new name. This action preserves the original file and creates a new file that you can modify.

**QUICK TIP**

The Save As command works identically in all Office programs, except Access; in Access, this command lets you save a copy of the current database object, such as a table or form, with a new name, but not a copy of the entire database.

5. **Navigate to the drive and folder where you store your Data Files if necessary, type OF A-Budget for Corporate Meeting in the File name text box, as shown in Figure A-11, then click Save**

   A copy of the existing workbook is created with the new name. The original file, Office A-1.xlsx, closes automatically.

6. **Click cell A19, type your name, then press [Enter], as shown in Figure A-12**

   In Excel, you enter data in cells, which are formed by the intersection of a row and a column. Cell A19 is at the intersection of column A and row 19. When you press [Enter], the cell pointer moves to cell A20.

7. **Click the Save button** 🖫 **on the Quick Access toolbar**

   Your name appears in the workbook, and your changes to the file are saved.

---

### Working in Compatibility Mode

Not everyone upgrades to the newest version of Office. As a general rule, new software versions are **backward compatible**, meaning that documents saved by an older version can be read by newer software. To open documents created in older Office versions, Office 2010 includes a feature called Compatibility Mode. When you use Office 2010 to open a file created in an earlier version of Office, "Compatibility Mode" appears in the title bar, letting you know the file was created in an earlier but usable version of the program. If you are working with someone who may not be using the newest version of the software, you can avoid possible incompatibility problems by saving your file in another, earlier format. To do this in an Office program, click the File tab, click Save As on the navigation bar, click the Save as type list arrow in the Save As dialog box, then click an option on the list. For example, if you're working in Excel, click Excel 97-2003 Workbook format in the Save as type list to save an Excel file so that it can be opened in Excel 97 or Excel 2003.

**FIGURE A-10:** Open dialog box

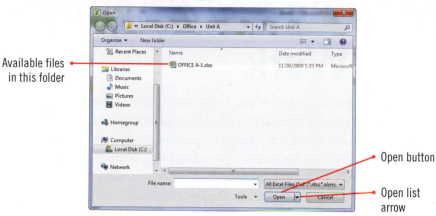

Available files in this folder

Open button

Open list arrow

**FIGURE A-11:** Save As dialog box

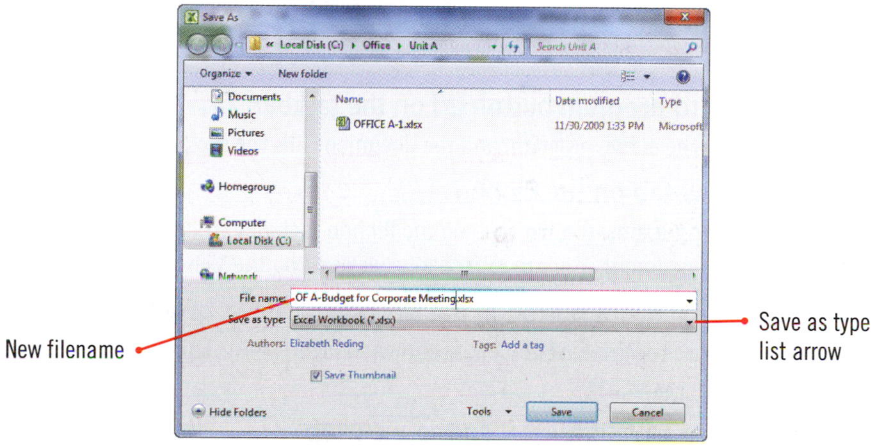

New filename

Save as type list arrow

**FIGURE A-12:** Your name added to the workbook

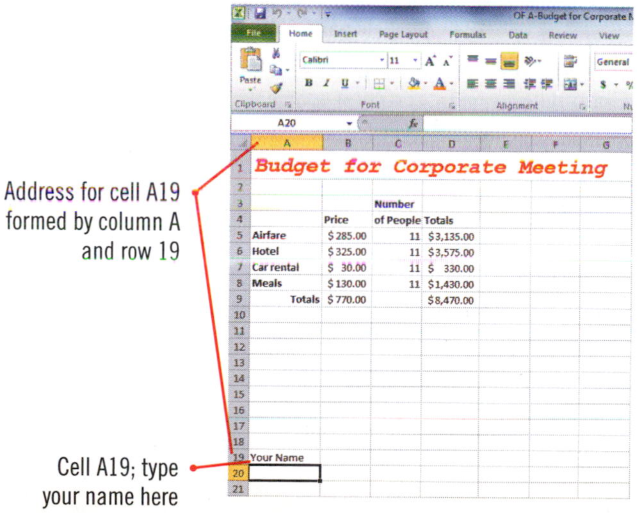

Address for cell A19 formed by column A and row 19

Budget for Corporate Meeting

| | Price | Number of People | Totals |
|---|---|---|---|
| Airfare | $285.00 | 11 | $3,135.00 |
| Hotel | $325.00 | 11 | $3,575.00 |
| Car rental | $30.00 | 11 | $330.00 |
| Meals | $130.00 | 11 | $1,430.00 |
| Totals | $770.00 | | $8,470.00 |

Cell A19; type your name here

Your Name

## Exploring File Open options

You might have noticed that the Open button on the Open dialog box includes an arrow. In a dialog box, if a button includes an arrow you can click the button to invoke the command, or you can click the arrow to choose from a list of related commands. The Open list arrow includes several related commands, including Open Read-Only and Open as Copy. Clicking Open Read-Only opens a file that you can only save with a new name; you cannot save changes to the original file. Clicking Open as Copy creates a copy of the file already saved and named with the word "Copy" in the title. Like the Save As command, these commands provide additional ways to use copies of existing files while ensuring that original files do not get changed by mistake.

# Viewing and Printing Your Work

Each Microsoft Office program lets you switch among various **views** of the document window to show more or fewer details or a different combination of elements that make it easier to complete certain tasks, such as formatting or reading text. Changing your view of a document does not affect the file in any way, it affects only the way it looks on screen. If your computer is connected to a printer or a print server, you can easily print any Office document using the Print button on the Print tab in Backstage view. Printing can be as simple as **previewing** the document to see exactly what a document will look like when it is printed and then clicking the Print button. Or, you can customize the print job by printing only selected pages or making other choices.  Experiment with changing your view of a Word document, and then preview and print your work.

## STEPS

1. **Click the Word program button** [W] **on the taskbar**

   Word becomes the active program, and the document fills the screen.

2. **Click the View tab on the Ribbon**

   In most Office programs, the View tab on the Ribbon includes groups and commands for changing your view of the current document. You can also change views using the View buttons on the status bar.

3. **Click the Web Layout button in the Document Views group on the View tab**

   The view changes to Web Layout view, as shown in Figure A-13. This view shows how the document will look if you save it as a Web page.

4. **Click the Print Layout button on the View tab**

   You return to Print Layout view, the default view in Word.

5. **Click the File tab, then click Print on the navigation bar**

   The Print tab opens in Backstage view. The preview pane on the right side of the window automatically displays a preview of how your document will look when printed, showing the entire page on screen at once. Compare your screen to Figure A-14. Options in the Settings section enable you to change settings such as margins, orientation, and paper size before printing. To change a setting, click it, and then click the new setting you want. For instance, to change from Letter paper size to Legal, click Letter in the Settings section, then click Legal on the menu that opens. The document preview is updated as you change the settings. You also can use the Settings section to change which pages to print and even the number of pages you print on each sheet of printed paper. If you have multiple printers from which to choose, you can change from one installed printer to another by clicking the current printer in the Printer section, then clicking the name of the installed printer you want to use. The Print section contains the Print button and also enables you to select the number of copies of the document to print.

6. **Click the Print button in the Print section**

   A copy of the document prints, and Backstage view closes.

> **QUICK TIP**
> You can add the Quick Print button [icon] to the Quick Access toolbar by clicking the Customize Quick Access Toolbar button, then clicking Quick Print. The Quick Print button prints one copy of your document using the default settings.

### Customizing the Quick Access toolbar

You can customize the Quick Access toolbar to display your favorite commands. To do so, click the Customize Quick Access Toolbar button [icon] in the title bar, then click the command you want to add. If you don't see the command in the list, click More Commands to open the Quick Access Toolbar tab of the current program's Options dialog box. In the Options dialog box, use the Choose commands from list to choose a category, click the desired command in the list on the left, click Add to add it to the Quick Access toolbar, then click

OK. To remove a button from the toolbar, click the name in the list on the right in the Options dialog box, then click Remove. To add a command to the Quick Access toolbar on the fly, simply right-click the button on the Ribbon, then click Add to Quick Access Toolbar on the shortcut menu. To move the Quick Access toolbar below the Ribbon, click the Customize Quick Access Toolbar button, and then click Show Below the Ribbon.

**FIGURE A-13:** Web Layout view

Web Layout button

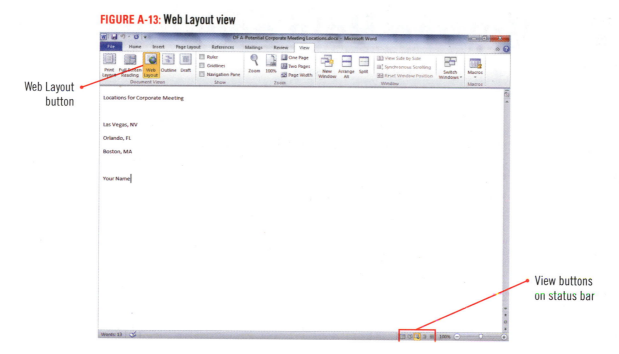

View buttons on status bar

**FIGURE A-14:** Print tab in Backstage view

Print button

Click to select a different installed printer

Settings section

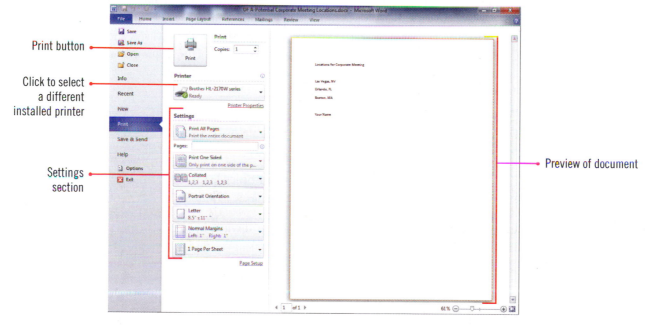

Preview of document

## Creating a screen capture

A **screen capture** is a digital image of your screen, as if you took a picture of it with a camera. For instance, you might want to take a screen capture if an error message occurs and you want Technical Support to see exactly what's on the screen. You can create a screen capture using features found in Windows 7 or Office 2010. Windows 7 comes with the Snipping Tool, a separate program designed to capture whole screens or portions of screens. To open the Snipping Tool, click it on the Start menu or click All Programs, click Accessories, then click Snipping Tool. After opening the Snipping Tool, drag the pointer on the screen to select the area of the screen you want to capture. When you release the mouse button, the screen capture opens in the Snipping Tool window, and

you can save, copy, or send it in an e-mail. In Word, Excel, and PowerPoint 2010, you can capture screens or portions of screens and insert them in the current document using the Screenshot button on the Insert tab. And finally, you can create a screen capture by pressing [PrtScn]. (Keyboards differ, but you may find the [PrtScn] button in or near your keyboard's function keys.) Pressing this key places a digital image of your screen in the Windows temporary storage area known as the **Clipboard**. Open the document where you want the screen capture to appear, click the Home tab on the Ribbon (if necessary), then click the Paste button on the Home tab. The screen capture is pasted into the document.

# Getting Help and Closing a File

You can get comprehensive help at any time by pressing [F1] in an Office program. You can also get help in the form of a ScreenTip by pointing to almost any icon in the program window. When you're finished working in an Office document, you have a few choices regarding ending your work session. You can close a file or exit a program by using the File tab or by clicking a button on the title bar. Closing a file leaves a program running, while exiting a program closes all the open files in that program as well as the program itself. In all cases, Office reminds you if you try to close a file or exit a program and your document contains unsaved changes. Explore the Help system in Microsoft Office, and then close your documents and exit any open programs.

## STEPS

**TROUBLE**

If the Table of Contents pane doesn't appear on the left in the Help window, click the Show Table of Contents button on the Help toolbar to show it.

1. **Point to the Zoom button on the View tab of the Ribbon**
   A ScreenTip appears that describes how the Zoom button works and explains where to find other zoom controls.

2. **Press [F1]**
   The Word Help window opens, as shown in Figure A-15, displaying the home page for help in Word on the right and the Table of Contents pane on the left. In both panes of the Help window, each entry is a hyperlink you can click to open a list of related topics. The Help window also includes a toolbar of useful Help commands and a Search field. The connection status at the bottom of the Help window indicates that the connection to Office.com is active. Office.com supplements the help content available on your computer with a wide variety of up-to-date topics, templates, and training. If you are not connected to the Internet, the Help window displays only the help content available on your computer.

**QUICK TIP**

You can also open the Help window by clicking the Microsoft Office Word Help button to the right of the tabs on the Ribbon.

3. **Click the Creating documents link in the Table of Contents pane**
   The icon next to Creating documents changes, and a list of subtopics expands beneath the topic.

4. **Click the Create a document link in the subtopics list in the Table of Contents pane**
   The topic opens in the right pane of the Help window, as shown in Figure A-16.

5. **Click Delete a document under "What do you want to do?" in the right pane**
   The link leads to information about deleting a document.

**QUICK TIP**

You can print the entire current topic by clicking the Print button on the Help toolbar, then clicking Print in the Print dialog box.

6. **Click the Accessibility link in the Table of Contents pane, click the Accessibility features in Word link, read the information in the right pane, then click the Help window Close button**

7. **Click the File tab, then click Close on the navigation bar; if a dialog box opens asking whether you want to save your changes, click Save**
   The Potential Corporate Meeting Locations document closes, leaving the Word program open.

8. **Click the File tab, then click Exit on the navigation bar**
   Word closes, and the Excel program window is active.

9. **Click the File tab, click Exit on the navigation bar to exit Excel, click the PowerPoint program button on the taskbar if necessary, click the File tab, then click Exit on the navigation bar to exit PowerPoint**
   Excel and PowerPoint both close.

**FIGURE A-15:** Word Help window

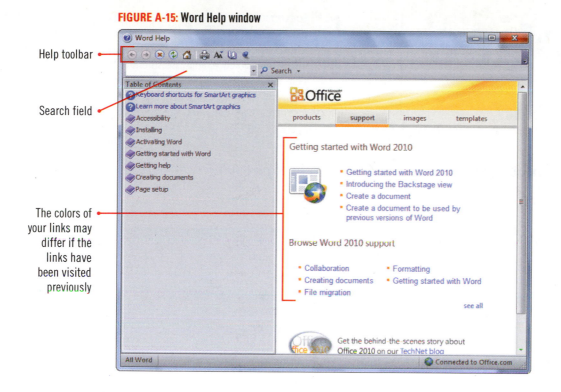

Help toolbar

Search field

The colors of
your links may
differ if the
links have
been visited
previously

**FIGURE A-16:** Create a document Help topic

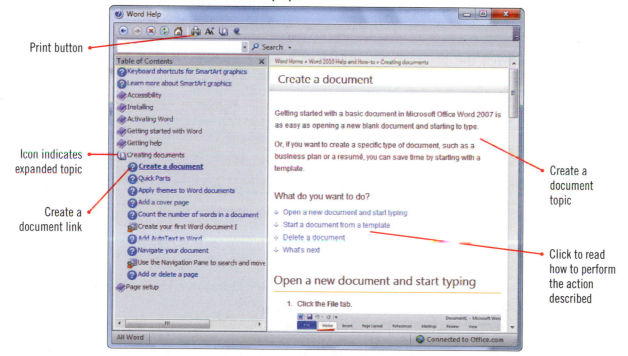

Print button

Icon indicates
expanded topic

Create a
document link

Create a
document
topic

Click to read
how to perform
the action
described

## Recovering a document

Each Office program has a built-in recovery feature that allows you to open and save files that were open at the time of an interruption such as a power failure. When you restart the program(s) after an interruption, the Document Recovery task pane opens on the left side of your screen displaying both original and recovered versions of the files that were open. If you're not sure which file to open (original or recovered), it's usually better to open the recovered file because it will contain the latest information. You can, however, open and review all versions of the file that were recovered and save the best one. Each file listed in the Document Recovery task pane displays a list arrow with options that allow you to open the file, save it as is, delete it, or show repairs made to it during recovery.

# Practice

**SAM**

For current SAM information, including versions and content details, visit SAM Central (http://www.cengage.com/samcentral). If you have a SAM user profile, you may have access to hands-on instruction, practice, and assessment of the skills covered in this unit. Since various versions of SAM are supported throughout the life of this text, check with your instructor for the correct instructions and URL/Web site for accessing assignments.

## Concepts Review

**Label the elements of the program window shown in Figure A-17.**

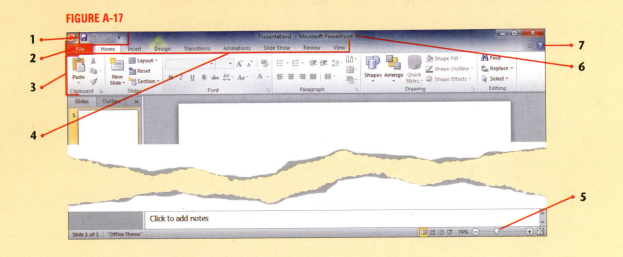

FIGURE A-17

**Match each project with the program for which it is best suited.**

8. Microsoft Access
9. Microsoft Excel
10. Microsoft Word
11. Microsoft PowerPoint

a. Corporate convention budget with expense projections
b. Business cover letter for a job application
c. Department store inventory
d. Presentation for city council meeting

# Independent Challenge 1

You just accepted an administrative position with a local independently owned produce vendor that has recently invested in computers and is now considering purchasing Microsoft Office for the company. You are asked to propose ways Office might help the business. You produce your document in Word.

a. Start Word, then save the document as **OF A-Microsoft Office Document** in the drive and folder where you store your Data Files.
b. Type **Microsoft Word**, press [Enter] twice, type **Microsoft Excel**, press [Enter] twice, type **Microsoft PowerPoint**, press [Enter] twice, type **Microsoft Access**, press [Enter] twice, then type your name.
c. Click the line beneath each program name, type at least two tasks suited to that program (each separated by a comma), then press [Enter].

### Advanced Challenge Exercise

- Press the [PrtScn] button to create a screen capture.
- Click after your name, press [Enter] to move to a blank line below your name, then click the Paste button in the Clipboard group on the Home tab.

d. Save the document, then submit your work to your instructor as directed.
e. Exit Word.

# Getting Started with Excel 2010

**Files You Will Need:**

EX A-1.xlsx
EX A-2.xlsx
EX A-3.xlsx
EX A-4.xlsx
EX A-5.xlsx

In this unit, you will learn how spreadsheet software helps you analyze data and make business decisions, even if you aren't a math pro. You'll become familiar with the different elements of a spreadsheet and learn your way around the Excel program window. You will also work in an Excel worksheet and make simple calculations.  You have been hired as an assistant at Quest Specialty Travel (QST), a company offering tours that immerse travelers in regional culture. You report to Grace Wong, the vice president of finance. As Grace's assistant, you create worksheets to analyze data from various divisions of the company, so you can help her make sound decisions on company expansion and investments.

**OBJECTIVES**

Understand spreadsheet software

Tour the Excel 2010 window

Understand formulas

Enter labels and values and use the Sum button

Edit cell entries

Enter and edit a simple formula

Switch worksheet views

Choose print options

# Understanding Spreadsheet Software

Microsoft Excel is the electronic spreadsheet program within the Microsoft Office suite. An **electronic spreadsheet** is an application you use to perform numeric calculations and to analyze and present numeric data. One advantage of spreadsheet programs over pencil and paper is that your calculations are updated automatically, so you can change entries without having to manually recalculate. Table A-1 shows some of the common business tasks people accomplish using Excel. In Excel, the electronic spreadsheet you work in is called a **worksheet**, and it is contained in a file called a **workbook**, which has the file extension .xlsx.  At Quest Specialty Travel, you use Excel extensively to track finances and manage corporate data.

## DETAILS

### When you use Excel, you have the ability to:

- **Enter data quickly and accurately**

  With Excel, you can enter information faster and more accurately than with pencil and paper. Figure A-1 shows a payroll worksheet created using pencil and paper. Figure A-2 shows the same worksheet created using Excel. Equations were added to calculate the hours and pay. You can use Excel to recreate this information for each week by copying the worksheet's structure and the information that doesn't change from week to week, then entering unique data and formulas for each week. You can also quickly create charts and other elements to help visualize how the payroll is distributed.

- **Recalculate data easily**

  Fixing typing errors or updating data is easy in Excel. In the payroll example, if you receive updated hours for an employee, you just enter the new hours and Excel recalculates the pay.

- **Perform what-if analysis**

  The ability to change data and quickly view the recalculated results gives you the power to make informed business decisions. For instance, if you're considering raising the hourly rate for an entry-level tour guide from $12.50 to $15.00, you can enter the new value in the worksheet and immediately see the impact on the overall payroll as well as on the individual employee. Any time you use a worksheet to ask the question "What if?" you are performing **what-if analysis**. Excel also includes a Scenario Manager where you can name and save different what-if versions of your worksheet.

- **Change the appearance of information**

  Excel provides powerful features for making information visually appealing and easier to understand. You can format text and numbers in different fonts, colors, and styles to make it stand out.

- **Create charts**

  Excel makes it easy to create charts based on worksheet information. Charts are updated automatically in Excel whenever data changes. The worksheet in Figure A-2 includes a 3-D pie chart.

- **Share information**

  It's easy for everyone at QST to collaborate in Excel using the company intranet, the Internet, or a network storage device. For example, you can complete the weekly payroll that your boss, Grace Wong, started creating. You can also take advantage of collaboration tools such as shared workbooks, so that multiple people can edit a workbook simultaneously.

- **Build on previous work**

  Instead of creating a new worksheet for every project, it's easy to modify an existing Excel worksheet. When you are ready to create next week's payroll, you can open the file for last week's payroll, save it with a new filename, and modify the information as necessary. You can also use predesigned, formatted files called **templates** to create new worksheets quickly. Excel comes with many templates that you can customize.

**FIGURE A-1:** Traditional paper worksheet

```
Quest Specialty Travel
Trip Advisor Division Payroll Calculator

                                        Reg      O/T      Gross
Name              Hours   O/T Hrs  Hrly Rate  Pay      Pay      Pay
Brueghel, Pieter    40      4      16–      640–     128–     768–
Cortona, Livia      35      0      10–      350–       0–     350–
Klimt, Gustave      40      2      12⁵⁰     500–      50–     550–
Le Pen, Jean-Marie  29      0      15–      435–       0–     435–
Martinez, Juan      37      0      12⁵⁰     462.50     0–     462.50
Mioshi, Keiko       39      0      20–      780–       0–     780–
Sherwood, Burton    40      0      16–      640–       0–     640–
Strano, Riccardo    40      8      15–      600–     240–     840–
Wadsworth, Alicia   40      5      12⁵⁰      5          625–
                    38      0      15
```

**FIGURE A-2:** Excel worksheet

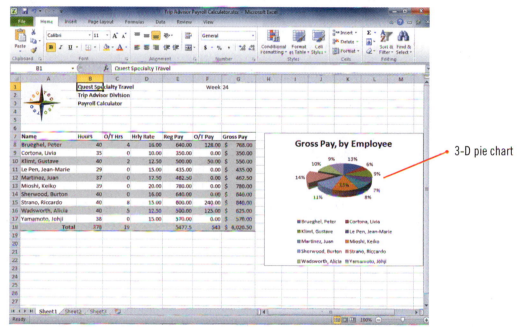

TABLE A-1: Business tasks you can accomplish using Excel

| you can use spreadsheets to: | by: |
|---|---|
| **Perform calculations** | Adding formulas and functions to worksheet data; for example, adding a list of sales results or calculating a car payment |
| **Represent values graphically** | Creating charts based on worksheet data; for example, creating a chart that displays expenses |
| **Generate reports** | Creating workbooks that combine information from multiple worksheets, such as summarized sales information from multiple stores |
| **Organize data** | Sorting data in ascending or descending order; for example, alphabetizing a list of products or customer names, or prioritizing orders by date |
| **Analyze data** | Creating data summaries and short lists using PivotTables or AutoFilters; for example, making a list of the top 10 customers based on spending habits |
| **Create what-if data scenarios** | Using variable values to investigate and sample different outcomes, such as changing the interest rate or payment schedule on a loan |

# Touring the Excel 2010 Window

To start Excel, Microsoft Windows must be running. Similar to starting any program in Office, you can use the Start button on the Windows taskbar, or you may have a shortcut on your desktop you prefer to use. If you need additional assistance, ask your instructor or technical support person.  You decide to start Excel and familiarize yourself with the worksheet window.

## STEPS

**QUICK TIP**

For more information on starting a program or opening and saving a file, see the unit "Getting Started with Microsoft Office 2010."

1. **Start Excel, click the File tab, then click Open on the navigation bar to open the Open dialog box**

2. **In the Open dialog box, navigate to the drive and folder where you store your Data Files, click EX A-1.xlsx, then click Open**

   The file opens in the Excel window.

3. **Click the File tab, then click Save As on the navigation bar to open the Save As dialog box**

**TROUBLE**

If you don't see the extension .xlsx on the filenames in the Save As dialog box, don't worry; Windows can be set up to display or not to display the file extensions.

4. **In the Save As dialog box, navigate to the drive and folder where you store your Data Files if necessary, type EX A-Trip Advisor Payroll Calculator in the File name text box, then click Save**

   Using Figure A-3 as a guide, identify the following items:
   - The **Name box** displays the active cell address. "A1" appears in the Name box.
   - The **formula bar** allows you to enter or edit data in the worksheet.
   - The worksheet window contains a grid of columns and rows. Columns are labeled alphabetically and rows are labeled numerically. The worksheet window can contain a total of 1,048,576 rows and 16,384 columns. The intersection of a column and a row is called a **cell**. Cells can contain text, numbers, formulas, or a combination of all three. Every cell has its own unique location or **cell address**, which is identified by the coordinates of the intersecting column and row.
   - The **cell pointer** is a dark rectangle that outlines the cell you are working in. This cell is called the **active cell**. In Figure A-3, the cell pointer outlines cell A1, so A1 is the active cell. The column and row headings for the active cell are highlighted, making it easier to locate.
   - **Sheet tabs** below the worksheet grid let you switch from sheet to sheet in a workbook. By default, a workbook file contains three worksheets—but you can use just one, or have as many as 255, in a workbook. The Insert Worksheet button to the right of Sheet 3 allows you to add worksheets to a workbook. **Sheet tab scrolling buttons** let you navigate to additional sheet tabs when available.
   - You can use the **scroll bars** to move around in a worksheet that is too large to fit on the screen at once.
   - The **status bar** is located at the bottom of the Excel window. It provides a brief description of the active command or task in progress. The **mode indicator** in the lower-left corner of the status bar provides additional information about certain tasks.

5. **Click cell A4**

   Cell A4 becomes the active cell. To activate a different cell, you can click the cell or press the arrow keys on your keyboard to move to it.

6. **Click cell B5, press and hold the mouse button, drag ✛ to cell B14, then release the mouse button**

   You selected a group of cells and they are highlighted, as shown in Figure A-4. A selection of two or more cells such as B5:B14 is called a **range**; you select a range when you want to perform an action on a group of cells at once, such as moving them or formatting them. When you select a range, the status bar displays the average, count (or number of items selected), and sum of the selected cells as a quick reference.

Getting Started with Excel 2010

**FIGURE A-3: Open workbook**

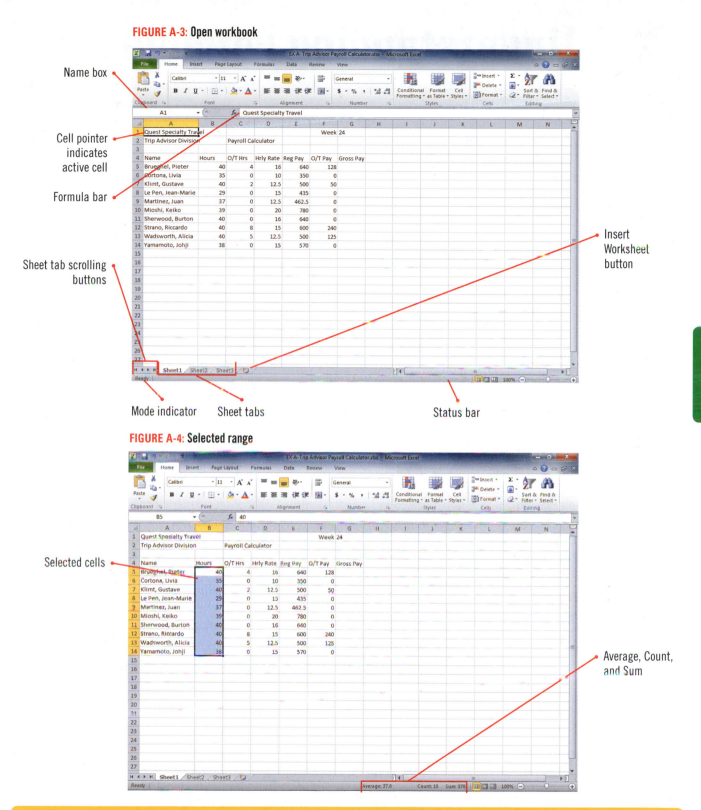

Name box

Cell pointer indicates active cell

Formula bar

Sheet tab scrolling buttons

Insert Worksheet button

Mode indicator

Sheet tabs

Status bar

Excel 2010

**FIGURE A-4: Selected range**

Selected cells

Average, Count, and Sum

---

## Windows Live and Microsoft Office Web Apps

All Office programs include the capability to incorporate feedback—called online collaboration—across the Internet or a company network. Using **cloud computing** (work done in a virtual environment), you can take advantage of Web programs called Microsoft Office Web Apps, which are simplified versions of the programs found in the Microsoft Office 2010 suite. Because these programs are online, they take up no computer disk space and are accessed using

Windows Live SkyDrive, a free service from Microsoft. Using Windows Live SkyDrive, you and your colleagues can create and store documents in a "cloud" and make the documents available to whomever you grant access. To use Windows Live SkyDrive, you need a free Windows Live ID, which you obtain at the Windows Live Web site. You can find more information in the "Working with Windows Live and Office Web Apps" appendix.

# Understanding Formulas

Excel is a truly powerful program because users at every level of mathematical expertise can make calculations with accuracy. To do so, you use formulas. A **formula** is an equation in a worksheet. You use formulas to make calculations as simple as adding a column of numbers, or as complex as creating profit-and-loss projections for a global corporation. To tap into the power of Excel, you should understand how formulas work.  Managers at QST use the Trip Advisor Payroll Calculator workbook to keep track of employee hours prior to submitting them to the Payroll Department. You'll be using this workbook regularly, so you need to understand the formulas it contains and how Excel calculates the results.

## STEPS

1. **Click cell E5**

   The active cell contains a formula, which appears on the formula bar. All Excel formulas begin with the equal sign ( = ). If you want a cell to show the result of adding 4 plus 2, the formula in the cell would look like this: =4+2. If you want a cell to show the result of multiplying two values in your worksheet, such as the values in cells B5 and D5, the formula would look like this: =B5*D5, as shown in Figure A-5. While you're entering a formula in a cell, the cell references and arithmetic operators appear on the formula bar. See Table A-2 for a list of commonly used arithmetic operators. When you're finished entering the formula, you can either click the Enter button on the formula bar or press [Enter].

2. **Click cell F5**

   An example of a more complex formula is the calculation of overtime pay. At QST, overtime pay is calculated at twice the regular hourly rate times the number of overtime hours. The formula used to calculate overtime pay for the employee in row 5 is:

   O/T Hrs times (2 times Hrly Rate)

   In the worksheet cell, you would enter: =C5*(2*D5), as shown in Figure A-6. The use of parentheses creates groups within the formula and indicates which calculations to complete first—an important consideration in complex formulas. In this formula, first the hourly rate is multiplied by 2, because that calculation is within the parentheses. Next, that value is multiplied by the number of overtime hours. Because overtime is calculated at twice the hourly rate, managers are aware that they need to closely watch this expense.

## DETAILS

**In creating calculations in Excel, it is important to:**

- **Know where the formulas should be**

  An Excel formula is created in the cell where the formula's results should appear. This means that the formula calculating Gross Pay for the employee in row 5 will be entered in cell G5.

- **Know exactly what cells and arithmetic operations are needed**

  Don't guess; make sure you know exactly what cells are involved before creating a formula.

- **Create formulas with care**

  Make sure you know exactly what you want a formula to accomplish before it is created. An inaccurate formula may have far-reaching effects if the formula or its results are referenced by other formulas.

- **Use cell references rather than values**

  The beauty of Excel is that whenever you change a value in a cell, any formula containing a reference to that cell is automatically updated. For this reason, it's important that you use cell references in formulas, rather than actual values, whenever possible.

- **Determine what calculations will be needed**

  Sometimes it's difficult to predict what data will be needed within a worksheet, but you should try to anticipate what statistical information may be required. For example, if there are columns of numbers, chances are good that both column and row totals should be present.

**FIGURE A-5:** Viewing a formula

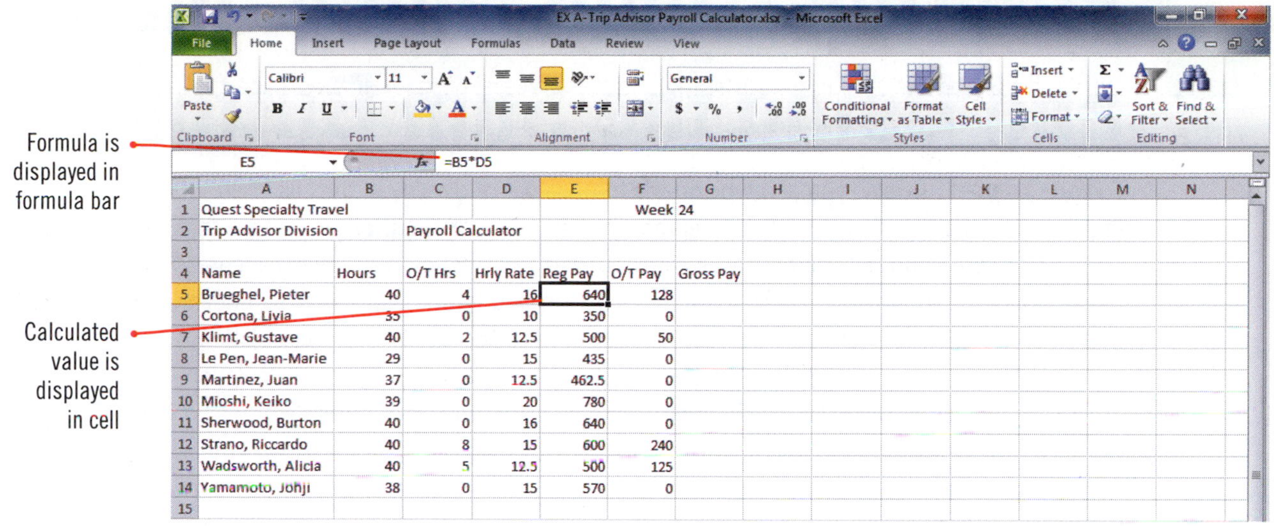

Formula is displayed in formula bar

Calculated value is displayed in cell

**FIGURE A-6:** Formula with multiple operators

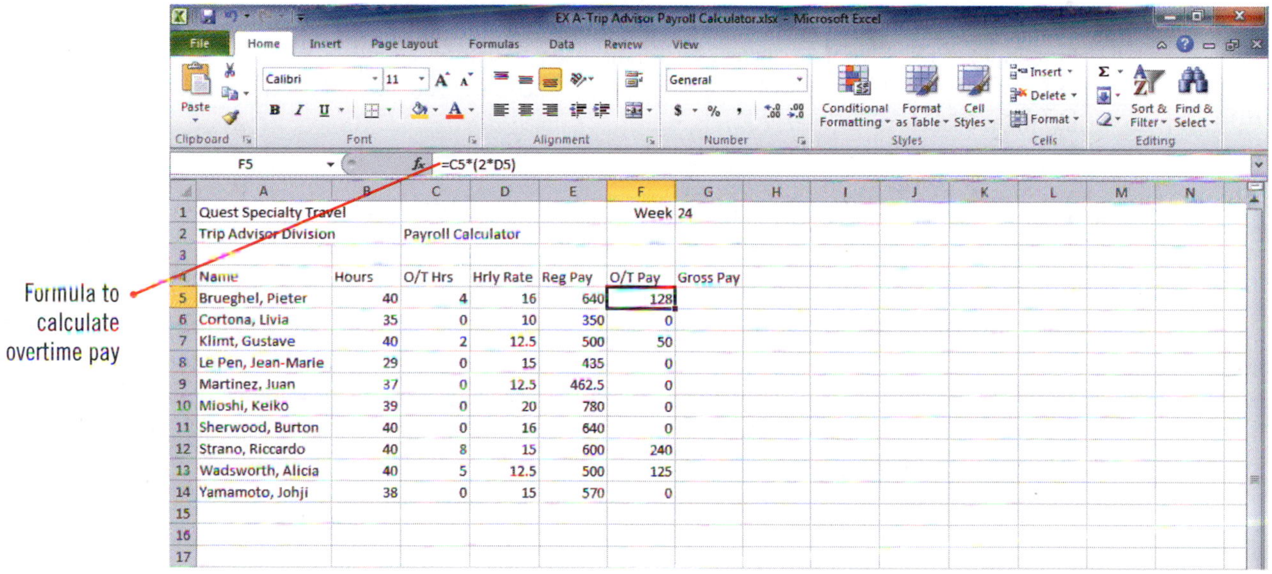

Formula to calculate overtime pay

**TABLE A-2:** Excel arithmetic operators

| operator | purpose | example |
|----------|---------|---------|
| + | Addition | =A5+A7 |
| - | Subtraction or negation | =A5-10 |
| * | Multiplication | =A5*A7 |
| / | Division | =A5/A7 |
| % | Percent | =35% |
| ^ (caret) | Exponent | =6^2 (same as $6^2$) |

Getting Started with Excel 2010

Excel 7

# Entering Labels and Values and Using the Sum Button

To enter content in a cell, you can type on the formula bar or directly in the cell itself. When entering content in a worksheet, you should start by entering all the labels first. **Labels** are entries that contain text and numerical information not used in calculations, such as "2011 Sales" or "Travel Expenses." Labels help you identify data in worksheet rows and columns, making your worksheet easier to understand. **Values** are numbers, formulas, and functions that can be used in calculations. To enter a calculation, you type an equal sign (=) plus the formula for the calculation; some examples of an Excel calculation are "=2+2" and "=C5+C6." Functions are Excel's built-in formulas; you learn more about them in the next unit.  You want to enter some information in the Trip Advisor Payroll Calculator workbook, and use a very simple function to total a range of cells.

1. **Click cell A15, then click in the formula bar**

   Notice that the **mode indicator** on the status bar now reads "Edit," indicating you are in Edit mode. You are in Edit mode any time you are entering or changing the contents of a cell.

   > **QUICK TIP**
   > If you change your mind and want to cancel an entry in the formula bar, click the Cancel button ☒ on the formula bar.

2. **Type Totals, then click the Enter button ☑ on the formula bar**

   Clicking the Enter button accepts the entry. The new text is left-aligned in the cell. Labels are left-aligned by default, and values are right-aligned by default. Excel recognizes an entry as a value if it is a number or it begins with one of these symbols: +, -, =, @, #, or $. When a cell contains both text and numbers, Excel recognizes it as a label.

3. **Click cell B15**

   You want this cell to total the hours worked by all the trip advisors. You might think you need to create a formula that looks like this: =B5+B6+B7+B8+B9+B10+B11+B12+B13+B14. However, there's an easier way to achieve this result.

4. **Click the Sum button Σ in the Editing group on the Home tab on the Ribbon**

   The SUM function is inserted in the cell, and a suggested range appears in parentheses, as shown in Figure A-7. A **function** is a built-in formula; it includes the **arguments** (the information necessary to calculate an answer) as well as cell references and other unique information. Clicking the Sum button sums the adjacent range (that is, the cells next to the active cell) above or to the left, though you can adjust the range if necessary by selecting a different range before accepting the cell entry. Using the SUM function is quicker than entering a formula, and using the range B5:B14 is more efficient than entering individual cell references.

   > **QUICK TIP**
   > You can create formulas in a cell even before you enter the values to be calculated; the results will be recalculated as soon as the data is entered.

5. **Click ☑ on the formula bar**

   Excel calculates the total contained in cells B5:B14 and displays the result, 378, in cell B15. The cell actually contains the formula =SUM(B5:B14), and the result is displayed.

6. **Click cell C13, type 6, then press [Enter]**

   The number 6 replaces the cell's contents, the cell pointer moves to cell C14, and the value in cell F13 changes.

   > **QUICK TIP**
   > You can also press [Tab] to complete a cell entry and move the cell pointer to the right.

7. **Click cell C18, type Average Gross Pay, then press [Enter]**

   The new label is entered in cell C18. The contents appear to spill into the empty cells to the right.

8. **Click cell B15, position the pointer on the lower-right corner of the cell (the fill handle) so that the pointer changes to ✛, drag the ✛ to cell G15, then release the mouse button**

   Dragging the fill handle across a range of cells copies the contents of the first cell into the other cells in the range. In the range B15:F15, each filled cell now contains a function that sums the range of cells above, as shown in Figure A-8.

9. **Save your work**

**FIGURE A-7:** Creating a formula using the Sum button

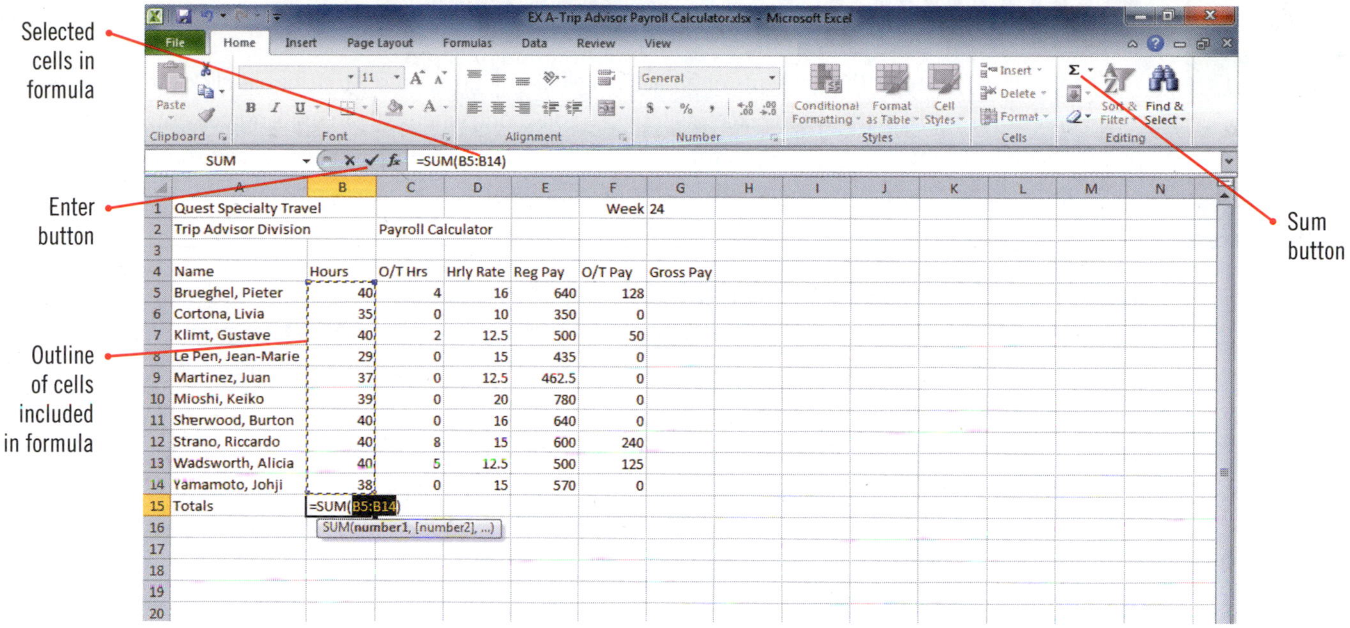

Selected cells in formula

Enter button

Outline of cells included in formula

Sum button

| | A | B | C | D | E | F | G | H | I | J | K | L | M | N |
|---|---|---|---|---|---|---|---|---|---|---|---|---|---|---|
| 1 | Quest Specialty Travel | | | | | Week | 24 | | | | | | | |
| 2 | Trip Advisor Division | | Payroll Calculator | | | | | | | | | | | |
| 3 | | | | | | | | | | | | | | |
| 4 | Name | Hours | O/T Hrs | Hrly Rate | Reg Pay | O/T Pay | Gross Pay | | | | | | | |
| 5 | Brueghel, Pieter | 40 | 4 | 16 | 640 | 128 | | | | | | | | |
| 6 | Cortona, Livia | 35 | 0 | 10 | 350 | 0 | | | | | | | | |
| 7 | Klimt, Gustave | 40 | 2 | 12.5 | 500 | 50 | | | | | | | | |
| 8 | Le Pen, Jean-Marie | 29 | 0 | 15 | 435 | 0 | | | | | | | | |
| 9 | Martinez, Juan | 37 | 0 | 12.5 | 462.5 | 0 | | | | | | | | |
| 10 | Mioshi, Keiko | 39 | 0 | 20 | 780 | 0 | | | | | | | | |
| 11 | Sherwood, Burton | 40 | 0 | 16 | 640 | 0 | | | | | | | | |
| 12 | Strano, Riccardo | 40 | 8 | 15 | 600 | 240 | | | | | | | | |
| 13 | Wadsworth, Alicia | 40 | 5 | 12.5 | 500 | 125 | | | | | | | | |
| 14 | Yamamoto, Johji | 38 | 0 | 15 | 570 | 0 | | | | | | | | |
| 15 | Totals | =SUM(B5:B14) | | | | | | | | | | | | |
| 16 | | SUM(number1, [number2], ...) | | | | | | | | | | | | |
| 17 | | | | | | | | | | | | | | |
| 18 | | | | | | | | | | | | | | |
| 19 | | | | | | | | | | | | | | |
| 20 | | | | | | | | | | | | | | |

Excel 2010

**FIGURE A-8:** Results of copied SUM functions

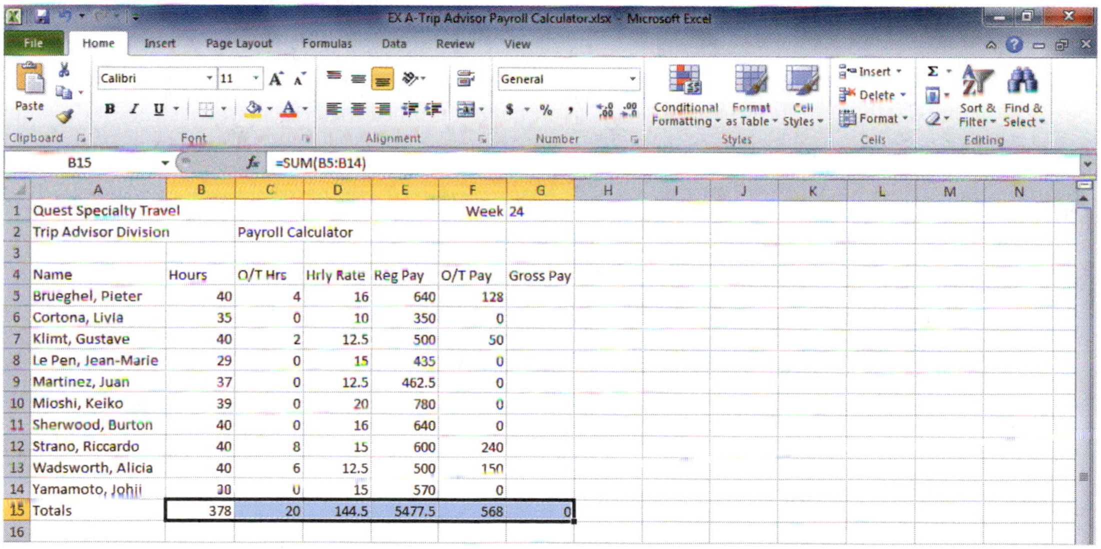

B15    =SUM(B5:B14)

| | A | B | C | D | E | F | G | H | I | J | K | L | M | N |
|---|---|---|---|---|---|---|---|---|---|---|---|---|---|---|
| 1 | Quest Specialty Travel | | | | | Week | 24 | | | | | | | |
| 2 | Trip Advisor Division | | Payroll Calculator | | | | | | | | | | | |
| 3 | | | | | | | | | | | | | | |
| 4 | Name | Hours | O/T Hrs | Hrly Rate | Reg Pay | O/T Pay | Gross Pay | | | | | | | |
| 5 | Brueghel, Pieter | 40 | 4 | 16 | 640 | 128 | | | | | | | | |
| 6 | Cortona, Livia | 35 | 0 | 10 | 350 | 0 | | | | | | | | |
| 7 | Klimt, Gustave | 40 | 2 | 12.5 | 500 | 50 | | | | | | | | |
| 8 | Le Pen, Jean-Marie | 29 | 0 | 15 | 435 | 0 | | | | | | | | |
| 9 | Martinez, Juan | 37 | 0 | 12.5 | 462.5 | 0 | | | | | | | | |
| 10 | Mioshi, Keiko | 39 | 0 | 20 | 780 | 0 | | | | | | | | |
| 11 | Sherwood, Burton | 40 | 0 | 16 | 640 | 0 | | | | | | | | |
| 12 | Strano, Riccardo | 40 | 8 | 15 | 600 | 240 | | | | | | | | |
| 13 | Wadsworth, Alicia | 40 | 6 | 12.5 | 500 | 150 | | | | | | | | |
| 14 | Yamamoto, Johji | 38 | 0 | 15 | 570 | 0 | | | | | | | | |
| 15 | Totals | 378 | 20 | 144.5 | 5477.5 | 568 | 0 | | | | | | | |
| 16 | | | | | | | | | | | | | | |

## Navigating a worksheet

With over a million cells available in a worksheet, it is important to know how to move around in, or **navigate**, a worksheet. You can use the arrow keys on the keyboard [↑],[↓], [→], or [←] to move one cell at a time, or press [Page Up] or [Page Down] to move one screen at a time. To move one screen to the left press [Alt][Page Up]; to move one screen to the right press [Alt][Page Down]. You can also use the mouse pointer to click the desired cell. If the desired cell is not visible in the worksheet window, use the scroll bars or use the Go To command by clicking the Find & Select button in the Editing group on the Home tab on the Ribbon. To quickly jump to the first cell in a worksheet press [Ctrl][Home]; to jump to the last cell, press [Ctrl][End].

# Editing Cell Entries

You can change, or **edit**, the contents of an active cell at any time. To do so, double-click the cell, click in the formula bar, or just start typing. Excel switches to Edit mode when you are making cell entries. Different pointers, shown in Table A-3, guide you through the editing process. You noticed some errors in the worksheet and want to make corrections. The first error is in cell A5, which contains a misspelled name.

**STEPS**

1. **Click cell A5, then click to the right of P in the formula bar**

   As soon as you click in the formula bar, a blinking vertical line called the **insertion point** appears on the formula bar at the location where new text will be inserted. See Figure A-9. The mouse pointer changes to I when you point anywhere in the formula bar.

2. **Press [Delete], then click the Enter button ✔ on the formula bar**

   Clicking the Enter button accepts the edit, and the spelling of the employee's first name is corrected. You can also press [Enter] or [Tab] to accept an edit. Pressing [Enter] to accept an edit moves the cell pointer down one cell, and pressing [Tab] to accept an edit moves the cell pointer one cell to the right.

> **QUICK TIP**
> On some keyboards, you might need to press an [F Lock] key to enable the function keys.

3. **Click cell B6, then press [F2]**

   Excel switches to Edit mode, and the insertion point blinks in the cell. Pressing [F2] activates the cell for editing directly in the cell instead of the formula bar. Whether you edit in the cell or the formula bar is simply a matter of preference; the results in the worksheet are the same.

> **QUICK TIP**
> The Undo button allows you to reverse up to 100 previous actions, one at a time.

4. **Press [Backspace], type 8, then press [Enter]**

   The value in the cell changes from 35 to 38, and cell B7 becomes the active cell. Did you notice that the calculations in cells B15 and E15 also changed? That's because those cells contain formulas that include cell B6 in their calculations. If you make a mistake when editing, you can click the Cancel button ✖ on the formula bar *before* pressing [Enter] to confirm the cell entry. The Enter and Cancel buttons appear only when you're in Edit mode. If you notice the mistake *after* you have confirmed the cell entry, click the Undo button ↻ on the Quick Access toolbar.

> **QUICK TIP**
> You can use the keyboard to select all cell contents by clicking to the right of the cell contents in the cell or formula bar, pressing and holding [Shift], then pressing [Home].

5. **Click cell A9, then double-click the word Juan in the formula bar**

   Double-clicking a word in a cell selects it.

6. **Type Javier, then press [Enter]**

   When text is selected, typing deletes it and replaces it with the new text.

7. **Double-click cell C12, press [Delete], type 4, then click ✔**

   Double-clicking a cell activates it for editing directly in the cell. Compare your screen to Figure A-10.

8. **Save your work**

   Your changes to the workbook are saved.

---

### Recovering unsaved changes to a workbook file

You can use Excel's AutoRecover feature to automatically save (Autosave) your work as often as you want. This means that if you suddenly lose power or if Excel closes unexpectedly while you're working, you can recover all or some of the changes you made since you saved it last. (Of course, this is no substitute for regularly saving your work: this is just added insurance.) To customize the AutoRecover settings, click the File tab, click Options, then click

Save. AutoRecover lets you decide how often and into which location it should Autosave files. When you restart Excel after losing power, a Document Recovery pane opens and provides access to the saved and Autosaved versions of the files that were open when Excel closed. You can also click the File tab, click Recent on the navigation bar, then click Recover Unsaved Workbooks to open Autosaved workbooks using the Open dialog box.

Active cell

Insertion point

Mode indicator

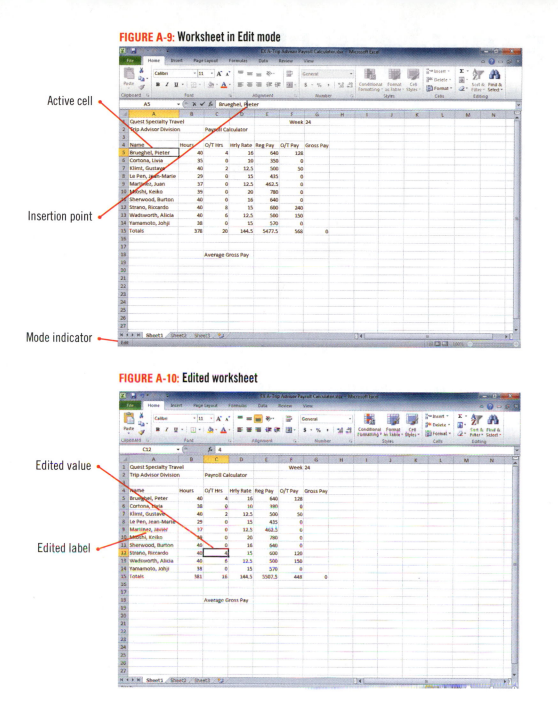

**FIGURE A-10:** Edited worksheet

Edited value

Edited label

**TABLE A-3:** Common pointers in Excel

| name | pointer | use to | visible over the |
|---|---|---|---|
| Normal | ✛ | Select a cell or range; indicates Ready mode | Active worksheet |
| Fill handle | ✚ | Copy cell contents to adjacent cells | Lower-right corner of the active cell or range |
| I-beam | I | Edit cell contents in active cell or formula bar | Active cell in Edit mode or over the formula bar |
| Move | ⬍ | Change the location of the selected cell(s) | Perimeter of the active cell(s) |
| Copy | ⬍⁺ | Create a duplicate of the selected cell(s) | Perimeter of the active cell(s) when [Ctrl] is pressed |
| Column resize | ↔ | Change the width of a column | Border between column heading indicators |

# Entering and Editing a Simple Formula

You use formulas in Excel to perform calculations such as adding, multiplying, and averaging. Formulas in an Excel worksheet start with the equal sign ( = ), also called the **formula prefix**, followed by cell addresses, range names, values, and calculation operators. **Calculation operators** indicate what type of calculation you want to perform on the cells, ranges, or values. They can include **arithmetic operators,** which perform mathematical calculations (see Table A-2 in the "Understanding Formulas" lesson); **comparison operators**, which compare values for the purpose of true/false results; **text concatenation operators**, which join strings of text in different cells; and **reference operators**, which enable you to use ranges in calculations. You want to create a formula in the worksheet that calculates gross pay for each employee.

**STEPS**

1. **Click cell G5**

   This is the first cell where you want to insert the formula. To calculate gross pay, you need to add regular pay and overtime pay. For employee Peter Brueghel, regular pay appears in cell E5 and overtime pay appears in cell F5.

**QUICK TIP**
You can reference a cell in a formula either by typing the cell reference or clicking the cell in the worksheet; when you click a cell to add a reference, the Mode indicator changes to "Point."

2. **Type =, click cell E5, type +, then click cell F5**

   Compare your formula bar to Figure A-11. The blue and green cell references in cell G5 correspond to the colored cell outlines. When entering a formula, it's a good idea to use cell references instead of values whenever you can. That way, if you later change a value in a cell (if, for example, Peter's regular pay changes to 615), any formula that includes this information reflects accurate, up-to-date results.

3. **Click the Enter button ✓ on the formula bar**

   The result of the formula =E5+F5, 768, appears in cell G5. This same value appears in cell G15 because cell G15 contains a formula that totals the values in cells G5:G14, and there are no other values now.

4. **Click cell F5**

   The formula in this cell calculates overtime pay by multiplying overtime hours (C5) times twice the regular hourly rate (2*D5). You want to edit this formula to reflect a new overtime pay rate.

5. **Click to the right of 2 in the formula bar, then type .5 as shown in Figure A-12**

   The formula that calculates overtime pay has been edited.

6. **Click ✓ on the formula bar**

   Compare your screen to Figure A-13. Notice that the calculated values in cells G5, F15, and G15 have all changed to reflect your edits to cell F5.

7. **Save your work**

---

### Understanding named ranges

It can be difficult to remember the cell locations of critical information in a worksheet, but using cell names can make this task much easier. You can name a single cell or range of contiguous, or touching, cells. For example, you might name a cell that contains data on average gross pay "AVG_GP" instead of trying to remember the cell address C18. A named range must begin with a letter or an underscore. It cannot contain any spaces or be the same as a built-in name, such as a function or another object (such as a different named range) in the workbook. To name a range, select the cell(s) you want to name, click the Name box in the formula bar, type the name you want to use, then press [Enter]. You can also name a range by clicking the Formulas tab, then clicking the Define Name button in the Defined Names group. Type the new range name in the Name text box in the New Name dialog box, verify the selected range, then click OK. When you use a named range in a formula, the named range appears instead of the cell address. You can also create a named range using the contents of a cell already in the range. Select the range containing the text you want to use as a name, then click the Create from Selection button in the Defined Names group. The Create Names from Selection dialog box opens. Choose the location of the name you want to use, then click OK.

FIGURE A-11: Simple formula in a worksheet

Cell outline color
corresponds to cell
reference

Referenced
cells are
inserted in
formula

Mode indicator
changes to Point

FIGURE A-12: Edited formula in a worksheet

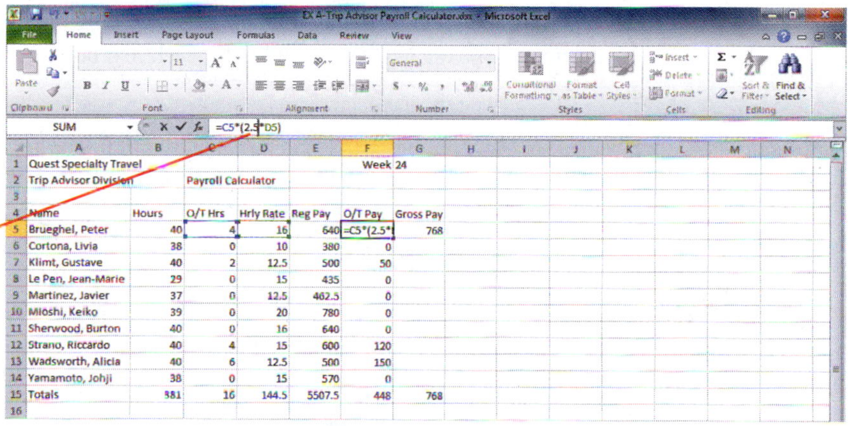

Edited value in
formula

FIGURE A-13: Edited formula with changes

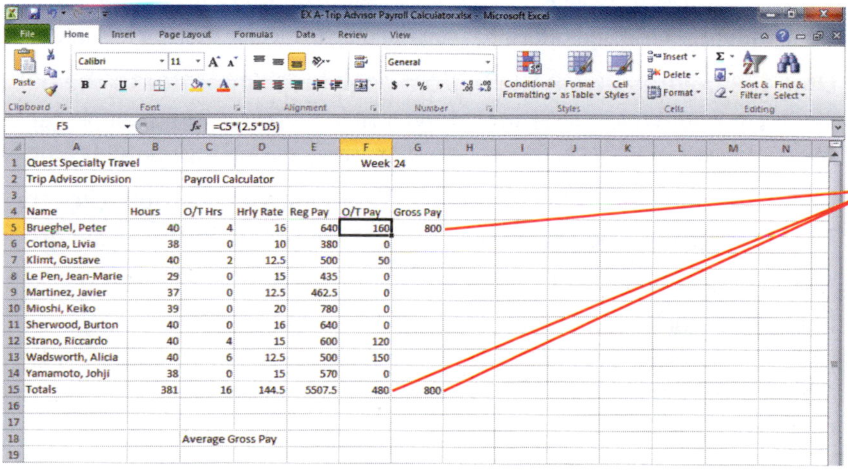

Edited formula
results in changes
to these other cells

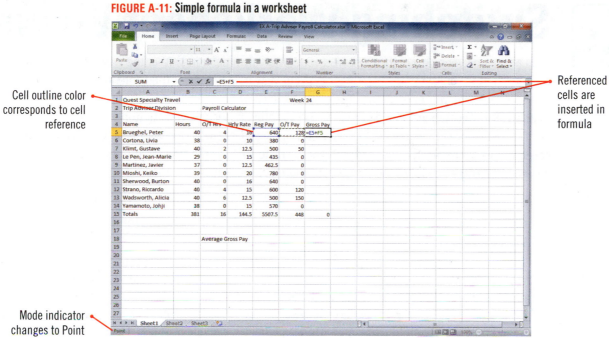

# Switching Worksheet Views

•You can change your view of the worksheet window at any time, using either the View tab on the Ribbon or the View buttons on the status bar. Changing your view does not affect the contents of a worksheet; it just makes it easier for you to focus on different tasks, such as entering content or preparing a worksheet for printing. The View tab includes a variety of viewing options, such as View buttons, zoom controls, and the ability to show or hide worksheet elements such as gridlines. The status bar offers fewer View options but can be more convenient to use. 🎨 You want to make some final adjustments to your worksheet, including adding a header so the document looks more polished.

## STEPS

> **QUICK TIP**
>
> Although a worksheet can contain more than a million rows and thousands of columns, the current document contains only as many pages as necessary for the current project.

1. **Click the View tab on the Ribbon, then click the Page Layout button in the Workbook Views group**

   The view switches from the default view, Normal, to Page Layout view. **Normal view** shows the worksheet without including certain details like headers and footers, or tools like rulers and a page number indicator; it's great for creating and editing a worksheet, but may not be detailed enough when you want to put the finishing touches on a document. **Page Layout view** provides a more accurate view of how a worksheet will look when printed, as shown in Figure A-14. The margins of the page are displayed, along with a text box for the header. A footer text box appears at the bottom of the page, but your screen may not be large enough to view it without scrolling. Above and to the left of the page are rulers. Part of an additional page appears to the right of this page, but it is dimmed, indicating that it does not contain any data. A page number indicator on the status bar tells you the current page and the total number of pages in this worksheet.

2. **Drag the pointer ⌖ over the header *without clicking***

   The header is made up of three text boxes: left, center, and right. Each text box is highlighted blue as you pass over it with the pointer.

> **QUICK TIP**
>
> You can change header and footer information using the Header & Footer Tools Design tab that opens on the Ribbon when a header or footer is active. For example, you can insert the date by clicking the Current Date button in the Header & Footer Elements group, or insert the time by clicking the Current Time button.

3. **Click the left header text box, type Quest Specialty Travel, click the center header text box, type Trip Advisor Payroll Calculator, click the right header text box, then type Week 24**

   The new text appears in the text boxes, as shown in Figure A-15.

4. **Select the range A1:G2, then press [Delete]**

   The duplicate information you just entered in the header is deleted from cells in the worksheet.

5. **Click the View tab if necessary, click the Ruler check box in the Show group, then click the Gridlines check box in the Show group**

   The rulers and the gridlines are hidden. By default, gridlines in a worksheet do not print, so hiding them gives you a more accurate image of your final document.

6. **Click the Page Break Preview button 🗔 on the status bar, then click OK in the Welcome to Page Break Preview dialog box, if necessary**

   Your view changes to **Page Break Preview**, which displays a reduced view of each page of your worksheet, along with page break indicators that you can drag to include more or less information on a page.

7. **Drag the pointer ↕ from the bottom page break indicator to the bottom of row 21**

   See Figure A-16. When you're working on a large worksheet with multiple pages, sometimes you need to adjust where pages break; in this worksheet, however, the information all fits comfortably on one page.

> **QUICK TIP**
>
> Once you view a worksheet in Page Break Preview, the page break indicators appear as dotted lines after you switch back to Normal view or Page Layout view.

8. **Click the Page Layout button in the Workbook Views group, click the Ruler check box in the Show group, then click the Gridlines check box in the Show group**

   The rulers and gridlines are no longer hidden. You can show or hide View tab items in any view.

9. **Save your work**

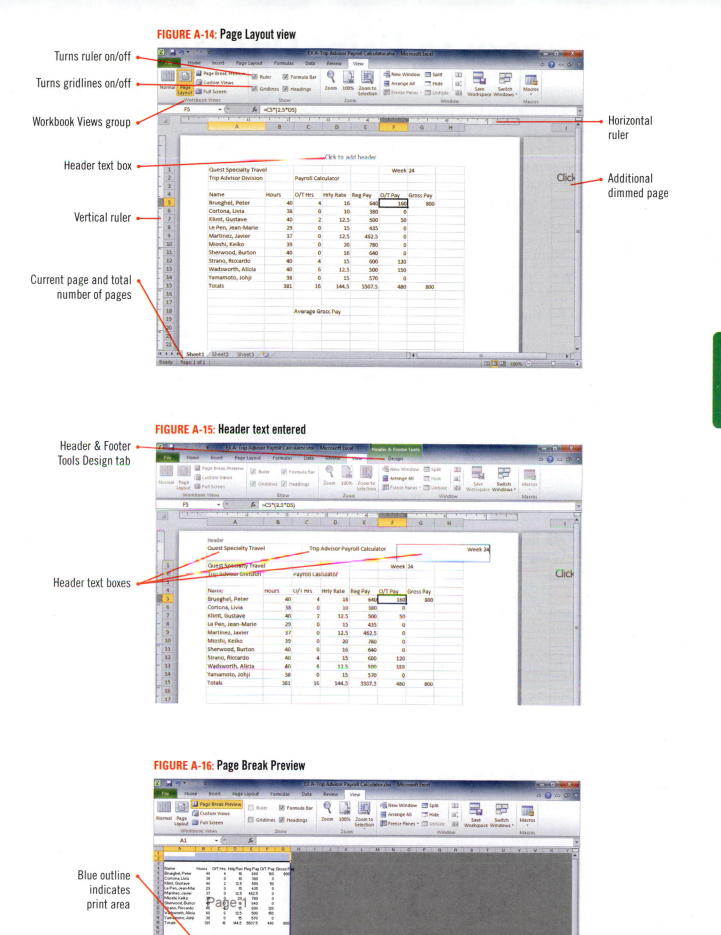

**FIGURE A-14:** Page Layout view

Turns ruler on/off

Turns gridlines on/off

Workbook Views group

Header text box

Vertical ruler

Current page and total number of pages

Horizontal ruler

Additional dimmed page

Click

**FIGURE A-15:** Header text entered

Header & Footer Tools Design tab

Header text boxes

**FIGURE A-16:** Page Break Preview

Blue outline indicates print area

Excel 2010

# Choosing Print Options

Before printing a document, you may want to review it using the Page Layout tab to fine-tune your printed output. You can use tools on the Page Layout tab to adjust print orientation (the direction in which the content prints across the page), paper size, and location of page breaks. You can also use the Scale to Fit options on the Page Layout tab to fit a large amount of data on a single page without making changes to individual margins, and to turn gridlines and column/row headings on and off. When you are ready to print, you can set print options such as the number of copies to print and the correct printer, and you can preview your document in Backstage view using the File tab. You can also adjust page layout settings from within Backstage view and immediately see the results in the document preview.  You are ready to prepare your worksheet for printing.

## STEPS

1. **Click cell A21, type your name, then press [Enter]**

2. **Click the Page Layout tab on the Ribbon**

   Compare your screen to Figure A-17. The dotted line indicates the default **print area**, the area to be printed.

> **QUICK TIP**
> You can use the Zoom slider on the status bar at any time to enlarge your view of specific areas of your worksheet.

3. **Click the Orientation button in the Page Setup group, then click Landscape**

   The paper orientation changes to **landscape**, so the contents will print across the length of the page instead of across the width.

4. **Click the Orientation button in the Page Setup group, then click Portrait**

   The orientation returns to **portrait**, so the contents will print across the width of the page.

5. **Click the Gridlines View check box in the Sheet Options group on the Page Layout tab, click the Gridlines Print check box to select it if necessary, then save your work**

   Printing gridlines makes the data easier to read, but the gridlines will not print unless the Gridlines Print check box is checked.

> **QUICK TIP**
> To change the active printer, click the current printer in the Printer section in Backstage view, then choose a different printer.

6. **Click the File tab, then click Print on the navigation bar**

   The Print tab in Backstage view displays a preview of your worksheet exactly as it will look when it is printed. To the left of the worksheet preview, you can also change a number of document settings and print options. To open the Page Setup dialog box and adjust page layout options, click the Page Setup link in the Settings section. Compare your preview screen to Figure A-18. You can print from this view by clicking the Print button, or return to the worksheet without printing by clicking the File tab again.

> **QUICK TIP**
> If the Quick Print button appears on the Quick Access Toolbar, you can print your worksheet using the default settings by clicking it.

7. **Compare your settings to Figure A-18, then click the Print button**

   One copy of the worksheet prints.

8. **Submit your work to your instructor as directed, then exit Excel**

---

### Printing worksheet formulas

Sometimes you need to keep a record of all the formulas in a worksheet. You might want to do this to see exactly how you came up with a complex calculation, so you can explain it to others. To prepare a worksheet to show formulas rather than results when printed, open the workbook containing the formulas you want to print. Click the Formulas tab, then click the Show Formulas button in the Formula Auditing group to select it. When the Show Formulas button is selected, formulas rather than resulting values are displayed in the worksheet on screen and when printed.

**FIGURE A-17:** Worksheet with portrait orientation

Dotted line
surrounds
print area

Your name
appears here

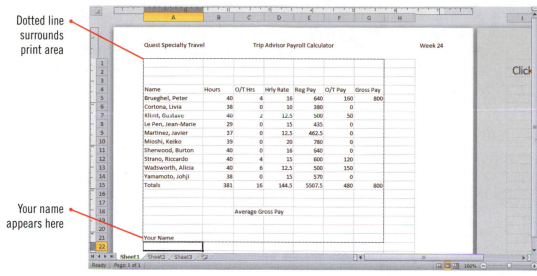

**FIGURE A-18:** Print tab in Backstage view

Click to change
number of copies

Print button

Active printer;
yours will be different

Choose which
pages to print

Click to select
scaling options

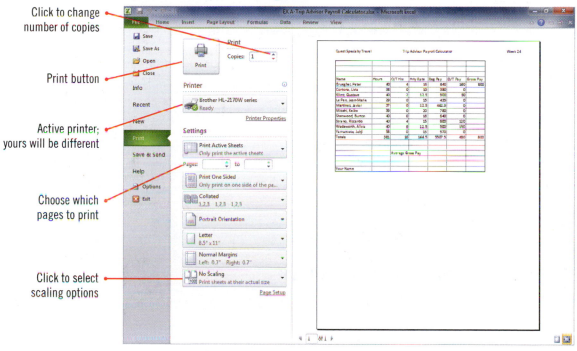

---

## Scaling to fit

If you have a large amount of data that you want to fit to a single sheet of paper, but you don't want to spend a lot of time trying to adjust the margins and other settings, you have several options. You can easily print your work on a single sheet by clicking the No Scaling list arrow in the Settings section on the Print tab in Backstage view, then clicking Fit Sheet on One Page. Another method for fitting worksheet content onto one page is to click the Page Layout tab, then change the Width and Height settings in the Scale to Fit group each to 1 Page. You can also use the Fit to option in the Page Setup dialog box to fit a worksheet on one page. To open the Page Setup dialog box, click the dialog box launcher in the Scale to Fit group on the Page Layout tab, or click the Page Setup link on the Print tab in Backstage view. Make sure the Page tab is selected in the Page Setup dialog box, then click the Fit to option button.

# Practice

**SAM** For current SAM information, including versions and content details, visit SAM Central (http://www.cengage.com/samcentral). If you have a SAM user profile, you may have access to hands-on instruction, practice, and assessment of the skills covered in this unit. Since various versions of SAM are supported throughout the life of this text, check with your instructor for the correct instructions and URL/Web site for accessing assignments.

## Concepts Review

**Label the elements of the Excel worksheet window shown in Figure A-19.**

FIGURE A-19

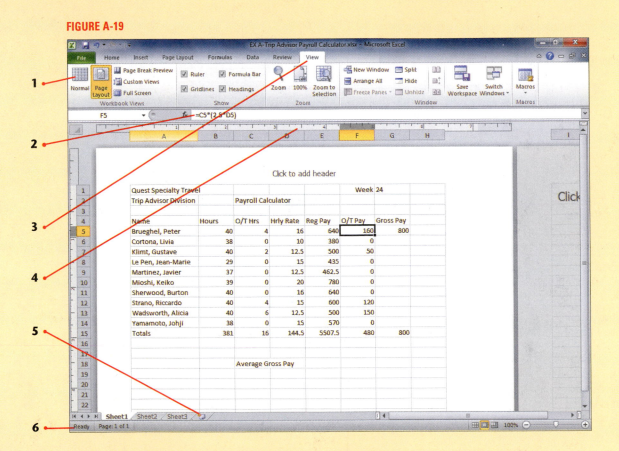

**Match each term with the statement that best describes it.**

7. **Formula prefix**

8. **Normal view**

9. **Name box**

10. **Cell**

11. **Orientation**

12. **Workbook**

a. Default view in Excel

b. Direction in which contents of page will print

c. Equal sign preceding a formula

d. File consisting of one or more worksheets

e. Intersection of a column and a row

f. Part of the Excel program window that displays the active cell address

**Select the best answer from the list of choices.**

13. **The maximum number of worksheets you can include in a workbook is:**
    - **a.** 3.
    - **b.** 250.
    - **c.** 255.
    - **d.** Unlimited.

14. **Using a cell address in a formula is known as:**
    - **a.** Formularizing.
    - **b.** Prefixing.
    - **c.** Cell referencing.
    - **d.** Cell mathematics.

15. **Which feature could be used to print a very long worksheet on a single sheet of paper?**
    - **a.** Show Formulas
    - **b.** Scale to fit
    - **c.** Page Break Preview
    - **d.** Named Ranges

16. **A selection of multiple cells is called a:**
    - **a.** Group.
    - **b.** Range.
    - **c.** Reference.
    - **d.** Package.

17. **Which worksheet view shows how your worksheet will look when printed?**
    - **a.** Page Layout
    - **b.** Data
    - **c.** Review
    - **d.** View

18. **Which key can you press to switch to Edit mode?**
    - **a.** [F1]
    - **b.** [F2]
    - **c.** [F4]
    - **d.** [F6]

19. **Which view shows you a reduced view of each page of your worksheet?**
    - **a.** Normal
    - **b.** Page Layout
    - **c.** Thumbnail
    - **d.** Page Break Preview

20. **In which area can you see a preview of your worksheet?**
    - **a.** Page Setup
    - **b.** Backstage view
    - **c.** Printer Setup
    - **d.** View tab

21. **In which view can you see the header and footer areas of a worksheet?**
    - **a.** Normal view
    - **b.** Page Layout view
    - **c.** Page Break Preview
    - **d.** Header/Footer view

## Skills Review

1. **Understand spreadsheet software.**
   - **a.** What is the difference between a workbook and a worksheet?
   - **b.** Identify five common business uses for electronic spreadsheets.
   - **c.** What is what-if analysis?

2. **Tour the Excel 2010 window.**
   - **a.** Start Excel.
   - **b.** Open the file EX A-2.xlsx from the drive and folder where you store your Data Files, then save it as **EX A-Weather Statistics**.
   - **c.** Locate the formula bar, the Sheet tabs, the mode indicator, and the cell pointer.

3. **Understand formulas.**
   - **a.** What is the average high temperature of the listed cities? (*Hint*: Select the range B5:G5 and use the status bar.)
   - **b.** What formula would you create to calculate the difference in altitude between Denver and Phoenix? Enter your answer (as an equation) in cell D13.

4. **Enter labels and values and use the Sum button.**
   - **a.** Click cell H8, then use the Sum button to calculate the total snowfall.
   - **b.** Click cell H7, then use the Sum button to calculate the total rainfall.
   - **c.** Save your changes to the file.

# Skills Review (continued)

### 5. Edit cell entries.

a. Use [F2] to correct the spelling of SanteFe in cell G3 (the correct spelling is Santa Fe).

b. Click cell A17, then type your name.

c. Save your changes.

### 6. Enter and edit a simple formula.

a. Change the value 41 in cell C8 to **52**.

b. Change the value 37 in cell D6 to **35.4**.

c. Select cell J4, then use the fill handle to copy the formula in cell J4 to cells J5:J8

d. Save your changes.

### 7. Switch worksheet views.

a. Click the View tab on the Ribbon, then switch to Page Layout view.

b. Add the header **Average Annual Weather Statistics** to the center header text box.

c. Add your name to the right header box.

d. Delete the contents of cell A1.

e. Delete the contents of cell A17.

f. Save your changes.

### 8. Choose print options.

a. Use the Page Layout tab to change the orientation to Portrait.

b. Turn off gridlines by deselecting both the Gridlines View and Gridlines Print check boxes (if necessary) in the Sheet Options group.

c. Scale the worksheet so all the information fits on one page. (*Hint*: Click the Width list arrow in the Scale to Fit group, click 1 page, click the Height list arrow in the Scale to Fit group, then click 1 page.) Compare your screen to Figure A-20.

d. Preview the worksheet in Backstage view, then print the worksheet.

e. Save your changes, submit your work to your instructor as directed, then close the workbook and exit Excel.

**FIGURE A-20**

| | Albany | Boston | Denver | Orlando | Phoenix | Santa Fe | Total | | Average |
|---|---|---|---|---|---|---|---|---|---|
| | | | | | | | | | |
| | | | | | | Average Annual Weather Statistics | | | Your Name |
| Altitude | 84 | 20 | 5286 | 91 | 1110 | 7000 | | | 2265.167 |
| High Temp | 71 | 69 | 64 | 82 | 86 | 70 | | | 73.66667 |
| Low Temp | -22 | 44 | 35.4 | 62 | 59 | 43 | | | 36.9 |
| Rain (in.) | 2.9 | 42.9 | 15.5 | 47.7 | 7.3 | 14 | 130.3 | | 21.71667 |
| Snow (in.) | 13.99 | 52 | 63 | 0 | 0 | 32 | 160.99 | | 26.83167 |
| | | | | | | | | | |
| Alt. Diff. -> | Denver vs. Phoenix | | 4176 | | | | | | |

## Independent Challenge 1

A local executive relocation company has hired you to help them make the transition to using Excel in their office. They would like to list their properties in a workbook. You've started a worksheet for this project that contains labels but no data.

If you have a SAM 2010 user profile, an autogradable SAM version of this assignment may be available at http://www.cengage.com/sam2010. Check with your instructor to confirm that this assignment is available in SAM. To use the SAM version of this assignment, log into the SAM 2010 Web site and download the instruction and start files.

a. Open the file EX A-3.xlsx from where you store your Data Files, then save it as **EX A-Property Listings**.

b. Enter the data shown in Table A-4 in columns A, C, D, and E (the property address information should spill into column B).

**TABLE A-4**

| Property Address | Price | Bedrooms | Bathrooms |
|---|---|---|---|
| 1507 Pinon Lane | 475000 | 4 | 2.5 |
| 32 Zanzibar Way | 325000 | 3 | 4 |
| 60 Pottery Lane | 475500 | 2 | 2 |
| 902 Excelsior Drive | 295000 | 4 | 3 |

# Independent Challenge 1 (continued)

**c.** Use Page Layout view to create a header with the following components: the title **Property Listings** in the center and your name on the right.

**d.** Create formulas for totals in cells C6:E6.

**e.** Save your changes, then compare your worksheet to Figure A-21.

**f.** Submit your work to your instructor as directed.

**g.** Close the worksheet and exit Excel.

**FIGURE A-21**

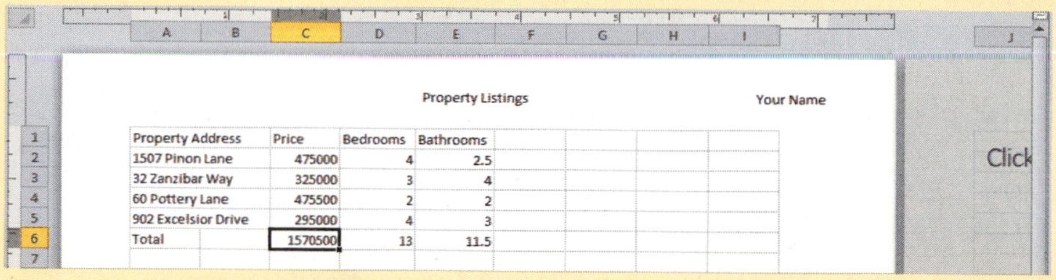

| Property Address | Price | Bedrooms | Bathrooms |
|---|---|---|---|
| 1507 Pinon Lane | 475000 | 4 | 2.5 |
| 32 Zanzibar Way | 325000 | 3 | 4 |
| 60 Pottery Lane | 475500 | 2 | 2 |
| 902 Excelsior Drive | 295000 | 4 | 3 |
| Total | 1570500 | 13 | 11.5 |

_Property Listings_ (center header)  _Your Name_ (right header)

# Independent Challenge 2

You are the General Manager for Prestige Import Motors, a small auto parts supplier. Although the company is just 5 years old, it is expanding rapidly, and you are continually looking for ways to save time. You recently began using Excel to manage and maintain data on inventory and sales, which has greatly helped you to track information accurately and efficiently.

**a.** Start Excel.

**b.** Save a new workbook as **EX A-Prestige Import Motors** in the drive and folder where you store your Data Files.

**c.** Switch to an appropriate view, then add a header that contains your name in the left header text box and the title **Prestige Import Motors** in the center header text box.

**d.** Using Figure A-22 as a guide, create labels for at least seven car manufacturers and sales for three months. Include other labels as appropriate. The car make should be in column A and the months should be in columns B, C, and D. A Total row should be beneath the data, and a Total column should be in column E.

**FIGURE A-22**

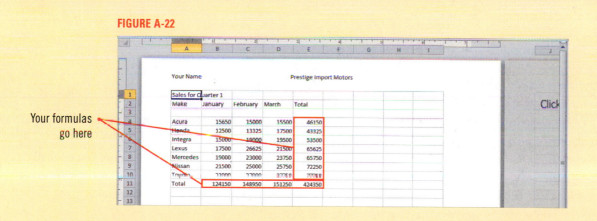

Your formulas go here

| Make | January | February | March | Total |
|---|---|---|---|---|
| Acura | 15650 | 15000 | 15500 | 46150 |
| Honda | 12500 | 13325 | 17500 | 43325 |
| Integra | 15000 | 19000 | 19500 | 53500 |
| Lexus | 17500 | 26625 | 21500 | 65625 |
| Mercedes | 19000 | 23000 | 23750 | 65750 |
| Nissan | 21500 | 25000 | 25750 | 72250 |
| Toyota | 23000 | 27000 | 27750 | 77750 |
| Total | 124150 | 148950 | 151250 | 424350 |

Sales for Quarter 1

**e.** Enter values of your choice for the monthly sales for each make.

**f.** Add formulas in the Total column to calculate total quarterly sales for each make. Add formulas at the bottom of each column of values to calculate the total for that column. Remember that you can use the Sum button and the fill handle to save time.

**g.** Save your changes, preview the worksheet in Backstage view, then submit your work to your instructor as directed.

# Independent Challenge 2 (continued)

**Advanced Challenge Exercise**

- Create a label two rows beneath the data in column A that says **15% increase**.
- Create a formula in each of cells B13, C13, and D13 that calculates monthly sales plus a 15% increase.
- Display the formulas in the worksheet, then print a copy of the worksheet with formulas displayed.
- Save the workbook.

**h.** Close the workbook and exit Excel.

# Independent Challenge 3

**This Independent Challenge requires an Internet connection.**

Your office is starting a branch in Paris, and you think it would be helpful to create a worksheet that can be used to convert Fahrenheit temperatures to Celsius, to help employees who are unfamiliar with this type of temperature measurement.

**a.** Start Excel, then save a blank workbook as **EX A-Temperature Conversions** in the drive and folder where you store your Data Files.

**b.** Create column headings using Figure A-23 as a guide. (*Hint*: You can widen column B by clicking cell B1, clicking the Format button in the Cells group on the Home tab, then clicking AutoFit Column Width.)

**FIGURE A-23**

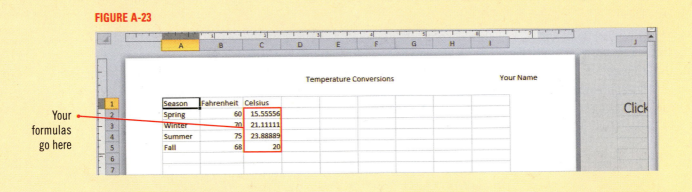

**c.** Create row labels for each of the seasons.

**d.** In the appropriate cells, enter what you determine to be a reasonable indoor temperature for each season.

**e.** Use your Web browser to find out the conversion rate for Fahrenheit to Celsius. (*Hint*: Use your favorite search engine to search on a term such as **temperature conversion formula**.)

**f.** In the appropriate cells, create a formula that calculates the conversion of the Fahrenheit temperature you entered into a Celsius temperature.

**g.** In Page Layout View, add your name and the title **Temperature Conversions** to the header.

**h.** Save your work, then submit your work to your instructor as directed.

**i.** Close the file, then exit Excel.

# Real Life Independent Challenge

You've decided to finally get your life organized. You're going to organize your personal finances so you can begin saving money, and you're going to use Excel to keep track of your expenses.

**a.** Start Excel, open the file EX A-4.xlsx from the drive and folder where you store your Data Files, then save it as **EX A-Personal Checkbook**.

**b.** Type check numbers (using your choice of a starting number) in cells A5 through A9.

**c.** Create sample data for the date, item, and amount in cells B5 through D9.

**d.** Save your work.

## Advanced Challenge Exercise

- Use Help to find out about creating a series of numbers.
- Delete the contents of cells A5:A9.
- Create a series of numbers in cells A5:A9.
- In cell C15, type a brief description of how you created the series.
- Save the workbook.

**e.** Create formulas in cells E5:E9 that calculate a running balance. (*Hint:* For the first check, the running balance equals the starting balance minus a check; for the following checks, the running balance equals the previous balance value minus each check value.)

**f.** Create a formula in cell D10 that totals the amount of the checks.

**g.** Enter your name in cell C12, then compare your screen to Figure A-24.

**h.** Save your changes to the file, submit your work to your instructor, then exit Excel.

**FIGURE A-24**

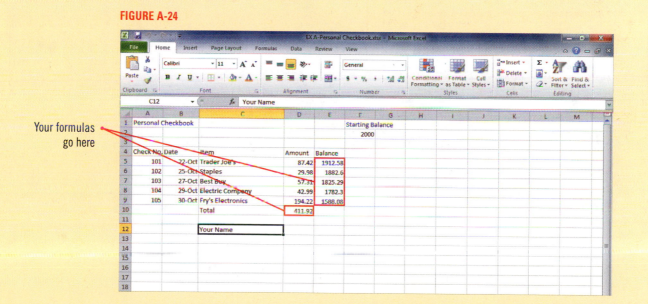

Your formulas go here

# Visual Workshop

Open the file EX A-5.xlsx from the drive and folder where you store your Data Files, then save it as **EX A-Inventory Items**. Using the skills you learned in this unit, modify your worksheet so it matches Figure A-25. Enter formulas in cells D4 through D13 and in cells B14 and C14. Use the Sum button and fill handle to make entering your formulas easier. Add your name in the left header text box, then print one copy of the worksheet with the formulas displayed.

**FIGURE A-25**

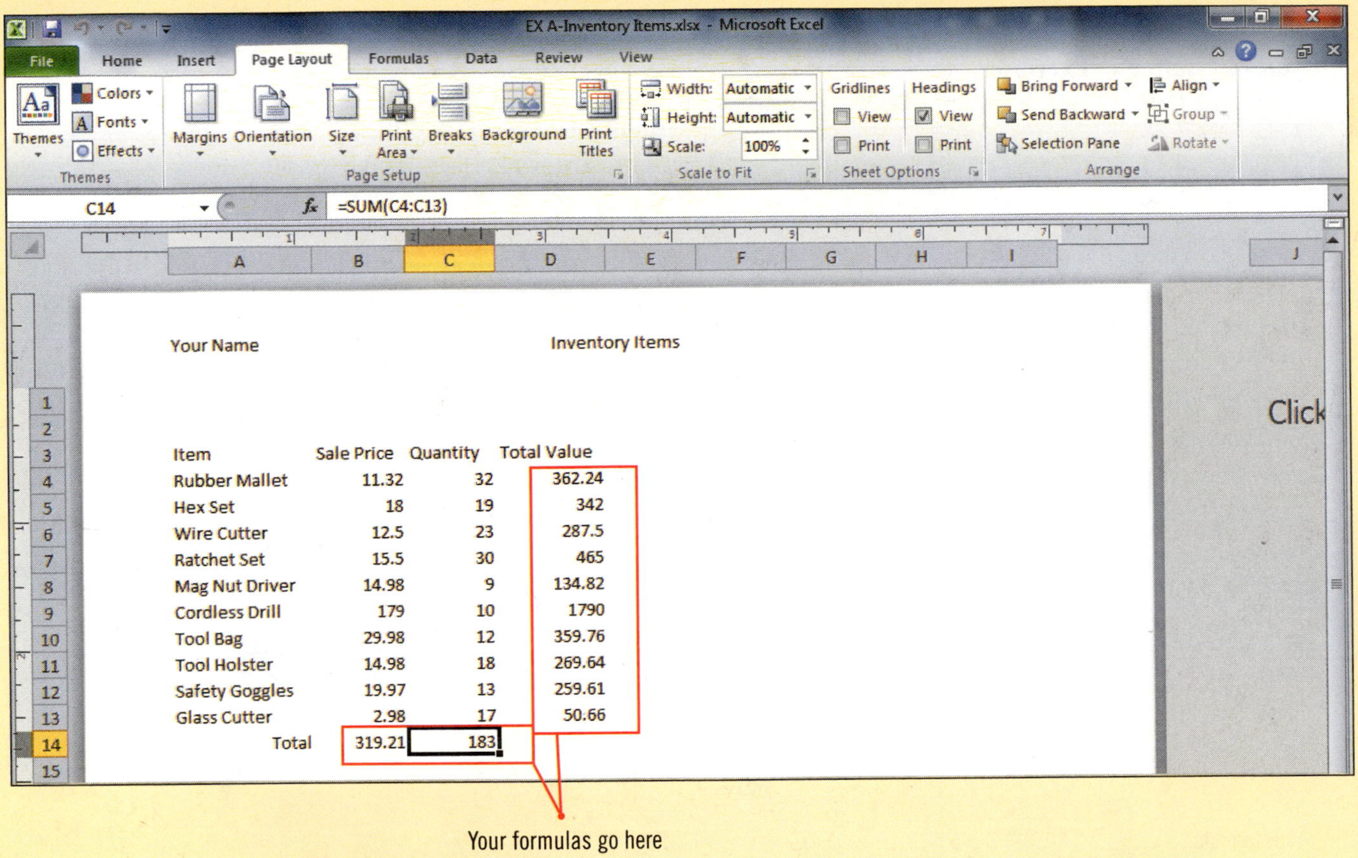

| Item | Sale Price | Quantity | Total Value |
|------|-----------|----------|-------------|
| Rubber Mallet | 11.32 | 32 | 362.24 |
| Hex Set | 18 | 19 | 342 |
| Wire Cutter | 12.5 | 23 | 287.5 |
| Ratchet Set | 15.5 | 30 | 465 |
| Mag Nut Driver | 14.98 | 9 | 134.82 |
| Cordless Drill | 179 | 10 | 1790 |
| Tool Bag | 29.98 | 12 | 359.76 |
| Tool Holster | 14.98 | 18 | 269.64 |
| Safety Goggles | 19.97 | 13 | 259.61 |
| Glass Cutter | 2.98 | 17 | 50.66 |
| Total | 319.21 | 183 | |

Your Name

Inventory Items

C14    =SUM(C4:C13)

Your formulas go here

# Working with Formulas and Functions

**Files You Will Need:**

EX B-1.xlsx

EX B-2.xlsx

EX B-3.xlsx

EX B-4.xlsx

Using your knowledge of Excel basics, you can develop your worksheets to include more complex formulas and functions. To work more efficiently, you can copy and move existing formulas into other cells instead of manually retyping the same information. When copying or moving, you can also control how cell references are handled so that your formulas always reference the intended cells.  Grace Wong, vice president of finance at Quest Specialty Travel, needs to analyze tour expenses for the current year. She has asked you to prepare a worksheet that summarizes this expense data and includes some statistical analysis. She would also like you to perform some what-if analysis, to see what quarterly expenses would look like with various projected increases.

**OBJECTIVES**

Create a complex formula

Insert a function

Type a function

Copy and move cell entries

Understand relative and absolute cell references

Copy formulas with relative cell references

Copy formulas with absolute cell references

Round a value with a function

# Creating a Complex Formula

A **complex formula** is one that uses more than one arithmetic operator. You might, for example, need to create a formula that uses addition and multiplication. In formulas containing more than one arithmetic operator, Excel uses the standard **order of precedence** rules to determine which operation to perform first. You can change the order of precedence in a formula by using parentheses around the part you want to calculate first. For example, the formula =4+2*5 equals 14, because the order of precedence dictates that multiplication is performed before addition. However, the formula =(4+2)*5 equals 30, because the parentheses cause 4+2 to be calculated first.  You want to create a formula that calculates a 20% increase in tour expenses.

## STEPS

1. **Start Excel, open the file EX B-1.xlsx from the drive and folder where you store your Data Files, then save it as EX B-Tour Expense Analysis**

**QUICK TIP**
When the mode indicator on the status bar says "Point," cells you click are added to the formula.

2. **Click cell B14, type =, click cell B12, then type +**
   In this first part of the formula, you are using a reference to the total expenses for Quarter 1.

3. **Click cell B12, then type *.2**
   The second part of this formula adds a 20% increase (B12*.2) to the original value of the cell (the total expenses for Quarter 1). Compare your worksheet to Figure B-1.

4. **Click the Enter button ☑ on the formula bar**
   The result, 41058.996, appears in cell B14.

5. **Press [Tab], type =, click cell C12, type +, click cell C12, type *.2, then click ☑**
   The result, 41096.916, appears in cell C14.

**QUICK TIP**
You can also copy the formulas by selecting the range C14:E14, clicking the Fill button 🔽 in the Editing group on the Home tab, then clicking Right.

6. **Drag the fill handle from cell C14 to cell E14**
   The calculated values appear in the selected range, as shown in Figure B-2. Dragging the fill handle on a cell copies the cell's contents or continues a series of data (such as Quarter 1, Quarter 2, etc.) into adjacent cells. This option is called **Auto Fill**.

7. **Save your work**

---

### Reviewing the order of precedence

When you work with formulas that contain more than one operator, the order of precedence is very important because it affects the final value. If a formula contains two or more operators, such as 4+.55/4000*25, Excel performs the calculations in a particular sequence based on the following rules: Operations inside parentheses are calculated before any other operations. Reference operators (such as ranges) are calculated first. Exponents are calculated next, then any multiplication and division—progressing from left to right.

Finally, addition and subtraction are calculated from left to right. In the example 4+.55/4000*25, Excel performs the arithmetic operations by first dividing 4000 into .55, then multiplying the result by 25, then adding 4. You can change the order of calculations by using parentheses. For example, in the formula (4+.55)/4000*25, Excel would first add 4 and .55, then divide that amount by 4000, then finally multiply by 25.

**FIGURE B-1:** Formula containing multiple arithmetic operators

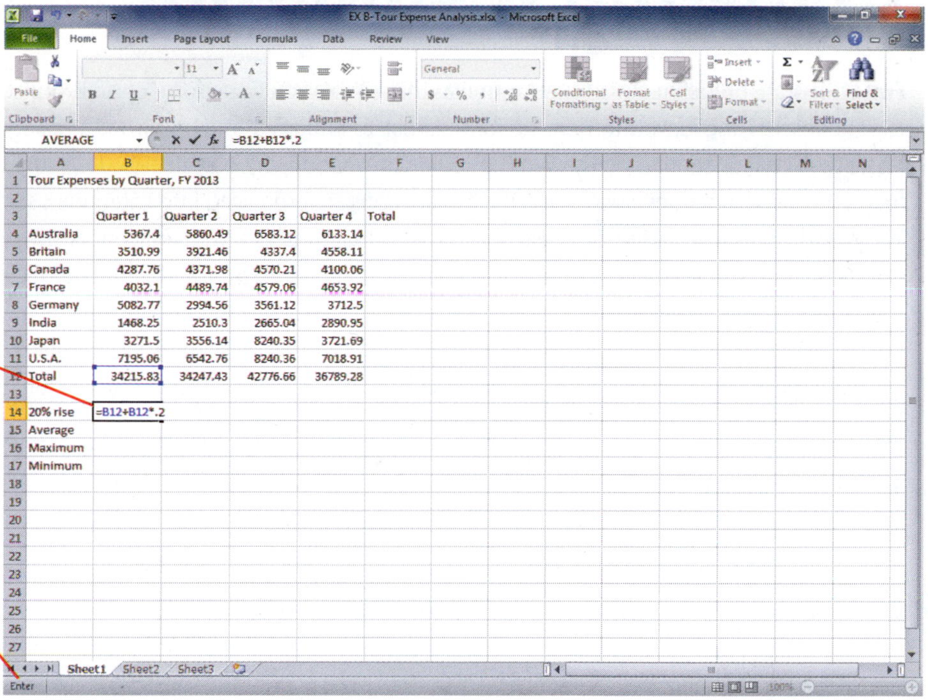

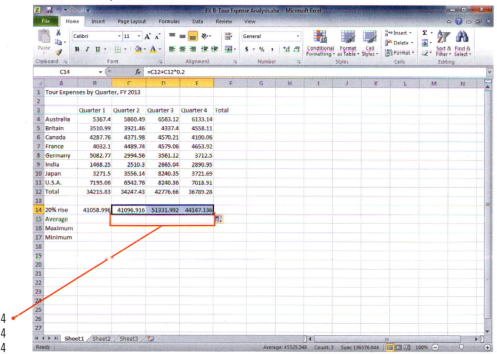

Complex formula

Mode indicator

**FIGURE B-2:** Complex formulas in worksheet

Formula in cell C14 copied to cells D14 and E14

# Inserting a Function

**Functions** are predefined worksheet formulas that enable you to perform complex calculations easily. You can use the Insert Function button on the formula bar to choose a function from a dialog box. You can quickly insert the SUM function using the Sum button on the Ribbon, or you can click the Sum list arrow to enter other frequently used functions, such as AVERAGE. Functions are organized into categories, such as Financial, Date & Time, and Statistical, based on their purposes. You can insert a function on its own or as part of another formula. For example, you have used the SUM function on its own to add a range of cells. You could also use the SUM function within a formula that adds a range of cells and then multiplies the total by a decimal. If you use a function alone, it always begins with an equal sign ( = ) as the formula prefix.  You need to calculate the average expenses for the first quarter of the year, and decide to use a function to do so.

## STEPS

1. **Click cell B15**

   This is the cell where you want to enter the calculation that averages expenses per country for the first quarter. You want to use the Insert Function dialog box to enter this function.

   > **QUICK TIP**
   > When using the Insert Function button or the Sum list arrow, it is not necessary to type the equal sign (=); Excel adds it as necessary.

2. ▶ **Click the Insert Function button $f_x$ on the formula bar**

   An equal sign ( = ) is inserted in the active cell and in the formula bar, and the Insert Function dialog box opens, as shown in Figure B-3. In this dialog box, you specify the function you want to use by clicking it in the Select a function list. The Select a function list initially displays recently used functions. If you don't see the function you want, you can click the Or select a category list arrow to choose the desired category. If you're not sure which category to choose, you can type the function name or a description in the Search for a function field. The AVERAGE function is a statistical function, but you don't need to open the Statistical category because this function already appears in the Most Recently Used category.

   > **QUICK TIP**
   > To learn about a function, click it in the Select a function list. The arguments and format required for the function appear below the list.

3. ▶ **Click AVERAGE in the Select a function list if necessary, read the information that appears under the list, then click OK**

   The Function Arguments dialog box opens, in which you define the range of cells you want to average.

   > **QUICK TIP**
   > When selecting a range, remember to select all the cells between and including the two references in the range.

4. ▶ **Click the Collapse button 🔲 in the Number1 field of the Function Arguments dialog box, select the range B4:B11 in the worksheet, then click the Expand button 🔲 in the Function Arguments dialog box**

   Clicking the Collapse button minimizes the dialog box so you can select cells in the worksheet. When you click the Expand button, the dialog box is restored, as shown in Figure B-4. You can also begin dragging in the worksheet to automatically minimize the dialog box; after you select the desired range, the dialog box is restored.

5. **Click OK**

   The Function Arguments dialog box closes, and the calculated value is displayed in cell B15. The average expenses per country for Quarter 1 is 4276.97875.

6. **Click cell C15, click the Sum list arrow $\Sigma$ ▾ in the Editing group on the Home tab, then click Average**

   A ScreenTip beneath cell C15 displays the arguments needed to complete the function. The text "number1" is shown in boldface type, telling you that the next step is to supply the first cell in the group you want to average. You want to average a range of cells.

7. **Select the range C4:C11 in the worksheet, then click the Enter button ✓ on the formula bar**

   The average expenses per country for the second quarter appears in cell C15.

8. **Drag the fill handle from cell C15 to cell E15**

   The formula in cell C15 is copied to the rest of the selected range, as shown in Figure B-5.

9. **Save your work**

Working with Formulas and Functions

**FIGURE B-3:** Insert Function dialog box

Search for a function field →

Or select a category list arrow

Select a function list; yours may differ →

Description of selected function

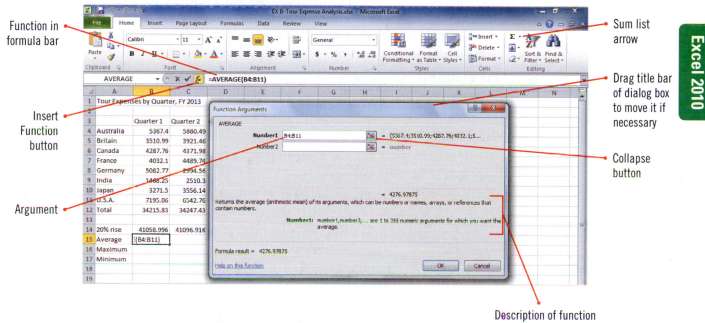

**Insert Function**

Search for a function:

Type a brief description of what you want to do and then click Go

Or select a category: Most Recently Used

Select a function:

SUM
AVERAGE
IF
HYPERLINK
COUNT
MAX
SIN

SUM(number1,number2,...)
Adds all the numbers in a range of cells.

Help on this function    OK    Cancel

**FIGURE B-4:** Expanded Function Arguments dialog box

Function in formula bar →

Insert Function button →

Argument →

Sum list arrow

Drag title bar of dialog box to move it if necessary

Collapse button

Description of function and arguments

**FIGURE B-5:** Average functions used in worksheet

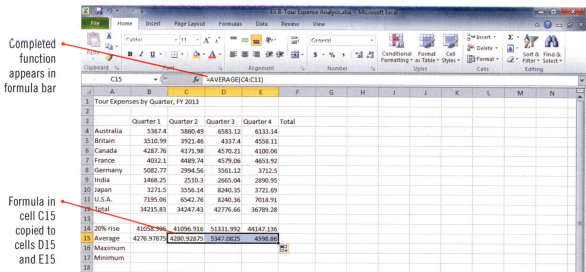

Completed function appears in formula bar →

Formula in cell C15 copied to cells D15 and E15 →

C15    =AVERAGE(C4:C11)

| | A | Quarter 1 | Quarter 2 | Quarter 3 | Quarter 4 | Total |
|---|---|---|---|---|---|---|
| 1 | Tour Expenses by Quarter, FY 2013 | | | | | |
| 2 | | | | | | |
| 3 | | Quarter 1 | Quarter 2 | Quarter 3 | Quarter 4 | Total |
| 4 | Australia | 5367.4 | 5860.49 | 6583.12 | 6133.14 | |
| 5 | Britain | 3510.99 | 3921.46 | 4337.4 | 4558.11 | |
| 6 | Canada | 4287.76 | 4371.98 | 4570.21 | 4100.06 | |
| 7 | France | 4032.1 | 4489.74 | 4579.06 | 4653.92 | |
| 8 | Germany | 5082.77 | 2994.56 | 3561.12 | 3712.5 | |
| 9 | India | 1468.25 | 2510.3 | 2665.04 | 2890.95 | |
| 10 | Japan | 3271.5 | 3556.14 | 8240.35 | 3721.69 | |
| 11 | U.S.A. | 7195.06 | 6542.76 | 8240.36 | 7018.91 | |
| 12 | Total | 34215.83 | 34247.43 | 42776.66 | 36789.28 | |
| 13 | | | | | | |
| 14 | 20% rise | 41058.996 | 41096.916 | 51331.992 | 44147.136 | |
| 15 | Average | 4276.97875 | 4280.92875 | 5347.0825 | 4598.66 | |
| 16 | Maximum | | | | | |
| 17 | Minimum | | | | | |
| 18 | | | | | | |

Working with Formulas and Functions

# Typing a Function

In addition to using the Insert Function dialog box, the Sum button, or the Sum list arrow on the Ribbon to enter a function, you can manually type the function into a cell and then complete the arguments needed. This method requires that you know the name and initial characters of the function, but it can be faster than opening several dialog boxes. Experienced Excel users often prefer this method, but it is only an alternative, not better or more correct than any other method. Excel's Formula AutoComplete feature makes it easier to enter function names by typing, because it suggests functions depending on the first letters you type.  You want to calculate the maximum and minimum quarterly expenses in your worksheet, and you decide to manually enter these statistical functions.

## STEPS

1.  **Click cell B16, type =, then type m**

    Because you are manually typing this function, it is necessary to begin with the equal sign ( = ). The Formula AutoComplete feature displays a list of function names beginning with "M" beneath cell B16. Once you type an equal sign in a cell, each letter you type acts as a trigger to activate the Formula AutoComplete feature. This feature minimizes the amount of typing you need to do to enter a function and reduces typing and syntax errors.

2.  **Click MAX in the list**

    Clicking any function in the Formula AutoComplete list opens a ScreenTip next to the list that describes the function.

3.  **Double-click MAX**

    The function is inserted in the cell, and a ScreenTip appears beneath the cell to help you complete the formula. See Figure B-6.

4.  **Select the range B4:B11, as shown in Figure B-7, then click the Enter button ✓ on the formula bar**

    The result, 7195.06, appears in cell B16. When you completed the entry, the closing parenthesis was automatically added to the formula.

5.  **Click cell B17, type =, type m, then double-click MIN in the list of function names**

    The MIN function appears in the cell.

6.  **Select the range B4:B11, then press [Enter]**

    The result, 1468.25, appears in cell B17.

7.  **Select the range B16:B17, then drag the fill handle from cell B17 to cell E17**

    The maximum and minimum values for all of the quarters appear in the selected range, as shown in Figure B-8.

8.  **Save your work**

---

### Using the COUNT and COUNTA functions

When you select a range, a count of cells in the range that are not blank appears in the status bar. For example, if you select the range A1:A5 and only cells A1 and A2 contain data, the status bar displays "Count: 2." To count nonblank cells more precisely, or to incorporate these calculations in a worksheet, you can use the COUNT and COUNTA functions. The COUNT function returns the number of cells in a range that contain numeric data, including numbers, dates, and formulas. The COUNTA function returns the number of cells in a range that contain any data at all, including numeric data, labels, and even a blank space. For example, the formula =COUNT(A1:A5) returns the number of cells in the range that contain numeric data, and the formula =COUNTA(A1:A5) returns the number of cells in the range that are not empty.

**FIGURE B-6:** MAX function in progress

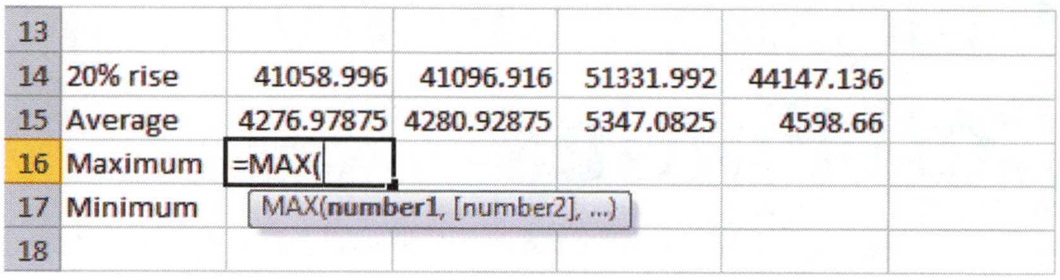

| 13 | | | | | | |
|----|----------|------------|------------|------------|------------|---|
| 14 | 20% rise | 41058.996 | 41096.916 | 51331.992 | 44147.136 | |
| 15 | Average | 4276.97875 | 4280.92875 | 5347.0825 | 4598.66 | |
| 16 | Maximum | =MAX( | | | | |
| 17 | Minimum | MAX(**number1**, [number2], ...) | | | | |
| 18 | | | | | | |

**FIGURE B-7:** Completing the MAX function

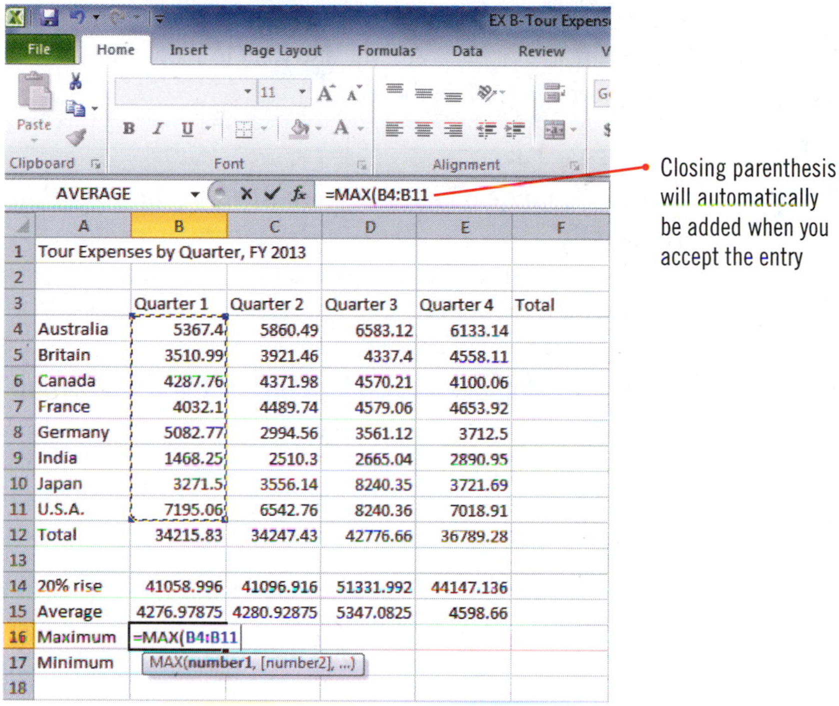

Closing parenthesis will automatically be added when you accept the entry

**FIGURE B-8:** Completed MAX and MIN functions

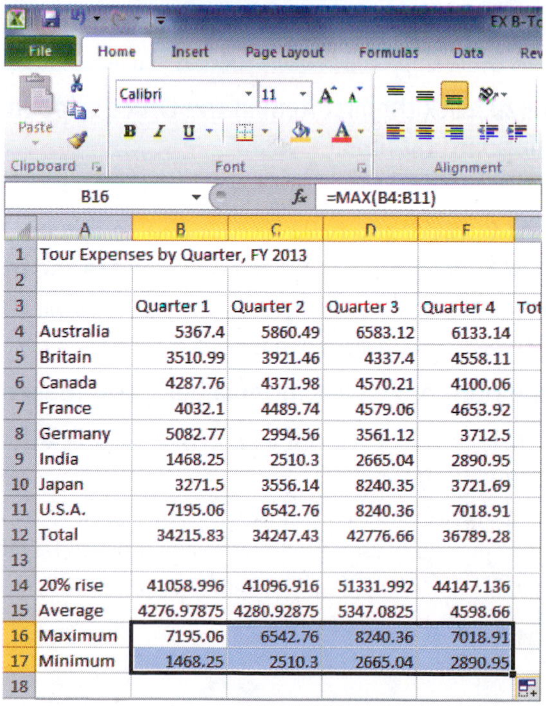

Working with Formulas and Functions

# Copying and Moving Cell Entries

There are three ways you can copy or move cells and ranges (or the contents within them) from one location to another: the Cut, Copy, and Paste buttons on the Home tab on the Ribbon; the fill handle in the lower-right corner of the active cell or range; or the drag-and-drop feature. When you copy cells, the original data remains in the original location; when you cut or move cells, the original data is deleted from its original location. You can also cut, copy, and paste cells or ranges from one worksheet to another.  In addition to the 20% rise in tour expenses, you also want to show a 30% rise. Rather than retype this information, you copy and move the labels in these cells.

## STEPS

> **QUICK TIP**
>
> To cut or copy selected cell contents, activate the cell, then select the characters within the cell that you want to cut or copy.

1. **Select the range B3:E3, then click the Copy button 🖹 in the Clipboard group on the Home tab**

   The selected range (B3:E3) is copied to the **Clipboard**, a temporary Windows storage area that holds the selections you copy or cut. A moving border surrounds the selected range until you press [Esc] or copy an additional item to the Clipboard.

2. **Click the dialog box launcher 🖿 in the Clipboard group**

   The Office Clipboard opens in the Clipboard task pane, as shown in Figure B-9. When you copy or cut an item, it is cut or copied both to the Clipboard provided by Windows and to the Office Clipboard. Unlike the Windows Clipboard, which holds just one item at a time, the Office Clipboard contains up to 24 of the most recently cut or copied items from any Office program. Your Clipboard task pane may contain more items than shown in the figure.

> **QUICK TIP**
>
> Once the Office Clipboard contains 24 items, the oldest existing item is automatically deleted each time you add an item.

3. **Click cell B19, then click the Paste button in the Clipboard group**

   A copy of the contents of range B3:E3 is pasted into the range B19:E19. When pasting an item from the Office Clipboard or Clipboard into a worksheet, you only need to specify the upper-left cell of the range where you want to paste the selection. Notice that the information you copied remains in the original range B3:E3; if you had cut instead of copied, the information would have been deleted from its original location once it was pasted.

4. **Press [Delete]**

   The selected cells are empty. You have decided to paste the cells in a different row. You can repeatedly paste an item from the Office Clipboard as many times as you like, as long as the item remains in the Office Clipboard.

> **QUICK TIP**
>
> You can also close the Office Clipboard pane by clicking the dialog box launcher in the Clipboard group.

5. **Click cell B20, click the first item in the Office Clipboard, then click the Close button ✖ on the Clipboard task pane**

   Cells B20:E20 contain the copied labels.

6. **Click cell A14 , press and hold [Ctrl], point to any edge of the cell until the pointer changes to ⬉, drag cell A14 to cell A21, release the mouse button, then release [Ctrl]**

   The copy pointer ⬉ continues to appear as you drag, as shown in Figure B-10. When you release the mouse button, the contents of cell A14 are copied to cell A21.

7. **Click to the right of 2 in the formula bar, press [Backspace], type 3, then press [Enter]**

8. **Click cell B21, type =, click cell B12, type *1.3, click the Enter button ☑ on the formula bar, then save your work**

   This new formula calculates a 30% increase of the expenses for Quarter 1, though using a different method from what you previously used. Anything you multiply by 1.3 returns an amount that is 130% of the original amount, or a 30% increase. Compare your screen to Figure B-11.

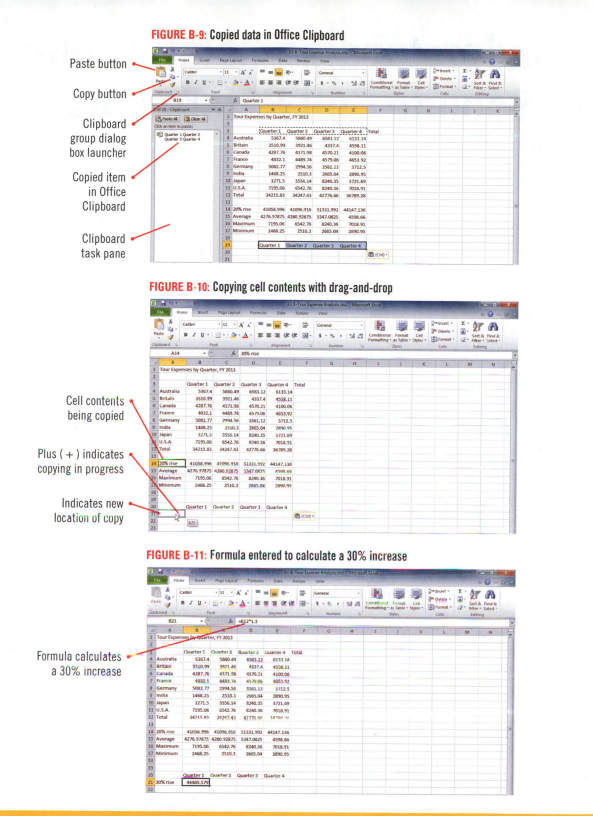

**FIGURE B-9:** Copied data in Office Clipboard

Paste button

Copy button

Clipboard group dialog box launcher

Copied item in Office Clipboard

Clipboard task pane

**FIGURE B-10:** Copying cell contents with drag-and-drop

Cell contents being copied

Plus ( + ) indicates copying in progress

Indicates new location of copy

**FIGURE B-11:** Formula entered to calculate a 30% increase

Formula calculates a 30% increase

Excel 2010

---

## Inserting and deleting selected cells

As you add formulas to your workbook, you may need to insert or delete cells. When you do this, Excel automatically adjusts cell references to reflect their new locations. To insert cells, click the Insert list arrow in the Cells group on the Home tab, then click Insert Cells. The Insert dialog box opens, asking if you want to insert a cell and move the current active cell down or to the right of the new one. To delete one or more selected cells, click the Delete list arrow in the

Cells group, click Delete Cells, and in the Delete dialog box, indicate which way you want to move the adjacent cells. When using this option, be careful not to disturb row or column alignment that may be necessary to maintain the accuracy of cell references in the worksheet. Click the Insert button or Delete button in the Cells group to insert or delete a single cell.

# Understanding Relative and Absolute Cell References

As you work in Excel, you may want to reuse formulas in different parts of a worksheet to reduce the amount of data you have to retype. For example, you might want to include a what-if analysis in one part of a worksheet showing a set of sales projections if sales increase by 10%. To include another analysis in another part of the worksheet showing projections if sales increase by 50%, you can copy the formulas from one section to another and simply change the "1" to a "5". But when you copy formulas, it is important to make sure that they refer to the correct cells. To do this, you need to understand the difference between relative and absolute cell references.  You plan to reuse formulas in different parts of your worksheets, so you want to understand relative and absolute cell references.

## DETAILS

### Consider the following when using relative and absolute cell references:

- **Use relative references when you want to preserve the relationship to the formula location**

  When you create a formula that references another cell, Excel normally does not "record" the exact cell address for the cell being referenced in the formula. Instead, it looks at the relationship that cell has to the cell containing the formula. For example, in Figure B-12, cell F5 contains the formula: =SUM(B5:E5). When Excel retrieves values to calculate the formula in cell F5, it actually looks for "the four cells to the left of the formula," which in this case is cells B5:E5. This way, if you copy the cell to a new location, such as cell F6, the results will reflect the new formula location, and will automatically retrieve the values in cells B6, C6, D6, and E6. These are **relative cell references**, because Excel is recording the input cells *in relation to* or *relative to* the formula cell.

  In most cases, you want to use relative cell references when copying or moving, so this is the Excel default. In Figure B-12, the formulas in F5:F12 and in B13:F13 contain relative cell references. They total the "four cells to the left of" or the "eight cells above" the formulas.

- **Use absolute cell references when you want to preserve the exact cell address in a formula**

  There are times when you want Excel to retrieve formula information from a specific cell, and you don't want the cell address in the formula to change when you copy it to a new location. For example, you might have a price in a specific cell that you want to use in all formulas, regardless of their location. If you use relative cell referencing, the formula results would be incorrect, because Excel would use a different cell every time you copy the formula. Therefore you need to use an **absolute cell reference**, which is a reference that does not change when you copy the formula.

  You create an absolute cell reference by placing a $ (dollar sign) in front of both the column letter and the row number of the cell address. You can either type the dollar sign when typing the cell address in a formula (for example, "=C12*$B$16"), or you can select a cell address on the formula bar and then press [F4] and the dollar signs are added automatically. Figure B-13 shows formulas containing both absolute and relative references. The formulas in cells B19 to E26 use absolute cell references to refer to a potential sales increase of 50%, shown in cell B16.

**FIGURE B-12:** Formulas containing relative references

Formula containing relative references →

Copied formulas adjust to preserve relationship of formula to referenced cells →

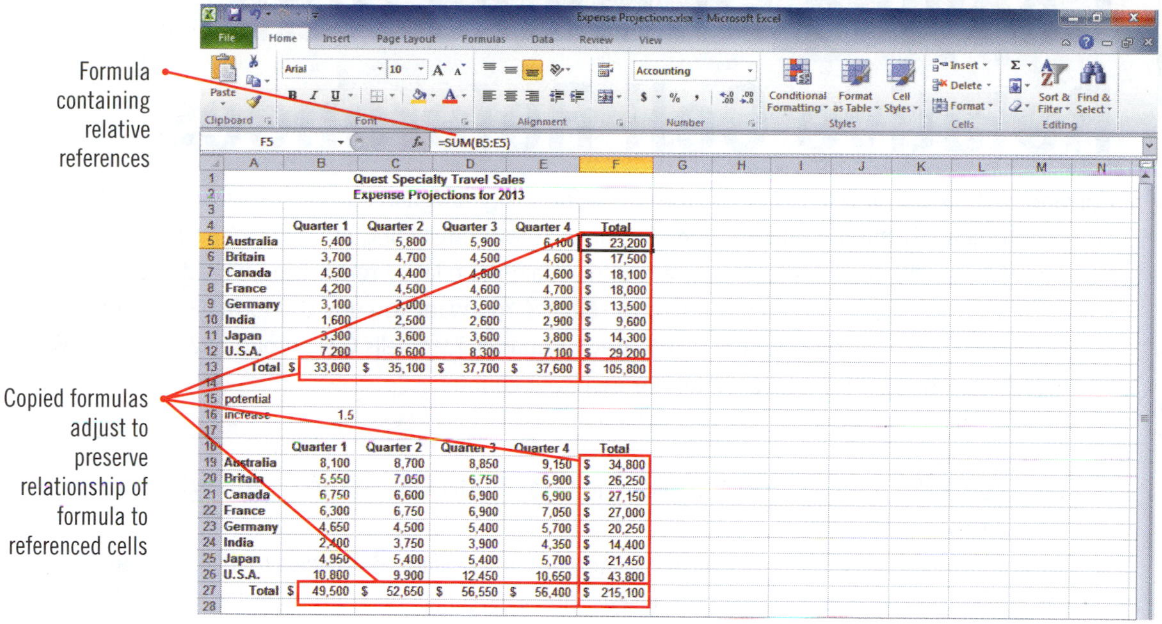

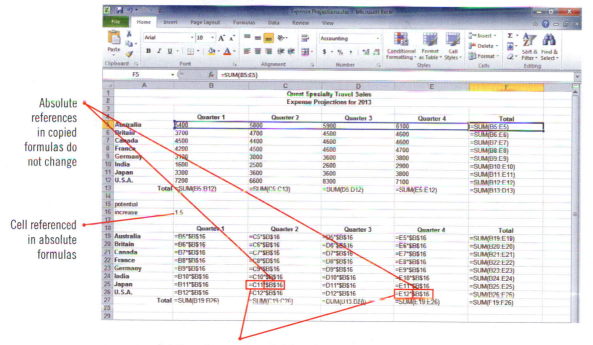

**FIGURE B-13:** Formulas containing absolute and relative references

Absolute references in copied formulas do not change →

Cell referenced in absolute formulas →

Relative references in copied formulas adjust to the new location

## Using a mixed reference

Sometimes when you copy a formula, you want to change the row reference, but keep the column reference the same. This type of cell referencing combines elements of both absolute and relative referencing and is called a **mixed reference**. For example, when copied, a formula containing the mixed reference C$14 would change the column letter relative to its new location, but not the row number. In the mixed reference $C14, the column letter would not change, but the row number would be updated relative to its location. Like an absolute reference, a mixed reference can be created by pressing the [F4] function key with the cell reference selected. With each press of the [F4] key, you cycle through all the possible combinations of relative, absolute, and mixed references ($C$14, C$14, $C14, and C14).

# Copying Formulas with Relative Cell References

Copying and moving a cell allows you to reuse a formula you've already created. Copying cells is usually faster than retyping the formulas in them and helps to prevent typing errors. If the cells you are copying contain relative cell references and you want to maintain the relative referencing, you don't need to make any changes to the cells before copying them.  You want to copy the formula in cell B21, which calculates the 30% increase in quarterly expenses for quarter 1, to cells C21 through E21. You also want to create formulas to calculate total expenses for each tour country.

## STEPS

1. **Click cell B21, if necessary, then click the Copy button 📋 in the Clipboard group on the Home tab**

   The formula for calculating the 30% expense increase during Quarter 1 is copied to the Clipboard. Notice that the formula =B12*1.3 appears in the formula bar, and a moving border surrounds the active cell.

**QUICK TIP**

To paste only specific components of a copied cell or range, click the Paste list arrow in the Clipboard group, then click Paste Special. You can selectively copy formulas, values, or other choices using options in the Paste Special dialog box.

2. **Click cell C21, then click the Paste button (not the list arrow) in the Clipboard group**

   The formula from cell B21 is copied into cell C21, where the new result of 44521.659 appears. Notice in the formula bar that the cell references have changed, so that cell C12 is referenced in the formula. This formula contains a relative cell reference, which tells Excel to substitute new cell references within the copied formulas as necessary. This maintains the same relationship between the new cell containing the formula and the cell references within the formula. In this case, Excel adjusted the formula so that cell C12—the cell reference nine rows above C21—replaced cell B12, the cell reference nine rows above B21.

3. **Drag the fill handle from cell C21 to cell E21**

   A formula similar to the one in cell C21 now appears in cells D21 and E21. After you use the fill handle to copy cell contents, the **Auto Fill Options button** appears, as seen in Figure B-14. You can use the Auto Fill Options button to fill the cells with only specific elements of the copied cell if you wish.

4. **Click cell F4, click the Sum button Σ in the Editing group, then click the Enter button ✓ on the formula bar**

5. **Click 📋 in the Clipboard group, select the range F5:F6, then click the Paste button**

   See Figure B-15. After you click the Paste button, the **Paste Options button** appears, which you can use to paste only specific elements of the copied selection if you wish. The formula for calculating total expenses for tours in Britain appears in the formula bar. You would like totals to appear in cells F7:F11. The Fill button in the Editing group can be used to copy the formula into the remaining cells.

6. **Select the range F6:F11**

7. **Click the Fill button 📊▾ in the Editing group, then click Down**

   The formulas containing relative references are copied to each cell. Compare your worksheet to Figure B-16.

8. **Save your work**

---

### Using Paste Preview

You can selectively copy formulas, values, or other choices using the Paste list arrow, and you can see how the pasted contents will look using the Paste Preview feature. When you click the Paste list arrow, a gallery of paste option icons opens. When you point to an icon, a preview of how the content will be pasted using that option is shown in the worksheet. Options include pasting values only, pasting values with number formatting, pasting formulas only, pasting formatting only, pasting transposed data so that column data appears in rows and row data appears in columns, and pasting with no borders (to remove any borders around pasted cells).

**FIGURE B-14:** Formula copied using the fill handle

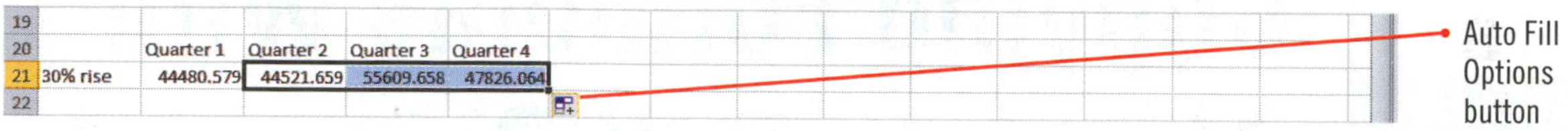

| | Quarter 1 | Quarter 2 | Quarter 3 | Quarter 4 | |
|---|---|---|---|---|---|
| 30% rise | 44480.579 | 44521.659 | 55609.658 | 47826.064 | |

Auto Fill Options button

**FIGURE B-15:** Formulas pasted in the range F5:F6

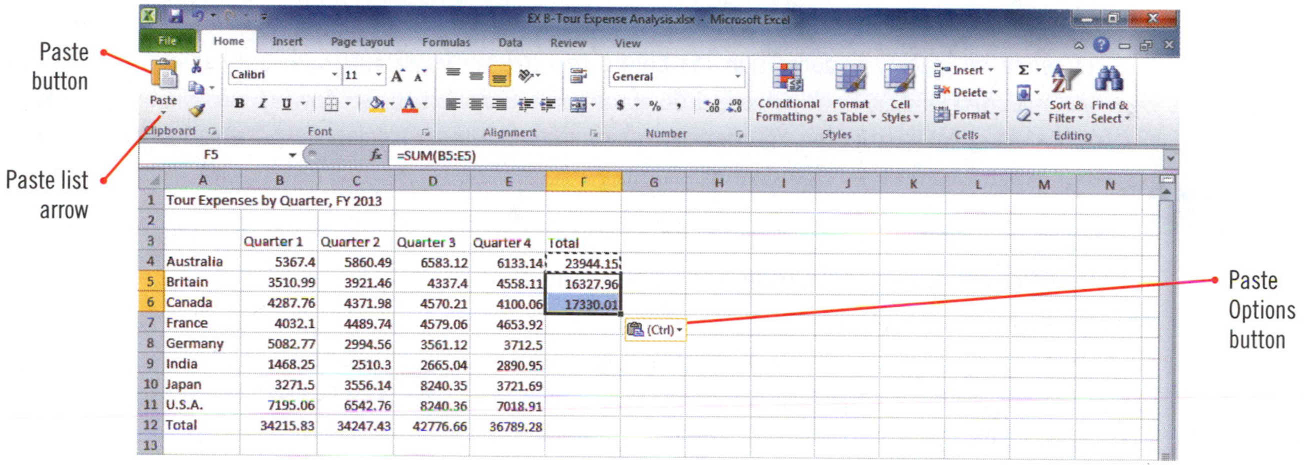

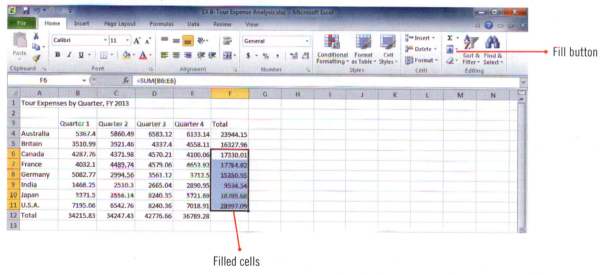

Paste button

Paste list arrow

Paste Options button

**FIGURE B-16:** Formula copied using Fill Down

Fill button

Filled cells

## Using Auto Fill options

When you use the fill handle to copy cells, the Auto Fill Options button appears. Auto Fill options differ depending on what you are copying. If you had selected cells containing a series (such as "Monday" and "Tuesday") and then used the fill handle, you would see options for continuing the series (such as "Wednesday" and "Thursday") or for simply pasting the copied cells. Clicking the Auto Fill Options button opens a list that lets you choose from the following options: Copy Cells, Fill Series (if applicable), Fill Formatting Only, or Fill Without Formatting. Choosing Copy Cells means that the cell's contents and its formatting will be copied. The Fill Formatting Only option copies only the formatting attributes, but not cell contents. The Fill Without Formatting option copies the cell contents, but no formatting attributes. Copy Cells is the default option when using the fill handle to copy a cell, so if you want to copy the cell's contents and its formatting, you can ignore the Auto Fill Options button.

Excel 2010

# Copying Formulas with Absolute Cell References

When copying formulas, you might want one or more cell references in the formula to remain unchanged in relation to the formula. In such an instance, you need to apply an absolute cell reference before copying the formula to preserve the specific cell address when the formula is copied. You create an absolute reference by placing a dollar sign ($) before the column letter and row number of the address (for example, $A$1).  You need to do some what-if analysis to see how various percentage increases might affect total expenses. You decide to add a column that calculates a possible increase in the total tour expenses, and then change the percentage to see various potential results.

## STEPS

1. **Click cell G1, type Change, then press [Enter]**

2. **Type 1.1, then press [Enter]**
   You store the increase factor that will be used in the what-if analysis in this cell (G2). The value 1.1 can be used to calculate a 10% increase: anything you multiply by 1.1 returns an amount that is 110% of the original amount.

3. **Click cell H3, type What if?, then press [Enter]**

4. **In cell H4, type =, click cell F4, type *, click cell G2, then click the Enter button ☑ on the formula bar**
   The result, 26338.57, appears in cell H4. This value represents the total annual expenses for Australia if there is a 10% increase. You want to perform a what-if analysis for all the tour countries.

   **QUICK TIP**
   Before you copy or move a formula, always check to see if you need to use an absolute cell reference.

5. **Drag the fill handle from cell H4 to cell H11**
   The resulting values in the range H5:H11 are all zeros, which is *not* the result you wanted. Because you used relative cell addressing in cell H4, the copied formula adjusted so that the formula in cell H5 is =F5*G3. Because there is no value in cell G3, the result is 0, an error. You need to use an absolute reference in the formula to keep the formula from adjusting itself. That way, it will always reference cell G2.

   **QUICK TIP**
   When changing a cell reference to an absolute reference, make sure the reference is selected or the insertion point is next to it in the cell before pressing [F4].

6. **Click cell H4, press [F2] to change to Edit mode, then press [F4]**
   When you press [F2], the range finder outlines the arguments of the equation in blue and green. The insertion point appears next to the G2 cell reference in cell H4. When you press [F4], dollar signs are inserted in the G2 cell reference, making it an absolute reference. See Figure B-17.

7. **Click ☑, then drag the fill handle from cell H4 to cell H11**
   Because the formula correctly contains an absolute cell reference, the correct values for a 10% increase appear in cells H4:H11. You now want to see what a 20% increase in expenses looks like.

8. **Click cell G2, type 1.2, then click ☑**
   The values in the range H4:H11 change to reflect the 20% increase. Compare your worksheet to Figure B-18.

9. **Save your work**

**FIGURE B-17:** Absolute reference created in formula

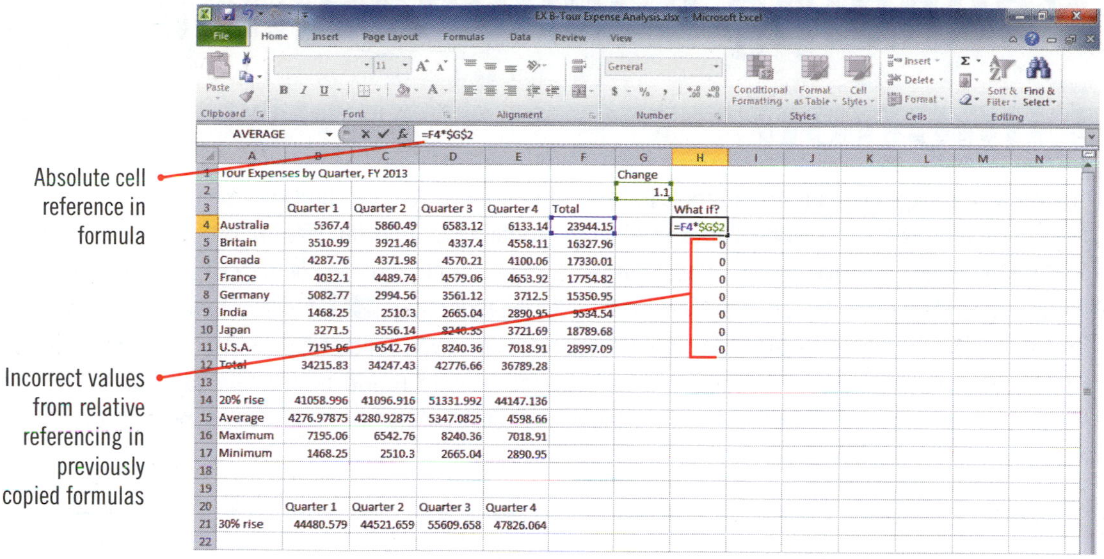

Absolute cell reference in formula

Incorrect values from relative referencing in previously copied formulas

**FIGURE B-18:** What-if analysis with modified change factor

Modified change factor

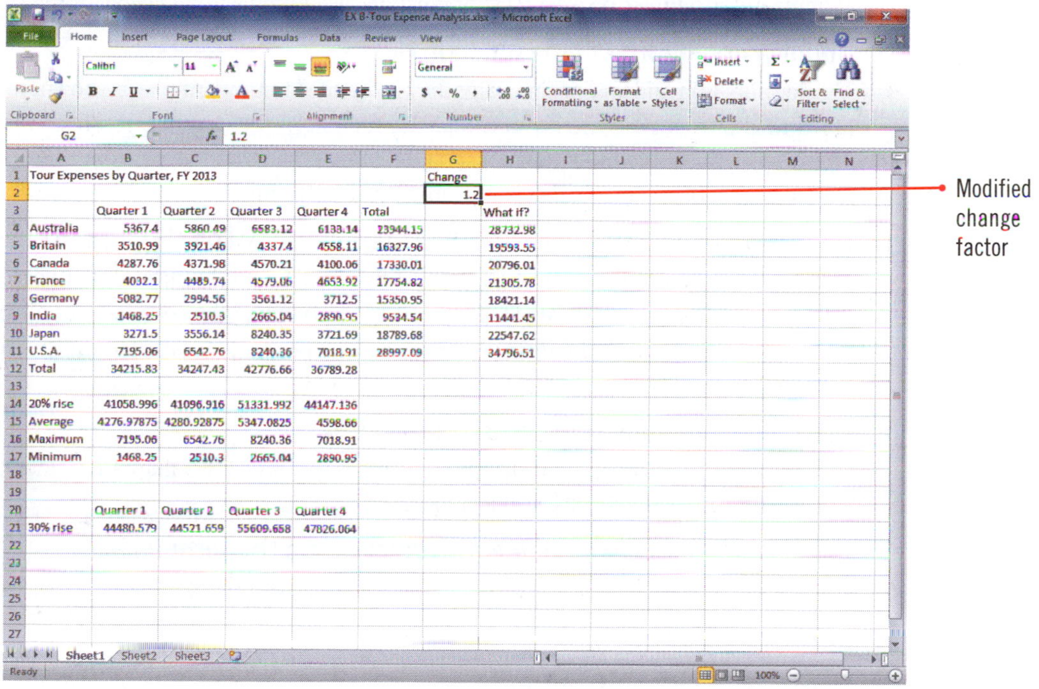

## Using the fill handle for sequential text or values

Often, you need to fill cells with sequential text: months of the year, days of the week, years, or text plus a number (Quarter 1, Quarter 2,...). For example, you might want to create a worksheet that calculates data for every month of the year. Using the fill handle, you can quickly and easily create labels for the months of the year just by typing "January" in a cell. Drag the fill handle from the cell containing "January" until you have all the monthly labels you need. You can also easily fill cells with a date sequence by dragging the fill handle on a single cell containing a date. You can fill cells with a number sequence (such as 1, 2, 3,...) by dragging the fill handle on a selection of two or more cells that contain the sequence. To create a number sequence using the value in a single cell, press and hold [Ctrl] as you drag the fill handle of the cell. As you drag the fill handle, Excel automatically extends the existing sequence into the additional cells. (The content of the last filled cell appears in the ScreenTip.) To examine all the fill series options for the current selection, click the Fill button in the Editing group on the Home tab, then click Series to open the Series dialog box.

Working with Formulas and Functions

# Rounding a Value with a Function

The more you explore features and tools in Excel, the more ways you'll find to simplify your work and convey information more efficiently. For example, cells containing financial data are often easier to read if they contain fewer decimal places than those that appear by default. You can round a value or formula result to a specific number of decimal places by using the ROUND function.  In your worksheet, you'd like to round the cells showing the 20% rise in expenses to show fewer digits; after all, it's not important to show cents in the projections, only whole dollars. You want Excel to round the calculated value to the nearest integer. You decide to edit cell B14 so it includes the ROUND function, and then copy the edited formula into the other formulas in this row.

## STEPS

1. **Click cell B14, then click to the right of = in the formula bar**

   You want to position the function at the beginning of the formula, before any values or arguments.

   **QUICK TIP**

   In the Insert Function dialog box, the ROUND function is in the Math & Trig category.

2. **Type RO**

   Formula AutoComplete displays a list of functions beginning with RO beneath the formula bar.

3. **Double-click ROUND in the functions list**

   The new function and an opening parenthesis are added to the formula, as shown in Figure B-19. A few additional modifications are needed to complete your edit of the formula. You need to indicate the number of decimal places to which the function should round numbers and you also need to add a closing parenthesis around the set of arguments that comes after the ROUND function.

   **TROUBLE**

   If you have too many or too few parentheses, the extraneous parenthesis is displayed in green, or a warning dialog box opens with a suggested solution to the error.

4. **Press [END], type ,0), then click the Enter button ☑ on the formula bar**

   The comma separates the arguments within the formula, and 0 indicates that you don't want any decimal places to appear in the calculated value. When you complete the edit, the parentheses at either end of the formula briefly become bold, indicating that the formula has the correct number of open and closed parentheses and is balanced.

5. **Drag the fill handle from cell B14 to cell E14**

   The formula in cell B14 is copied to the range C14:E14. All the values are rounded to display no decimal places. Compare your worksheet to Figure B-20.

6. **Click cell A25, type your name, then click ☑ on the formula bar**

7. **Save your work, preview the worksheet in Backstage view, then submit your work to your Instructor as directed**

8. **Exit Excel**

ROUND function and opening parenthesis inserted in formula

Screentip indicates needed arguments

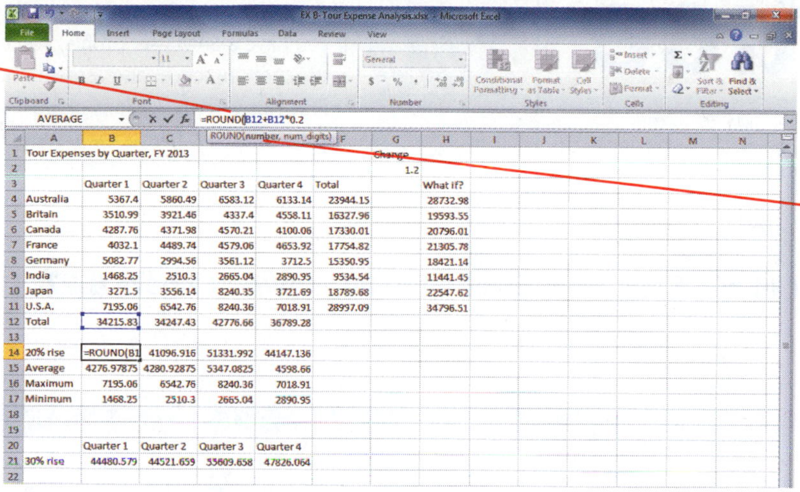

FIGURE B-20: Completed worksheet

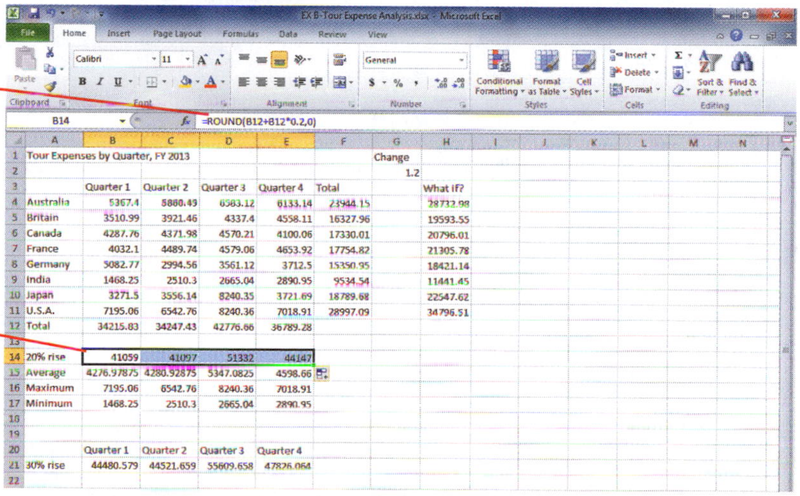

Function surrounds existing formula

Calculated values with no decimals

## Creating a new workbook using a template

Excel **templates** are predesigned workbook files intended to save time when you create common documents such as balance sheets, budgets, or time cards. Templates contain labels, values, formulas, and formatting, so all you have to do is customize them with your own information. Excel comes with many templates, and you can also create your own or find additional templates on the Web. Unlike a typical workbook, which has the file extension .xlsx, a template has the extension .xltx. To create a workbook using a template, click the File tab, then click New on the navigation bar. The Available Templates pane in Backstage view lists templates installed on your computer and templates available through Office.com. The Blank Workbook template is selected by default and is used to create a blank workbook with no content or special formatting. A preview of the selected template appears to the right of the Available Templates pane. To select a template, click a category in the Available Templates pane, select the template you want in the category, then click Create (if you've selected an installed template) or Download (if you've selected an Office.com template). Figure B-21 shows a template selected in the Budgets category of Office.com templates. (Your list of templates may differ.) When you click Create or

Download, a new workbook is created based on the template; when you save the new file in the default format, it has the regular .xlsx extension. To save a workbook of your own as a template, open the Save As dialog box, click the Save as type list arrow, then change the file type to Excel Template.

FIGURE B-21: Budget template selected in Backstage view

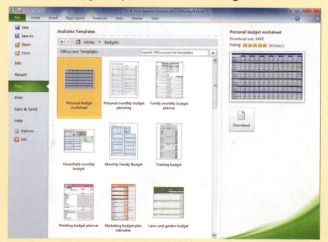

Excel 2010

# Practice

**SAM**

For current SAM information, including versions and content details, visit SAM Central (http://www.cengage.com/samcentral). If you have a SAM user profile, you may have access to hands-on instruction, practice, and assessment of the skills covered in this unit. Since various versions of SAM are supported throughout the life of this text, check with your instructor for the correct instructions and URL/Web site for accessing assignments.

## Concepts Review

**Label each element of the Excel worksheet window shown in Figure B-22.**

FIGURE B-22

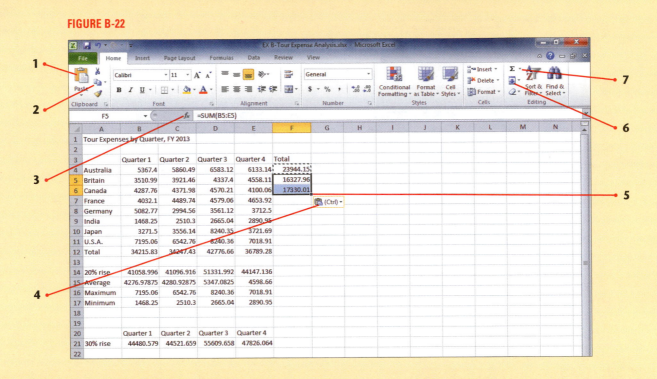

**Match each term or button with the statement that best describes it.**

8. Fill handle
9. Dialog box launcher
10. Drag-and-drop method
11. [Delete]
12. Formula AutoComplete

a. Clears the contents of selected cells
b. Item on the Ribbon that opens a dialog box or task pane
c. Lets you move or copy data from one cell to another without using the Clipboard
d. Displays an alphabetical list of functions from which you can choose
e. Lets you copy cell contents or continue a series of data into a range of selected cells

**Select the best answer from the list of choices.**

13. **Which key do you press to copy while dragging and dropping selected cells?**
    a. [Alt]
    b. [Ctrl]
    c. [F2]
    d. [Tab]

14. **What type of cell reference is C$19?**
    a. Relative
    b. Absolute
    c. Mixed
    d. Certain

15. **What type of cell reference changes when it is copied?**
    a. Circular
    b. Absolute
    c. Relative
    d. Specified

16. **Which key do you press to convert a relative cell reference to an absolute cell reference?**
    a. [F2]
    b. [F4]
    c. [F5]
    d. [F6]

17. **You can use any of the following features to enter a function *except*:**
    a. Insert Function button.
    b. Formula AutoComplete.
    c. Sum list arrow.
    d. Clipboard.

## Skills Review

1. **Create a complex formula.**
    a. Open the file EX B-2.xlsx from the drive and folder where you store your Data Files, then save it as **EX B-Baking Supply Company Inventory**.
    b. In cell B11, create a complex formula that calculates a 30% decrease in the total number of cases of cake pans.
    c. Use the fill handle to copy this formula into cell C11 through cell E11.
    d. Save your work.

2. **Insert a function.**
    a. Use the Sum list arrow to create a formula in cell B13 that averages the number of cases of cake pans in each storage area.
    b. Use the Insert Function button to create a formula in cell B14 that calculates the maximum number of cases of cake pans in a storage area.
    c. Use the Sum list arrow to create a formula in cell B15 that calculates the minimum number of cases of cake pans in a storage area.
    d. Save your work.

3. **Type a function.**
    a. In cell C13, type a formula that includes a function to average the number of cases of pie pans in each storage area. (*Hint*: Use Formula AutoComplete to enter the function.)
    b. In cell C14, type a formula that includes a function to calculate the maximum number of cases of pie pans in a storage area.
    c. In cell C15, type a formula that includes a function to calculate the minimum number of cases of pie pans in a storage area.
    d. Save your work.

# Skills Review (continued)

**4. Copy and move cell entries.**

    **a.** Select the range B3:F3.

    **b.** Copy the selection to the Clipboard.

    **c.** Open the Clipboard task pane, then paste the selection into cell B17.

    **d.** Close the Clipboard task pane, then select the range A4:A9.

    **e.** Use the drag-and-drop method to copy the selection to cell A18. (*Hint*: The results should fill the range A18:A23.)

    **f.** Save your work.

**5. Understand relative and absolute cell references.**

    **a.** Write a brief description of the difference between relative and absolute references.

    **b.** List at least three situations in which you think a business might use an absolute reference in its calculations. Examples can include calculations for different types of worksheets, such as time cards, invoices, and budgets.

**6. Copy formulas with relative cell references.**

    **a.** Calculate the total in cell F4.

    **b.** Use the Fill button to copy the formula in cell F4 down to cells F5:F8.

    **c.** Select the range C13:C15.

    **d.** Use the fill handle to copy these cells to the range D13:F15.

    **e.** Save your work.

**7. Copy formulas with absolute cell references.**

    **a.** In cell H1, enter the value **1.575**.

    **b.** In cell H4, create a formula that multiplies F4 and an absolute reference to cell H1.

    **c.** Use the fill handle to copy the formula in cell H4 to cells H5 and H6.

    **d.** Use the Copy and Paste buttons to copy the formula in cell H4 to cells H7 and H8.

    **e.** Change the amount in cell H1 to **2.3**.

    **f.** Save your work.

**8. Round a value with a function.**

    **a.** Click cell H4.

    **b.** Edit this formula to include the ROUND function showing zero decimal places.

    **c.** Use the fill handle to copy the formula in cell H4 to the range H5:H8.

    **d.** Enter your name in cell A25, then compare your work to Figure B-23.

    **e.** Save your work, preview the worksheet in Backstage view, then submit your work to your instructor as directed.

    **f.** Close the workbook, then exit Excel.

**FIGURE B-23**

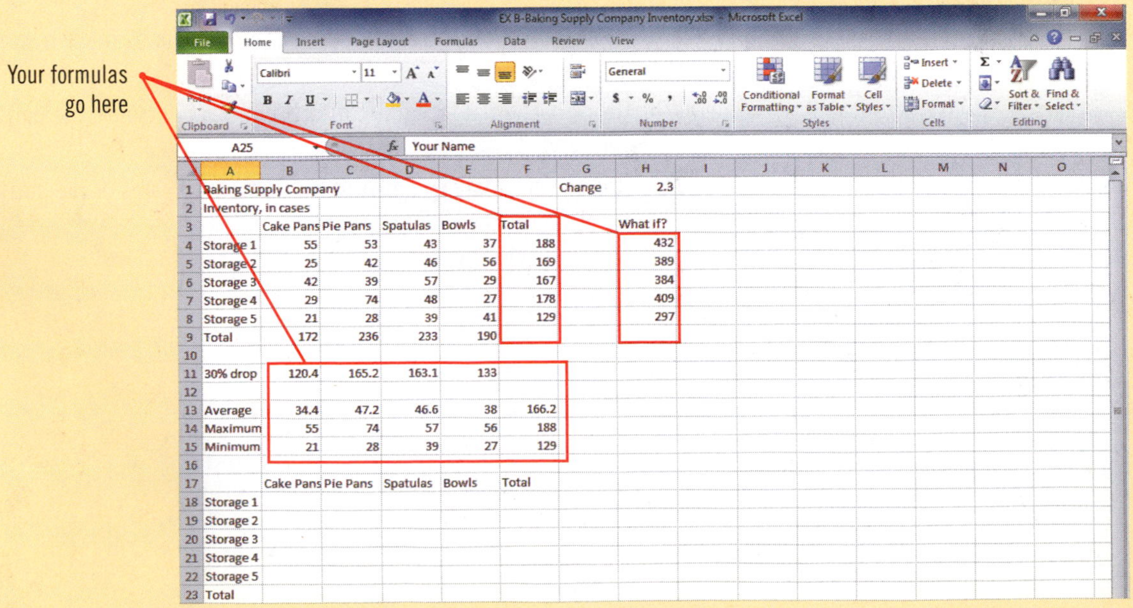

Your formulas go here

Working with Formulas and Functions

# Independent Challenge 1

You are thinking of starting a small express oil change service center. Before you begin, you need to evaluate what you think your monthly expenses will be. You've started a workbook, but need to complete the entries and add formulas.

If you have a SAM 2010 user profile, an autogradable SAM version of this assignment may be available at http://www.cengage.com/sam2010. Check with your instructor to confirm that this assignment is available in SAM. To use the SAM version of this assignment, log into the SAM 2010 Web site and download the instruction and start files.

a. Open the file EX B-3.xlsx from the drive and folder where you store your Data Files, then save it as **EX B-Express Oil Change Expenses**.

b. Make up your own expense data, and enter it in cells B4:B10. (Monthly sales are already included in the worksheet.)

c. Create a formula in cell C4 that calculates the annual rent.

d. Copy the formula in cell C4 to the range C5:C10.

e. Move the label in cell A15 to cell A14.

f. Create formulas in cells B11 and C11 that total the monthly and annual expenses.

g. Create a formula in cell C13 that calculates annual sales.

h. Create a formula in cell B14 that determines whether you will make a profit or loss, then copy the formula into cell C14.

i. Copy the labels in cells B3:C3 to cells E3:F3.

j. Type **Projected Increase** in cell G1, then type **.2** in cell H2.

k. Create a formula in cell E4 that calculates an increase in the monthly rent by the amount in cell H2. You will be copying this formula to other cells, so you'll need to use an absolute reference.

l. Create a formula in cell F4 that calculates the increased annual rent expense based on the calculation in cell E4.

m. Copy the formulas in cells E4:F4 into cells E5:F10 to calculate the remaining monthly and annual expenses.

n. Create a formula in cell E11 that calculates the total monthly expenses, then copy that formula to cell F11.

o. Copy the contents of cells B13:C13 into cells E13:F13.

p. Create formulas in cells E14 and F14 that calculate profit/loss based on the projected increase in monthly and annual expenses.

q. Change the projected increase to **.15**, then compare your work to the sample in Figure B-24.

r. Enter your name in a cell in the worksheet.

s. Save your work, preview the worksheet in Backstage view, submit your work to your instructor as directed, close the workbook, and exit Excel.

**FIGURE B-24**

Your formulas go here (your formula results will differ)

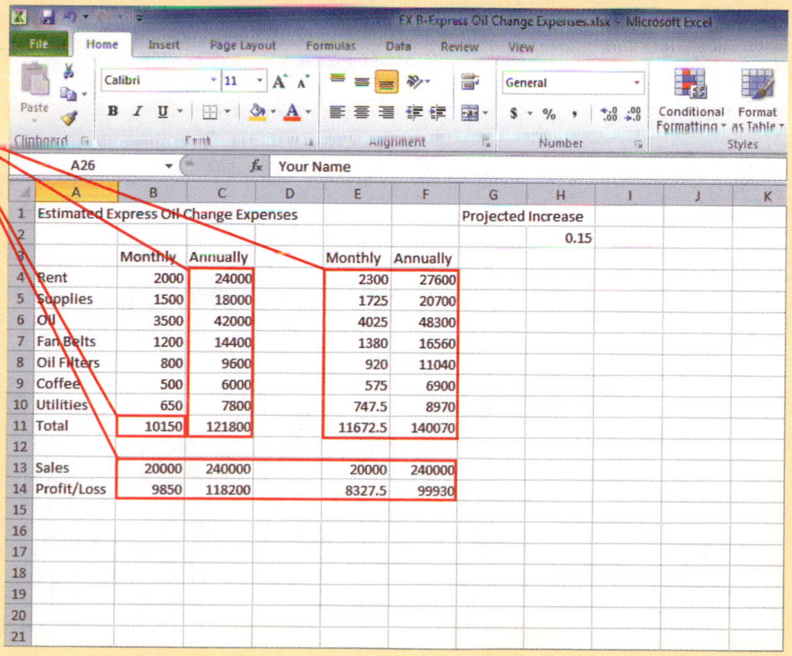

| | A | B | C | D | E | F | G | H |
|---|---|---|---|---|---|---|---|---|
| 1 | Estimated Express Oil Change Expenses | | | | | | Projected Increase | |
| 2 | | | | | | | | 0.15 |
| 3 | | Monthly | Annually | | Monthly | Annually | | |
| 4 | Rent | 2000 | 24000 | | 2300 | 27600 | | |
| 5 | Supplies | 1500 | 18000 | | 1725 | 20700 | | |
| 6 | Oil | 3500 | 42000 | | 4025 | 48300 | | |
| 7 | Fan Belts | 1200 | 14400 | | 1380 | 16560 | | |
| 8 | Oil Filters | 800 | 9600 | | 920 | 11040 | | |
| 9 | Coffee | 500 | 6000 | | 575 | 6900 | | |
| 10 | Utilities | 650 | 7800 | | 747.5 | 8970 | | |
| 11 | Total | 10150 | 121800 | | 11672.5 | 140070 | | |
| 12 | | | | | | | | |
| 13 | Sales | 20000 | 240000 | | 20000 | 240000 | | |
| 14 | Profit/Loss | 9850 | 118200 | | 8327.5 | 99930 | | |

# Independent Challenge 2

The Dog Days Daycare Center is a small, growing pet care center that has hired you to organize its accounting records using Excel. The owners want you to track the company's expenses. Before you were hired, one of the bookkeepers began entering last year's expenses in a workbook, but the analysis was never completed.

**a.** Start Excel, open the file EX B-4.xlsx from the drive and folder where you store your Data Files, then save it as **EX B-Dog Days Daycare Center Finances**. The worksheet includes labels for functions such as the average, maximum, and minimum amounts of each of the expenses in the worksheet.

**b.** Think about what information would be important for the bookkeeping staff to know.

**c.** Using the SUM function, create formulas for each expense in the Total column and each quarter in the Total row.

**d.** Create formulas for each expense and each quarter in the Average, Maximum, and Minimum columns and rows using the method of your choice.

**e.** Save your work, then compare your worksheet to the sample shown in Figure B-25.

**FIGURE B-25**

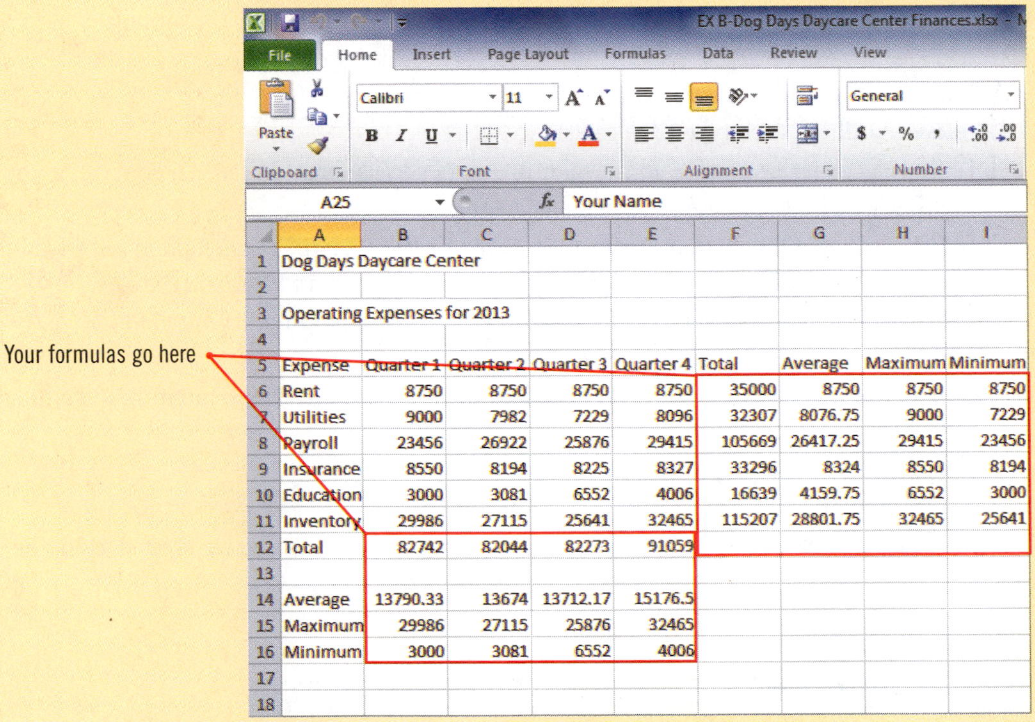

Your formulas go here →

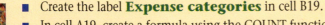

| | A | B | C | D | E | F | G | H | I |
|---|---|---|---|---|---|---|---|---|---|
| 1 | Dog Days Daycare Center | | | | | | | | |
| 2 | | | | | | | | | |
| 3 | Operating Expenses for 2013 | | | | | | | | |
| 4 | | | | | | | | | |
| 5 | Expense | Quarter 1 | Quarter 2 | Quarter 3 | Quarter 4 | Total | Average | Maximum | Minimum |
| 6 | Rent | 8750 | 8750 | 8750 | 8750 | 35000 | 8750 | 8750 | 8750 |
| 7 | Utilities | 9000 | 7982 | 7229 | 8096 | 32307 | 8076.75 | 9000 | 7229 |
| 8 | Payroll | 23456 | 26922 | 25876 | 29415 | 105669 | 26417.25 | 29415 | 23456 |
| 9 | Insurance | 8550 | 8194 | 8225 | 8327 | 33296 | 8324 | 8550 | 8194 |
| 10 | Education | 3000 | 3081 | 6552 | 4006 | 16639 | 4159.75 | 6552 | 3000 |
| 11 | Inventory | 29986 | 27115 | 25641 | 32465 | 115207 | 28801.75 | 32465 | 25641 |
| 12 | Total | 82742 | 82044 | 82273 | 91059 | | | | |
| 13 | | | | | | | | | |
| 14 | Average | 13790.33 | 13674 | 13712.17 | 15176.5 | | | | |
| 15 | Maximum | 29986 | 27115 | 25876 | 32465 | | | | |
| 16 | Minimum | 3000 | 3081 | 6552 | 4006 | | | | |
| 17 | | | | | | | | | |
| 18 | | | | | | | | | |

## Advanced Challenge Exercise

- Create the label **Expense categories** in cell B19.
- In cell A19, create a formula using the COUNT function that determines the total number of expense categories listed per quarter.
- Save the workbook.

**f.** Enter your name in cell A25.

**g.** Preview the worksheet, then submit your work to your instructor as directed.

**h.** Close the workbook and exit Excel.

Working with Formulas and Functions

# Independent Challenge 3

As the accounting manager of a locally owned business, it is your responsibility to calculate accrued sales tax payments on a monthly basis and then submit the payments to the state government. You've decided to use an Excel workbook to make these calculations.

**a.** Start Excel, then save a new, blank workbook to the drive and folder where you store your Data Files as **EX B-Sales Tax Calculations**.

**b.** Decide on the layout for all columns and rows. The worksheet will contain data for six stores, which you can name by store number, neighborhood, or another method of your choice. For each store, you will calculate total sales tax based on the local sales tax rate. You'll also calculate total tax owed for all six stores.

**c.** Make up sales data for all six stores.

**d.** Enter the rate to be used to calculate the sales tax, using your own local rate.

**e.** Create formulas to calculate the sales tax owed for each store. If you don't know the local tax rate, use **6.5%**.

**f.** Create a formula to total all the owed sales tax, then compare your work to the sample shown in Figure B-26.

**FIGURE B-26**

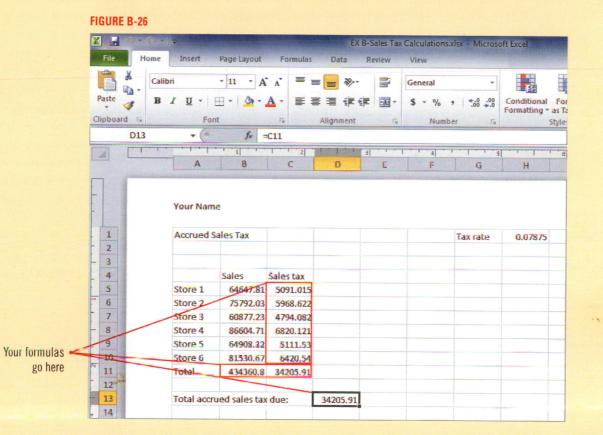

## Advanced Challenge Exercise

- Use the ROUND function to eliminate any decimal places in the sales tax figures for each store and the total due.
- Save the workbook.

**g.** Add your name to the header.

**h.** Save your work, preview the worksheet, and submit your work to your instructor as directed.

**i.** Close the workbook and exit Excel.

# Real Life Independent Challenge

Since your recent promotion at work, you have started thinking about purchasing a home. As you begin the round of open houses and realtors' listings, you notice that there are many fees associated with buying a home. Some fees are based on a percentage of the purchase price, and others are a flat fee; overall, they seem to represent a substantial amount above the purchase prices you see listed. You've seen five houses so far that interest you; one is easily affordable, and the remaining four are all nice, but increasingly more expensive. Although you will be financing the home, the bottom line is still important to you, so you decide to create an Excel workbook to figure out the real cost of buying each one.

   **a.** Find out the typical cost or percentage rate of at least three fees that are usually charged when buying a home and taking out a mortgage. (*Hint*: If you have access to the Internet you can research the topic of home buying on the Web, or you can ask friends about standard rates or percentages for items such as title insurance, credit reports, and inspection fees.)

   **b.** Start Excel, then save a new, blank workbook to the drive and folder where you store your Data Files as **EX B-Home Purchase Costs**.

   **c.** Create labels and enter data for at least three homes. If you enter this information across the columns in your worksheet, you should have one column for each house, with the purchase price in the cell below each label. Be sure to enter a different purchase price for each house.

   **d.** Create labels for the Fees column and for an Amount or Rate column. Enter the information for each of the fees you have researched.

   **e.** In each house column, enter formulas that calculate the fee for each item. The formulas (and use of absolute or relative referencing) will vary depending on whether the charges are a flat fee or based on a percentage of the purchase price.

# Real Life Independent Challenge (continued)

**f.** Total the fees for each house, then create formulas that add the total fees to the purchase price. A sample of what your workbook might look like is shown in Figure B-27.

**g.** Enter a title for the worksheet in the header.

**h.** Enter your name in the header, save your work, preview the worksheet, then submit your work to your instructor as directed.

**i.** Close the file and exit Excel.

**FIGURE B-27**

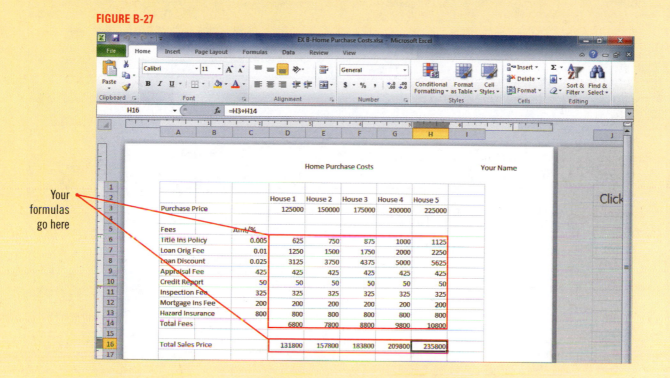

# Visual Workshop

Create the worksheet shown in Figure B-28 using the skills you learned in this unit. Save the workbook as **EX B-Expense Analysis** to the drive and folder where you store your Data Files. Enter your name in the header as shown, hide the gridlines, preview the worksheet, and then submit your work to your instructor as directed.

**FIGURE B-28**

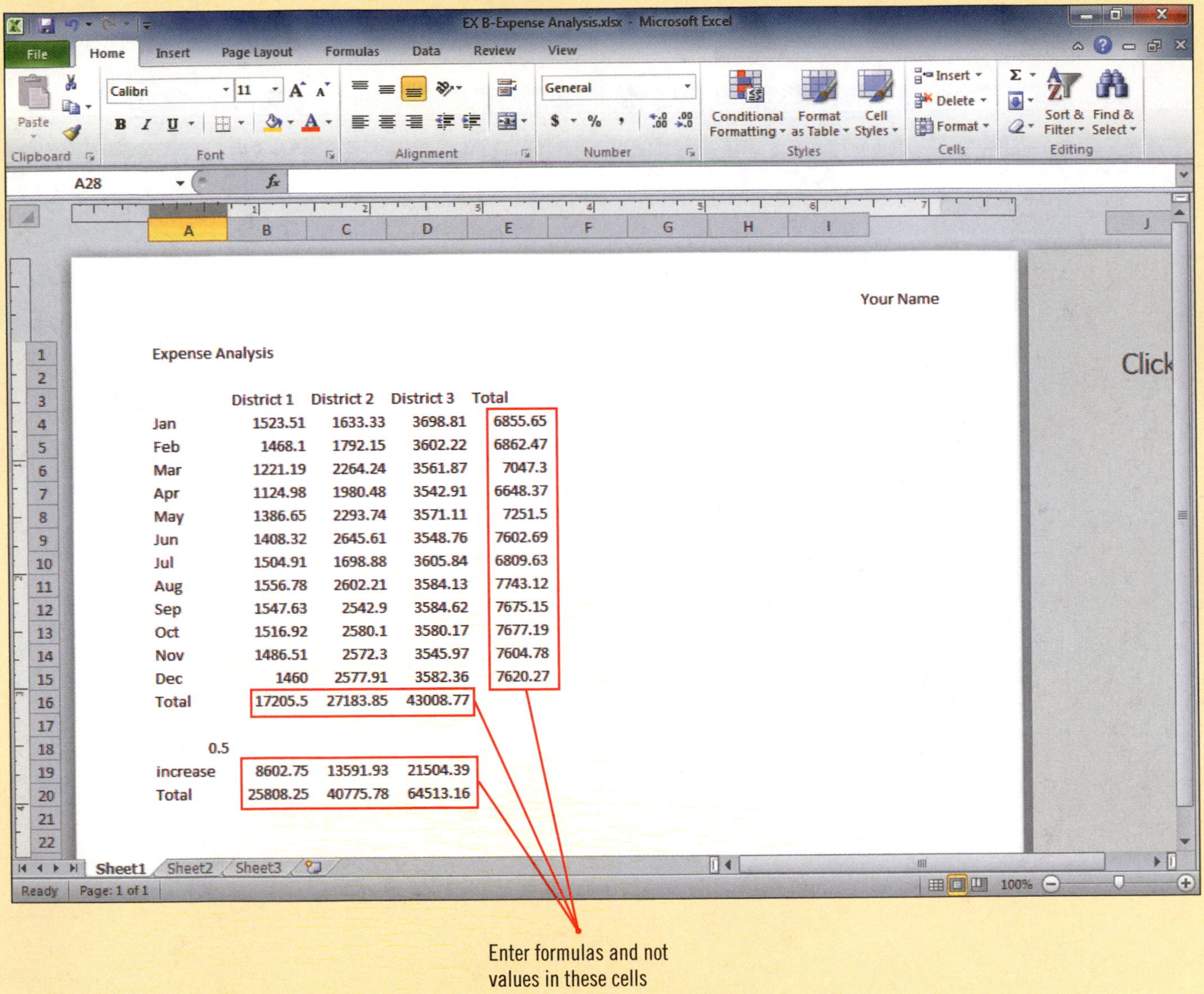
EX B-Expense Analysis.xlsx - Microsoft Excel
File Home Insert Page Layout Formulas Data Review View
A28
Your Name
Expense Analysis
District 1 District 2 District 3 Total
Jan 1523.51 1633.33 3698.81 6855.65
Feb 1468.1 1792.15 3602.22 6862.47
Mar 1221.19 2264.24 3561.87 7047.3
Apr 1124.98 1980.48 3542.91 6648.37
May 1386.65 2293.74 3571.11 7251.5
Jun 1408.32 2645.61 3548.76 7602.69
Jul 1504.91 1698.88 3605.84 6809.63
Aug 1556.78 2602.21 3584.13 7743.12
Sep 1547.63 2542.9 3584.62 7675.15
Oct 1516.92 2580.1 3580.17 7677.19
Nov 1486.51 2572.3 3545.97 7604.78
Dec 1460 2577.91 3582.36 7620.27
Total 17205.5 27183.85 43008.77
0.5
increase 8602.75 13591.93 21504.39
Total 25808.25 40775.78 64513.16
Sheet1 Sheet2 Sheet3
Ready Page: 1 of 1
Enter formulas and not values in these cells

# Formatting a Worksheet

**Files You Will Need:**

EX C-1.xlsx
EX C-2.xlsx
EX C-3.xlsx
EX C-4.xlsx
EX C-5.xlsx

You can use formatting features to make a worksheet more attractive or easier to read, and to emphasize key data. You can apply different formatting attributes such as colors, font styles, and font sizes to the cell contents; you can adjust column width and row height; and you can insert or delete columns and rows. You can also apply conditional formatting so that cells meeting certain conditions are formatted differently from other cells. This makes it easy to emphasize selected information, such as sales that exceed or fall below a certain threshold. The corporate marketing managers at QST have requested data from all QST locations for advertising expenses incurred during the first quarter of this year. Grace Wong has created a worksheet listing this information. She asks you to format the worksheet to make it easier to read and to call attention to important data.

**OBJECTIVES**

Format values

Change font and font size

Change font styles and alignment

Adjust column width

Insert and delete rows and columns

Apply colors, patterns, and borders

Apply conditional formatting

Rename and move a worksheet

Check spelling

# Formatting Values

The **format** of a cell determines how the labels and values look—for example, whether the contents appear boldfaced, italicized, or with dollar signs and commas. Formatting changes only the appearance of a value or label; it does not alter the actual data in any way. To format a cell or range, first you select it, then you apply the formatting using the Ribbon, Mini toolbar, or a keyboard shortcut. You can apply formatting before or after you enter data in a cell or range. 🎨 Grace has provided you with a worksheet that lists individual advertising expenses, and you're ready to improve its appearance and readability. You decide to start by formatting some of the values so they are displayed as currency, percentages, and dates.

**STEPS**

1. **Start Excel, open the file EX C-1.xlsx from the drive and folder where you store your Data Files, then save it as EX C-QST Advertising Expenses**

   This worksheet is difficult to interpret because all the information is crowded and looks the same. In some columns, the contents appear cut off because there is too much data to fit given the current column width. You decide not to widen the columns yet, because the other changes you plan to make might affect column width and row height. The first thing you want to do is format the data showing the cost of each ad.

   **QUICK TIP**

   You can use a different type of currency, such as Euros or British pounds, by clicking the Accounting Number Format list arrow, then clicking a different currency type.

2. **Select the range D4:D32, then click the Accounting Number Format button $ in the Number group on the Home tab**

   The default Accounting **number format** adds dollar signs and two decimal places to the data, as shown in Figure C-1. Formatting this data in Accounting format makes it clear that its values are monetary values. Excel automatically resizes the column to display the new formatting. The Accounting and Currency number formats are both used for monetary values, but the Accounting format aligns currency symbols and decimal points of numbers in a column.

   **QUICK TIP**

   Select any range of contiguous cells by clicking the upper-left cell of the range, pressing and holding [Shift], then clicking the lower-right cell of the range. Add a row to the selected range by continuing to hold down [Shift] and pressing ↓; add a column by pressing →.

3. **Select the range F4:H32, then click the Comma Style button , in the Number group**

   The values in columns F, G, and H display the Comma Style format, which does not include a dollar sign but can be useful for some types of accounting data.

4. **Select the range J4:J32, click the Number Format list arrow, click Percentage, then click the Increase Decimal button .00 in the Number group**

   The data in the % of Total column is now formatted with a percent sign ( % ) and three decimal places. The Number Format list arrow lets you choose from popular number formats and shows an example of what the selected cell or cells would look like in each format (when multiple cells are selected, the example is based on the first cell in the range). Each time you click the Increase Decimal button, you add one decimal place; clicking the button twice would add two decimal places.

5. **Click the Decrease Decimal button .00 in the Number group twice**

   Two decimal places are removed from the percentage values in column J.

6. **Select the range B4:B31, then click the dialog box launcher ⌐ in the Number group**

   The Format Cells dialog box opens with the Date category already selected on the Number tab.

7. **Select the first 14-Mar-01 format in the Type list box as shown in Figure C-2, then click OK**

   The dates in column B appear in the 14-Mar-01 format. The second 14-Mar-01 format in the list displays all days in two digits (it adds a leading zero if the day is only a single-digit number), while the one you chose displays single-digit days without a leading zero.

   **QUICK TIP**

   Make sure you examine formatted data to confirm that you have applied the appropriate formatting; for example, dates should not have a currency format, and monetary values should not have a date format.

8. **Select the range C4:C31, right-click the range, click Format Cells on the shortcut menu, click 14-Mar in the Type list box in the Format Cells dialog box, then click OK**

   Compare your worksheet to Figure C-3.

9. **Press [Ctrl][Home], then save your work**

**FIGURE C-1:** Accounting number format applied to range

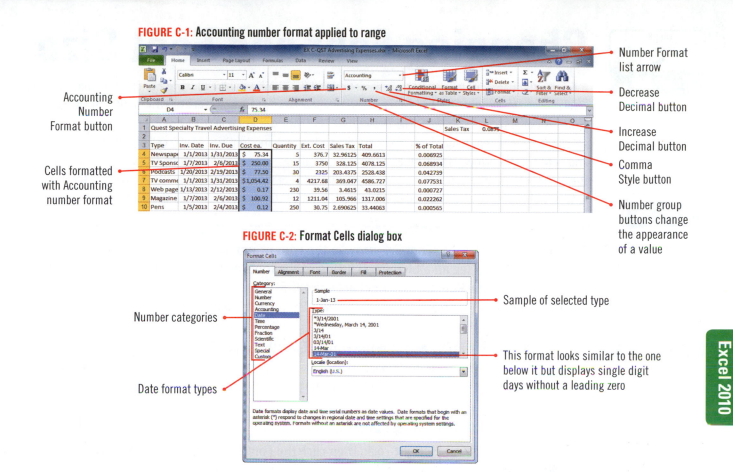

Number Format list arrow

Accounting Number Format button

Cells formatted with Accounting number format

Decrease Decimal button

Increase Decimal button

Comma Style button

Number group buttons change the appearance of a value

**FIGURE C-2:** Format Cells dialog box

Number categories

Date format types

Sample of selected type

This format looks similar to the one below it but displays single digit days without a leading zero

**FIGURE C-3:** Worksheet with formatted values

New format displayed in Number Format box

Date formats appear without year

## Formatting as a table

Excel includes 60 predefined **table styles** to make it easy to format selected worksheet cells as a table. You can apply table styles to any range of cells that you want to format quickly, or even to an entire worksheet, but they're especially useful for those ranges with labels in the left column and top row, and totals in the bottom row or right column. To apply a table style, select the data to be formatted or click anywhere within the intended range (Excel can automatically detect a range of cells filled with data), click the Format as Table button in the Styles group on the Home tab, then click a style in the gallery, as shown in Figure C-4. Table styles are organized in three categories: Light, Medium, and Dark. Once you click a style, Excel asks you to confirm the range selection, then applies the style. Once you have formatted a range as a table, you can use Live Preview to preview the table in other styles by pointing to any style in the Table Styles gallery.

**FIGURE C-4:** Table Styles gallery

Excel 2010

# Changing Font and Font Size

A **font** is the name for a collection of characters (letters, numbers, symbols, and punctuation marks) with a similar, specific design. The **font size** is the physical size of the text, measured in units called points. A **point** is equal to $\frac{1}{72}$ of an inch. The default font and font size in Excel is 11-point Calibri. Table C-1 shows several fonts in different font sizes. You can change the font and font size of any cell or range using the Font and Font Size list arrows. The Font and Font Size list arrows appear on the Home tab on the Ribbon and on the Mini toolbar, which opens when you right-click a cell or range.  You want to change the font and font size of the labels and the worksheet title so that they stand out more from the data.

## STEPS

**QUICK TIP**

To quickly move to a font in the Font list, type the first few characters of its name.

1. **Click cell A1, click the Font list arrow in the Font group on the Home tab, scroll down in the Font list to see an alphabetical listing of the fonts available on your computer, then click Times New Roman, as shown in Figure C-5**

   The font in cell A1 changes to Times New Roman. Notice that the font names on the list are displayed in the font they represent.

**QUICK TIP**

When you point to an option in the Font or Font Size list, Live Preview shows the selected cells with the option temporarily applied.

2. **Click the Font Size list arrow in the Font group, then click 20**

   The worksheet title appears in 20-point Times New Roman, and the Font and Font Size list boxes on the Home tab display the new font and font size information.

3. **Click the Increase Font Size button** A⁺ **in the Font group twice**

   The font size of the title increases to 24 point.

4. **Select the range A3:J3, right-click, then click the Font list arrow in the Font group on the Mini toolbar**

   The Mini toolbar includes the most commonly used formatting tools, so it's great for making quick formatting changes.

**QUICK TIP**

You can format an entire row by clicking the row indicator button to select the row before formatting (or select an entire column by clicking the column indicator button before formatting).

5. **Scroll down in the Font list and click Times New Roman, click the Font Size list arrow on the Mini toolbar, then click 14**

   The Mini toolbar closes when you move the pointer away from the selection. Compare your worksheet to Figure C-6. Notice that some of the column labels are now too wide to appear fully in the column. Excel does not automatically adjust column widths to accommodate cell formatting; you have to adjust column widths manually. You'll learn to do this in a later lesson.

6. **Save your work**

**TABLE C-1:** Examples of fonts and font sizes

| font | 12 point | 24 point |
|---|---|---|
| Calibri | Excel | Excel |
| Playbill | Excel | Excel |
| Comic Sans MS | Excel | Excel |
| Times New Roman | Excel | Excel |

Formatting a Worksheet

**FIGURE C-5:** Font list

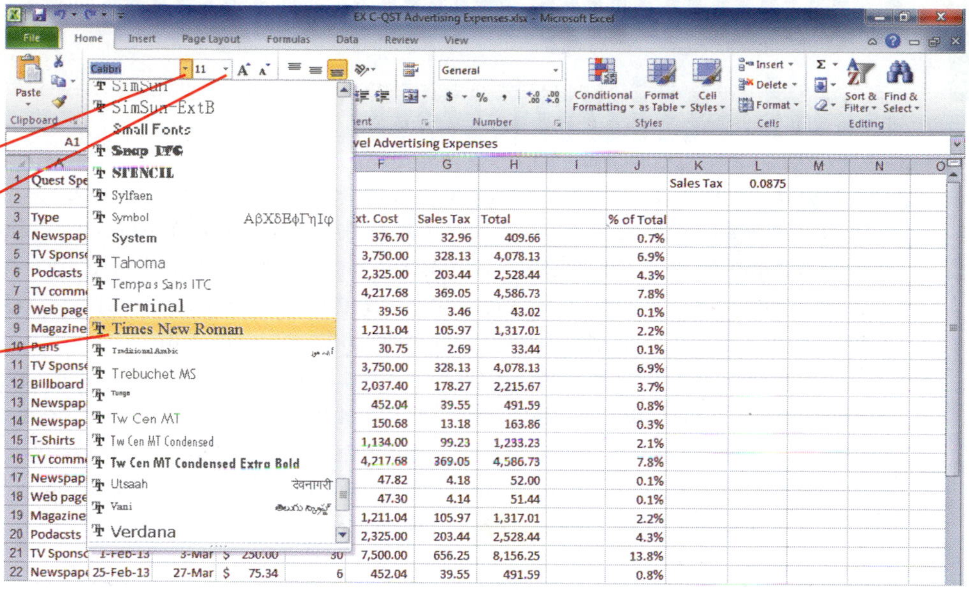

Font list arrow

Font Size list arrow

Click a font to apply it to the selected cell

**FIGURE C-6:** Worksheet with formatted title and column labels

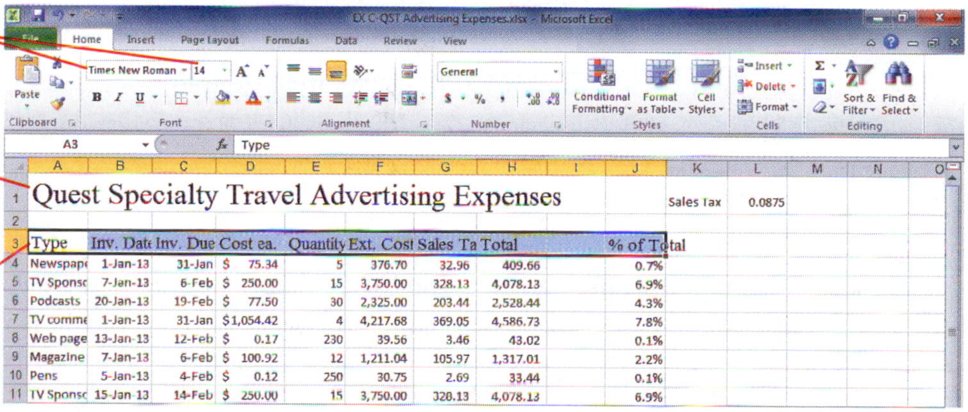

Font and font size of active cell or range

Title appears in 24-point Times New Roman

Column labels are now 14-point Times New Roman

## Inserting and adjusting clip art and other images

You can illustrate your worksheets using clip art and other images. A **clip** is an individual media file, such as a graphic, sound, animation, or a movie. **Clip art** refers to images such as a corporate logo, a picture, or a photo. Microsoft Office comes with many clips available for your use. To add a clip to a worksheet, click the Clip Art button in the Illustrations group on the Insert tab. The Clip Art task pane opens. Here you can search for clips by typing one or more keywords (words related to your subject) in the Search for text box, then click Go. Clips that relate to your keywords appear in the Clip Art task pane, as shown in Figure C-7. (If you have a standard Office installation and an active Internet connection, click the Include Office.com content check box to see clips available through Office.com in addition to those on your computer.) When you click the image you want in the Clip Art task pane, the image is inserted at the location of the active cell. To add your own images to a worksheet, click the Insert tab on the Ribbon, then click the Picture button. Navigate to the file you want, then click Insert. To resize an image, drag any corner sizing handle. To move an image, point inside the clip until the pointer changes to ⊹, then drag it to a new location.

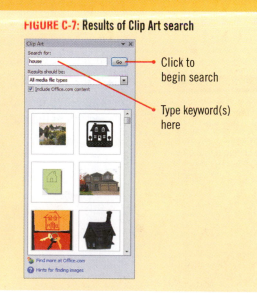

**FIGURE C-7:** Results of Clip Art search

Click to begin search

Type keyword(s) here

Formatting a Worksheet

# Changing Font Styles and Alignment

**Font styles** are formats such as bold, italic, and underlining that you can apply to affect the way text and numbers look in a worksheet. You can also change the **alignment** of labels and values in cells to position them in relation to the cells' edges—such as left-aligned, right-aligned, or centered. You can apply font styles and alignment options using the Home tab, the Format Cells dialog box, or the Mini toolbar. See Table C-2 for a description of common font style and alignment buttons that are available on the Home tab and the Mini toolbar. Once you have formatted a cell the way you want it, you can "paint" or copy the cell's formats into other cells by using the Format Painter button in the Clipboard group on the Home tab. This is similar to using copy and paste, but instead of copying cell contents, it copies only the cell's formatting. You want to further enhance the worksheet's appearance by adding bold and underline formatting and centering some of the labels.

## STEPS

**QUICK TIP**

You can use the following keyboard shortcuts to format a selected cell or range: [Ctrl][B] to bold, [Ctrl][I] to italicize, and [Ctrl][U] to underline.

1. **Press [Ctrl][Home], then click the Bold button B in the Font group on the Home tab**

   The title in cell A1 appears in bold.

2. **Click cell A3, then click the Underline button U in the Font group**

   The column label is now underlined, though this may be difficult to see with the cell selected.

3. **Click the Italic button I in the Font group, then click B**

   The heading now appears in boldface, underlined, italic type. Notice that the Bold, Italic, and Underline buttons in the Font group are all selected.

**QUICK TIP**

Overuse of any font style and random formatting can make a workbook difficult to read. Be consistent and add the same formatting to similar items throughout a worksheet or in related worksheets.

4. **Click the Italic button I to deselect it**

   The italic font style is removed from cell A3, but the bold and underline font styles remain.

5. **Click the Format Painter button in the Clipboard group, then select the range B3:J3**

   The formatting in cell A3 is copied to the rest of the column labels. To paint the formats on more than one selection, double-click the Format Painter button to keep it activated until you turn it off. You can turn off the Format Painter by pressing [Esc] or by clicking . You decide the title would look better if it were centered over the data columns.

6. **Select the range A1:H1, then click the Merge & Center button in the Alignment group**

   The Merge & Center button creates one cell out of the eight cells across the row, then centers the text in that newly created, merged cell. The title "Quest Specialty Travel Advertising Expenses" is centered across the eight columns you selected. To split a merged cell into its original components, select the merged cell, then click the Merge & Center button to deselect it. The merged and centered text might look awkward now, but you'll be changing the column widths shortly.

**QUICK TIP**

To clear all formatting from a selected range, click the Clear button in the Editing group on the Home tab, then click Clear Formats.

7. **Select the range A3:J3, right-click, then click the Center button on the Mini toolbar**

   Compare your screen to Figure C-8. Although they may be difficult to read, notice that all the headings are centered within their cells.

8. **Save your work**

**FIGURE C-8:** Worksheet with font styles and alignment applied

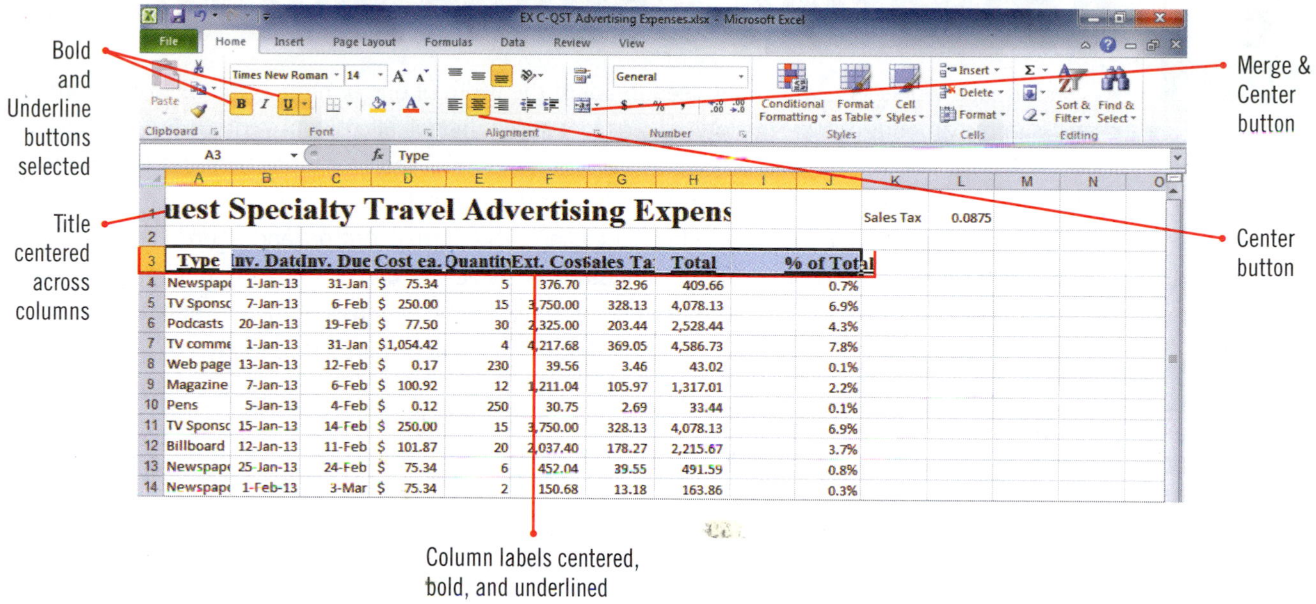

Bold and Underline buttons selected

Title centered across columns

Merge & Center button

Center button

Column labels centered, bold, and underlined

**TABLE C-2:** Common font style and alignment buttons

| button | description | button | description |
|--------|-------------|--------|-------------|
| **B** | Bolds text | | Aligns text at the left edge of the cell |
| *I* | Italicizes text | | Centers text horizontally within the cell |
| U | Underlines text | | Aligns text at the right edge of the cell |
| | Centers text across columns, and combines two or more selected, adjacent cells into one cell | | |

## Rotating and indenting cell entries

In addition to applying fonts and font styles, you can rotate or indent data within a cell to further change its appearance. You can rotate text within a cell by altering its alignment. To change alignment, select the cells you want to modify, then click the dialog box launcher in the Alignment group to open the Alignment tab of the Format Cells dialog box. Click a position in the Orientation box or type a number in the Degrees text box to rotate text from its default horizontal orientation, then click OK. You can indent cell contents using the Increase Indent button in the Alignment group, which moves cell contents to the right one space, or the Decrease Indent button, which moves cell contents to the left one space.

# Adjusting Column Width

As you format a worksheet, you might need to adjust the width of one or more columns to accommodate changes in the amount of text, the font size, or font style. The default column width is 8.43 characters, a little less than 1". With Excel, you can adjust the width of one or more columns by using the mouse, the Format button in the Cells group on the Home tab, or the shortcut menu. Using the mouse, you can drag or double-click the right edge of a column heading. The Format button and shortcut menu include commands for making more precise width adjustments. Table C-3 describes common column formatting commands. 🎨 You have noticed that some of the labels in columns A through J don't fit in the cells. You want to adjust the widths of the columns so that the labels appear in their entirety.

## STEPS

1. **Position the mouse pointer on the line between the column A and column B headings until it changes to ✛**

   See Figure C-9. The **column heading** is the box at the top of each column containing a letter. Before you can adjust column width using the mouse, you need to position the pointer on the right edge of the column heading for the column you want to adjust. The cell entry "TV commercials" is the widest in the column.

> **QUICK TIP**
>
> If "#######" appears after you adjust a column of values, the column is too narrow to display the values completely; increase the column width until the values appear.

2. **Click and drag the ✛ to the right until the column displays the "TV commercials" cell entries fully (approximately 13.86 characters, 1.06", or 102 pixels)**

   As you change the column width, a ScreenTip is displayed listing the column width. In Normal view, the ScreenTip lists the width in characters and pixels; in Page Layout view, the ScreenTip lists the width in inches and pixels.

3. **Position the pointer on the line between columns B and C until it changes to ✛, then double-click**

   Double-clicking the right edge of a column heading activates the **AutoFit** feature, which automatically resizes the column to accommodate the widest entry in the column. Column B automatically widens to fit the widest entry, which is the column label "Inv. Date".

4. **Use AutoFit to resize columns C, D, and J**

5. **Select the range E5:H5**

   You can change the width of multiple columns at once, by first selecting either the column headings or at least one cell in each column.

> **QUICK TIP**
>
> If an entire column rather than a column cell is selected, you can change the width of the column by right-clicking the column heading, then clicking Column Width on the shortcut menu.

6. **Click the Format button in the Cells group, then click Column Width**

   The Column Width dialog box opens. Column width measurement is based on the number of characters that will fit in the column when formatted in the Normal font and font size (in this case, 11 pt Calibri).

7. **Drag the dialog box by its title bar if its placement obscures your view of the worksheet, type 11 in the Column width text box, then click OK**

   The widths of columns E, F, G, and H change to reflect the new setting. See Figure C-10.

8. **Save your work**

**TABLE C-3: Common column formatting commands**

| command | description | available using |
|---|---|---|
| Column Width | Sets the width to a specific number of characters | Format button; shortcut menu |
| AutoFit Column Width | Fits to the widest entry in a column | Format button; mouse |
| Hide & Unhide | Hides or displays hidden column(s) | Format button; shortcut menu |
| Default Width | Resets column to worksheet's default column width | Format button |

**FIGURE C-9:** Preparing to change the column width

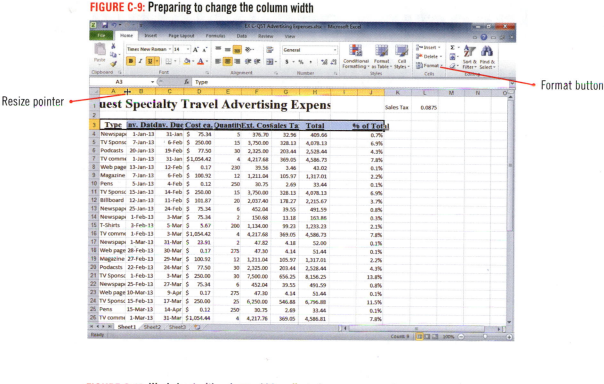

Resize pointer

Format button

**FIGURE C-10:** Worksheet with column widths adjusted

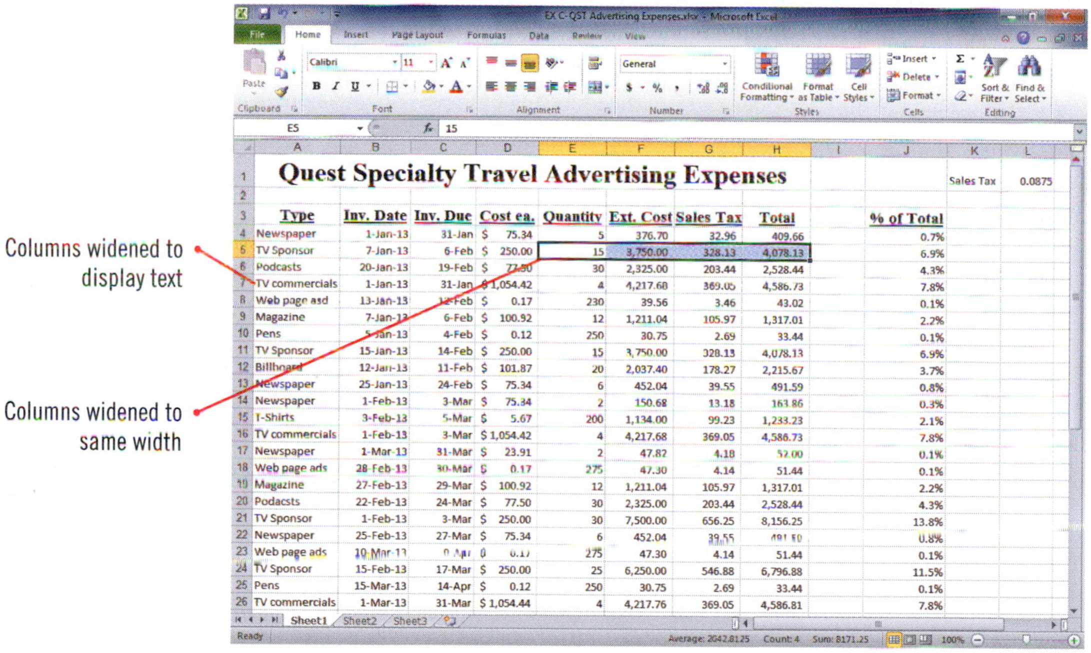

Columns widened to display text

Columns widened to same width

## Changing row height

Changing row height is as easy as changing column width. Row height is calculated in points, the same units of measure used for fonts. The row height must exceed the size of the font you are using. Normally, you don't need to adjust row heights manually, because row heights adjust automatically to accommodate font size changes. If you format something in a row to be a larger point size, Excel adjusts the row to fit the largest point size in the row. However, you have just as many options for changing row height as you do

column width. Using the mouse, you can place the ✛ pointer on the line dividing a row heading from the heading below, and then drag to the desired height; double-clicking the line AutoFits the row height where necessary. You can also select one or more rows, then use the Row Height command on the shortcut menu, or click the Format button on the Home tab and click the Row Height or AutoFit Row Height command.

# Inserting and Deleting Rows and Columns

As you modify a worksheet, you might find it necessary to insert or delete rows and columns to keep your worksheet current. For example, you might need to insert rows to accommodate new inventory products or remove a column of yearly totals that are no longer necessary. When you insert a new row, the row is inserted above the cell pointer and the contents of the worksheet shift down from the newly inserted row. When you insert a new column, the column is inserted to the left of the cell pointer and the contents of the worksheet shift to the right of the new column. To insert multiple rows, select the same number of row headings as you want to insert before using the Insert command.  You want to improve the overall appearance of the worksheet by inserting a row between the last row of data and the totals. Also, you have learned that row 27 and column J need to be deleted from the worksheet.

## STEPS

**QUICK TIP**

To insert a single row or column, right-click the row heading immediately below where you want the new row, or right-click the column heading to the right of where you want the new column, then click Insert on the shortcut menu.

1. **Right-click cell A32, then click Insert on the shortcut menu**

   The Insert dialog box opens. See Figure C-11. You can choose to insert a column or a row; insert a single cell and shift the cells in the active column to the right; or insert a single cell and shift the cells in the active row down. An additional row between the last row of data and the totals will visually separate the totals.

2. **Click the Entire row option button, then click OK**

   A blank row appears between the Billboard data and the totals, and the formula result in cell E33 has not changed. The Insert Options button 🖌 appears beside cell A33. Pointing to the button displays a list arrow, which you can click and then choose from the following options: Format Same As Above (the default setting, already selected), Format Same As Below, or Clear Formatting.

3. **Click the row 27 heading**

   All of row 27 is selected, as shown in Figure C-12.

**QUICK TIP**

If you inadvertently click the Delete list arrow instead of the button itself, click Delete Sheet Rows in the menu that opens.

4. **Click the Delete button in the Cells group; *do not click the list arrow***

   Excel deletes row 27, and all rows below it shift up one row. You must use the Delete button or the Delete command on the shortcut menu to delete a row or column; pressing [Delete] on the keyboard removes only the *contents* of a selected row or column.

5. **Click the column J heading**

   The percentage information is calculated elsewhere and is no longer necessary in this worksheet.

**QUICK TIP**

After inserting or deleting rows or columns in a worksheet, be sure to proof formulas that contain relative cell references.

6. **Click the Delete button in the Cells group**

   Excel deletes column J. The remaining columns to the right shift left one column.

7. **Save your work**

---

### Hiding and unhiding columns and rows

When you don't want data in a column or row to be visible, but you don't want to delete it, you can hide the column or row. To hide a selected column, click the Format button in the Cells group on the Home tab, point to Hide & Unhide, then click Hide Columns. A hidden column is indicated by a dark black vertical line in its original position. This black line disappears when you click elsewhere in the worksheet. You can display a hidden column by selecting the columns on either side of the hidden column, clicking the Format button in the Cells group, pointing to Hide & Unhide, and then clicking Unhide Columns. (To hide or unhide one or more rows, substitute Hide Rows and Unhide Rows for the Hide Columns and Unhide Columns commands.)

Formatting a Worksheet

FIGURE C-11: Insert dialog box

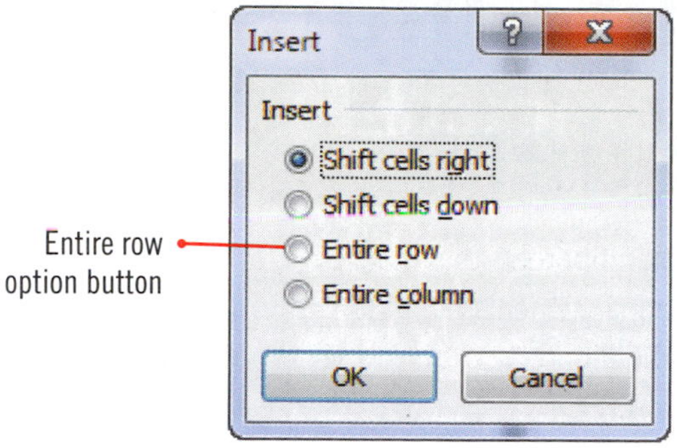

Entire row option button

FIGURE C-12: Worksheet with row 27 selected

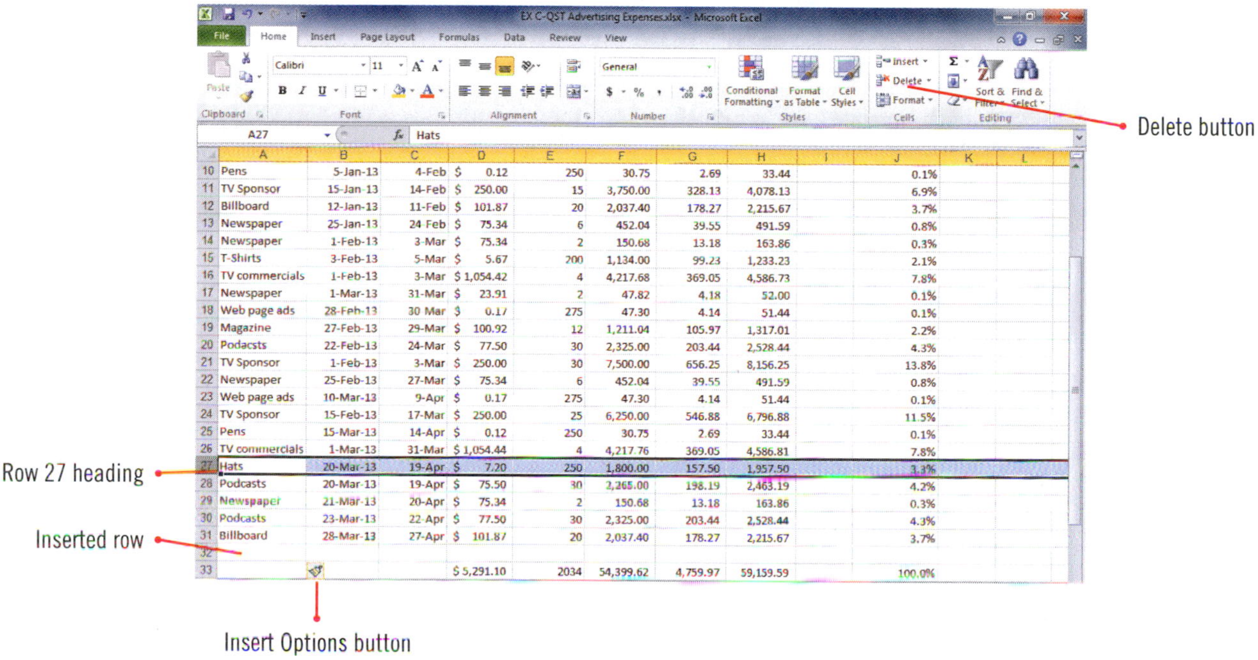

Delete button

Row 27 heading

Inserted row

Insert Options button

## Adding and editing comments

Much of your work in Excel may be in collaboration with teammates with whom you share worksheets. You can share ideas with other worksheet users by adding comments within selected cells. To include a comment in a worksheet, click the cell where you want to place the comment, click the Review tab on the Ribbon, then click the New Comment button in the Comments group. You can type your comments in the resizable text box that opens containing the computer user's name. A small, red triangle appears in the upper-right corner of a cell containing a comment. If comments are not already displayed in a workbook, other users can point to the triangle to display the comment. To see all worksheet comments, as shown in Figure C-13, click the Show All Comments button in the Comments group. To edit a comment, click the cell containing the comment, then click the Edit Comment button in the Comments group. To delete a comment, click the cell containing the comment, then click the Delete button in the Comments group.

FIGURE C-13: Comments displayed in a worksheet

Excel 2010

# Applying Colors, Patterns, and Borders

You can use colors, patterns, and borders to enhance the overall appearance of a worksheet and make it easier to read. You can add these enhancements by using the Borders, Font Color, and Fill Color buttons in the Font group on the Home tab of the Ribbon and on the Mini toolbar, or by using the Fill tab and the Border tab in the Format Cells dialog box. You can open the Format Cells dialog box by clicking the dialog box launcher in the Font, Alignment, or Number group on the Home tab, or by right-clicking a selection, then clicking Format Cells on the shortcut menu. You can apply a color to the background of a cell or a range or to cell contents (such as letters and numbers), and you can apply a pattern to a cell or range. You can apply borders to all the cells in a worksheet or only to selected cells to call attention to selected information. To save time, you can also apply **cell styles**, predesigned combinations of formats. 🎨 You want to add a pattern, a border, and color to the title of the worksheet to give the worksheet a more professional appearance.

## STEPS

1. **Select cell A1, click the Fill Color list arrow** 🖌️▾ **in the Font group, then hover the pointer over the Turquoise, Accent 2 color (first row, sixth column from the left)**

   See Figure C-14. Live Preview shows you how the color will look *before* you apply it. (Remember that cell A1 spans columns A through H because the Merge & Center command was applied.)

2. **Click the Turquoise, Accent 2 color**

   The color is applied to the background (or fill) of this cell. When you change fill or font color, the color on the Fill Color or Font Color button changes to the last color you selected.

3. **Right-click cell A1, then click Format Cells on the shortcut menu**

   The Format Cells dialog box opens.

**QUICK TIP**

Use fill colors and patterns sparingly. Too many colors can be distracting or make it hard to see which information is important.

4. **Click the Fill tab, click the Pattern Style list arrow, click the 6.25% Gray style (first row, sixth column from the left), then click OK**

**QUICK TIP**

You can also create custom cell borders. Click the Borders list arrow in the Font group, click More Borders, then click the individual border buttons to apply the borders you want to the selected cell(s).

5. **Click the Borders list arrow** ▦▾ **in the Font group, then click Thick Bottom Border**

   Unlike underlining, which is a text-formatting tool, borders extend to the width of the cell, and can appear at the bottom of the cell, at the top, on either side, or on any combination of the four sides. It can be difficult to see a border when the cell is selected.

6. **Select the range A3:H3, click the Font Color list arrow** 🅰️▾ **in the Font group, then click the Blue, Accent 1 color (first Theme color row, fifth column from the left) on the palette**

   The new color is applied to the labels in the selected range.

7. **Select the range J1:K1, click the Cell Styles button in the Styles group, then click the Neutral cell style (first row, fourth column from the left) in the gallery**

   The font and color change in the range, as shown in Figure C-15.

8. **Save your work**

**FIGURE C-14:** Live Preview of fill color

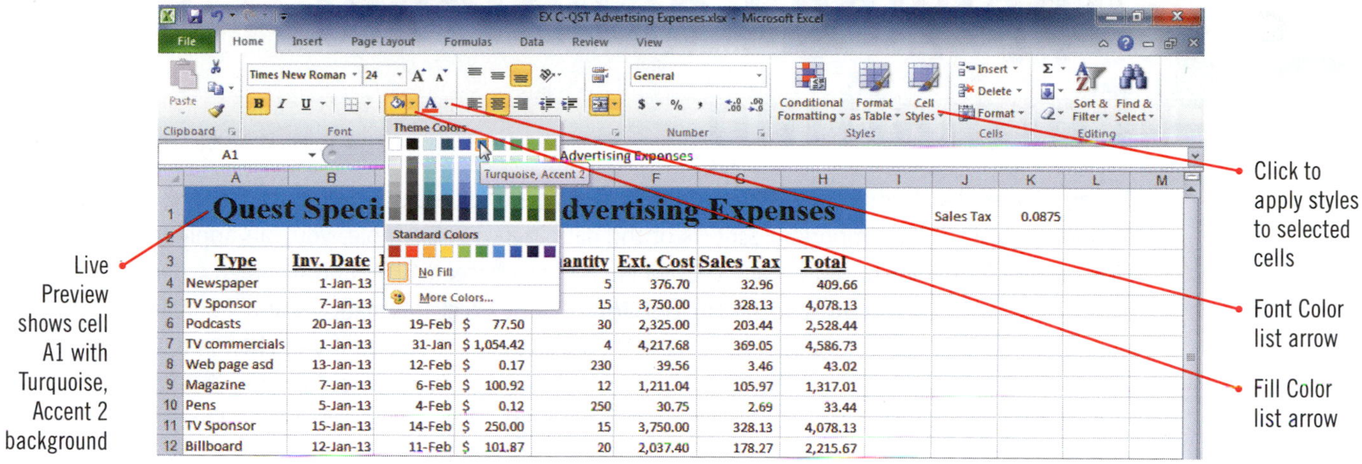

Live Preview shows cell A1 with Turquoise, Accent 2 background

Turquoise, Accent 2

Click to apply styles to selected cells

Font Color list arrow

Fill Color list arrow

**FIGURE C-15:** Worksheet with color, patterns, border, and cell style applied

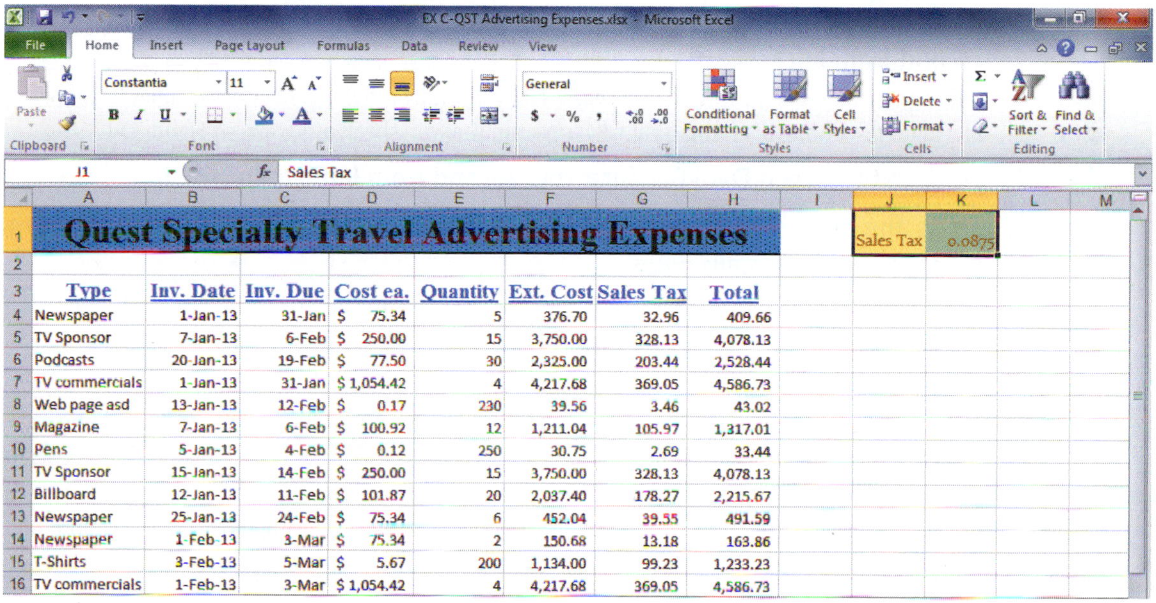

| | Quest Specialty Travel Advertising Expenses | | | | | | | | | | Sales Tax | 0.0875 |
|---|---|---|---|---|---|---|---|---|---|---|---|---|
| | **Type** | **Inv. Date** | **Inv. Due** | **Cost ea.** | **Quantity** | **Ext. Cost** | **Sales Tax** | **Total** | | | | |
| 4 | Newspaper | 1-Jan-13 | 31-Jan | $ 75.34 | 5 | 376.70 | 32.96 | 409.66 | | | | |
| 5 | TV Sponsor | 7-Jan-13 | 6-Feb | $ 250.00 | 15 | 3,750.00 | 328.13 | 4,078.13 | | | | |
| 6 | Podcasts | 20-Jan-13 | 19-Feb | $ 77.50 | 30 | 2,325.00 | 203.44 | 2,528.44 | | | | |
| 7 | TV commercials | 1-Jan-13 | 31-Jan | $ 1,054.42 | 4 | 4,217.68 | 369.05 | 4,586.73 | | | | |
| 8 | Web page asd | 13-Jan-13 | 12-Feb | $ 0.17 | 230 | 39.56 | 3.46 | 43.02 | | | | |
| 9 | Magazine | 7-Jan-13 | 6-Feb | $ 100.92 | 12 | 1,211.04 | 105.97 | 1,317.01 | | | | |
| 10 | Pens | 5-Jan-13 | 4-Feb | $ 0.12 | 250 | 30.75 | 2.69 | 33.44 | | | | |
| 11 | TV Sponsor | 15-Jan-13 | 14-Feb | $ 250.00 | 15 | 3,750.00 | 328.13 | 4,078.13 | | | | |
| 12 | Billboard | 12-Jan-13 | 11-Feb | $ 101.87 | 20 | 2,037.40 | 178.27 | 2,215.67 | | | | |
| 13 | Newspaper | 25-Jan-13 | 24-Feb | $ 75.34 | 6 | 452.04 | 39.55 | 491.59 | | | | |
| 14 | Newspaper | 1-Feb-13 | 3-Mar | $ 75.34 | 2 | 150.68 | 13.18 | 163.86 | | | | |
| 15 | T-Shirts | 3-Feb-13 | 5-Mar | $ 5.67 | 200 | 1,134.00 | 99.23 | 1,233.23 | | | | |
| 16 | TV commercials | 1-Feb-13 | 3-Mar | $ 1,054.42 | 4 | 4,217.68 | 369.05 | 4,586.73 | | | | |

## Working with themes and cell styles

Using themes and cell styles makes it easier to ensure that your worksheets are consistent. A **theme** is a predefined set of formats that gives your Excel worksheet a professional look. Formatting choices included in a theme are colors, fonts, and line and fill effects. To apply a theme, click the Themes button in the Themes group on the Page Layout tab to open the Themes gallery, as shown in Figure C-16, then click a theme in the gallery. **Cell styles** are sets of cell formats based on themes, so they are automatically updated if you change a theme. For example, if you apply the 20% - Accent1 cell style to cell A1 in a worksheet that has no theme applied, the fill color changes to light blue and the font changes to Constantia. If you change the theme of the worksheet to Metro, cell A1's fill color changes to light green and the font changes to Corbel, because these are the new theme's associated formats.

**FIGURE C-16:** Themes gallery

Formatting a Worksheet

Excel 63

Excel 2010

# Applying Conditional Formatting

So far, you've used formatting to change the appearance of different types of data, but you can also use formatting to highlight important aspects of the data itself. For example, you can apply formatting that changes the font color to red for any cells where ad costs exceed $100 and to green where ad costs are below $50. This is called **conditional formatting** because Excel automatically applies different formats to data if the data meets conditions you specify. The formatting is updated if you change data in the worksheet. You can also copy conditional formats the same way you copy other formats. Grace is concerned about advertising costs exceeding the yearly budget. You decide to use conditional formatting to highlight certain trends and patterns in the data so that it's easy to spot the most expensive advertising.

## STEPS

1. **Select the range H4:H30, click the Conditional Formatting button in the Styles group on the Home tab, point to Data Bars, then point to the Light Blue Data Bar (second row, second from left)**

   Data bars are colored horizontal bars that visually illustrate differences between values in a range of cells. Live Preview shows how this formatting will appear in the worksheet, as shown in Figure C-17.

**QUICK TIP**

You can apply an Icon Set to a selected range by clicking the Conditional Formatting button in the Styles group, then pointing to Icon Sets; icons appear within the cells to illustrate differences in values.

2. **Point to the Green Data Bar (first row, second from left), then click it**

3. **Select the range F4:F30, click the Conditional Formatting button in the Styles group, then point to Highlight Cells Rules**

   The Highlight Cells Rules submenu displays choices for creating different formatting conditions. For example, you can create a rule for values that are greater than or less than a certain amount, or between two amounts.

4. **Click Between on the submenu**

   The Between dialog box opens, displaying input boxes you can use to define the condition and a default format (Light Red Fill with Dark Red Text) selected for cells that meet that condition. Depending on the condition you select in the Highlight Cells Rules submenu (such as "Greater Than" or "Less Than"), this dialog box displays different input boxes. You define the condition using the input boxes and then assign the formatting you want to use for cells that meet that condition. Values used in input boxes for a condition can be constants, formulas, cell references, or dates.

**QUICK TIP**

To define custom formatting for data that meets the condition, click Custom Format at the bottom of the with list, and then use the Format Cells dialog box to set the formatting to be applied.

5. **Type 2000 in the first text box, type 4000 in the second text box, click the with list arrow, click Light Red Fill, compare your settings to Figure C-18, then click OK**

   All cells with values between 2000 and 4000 in column F appear with a light red fill.

6. **Click cell F7, type 3975.55, then press [Enter]**

   When the value in cell F7 changes, the formatting also changes because the new value meets the condition you set. Compare your results to Figure C-19.

7. **Press [Ctrl][Home] to select cell A1, then save your work**

---

### Managing conditional formatting rules

If you create a conditional formatting rule and then want to change the condition to reflect a different value or format, you don't need to create a new rule; instead, you can modify the rule using the Rules Manager. Select the cell(s) containing conditional formatting, click the Conditional Formatting button in the Styles group, then click Manage Rules. The Conditional Formatting Rules Manager dialog box opens. Select the rule you want to edit, click Edit Rule, and then modify the settings in the Edit the Rule Description area in the Edit Formatting Rule dialog box. To change the formatting for a rule, click the Format button in the Edit the Rule Description area, select the formatting styles you want the text to have, then click OK three times to close the Format Cells dialog box, the Edit Formatting Rule dialog box, and then the Conditional Formatting Rules Manager dialog box. The rule is modified, and the new conditional formatting is applied to the selected cells. To delete a rule, select the rule in the Conditional Formatting Rules Manager dialog box, then click the Delete Rule button.

FIGURE C-17: Previewing data bars in a range

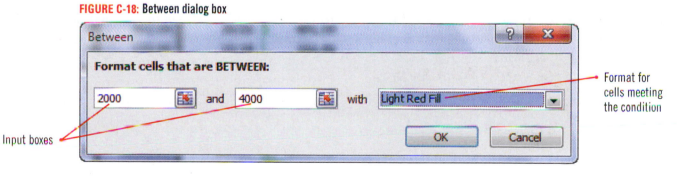

FIGURE C-17: Previewing data bars in a range

Live Preview shows data bars
displayed in selected range

FIGURE C-18: Between dialog box

Between

Format cells that are BETWEEN:

2000    and    4000    with    Light Red Fill

Input boxes

Format for
cells meeting
the condition

OK    Cancel

FIGURE C-19: Worksheet with conditional formatting

| Type | Inv. Date | Inv. Due | Cost ea. | Quantity | Ext. Cost | Sales Tax | Total |
|---|---|---|---|---|---|---|---|
| Newspaper | 1-Jan-13 | 31-Jan | $ 75.34 | 5 | 376.70 | 32.96 | 409.66 |
| TV Sponsor | 7-Jan-13 | 6-Feb | $ 250.00 | 15 | 3,750.00 | 328.13 | 4,078.13 |
| Podcasts | 20-Jan-13 | 19-Feb | $ 77.50 | 30 | 2,325.00 | 203.44 | 2,528.44 |
| TV commercials | 1-Jan-13 | 31-Jan | $ 1,054.42 | 4 | 3,975.55 | 347.86 | 4,323.41 |
| Web page asd | 13-Jan-13 | 12-Feb | $ 0.17 | 230 | 39.56 | 3.46 | 43.02 |
| Magazine | 7-Jan-13 | 6-Feb | $ 100.92 | 12 | 1,211.04 | 105.97 | 1,317.01 |
| Pens | 5-Jan-13 | 4-Feb | $ 0.12 | 250 | 30.75 | 2.69 | 33.44 |
| TV Sponsor | 15-Jan-13 | 14-Feb | $ 250.00 | 15 | 3,750.00 | 328.13 | 4,078.13 |
| Billboard | 12-Jan-13 | 11-Feb | $ 101.87 | 20 | 2,037.40 | 178.27 | 2,215.67 |

Sales Tax   0.0875

Excel 2010

**UNIT**
**C**
Excel 2010

# Renaming and Moving a Worksheet

By default, an Excel workbook initially contains three worksheets, named Sheet1, Sheet2, and Sheet3. Each sheet name appears on a sheet tab at the bottom of the worksheet. When you open a new workbook, the first worksheet, Sheet1, is the active sheet. To move from sheet to sheet, you can click any sheet tab at the bottom of the worksheet window. The sheet tab scrolling buttons, located to the left of the sheet tabs, are useful when a workbook contains too many sheet tabs to display at once. To make it easier to identify the sheets in a workbook, you can rename each sheet and add color to the tabs. You can also organize them in a logical way. For instance, to better track performance goals, you could name each workbook sheet for an individual salesperson, and you could move the sheets so they appear in alphabetical order. In the current worksheet, Sheet1 contains information about actual advertising expenses. Sheet2 contains an advertising budget, and Sheet3 contains no data. You want to rename the two sheets in the workbook to reflect their contents, add color to a sheet tab to easily distinguish one from the other, and change their order.

## STEPS

> **QUICK TIP**
>
> You can also rename a sheet by right-clicking the tab, clicking Rename on the shortcut menu, typing the new name, then pressing [Enter].

1. **Click the Sheet2 tab**

   Sheet2 becomes active, appearing in front of the Sheet1 tab; this is the worksheet that contains the budgeted advertising expenses. See Figure C-20.

2. **Click the Sheet1 tab**

   Sheet1, which contains the actual advertising expenses, becomes active again.

> **QUICK TIP**
>
> To delete a sheet, click its tab, click the Delete list arrow in the Cells group, then click Delete Sheet. To insert a worksheet, click the Insert Worksheet button 📄 to the right of the sheet tabs.

3. **Double-click the Sheet2 tab, type Budget, then press [Enter]**

   The new name for Sheet2 automatically replaces the default name on the tab. Worksheet names can have up to 31 characters, including spaces and punctuation.

4. **Right-click the Budget tab, point to Tab Color on the shortcut menu, then click the Bright Green, Accent 4, Lighter 80% color (second row, third column from the right) as shown in Figure C-21**

5. **Double-click the Sheet1 tab, type Actual, then press [Enter]**

   Notice that the color of the Budget tab changes depending on whether it is the active tab; when the Actual tab is active, the color of the Budget tab changes to the green tab color you selected. You decide to rearrange the order of the sheets, so that the Budget tab is to the left of the Actual tab.

> **QUICK TIP**
>
> If you have more sheet tabs than are visible, you can move between sheets by using the tab scrolling buttons to the left of the sheet tabs: the First Worksheet button ⏮ ; the Last Worksheet button ⏭ ; the Previous Worksheet button ◀ ; and the Next Worksheet button ▶ .

6. **Click the Budget tab, hold down the mouse button, drag it to the left of the Actual tab, as shown in Figure C-22, then release the mouse button**

   As you drag, the pointer changes to ▨, the sheet relocation pointer, and a small, black triangle just above the tabs shows the position the moved sheet will be in when you release the mouse button. The first sheet in the workbook is now the Budget sheet. See Figure C-23.

7. **Click the Actual sheet tab, click the Page Layout button 🔲 on the status bar to open Page Layout view, enter your name in the left header text box, then click anywhere in the worksheet to deselect the header**

8. **Click the Page Layout tab on the Ribbon, click the Orientation button in the Page Setup group, then click Landscape**

9. **Press [Ctrl][Home], then save your work**

Formatting a Worksheet

**FIGURE C-20:** Sheet tabs in workbook

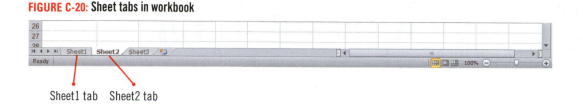

Sheet1 tab      Sheet2 tab

**FIGURE C-21:** Tab Color palette

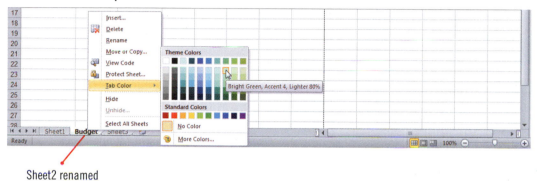

Sheet2 renamed

**FIGURE C-22:** Moving the Budget sheet

Sheet relocation pointer

**FIGURE C-23:** Reordered sheets

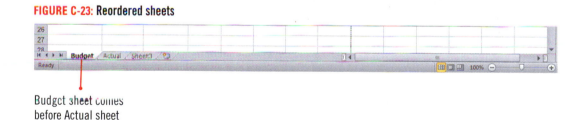

Budget sheet comes
before Actual sheet

Excel 2010

## Copying worksheets

There are times when you may want to copy a worksheet. For example, a workbook might contain a sheet with Quarter 1 expenses, and you want to use that sheet as the basis for a sheet containing Quarter 2 expenses. To copy a sheet within the same workbook, press and hold [Ctrl], drag the sheet tab to the desired tab location, release the mouse button, then release [Ctrl]. A duplicate sheet appears with the same name as the copied sheet followed by "(2)" indicating it is a copy. You can then rename the sheet to a more meaningful name. To copy a sheet to a different workbook, both the source and destination workbooks must be open. Select the sheet to copy or move, right-click the sheet tab, then click Move or Copy in the shortcut menu. Complete the information in the Move or Copy dialog box. Be sure to click the Create a copy check box if you are copying rather than moving the worksheet. Carefully check your calculation results whenever you move or copy a worksheet.

# Checking Spelling

Excel includes a spell checker to help you ensure that the words in your worksheet are spelled correctly. The spell checker scans your worksheet, displays words it doesn't find in its built-in dictionary, and suggests replacements when they are available. To check all of the sheets in a multiple-sheet workbook, you need to display each sheet individually and run the spell checker for each one. Because the built-in dictionary cannot possibly include all the words that anyone needs, you can add words to the dictionary, such as your company name, an acronym, or an unusual technical term. Once you add a word or term, the spell checker no longer considers that word misspelled. Any words you've added to the dictionary using Word, Access, or PowerPoint are also available in Excel. **[image]** Before you distribute this workbook to Grace and the marketing managers, you check its spelling.

## STEPS

**QUICK TIP**

The Spelling dialog box lists the name of the language currently being used in its title bar.

1. **Click the Review tab on the Ribbon, then click the Spelling button in the Proofing group**

   The Spelling: English (U.S.) dialog box opens, as shown in Figure C-24, with "asd" selected as the first misspelled word in the worksheet, and with "ads" selected in the Suggestions list as a possible replacement. For any word, you have the option to Ignore this case of the flagged word, Ignore All cases of the flagged word, Change the word to the selected suggestion, Change All instances of the flagged word to the selected suggestion, or add the flagged word to the dictionary using Add to Dictionary.

2. **Click Change**

   Next, the spell checker finds the word "Podacsts" and suggests "Podcasts" as an alternative.

3. **Verify that the word Podcasts is selected in the Suggestions list, then click Change**

   When no more incorrect words are found, Excel displays a message indicating that the spell check is complete.

4. **Click OK**

5. **Click the Home tab, click Find & Select in the Editing group, then click Replace**

   The Find and Replace dialog box opens. You can use this dialog box to replace a word or phrase. It might be a misspelling of a proper name that the spell checker didn't recognize as misspelled, or it could simply be a term that you want to change throughout the worksheet. Grace has just told you that each instance of "Billboard" in the worksheet should be changed to "Sign".

6. **Type Billboard in the Find what text box, press [Tab], then type Sign in the Replace with text box**

   Compare your dialog box to Figure C-25.

7. **Click Replace All, click OK to close the Microsoft Excel dialog box, then click Close to close the Find and Replace dialog box**

   Excel has made two replacements.

8. **Click the File tab, click Print on the navigation bar, click the No Scaling setting in the Settings section on the Print tab, then click Fit Sheet on One Page**

9. **Click the File tab to return to your worksheet, save your work, submit it to your instructor as directed, close the workbook, then exit Excel**

   The completed worksheet is shown in Figure C-26.

---

### E-mailing a workbook

You can send an entire workbook from within Excel using your installed e-mail program, such as Microsoft Outlook. To send a workbook as an e-mail message attachment, open the workbook, click the File tab, then click Save & Send on the navigation bar. With the Send Using E-mail option selected in the Save & Send section in Backstage view, click Send as Attachment in the right pane. An e-mail message opens in your default e-mail program with the workbook automatically attached; the filename appears in the Attached field. Complete the To and optional Cc fields, include a message if you wish, then click Send.

**FIGURE C-24:** Spelling: English (U.S.) dialog box

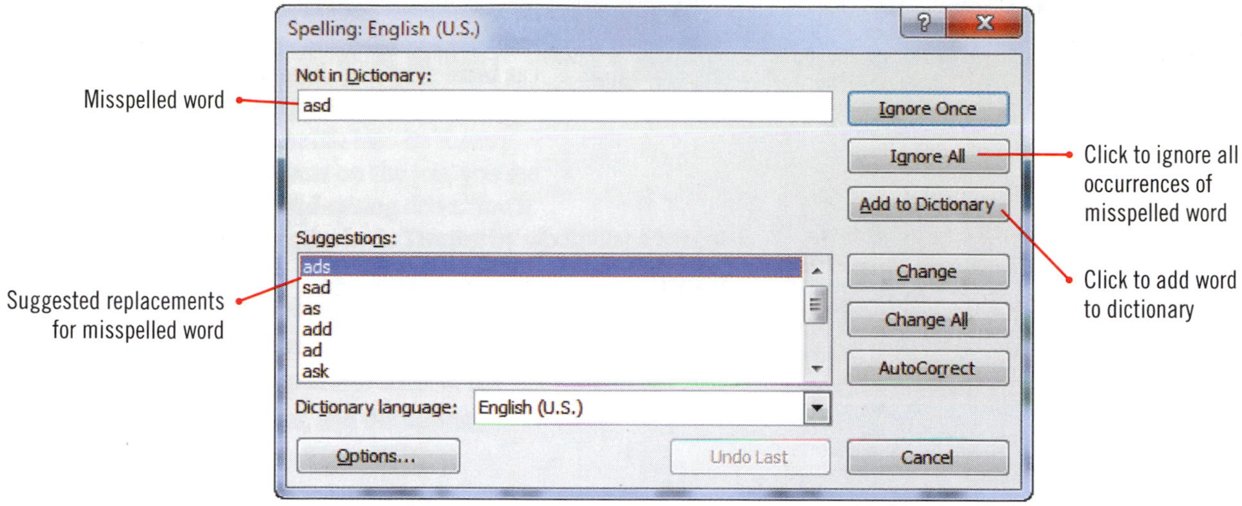

Misspelled word →

Suggested replacements
for misspelled word →

Click to ignore all
occurrences of
misspelled word

Click to add word
to dictionary

**FIGURE C-25:** Find and Replace dialog box

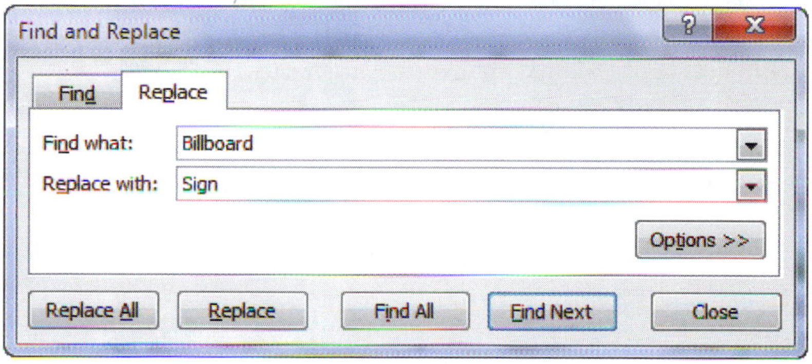

**FIGURE C-26:** Completed worksheet

Your Name

## Quest Specialty Travel Advertising Expenses

Sales Tax 0.0875

| Type | Inv. Date | Inv. Due | Cost ea. | Quantity | Ext. Cost | Sales Tax | Total |
|------|-----------|----------|----------|----------|-----------|-----------|-------|
| Newspaper | 1-Jan-13 | 31-Jan | $ 75.34 | 5 | 376.70 | 32.96 | 409.66 |
| TV Sponsor | 7-Jan-13 | 6-Feb | $ 250.00 | 15 | 3,750.00 | 328.13 | 4,078.13 |
| Podcasts | 20-Jan-13 | 19-Feb | $ 77.50 | 30 | 2,325.00 | 203.44 | 2,528.44 |
| TV commercials | 1 Jan 13 | 31-Jan | $ 1,054.42 | 4 | 3,975.55 | 347.86 | 4,323.41 |
| Web page ads | 13-Jan-13 | 12-Feb | $ 0.17 | 230 | 39.56 | 3.46 | 43.02 |
| Magazine | 7-Jan-13 | 6-Feb | $ 100.92 | 12 | 1,211.04 | 105.97 | 1,317.01 |
| Pens | 5-Jan-13 | 4-Feb | $ 0.12 | 250 | 30.75 | 2.69 | 33.44 |
| TV Sponsor | 15-Jan-13 | 14-Feb | $ 250.00 | 15 | 3,750.00 | 328.13 | 4,078.13 |
| Sign | 12-Jan-13 | 11-Feb | $ 101.87 | 20 | 2,037.40 | 178.27 | 2,215.67 |
| Newspaper | 25-Jan-13 | 24-Feb | $ 75.34 | 6 | 452.04 | 39.55 | 491.59 |
| Newspaper | 1-Feb-13 | 3-Mar | $ 75.34 | 2 | 150.68 | 13.18 | 163.86 |
| T-Shirts | 3-Feb-13 | 5-Mar | $ 5.67 | 200 | 1,134.00 | 99.23 | 1,233.23 |
| TV commercials | 1-Feb-13 | 3-Mar | $ 1,054.42 | 4 | 4,217.68 | 369.05 | 4,586.73 |
| Newspaper | 1-Mar-13 | 31-Mar | $ 23.91 | 2 | 47.82 | 4.18 | 52.00 |
| Web page ads | 28-Feb-13 | 30-Mar | $ 0.17 | 275 | 47.30 | 4.14 | 51.44 |
| Magazine | 27-Feb-13 | 29-Mar | $ 100.92 | 12 | 1,211.04 | 105.97 | 1,317.01 |
| Podcasts | 22-Feb-13 | 24-Mar | $ 77.50 | 30 | 2,325.00 | 203.44 | 2,528.44 |
| TV Sponsor | 1-Feb-13 | 3-Mar | $ 250.00 | 30 | 7,500.00 | 656.25 | 8,156.25 |
| Newspaper | 25-Feb-13 | 27-Mar | $ 75.34 | 6 | 452.04 | 39.55 | 491.59 |
| Web page ads | 10-Mar-13 | 9-Apr | $ 0.17 | 275 | 47.30 | 4.14 | 51.44 |
| TV Sponsor | 15-Feb-13 | 17-Mar | $ 250.00 | 25 | 6,250.00 | 546.88 | 6,796.88 |
| Pens | 15-Mar-13 | 14-Apr | $ 0.12 | 250 | 30.75 | 2.69 | 33.44 |
| TV commercials | 1-Mar-13 | 31-Mar | $ 1,054.44 | 4 | 4,217.76 | 369.05 | 4,586.81 |
| Podcasts | 20-Mar-13 | 19-Apr | $ 75.50 | 30 | 2,265.00 | 198.19 | 2,463.19 |
| Newspaper | 21-Mar-13 | 20-Apr | $ 75.34 | 2 | 150.68 | 13.18 | 163.86 |
| Podcasts | 23-Mar-13 | 22-Apr | $ 77.50 | 30 | 2,325.00 | 203.44 | 2,528.44 |
| Sign | 28-Mar-13 | 27-Apr | $ 101.87 | 20 | 2,037.40 | 178.27 | 2,215.67 |
|  |  |  | $ 5,283.90 | 1784 | 52,357.49 | 4,581.28 | 56,938.77 |

# Practice

SAM

For current SAM information, including versions and content details, visit SAM Central (http://www.cengage.com/samcentral). If you have a SAM user profile, you may have access to hands-on instruction, practice, and assessment of the skills covered in this unit. Since various versions of SAM are supported throughout the life of this text, check with your instructor for the correct instructions and URL/Web site for accessing assignments.

## Concepts Review

**Label each element of the Excel worksheet window shown in Figure C-27.**

FIGURE C-27

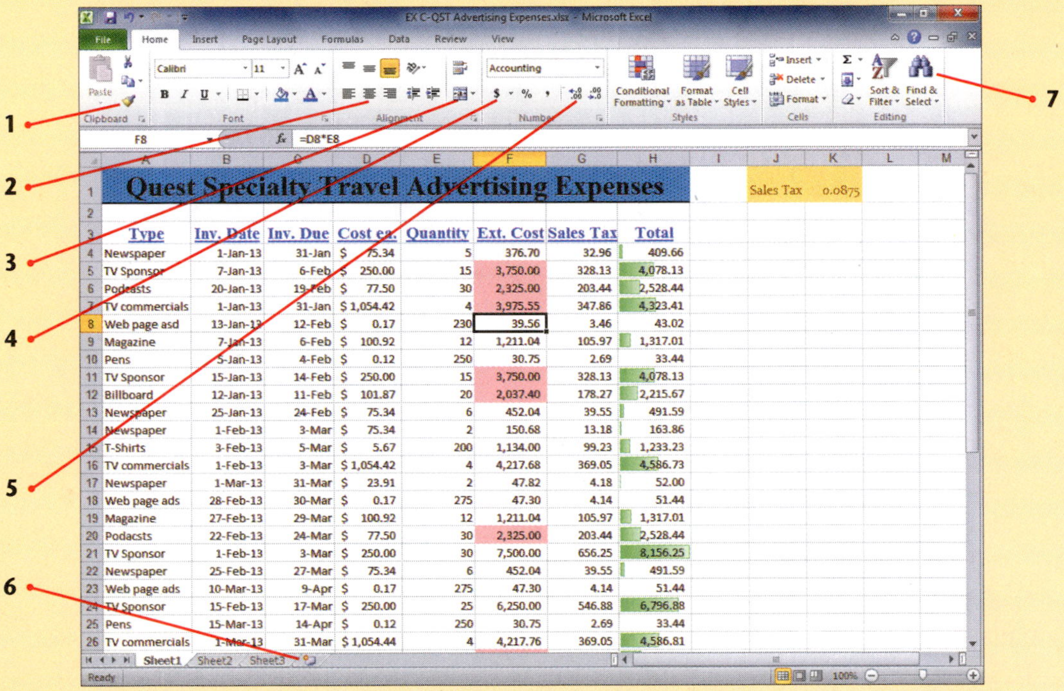

**Match each command or button with the statement that best describes it.**

8. **Conditional formatting**

9. [icon]

10. **Spelling button**

11. **[Ctrl][Home]**

12.  [icon]

13. **$**

a. Centers cell contents over multiple cells

b. Adds dollar signs and two decimal places to selected data

c. Changes formatting of a cell that meets a certain rule

d. Displays background color options for a cell

e. Moves cell pointer to cell A1

f. Checks for apparent misspellings in a worksheet

**Select the best answer from the list of choices.**

14. Which of the following is an example of Accounting number format?
    a. 5555
    c. 55.55%
    b. $5,555.55
    d. 5,555.55

15. What feature is used to delete a conditional formatting rule?
    a. Rules Reminder
    c. Condition Manager
    b. Conditional Formatting Rules Manager
    d. Format Manager

16. Which button removes the italic font style from selected cells?
    a. *I*
    c. ✔
    b. **B**
    d. *I*

17. What is the name of the feature used to resize a column to accommodate its widest entry?
    a. AutoFormat
    c. AutoResize
    b. AutoFit
    d. AutoRefit

18. Which button increases the number of decimal places in selected cells?
    a. (button icon)
    c. (button icon)
    b. (button icon)
    d. (button icon)

19. Which button copies multiple formats from selected cells to other cells?
    a. (button icon)
    c. (button icon)
    b. (button icon)
    d. (button icon)

## Skills Review

1. **Format values.**
   a. Start Excel, open the file EX C-2.xlsx from the drive and folder where you store your Data Files, then save it as **EX C-Life Insurance Premiums**.
   b. Enter a formula in cell B10 that totals the number of employees.
   c. Create a formula in cell C5 that calculates the monthly insurance premium for the accounting department. (*Hint*: Make sure you use the correct type of cell reference in the formula. To calculate the department's monthly premium, multiply the number of employees by the monthly premium in cell C14.)
   d. Copy the formula in cell C5 to the range C6:C10.
   e. Format the range C5:C10 using Accounting number format.
   f. Change the format of the range C6:C9 to the Comma Style.
   g. Reduce the number of decimals in cell B14 to 0 using a button in the Number group on the Home tab.
   h. Save your work.

2. **Change font and font sizes.**
   a. Select the range of cells containing the column labels (in row 4).
   b. Change the font of the selection to Times New Roman.
   c. Increase the font size of the selection to 12 points.
   d. Increase the font size of the label in cell A1 to 14 points.
   e. Save your changes.

3. **Change font styles and alignment.**
   a. Apply the bold and italic font styles to the worksheet title in cell A1.
   b. Use the Merge & Center button to center the Life Insurance Premiums label over columns A through C.
   c. Apply the italic font style to the Life Insurance Premiums label.
   d. Add the bold font style to the labels in row 4.
   e. Use the Format Painter to copy the format in cell A4 to the range A5:A10.
   f. Apply the format in cell C10 to cell B14.

# Skills Review (continued)

g. Change the alignment of cell A10 to Align Right using a button in the Alignment group.

h. Select the range of cells containing the column labels, then center them.

i. Remove the italic font style from the Life Insurance Premiums label, then increase the font size to 14.

j. Move the Life Insurance Premiums label to cell A3, then add the bold and underline font styles.

k. Save your changes.

4. **Adjust column width.**

a. Resize column C to a width of 10.71 characters.

b. Use the AutoFit feature to resize columns A and B.

c. Clear the contents of cell A13 (do not delete the cell).

d. Change the text in cell A14 to **Monthly Insurance Premium**, then change the width of the column to 25 characters.

e. Save your changes.

5. **Insert and delete rows and columns.**

a. Insert a new row between rows 5 and 6.

b. Add a new department, **Charity**, in the newly inserted row. Enter **6** as the number of employees in the department.

c. Copy the formula in cell C7 to C6.

d. Add the following comment to cell A6: **New department**. Display the comment, then drag to move it out of the way, if necessary.

e. Add a new column between the Department and Employees columns with the title **Family Coverage**, then resize the column using AutoFit.

f. Delete the Legal row from the worksheet.

g. Move the value in cell C14 to cell B14.

h. Save your changes.

6. **Apply colors, patterns, and borders.**

a. Add Outside Borders around the range A4:D10.

b. Add a Bottom Double Border to cells C9 and D9 (above the calculated employee and premium totals).

c. Apply the Aqua, Accent 5, Lighter 80% fill color to the labels in the Department column (do not include the Total label).

d. Apply the Orange, Accent 6, Lighter 60% fill color to the range A4:D4.

e. Change the color of the font in the range A4:D4 to Red, Accent 2, Darker 25%.

f. Add a 12.5% Gray pattern style to cell A1.

g. Format the range A14:B14 with a fill color of Dark Blue, Text 2, Lighter 40%, change the font color to White, Background 1, then apply the bold font style.

h. Save your changes.

7. **Apply conditional formatting.**

a. Select the range D5:D9, then create a conditional format that changes cell contents to green fill with dark green text if the value is between 150 and 275.

b. Select the range C5:C9, then create a conditional format that changes cell contents to red text if the number of employees exceeds 10.

c. Apply a blue gradient-filled data bar to the range C5:C9. (*Hint*: Click Blue Data Bar in the Gradient Fill section.)

d. Use the Rules Manager to modify the conditional format in cells C5:C9 to display values greater than 10 in bold dark red text.

e. Merge and center the title (cell A1) over columns A through D.

f. Save your changes.

8. **Rename and move a worksheet.**

a. Name the Sheet1 tab **Insurance Data**.

b. Name the Sheet3 tab **Employee Data**.

c. Change the Insurance Data tab color to Red, Accent 2, Lighter 40%.

d. Change the Employee Data tab color to Aqua, Accent 5, Lighter 40%.

e. Move the Employee Data sheet so it comes after (to the right of) the Insurance Data sheet.

f. Make the Insurance Data sheet active, enter your name in cell A20, then save your work.

# Skills Review (continued)

9. **Check spelling.**

   a. Move the cell pointer to cell A1.

   b. Use the Find & Select feature to replace the Accounting label in cell A5 with Accounting/Legal.

   c. Check the spelling in the worksheet using the spell checker, and correct any spelling errors if necessary.

   d. Save your changes, then compare your Insurance Data sheet to Figure C-28.

   e. Preview the Insurance Data sheet in Backstage view, submit your work to your instructor as directed, then close the workbook and exit Excel.

**FIGURE C-28**

Your formulas
go here

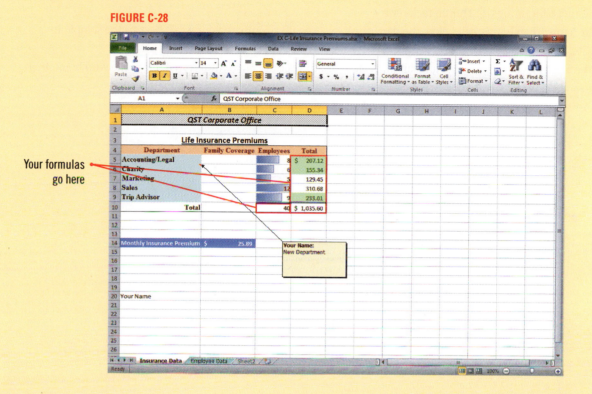

## Independent Challenge 1

You run a freelance accounting business, and one of your newest clients is Pen & Paper, a small office supply store. Now that you've converted the store's accounting records to Excel, the manager would like you to work on an analysis of the inventory. Although more items will be added later, the worksheet has enough items for you to begin your modifications.

If you have a SAM 2010 user profile, an autogradable SAM version of this assignment may be available at http://www.cengage.com/sam2010. Check with your instructor to confirm that this assignment is available in SAM. To use the SAM version of this assignment, log into the SAM 2010 Web site and download the instruction and start files.

a. Start Excel, open the file EX C-3.xlsx from the drive and folder where you store your Data Files, then save it as **EX C-Pen & Paper Office Supply Inventory**.

b. Create a formula in cell E4 that calculates the value of the items in stock based on the price paid per item in cell B4. Format the cell in the Comma Style.

c. In cell F4, calculate the sale price of the items in stock using an absolute reference to the markup value shown in cell H1.

d. Copy the formulas created above into the range E5:F14; first convert any necessary cell references to absolute so that the formulas work correctly.

e. Apply bold to the column labels, and italicize the inventory items in column A.

f. Make sure all columns are wide enough to display the data and labels.

g. Format the values in the Sale Price column as Accounting number format with two decimal places.

h. Format the values in the Price Paid column as Comma Style with two decimal places.

# Independent Challenge 1 (continued)

**i.** Add a row under #2 Pencils for **Digital cordless telephones**, price paid **53.45**, sold individually (**each**), with **23** on hand. Copy the appropriate formulas to cells E7:F7.

**j.** Verify that all the data in the worksheet is visible and formulas are correct. Adjust any items as needed, and check the spelling of the entire worksheet.

**k.** Use conditional formatting to apply yellow fill with dark yellow text to items with a quantity of less than 25 on hand.

**l.** Use an icon set of your choosing in the range D4:D15 to illustrate the relative differences between values in the range.

**m.** Add an outside border around the data in the Item column (do not include the Item column label).

**n.** Delete the row containing the Thumb tacks entry.

**o.** Enter your name in an empty cell below the data, then save the file. Compare your worksheet to the sample in Figure C-29.

**p.** Preview the worksheet in Backstage view, submit your work to your instructor as directed, close the workbook, then exit Excel.

**FIGURE C-29**

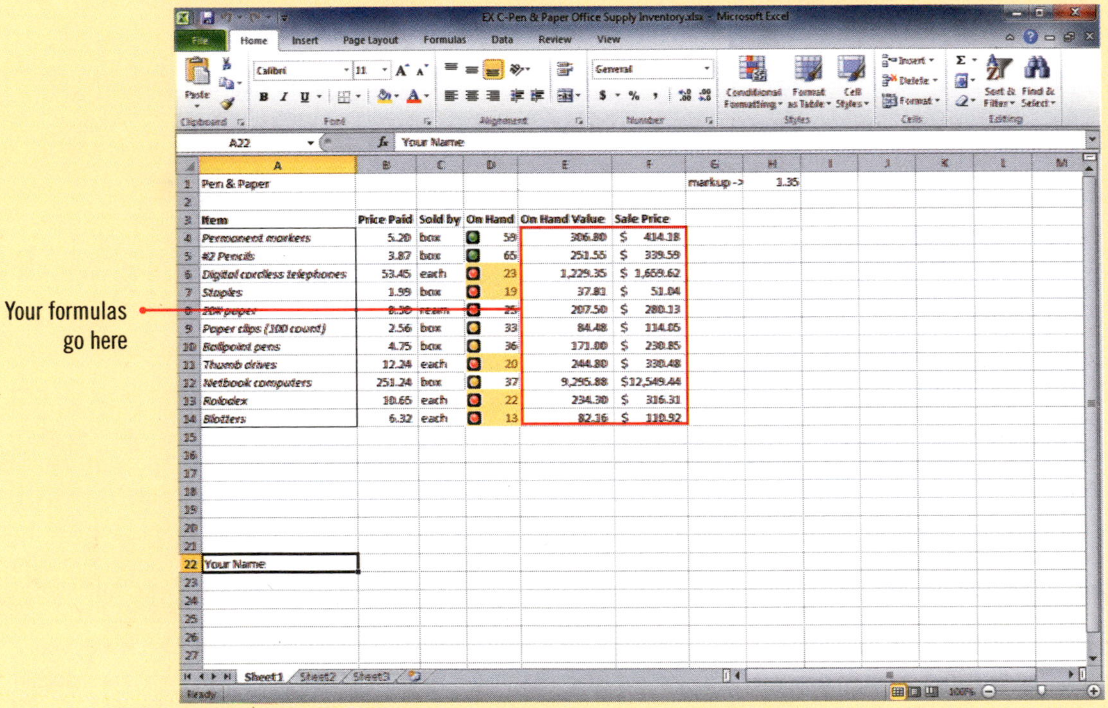

# Independent Challenge 2

You volunteer several hours each week with the Assistance League of Boise, and you are in charge of maintaining the membership list. You're currently planning a mailing campaign to members in certain regions of the city. You also want to create renewal letters for members whose membership expires soon. You decide to format the list to enhance the appearance of the worksheet and make your upcoming tasks easier to plan.

**a.** Start Excel, open the file EX C-4.xlsx from the drive and folder where you store your Data Files, then save it as **EX C-Boise Assistance League**.

**b.** Remove any blank columns.

**c.** Create a conditional format in the Zip Code column so that entries greater than 83749 appear in light red fill with dark red text.

**d.** Make all columns wide enough to fit their data and labels.

**e.** Use formatting enhancements, such as fonts, font sizes, font styles, and fill colors, to make the worksheet more attractive.

**f.** Center the column labels.

# Independent Challenge 2 (continued)

g. Use conditional formatting so that entries for Year of Membership Expiration that are between 2014 and 2017 appear in green fill with bold black text. (*Hint*: Create a custom format for cells that meet the condition.)

**FIGURE C-30**

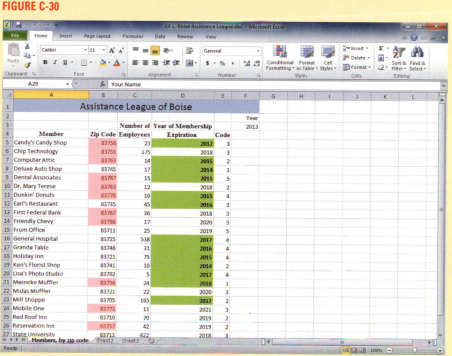

h. Adjust any items as necessary, then check the spelling.

i. Change the name of the Sheet1 tab to one that reflects the sheet's contents, then add a tab color of your choice.

j. Enter your name in an empty cell, then save your work.

k. Preview the worksheet in Backstage view, make any final changes you think necessary, then submit your work to your instructor as directed. Compare your work to the sample shown in Figure C-30.

l. Close the workbook, then exit Excel.

# Independent Challenge 3

Prestige Press is a Boston-based publisher that manufactures children's books. As the finance manager for the company, one of your responsibilities is to analyze the monthly reports from the five district sales offices. Your boss, Joanne Bennington, has just asked you to prepare a quarterly sales report for an upcoming meeting. Because several top executives will be attending this meeting, Joanne reminds you that the report must look professional. In particular, she asks you to emphasize the company's surge in profits during the last month and to highlight the fact that the Northeastern district continues to outpace the other districts.

a. Plan a worksheet that shows the company's sales during the first quarter. Assume that all books are the same price. Make sure you include the following:

- The number of books sold (units sold) and the associated revenues (total sales) for each of the five district sales offices. The five sales districts are Northeastern, Midwestern, Southeastern, Southern, and Western.
- Calculations that show month-by-month totals for January, February, and March, and a 3-month cumulative total.
- Calculations that show each district's share of sales (percent of Total Sales).
- Labels that reflect the month-by-month data as well as the cumulative data.
- Formatting enhancements and data bars that emphasize the recent month's sales surge and the Northeastern district's sales leadership.

b. Ask yourself the following questions about the organization and formatting of the worksheet: What worksheet title and labels do you need, and where should they appear? How can you calculate the totals? What formulas can you copy to save time and keystrokes? Do any of these formulas need to use an absolute reference? How do you show dollar amounts? What information should be shown in bold? Do you need to use more than one font? Should you use more than one point size?

c. Start Excel, then save a new, blank workbook as **EX C-Prestige Press** to the drive and folder where you store your Data Files.

# Independent Challenge 3 (continued)

**d.** Build the worksheet with your own price and sales data. Enter the titles and labels first, then enter the numbers and formulas. You can use the information in Table C-4 to get started.

**TABLE C-4**

### Prestige Press

#### 1st Quarter Sales Report

| Office | Price | January Units Sold | January Sales | February Units Sold | February Sales | March Units Sold | March Sales | Total Units Sold | Total Sales | Total % of Sales |
|---|---|---|---|---|---|---|---|---|---|---|
| Northeastern | | | | | | | | | | |
| Midwestern | | | | | | | | | | |
| Southeastern | | | | | | | | | | |
| Southern | | | | | | | | | | |
| Western | | | | | | | | | | |

**e.** Add a row beneath the data containing the totals for each column.

**f.** Adjust the column widths as necessary.

**g.** Change the height of row 1 to 33 points.

**h.** Format labels and values to enhance the look of the worksheet, and change the font styles and alignment if necessary.

**i.** Resize columns and adjust the formatting as necessary.

**j.** Add data bars for the monthly Units Sold columns.

**k.** Add a column that calculates a 25% increase in total sales dollars. Use an absolute cell reference in this calculation.
(*Hint*: Make sure the current formatting is applied to the new information.)

### Advanced Challenge Exercise

- Delete the contents of cells J4:K4 if necessary, then merge and center cell I4 over column I:K.
- Insert a clip art image related to books in an appropriate location, adjusting its size and position as necessary.
- Save your work.

**l.** Enter your name in an empty cell.

**m.** Check the spelling in the workbook, change to a landscape orientation, save your work, then compare your work to Figure C-31.

**n.** Preview the worksheet in Backstage view, then submit your work to your instructor as directed.

**o.** Close the workbook file, then exit Excel.

**FIGURE C-31**

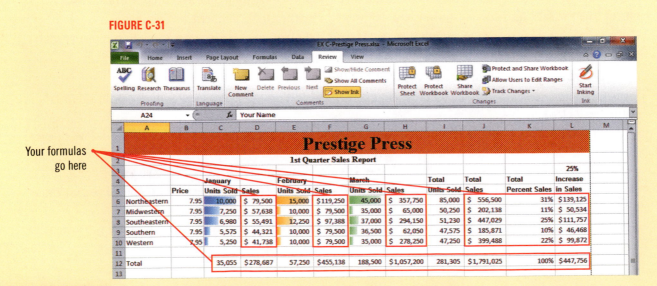

# Real Life Independent Challenge

**This project requires an Internet connection.**

You are saving money to take an international trip you have always dreamed about. You plan to visit seven different countries over the course of 2 months, and you have budgeted an identical spending allowance in each country. You want to create a worksheet that calculates the amount of native currency you will have in each country based on the budgeted amount. You want the workbook to reflect the currency information for each country.

a. Start Excel, then save a new, blank workbook as **EX C-World Tour Budget** to the drive and folder where you store your Data Files.

b. Add a title at the top of the worksheet.

c. Think of seven countries you would like to visit, then enter column and row labels for your worksheet. (*Hint*: You may wish to include row labels for each country, plus column labels for the country, the $1 equivalent in native currency, the total amount of native currency you'll have in each country, and the name of each country's monetary unit.)

d. Decide how much money you want to bring to each country (for example, $1,000), and enter that in the worksheet.

e. Use your favorite search engine to find your own information sources on currency conversions for the countries you plan to visit.

f. Enter the cash equivalent to $1 in U.S. dollars for each country in your list.

g. Create an equation that calculates the amount of native currency you will have in each country, using an absolute cell reference in the formula.

h. Format the entries in the column containing the native currency $1 equivalent as Number number format with three decimal places, and format the column containing the total native currency budget with two decimal places, using the correct currency number format for each country. (*Hint*: Use the Number tab in the Format cells dialog box; choose the appropriate currency number format from the Symbol list.)

i. Create a conditional format that changes the font style and color of the calculated amount in the $1,000 US column to light red fill with dark red text if the amount exceeds **1000** units of the local currency.

j. Merge and center the worksheet title over the column headings.

k. Add any formatting you want to the column headings, and resize the columns as necessary.

l. Add a background color to the title.

## Advanced Challenge Exercise

- Modify the conditional format in the $1,000 US column so that entries between 1500 and 3999 are displayed in red, boldface type; and entries above 4000 appear in blue, boldface type with a light red background.
- Delete all the unused sheets in the workbook.
- Save your work as **EX C-World Tour Budget ACE** to the drive and folder where you store your Data Files.
- If you have access to an e-mail account, e-mail this workbook to your instructor as an attachment.

m. Enter your name in the header of the worksheet.

n. Spell check the worksheet, save your changes, compare your work to Figure C-32, then preview the worksheet in Backstage view, and submit your work to your instructor as directed.

o. Close the workbook and exit Excel.

**FIGURE C-32**

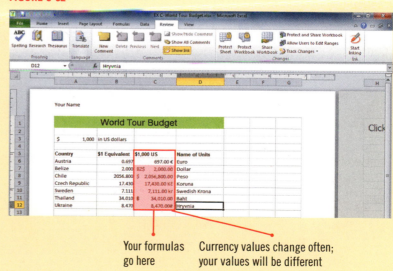

Your formulas go here

Currency values change often; your values will be different

# Visual Workshop

Open the file EX C-5.xlsx from the drive and folder where you store your Data Files, then save it as **EX C-Tip-Top Temps**. Use the skills you learned in this unit to format the worksheet so it looks like the one shown in Figure C-33. Create a conditional format in the Level column so that entries greater than 3 appear in red text. Create an additional conditional format in the Review Cycle column so that any value equal to 3 appears in green bold text. Replace the Accounting department label with **Legal**. (*Hint*: The only additional font used in this exercise is 16-point Times New Roman in row 1.) Enter your name in cell A25, check the spelling in the worksheet, save your changes, then submit your work to your instructor as directed.

FIGURE C-33

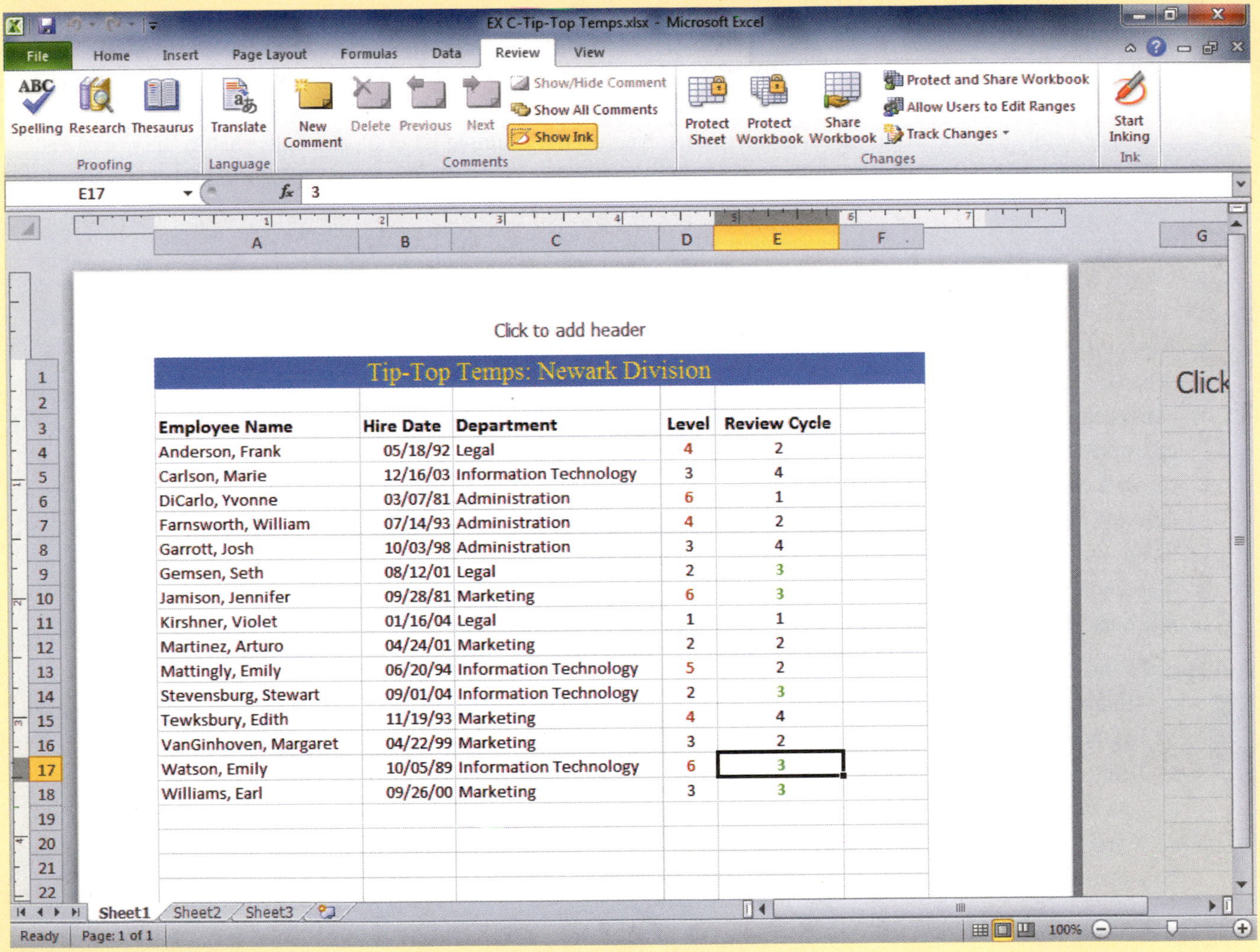


| Employee Name | Hire Date | Department | Level | Review Cycle |
|---|---|---|---|---|
| Anderson, Frank | 05/18/92 | Legal | 4 | 2 |
| Carlson, Marie | 12/16/03 | Information Technology | 3 | 4 |
| DiCarlo, Yvonne | 03/07/81 | Administration | 6 | 1 |
| Farnsworth, William | 07/14/93 | Administration | 4 | 2 |
| Garrott, Josh | 10/03/98 | Administration | 3 | 4 |
| Gemsen, Seth | 08/12/01 | Legal | 2 | 3 |
| Jamison, Jennifer | 09/28/81 | Marketing | 6 | 3 |
| Kirshner, Violet | 01/16/04 | Legal | 1 | 1 |
| Martinez, Arturo | 04/24/01 | Marketing | 2 | 2 |
| Mattingly, Emily | 06/20/94 | Information Technology | 5 | 2 |
| Stevensburg, Stewart | 09/01/04 | Information Technology | 2 | 3 |
| Tewksbury, Edith | 11/19/93 | Marketing | 4 | 4 |
| VanGinhoven, Margaret | 04/22/99 | Marketing | 3 | 2 |
| Watson, Emily | 10/05/89 | Information Technology | 6 | 3 |
| Williams, Earl | 09/26/00 | Marketing | 3 | 3 |

# Working with Charts

**Files You Will Need:**

EX D-1.xlsx
EX D-2.xlsx
EX D-3.xlsx
EX D-4.xlsx
EX D-5.xlsx
EX D-6.xlsx

Worksheets provide an effective layout for calculating and organizing data, but the grid layout is not always the best format for presenting your work to others. To display information so it's easier to interpret, you can create a chart. **Charts**, sometimes called graphs, present information in a graphic format, making it easier to see patterns, trends, and relationships. In this unit, you learn how to create a chart, how to edit the chart and change the chart type, how to add text annotations and arrows, and how to preview and print the chart. At the upcoming annual meeting, Grace Wong wants to emphasize spending patterns at Quest Specialty Travel. She asks you to create a chart showing the trends in company expenses over the past four quarters.

**OBJECTIVES**

Plan a chart

Create a chart

Move and resize a chart

Change the chart design

Change the chart layout

Format a chart

Annotate and draw on a chart

Create a pie chart

# Planning a Chart

Before creating a chart, you need to plan the information you want your chart to show and how you want it to look. Planning ahead helps you decide what type of chart to create and how to organize the data. Understanding the parts of a chart makes it easier to format and to change specific elements so that the chart best illustrates your data.  In preparation for creating the chart for Grace's presentation, you identify your goals for the chart and plan its layout.

## Use the following guidelines to plan the chart:

- **Determine the purpose of the chart, and identify the data relationships you want to communicate graphically**

  You want to create a chart that shows quarterly tour expenses for each country where Quest Specialty Travel provides tours. This worksheet data is shown in Figure D-1. You also want the chart to illustrate whether the quarterly expenses for each country increased or decreased from quarter to quarter.

- **Determine the results you want to see, and decide which chart type is most appropriate**

  Different chart types display data in distinctive ways. For example, a pie chart compares parts to the whole, so it's useful for showing what proportion of a budget amount was spent on tours in one country relative to what was spent on tours in other countries. A line chart, in contrast, is best for showing trends over time. To choose the best chart type for your data, you should first decide how you want your data displayed and interpreted. Table D-1 describes several different types of charts you can create in Excel and their corresponding buttons on the Insert tab on the Ribbon. Because you want to compare QST tour expenses in multiple countries over a period of four quarters, you decide to use a column chart.

- **Identify the worksheet data you want the chart to illustrate**

  Sometimes you use all the data in a worksheet to create a chart, while at other times you may need to select a range within the sheet. The worksheet from which you are creating your chart contains expense data for each of the past four quarters and the totals for the past year. You will need to use all the quarterly data contained in the worksheet except the quarterly totals.

- **Understand the elements of a chart**

  The chart shown in Figure D-2 contains basic elements of a chart. In the figure, QST tour countries are on the horizontal axis (also called the **x-axis**) and expense dollar amounts are on the vertical axis (also called the **y-axis**). The horizontal axis is also called the **category axis** because it often contains the names of data groups, such as locations, months, or years. The vertical axis is also called the **value axis** because it often contains numerical values that help you interpret the size of chart elements. (3-D charts also contain a **z-axis**, for comparing data across both categories and values.) The area inside the horizontal and vertical axes is the **plot area**. The **tick marks**, on the vertical axis, and **gridlines** (extending across the plot area) create a scale of measure for each value. Each value in a cell you select for your chart is a **data point**. In any chart, a **data marker** visually represents each data point, which in this case is a column. A collection of related data points is a **data series**. In this chart, there are four data series (Quarter 1, Quarter 2, Quarter 3, and Quarter 4). Each is made up of column data markers of a different color, so a **legend** is included to make it easy to identify them.

FIGURE D-1 worksheet:

| | A | B | C | D | E | F |
|---|---|---|---|---|---|---|
| 1 | **Quest Specialty Travel** | | | | | |
| 2 | FY 2013 Quarterly Tour Expenses | | | | | |
| 3 | | | | | | |
| 4 | | Quarter 1 | Quarter 2 | Quarter 3 | Quarter 4 | Total |
| 5 | **Australia** | 5,367.40 | 5,860.49 | 6,583.12 | 6,133.14 | $ 23,944.15 |
| 6 | **Britain** | 3,510.99 | 3,921.46 | 4,337.40 | 4,558.11 | $ 16,327.96 |
| 7 | **Canada** | 4,287.76 | 4,371.98 | 4,570.21 | 4,100.06 | $ 17,330.01 |
| 8 | **France** | 4,032.10 | 4,489.74 | 4,579.06 | 4,653.92 | $ 17,754.82 |
| 9 | **Germany** | 5,082.77 | 2,994.56 | 3,561.12 | 3,712.50 | $ 15,350.95 |
| 10 | **India** | 1,468.25 | 2,510.30 | 2,665.04 | 2,890.95 | $ 9,534.54 |
| 11 | **Japan** | 3,271.50 | 3,556.14 | 8,240.35 | 3,721.69 | $ 18,789.68 |
| 12 | **U.S.A.** | 7,195.06 | 6,542.76 | 8,240.36 | 7,018.91 | $ 28,997.09 |
| 13 | **Total** | $ 34,215.83 | $ 34,247.43 | $ 42,776.66 | $ 36,789.28 | $ 148,029.20 |
| 14 | | | | | | |

FIGURE D-2: Chart elements

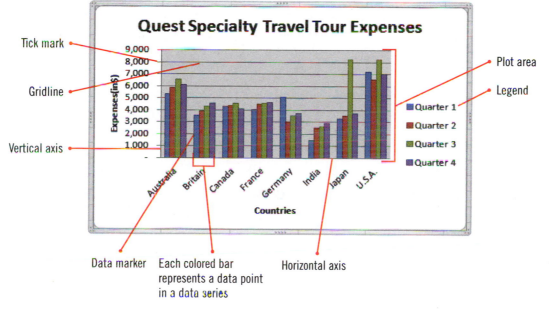

TABLE D-1: Common chart types

| type | button | description |
|---|---|---|
| **Column** | | Compares data using columns; the Excel default; sometimes referred to as a bar chart in other spreadsheet programs |
| **Line** | | Compares trends over even time intervals; looks similar to an area chart, but does not emphasize total |
| **Pie** | | Compares sizes of pieces as part of a whole; used for a single series of numbers |
| **Bar** | | Compares data using horizontal bars; sometimes referred to as a horizontal bar chart in other spreadsheet programs |
| **Area** | | Shows how individual volume changes over time in relation to total volume |
| **Scatter** | | Compares trends over uneven time or measurement intervals; used in scientific and engineering disciplines for trend spotting and extrapolation |

# Creating a Chart

To create a chart in Excel, you first select the range in a worksheet containing the data you want to chart. Once you've selected a range, you can use buttons on the Insert tab on the Ribbon to create a chart based on the data in the range.  Using the worksheet containing the quarterly expense data, you create a chart that shows how the expenses in each country varied across the quarters.

## STEPS

**QUICK TIP**

When charting data for a particular time period, make sure all series are for the same time period.

1. **Start Excel, open the file EX D-1.xlsx from the drive and folder where you store your Data Files, then save it as EX D-Quarterly Tour Expenses**

   You want the chart to include the quarterly tour expenses values, as well as quarter and country labels. You don't include the Total column and row because the figures in these cells would skew the chart.

2. **Select the range A4:E12, then click the Insert tab on the Ribbon**

   The Insert tab contains groups for inserting various types of objects, including charts. The Charts group includes buttons for each major chart type, plus an Other Charts button for additional chart types, such as stock charts for charting stock market data.

**QUICK TIP**

To base a chart on data in nonadjacent ranges, press and hold [Ctrl] while selecting each range, then use the Insert tab to create the chart.

3. **Click the Column button in the Charts group, then click Clustered Column under 2-D Column in the Column chart gallery, as shown in Figure D-3**

   The chart is inserted in the center of the worksheet, and three contextual Chart Tools tabs appear on the Ribbon: Design, Layout, and Format. On the Design tab, which is currently in front, you can quickly change the chart type, chart layout, and chart style, and you can swap how the columns and rows of data in the worksheet are represented in the chart. Currently, the countries are charted along the horizontal x-axis, with the quarterly expense dollar amounts charted along the y-axis. This lets you easily compare the quarterly expenses for each country.

4. **Click the Switch Row/Column button in the Data group on the Chart Tools Design tab**

   The quarters are now charted along the x-axis. The expense amounts per country are charted along the y-axis, as indicated by the updated legend. See Figure D-4.

5. **Click the Undo button on the Quick Access toolbar**

   The chart returns to its original design.

6. **Click the Chart Tools Layout tab, click the Chart Title button in the Labels group, then click Above Chart**

   A title placeholder appears above the chart.

**QUICK TIP**

You can also triple-click to select the chart title text.

7. **Click anywhere in the Chart Title text box, press [Ctrl][A] to select the text, type Quarterly Tour Expenses, then click anywhere in the chart to deselect the title**

   Adding a title helps identify the chart. The border around the chart and the chart's **sizing handles**, the small series of dots at the corners and sides of the chart's border, indicate that the chart is selected. See Figure D-5. Your chart might be in a different location on the worksheet and may look slightly different; you will move and resize it in the next lesson. Any time a chart is selected, as it is now, a blue border surrounds the worksheet data range on which the chart is based, a purple border surrounds the cells containing the category axis labels, and a green border surrounds the cells containing the data series labels. This chart is known as an **embedded chart** because it is inserted directly in the current worksheet and doesn't exist in a separate file. Embedding a chart in the current sheet is the default selection when creating a chart, but you can also embed a chart on a different sheet in the workbook, or on a newly created chart sheet. A **chart sheet** is a sheet in a workbook that contains only a chart that is linked to the workbook data.

8. **Save your work**

FIGURE D-3: Column chart gallery

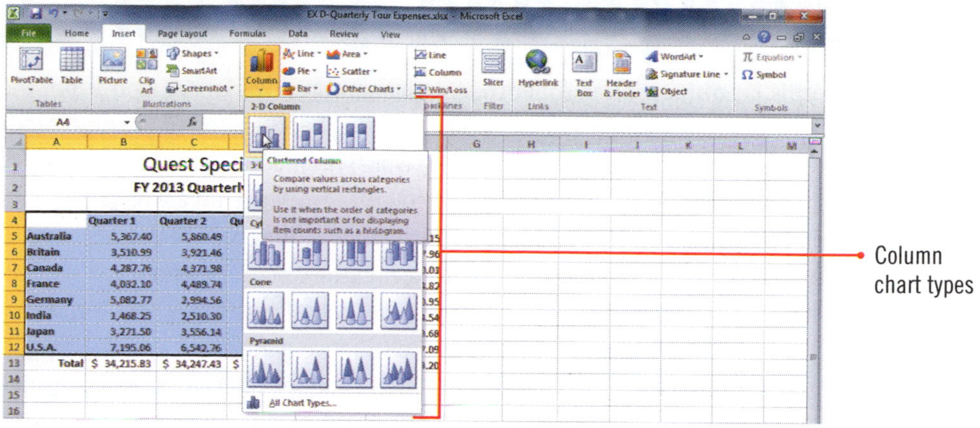

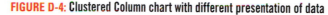

Column
chart types

FIGURE D-4: Clustered Column chart with different presentation of data

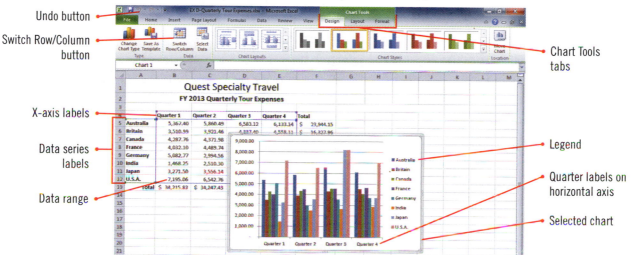

Undo button
Switch Row/Column
button
X-axis labels
Data series
labels
Data range
Chart Tools
tabs
Legend
Quarter labels on
horizontal axis
Selected chart
Quest Specialty Travel
FY 2013 Quarterly Tour Expenses

FIGURE D-5: Chart with rows and columns restored and title added

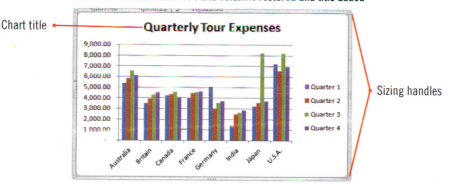

Chart title
Quarterly Tour Expenses
Quarter 1
Quarter 2
Quarter 3
Quarter 4
Australia
Britain
Canada
France
Germany
India
Japan
U.S.A.
Sizing handles

## Creating sparklines

You can quickly create a miniature chart called a **sparkline** that serves as a visual indicator of data trends. To do this, select a range of data, click the Insert tab, then click the Line, Column, or Win/Loss button in the Sparklines group. In the Create Sparklines dialog box that opens, enter the cell in which you want the sparkline to appear, then click OK. Figure D-6 shows four sparklines created in four different cells. Any changes to data in the range are reflected in the sparkline. To delete a selected sparkline from a cell, click the Clear button in the Group group on the Sparkline Tools Design tab.

FIGURE D-6: Sparklines in cells

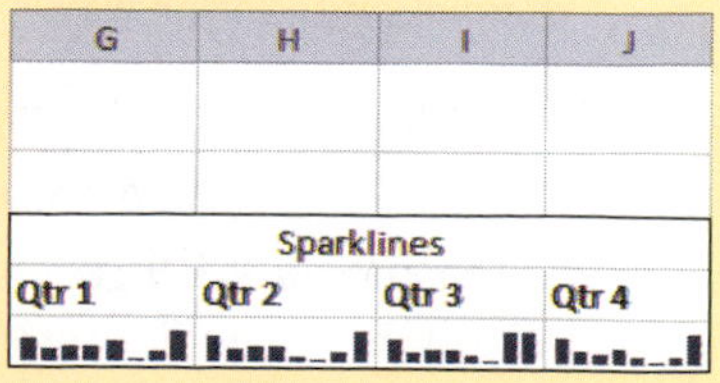

G
H
I
J
Sparklines
Qtr 1
Qtr 2
Qtr 3
Qtr 4

# Moving and Resizing a Chart

A chart is an **object**, or an independent element on a worksheet, and is not located in a specific cell or range. You can select an object by clicking it; sizing handles around the object indicate it is selected. (When a chart is selected in Excel, the Name box, which normally tells you the address of the active cell, tells you the chart number.) You can move a selected chart anywhere on a worksheet without affecting formulas or data in the worksheet. However, any data changed in the worksheet is automatically updated in the chart. You can even move a chart to a different sheet in the workbook, and it will still reflect the original data. You can resize a chart to improve its appearance by dragging its sizing handles. A chart contains chart objects, such as a title and legend, which you can also move and resize. You can reposition chart objects to pre-defined locations using commands on the Layout tab, or you can freely move any chart object by dragging it or by cutting and pasting it to a new location. When you point to a chart object, the name of the object appears as a ScreenTip.  You want to resize the chart, position it below the worksheet data, and move the legend.

## STEPS

**QUICK TIP**

To delete a selected chart, press [Delete].

1. **Make sure the chart is still selected, then position the pointer over the chart**

   The pointer shape ⁺↕ indicates that you can move the chart. For a table of commonly used object pointers, refer to Table D-2.

**TROUBLE**

If you do not drag a blank area on the chart, you might inadvertently move a chart element instead of the whole chart; if this happens, undo the action and try again.

2. **Position ⁺↕ on a blank area near the upper-left edge of the chart, press and hold the left mouse button, drag the chart until its upper-left corner is at the upper-left corner of cell A16, then release the mouse button**

   As you drag the chart, you can see an outline representing the chart's perimeter. The chart appears in the new location.

3. **Position the pointer on the right-middle sizing handle until it changes to ⟷, then drag the right border of the chart to the right edge of column G**

   The chart is widened. See Figure D-7.

**QUICK TIP**

To resize a selected chart to an exact specification, click the Chart Tools Format tab, then enter the desired height and width in the Size group.

4. **Position the pointer over the upper-middle sizing handle until it changes to ↕, then drag the top border of the chart to the top edge of row 15**

5. **Scroll down if necessary so row 30 is visible, position the pointer over the lower-middle sizing handle until it changes to ↕, then drag the bottom border of the chart to the bottom border of row 26**

   You can move any object on a chart. You want to align the top of the legend with the top of the plot area.

**QUICK TIP**

You can move a legend to the right, top, left, or bottom of a chart by clicking the Legend button in the Labels group on the Chart Tools Layout tab, then clicking a location option.

6. **Click the legend to select it, press and hold [Shift], drag the legend up using ⁺↕ so the dotted outline is approximately 1/4" above the top of the plot area, then release [Shift]**

   When you click the legend, sizing handles appear around it and "Legend" appears as a ScreenTip when the pointer hovers over the object. As you drag, a dotted outline of the legend border appears. Pressing and holding the [Shift] key holds the horizontal position of the legend as you move it vertically. Although the sizing handles on objects within a chart look different from the sizing handles that surround a chart, they function the same way.

7. **Click cell A12, type United States, click the Enter button ✓ on the formula bar, use AutoFit to resize column A, then press [Ctrl][Home]**

   The axis label changes to reflect the updated cell contents, as shown in Figure D-8. Changing any data in the worksheet modifies corresponding text or values in the chart. Because the chart is no longer selected, the Chart Tools tabs no longer appear on the Ribbon.

8. **Save your work**

**FIGURE D-7:** Moved and resized chart

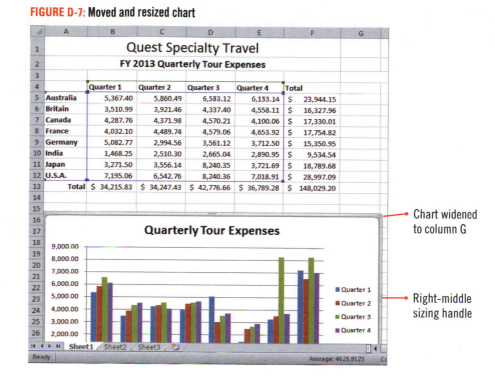

Chart widened to column G

Right-middle sizing handle

**FIGURE D-8:** Worksheet with modified legend and label

Modified text

Plot area

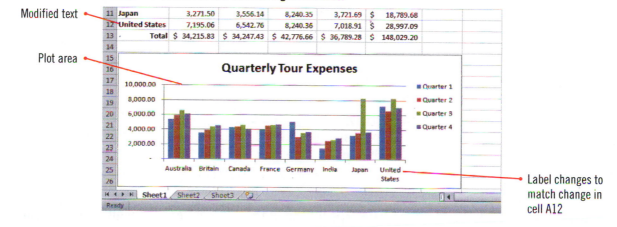

Label changes to match change in cell A12

**TABLE D-2:** Common object pointers

| name | pointer | use | name | pointer | use |
|------|---------|-----|------|---------|-----|
| Diagonal resizing | ⤢ or ⤡ | Change chart shape from corners | I-beam | I | Edit object text |
| Draw | + | Draw an object | Move | ⁺⇱ | Move object |
| Horizontal resizing | ⇔ | Change object width | Vertical resizing | ↕ | Change object height |

## Moving an embedded chart to a sheet

Suppose you have created an embedded chart that you decide would look better on a chart sheet or in a different worksheet. You can make this change without recreating the entire chart. To do so, first select the chart, click the Chart Tools Design tab, then click the Move Chart button in the Location group. The Move Chart dialog box opens. To move the chart to its own chart sheet, click the New sheet option button, type a name for the new sheet if desired, then click OK. If the chart is already on its own sheet, click the Object in option button, select the worksheet to where you want to move it, then click OK.

# Changing the Chart Design

Once you've created a chart, it's easy to modify the design using the Chart Tools Design tab. You can change the chart type, modify the data range and column/row configuration, apply a different chart style, and change the layout of objects in the chart. The layouts in the Chart Layouts group on the Chart Tools Design tab offer preconfigured arrangements of objects in your chart, such as its legend, title, or gridlines; choosing one of these layouts is an alternative to manually changing how objects are arranged in a chart. You look over your worksheet and realize the data for Japan and the United States in Quarter 3 is incorrect. After you correct this data, you want to see how the corrected data looks using different chart layouts and types.

## STEPS

1. **Click cell D11, type 4568.92, press [Enter], type 6107.09, then press [Enter]**

   In the chart, the Quarter 3 data markers for Japan and the United States reflect the adjusted expense figures. See Figure D-9.

   > **QUICK TIP**
   > You can see more layout choices by clicking the More button ⊟ in the Chart Layouts group.

2. **Select the chart by clicking a blank area within the chart border, click the Chart Tools Design tab on the Ribbon, then click Layout 3 in the Chart Layouts group**

   The legend moves to the bottom of the chart. You prefer the original layout.

3. **Click the Undo button � on the Quick Access toolbar, then click the Change Chart Type button in the Type group**

   The Change Chart Type dialog box opens, as shown in Figure D-10. The left pane of the dialog box lists the available categories, and the right pane shows the individual chart types. An orange border surrounds the currently selected chart type.

4. **Click Bar in the left pane of the Change Chart Type dialog box, confirm that the Clustered Bar chart type is selected in the right pane, then click OK**

   The column chart changes to a clustered bar chart. See Figure D-11. You look at the bar chart, then decide to see how the data looks in a three-dimensional column chart.

5. **Click the Change Chart Type button in the Type group, click Column in the left pane of the Change Chart Type dialog box, click 3-D Clustered Column (fourth from the left in the first row) in the right pane, then click OK**

   A three-dimensional column chart appears. You notice that the three-dimensional column format gives you a sense of volume, but it is more crowded than the two-dimensional column format.

   > **QUICK TIP**
   > If you plan to print a chart on a black-and-white printer, you may wish to apply a black-and-white chart style to your chart so you can see how the output will look as you work.

6. **Click the Change Chart Type button in the Type group, click Clustered Column (first from the left in the first row) in the right pane of the Change Chart Type dialog box, then click OK**

7. **Click the Style 3 chart style in the Chart Styles group**

   The columns change to shades of blue. You prefer the previous chart style's color scheme.

8. **Click ↪ on the Quick Access toolbar, then save your work**

---

### Creating a combination chart

A **combination chart** is two charts in one; a column chart with a line chart, for example. This type of chart (which cannot be used with all data) is helpful when charting dissimilar but related data. For example, you can create a combination chart based on home price and home size data, showing home prices in a column chart, and related home sizes in a line chart. In such a combination chart, a **secondary axis** (such as a vertical axis on the right side of the chart) would supply the scale for the home sizes. To create a combination chart, you can apply a chart type to a data series in an existing chart. Select the chart data series that you want plotted on a secondary axis, then click Format Selection in the Current Selection group on the Chart Tools Layout tab or Format tab to open the Format Data Series dialog box. In the dialog box, click Series Options if necessary, click the Secondary Axis option button under Plot Series On, then click Close. Click the Chart Tools Layout tab if necessary, click the Axes button in the Axes group, then click the type of secondary axis you want and where you want it to appear. To finish, click the Change Chart Type button in the Type group on the Design tab, then select a chart type for the data series.

**FIGURE D-9:** Worksheet with modified data

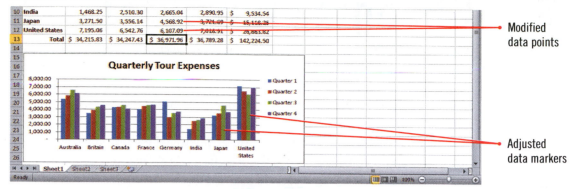

Modified data points

Adjusted data markers

**FIGURE D-10:** Change Chart Type dialog box

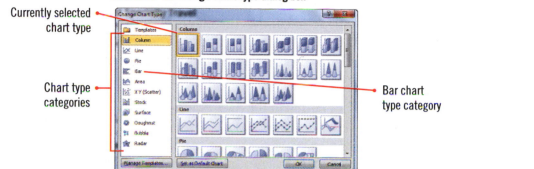

Currently selected chart type

Chart type categories

Bar chart type category

**FIGURE D-11:** Column chart changed to bar chart

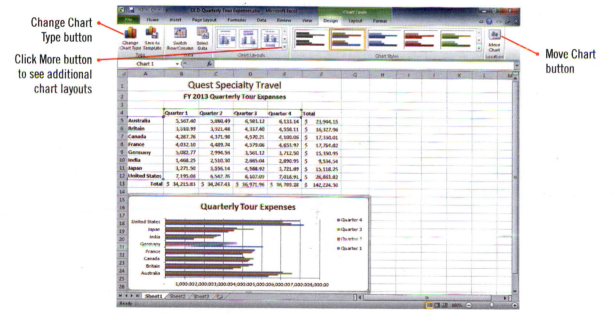

Change Chart Type button

Click More button to see additional chart layouts

Move Chart button

Excel 2010

---

## Working with a 3-D chart

Excel includes two kinds of 3-D chart types. In a true 3-D chart, a third axis, called the **z-axis**, lets you compare data points across both categories and values. The z-axis runs along the depth of the chart, so it appears to advance from the back of the chart. To create a true 3-D chart, look for chart types that begin with "3-D," such as 3-D Column. Charts that are formatted in 3-D, but are not true 3-D, contain only two axes but their graphics give the illusion of three-dimensionality. To create a chart that is only formatted in 3-D, look for chart types that end with "in 3-D." In any 3-D chart, data series can sometimes obscure other columns or bars in the same chart, but you can rotate the chart to obtain a better view. Right-click the chart, then click 3-D Rotation. The Format Chart Area dialog box opens with the 3-D Rotation category active. The 3-D Rotation options let you change the orientation and perspective of the chart area, plot area, walls, and floor. The 3-D Format category lets you apply three-dimensional effects to selected chart objects. (Not all 3-D Rotation and 3-D Format options are available on all charts.)

# Changing the Chart Layout

While the Chart Tools Design tab contains preconfigured chart layouts you can apply to a chart, the Chart Tools Layout tab makes it easy to add, remove, and modify individual chart objects such as a chart title or legend. Using buttons on this tab, you can also add shapes, pictures, and additional text to a chart, add and modify labels, change the display of axes, modify the fill behind the plot area, create titles for the horizontal and vertical axes, and eliminate or change the look of gridlines. You can format the text in a chart object using the Home tab or the Mini toolbar, just as you would the text in a worksheet.  You want to change the layout of the chart by creating titles for the horizontal and vertical axes. To improve the chart's appearance, you'll add a drop shadow to the chart title.

## STEPS

1. **With the chart still selected, click the Chart Tools Layout tab on the Ribbon, click the Gridlines button in the Axes group, point to Primary Horizontal Gridlines, then click None**

   The gridlines that extend from the value axis tick marks across the chart's plot area are removed from the chart, as shown in Figure D-12.

2. **Click the Gridlines button in the Axes group, point to Primary Horizontal Gridlines, then click Major & Minor Gridlines**

   Both major and minor gridlines now appear in the chart. **Major gridlines** represent the values at the value axis tick marks, and **minor gridlines** represent the values between the tick marks.

> **QUICK TIP**
> You can move any title to a new position by clicking one of its edges, then dragging it.

3. **Click the Axis Titles button in the Labels group, point to Primary Horizontal Axis Title, click Title Below Axis, triple-click the axis title, then type Tour Countries**

   Descriptive text on the category axis helps readers understand the chart.

4. **Click the Axis Titles button in the Labels group, point to Primary Vertical Axis Title, then click Rotated Title**

   A placeholder for the vertical axis title is added to the left of the vertical axis.

> **QUICK TIP**
> You can also edit text in a chart or axis title by positioning the pointer over the selected title until it changes to I, clicking the title, then editing the text.

5. **Triple-click the vertical axis title, then type Expenses (in $)**

   The text "Expenses (in $)" appears to the left of the vertical axis, as shown in Figure D-13.

6. **Right-click the horizontal axis labels ("Australia", "Britain", etc.), click the Font list arrow on the Mini toolbar, click Times New Roman, click the Font Size list arrow on the Mini toolbar, then click 8**

   The font of the horizontal axis labels changes to Times New Roman, and the font size decreases, making more of the plot area visible.

> **QUICK TIP**
> You can also apply a border to a selected chart object by clicking the Shape Outline list arrow on the Chart Tools Format tab, and then selecting from the available options.

7. **Right-click the vertical axis labels, click the Font list arrow on the Mini toolbar, click Times New Roman, click the Font Size list arrow on the Mini toolbar, then click 8**

8. **Right-click the chart title ("Quarterly Tour Expenses"), click Format Chart Title on the shortcut menu, click Border Color in the left pane of the Format Chart Title dialog box, then click the Solid line option button in the right pane**

   A solid border will appear around the chart title with the default blue color.

> **QUICK TIP**
> You can also apply a shadow to a selected chart object by clicking the Shape Effects button on the Chart Tools Layout tab, pointing to Shadow, and then clicking a shadow effect.

9. **Click Shadow in the left pane of the Format Chart Title dialog box, click the Presets list arrow, click Offset Diagonal Bottom Right in the Outer group (first row, first from the left), click Close, then save your work**

   A blue border with a drop shadow surrounds the title. Compare your work to Figure D-14.

Working with Charts

Chart Tools
Layout tab

Axis Titles
button

Gridlines
button

Chart with-
out gridlines

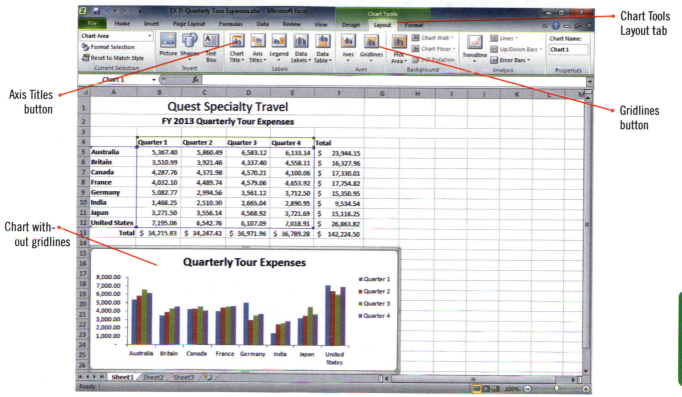

**FIGURE D-13:** Axis titles added to chart

Chart title

Vertical
axis title

Horizontal
axis labels

Vertical
axis labels

Horizontal
axis title

**FIGURE D-14:** Enhanced chart

Border and
shadow
added to
chart title

Modified
axis labels

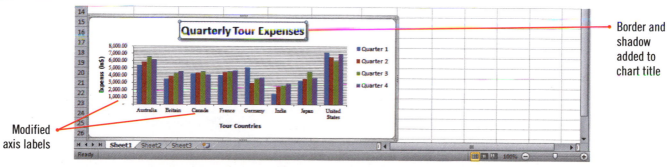

Excel 2010

## Adding data labels to a chart

There are times when your audience might benefit by seeing data labels on a chart. These labels appear next to the data markers in the chart and can indicate the series name, category name, and/or the value of one or more data points. Once your chart is selected, you can add this information to your chart by clicking the Data Labels button in the Labels group on the Chart Tools Layout tab, and then clicking a display option for the data labels. Once you have added the data labels, you can format them or delete individual data labels. To delete a data label, select it and then press [Delete].

# Formatting a Chart

Formatting a chart can make it easier to read and understand. Many formatting enhancements can be made using the Chart Tools Format tab. You can change the fill color for a specific data series, or you can apply a shape style to a title or a data series using the Shape Styles group. Shape styles make it possible to apply multiple formats, such as an outline, fill color, and text color, all with a single click. You can also apply different fill colors, outlines, and effects to chart objects using arrows and buttons in the Shape Styles group.  You want to use a different color for one data series in the chart and apply a shape style to another to enhance the look of the chart.

## STEPS

1. **With the chart selected, click the Chart Tools Format tab on the Ribbon, then click any column in the Quarter 4 data series**

   The Chart Tools Format tab opens, and handles appear on each column in the Quarter 4 data series, indicating that the entire series is selected.

2. **Click the Shape Fill list arrow in the Shape Styles group on the Chart Tools Format tab**

3. **Click Orange, Accent 6 (first row, 10th from the left) as shown in Figure D-15**

   All the columns for the series become orange, and the legend changes to match the new color. You can also change the color of selected objects by applying a shape style.

4. **Click any column in the Quarter 3 data series**

   Handles appear on each column in the Quarter 3 data series.

5. **Click the More button ⊡ on the Shape Styles gallery, then hover the pointer over the Moderate Effect – Olive Green, Accent 3 shape style (fifth row, fourth from the left) in the gallery, as shown in Figure D-16**

   Live Preview shows the data series in the chart with the shape style applied.

**QUICK TIP**

To apply a WordArt style to a text object (such as the chart title), select the object, then click a style in the WordArt Styles group on the Chart Tools Format tab.

6. **Click the Subtle Effect – Olive Green, Accent 3 shape style (fourth row, fourth from the left) in the gallery**

   The style for the data series changes, as shown in Figure D-17.

7. **Save your work**

---

### Changing alignment and angle in axis labels and titles

The buttons on the Chart Tools Layout tab provide a few options for positioning axis labels and titles, but you can customize their position and rotation to exact specifications using the Format Axis dialog box or Format Axis Title dialog box. With a chart selected, right-click the axis text you want to modify, then click Format Axis or Format Axis Title on the shortcut menu. In the dialog box that opens, click Alignment, then select the appropriate Text layout option. You can also create a custom angle by clicking the Custom angle up and down arrows. When you have made the desired changes, click Close.

**FIGURE D-15:** New shape fill applied to data series

Shape Fill list arrow

**FIGURE D-16:** Live Preview of new style applied to data series

Subtle Effect —
Olive Green,
Accent 3

Moderate Effect —
Olive Green, Accent 3

Live Preview of
current style

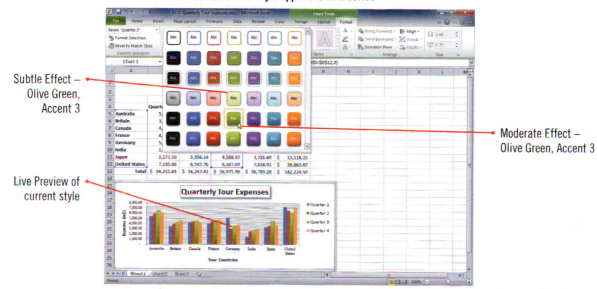

**FIGURE D-17:** Style of data series changed

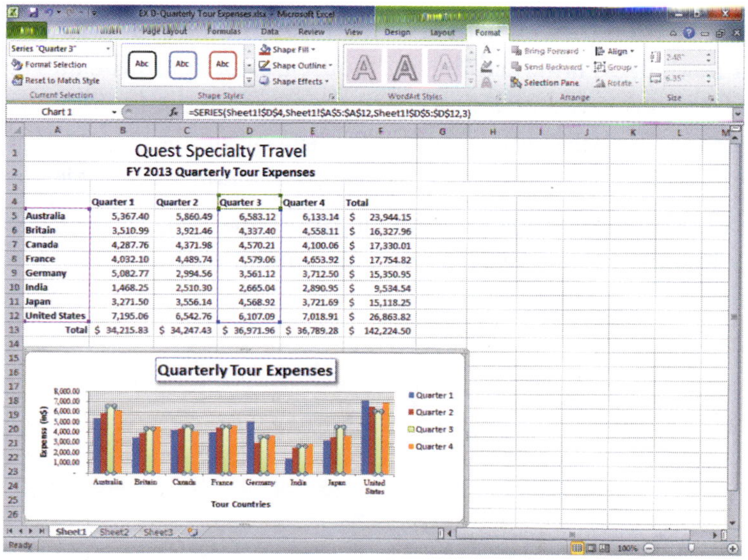

# Annotating and Drawing on a Chart

You can use text annotations and graphics to point out critical information in a chart. **Text annotations** are labels that further describe your data. You can also draw lines and arrows that point to the exact locations you want to emphasize. Shapes such as arrows and boxes can be added from the Illustrations group on the Insert tab or from the Insert group on the Chart Tools Layout group on the Ribbon. These groups are also used to insert pictures and clip art into worksheets and charts.  You want to call attention to the Germany tour expense decrease, so you decide to add a text annotation and an arrow to this information in the chart.

**STEPS**

1. **Make sure the chart is selected, click the Chart Tools Layout tab, click the Text Box button in the Insert group, then move the pointer over the worksheet**

   The pointer changes to ↓, indicating that you will insert a text box where you next click.

**QUICK TIP**

You can also insert a text box by clicking the Text Box button in the Text group in the Insert tab, then clicking in the worksheet.

2. **Click to the right of the chart (anywhere *outside* the chart boundary)**

   A text box is added to the worksheet, and the Drawing Tools Format tab appears on the Ribbon so that you can format the new object. First you need to type the text.

3. **Type Great improvement**

   The text appears in a selected text box on the worksheet, and the chart is no longer selected, as shown in Figure D-18. Your text box may be in a different location; this is not important, because you'll move the annotation in the next step.

4. **Point to an edge of the text box so that the pointer changes to ⌖, drag the text box into the chart to the left of the chart title, as shown in Figure D-19, then release the mouse button**

   The text box is a text annotation for the chart. You also want to add a simple arrow shape in the chart.

**QUICK TIP**

To annotate a chart using a callout, click the Shapes button in either the Illustrations group on the Insert tab or the Insert group on the Chart Tools Layout tab, then click a shape in the Callouts category of the Shapes gallery.

5. **Click the chart to select it, click the Chart Tools Layout tab, click the Shapes button in the Insert group, click the Arrow shape in the Lines category, then move the pointer over the text box on the chart**

   The pointer changes to +, and the status bar displays "Click and drag to insert an AutoShape." When + is over the text box, red handles appear around the text in the text box. A red handle can act as an anchor for the arrow.

6. **Position + on the red handle to the right of the "t" in the word "improvement" (in the text box), press and hold the left mouse button, drag the line to the Quarter 2 column for the Germany category in the chart, then release the mouse button**

   An arrow points to the Quarter 2 expense for Germany, and the Drawing Tools Format tab displays options for working with the new arrow object. You can resize, format, or delete it just like any other object in a chart.

7. **Click the Shape Outline list arrow in the Shape Styles group, click the Automatic color, click the Shape Outline list arrow again, point to Weight, then click 1½ pt**

   Compare your finished chart to Figure D-20.

8. **Save your work**

**FIGURE D-18:** Text box added

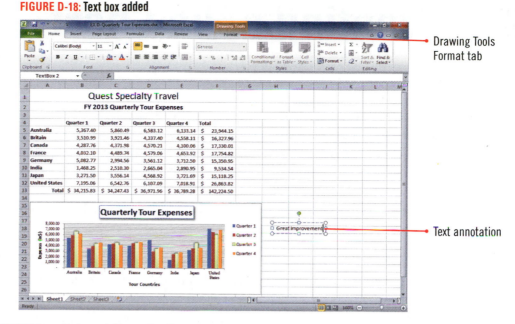

Drawing Tools
Format tab

Text annotation

**FIGURE D-19:** Text annotation on the chart

Text annotation

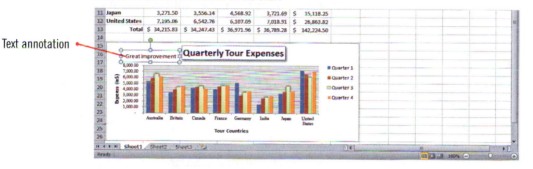

**FIGURE D-20:** Arrow shape added to chart

Arrow drawn
and formatted

## Adding SmartArt graphics

In addition to charts, annotations, and drawn objects, you can create a variety of diagrams using SmartArt graphics. **SmartArt graphics** are available in List, Process, Cycle, Hierarchy, Relationship, Matrix, and Pyramid categories. To insert SmartArt, click the SmartArt button in the Illustrations group on the Insert tab to open the Choose a SmartArt Graphic dialog box. Click a SmartArt category in the left pane, then click the layout for the graphic in the center pane. The right pane shows a sample of the selected SmartArt layout, as shown in Figure D-21. The SmartArt graphic appears in the worksheet as an embedded object with sizing handles. Click the Text Pane button on the SmartArt Tools Design tab to open a text pane next to the graphic; you can enter text into the graphic using the text pane or by typing directly in the shapes in the diagram.

**FIGURE D-21:** Choose a SmartArt Graphic dialog box

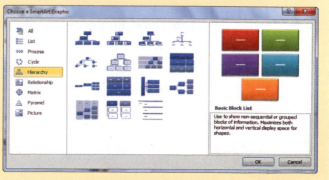

# Creating a Pie Chart

You can create multiple charts based on the same worksheet data. While a column chart may illustrate certain important aspects of your worksheet data, you may find you want to create an additional chart to emphasize a different point. Depending on the type of chart you create, you have additional options for calling attention to trends and patterns. For example, if you create a pie chart, you can emphasize one data point by **exploding**, or pulling that slice away from, the pie chart. When you're ready to print a chart, you can preview it just as you do a worksheet to check the output before committing it to paper. You can print a chart by itself or as part of the worksheet.  At an upcoming meeting, Grace plans to discuss the total tour expenses and which countries need improvement. You want to create a pie chart she can use to illustrate total expenses. Finally, you want to fit the worksheet and the charts onto one worksheet page.

## STEPS

**QUICK TIP**

The Exploded pie in 3-D button creates a pie chart in which all slices are exploded.

1. **Select the range A5:A12, press and hold [Ctrl], select the range F5:F12, click the Insert tab, click the Pie button in the Charts group, then click Pie in 3-D in the Pie chart gallery**

   The new chart appears in the center of the worksheet. You can move the chart and quickly format it using a chart layout.

2. **Drag the chart so its upper-left corner is at the upper-left corner of cell G1, then click Layout 2 in the Chart Layouts group**

   The chart is repositioned on the page, and its layout changes so that a chart title is added and the legend appears just below the chart title.

3. **Select the chart title text, then type Total Expenses, by Country**

**TROUBLE**

If the Format Data Series command appears on the shortcut menu instead of Format Data Point, double-click the slice you want to explode to make sure it is selected by itself, then right-click it again.

4. **Click the slice for the India data point, click it again so it is the only slice selected, right-click it, then click Format Data Point**

   The Format Data Point dialog box opens, as shown in Figure D-22. You can use the Point Explosion slider to control the distance a pie slice moves away from the pie, or you can type a value in the Point Explosion text box.

5. **Double-click 0 in the Point Explosion text box, type 40, then click Close**

   Compare your chart to Figure D-23. You decide to preview the chart and data before you print.

6. **Click cell A1, switch to Page Layout view, type your name in the left header text box, then click cell A1**

   You decide the chart and data would fit better on the page if they were printed in landscape orientation.

7. **Click the Page Layout tab, click the Orientation button in the Page Setup group, then click Landscape**

8. **Click the File tab, click Print on the navigation bar, click the No Scaling setting in the Settings section on the Print tab, then click Fit Sheet on One Page**

   The data and chart are positioned horizontally on a single page, as shown in Figure D-24. The printer you have selected may affect the appearance of your preview screen.

9. **Save and close the workbook, submit your work to your instructor as directed, then exit Excel**

### Previewing a chart

To print or preview just a chart, select the chart (or make the chart sheet active), click the File tab, then click Print on the navigation bar. To reposition a chart by changing the page's margins, click the Show Margins button ▦ in the lower-right corner of the Print tab to display the margins in the preview. You can drag the margin lines to the exact settings you want; as the margins change, the size and placement of the chart on the page changes too.

Point Explosion slider

Point Explosion text box

FIGURE D-23: Exploded pie slice

FIGURE D-24: Preview of worksheet with charts in Backstage view

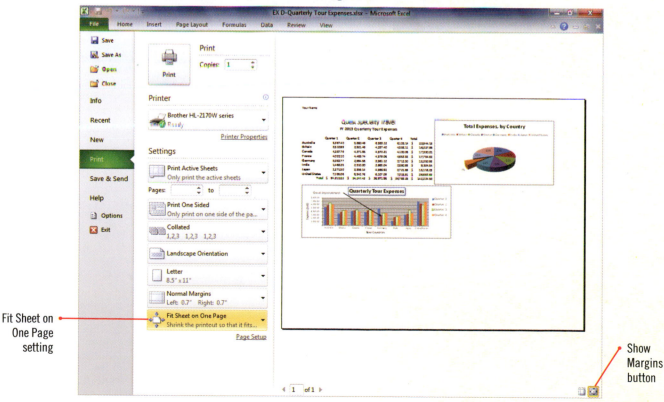

Fit Sheet on One Page setting

Show Margins button

# Practice

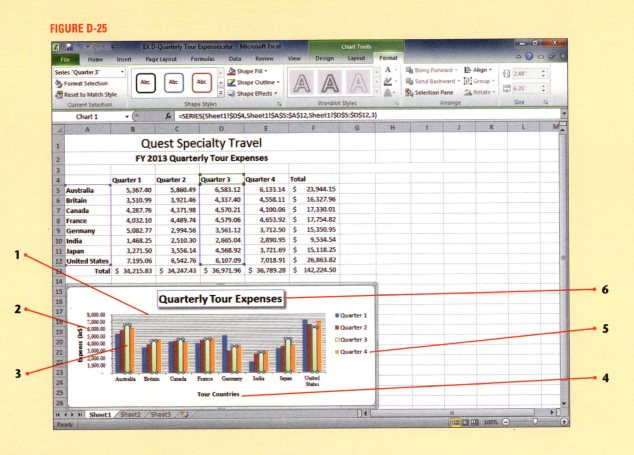

**SAM**

For current SAM information, including versions and content details, visit SAM Central (http://www.cengage.com/samcentral). If you have a SAM user profile, you may have access to hands-on instruction, practice, and assessment of the skills covered in this unit. Since various versions of SAM are supported throughout the life of this text, check with your instructor for the correct instructions and URL/Web site for accessing assignments.

## Concepts Review

**Label each element of the Excel chart shown in Figure D-25.**

FIGURE D-25

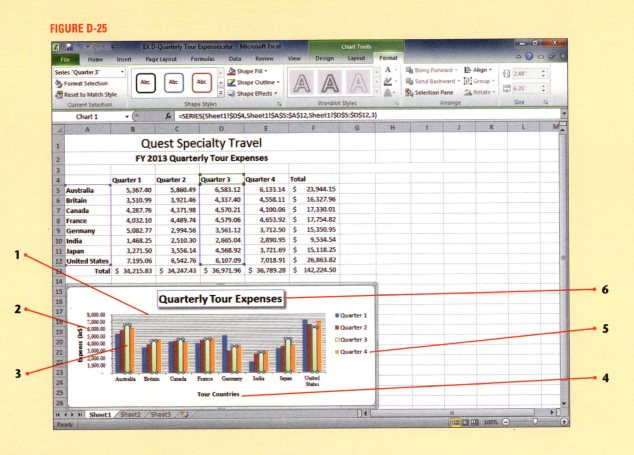

**Match each chart type with the statement that best describes it.**

7. Column
8. Line
9. Combination
10. Pie
11. Area

a. Displays a column and line chart using different scales of measurement
b. Compares trends over even time intervals
c. Compares data using columns
d. Compares data as parts of a whole
e. Shows how volume changes over time

**Select the best answer from the list of choices.**

12. **Which pointer do you use to resize a chart?**
    a.  ┼
    b.  I
    c.  ↕
    d.  ↔

13. **The object in a chart that identifies the colors used for each data series is a(n):**
    a.  Data marker.
    b.  Data point.
    c.  Organizer.
    d.  Legend.

14. **Which tab appears only when a chart is selected?**
    a.  Insert
    b.  Chart Tools Format
    c.  Review
    d.  Page Layout

15. **How do you move an embedded chart to a chart sheet?**
    a.  Click a button on the Chart Tools Design tab.
    b.  Drag the chart to the sheet tab.
    c.  Delete the chart, switch to a different sheet, then create a new chart.
    d.  Use the Copy and Paste buttons on the Ribbon.

16. **Which tab on the Ribbon do you use to create a chart?**
    a.  Design
    b.  Insert
    c.  Page Layout
    d.  Format

17. **A collection of related data points in a chart is called a:**
    a.  Data series.
    b.  Data tick.
    c.  Cell address.
    d.  Value title.

## Skills Review

1.  **Plan a chart.**
    a.  Start Excel, open the Data File EX D-2.xlsx from the drive and folder where you store your Data Files, then save it as **EX D-Departmental Software Usage**.
    b.  Describe the type of chart you would use to plot this data.
    c.  What chart type would you use to compare the number of Excel users in each department?

2.  **Create a chart.**
    a.  In the worksheet, select the range containing all the data and headings.
    b.  Click the Insert tab.
    c.  Create a Clustered Column chart, then add the chart title **Software Usage, by Department** above the chart.
    d.  Save your work.

If you have a SAM 2010 user profile, an autogradable SAM version of this assignment may be available at http://www.cengage.com/sam2010. Check with your instructor to confirm that this assignment is available in SAM. To use the SAM version of this assignment, log into the SAM 2010 Web site and download the instruction and start files.

# Skills Review (continued)

**3. Move and resize a chart.**

  **a.** Make sure the chart is still selected.

  **b.** Move the chart beneath the worksheet data.

  **c.** Widen the chart so it extends to the right edge of column H.

  **d.** Use the Chart Tools Layout tab to move the legend below the charted data. (*Hint*: Click the Legend button, then click Show Legend at Bottom.)

  **e.** Resize the chart so its bottom edge is at the top of row 25.

  **f.** Save your work.

**4. Change the chart design.**

  **a.** Change the value in cell B3 to **15**. Observe the change in the chart.

  **b.** Select the chart.

  **c.** Use the Chart Layouts group on the Chart Tools Design tab to apply the Layout 7 layout to the chart, then undo the change.

  **d.** Use the Change Chart Type button on the Chart Tools Design tab to change the chart to a Clustered Bar chart.

  **e.** Change the chart to a 3-D Clustered Column chart, then change it back to a Clustered Column chart.

  **f.** Save your work.

**5. Change the chart layout.**

  **a.** Use the Chart Tools Layout tab to turn off the major horizontal gridlines in the chart.

  **b.** Change the font used in the horizontal and vertical axes labels to Times New Roman.

  **c.** Turn on the major gridlines for both the horizontal and vertical axes.

  **d.** Change the chart title's font to Times New Roman if necessary, with a font size of 20.

  **e.** Insert **Departments** as the horizontal axis title.

  **f.** Insert **Number of Users** as the vertical axis title.

  **g.** Change the font size of the horizontal and vertical axis titles to 10 and the font to Times New Roman, if necessary.

  **h.** Change "Personnel" in the worksheet column heading to **Human Resources**, then AutoFit column E.

  **i.** Change the font size of the legend to 14.

  **j.** Add a solid line border in the default color and an Offset Diagonal Bottom Right shadow to the chart title.

  **k.** Save your work.

**6. Format a chart.**

  **a.** Make sure the chart is selected, then select the Chart Tools Format tab, if necessary.

  **b.** Change the shape fill of the Excel data series to Dark Blue, Text 2.

  **c.** Change the shape style of the Excel data series to Subtle Effect Orange, Accent 6.

  **d.** Save your work.

**7. Annotate and draw on a chart.**

  **a.** Make sure the chart is selected, then create the text annotation **Needs more users**.

  **b.** Position the text annotation so the word "Needs" is just below the word "Software" in the chart title.

  **c.** Select the chart, then use the Chart Tools Layout tab to create a 1½ pt weight arrow that points from the bottom center of the text box to the Excel users in the Design department.

  **d.** Deselect the chart.

  **e.** Save your work.

# Skills Review (continued)

**8. Create a pie chart.**

   **a.** Select the range A1:F2, then create a Pie in 3-D chart.

   **b.** Drag the 3-D pie chart beneath the existing chart.

   **c.** Change the chart title to **Excel Users**.

   **d.** Apply the Style 42 chart style to the chart.

   **e.** Explode the Human Resources slice from the pie chart at **25%**.

   **f.** In Page Layout view, enter your name in the left section of the worksheet header.

   **g.** Preview the worksheet and charts in Backstage view, make sure all the contents fit on one page, then submit your work to your instructor as directed. When printed, the worksheet should look like Figure D-26.

   **h.** Save your work, close the workbook, then exit Excel.

**FIGURE D-26**

The position of your annotation may vary

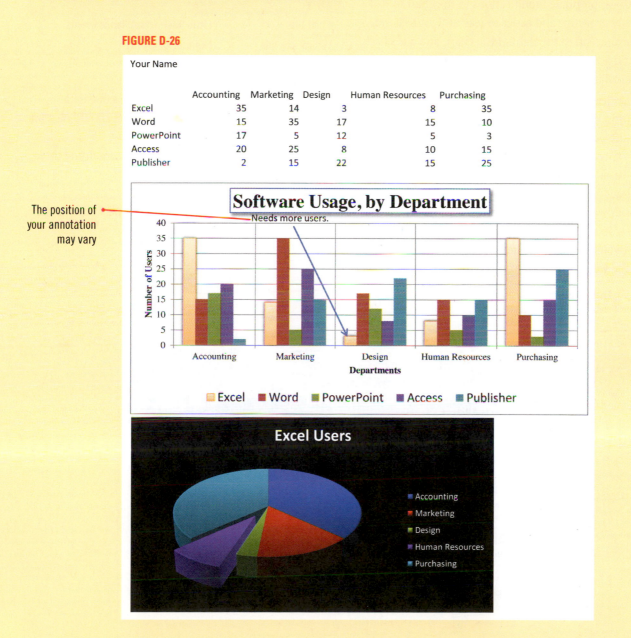

# Independent Challenge 1

You are the operations manager for the Little Rock Arts Alliance in Arkansas. Each year the group applies to various state and federal agencies for matching funds. For this year's funding proposal, you need to create charts to document the number of productions in previous years.

a. Start Excel, open the file EX D-3.xlsx from the drive and folder where you store your Data Files, then save it as **EX D-Little Rock Arts Alliance**.

b. Take some time to plan your charts. Which type of chart or charts might best illustrate the information you need to display? What kind of chart enhancements do you want to use? Will a 3-D effect make your chart easier to understand?

c. Create a Clustered Column chart for the data.

d. Change at least one of the colors used in a data series.

e. Make the appropriate modifications to the chart to make it visually attractive and easier to read and understand. Include a legend to the right of the chart, and add chart titles and horizontal and vertical axis titles using the text shown in Table D-3.

**TABLE D-3**

| title | text |
|-------|------|
| Chart title | **Little Rock Arts Alliance Events** |
| Vertical axis title | **Number of Events** |
| Horizontal axis title | **Types of Events** |

f. Create at least two additional charts for the same data to show how different chart types display the same data. Reposition each new chart so that all charts are visible in the worksheet. One of the additional charts should be a pie chart; the other is up to you.

g. Modify each new chart as necessary to improve its appearance and effectiveness. A sample worksheet containing three charts based on the worksheet data is shown in Figure D-27.

h. Enter your name in the worksheet header.

i. Save your work. Before printing, preview the worksheet in Backstage view, then adjust any settings as necessary so that all the worksheet data and charts print on a single page.

j. Submit your work to your instructor as directed.

k. Close the workbook, then exit Excel.

**FIGURE D-27**

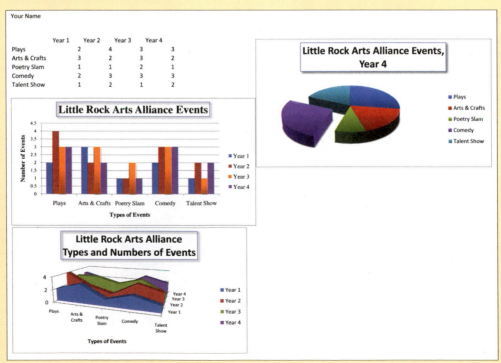

# Independent Challenge 2

You work at Bark Bark Bark, a locally owned day spa for dogs. One of your responsibilities at the day spa is to manage the company's sales and expenses using Excel. Another is to convince the current staff that Excel can help them make daily operating decisions more easily and efficiently. To do this, you've decided to create charts using the previous year's operating expenses including rent, utilities, and payroll. The manager will use these charts at the next monthly meeting.

a. Start Excel, open the Data File EX D-4.xlsx from the drive and folder where you store your Data Files, then save it as **EX D-Bark Bark Bark Doggie Day Spa Analysis**.

b. Decide which data in the worksheet should be charted. What chart types are best suited for the information you need to show? What kinds of chart enhancements are necessary?

c. Create a 3-D Clustered Column chart in the worksheet showing the expense data for all four quarters. (*Hint:* The expense categories should appear on the x-axis. Do not include the totals.)

d. Change the vertical axis labels (Expenses data) so that no decimals are displayed. (*Hint:* Right-click the axis labels you want to modify, click Format Axis, click the Number category in the Format Axis dialog box, change the number of decimal places, then click Close.)

e. Using the sales data, create two charts on this worksheet that compare the sales amounts. (*Hint:* Move each chart to a new location on the worksheet, then deselect it before creating the next one.)

f. In one chart of the sales data, add data labels, then add chart titles as you see fit.

g. Make any necessary formatting changes to make the charts look more attractive, then enter your name in a worksheet cell.

h. Save your work.

i. Preview each chart in Backstage view, and adjust any items as needed. Fit the worksheet to a single page, then submit your work to your instructor as directed. A sample of a printed worksheet is shown in Figure D-28.

j. Close the workbook, then exit Excel.

**FIGURE D-28**

## Bark Bark Bark Doggie Day Spa

Sales and Expenses for 2012

| Expenses | Quarter 1 | Quarter 2 | Quarter 3 | Quarter 4 | Total |
|---|---|---|---|---|---|
| Rent | 2,750.00 | 2,500.00 | 2,500.00 | 2,500.00 | $ 10,250.00 |
| Utilities | 325.12 | 309.05 | 287.98 | 352.64 | $ 1,274.79 |
| Payroll | 10,532.97 | 11,299.87 | 9,364.81 | 15,226.47 | $ 46,424.12 |
| Insurance | 253.62 | 253.62 | 253.62 | 253.62 | $ 1,014.48 |
| Supplies | 1,568.92 | 1,790.84 | 1,706.77 | 1,628.13 | $ 6,694.66 |
| Total | $ 15,430.63 | $ 16,153.38 | $ 14,113.18 | $ 19,960.86 | |

| Sales | Quarter 1 | Quarter 2 | Quarter 3 | Quarter 4 | Total |
|---|---|---|---|---|---|
| Catering | 14,562.87 | 16,247.72 | 12,184.65 | 19,895.60 | $ 62,890.84 |
| Treats | 423.90 | 506.18 | 480.01 | 789.66 | $ 2,199.75 |
| Accessories | 1,228.09 | 1,287.16 | 1,494.67 | 1,982.64 | $ 5,992.56 |
| Total | $ 16,214.86 | $ 18,041.06 | $ 14,159.33 | $ 22,667.90 | |

| Net | $ 784.23 | $ 1,887.68 | $ 46.15 | $ 2,707.04 | $ 5,425.10 |

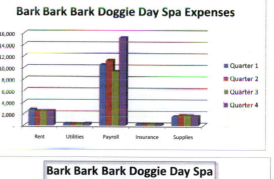

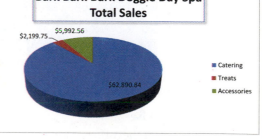

Your Name

# Independent Challenge 3

You are working as an account representative at a magazine called *Creativity*. You have been examining the expenses incurred recently. The CEO wants to examine expenses designed to increase circulation and has asked you to prepare charts that can be used in this evaluation. In particular, you want to see how dollar amounts compare among the different expenses, and you also want to see how expenses compare with each other proportional to the total budget.

**a.** Start Excel, open the Data File EX D-5.xlsx from the drive and folder where you store your Data Files, then save it as **EX D-Creativity Magazine**.

**b.** Identify three types of charts that seem best suited to illustrate the data in the range A16:B24. What kinds of chart enhancements are necessary?

**c.** Create at least two different types of charts that show the distribution of circulation expenses. (*Hint*: Move each chart to a new location on the same worksheet.) One of the charts should be a 3-D pie chart.

**d.** In at least one of the charts, add annotated text and arrows highlighting important data, such as the largest expense.

**e.** Change the color of at least one data series in at least one of the charts.

**f.** Add chart titles and category and value axis titles where appropriate. Format the titles with a font of your choice. Apply a shadow to the chart title in at least one chart.

**g.** Add your name to a section of the header, then save your work.

**h.** Preview the worksheet in Backstage view. Adjust any items as needed. Be sure the charts are all visible on one page. Compare your work to the sample in Figure D-29.

**FIGURE D-29**

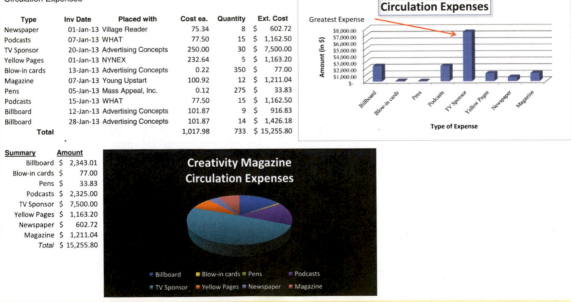

## Advanced Challenge Exercise

- Explode a slice from the 3-D pie chart.
- Add a data label to the exploded pie slice.
- Change the number format of labels in the non-pie chart so no decimals are displayed.
- Save your work, then preview it in Backstage view.

**i.** Submit your work to your instructor as directed, close the workbook, then exit Excel.

# Real Life Independent Challenge

**This project requires an Internet connection.**

A cash inheritance from a distant relative has finally been deposited in your bank account, and you have decided to purchase a home. You have a good idea where you'd like to live, and you decide to use the Web to find out more about houses that are currently available.

a. Start Excel, then save a new, blank workbook as **EX D-My Dream House** to the drive and folder where you save your Data Files.

b. Decide on where you would like to live, and use your favorite search engine to find information sources on homes for sale in that area. (*Hint*: Try using realtor.com or other realtor-sponsored sites.)

c. Determine a price range and features within the home. Find data for at least five homes that meet your location and price requirements, and enter them in the worksheet. See Table D-4 below for a suggested data layout.

**TABLE D-4**

| suggested data layout | | | | | |
|---|---|---|---|---|---|
| Location | | | | | |
| Price range | | | | | |
| | House 1 | House 2 | House 3 | House 4 | House 5 |
| Asking price | | | | | |
| Bedrooms | | | | | |
| Bathrooms | | | | | |
| Year built | | | | | |
| Size (in sq. ft.) | | | | | |

d. Format the data so it looks attractive and professional.

e. Create any type of column chart using only the House and Asking Price data. Place it on the same worksheet as the data. Include a descriptive title.

f. Change the colors in the chart using the chart style of your choice.

g. Enter your name in a section of the header.

h. Save the workbook. Preview the worksheet in Backstage view and make adjustments if necessary to fit all of the information on one page. See Figure D-30 for an example of what your worksheet might look like.

i. Submit your work to your instructor as directed.

**FIGURE D-30**

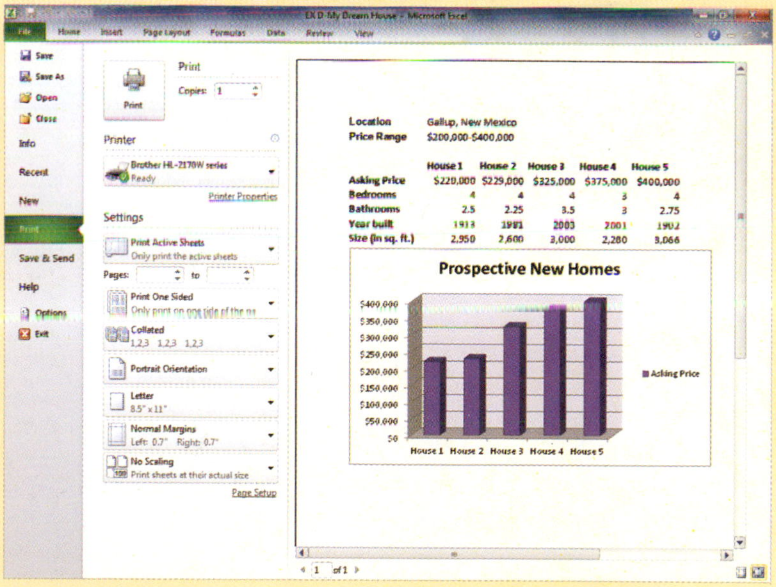

## Advanced Challenge Exercise

- If necessary, change the chart type to a Clustered Column chart.
- Change the data used for the chart to include the size data in cells A9:F9.
- Create a combination chart that plots the asking price on one axis and the size of the home on the other axis. (*Hint*: Use Help to get tips on how to chart with a secondary axis.)

j. Close the workbook, then exit Excel.

# Visual Workshop

Open the Data File EX D-6.xlsx from the drive and folder where you store your Data Files, then save it as **EX D-Projected Project Expenses**. Format the worksheet data so it looks like Figure D-31, then create and modify two charts to match the ones shown in the figure. You will need to make formatting, layout, and design changes once you create the charts. (*Hint*: The shadow used in the 3-D pie chart title is made using the Outer Offset Diagonal Top Right shadow.) Enter your name in the left text box of the header, then save and preview the worksheet. Submit your work to your instructor as directed, then close the workbook and exit Excel.

**FIGURE D-31**

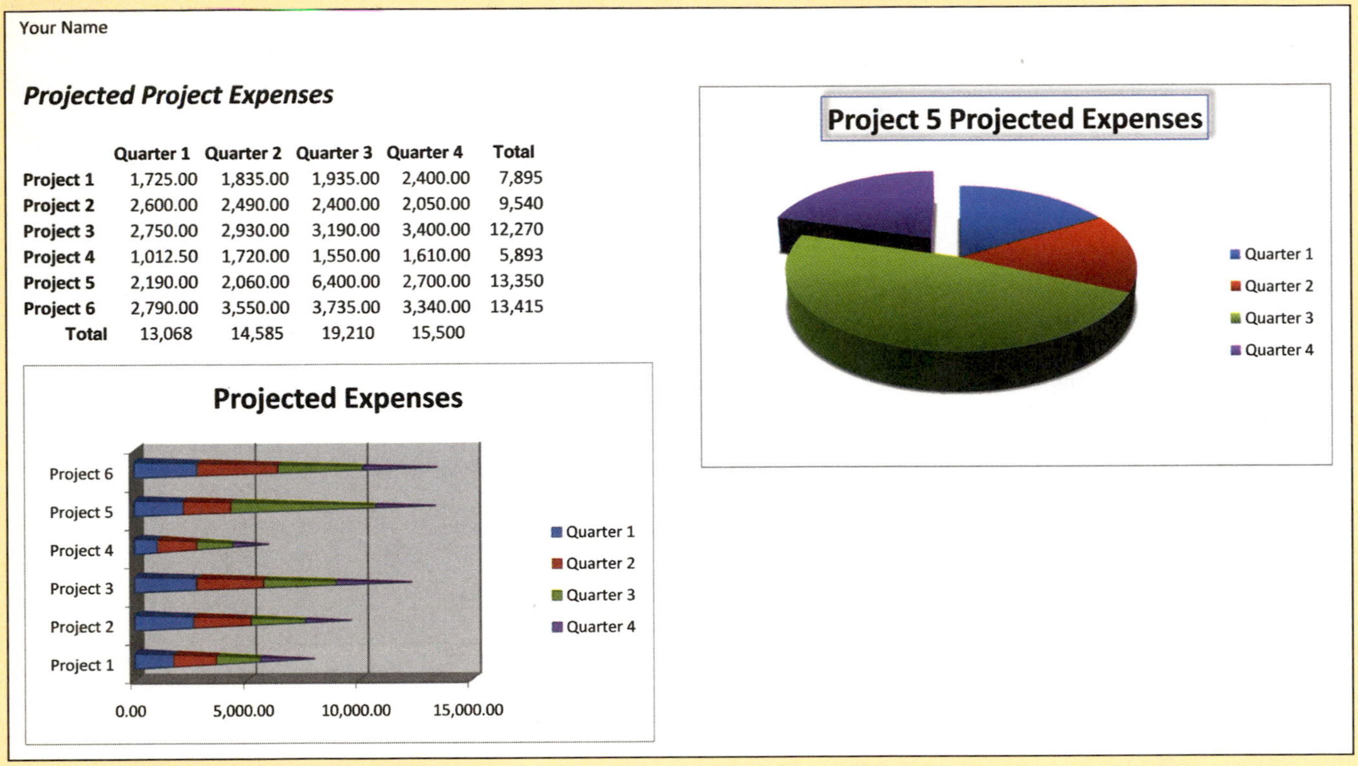
Your Name
Projected Project Expenses
Quarter 1 Quarter 2 Quarter 3 Quarter 4 Total
Project 1 1,725.00 1,835.00 1,935.00 2,400.00 7,895
Project 2 2,600.00 2,490.00 2,400.00 2,050.00 9,540
Project 3 2,750.00 2,930.00 3,190.00 3,400.00 12,270
Project 4 1,012.50 1,720.00 1,550.00 1,610.00 5,893
Project 5 2,190.00 2,060.00 6,400.00 2,700.00 13,350
Project 6 2,790.00 3,550.00 3,735.00 3,340.00 13,415
Total 13,068 14,585 19,210 15,500
Project 5 Projected Expenses
Quarter 1
Quarter 2
Quarter 3
Quarter 4
Projected Expenses
Project 6
Project 5
Project 4
Project 3
Project 2
Project 1
0.00
5,000.00
10,000.00
15,000.00
Quarter 1
Quarter 2
Quarter 3
Quarter 4

# Analyzing Data Using Formulas

**Files You Will Need:**

EX E-1.xlsx
EX E-2.xlsx
EX E-3.xlsx
EX E-4.xlsx
EX E-5.xlsx
EX E-6.xlsx
EX E-7.xlsx

As you have learned, formulas and functions help you to analyze worksheet data. As you learn how to use different types of formulas and functions, you will discover more valuable uses for Excel. In this unit, you will gain a deeper understanding of Excel formulas and learn how to use several Excel functions.  Kate Morgan, Quest's vice president of sales, uses Excel formulas and functions to analyze sales data for the U.S. region and to consolidate sales data from several worksheets. Because management is considering adding a new regional branch, Kate asks you to estimate the loan costs for a new office facility and to compare tour sales in the existing U.S. offices.

## OBJECTIVES

Format data using text functions
Sum a data range based on conditions
Consolidate data using a formula
Check formulas for errors
Construct formulas using named ranges
Build a logical formula with the IF function
Build a logical formula with the AND function
Calculate payments with the PMT function

# Formatting Data Using Text Functions

Often, you need to import data into Excel from an outside source, such as another program or the Internet. Sometimes you need to reformat this data to make it understandable and attractive. Instead of handling these tasks manually in each cell, you can save time by using Excel text functions to perform these tasks automatically for a range of cell data. The Convert Text to Columns feature breaks data fields in one column into separate columns. The text function PROPER capitalizes the first letter in a string of text as well as any text following a space. You can use the CONCATENATE function to join two or more strings into one text string. Kate has received the U.S. sales representatives' data from the Human Resources Department. She asks you to use text formulas to format the data into a more useful layout.

## STEPS

1. **Start Excel, open the file EX E-1.xlsx from the drive and folder where you store your Data Files, then save it as EX E-Sales**

2. **On the Sales Reps sheet, select the range A4:A15, click the Data tab, then click the Text to Columns button in the Data Tools group**

   The Convert Text to Columns Wizard opens, as shown in Figure E-1. The data fields on your worksheet are separated by commas, which will act as delimiters. A **delimiter** is a separator, such as a space, comma, or semicolon that should separate your data. Excel separates your data into columns at the delimiter.

3. **If necessary, click the Delimited option button to select it, click Next, in the Delimiters area of the dialog box click the Comma check box to select it if necessary, click any other selected check boxes to deselect them, then click Next**

   You instructed Excel to separate your data at the comma delimiter.

4. **Click the Text option button in the Column data format area, click the second column with the city data to select it in the Data preview area, click the Text option button again in the Column data format area, observe the column headings and data in the Data preview area, then click Finish**

   The data are separated into three columns of text. You want to format the letters in the names and cities to the correct cases.

> **QUICK TIP**
> You can move the Function Arguments dialog box if it overlaps a cell or range that you need to click. You can also click the Collapse Dialog Box button [icon], select the cell or range, then click the Expand Dialog box button [icon] to return to the Function Arguments dialog box.

5. **Click cell D4, click the Formulas tab, click the Text button in the Function Library group, click PROPER, with the insertion point in the Text text box, click cell A4, then click OK**

   The name is copied from cell A4 to cell D4 with the correct uppercase letters for proper names. The remaining names and the cities are still in lowercase letters.

6. **Drag the fill handle to copy the formula in cell D4 to cell E4, then copy the formulas in cells D4:E4 into the range D5:E15**

   You want to format the years data to be more descriptive.

> **QUICK TIP**
> Excel automatically inserts quotation marks to enclose the space and the Years text.

7. **Click cell F4, click the Text button in the Function Library group, click CONCATENATE, with the insertion point in the Text1 text box, click cell C4, press [Tab], with the insertion point in the Text2 text box, press [Spacebar], type Years, then click OK**

8. **Copy the formula in cell F4 into the range F5:F15, compare your work to Figure E-2, click the Insert tab, click the Header & Footer button in the Text group, click the Go to Footer button in the Navigation group, enter your name in the center text box, click on the worksheet, scroll up and click cell A1, then click the Normal button [icon] in the status bar**

9. **Save your file, then preview the worksheet**

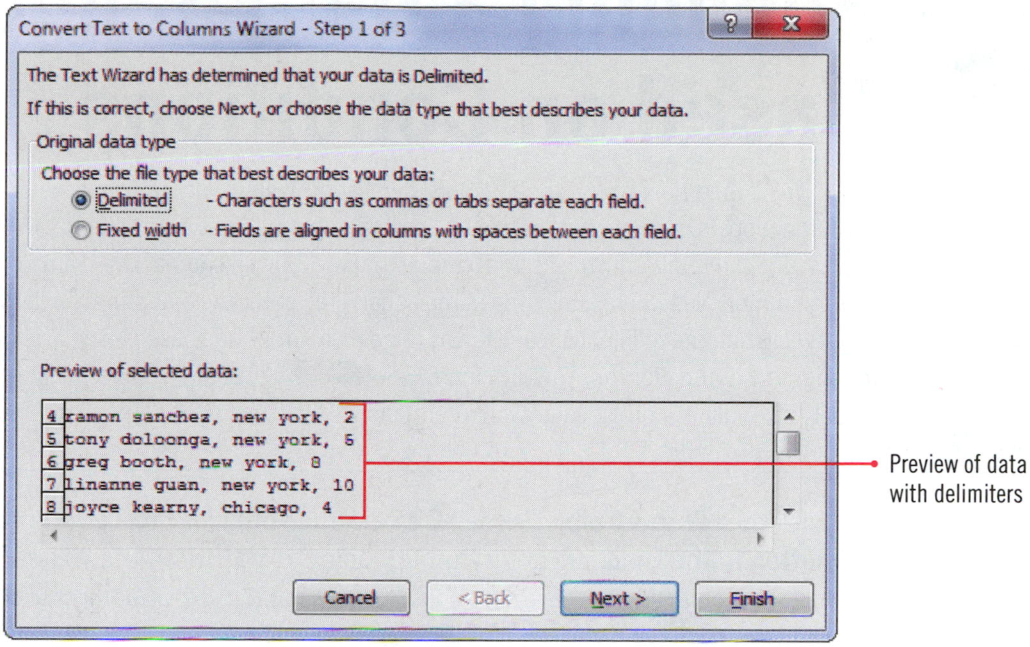

**FIGURE E-2:** Worksheet with data formatted in columns

| | A | B | C | D | E | F |
|---|---|---|---|---|---|---|
| 1 | | | | | Quest | |
| 2 | | | | | Sales Representatives | |
| 3 | | | | Name | Office | Years of Service |
| 4 | ramon sanchez | new york | 2 | Ramon Sanchez | New York | 2 Years |
| 5 | tony doloonga | new york | 5 | Tony Doloonga | New York | 5 Years |
| 6 | greg booth | new york | 8 | Greg Booth | New York | 8 Years |
| 7 | linanne guan | new york | 10 | Linanne Guan | New York | 10 Years |
| 8 | joyce kearny | chicago | 4 | Joyce Kearny | Chicago | 4 Years |
| 9 | garrett cunnea | chicago | 7 | Garrett Cunnea | Chicago | 7 Years |
| 10 | kathy jaques | chicago | 5 | Kathy Jaques | Chicago | 5 Years |
| 11 | alyssa maztta | chicago | 4 | Alyssa Maztta | Chicago | 4 Years |
| 12 | ann tadka | miami | 6 | Ann Tadka | Miami | 6 Years |
| 13 | jose costello | miami | 7 | Jose Costello | Miami | 7 Years |
| 14 | joan hanley | miami | 4 | Joan Hanley | Miami | 4 Years |
| 15 | spring zola | miami | 7 | Spring Zola | Miami | 7 Years |
| 16 | | | | | | |

## Using text functions

Other useful text functions include UPPER, LOWER, and SUBSTITUTE. The UPPER function converts text to all uppercase letters, the LOWER function converts text to all lowercase letters, and SUBSTITUTE replaces text in a text string. For example, if cell A1 contains the text string "Today is Wednesday", then =LOWER(A1) would produce "today is wednesday"; =UPPER(A1) would produce "TODAY IS WEDNESDAY"; and =SUBSTITUTE(A1, "Wednesday", "Tuesday") would result in "Today is Tuesday".

If you want to copy and paste data that you have formatted using text functions, you need to select Values Only from the Paste Options drop-down list to paste the cell values rather than the text formulas.

Excel 2010

# Summing a Data Range Based on Conditions

You have learned how to use the SUM, COUNT, and AVERAGE functions for data ranges. You can also use Excel functions to sum, count, and average data in a range based on criteria, or conditions, you set. The SUMIF function totals only the cells in a range that meet given criteria. For example, you can total the values in a column of sales where a sales rep name equals Joe Smith (the criterion). Similarly, the COUNTIF function counts cells and the AVERAGEIF function averages cells in a range based on a specified condition. The format for the SUMIF function appears in Figure E-3.  Kate asks you to analyze the New York branch's January sales data to provide her with information about each tour.

**STEPS**

1. **Click the NY sheet tab, click cell G7, click the Formulas tab, click the More Functions button in the Function Library group, point to Statistical, then click COUNTIF**

   The Function Arguments dialog box opens, as shown in Figure E-4. You want to count the number of times Pacific Odyssey appears in the Tour column. The formula you use will say, in effect, "Examine the range I specify, then count the number of cells in that range that contain "Pacific Odyssey." You will specify absolute addresses for the range so you can copy the formula.

2. **With the insertion point in the Range text box, select the range A6:A25, press [F4], press [Tab], with the insertion point in the Criteria text box, click cell F7, then click OK**

   Your formula asks Excel to search the range A6:A25, and where it finds the value shown in cell F7 (that is, when it finds the value "Pacific Odyssey"), add one to the total count. The number of Pacific Odyssey tours, 4, appears in cell G7. You want to calculate the total sales revenue for the Pacific Odyssey tours.

**QUICK TIP**
You can also sum, count, and average ranges with multiple criteria using the functions SUMIFS, COUNTIFS, and AVERAGEIFS

3. **Click cell H7, click the Math & Trig button in the Function Library group, scroll down the list of functions, then click SUMIF**

   The Function Arguments dialog box opens. You want to enter two ranges and a criterion; the first range is the one where you want Excel to search for the criteria entered. The second range contains the corresponding cells that Excel will total when it finds the criterion you specify in the first range.

4. **With the insertion point in the Range text box, select the range A6:A25, press [F4], press [Tab], with the insertion point in the Criteria text box, click cell F7, press [Tab], with the insertion point in the Sum_range text box, select the range B6:B25, press [F4], then click OK**

   Your formula asks Excel to search the range A6:A25, and where it finds the value shown in cell F7 (that is, when it finds the value "Pacific Odyssey"), add the corresponding amounts from column B. The revenue for the Pacific Odyssey tours, $4,403, appears in cell H7. You want to calculate the average price paid for the Pacific Odyssey tours.

5. **Click cell I7, click the More Functions button in the Function Library group, point to Statistical, then click AVERAGEIF**

6. **With the insertion point in the Range text box, select the range A6:A25, press [F4], press [Tab], with the insertion point in the Criteria text box, click cell F7, press [Tab], with the insertion point in the Average_range text box, select the range B6:B25, press [F4], then click OK**

   The average price paid for the Pacific Odyssey tours, $1,101, appears in cell I7.

**TROUBLE**
Follow the same steps that you used to add a footer to the Sales Reps worksheet in the previous lesson.

7. **Select the range G7:I7, then drag the fill handle to fill the range G8:I10**

   Compare your results with those in Figure E-5.

8. **Add your name to the center of the footer, save the workbook, then preview the worksheet**

$$\text{SUMIF}(\underline{\text{range}}, \underline{\text{criteria}}, \underline{[\text{sum\_range}]})$$

The range the function searches

The condition that must be satisfied in the range

The range where the cells that meet the condition will be totaled

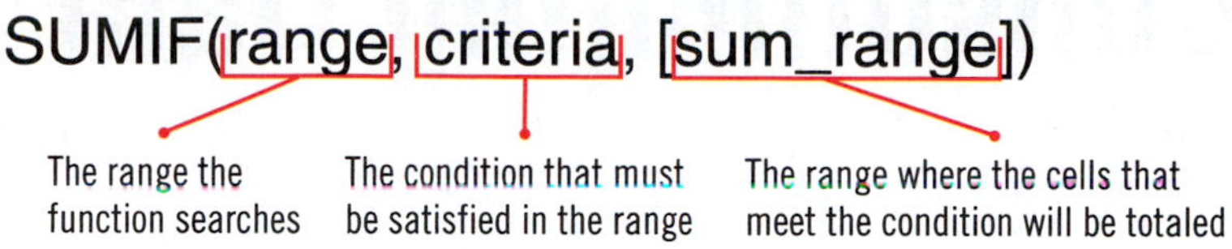

**FIGURE E-4:** COUNTIF function in the Function Arguments dialog box

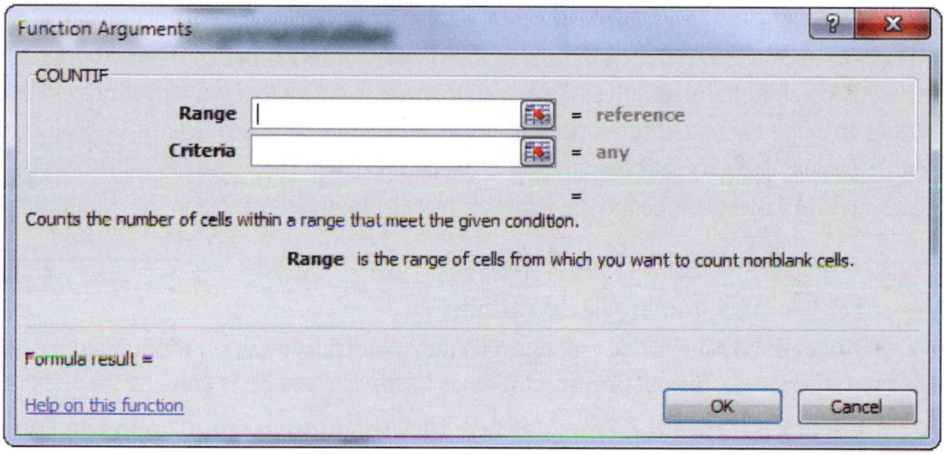

Function Arguments

COUNTIF

Range | = reference

Criteria | = any

=

Counts the number of cells within a range that meet the given condition.

**Range** is the range of cells from which you want to count nonblank cells.

Formula result =

Help on this function

OK    Cancel

Excel 2010

**FIGURE E-5:** Worksheet with conditional statistics

| Tour | Tours Sold | Revenue | Average Price |
|------|-----------|---------|---------------|
| Pacific Odyssey | 4 | $ 4,403 | $ 1,101 |
| Old Japan | 5 | $ 5,503 | $ 1,101 |
| Costa Rica | 5 | $ 9,016 | $ 1,803 |
| Yellowstone | 6 | $ 5,862 | $ 977 |

Sales Reps | NY | Chicago | Miami | US Summary Jan

Conditional statistics

Analyzing Data Using Formulas

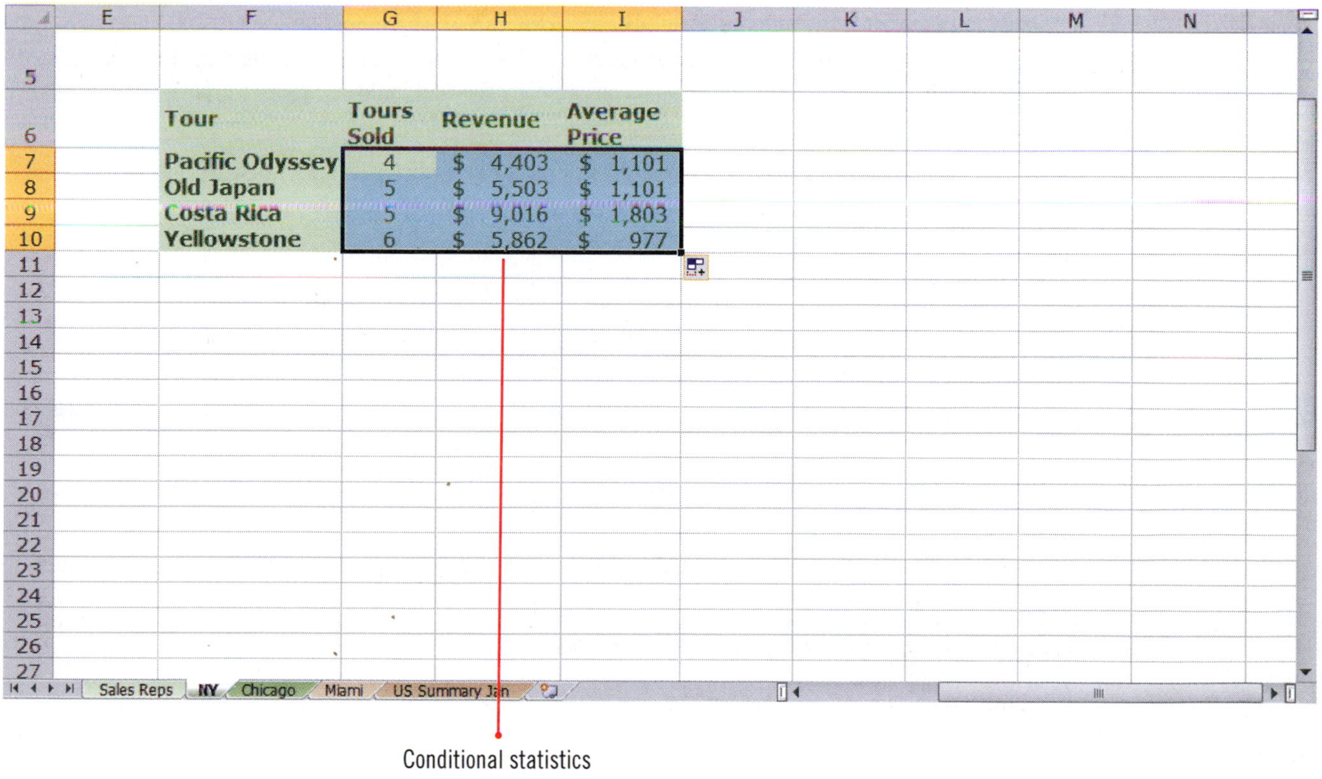

# Consolidating Data Using a Formula

When you want to summarize similar data that exists in different sheets or workbooks, you can **consolidate**, or combine and display, the data in one sheet. For example, you might have entered departmental sales figures on four different store sheets that you want to consolidate on one summary sheet, showing total departmental sales for all stores. Or, you may have quarterly sales data on separate sheets that you want to total for yearly sales on a summary sheet. The best way to consolidate data is to use cell references to the various sheets on a consolidation, or summary, sheet. Because they reference other sheets that are usually behind the summary sheet, such references effectively create another dimension in the workbook and are called **3-D references**, as shown in Figure E-6. You can reference, or **link** to, data in other sheets and in other workbooks. Linking to a worksheet or workbook is better than retyping calculated results from another worksheet or workbook because the data values that the calculated totals depend on might change. If you reference the values, any changes to the original values are automatically reflected in the consolidation sheet.  Kate asks you to prepare a January sales summary sheet comparing the total U.S. revenue for the tours sold in the month.

**STEPS**

1. **Click the US Summary Jan sheet tab**

   Because the US Summary Jan sheet (which is the consolidation sheet) will contain the reference to the data in the other sheets, the cell pointer must reside there when you begin entering the reference.

2. **Click cell B7, click the Formulas tab, click the AutoSum button in the Function Library group, click the NY sheet tab, press and hold [Shift] and click the Miami sheet tab, scroll up if necessary and click cell G7, then click the Enter button ✓ on the formula bar**

   The US Summary Jan sheet becomes active, and the formula bar reads =SUM(NY:Miami!G7), as shown in Figure E-7. "NY:Miami" references the NY, Chicago, and Miami sheets. The exclamation point ( ! ) is an **external reference indicator**, meaning that the cells referenced are outside the active sheet; G7 is the actual cell reference you want to total in the external sheets. The result, 12, appears in cell B7 of the US Summary Jan sheet; it is the sum of the number of Pacific Odyssey tours sold and referenced in cell G7 of the NY, Chicago, and Miami sheets. Because the Revenue data is in the column to the right of the Tours Sold column on the NY, Chicago, and Miami sheets, you can copy the tours sold summary formula, with its relative addresses, into the cell that holds the revenue summary information.

3. **Drag the fill handle to copy the formula in cell B7 to cell C7, click the Auto Fill options list arrow 📋▾, then click the Fill Without Formatting option button**

   The result, $13,404, appears in cell C7 of the US Summary Jan sheet, showing the sum of the Pacific Odyssey tour revenue referenced in cell H7 of the NY, Chicago, and Miami sheets.

4. **In the US Summary Jan sheet, with the range B7:C7 selected, drag the fill handle to fill the range B8:C10**

   You can test a consolidation reference by changing one cell value on which the formula is based and seeing if the formula result changes.

5. **Click the Chicago sheet tab, edit cell A6 to read Pacific Odyssey, then click the US Summary Jan sheet tab**

   The number of Pacific Odyssey tours sold is automatically updated to 13, and the revenue is increased to $15,279, as shown in Figure E-8.

6. **Save the workbook, then preview the worksheet**

**QUICK TIP**

You can preview your worksheet with the worksheet gridlines and column and row headings for printing at a later time. Click the Print check boxes under Gridlines and Headings in the Sheet Options group of the Page Layout tab.

**FIGURE E-6:** Consolidating data from three worksheets

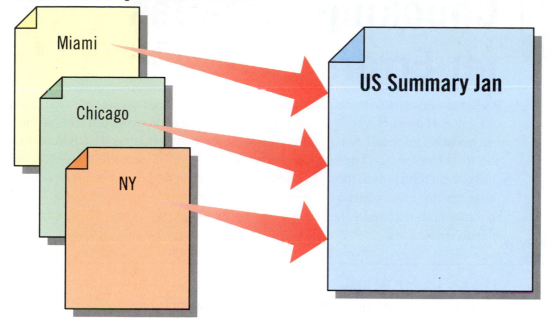

**FIGURE E-7:** Worksheet showing total Pacific Odyssey tours sold

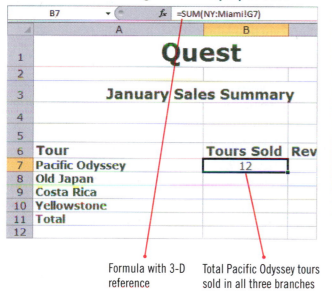

Formula with 3-D reference

Total Pacific Odyssey tours sold in all three branches

**FIGURE E-8:** US Summary Jan worksheet with updated totals

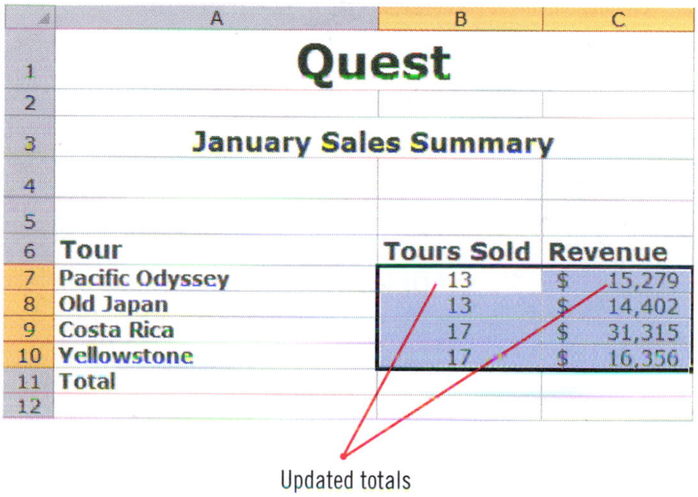

Updated totals

---

### Linking data between workbooks

Just as you can link data between cells in a worksheet and between sheets in a workbook, you can link workbooks so that changes made in referenced cells in one workbook are reflected in the consolidation sheet in the other workbook. To link a single cell between workbooks, open both workbooks, select the cell to receive the linked data, type the equal sign ( = ), select the cell in the other workbook containing the data to be linked, then press [Enter]. Excel automatically inserts the name of the referenced workbook in the cell reference. For example, if the linked data is contained in cell C7 of the Sales worksheet in the Product workbook, the cell entry reads =[Product.xlsx]Sales!$C$7. To perform calculations, enter formulas on the consolidation sheet using cells in the supporting sheets.

# Checking Formulas for Errors

When formulas result in errors, Excel displays an error value based on the error type. See Table E-1 for a description of the error types and error codes that might appear in worksheets. One way to check formulas in a worksheet for errors is to display the formulas on the worksheet rather than the formula results. You can also check for errors when entering formulas by using the IFERROR function. The IFERROR function simplifies the error-checking process for your worksheets. This function displays a message or value that you specify, rather than the one automatically generated by Excel, if there is an error in a formula.  Kate asks you to use formulas to compare the tour revenues for January. You will use the IFERROR function to help catch formula errors.

## STEPS

1. **Click cell B11, click the Formulas tab, click the AutoSum button in the Function Library group, then click the Enter button ✔ on the formula bar**

   The number of tours sold, 60, appears in cell B11.

2. **Drag the fill handle to copy the formula in cell B11 into cell C11, click the Auto Fill options list arrow ⊞▾, then click the Fill Without Formatting option button**

   The tour revenue total of $77,352 appears in cell C11. You decide to enter a formula to calculate the percentage of revenue the Pacific Odyssey tour represents by dividing the individual tour revenue figures by the total revenue figure. To help with error checking, you decide to enter the formula using the IFERROR function.

3. **Click cell D7, click the Logical button in the Function Library group, click IFERROR, with the insertion point in the Value text box, click cell C7, type /, click cell C11, press [Tab], in the Value_if_error text box, type ERROR, then click OK**

   The Pacific Odyssey tour revenue percentage of 19.75% appears in cell D7. You want to be sure that your error message will be displayed properly, so you decide to test it by intentionally creating an error. You copy and paste the formula—which has a relative address in the denominator, where an absolute address should be used.

   **TROUBLE**
   You will fix the ERROR codes in cells D8:D10 in the next step.

4. **Drag the fill handle to copy the formula in cell D7 into the range D8:D10**

   The ERROR value appears in cells D8:D10, as shown in Figure E-9. The errors are a result of the relative address for C11 in the denominator of the copied formula. Changing the relative address of C11 in the copied formula to an absolute address of $C$11 will correct the errors.

   **QUICK TIP**
   You can also check formulas for errors using the buttons in the Formula Auditing group on the Formulas tab.

5. **Double-click cell D7, select C11 in the formula, press [F4], then click ✔ on the formula bar**

   The formula now contains an absolute reference to cell C11.

6. **Copy the corrected formula in cell D7 into the range D8:D10**

   The tour revenue percentages now appear in all four cells, without error messages, as shown in Figure E-10. You want to check all of your worksheet formulas by displaying them on the worksheet.

   **QUICK TIP**
   You can also display worksheet formulas by holding [Ctrl] and pressing [`].

7. **Click the Show Formulas button in the Formula Auditing group**

   The formulas appear in columns B, C, and D. You want to display the formula results again. The Show Formulas button works as a toggle, turning the feature on and off with each click.

8. **Click the Show Formulas button in the Formula Auditing group**

   The formula results appear on the worksheet.

9. **Add your name to the center section of the footer, save the workbook, preview the worksheet, close the workbook, then submit the workbook to your instructor**

**FIGURE E-9:** Worksheet with error codes

FIGURE E-9: Worksheet with error codes

D7    fx =IFERROR(C7/C11,"ERROR")

**Quest**

**January Sales Summary**

| Tour | Tours Sold | Revenue | Percentage |
|------|-----------|---------|-----------|
| Pacific Odyssey | 13 | $ 15,279 | 19.75% |
| Old Japan | 13 | $ 14,402 | ERROR |
| Costa Rica | 17 | $ 31,315 | ERROR |
| Yellowstone | 17 | $ 16,356 | ERROR |
| Total | 60 | $ 77,352 | |

Relative reference to cell C11

Error values

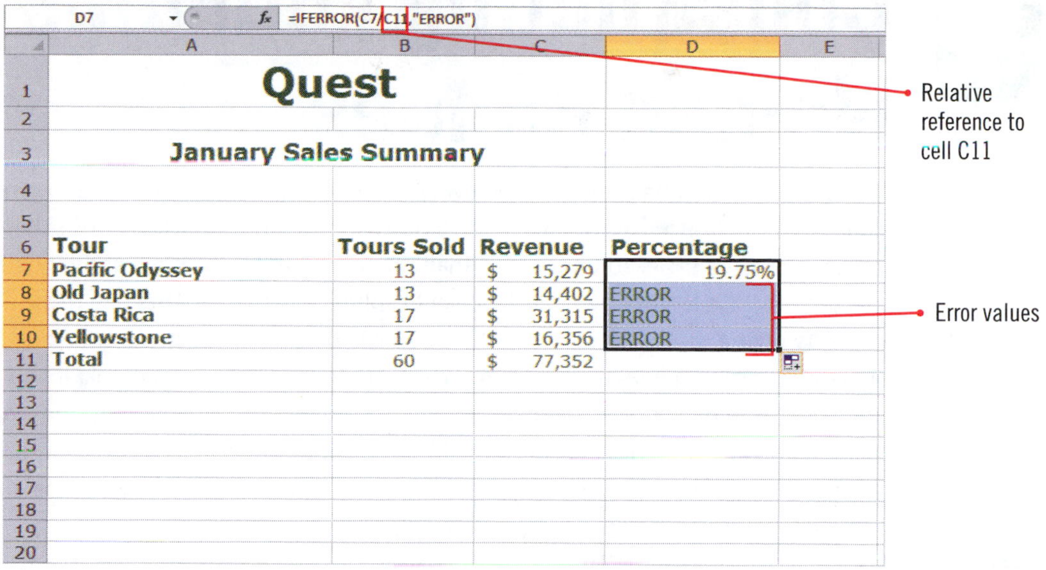

FIGURE E-10: Worksheet with tour percentages

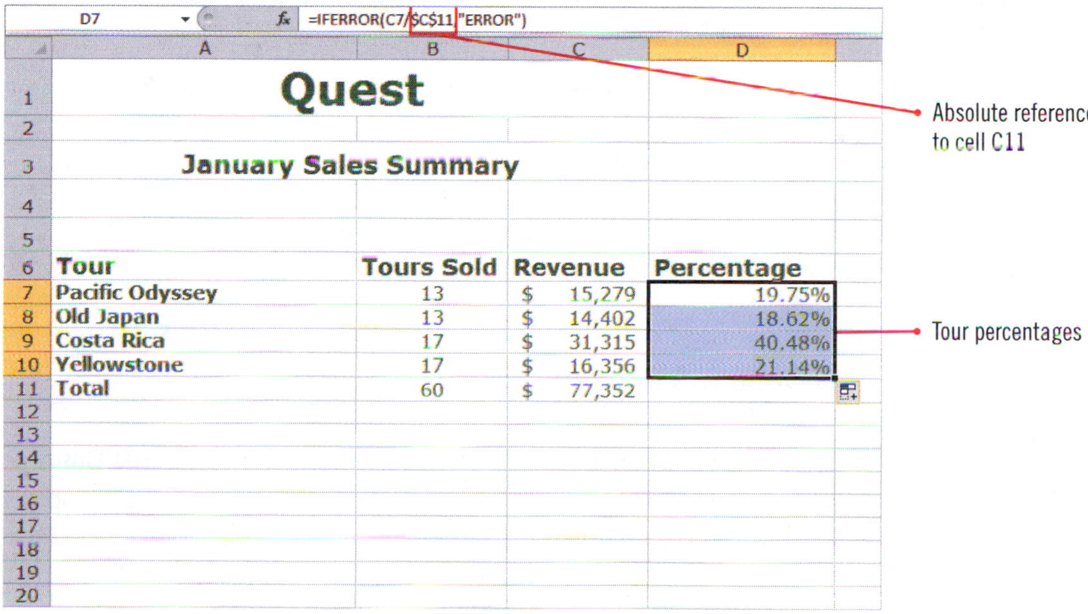

D7    fx =IFERROR(C7/$C$11,"ERROR")

**Quest**

**January Sales Summary**

| Tour | Tours Sold | Revenue | Percentage |
|------|-----------|---------|-----------|
| Pacific Odyssey | 13 | $ 15,279 | 19.75% |
| Old Japan | 13 | $ 14,402 | 18.62% |
| Costa Rica | 17 | $ 31,315 | 40.48% |
| Yellowstone | 17 | $ 16,356 | 21.14% |
| Total | 60 | $ 77,352 | |

Absolute reference to cell C11

Tour percentages

TABLE E-1: Understanding error values

| error value | cause of error | error value | cause of error |
|------|------|------|------|
| #DIV/0! | A number is divided by 0 | #NAME? | Formula contains text error |
| #NA | A value in a formula is not available | #NULL! | Invalid intersection of areas |
| #NUM! | Invalid use of a number in a formula | #REF! | Invalid cell reference |
| #VALUE! | Wrong type of formula argument or operand | ##### | Column is not wide enough to display data |

## Correcting circular references

A cell with a circular reference contains a formula that refers to its own cell location. If you accidentally enter a formula with a circular reference, a warning box opens, alerting you to the problem. Click OK to open a Help window explaining how to find the circular reference. In simple formulas, a circular reference is easy to spot. To correct it, edit the formula to remove any reference to the cell where the formula is located.

# Constructing Formulas Using Named Ranges

To make your worksheet easier to follow, you can assign names to cells and ranges. You can also use names in formulas to make them easier to build and to reduce formula errors. For example, the formula "revenue-cost" is easier to understand than the formula "A5-A8". Cell and range names can use upper-case or lowercase letters as well as digits, but cannot have spaces. After you name a cell or range, you can define its **scope**, or the worksheets where you will be able to use it. When defining a name's scope, you can limit its use to a worksheet or make it available to the entire workbook. If you move a named cell or range, its name moves with it, and if you add or remove rows or column to the worksheet the ranges are adjusted to their new position in the worksheet. When used in formulas, names become absolute cell references by default. Kate asks you to calculate the number of days before each tour departs. You will use range names to construct the formula.

## STEPS

**QUICK TIP**

You can create range names by selecting a cell or range, typing a name in the Name Box, then pressing [Enter]. By default, its scope will be the workbook.

1. **Open the file EX E-2.xlsx from the drive and folder where you store your Data Files, then save it as EX E-Tours**

2. **Click cell B4, click the Formulas tab if necessary, click the Define Name button in the Defined Names group**

    The New Name dialog box opens, as shown in Figure E-11. You can give a cell that contains a date a name that will make it easier to build formulas that perform date calculations.

**QUICK TIP**

Because names cannot contain spaces, underscores are often used between words to replace spaces.

3. **Type current_date in the Name text box, click the Scope list arrow, click April Tours, then click OK**

    The name assigned to cell B4, current_date, appears in the Name Box. Because its scope is the April Tours worksheet, the range name current_date will appear on the name list only on that worksheet. You can also name ranges that contain dates.

4. **Select the range B7:B13, click the Define Name button in the Defined Names group, enter tour_date in the Name text box, click the Scope list arrow, click April Tours, then click OK**

    Now you can use the named cell and named range in a formula. The formula =tour_date–current_date is easier to understand than =B7-$B$4.

**QUICK TIP**

Named cells and ranges can be used as a navigational tool in a worksheet by selecting the name in the Name Box. The named cell or range becomes active.

5. **Click cell C7, type =, click the Use in Formula button in the Defined Names group, click tour_date, type –, click the Use in Formula button, click current_date, then click the Enter button ✓ on the formula bar**

    The number of days before the Costa Rica tour departs, 10, appears in cell C7. You can use the same formula to calculate the number of days before the other tours depart.

6. **Drag the fill handle to copy the formula in cell C7 into the range C8:C13, then compare your formula results with those in Figure E-12**

7. **Save the workbook**

---

### Consolidating data using named ranges

You can consolidate data using named cells and ranges. For example, you might have entered team sales figures using the names team1, team2, and team3 on different sheets that you want to consolidate on one summary sheet. As you enter the summary formula you can click the Formulas tab, click the Use in Formula button in the Defined Names group, and select the cell or range name.

**FIGURE E-11: New Name dialog box**

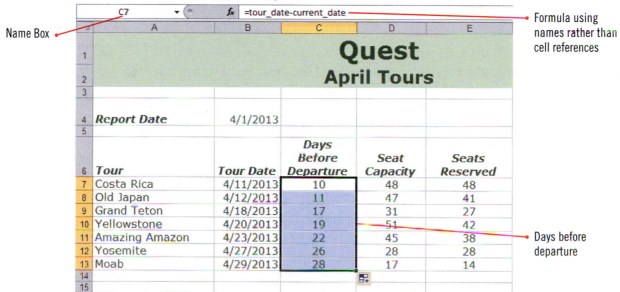

Enter cell or range name here

**FIGURE E-12: Worksheet with days before departure**

Name Box

Formula using names rather than cell references

Days before departure

| | A | B | C | D | E |
|---|---|---|---|---|---|
| 1 | | | **Quest** | | |
| 2 | | | **April Tours** | | |
| 3 | | | | | |
| 4 | **Report Date** | 4/1/2013 | | | |
| 5 | | | | | |
| 6 | **Tour** | **Tour Date** | **Days Before Departure** | **Seat Capacity** | **Seats Reserved** |
| 7 | Costa Rica | 4/11/2013 | 10 | 48 | 48 |
| 8 | Old Japan | 4/12/2013 | 11 | 47 | 41 |
| 9 | Grand Teton | 4/18/2013 | 17 | 31 | 27 |
| 10 | Yellowstone | 4/20/2013 | 19 | 51 | 42 |
| 11 | Amazing Amazon | 4/23/2013 | 22 | 45 | 38 |
| 12 | Yosemite | 4/27/2013 | 26 | 28 | 28 |
| 13 | Moab | 4/29/2013 | 28 | 17 | 14 |
| 14 | | | | | |
| 15 | | | | | |

C7  =tour_date-current_date

## Managing workbook names

You can use the Name Manager to create, delete, and edit names in a workbook. Click the Name Manager button in the Defined Names group on the Formulas tab to open the Name Manager dialog box, as shown in Figure E-13. Click the New button to create a new named cell or range, click Edit to change a highlighted cell name, and click Delete to remove a highlighted name. Click Filter to see options for displaying specific criteria for displaying names.

**FIGURE E-13: Name Manager dialog box**

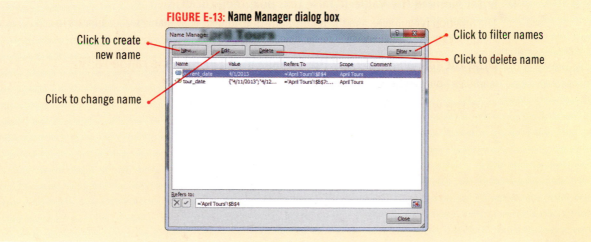

Click to create new name

Click to filter names

Click to delete name

Click to change name

# Building a Logical Formula with the IF Function

You can build a logical formula using an IF function. A **logical formula** makes calculations based on criteria that you create, called **stated conditions**. For example, you can build a formula to calculate bonuses based on a person's performance rating. If a person is rated a 5 (the stated condition) on a scale of 1 to 5, with 5 being the highest rating, he or she receives an additional 10% of his or her salary as a bonus; otherwise, there is no bonus. A condition that can be answered with a true or false response is called a **logical test**. The IF function has three parts, separated by commas: a condition or logical test, an action to take if the logical test or condition is true, and an action to take if the logical test or condition is false. Another way of expressing this is: IF(test_cond,do_this,else_this). Translated into an Excel IF function, the formula to calculate bonuses might look like this: IF(Rating=5,Salary*0.10,0). In other words, if the rating equals 5, multiply the salary by 0.10 (the decimal equivalent of 10%), then place the result in the selected cell; if the rating does not equal 5, place a 0 in the cell. When entering the logical test portion of an IF statement, you typically use some combination of the comparison operators listed in Table E-2.  Kate asks you to use an IF function to calculate the number of seats available for each tour in April.

## STEPS

1. **Click cell F7, on the Formulas tab, click the Logical button in the Function Library group, then click IF**

   The Function Arguments dialog box opens. You want the function to calculate the seats available as follows: If the seat capacity is greater than the number of seats reserved, calculate the number of seats that are available (capacity minus number reserved), and place the result in cell F7; otherwise, place the text "None" in the cell.

2. **With the insertion point in the Logical_test text box, click cell D7, type >, click cell E7, then press [Tab]**

   The symbol ( > ) represents "greater than." So far, the formula reads "If the seating capacity is greater than the number of reserved seats,". The next part of the function tells Excel the action to take if the capacity exceeds the reserved number of seats.

3. **With the insertion point in the Value_if_true text box, click cell D7, type –, click cell E7, then press [Tab]**

   This part of the formula tells the program what you want it to do if the logical test is true. Continuing the translation of the formula, this part means "Subtract the number of reserved seats from the seat capacity." The last part of the formula tells Excel the action to take if the logical test is false (that is, if the seat capacity does not exceed the number of reserved seats).

4. **Enter None in the Value_if_false text box, then click OK**

   The function is complete, and the result, None (the number of available seats), appears in cell F7, as shown in Figure E-14.

5. **Drag the fill handle to copy the formula in cell F7 into the range F8:F13**

   Compare your results with Figure E-15.

6. **Save the workbook**

**FIGURE E-14:** Worksheet with IF function

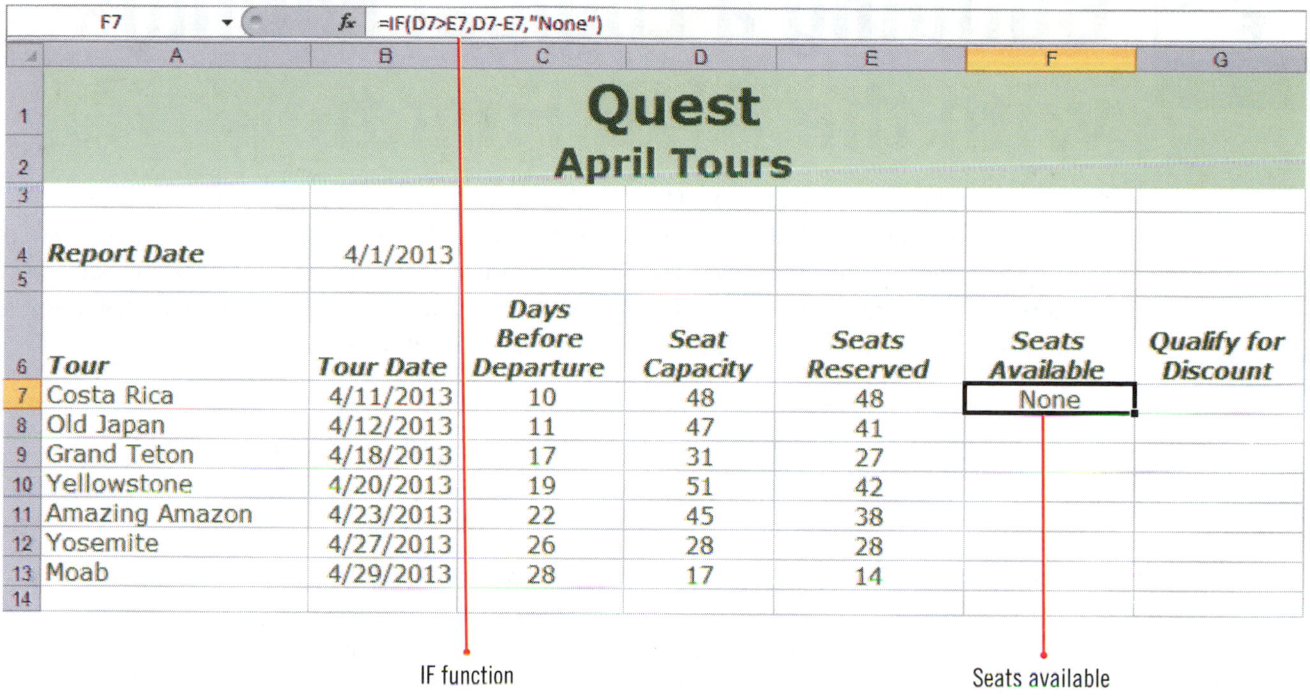

| | F7 | ▼ | $f_x$ | =IF(D7>E7,D7-E7,"None") | | |

| | A | B | C | D | E | F | G |
|---|---|---|---|---|---|---|---|
| 1 | | | | **Quest** | | | |
| 2 | | | | **April Tours** | | | |
| 3 | | | | | | | |
| 4 | **Report Date** | 4/1/2013 | | | | | |
| 5 | | | | | | | |
| 6 | **Tour** | **Tour Date** | **Days Before Departure** | **Seat Capacity** | **Seats Reserved** | **Seats Available** | **Qualify for Discount** |
| 7 | Costa Rica | 4/11/2013 | 10 | 48 | 48 | None | |
| 8 | Old Japan | 4/12/2013 | 11 | 47 | 41 | | |
| 9 | Grand Teton | 4/18/2013 | 17 | 31 | 27 | | |
| 10 | Yellowstone | 4/20/2013 | 19 | 51 | 42 | | |
| 11 | Amazing Amazon | 4/23/2013 | 22 | 45 | 38 | | |
| 12 | Yosemite | 4/27/2013 | 26 | 28 | 28 | | |
| 13 | Moab | 4/29/2013 | 28 | 17 | 14 | | |
| 14 | | | | | | | |

IF function      Seats available

Excel 2010

**FIGURE E-15:** Worksheet showing seats available

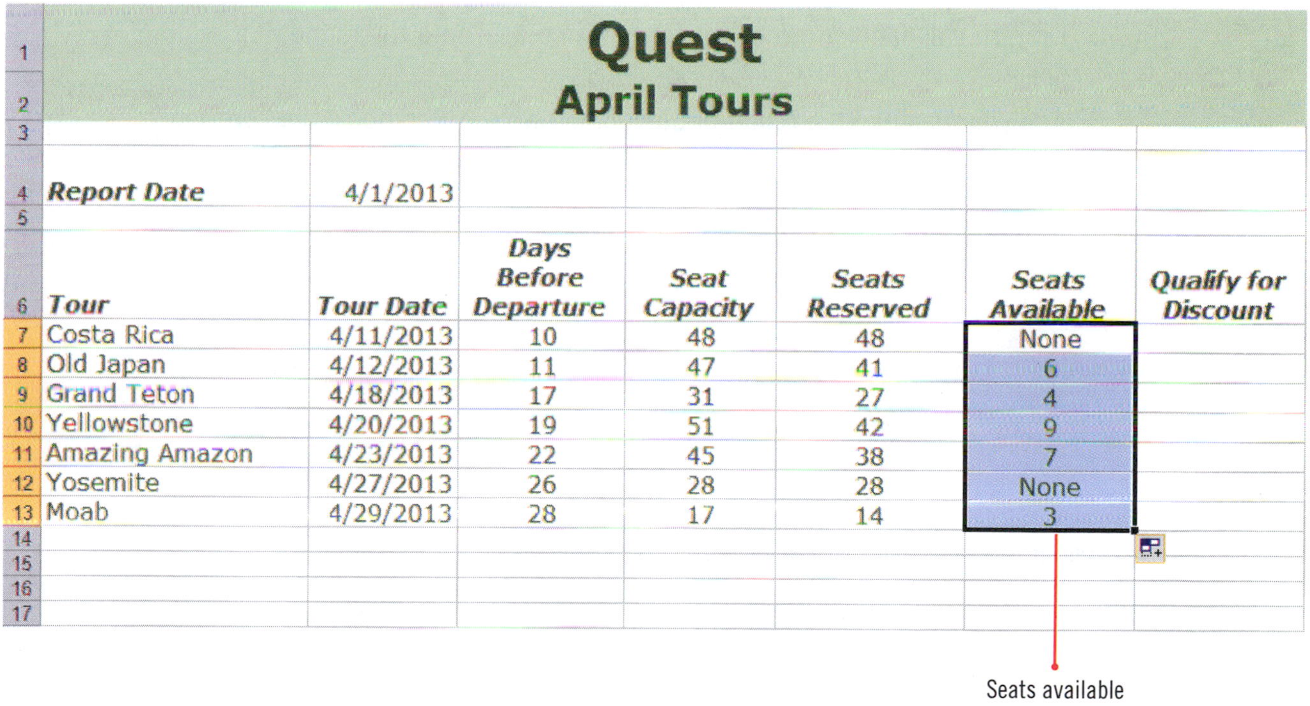

| | A | B | C | D | E | F | G |
|---|---|---|---|---|---|---|---|
| 1 | | | | **Quest** | | | |
| 2 | | | | **April Tours** | | | |
| 3 | | | | | | | |
| 4 | **Report Date** | 4/1/2013 | | | | | |
| 5 | | | | | | | |
| 6 | **Tour** | **Tour Date** | **Days Before Departure** | **Seat Capacity** | **Seats Reserved** | **Seats Available** | **Qualify for Discount** |
| 7 | Costa Rica | 4/11/2013 | 10 | 48 | 48 | None | |
| 8 | Old Japan | 4/12/2013 | 11 | 47 | 41 | 6 | |
| 9 | Grand Teton | 4/18/2013 | 17 | 31 | 27 | 4 | |
| 10 | Yellowstone | 4/20/2013 | 19 | 51 | 42 | 9 | |
| 11 | Amazing Amazon | 4/23/2013 | 22 | 45 | 38 | 7 | |
| 12 | Yosemite | 4/27/2013 | 26 | 28 | 28 | None | |
| 13 | Moab | 4/29/2013 | 28 | 17 | 14 | 3 | |
| 14 | | | | | | | |
| 15 | | | | | | | |
| 16 | | | | | | | |
| 17 | | | | | | | |

Seats available

**TABLE E-2:** Comparison operators

| operator | meaning | operator | meaning |
|---|---|---|---|
| < | Less than | <= | Less than or equal to |
| > | Greater than | >= | Greater than or equal to |
| = | Equal to | <> | Not equal to |

# Building a Logical Formula with the AND Function

You can also build a logical function using the AND function. The AND function evaluates all of its arguments and **returns**, or displays, TRUE if every logical test in the formula is true. The AND function returns a value of FALSE if one or more of its logical tests is false. The AND function arguments can include text, numbers, or cell references.  Kate wants you to analyze the tour data to find tours that qualify for discounting. You will use the AND function to check for tours with seats available and that depart within 21 days.

## STEPS

1. **Click cell G7, click the Logical button in the Function Library group, then click AND**

   The Function Arguments dialog box opens. You want the function to evaluate the discount qualification as follows: There must be seats available, and the tour must depart within 21 days.

   > **TROUBLE**
   > If you get a formula error, check to be sure that you typed the quotation marks around None.

2. **With the insertion point in the Logical1 text box, click cell F7, type < >, type "None", then press [Tab]**

   The symbol ( <> ) represents "not equal to." So far, the formula reads "If the number of seats available is not equal to None,"—in other words, if it is an integer. The next logical test checks the number of days before the tour departs.

3. **With the insertion point in the Logical2 text box, click cell C7, type <21, then click OK**

   The function is complete, and the result, FALSE, appears in cell G7, as shown in Figure E-16.

4. **Drag the fill handle to copy the formula in cell G7 into the range G8:G13**

   Compare your results with Figure E-17.

5. **Add your name to the center of the footer, save the workbook, then preview the worksheet**

**TABLE E-3:** Examples of AND, OR, and NOT functions with cell values A1=10 and B1=20

| function | formula | result |
|---|---|---|
| AND | =AND(A1>5,B1>25) | FALSE |
| OR | =OR(A1>5,B1>25) | TRUE |
| NOT | =NOT(A1=0) | TRUE |

### Using the OR and NOT logical functions

The OR logical function has the same syntax as the AND function, but rather than returning TRUE if every argument is true, the OR function will return TRUE if any of its arguments are true. It will only return FALSE if all of its arguments are false. The NOT logical function reverses the value of its argument. For example NOT(TRUE) reverses its argument of TRUE and returns FALSE. This can be used in a worksheet to ensure that a cell is not equal to a particular value. See Table E-3 for examples of the AND, OR, and NOT functions.

Excel 2010

**FIGURE E-16:** Worksheet with AND function

| | A | B | C | D | E | F | G |
|---|---|---|---|---|---|---|---|
| | G7 | | fx | =AND(F7<>"None",C7<21) | | | |
| 5 | | | | | | | |
| 6 | Tour | Tour Date | Days Before Departure | Seat Capacity | Seats Reserved | Seats Available | Qualify for Discount |
| 7 | Costa Rica | 4/11/2013 | 10 | 48 | 48 | None | FALSE |
| 8 | Old Japan | 4/12/2013 | 11 | 47 | 41 | 6 | |
| 9 | Grand Teton | 4/18/2013 | 17 | 31 | 27 | 4 | |
| 10 | Yellowstone | 4/20/2013 | 19 | 51 | 42 | 9 | |
| 11 | Amazing Amazon | 4/23/2013 | 22 | 45 | 38 | 7 | |
| 12 | Yosemite | 4/27/2013 | 26 | 28 | 28 | None | |
| 13 | Moab | 4/29/2013 | 28 | 17 | 14 | 3 | |
| 14 | | | | | | | |
| 15 | | | | | | | |
| 16 | | | | | | | |
| 17 | | | | | | | |
| 18 | | | | | | | |
| 19 | | | | | | | |
| 20 | | | | | | | |
| 21 | | | | | | | |
| 22 | | | | | | | |

AND function

Result of AND function

**FIGURE E-17:** Worksheet with discount status evaluated

| | A | B | C | D | E | F | |
|---|---|---|---|---|---|---|---|
| | G7 | | fx | =AND(F7<>"None",C7<21) | | | Formula Bar |
| 5 | | | | | | | |
| 6 | Tour | Tour Date | Days Before Departure | Seat Capacity | Seats Reserved | Seats Available | Qualify for Discount |
| 7 | Costa Rica | 4/11/2013 | 10 | 48 | 48 | None | FALSE |
| 8 | Old Japan | 4/12/2013 | 11 | 47 | 41 | 6 | TRUE |
| 9 | Grand Teton | 4/18/2013 | 17 | 31 | 27 | 4 | TRUE |
| 10 | Yellowstone | 4/20/2013 | 19 | 51 | 42 | 9 | TRUE |
| 11 | Amazing Amazon | 4/23/2013 | 22 | 45 | 38 | 7 | FALSE |
| 12 | Yosemite | 4/27/2013 | 26 | 28 | 28 | None | FALSE |
| 13 | Moab | 4/29/2013 | 28 | 17 | 14 | 3 | FALSE |
| 14 | | | | | | | |
| 15 | | | | | | | |
| 16 | | | | | | | |
| 17 | | | | | | | |
| 18 | | | | | | | |
| 19 | | | | | | | |
| 20 | | | | | | | |
| 21 | | | | | | | |
| 22 | | | | | | | |

## Inserting an equation into a worksheet

If your worksheet contains formulas, you might want to place an equation on the worksheet to document how you arrived at your results. First create a text box to hold the equation: Click the Insert tab, click the Text box button in the Text group, then click on the worksheet location where you want the equation to appear. To place the equation in the text box, click the Insert tab again, then click the Equation button in the Symbols group. When you see "Type equation here," you can build an equation by clicking the mathematical symbols in the Structures group of the Equation Tools Design tab. For example, if you wanted to enter a fraction of 2/7, you click the Fraction button, choose the first option, click the top box, enter 2, press [Tab], enter 7, then click outside of the fraction. To insert the symbol $x^2$ into a text box, click the Script list arrow in the Structures group of the Equation Tools Design tab, click the first option, click in the lower-left box and enter "x", press [Tab], enter 2 in the upper-right box, then click to the right of the boxes to exit the symbol. You can also add built-in equations to a text box: On the Equation Tools Design tab, click the Equation list arrow in the Tools group, then select the equation. Built-in equations include the equation for the area of a circle, the binomial theorem, Pythagorean theorem, and the quadratic equation.

# Calculating Payments with the PMT Function

PMT is a financial function that calculates the periodic payment amount for money borrowed. For example, if you want to borrow money to buy a car, and you know the principal amount, interest rate, and loan term, the PMT function can calculate your monthly payment. Say you want to borrow $20,000 at 6.5% interest and pay the loan off in 5 years. The Excel PMT function can tell you that your monthly payment will be $391.32. The main parts of the PMT function are PMT(rate, nper, pv). See Figure E-18 for an illustration of a PMT function that calculates the monthly payment in the car loan example.  For several months, QST's United States region has been discussing opening a new branch in San Francisco. Kate has obtained quotes from three different lenders on borrowing $359,000 to begin the expansion. She obtained loan quotes from a commercial bank, a venture capitalist, and an investment banker. She wants you to summarize the information using the Excel PMT function.

**STEPS**

1. Click the **Loan sheet tab**, click cell **F5**, click the **Formulas tab**, click the **Financial button** in the Function Library group, scroll down the list of functions, then click **PMT**

2. With the insertion point in the Rate text box, click cell **D5** on the worksheet, type **/12**, then press **[Tab]**

   You must divide the annual interest by 12 because you are calculating monthly, not annual, payments. You need to be consistent about the units you use for rate and nper. If you express nper as the number of monthly payments, then you must express the interest rate as a monthly rate.

**QUICK TIP**

The Fv and Type arguments are optional: The argument Fv is the future value, or the total amount you want to obtain after all payments. If you omit it, Excel assumes you want to pay off the loan completely, so the default Fv is 0. The Type argument indicates when the payments are made; 0 is the end of the period, and 1 is the beginning of the period. The default is the end of the period.

3. With the insertion point in the Nper text box, click cell **E5**; click the **Pv text box**, click cell **B5**, then click **OK**

   The payment of ($7,460.96) in cell F5 appears in red, indicating that it is a negative amount. Excel displays the result of a PMT function as a negative value to reflect the negative cash flow the loan represents to the borrower. To show the monthly payment as a positive number, you can place a minus sign in front of the Pv cell reference in the function.

4. Double-click cell **F5** and edit it so it reads **=PMT(D5/12,E5,-B5)**, then click the **Enter button** on the formula bar

   A positive value of $7,460.96 now appears in cell F5, as shown in Figure E-19. You can use the same formula to generate the monthly payments for the other loans.

5. With cell **F5** selected, drag the fill handle to fill the range **F6:F7**

   A monthly payment of $11,457.92 for the venture capitalist loan appears in cell F6. A monthly payment of $16,425.54 for the investment banker loan appears in cell F7. The loans with shorter terms have much higher monthly payments. But you will not know the entire financial picture until you calculate the total payments and total interest for each lender.

**QUICK TIP**

You can use the keyboard shortcut of [Ctrl][Enter] rather than clicking the Enter button. This enters the formula and leaves the cell selected.

6. Click cell **G5**, type **=**, click cell **E5**, type **\***, click cell **F5**, then press **[Tab]**, in cell **H5**, type **=**, click cell **G5**, type **–**, click cell **B5**, then click ✓

7. Copy the formulas in cells **G5:H5** into the range **G6:H7**, then click cell **A1**

   You can experiment with different interest rates, loan amounts, or terms for any one of the lenders; the PMT function generates a new set of values automatically.

8. Add your name to the center section of the footer, save the workbook, preview the worksheet, then submit the workbook to your instructor

   Your worksheet appears as shown in Figure E-20.

9. Close the workbook and exit Excel

**FIGURE E-18:** Example of PMT function for car loan

$$PMT(0.065/12, 60, 20000) = \$391.32$$

Interest rate per month (rate)    Number of monthly payments    Present value of loan amount (pv)    Monthly payment calculated

**FIGURE E-19:** PMT function calculating monthly loan payment

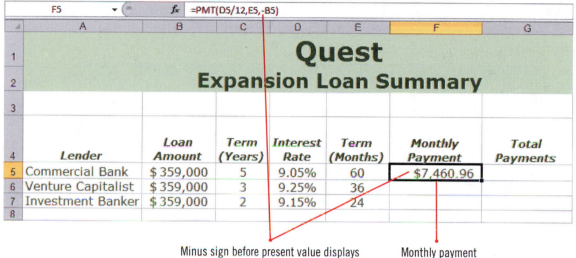

| | Lender | Loan Amount | Term (Years) | Interest Rate | Term (Months) | Monthly Payment | Total Payments |
|---|---|---|---|---|---|---|---|
| 5 | Commercial Bank | $ 359,000 | 5 | 9.05% | 60 | $7,460.96 | |
| 6 | Venture Capitalist | $ 359,000 | 3 | 9.25% | 36 | | |
| 7 | Investment Banker | $ 359,000 | 2 | 9.15% | 24 | | |

Formula bar: =PMT(D5/12,E5,-B5)

Minus sign before present value displays payment as a positive amount

Monthly payment calculated

**FIGURE E-20:** Completed worksheet

## Quest
### Expansion Loan Summary

| Lender | Loan Amount | Term (Years) | Interest Rate | Term (Months) | Monthly Payment | Total Payments | Total Interest |
|---|---|---|---|---|---|---|---|
| Commercial Bank | $ 359,000 | 5 | 9.05% | 60 | $7,460.96 | $ 447,657.85 | $ 88,657.85 |
| Venture Capitalist | $ 359,000 | 3 | 9.25% | 36 | $11,457.92 | $ 412,485.14 | $ 53,485.14 |
| Investment Banker | $ 359,000 | 2 | 9.15% | 24 | $16,425.54 | $ 394,212.98 | $ 35,212.98 |

Copied formula calculates total payments and interest for remaining two loan options

### Calculating future value with the FV function

You can use the FV (Future Value) function to determine the amount of money a given monthly investment will amount to, at a given interest rate, after a given number of payment periods. The syntax is similar to that of the PMT function: FV(rate,nper,pmt,pv,type). The rate is the interest paid by the financial institution, the nper is the number of periods, and the pmt is the amount that you deposit. For example, suppose you want to invest $1,000 every month for the next 12 months into an account that pays 2% a year, and you want to know how much you will have at the end of 12 months (that is, its future value). You enter the function FV(.02/12,12,-1000), and Excel returns the value $12,110.61 as the future value of your investment. As with the PMT function, the units for the rate and nper must be consistent.

Excel 2010

# Practice

**SAM** For current SAM information, including versions and content details, visit SAM Central (http://www.cengage.com/samcentral). If you have a SAM user profile, you may have access to hands-on instruction, practice, and assessment of the skills covered in this unit. Since various versions of SAM are supported throughout the life of this text, check with your instructor for the correct instructions and URL/Web site for accessing assignments.

## Concepts Review

**FIGURE E-21**

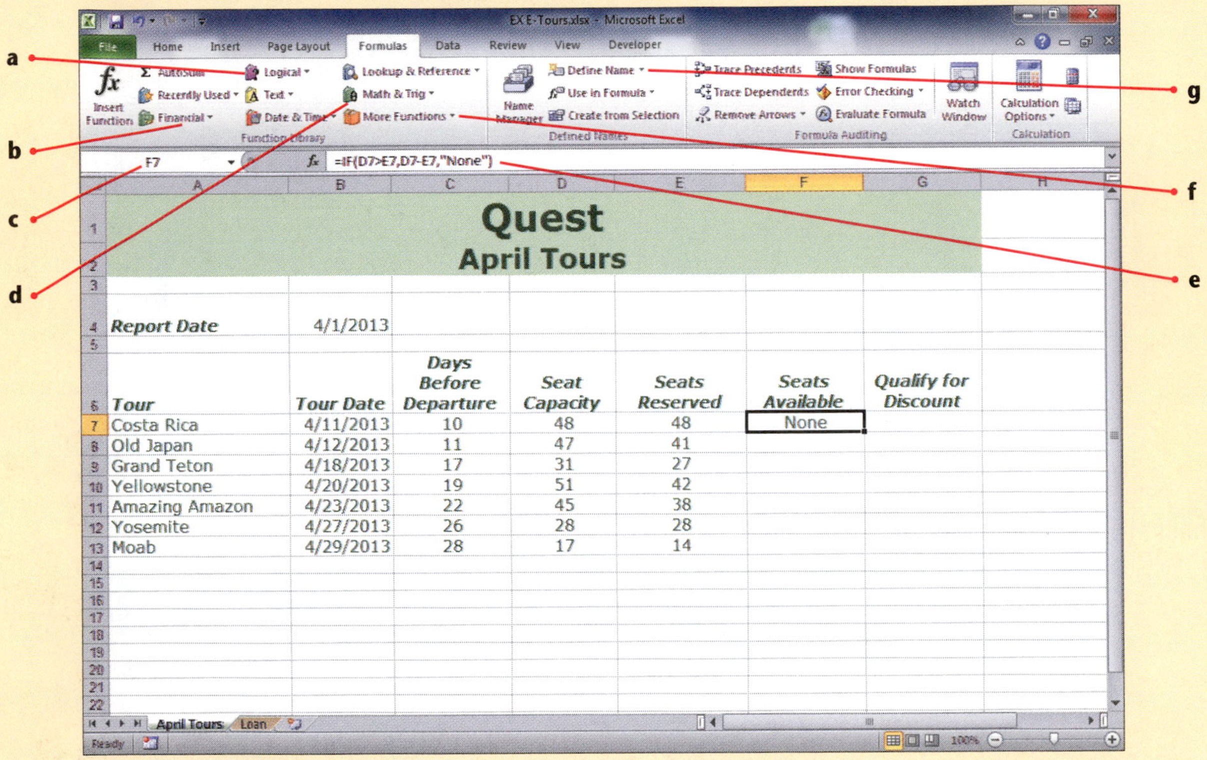

1. **Which element do you click to name a cell or range?**
2. **Which element do you click to add a statistical function to a worksheet?**
3. **Which element points to a logical formula?**
4. **Which element points to the area where the name of a selected cell or range appears?**
5. **Which element do you click to insert a PMT function into a worksheet?**
6. **Which element do you click to add a SUMIF function to a worksheet?**
7. **Which element do you click to add an IF function to a worksheet?**

## Match each term with the statement that best describes it.

8. **FV**
9. **PV**
10. **SUMIF**
11. **PROPER**
12. **test_cond**

a. Function used to change the first letter of a string to uppercase
b. Function used to determine the future amount of an investment
c. Part of the PMT function that represents the loan amount
d. Part of the IF function that the conditions are stated in
e. Function used to conditionally total cells

**Select the best answer from the list of choices.**

**13. When you enter the rate and nper arguments in a PMT function, you must:**

a. Multiply both units by 12.

b. Be consistent in the units used.

c. Divide both values by 12.

d. Always use annual units.

**14. To express conditions such as less than or equal to, you can use a:**

a. Comparison operator.

b. Text formula.

c. PMT function.

d. Statistical function.

# Skills Review

## 1. Format data using text functions.

a. Start Excel, open the file EX E-3.xlsx from the drive and folder where you store your Data Files, then save it as **EX E-Reviews**.

b. On the Managers worksheet, select the range A2:A9 and, using the Text to Columns button on the Data tab, separate the names into two text columns. (*Hint*: The delimiter is a space.)

c. In cell D2, enter the text formula to convert the first letter of the department in cell C2 to uppercase, then copy the formula in cell D2 into the range D3:D9.

d. In cell E2, enter the text formula to convert all letters of the department in cell C2 to uppercase, then copy the formula in cell E2 into the range E3:E9.

e. In cell F2, use the text formula to convert all letters of the department in cell C2 to lowercase, then copy the formula in cell F2 into the range F3:F9.

f. In cell G2, use the text formula to substitute "Human Resources" for "hr" if that text exists in cell F2. (*Hint*: In the Function Arguments dialog box, Text is F2, Old_text is "hr", and New_text is "Human Resources".) Copy the formula in cell G2 into the range G3:G9 to change the other cells containing "hr" to "Human Resources". (The marketing and sales entries will not change because the formula searches for the text "hr".)

g. Save your work, then enter your name in the worksheet footer. Compare your screen to Figure E-22.

h. Display the formulas in the worksheet.

i. Redisplay the formula results.

**FIGURE E-22**

| | A | B | C | D | E | F | G |
|---|---|---|---|---|---|---|---|
| 1 | Name | | Department | PROPER | UPPER | LOWER | SUBSTITUTE |
| 2 | Kathy | Kirk | MarKEting | Marketing | MARKETING | marketing | marketing |
| 3 | Sallie | Story | hR | Hr | HR | hr | Human Resources |
| 4 | Kim | Craven | MarKeting | Marketing | MARKETING | marketing | marketing |
| 5 | Albert | Meng | hR | Hr | HR | hr | Human Resources |
| 6 | Roberto | Delgado | saLEs | Sales | SALES | sales | sales |
| 7 | Harry | Desus | saleS | Sales | SALES | sales | sales |
| 8 | Mary | Abbott | hR | Hr | HR | hr | Human Resources |
| 9 | Jody | Williams | MarKeTing | Marketing | MARKETING | marketing | marketing |

## 2. Sum a data range based on conditions.

a. Make the HR sheet active.

b. In cell B20, use the COUNTIF function to count the number of employees with a rating of 5.

c. In cell B21, use the AVERAGEIF function to average the salaries of those with a rating of 5.

d. In cell B22, enter the SUMIF function that totals the salaries of employees with a rating of 5.

e. Format cells B21 and B22 with the Number format using commas and no decimals. Save your work, then compare your formula results to Figure E-23.

**FIGURE E-23**

| 17 | | |
|---|---|---|
| 18 | Department Statistics | |
| 19 | Top Rating | |
| 20 | Number | 5 |
| 21 | Average Salary | 31,180 |
| 22 | Total Salary | 155,900 |
| 23 | | |

## 3. Consolidate data using a formula.

a. Make the Summary sheet active.

b. In cell B4, use the AutoSum function to total cell F15 on the HR and Accounting sheets.

c. Format cell B4 with the Accounting Number format if necessary.

d. Enter your name in the worksheet footer, then save your work. Compare your screen to Figure E-24.

e. Display the formula in the worksheet, then redisplay the formula results in the worksheet.

**FIGURE E-24**

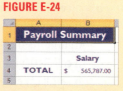

| | A | B |
|---|---|---|
| 1 | Payroll Summary | |
| 2 | | |
| 3 | | Salary |
| 4 | TOTAL | $ 565,787.00 |
| 5 | | |

## 4. Check formulas for errors.

a. Make the HR sheet active.

b. In cell I6, use the IFERROR function to display "ERROR" in the event that the formula F6/F15 results in a formula error. (*Note*: This formula will generate an intentional error after the next step, which you will correct in a moment.)

## Skills Review (continued)

**c.** Copy the formula in cell I6 into the range I7:I14.

**d.** Correct the formula in cell I6 by making the denominator, F15, an absolute address.

**e.** Copy the new formula in cell I6 into the range I7:I14, then save your work.

**5. Construct formulas using named ranges.**

**a.** On the HR sheet, name the range C6:C14 **review_date**, and limit the scope of the name to the HR worksheet.

**b.** In cell E6, enter the formula **=review_date+183**, using the Use in Formula button to enter the cell name.

**c.** Copy the formula in cell E6 into the range E7:E14.

**d.** Use the Name Manager to add a comment of **Date of last review** to the review_date name. (*Hint*: In the Name Manager dialog box, click the review_date name, then click Edit to enter the comment.) Save your work.

**6. Build a logical formula with the IF function.**

**a.** In cell G6, use the Function Arguments dialog box to enter the formula **=IF(D6=5,F6*0.05,0)**.

**b.** Copy the formula in cell G6 into the range G7:G14.

**c.** In cell G15, use AutoSum to total the range G6:G14.

**d.** Format the range G6:G15 with the Currency number format, using the $ symbol and no decimal places.

**e.** Save your work.

**7. Build a logical formula with the AND function.**

**a.** In cell H6, use the Function Arguments dialog box to enter the formula **=AND(G6>0,B6>5)**.

**b.** Copy the formula in cell H6 into the range H7:H14.

**c.** Enter your name in the worksheet footer, save your work, then compare your worksheet to Figure E-25.

**d.** Make the Accounting sheet active.

**e.** In cell H6, indicate if the employee needs more development hours to reach the minimum of 5. Use the Function Arguments dialog box for the NOT function to enter **B6>5** in the Logical text box. Copy the formula in cell H6 into the range H7:H14.

**f.** In cell I6, indicate if the employee needs to enroll in a quality class, as indicated by a rating less than 5 or having fewer than 5 development hours. Use the Function Arguments dialog box for the OR function to enter **D6<5** in the Logical1 text box and **B6<5** in the Logical2 text box. Copy the formula in cell I6 into the range I7:I14.

**g.** Enter your name in the worksheet footer, save your work, then compare your screen to Figure E-26.

**8. Calculate payments with the PMT function.**

**a.** Make the Loan sheet active.

**b.** In cell B9, determine the monthly payment using the loan information shown: Use the Function Arguments dialog box to enter the formula **=PMT(B5/12,B6,-B4)**.

**c.** In cell B10, enter a formula that multiplies the number of payments by the monthly payment.

**d.** In cell B11, enter the formula that subtracts the loan amount from the total payment amount, then compare your screen to Figure E-27.

**FIGURE E-25**

| Last Name | Professional Development Hours | Review Date | Rating | Next Review | Salary | Bonus | Pay Bonus | Percentage of Total |
|---|---|---|---|---|---|---|---|---|
| Human Resources Department | | | | | | | | |
| Merit Pay | | | | | | | | |
| Brack | 6 | 1/5/2013 | 2 | 7/7/2013 | $ 19,840.00 | $0 | FALSE | 7.21% |
| Casey | 8 | 4/1/2013 | 5 | 10/1/2013 | $ 26,700.00 | $1,335 | TRUE | 9.71% |
| Donnely | 1 | 7/1/2013 | 4 | 12/31/2013 | $ 33,200.00 | $0 | FALSE | 12.07% |
| Hemsley | 3 | 4/1/2013 | 5 | 10/1/2013 | $ 25,500.00 | $1,275 | FALSE | 9.27% |
| Kirn | 10 | 3/1/2013 | 5 | 8/31/2013 | $ 37,500.00 | $1,875 | TRUE | 13.63% |
| Maaley | 7 | 5/1/2013 | 5 | 10/31/2013 | $ 36,500.00 | $1,825 | TRUE | 13.27% |
| Merry | 10 | 6/1/2013 | 4 | 12/1/2013 | $ 37,500.00 | $0 | FALSE | 13.63% |
| Smith | 7 | 1/1/2013 | 3 | 7/3/2013 | $ 28,600.00 | $0 | FALSE | 10.40% |
| Storey | 3 | 7/1/2013 | 5 | 12/31/2013 | $ 29,700.00 | $1,485 | FALSE | 10.80% |
| Totals | | | | | $ 275,040.00 | $7,795 | | |

**FIGURE E-26**

| Last Name | Professional Development Hours | Review Date | Rating | Next Review | Salary | Bonus | Hours Required | Enroll in Quality Class |
|---|---|---|---|---|---|---|---|---|
| Accounting Department | | | | | | | | |
| Merit Pay | | | | | | | | |
| Allenson | 8 | 3/10/2013 | 2 | 9/9/2013 | $ 21,647.00 | $0.00 | FALSE | TRUE |
| Greeley | 2 | 5/1/2013 | 5 | 10/31/2013 | $ 28,600.00 | $1,430.00 | TRUE | TRUE |
| LaForte | 6 | 8/1/2013 | 3 | 1/31/2014 | $ 33,200.00 | $0.00 | FALSE | TRUE |
| Henley | 7 | 6/1/2013 | 4 | 12/1/2013 | $ 35,500.00 | $0.00 | FALSE | TRUE |
| Gosselin | 9 | 3/8/2013 | 5 | 9/7/2013 | $ 39,500.00 | $1,975.00 | FALSE | FALSE |
| Ramerez | 6 | 5/1/2013 | 5 | 10/31/2013 | $ 36,500.00 | $1,825.00 | FALSE | FALSE |
| Marton | 10 | 6/1/2013 | 4 | 12/1/2013 | $ 36,500.00 | $0.00 | FALSE | TRUE |
| Suille | 6 | 1/1/2013 | 5 | 7/3/2013 | $ 29,600.00 | $1,480.00 | FALSE | FALSE |
| Zen | 6 | 9/15/2013 | 1 | 3/17/2014 | $ 29,700.00 | $0.00 | FALSE | TRUE |
| Totals | | | | | $ 290,747.00 | $6,710.00 | | |

**FIGURE E-27**

| Human Resources | |
|---|---|
| Loan Quote for Inforr | |
| Loan Amount | $ 169,000.00 |
| Interest Rate | 8.25% |
| Term in Months | 36 |
| Monthly Payment: | $5,315.36 |
| Total Payments: | $ 191,352.89 |
| Total Interest: | $ 22,352.89 |

# Skills Review (continued)

**e.** Enter your name in the worksheet footer, save the workbook, then submit your workbook to your instructor.

**f.** Close the workbook, then exit Excel.

## Independent Challenge 1

As the accounting manager of World Travel, a travel insurance company, you are reviewing the accounts payable information for your advertising accounts and prioritizing the overdue invoices for your collections service. You will analyze the invoices and use logical functions to emphasize priority accounts.

**a.** Start Excel, open the file EX E-4.xlsx from the drive and folder where you store your Data Files, then save it as **EX E-Accounts**.

**b.** Name the range B7:B13 **invoice_date**, and give the name a scope of the accounts payable worksheet.

**c.** Name the cell B4 **current_date**, and give the name a scope of the accounts payable worksheet.

**d.** Enter a formula using the named range invoice_date in cell E7 that calculates the invoice due date by adding 30 to the invoice date.

**e.** Copy the formula in cell E7 to the range E8:E13.

**f.** In cell F7, enter a formula using the named range invoice_date and the named cell current_date that calculates the invoice age by subtracting the invoice date from the current date.

**g.** Copy the formula in cell F7 to the range F8:F13.

**h.** In cell G7, enter an IF function that calculates the number of days an invoice is overdue, assuming that an invoice must be paid in 30 days. (*Hint*: The Logical_test should check to see if the age of the invoice is greater than 30, the Value_if_true should calculate the current date minus the invoice due date, and the Value_if_false should be 0.) Copy the IF function into the range G8:G13.

**i.** In cell H7, enter an AND function to prioritize the overdue invoices that are more than $1,000 for collection services. (*Hint*: The Logical1 condition should check to see if the number of days overdue is more than 0, and the Logical2 condition should check if the amount is more than 1,000.) Copy the AND function into the range H8:H13.

**j.** Enter your name in the worksheet footer, save the workbook, preview the worksheet, then submit the workbook to your instructor.

### Advanced Challenge Exercise

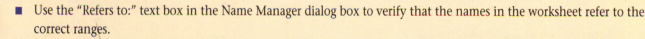

- Use the "Refers to:" text box in the Name Manager dialog box to verify that the names in the worksheet refer to the correct ranges.
- Use the Filter button in the Name Manager dialog box to verify that your names are scoped to the worksheet and not the workbook.
- Use the Filter button in the Name Manager dialog box to verify that your names are defined, free of errors, and not part of a table. If necessary, clear the Filter.

**k.** Close the workbook, then exit Excel.

## Independent Challenge 2

You are an auditor with a certified public accounting firm. The Green Home, an online seller of environmentally friendly home products, has contacted you to audit its first-quarter sales records. The management is considering expanding and needs its sales records audited to prepare the business plan. Specifically, they want to show what percent of annual sales each category represents. You will use a formula on a summary worksheet to summarize the sales for January, February, and March and to calculate the overall first-quarter percentage of the sales categories.

**a.** Start Excel, open the file EX E-5.xlsx from the drive and folder where you store your Data Files, then save it as **EX E-Products**.

**b.** In cell B10 of the Jan, Feb, and Mar sheets, enter the formulas to calculate the sales totals for the month.

# Independent Challenge 2 (continued)

c. For each month, in cell C5, create a formula calculating the percent of sales for the Compost Bins sales category. Use a function to display "INCORRECT" if there is a mistake in the formula. Verify that the percent appears with two decimal places. Copy this formula as necessary to complete the % of sales for all sales categories on all sheets. If any cells display "INCORRECT", fix the formulas in those cells.

d. In column B of the Summary sheet, use formulas to total the sales categories for the Jan, Feb, and Mar worksheets.

e. Enter the formula to calculate the first quarter sales total in cell B10 using the sales totals on the Jan, Feb, and Mar worksheets. Calculate the percent of each sales category on the Summary sheet. Use a function to display **MISCALCULATION** if there is a mistake in the formula. Copy this formula as necessary. If any cells display **MISCALCULATION,** fix the formulas in those cells.

f. Enter your name in the Summary worksheet footer, save the workbook, preview the worksheet, then submit it to your instructor.

g. On the Products sheet, separate the product list in cell A1 into separate columns of text data. (*Hint*: The products are delimited with commas.) Widen the columns as necessary. Use the second row to display the products with the first letter of each word in uppercase, as shown in Figure E-28.

**FIGURE E-28**

| | A | B | C | D | E |
|---|---|---|---|---|---|
| 1 | compost bins | green furniture | green bags | solar education materials | natural hot tubs |
| 2 | Compost Bins | Green Furniture | Green Bags | Solar Education Materials | Natural Hot Tubs |
| 3 | | | | | |

h. Enter your name in the Products worksheet footer, save the workbook, preview the worksheet, then submit the workbook to your instructor.

### Advanced Challenge Exercise

- Add a new sheet to the workbook and name it **Equations**.
- Use the built-in equations to enter the Pythagorean theorem in a text box on the worksheet. (*Hint*: Click the Equation list arrow in the Tools group of the Equation Tools Design tab and click Pythagorean Theorem. Also, see the Clues to Use "Inserting an equation into a worksheet" for more information about adding equations.)
- In a new text box, build the Pythagorean theorem using the mathematical symbols below the built-in equation. (*Hint*: To insert $a^2$ into a text box, click the Script list arrow in the Structures group of the Equation Tools Design tab, click the first option, click in the lower-left box and enter **a**, press [Tab], enter **2** in the upper-right box, then click to the right of the boxes to exit the symbol.)
- Enter your name in the Equations worksheet footer, save the workbook, preview the worksheet, then submit the workbook to your instructor.

i. Close the workbook, then exit Excel.

# Independent Challenge 3

As the owner of Digital Designs, a Web and graphic design firm, you are planning to expand your business. Because you will have to purchase additional equipment and hire a new part-time designer, you decide to take out a $50,000 loan to finance your expansion expenses. You check three loan sources: the Small Business Administration (SBA), your local bank, and a consortium of investors. The SBA will lend you the money at 6.5% interest, but you have to pay it off in 3 years. The local bank offers you the loan at 7.75% interest over 4 years. The consortium offers you an 8% loan, but they require you to pay it back in 2 years. To analyze all three loan options, you decide to build a loan summary worksheet. Using the loan terms provided, build a worksheet summarizing your options.

a. Start Excel, open a new workbook, save it as **EX E-Loan**, then rename Sheet1 **Loan Summary**.

b. Using Figure E-29 as a guide, enter labels and worksheet data for the three loan sources in columns A through D. (*Hint*: The worksheet in the figure uses the

**FIGURE E-29**

| | | | | | | | |
|---|---|---|---|---|---|---|---|
| 1 | | | Digital Designs | | | | |
| 2 | | | Loan Options | | | | |
| 3 | | | | | | | |
| 4 | Loan Source | Loan Amount | Interest Rate | # Payments | Monthly Payment | Total Payments | Total Interest |
| 5 | SBA | $ 50,000.00 | 6.50% | 36 | $ 1,532.45 | $ 55,168.21 | $ 5,168.21 |
| 6 | Bank | $ 50,000.00 | 7.75% | 48 | $ 1,214.79 | $ 58,309.78 | $ 8,309.78 |
| 7 | Investors | $ 50,000.00 | 8.00% | 24 | $ 2,261.36 | $ 54,272.75 | $ 4,272.75 |
| 8 | | | | | | | |

Your formulas go here

# Independent Challenge 3 (continued)

Median theme with Orange, Accent 2, Lighter 60%, as the fill color in the first two rows. Rows 1, 2 and 4 are bolded. The labels in column A are also bolded. The worksheet text color is orange, Accent 2, Darker 50%.)

c. Enter the monthly payment formula for your first loan source (making sure to show the payment as a positive amount), copy the formula as appropriate, then name the range containing the monthly payment formulas **Monthly_Payment** with a scope of the workbook.

d. Name the cell range containing the number of payments **Number_Payments** with the scope of the workbook.

e. Enter the formula for total payments for your first loan source using the named ranges Monthly_Payment and Number_Payments, then copy the formula as necessary.

f. Name the cell range containing the formulas for Total payments **Total_Payments**. Name the cell range containing the loan amounts **Loan_Amount**. Each name should have the workbook as its scope.

g. Enter the formula for total interest for your first loan source using the named ranges Total_Payments and Loan_Amount, then copy the formula as necessary.

h. Format the worksheet using appropriate formatting, then enter your name in the worksheet footer.

i. Save the workbook, preview the worksheet and change it to landscape orientation on a single page, then submit the workbook to your instructor.

### Advanced Challenge Exercise

- Turn on the print gridlines option for the sheet, then turn on printing of row and column headings.
- Display the worksheet formulas, save the workbook and submit it to your instructor.

j. Close the workbook then exit Excel.

## Real Life Independent Challenge

You decide to create a weekly log of your daily aerobic exercise. As part of this log, you record your aerobic activity along with the number of minutes spent working out. If you do more than one activity in a day, for example, if you bike and walk, record each as a separate event. Along with each activity, you record the location where you exercise. For example, you may walk in the gym or outdoors. You will use the log to analyze the amount of time that you spend on each type of exercise.

a. Start Excel, open the file EX E-6.xlsx from the drive and folder where you store your Data Files, then save it as **EX E-Workout**.

b. Use the structure of the worksheet to record your aerobic exercise activities. Change the data in columns A, B, C, D, and F to reflect your activities, locations, and times. If you do not have any data to enter, use the provided worksheet data.

c. Use a SUMIF function in the column G cells to calculate the total minutes spent on each activity.

d. Enter an AVERAGEIF function in the column H cells to average the number of minutes spent on each activity.

e. Enter a COUNTIF function in the column I cells to calculate the number of times each activity was performed. (*Hint*: The Range of cells to count is $B$2:$B$12 and the criteria is in cell F3.)

f. Format the Average Minutes column as number with two decimal places.

### Advanced Challenge Exercise

- Enter one of your activities with a specific location, such as Walk Outdoors, in a column F cell, then enter the SUMIFS function in the adjacent column G cell that calculates the total number of minutes spent on that activity in the specific location.
- Enter the AVERAGEIFS function in the corresponding column H cell that calculates the average number of minutes spent on the activity in the specified location.
- Enter the COUNTIFS function in the corresponding column I cell that calculates the number of days spent on the activity in the specific location.

g. Enter your name in the worksheet footer, save the workbook, preview the worksheet, then submit it to your instructor.

h. Close the workbook, then exit Excel.

# Visual Workshop

Open the file EX E-7.xlsx from the drive and folder where you store your Data Files, then save it as **EX E-Summary**. Create the worksheet shown in Figure E-30 using the data in columns B, C, and D along with the following criteria:

- The employee is eligible for a bonus if:

  - The employee has a performance rating of seven or higher.

  AND

  - The employee has sales that exceed the sales quota.

- If the employee is eligible for a bonus, the bonus amount is calculated as one percent of the sales amount. Otherwise the bonus amount is 0.

Enter your name in the worksheet footer, save the workbook, preview the worksheet, then submit the worksheet to your instructor.

(*Hint*: Use an AND formula to determine if a person is eligible for a bonus, and use an IF formula to check eligibility and to enter the bonus amount.)

**FIGURE E-30**

| | A | B | C | D | E | F |
|---|---|---|---|---|---|---|
| 1 | | | | Bonus Pay Summary | | |
| 2 | | | | | | |
| 3 | Last Name | Quota | Sales | Performance Rating | Eligible | Bonus Amount |
| 4 | Andrews | $175,000 | $182,557 | 7 | TRUE | $1,826 |
| 5 | Green | $95,774 | $94,223 | 3 | FALSE | $0 |
| 6 | Grey | $102,663 | $99,887 | 9 | FALSE | $0 |
| 7 | Hanley | $145,335 | $151,887 | 5 | FALSE | $0 |
| 8 | Kelly | $145,000 | $151,228 | 8 | TRUE | $1,512 |
| 9 | Medway | $130,000 | $152,774 | 5 | FALSE | $0 |
| 10 | Merkel | $152,885 | $160,224 | 7 | TRUE | $1,602 |
| 11 | Star | $98,000 | $87,224 | 3 | FALSE | $0 |
| 12 | Sealey | $90,000 | $86,700 | 9 | FALSE | $0 |

# Managing Workbook Data

**Files You Will Need:**

EX F-1.xlsx
EX F-2.xlsx
EX F-3.gif
EX F-4.xlsx
EX F-5.xlsx
EX F-6.xlsx
EX F-7.gif
EX F-Classifications.
   xlsx
EX F-Expenses.xlsx
EX F-Hardware.xlsx
EX F-Logo.gif
EX F-Price
   Information.xlsx
EX F-Toronto
   Sales.xlsx

As you analyze data using Excel, you will find that your worksheets and workbooks become more complex. In this unit, you will learn several Excel features to help you manage workbook data. In addition, you will want to share workbooks with coworkers, but you need to ensure that they can view your data while preventing unwarranted changes. You will learn how to save workbooks in different formats and how to prepare workbooks for distribution. Kate Morgan, the vice president of sales at Quest Specialty Travel, asks for your help in analyzing yearly sales data from the Canadian branches. When the analysis is complete, she will distribute the workbook for branch managers to review.

**OBJECTIVES**

View and arrange worksheets

Protect worksheets and workbooks

Save custom views of a worksheet

Add a worksheet background

Prepare a workbook for distribution

Insert hyperlinks

Save a workbook for distribution

Group worksheets

# Viewing and Arranging Worksheets

As you work with workbooks made up of multiple worksheets, you might need to compare data in the various sheets. To do this, you can view each worksheet in its own workbook window, called an **instance**, and display the windows in an arrangement that makes it easy to compare data. When you work with worksheets in separate windows, you are working with different views of the same workbook; the data itself remains in one file.  Kate asks you to compare the monthly store sales totals for the Toronto and Vancouver branches. Because the sales totals are on different worksheets, you want to arrange the worksheets side by side in separate windows.

**STEPS**

1. **Start Excel, open the file EX F-1.xlsx from the drive and folder where you store your Data Files, then save it as EX F-Store Sales**

2. **With the Toronto sheet active, click the View tab, then click the New Window button in the Window group**

   There are now two instances of the Store Sales workbook open. You can see them when you place the mouse pointer over the Excel icon on the task bar: EX F-Store Sales.xlsx:1 and EX F-Store Sales.xlsx:2. The Store Sales.xlsx:2 window is active—you can see its name on the title bar.

3. **Click the Vancouver sheet tab, click the Switch Windows button in the Window group, then click EX F-Store Sales.xlsx:1**

   The EX F-Store Sales.xlsx:1 instance is active. The Toronto sheet is active in the EX F-Store Sales.xlsx:1 workbook, and the Vancouver sheet is active in the EX F-Store Sales.xlsx:2 workbook.

**QUICK TIP**

You can use the View Side by Side button in the Window group to arrange the windows in their previous configuration. The Synchronous Scrolling button below the View Side by Side button is active by default, allowing you to scroll through the arranged worksheets simultaneously.

4. **Click the Arrange All button in the Window group**

   The Arrange Windows dialog box, shown in Figure F-1, lets you choose how to display the instances. You want to view the workbooks next to each other.

5. **Click the Vertical option button to select it, then click OK**

   The windows are arranged next to each other, as shown in Figure F-2. You can activate a workbook by clicking one of its cells. You can also view only one of the workbooks by hiding the one you do not wish to see.

6. **Scroll horizontally to view the data in the EX F-Store Sales.xlsx:1 workbook, click anywhere in the EX F-Store Sales.xlsx:2 workbook, scroll horizontally to view the data in the EX F-Store Sales.xlsx:2 workbook, then click the Hide button in the Window group**

   When you hide the second instance, only the EX F-Store Sales.xlsx:1 workbook is visible.

**QUICK TIP**

You can also hide a worksheet by right-clicking its sheet tab and clicking Hide on the shortcut menu. To display the hidden sheet, right-click any sheet tab, click Unhide, in the Unhide dialog box, select the sheet, then click OK.

7. **Click the Unhide button in the Window group; click EX F-Store Sales.xlsx:2, if necessary, in the Unhide dialog box; then click OK**

   The EX F-Store Sales.xlsx:2 book reappears.

8. **Close the EX F-Store Sales.xlsx:2 instance, then maximize the Toronto worksheet in the EX F-Store Sales.xlsx workbook**

   Closing the EX F-Store Sales.xlsx:2 instance leaves only the first instance open. Its name in the title bar returns to EX F-Store Sales.xlsx.

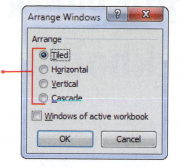

Click to select the window configuration options

FIGURE F-2: Windows displayed vertically

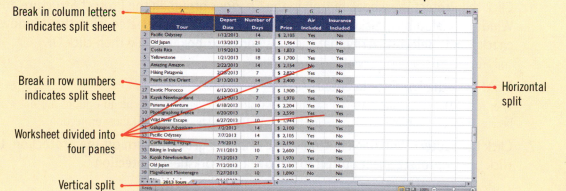

EX F-Store Sales.xlsx:1

EX F-Store Sales.xlsx:2

## Splitting the worksheet into multiple panes

Excel lets you split the worksheet area into vertical and/or horizontal panes, so that you can click inside any one pane and scroll to locate information in that pane while the other panes remain in place, as shown in Figure F-3. To split a worksheet area into multiple panes, drag a split box (the small box at the top of the vertical scroll bar or

at the right end of the horizontal scroll bar) in the direction you want the split to appear. To remove the split, move the pointer over the split until the pointer changes to a double-headed arrow, then double-click.

FIGURE F-3: Worksheet split into two horizontal and two vertical panes

Break in column letters indicates split sheet

Break in row numbers indicates split sheet

Worksheet divided into four panes

Vertical split

Horizontal split

Excel 2010

# Protecting Worksheets and Workbooks

To protect sensitive information, Excel lets you **lock** one or more cells so that other people can view the values and formulas in those cells, but not change it. Excel locks all cells by default, but this locking does not take effect until you activate the protection feature. A common worksheet protection strategy is to unlock cells in which data will be changed, sometimes called the **data entry area**, and to lock cells in which the data should not be changed. Then, when you protect the worksheet, the unlocked areas can still be changed.  Because the Toronto sales figures for January through March have been finalized, Kate asks you to protect that worksheet area. That way, users cannot change the figures for those months.

**STEPS**

1. **On the Toronto sheet, select the range E3:M6, click the Home tab, click the Format button in the Cells group, click Format Cells, then in the Format Cells dialog box click the Protection tab**

   The Locked check box in the Protection tab is already checked, as shown in Figure F-4. All the cells in a new workbook start out locked. The protection feature is inactive by default. Because the April through December sales figures have not yet been confirmed as final and may need to be changed, you do not want those cells to be locked when the protection feature is activated. You decide to unlock the cell range and protect the worksheet.

**QUICK TIP**

To hide any formulas that you don't want to be visible, select the cells that contain formulas that you want to hide, then click the Hidden check box on the Protection tab of the Format Cells dialog box to select it. The formula will be hidden after the worksheet is protected.

2. **Click the Locked check box to deselect it, click OK, click the Review tab, then click the Protect Sheet button in the Changes group**

   The Protect Sheet dialog box opens, as shown in Figure F-5. In the "Allow users of this worksheet to" list, you can select the actions that you want your worksheet users to be able to perform. The default options protect the worksheet while allowing users to select locked or unlocked cells only. You choose not to use a password.

3. **Verify that Protect worksheet and contents of locked cells is checked, that the password text box is blank, and that Select locked cells and Select unlocked cells are checked, then click OK**

   You are ready to test the new worksheet protection.

4. **In cell B3, type 1 to confirm that locked cells cannot be changed, click OK, click cell F3, type 1, notice that Excel lets you begin the entry, press [Esc] to cancel the entry, then save your work**

   When you try change a locked cell, a dialog box, shown in Figure F-6, reminds you of the protected cell's read-only status. **Read-only format** means that users can view but not change the data. Because you unlocked the cells in columns E through M before you protected the worksheet, you can change these cells. You decide to protect the workbook from these changes to the workbook's structure, but decide not to require a password.

5. **Click the Protect Workbook button in the Changes group, in the Protect Structure and Windows dialog box, make sure the Structure check box is selected, click the Windows check box to select it, verify that the password text box is blank, then click OK**

   You are ready to test the new workbook protection.

6. **Right-click the Toronto sheet tab**

   The Insert, Delete, Rename, Move or Copy, Tab Color, Hide, and Unhide menu options are not available because the sheet is protected. You decide to remove the workbook and worksheet protections.

7. **Click the Protect Workbook button in the Changes group to turn off the protection, then click the Unprotect Sheet button to remove the worksheet protection**

**FIGURE F-4:** Protection tab in Format Cells dialog box

Click to remove
check mark

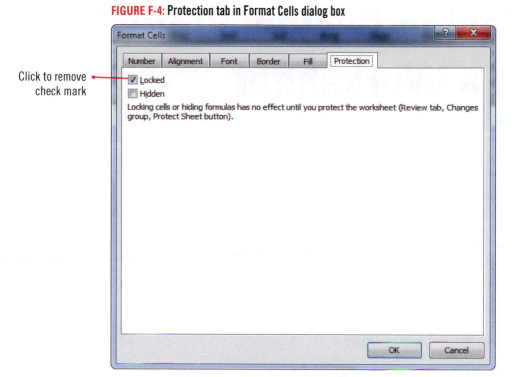

**FIGURE F-5:** Protect Sheet dialog box

Protects locked cells
from changes

Allows users to select
worksheet cells

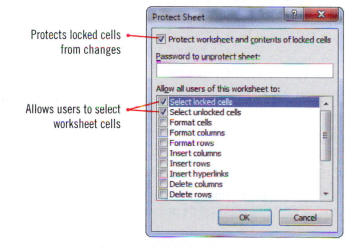

**FIGURE F-6:** Reminder of protected cell's read-only status

Microsoft Excel

The cell or chart that you are trying to change is protected and therefore read-only.

To modify a protected cell or chart, first remove protection using the Unprotect Sheet command (Review tab, Changes group). You may be prompted for a password.

OK

## Freezing rows and columns

As the rows and columns of a worksheet fill up with data, you might need to scroll through the worksheet to add, delete, change, and view information. You can temporarily freeze columns and rows so you can keep column or row labels in view as you scroll. **Panes** are the columns and rows that **freeze**, or remain in place, while you scroll through your worksheet. To freeze panes, click the first cell in the area you want to scroll, click the View tab, click the Freeze Panes button in the Window group, then click Freeze Panes. Excel freezes the columns to the left and the rows above the selected cell. You can also select Freeze Top Row or Freeze First Column to freeze the top row or left worksheet column.

# Saving Custom Views of a Worksheet

A **view** is a set of display and/or print settings that you can name and save, then access at a later time. By using the Excel Custom Views feature, you can create several different views of a worksheet without having to create separate sheets. For example, if you often hide columns in a worksheet, you can create two views, one that displays all of the columns and another with the columns hidden. You set the worksheet display first, then name the view.  Because Kate wants to generate a sales report from the final sales data for January through March, she asks you to save the first-quarter sales data as a custom view. You begin by creating a view showing all of the worksheet data.

## STEPS

1. **With the Toronto sheet active, click the View tab, then click the Custom Views button in the Workbook Views group**

   The Custom Views dialog box opens. Any previously defined views for the active worksheet appear in the Views box. No views are defined for the Toronto worksheet. You decide to add a named view for the current view, which shows all the worksheet columns. That way, you can easily return to it from any other views you create.

**QUICK TIP**

To delete views from the active worksheet, select the view in the Custom Views dialog box, then click Delete.

2. **Click Add**

   The Add View dialog box opens, as shown in Figure F-7. Here, you enter a name for the view and decide whether to include print settings and hidden rows, columns, and filter settings. You want to include the selected options.

3. **In the Name box, type Year Sales, then click OK**

   You have created a view called Year Sales that shows all the worksheet columns. You want to set up another view that will hide the April through December columns.

4. **Drag across the column headings to select columns E through M, right-click the selected area, then click Hide on the shortcut menu**

   You are ready to create a custom view of the January through March sales data.

5. **Click cell A1, click the Custom Views button in the Workbook Views group, click Add, in the Name box type First Quarter, then click OK**

   You are ready to test the two custom views.

**TROUBLE**

If you receive the message "Some view settings could not be applied", turn off worksheet protection by clicking the Unprotect Sheet button in the Changes group of the Review tab.

6. **Click the Custom Views button in the Workbook Views group, click Year Sales in the Views list, then click Show**

   The Year Sales custom view displays all of the months' sales data. Now you are ready to test the First Quarter custom view.

7. **Click the Custom Views button in the Workbook Views group, then with First Quarter in the Custom Views dialog box selected, click Show**

   Only the January through March sales figures appear on the screen, as shown in Figure F-8.

8. **Return to the Year Sales view, then save your work**

FIGURE F-7: Add View dialog box

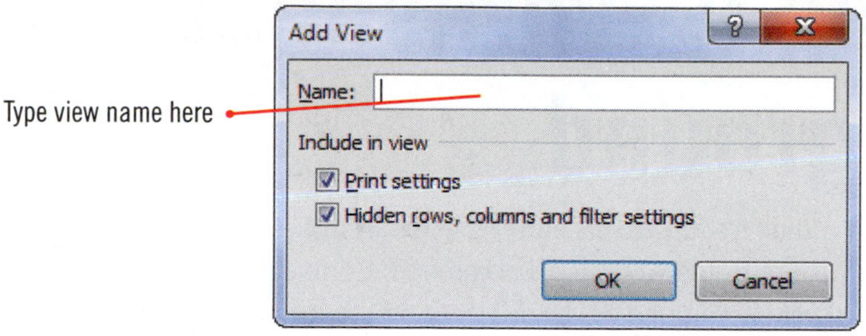

Type view name here

FIGURE F-8: First Quarter view

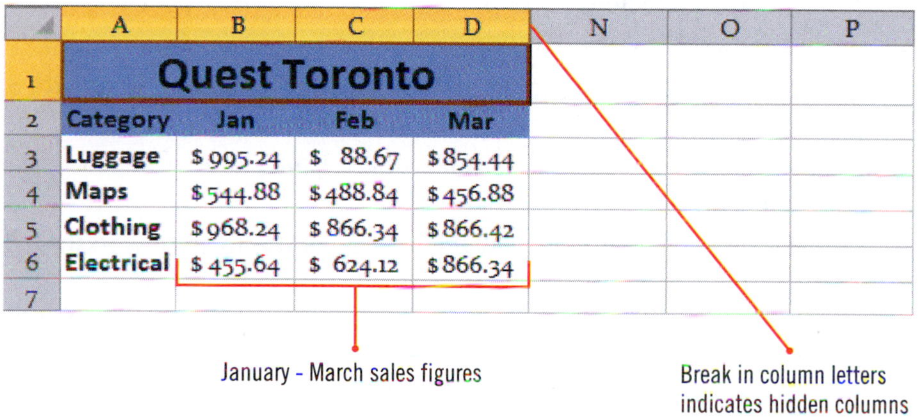

January - March sales figures

Break in column letters indicates hidden columns

## Using Page Break Preview

The vertical and horizontal dashed lines in the Normal view of worksheets represent page breaks. Excel automatically inserts a page break when your worksheet data doesn't fit on one page. These page breaks are **dynamic**, which means they adjust automatically when you insert or delete rows and columns and when you change column widths or row heights. Everything to the left of the first vertical dashed line and above the first horizontal dashed line is printed on the first page. You can manually add or remove page breaks by clicking the Page Layout tab, clicking the Breaks button in the Page Setup group, then clicking the appropriate command. You can also view and change page breaks manually by clicking the View tab, then clicking the Page Break Preview button in the Workbook Views group, or by clicking the Page Break Preview button 🔲 on the status bar, then clicking OK. You can drag the blue page break lines to the desired location, as shown in Figure F-9. Some cells may temporarily display ##### while you are in Page Break Preview. If you drag a page break to the right to include more data on a page, Excel shrinks the type to fit the data on that page. To exit Page Break Preview, click the Normal button in the Workbook Views group.

FIGURE F-9: Page Break Preview window

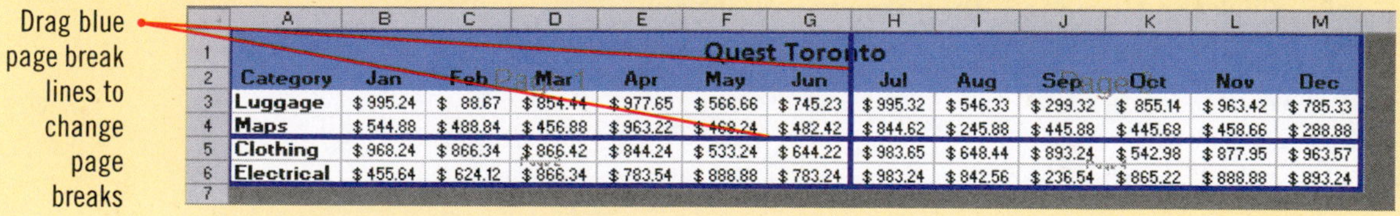

Drag blue page break lines to change page breaks

Excel 2010

# Adding a Worksheet Background

In addition to using a theme's font colors and fills, you can make your Excel data more attractive on the screen by adding a picture to the worksheet background. Companies often use their logo as a worksheet background. A worksheet background will be displayed on the screen but will not print with the worksheet. If you want to add a worksheet background that appears on printouts, you can add a **watermark**, a translucent background design that prints behind your data. To add a watermark, you add the image to the worksheet header or footer.  Kate asks you to add the Quest logo to the printed background of the Toronto worksheet. But first she wants to see it as a nonprinting background.

**STEPS**

1. **With the Toronto sheet active, click the Page Layout tab, then click the Background button in the Page Setup group**

   The Sheet Background dialog box opens.

2. **Navigate to the drive and folder where you store your Data Files, click EX F-Logo.gif, then click Insert**

   The Quest logo appears behind the worksheet data. It appears twice because the graphic is **tiled**, or repeated, to fill the background.

3. **Click the File tab, click Print, view the preview of the Toronto worksheet, then click the Page Layout tab**

   Because the logo is only for display purposes, it will not print with the worksheet, so is not visible in the Print preview. You want the logo to print with the worksheet, so you decide to remove the background and add the logo to the worksheet header.

4. **Click the Delete Background button in the Page Setup group, click the Insert tab, then click the Header & Footer button in the Text group**

   The Header & Footer Tools Design tab appears, as shown in Figure F-10. The Header & Footer group buttons add preformatted headers and footers to a worksheet. The Header & Footer Elements buttons let you add page numbers, the date, the time, the file location, names, and pictures to the header or footer. The Navigation group buttons move the insertion point from the header to the footer and back. You want to add a picture to the header.

5. **With the insertion point in the center section of the header, click the Picture button in the Header & Footer Elements group, navigate to the drive and folder where you store your Data Files, click EX F-Logo.gif, then click Insert**

   A code representing a picture, "&[Picture]", appears in the center of the header.

6. **Click cell A1, then click the Normal button ⊞ on the Status Bar**

   You want to scale the worksheet data to print on one page.

**QUICK TIP**
You can also scale the worksheet to fit on one page by clicking the File tab, clicking Print, clicking the No Scaling list arrow, then clicking Fit Sheet on One Page.

7. **Click the Page Layout tab, click the Width list arrow in the Scale to Fit group, click 1 page, click the Height list arrow in the Scale to Fit group, click 1 page, then preview the worksheet**

   Your worksheet should look like Figure F-11.

8. **Click the Home tab, then save the workbook**

**FIGURE F-10: Design tab of the Header & Footer tools**

Click these buttons to customize the header and footer

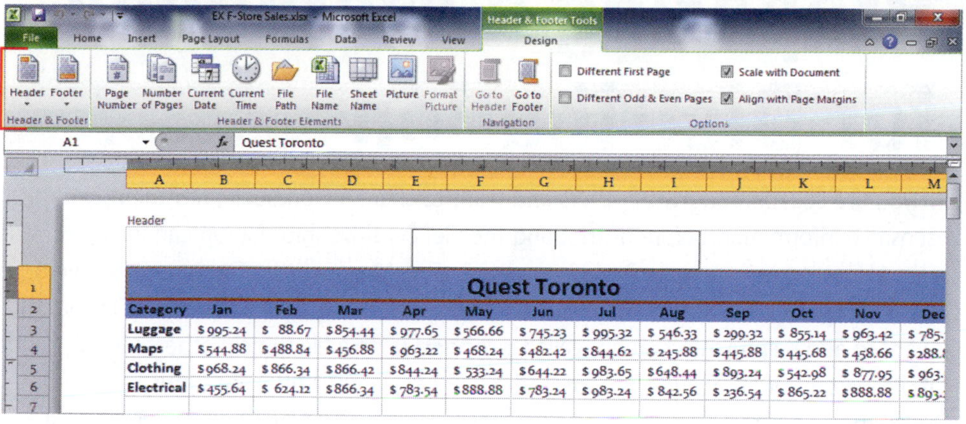


**FIGURE F-11: Preview of Toronto worksheet with logo in the background**

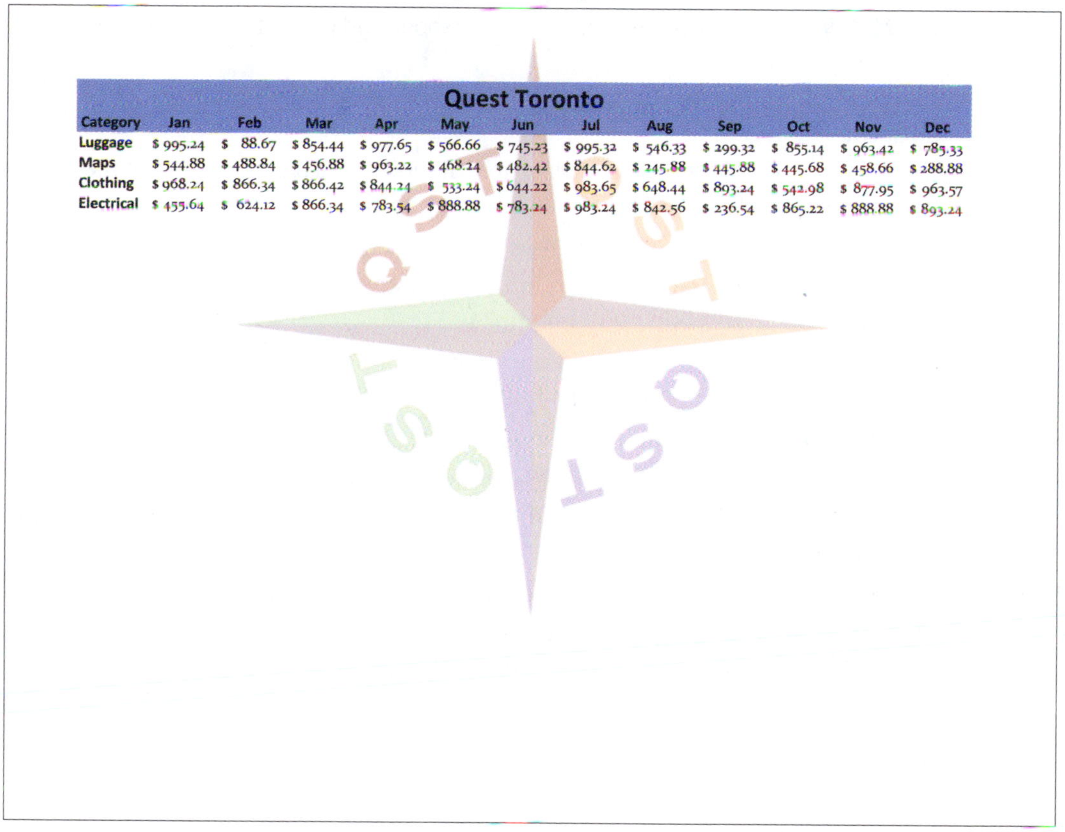


## Clipping Screens in Excel

You can paste an image of an open file into an Excel workbook or another Office document. This pastes the screenshot into your document as an image that you can move, copy, or edit. To insert a screenshot, click the Insert tab, click the Screenshot button in the Illustrations group, then click on one of the available windows in the gallery. This pastes a screen shot of the window you clicked into the current Excel document. You can also click the Screen Clipping button in the gallery to select and paste an area from an open window. After you paste an image on your worksheet, you can also cut or copy and paste in another program or in an e-mail. In addition to pasting screenshots from other windows into Excel, you can use the Screenshot feature to paste Excel screens into other programs such as Word, PowerPoint, and Outlook. This is helpful if you are having a problem with an Excel worksheet and want to e-mail your screen image to a Help Desk.

# Preparing a Workbook for Distribution

If you are collaborating with others and want to share a workbook with them, you might want to remove sensitive information before distributing the file. Sensitive information can include headers, footers, or hidden elements. You can use Backstage view in Excel to open the Document Inspector, which finds hidden data and personal information in your workbooks and helps you remove it. On the other hand, you might want to add helpful information, called **properties**, to a file to help others identify, understand, and locate it. Properties might include keywords, the author's name, a title, the status, and comments. **Keywords** are terms users can search for that will help them locate your workbook. Properties are a form of **metadata**, information that describes data and is used in Microsoft Windows document searches. You enter properties in the Document Properties Panel. In addition, to ensure that others do not make unauthorized changes to your workbook, you can mark a file as final. This makes it a read-only file, which others can open but not change.  Kate wants you to protect the workbook and prepare it for distribution.

## STEPS

1. **Click the File tab**

   Backstage view opens, with the Info tab in front. It shows you a preview of your printed worksheet and information about your file. This information includes who has permission to open, copy, or change your workbook. It also includes tools you can use to check for security issues.

2. **Click the Check for Issues button in the Prepare for Sharing area, then click Inspect Document**

   The Document Inspector dialog box opens, as shown in Figure F-12. It lists items from which you can have Excel evaluate hidden or personal information. All the options are selected by default.

3. **Click Inspect**

   After inspecting your document, the inspector displays its results. Areas with personal information have a "!" in front of them. Headers and footers is also flagged. You want to keep the file's header and footer and remove personal information.

   > **QUICK TIP**
   > You can view a file's summary information by clicking the File Tab and reviewing the information on the right side of the information area.

4. **Click Remove All next to Document Properties and Personal Information, then click Close**

   You decide to add keywords to help the sales managers find the worksheet. The search words "Toronto" or "Vancouver" would be good keywords for this workbook.

5. **Click the Properties list arrow on the right side of Backstage view, then click Show Document Panel**

   The Document Properties Panel appears at the top of the worksheet, as shown in Figure F-13. You decide to add a title, status, keywords, and comments.

   > **QUICK TIP**
   > If you have access to an Information Rights Management server, you can use the Information Rights Management (IRM) feature to specify access permissions to your files. You can also access this service through Windows Live ID.

6. **In the Title text box type Store Sales, in the Keywords text box type Toronto Vancouver store sales, in the Status text box type DRAFT, then in the Comments text box type The first-quarter figures are final., then click the Close button on the Document Properties Panel**

   You are ready to mark the workbook as final.

7. **Click the File tab, click the Protect Workbook button in the Permissions area, click Mark as Final, click OK, then click OK again**

   "[Read-Only]" appears in the title bar indicating the workbook is saved as a read-only file.

8. **Click the Home tab, click cell B3, type 1 to confirm that the cell cannot be changed, then click the Edit Anyway button above the formula bar**

   Marking a workbook as final is not a strong form of workbook protection because a workbook recipient can remove this Final status. Removing the read-only status makes it editable again.

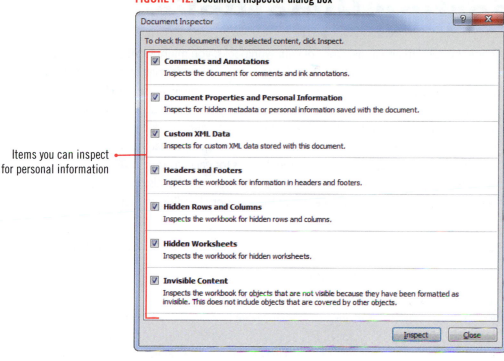

Items you can inspect for personal information

Add file information in text boxes

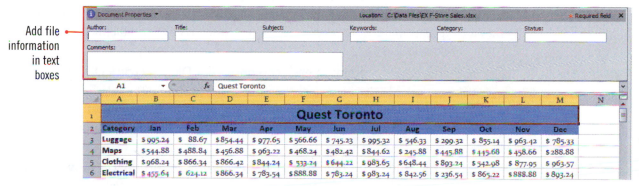

## Sharing a workbook

You can make an Excel file a **shared workbook** so that several users can open and modify it at the same time. Click the Review tab, click the Share Workbook button in the Changes group, then on the Editing tab of the Share Workbook dialog box click "Allow changes by more than one user at the same time. This also allows workbook merging.", then click OK. If you get an error that the workbook cannot be shared because privacy is enabled, click the File tab, click Options in the left section, click the Trust Center category on the left side of the dialog box, click Trust Center Settings, click Privacy Options in the list on the left, click the "Remove personal information from file properties on save" check box to deselect it, then click OK twice. When you share workbooks, it is often helpful to **track** modifications, or identify who made which changes. You can track all changes to a workbook by clicking the Track Changes button in the Changes group, and then clicking Highlight Changes. To view all changes that have been tracked in a workbook, click the Review tab, click the Track Changes button in the Changes group, click Highlight Changes, select the When check box in the Highlight Changes dialog box, click the When text box list arrow, then select All in the list. To resolve the tracked changes in a workbook, click the Track Changes button, then click Accept/Reject Changes. The changes are displayed one by one. You can accept the change or, if you disagree with any of the changes, you can reject them.

Excel 2010

# Inserting Hyperlinks

As you manage the content and appearance of your workbooks, you might want the workbook user to view information that exists in another location. It might be nonessential information or data that is too detailed to place in the workbook itself. In these cases, you can create a hyperlink. A **hyperlink** is an object (a file-name, word, phrase, or graphic) in a worksheet that, when you click it, displays, or "jumps to," another location, called the **target**. The target can also be a worksheet, another document, or a site on the World Wide Web. For example, in a worksheet that lists customer invoices, at each customer's name, you might create a hyperlink to an Excel file containing payment terms for each customer.  Kate wants managers who view the Store Sales workbook to be able to view the item totals for each sales category in the Toronto sheet. She asks you to create a hyperlink at the Category heading so that users can click the hyperlink to view the items for each category.

## STEPS

1. **Click cell A2 on the Toronto worksheet**

2. **Click the Insert tab, then click the Hyperlink button in the Links group**

    The Insert Hyperlink dialog box opens, as shown in Figure F-14. The icons under "Link to" on the left side of the dialog box let you select the type of location to where you want the link jump: an existing file or Web page, a place in the same document, a new document, or an e-mail address. Because you want the link to display an already-existing document, the selected first icon, Existing File or Web Page, is correct, so you won't have to change it.

3. **Click the Look in list arrow, navigate to the location where you store your Data Files if necessary, then click EX F-Toronto Sales.xlsx in the file list**

    The filename you selected and its path appear in the Address text box. This is the document users will see when they click the hyperlink. You can also specify the ScreenTip that users see when they hold the pointer over the hyperlink.

**QUICK TIP**

To remove a hyper-link or change its target, right-click it, then click Remove Hyperlink or Edit Hyperlink.

4. **Click the ScreenTip button, type Items in each category, click OK, then click OK again**

    Cell A2 now contains underlined yellow text, indicating that it is a hyperlink. The color of a hyperlink depends on the worksheet theme colors. You need to change the text color of the hyperlink text so it is visible on the dark background. After you create a hyperlink, you should check it to make sure that it jumps to the correct destination.

**QUICK TIP**

If you link to a Web page, you must be connected to the Internet to test the link.

5. **Click the Home tab, click the Font Color list arrow** ![A] **in the Font group, click the White, Background 1 color (first color in the Theme Colors), move the pointer over the Category text, view the ScreenTip, then click once**

    After you click, the EX F-Toronto Sales workbook opens, displaying the Sales sheet, as shown in Figure F-15.

6. **Close the EX F-Toronto Sales workbook, click Don't Save, then save the EX F-Store Sales workbook**

---

### Returning to your document

After you click a hyperlink and view the destination document, you will often want to return to your original document that contains the hyperlink. To do this, you can add the Back button to the Quick Access toolbar. However, the Back button does not appear in the Quick Access toolbar by default; you need to customize the toolbar. (If you are using a computer in a lab, check with your system administrator to see if you have permission to do this.) To customize the Quick Access toolbar, click the Customize Quick Access Toolbar arrow, click More Commands, click the Choose Commands from list arrow, select All Commands, scroll down, click the Back button, click Add, then click OK.

**FIGURE F-14:** Insert Hyperlink dialog box

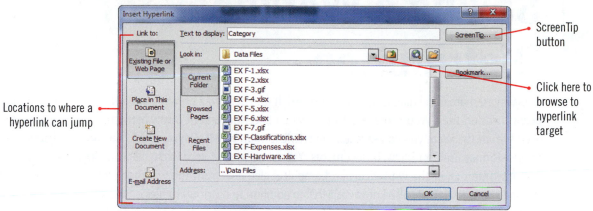

Locations to where a hyperlink can jump

ScreenTip button

Click here to browse to hyperlink target

**FIGURE F-15:** Target document

| | A | B | | C |
|---|---|---|---|---|
| 1 | Quest Toronto | | | |
| 2 | Travel Store Sales | | | |
| 3 | **Item** | **Total Sales** | | **Category** |
| 4 | PopOut Maps | $ | 1,619.81 | Maps |
| 5 | Smart Packing Books | $ | 3,934.77 | Maps |
| 6 | Airport Guides | $ | 4,941.61 | Maps |
| 7 | Pack It Guides | $ | 1,114.65 | Maps |
| 8 | Computer Case | $ | 1,855.65 | Luggage |
| 9 | Backpack | $ | 1,836.91 | Luggage |
| 10 | Plane Slippers | $ | 1,099.15 | Clothing |
| 11 | Travel Socks | $ | 1,108.16 | Clothing |
| 12 | Men's Sandals | $ | 1,103.14 | Clothing |
| 13 | Women's Sandals | $ | 1,954.19 | Clothing |
| 14 | Hats | $ | 975.44 | Clothing |
| 15 | Men's T-Shirts | $ | 3,111.76 | Clothing |
| 16 | Women's T-Shirts | $ | 1,108.41 | Clothing |
| 17 | Converter | $ | 1,798.53 | Electrical |
| 18 | Phone Charger | $ | 1,108.41 | Electrical |
| 19 | | | | |
| 20 | | | | |
| 21 | | | | |
| 22 | | | | |

Sales / Sheet2 / Sheet3

Ready

## Using research tools

You can access resources online and locally on your computer using the Research task pane. To open the Research task pane, click the Review tab, then click the Research button in the Proofing group. The Search for text box in the Research pane lets you specify a research topic. The Research pane has a drop-down list of the resources available to search for your topic. You can use this list to access resources such as a thesaurus, a dictionary, financial web sites, and research web sites. You can also quickly access the thesaurus in the Research task pane using the Thesaurus button on the Review tab in the Proofing group.

# Saving a Workbook for Distribution

One way to share Excel data is to place, or **publish**, the data on a network or on the Web so that others can access it using their Web browsers. To publish an Excel document to an **intranet** (a company's internal Web site) or the Web, you can save it in an HTML format. **HTML (Hypertext Markup Language)**, is the coding format used for all Web documents. You can also save your Excel file as a **single-file Web page** that integrates all of the worksheets and graphical elements from the workbook into a single file. This file format is called MHTML, also known as MHT. In addition to distributing files on the Web, you might need to distribute your files to people working with an earlier version of Excel. You can do this by saving your files as Excel 97-2003 workbooks. See Table F-1 for a list of the most popular formats.  Kate asks you to create a workbook version that managers running an earlier Excel version can use. She also asks you to save the EX F-Store Sales workbook in MHT format so she can publish it on the Quest intranet.

**STEPS**

1. **Click the** File tab, **click** Save As, **click the** Save as type list arrow **in the Save As dialog box, click** Excel 97-2003 Workbook (*.xls), **navigate to the drive and folder where you store your Data Files if necessary, then click** Save

   The Compatibility Checker dialog box opens. It alerts you to the features that will be lost or converted by saving in the earlier format. Some Excel 2010 features are not available in earlier versions of Excel.

**QUICK TIP**

To ensure that your workbook is displayed the same way on different computer platforms and screen settings, you can publish it in PDF format.

2. **Click** Continue, **close the workbook, then reopen the EX F-Store Sales.xls workbook**

   "[Compatibility Mode]" appears in the title bar, as shown in Figure F-16. Compatibility mode prevents you from including Excel features in your workbook that are not supported in Excel 97-2003 workbooks. To exit compatibility mode, you need to save your file in one of the Excel 2010 formats and reopen the file.

3. **Click the** File tab, **click** Save As, **click the** Save as type list arrow **in the Save As dialog box, click** Excel Workbook (*.xlsx); **if necessary, navigate to the drive and folder where you store your Data Files, click** Save, **then click** Yes **when you are asked if you want to replace the existing file**

   "[Compatibility Mode]" remains displayed in the title bar. You decide to close the file and reopen it to exit compatibility mode.

**QUICK TIP**

You can convert an .xls file to an .xlsx file when opening it in Excel 2010 by clicking the File tab and clicking Convert in the information pane. Note that this deletes the original .xls file.

4. **Close the workbook, then reopen the EX F-Store Sales.xlsx workbook**

   The title bar no longer displays "[Compatibility mode]". You still need to save the file for Web distribution.

5. **Click the** File tab, **click** Save As, **in the Save As dialog box navigate to the drive and folder where you store your Data Files if necessary, change the filename to** sales, **then click the** Save as type list arrow **and click** Single File Web Page (*.mht, *.mhtml)

   The Save as type list box indicates that the workbook is to be saved as a Single File Web Page, which is in MHTML or MHT format. To avoid problems when publishing your pages to a Web server, it is best to use lowercase characters, omit special characters and spaces, and limit your filename to eight characters with an additional three-character extension.

6. **Click** Save, **then click** Yes

   The dialog box indicated that some features may not be retained in the Web page file. Excel saves the workbook as an MHT file in the location you specified. The MHT file is open on your screen. See Figure F-17. It's a good idea to open an MHT file in your browser to see how it will look to viewers.

**TROUBLE**

The message above your workbook in the browser tells you that active content is restricted. Active content is interactive and usually in the form of small programs. These programs can present a security threat, and you should allow the active content only if you trust the source of the file.

7. **Close the** sales.mht **file in Excel, start your browser, open the** sales.mht **file by double-clicking it in the folder where you store your Data Files, click the** Vancouver sheet tab, **then close your browser window**

Managing Workbook Data

**FIGURE F-16:** Workbook in compatibility mode

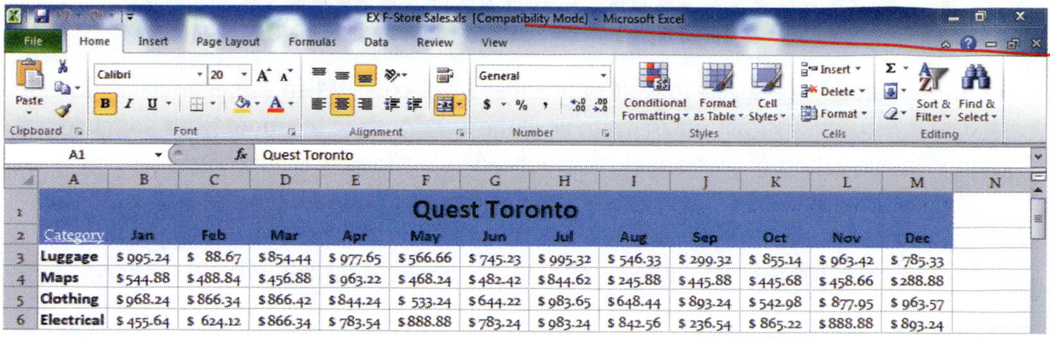

File is marked as using compatibility mode

**FIGURE F-17:** Workbook saved as a single file Web page

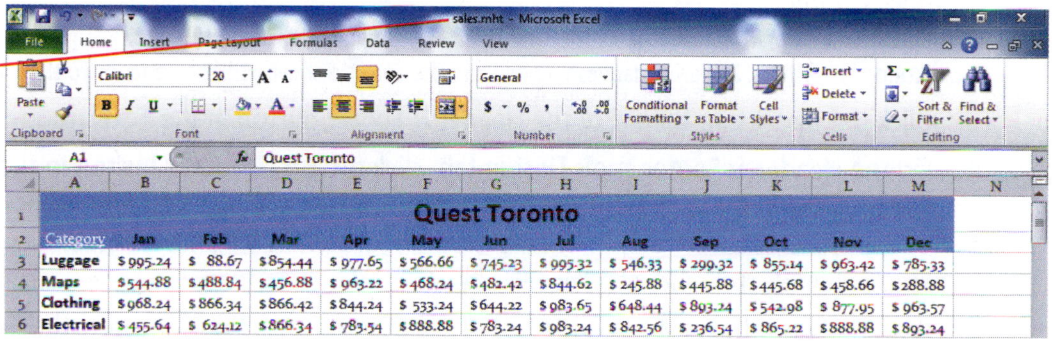

Web file with new name

**TABLE F-1:** Workbook formats

| type of file | file extension(s) | used for |
|---|---|---|
| Macro-enabled workbook | .xlsm | Files that contain macros |
| Excel 97 – 2003 workbook | .xls | Working with people using older versions of Excel |
| Single file Web page | .mht, .mhtml | Web sites with multiple pages and graphics |
| Web page | .htm, .html | Simple single-page Web sites |
| Excel template | .xltx | Excel files that will be reused with small changes |
| Excel macro-enabled template | .xltm | Excel files that will be used again and contain macros |
| Portable document format | .pdf | Files with formatting that needs to be preserved |
| XML paper specification | .xps | Files with formatting that needs to be preserved and files that need to be shared |
| OpenDocument spreadsheet | .ods | Files created with OpenOffice |

### Understanding Excel file formats

The default file format for Excel 2010 files is the Office Open XML format, which supports all Excel features. This has been the default file format of Office files since Microsoft Office 2007. This format stores Excel files in small XML components that are zipped for compression making the files smaller. The most often used format, .xlsx, does not support macros. **Macros**, programmed instructions that perform tasks, can be a security risk. If your worksheet contains macros, you need to save it with an extension of .xlsm so the macros can function in the workbook. If you use a workbook's text and formats repeatedly, you might want to save it as a template with the extension .xltx. If your template contains macros, you need to save it with the .xltm extension.

# Grouping Worksheets

You can group worksheets to work on them as a collection. When you enter data into one worksheet, that data is also automatically entered into all of the worksheets in the group. This is useful for data that is common to every sheet of a workbook, such as headers and footers, or for column headings that will apply to all monthly worksheets in a yearly summary. Grouping worksheets can also be used to print multiple worksheets at one time.  Kate asks you to add the text "Quest" to the footer of both the Toronto and Vancouver worksheets. You will also add 1-inch margins to the top of both worksheets.

**STEPS**

1. **Open the EX F-Store Sales.xlsx file from the drive and folder where you store your Data Files**

**QUICK TIP**

You can group non-contiguous worksheets by pressing and holding [Ctrl] while clicking the sheet tabs that you want to group.

2. **With the Toronto sheet active, press and hold [Shift], click the Vancouver sheet, then release [Shift]**

   Both sheet tabs are selected, and the title bar now contains "[Group]", indicating that the worksheets are grouped together. Now any changes you make to the Toronto sheet will also be made to the Vancouver sheet.

3. **Click the Insert tab, then click the Header & Footer button in the Text group**

4. **On the Header & Footer Tools Design tab, click the Go to Footer button in the Navigation group, type Quest in the center section of the footer, enter your name in the left section of the footer, click cell A1, then click the Normal button 🖼 on the Status Bar**

   You decide to check the footers in Print Preview.

5. **With the worksheets still grouped, click the File tab, click Print, preview the first page, then click the Next Page button ▶ to preview the second page**

   Because the worksheets are grouped, both pages contain the footer with "Quest" and your name. The worksheets would look better with a wider top margin.

6. **Click the Normal Margins list arrow, click Custom Margins, in the Top text box on the Margins tab of the Page Setup dialog box type 1, then click OK**

   You decide to ungroup the worksheets.

7. **Click the Home tab, right-click the Toronto worksheet sheet tab, then click Ungroup Sheets**

8. **Save and close the workbook, exit Excel, then submit the workbook to your instructor**

9. **The completed worksheets are shown in Figures F-18 and F-19.**

---

### Adding a digital signature to a workbook

You can digitally sign a workbook to establish its validity and prevent it from being changed. You can obtain a valid certificate from a certificate authority to authenticate the workbook or you can create your own digital signature. To add a signature line in a workbook, click the Insert tab, click the Signature Line button in the Text group, then click OK. In the Signature Setup dialog box, enter information about the signer of the worksheet and then click OK. To add a signature, double-click the signature line, click OK; if prompted, in the Get a Digital ID dialog box, click the Create your own digital ID option button, then click OK. Click Create, in the Sign dialog box, click Select Image next to the sign box, browse to the location where your signature is saved, click Sign, then click OK. To add the certificate authenticating the workbook, click the File tab, click the Protect Workbook button, click Add a Digital Signature, then click OK. In the Sign dialog box click Sign, then click OK. The workbook will be saved as read-only, and it will not be able to be changed by other users.

**FIGURE F-18:** Toronto worksheet

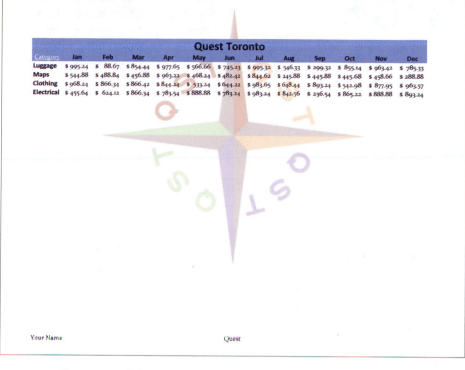

| Category | Jan | Feb | Mar | Apr | May | Jun | Jul | Aug | Sep | Oct | Nov | Dec |
|---|---|---|---|---|---|---|---|---|---|---|---|---|
| **Luggage** | $995.24 | $88.67 | $854.44 | $977.65 | $566.66 | $745.23 | $995.32 | $546.33 | $299.32 | $855.14 | $963.42 | $785.33 |
| **Maps** | $544.88 | $488.84 | $456.88 | $963.22 | $468.24 | $482.42 | $844.62 | $245.88 | $445.88 | $445.68 | $458.66 | $288.88 |
| **Clothing** | $968.24 | $866.34 | $866.42 | $844.24 | $533.24 | $644.22 | $983.65 | $648.44 | $893.24 | $542.98 | $877.95 | $963.57 |
| **Electrical** | $455.64 | $624.12 | $866.34 | $783.54 | $888.88 | $783.24 | $983.24 | $842.56 | $236.54 | $865.22 | $888.88 | $893.24 |

Your Name        Quest

**FIGURE F-19:** Vancouver worksheet

**Quest Vancouver**

| Category | Jan | Feb | Mar | Apr | May | Jun | Jul | Aug | Sep | Oct | Nov | Dec |
|---|---|---|---|---|---|---|---|---|---|---|---|---|
| **Luggage** | $863.54 | $869.54 | $844.32 | $951.55 | $877.34 | $963.54 | $951.53 | $782.54 | $445.32 | $951.55 | $963.54 | $456.37 |
| **Maps** | $863.98 | $863.54 | $458.35 | $874.21 | $125.68 | $822.31 | $117.36 | $185.67 | $136.24 | $536.54 | $959.77 | $999.99 |
| **Clothing** | $915.73 | $951.35 | $752.21 | $453.21 | $933.35 | $124.84 | $745.21 | $526.68 | $158.69 | $752.36 | $422.31 | $231.58 |
| **Electrical** | $899.48 | $532.54 | $785.34 | $423.36 | $744.35 | $425.36 | $455.62 | $953.57 | $855.47 | $975.11 | $999.99 | $963.24 |

Your Name        Quest

## Creating a workspace

If you work with several workbooks at a time in a particular arrangement on the screen, you can group them so that you can open them in one step by creating a workspace. A **workspace** is a file with an .xlw extension. Then, instead of opening each workbook individually, you can open the workspace. To create a workspace, open the workbooks you wish to group, then position and size them as you would like them to appear. Click the View tab, click the Save Workspace button in the Window group, type a name for the workspace file, navigate to the location where you want to store it, then click Save. The workspace file does not contain the workbooks themselves, however. You still have to save any changes you make to the original workbook files. If you work at another computer, you need to have the workspace file and all of the workbook files that are part of the workspace.

# Practice

## Concepts Review

For current SAM information, including versions and content details, visit SAM Central (http://www.cengage.com/samcentral). If you have a SAM user profile, you may have access to hands-on instruction, practice, and assessment of the skills covered in this unit. Since various versions of SAM are supported throughout the life of this text, check with your instructor for the correct instructions and URL/Web site for accessing assignments.

**FIGURE F-20**

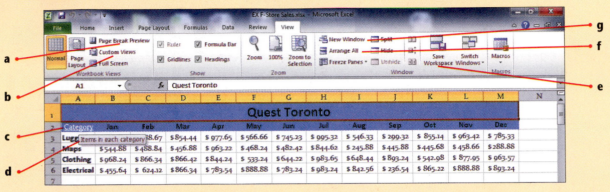

1. Which element do you click to view and change the way worksheet data is distributed on printed pages?
2. Which element do you click to group workbooks so that they open together as a unit?
3. Which element do you click to name and save a set of display and/or print settings?
4. Which element do you click to open the active worksheet in a new window?
5. Which element points to a hyperlink?
6. Which element points to a ScreenTip for a hyperlink?
7. Which element do you click to organize windows in a specific configuration?

## Match each term with the statement that best describes it.

8. Dynamic page breaks
9. HTML
10. Watermark
11. Hyperlink
12. Data entry area

a. Web page format
b. Portion of a worksheet that can be changed
c. Translucent background design on a printed worksheet
d. An object that when clicked displays another worksheet or a Web page
e. Adjusted automatically when rows and columns are inserted or deleted

**Select the best answer from the list of choices.**

**13.** You can establish the validity of a workbook by adding a:

    **a.** Template.
    **c.** Custom View.

    **b.** Digital signature.
    **d.** Keyword.

**14.** So that they can be opened together rather than individually, you can group several workbooks in a:

    **a.** Workspace.
    **c.** Workgroup.

    **b.** Consolidated workbook.
    **d.** Work unit.

## Skills Review

**1. View and arrange worksheets.**

  **a.** Start Excel, open the file EX F-2.xlsx from the drive and folder where you store your Data Files, then save it as **EX F-Dolce**.

  **b.** Activate the 2013 sheet if necessary, then open the 2014 sheet in a new window.

  **c.** Activate the 2013 sheet in the EX F-Dolce.xlsx:1 workbook. Activate the 2014 sheet in the EX F-Dolce.xlsx:2 workbook.

  **d.** View the EX F-Dolce.xlsx:1 and EX F-Dolce.xlsx:2 workbooks tiled horizontally. View the workbooks in a vertical arrangement.

  **e.** Hide the EX F-Dolce.xlsx:2 instance, then unhide the instance. Close the EX F-Dolce.xlsx:2 instance, and maximize the EX F-Dolce.xlsx workbook.

  **f.** Split the 2013 sheet into two horizontal panes. (*Hint*: Drag the Horizontal split box.) Remove the split by double-clicking it, then save your work.

**2. Protect worksheets and workbooks.**

  **a.** On the 2013 sheet, unlock the expense data in the range B12:F19.

  **b.** Protect the sheet without using a password.

  **c.** To make sure the other cells are locked, attempt to make an entry in cell D4 and verify that you receive an error message.

  **d.** Change the first-quarter mortgage expense in cell B12 to 5500.

  **e.** Protect the workbook's structure and windows without applying a password. Right-click the 2013 and 2014 sheet tabs to verify that you cannot insert, delete, rename, move, copy, hide, or unhide the sheets, or change their tab color.

  **f.** Unprotect the workbook. Unprotect the 2013 worksheet.

  **g.** Save the workbook.

**3. Save custom views of a worksheet**

  **a.** Using the 2013 sheet, create a custom view of the entire worksheet called **Entire 2013 Budget**.

  **b.** Hide rows 10 through 23, then create a new view called **Income** showing only the income data.

  **c.** Use the Custom Views dialog box to display all of the data on the 2013 worksheet.

  **d.** Use the Custom Views dialog box to display only the income data on the 2013 worksheet.

  **e.** Use the Custom Views dialog box to return to the Entire 2013 Budget view.

  **f.** Save the workbook.

**4. Add a worksheet background.**

  **a.** Use EX F-3.gif as a worksheet background for the 2013 sheet, then delete it.

  **b.** Add EX F-3.gif to the 2013 header, then preview the sheet to verify that the background will print.

  **c.** Add your name to the center section of the 2013 worksheet footer, then save the workbook.

**5. Prepare a workbook for distribution.**

  **a.** Inspect the workbook and remove any properties, personal data, and header and footer information.

  **b.** Use the Document Properties Panel to add a title of **Quarterly Budget** and the keywords **dolce** and **coffee**.

  **c.** Mark the workbook as final and verify that "[Read-Only]" is in the title bar.

  **d.** Remove the final status, then save the workbook.

**6. Insert hyperlinks.**

  **a.** On the 2013 worksheet, make cell A11 a hyperlink to the file **EX F-Expenses.xlsx** in your Data Files folder.

  **b.** Test the link and verify that Sheet1 of the target file displays expense details.

# Skills Review (continued)

   **c.** Return to the EX F-Dolce.xlsx workbook, edit the hyperlink in cell A11, adding a ScreenTip that reads **Expense Details**, then verify that the ScreenTip appears.

   **d.** On the 2014 worksheet, enter the text **Based on 2013 budget** in cell A25.

   **e.** Make the text in cell A25 a hyperlink to cell A1 in the 2013 worksheet. (*Hint*: Use the Place in This Document button and note the cell reference in the Type the cell reference text box.)

   **f.** Test the hyperlink. Remove the hyperlink in cell A25 of the 2014 worksheet, then save the workbook.

**7. Save a workbook for distribution.**

   **a.** Save the EX F-Dolce.xlsx workbook as a single file Web page with the name **dolce.mht**. Close the dolce.mht file that is open in Excel, then open the dolce.mht file in your Web browser. (The Information bar at the top of the Web page notifies you about blocked content. Your Web page doesn't contain any scripts that need to run so you can ignore the Information bar.) Close your browser window, and reopen EX F-Dolce.xlsx.

   **b.** Save the EX F-Dolce.xlsx workbook with the 2013 sheet active as a PDF file. Close the file EX F-Dolce.pdf.

   **c.** Save the EX F-Dolce workbook as an Excel 97-2003 workbook, and review the results of the Compatibility Checker.

   **d.** Close the EX F-Dolce.xls file, and reopen the EX F-Dolce.xlsx file.

   **e.** Save the workbook as a macro-enabled template in the drive and folder where you store your Data Files. (*Hint*: Select the type Excel Macro-Enabled Template (*.xltm) in the Save as type list.)

   **f.** Close the template file, then reopen the EX F-Dolce.xlsx file.

**8. Grouping worksheets.**

   **a.** Group the 2013 and 2014 worksheets, then add your name to the center footer section of the worksheets.

   **b.** Save the workbook, preview both sheets, comparing your worksheets to Figure F-21, then ungroup the sheets.

   **c.** Submit your EX F-Dolce.xlsx workbook to your instructor, close all open files, and exit Excel.

**FIGURE F-21**

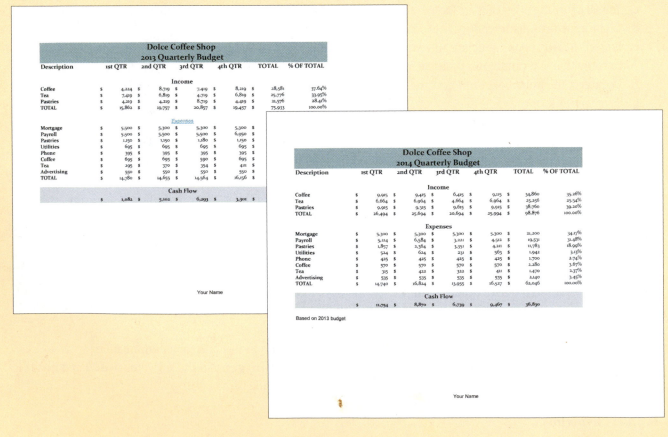

# Independent Challenge 1

You manage Shore Road Rugs, a wholesale supplier to retail stores. You are organizing your first-quarter sales in an Excel worksheet. Because the sheet for the month of January includes the same type of information you need for February and March, you decide to enter the headings for all of the first-quarter months at the same time. You use a separate worksheet for each month and create data for 3 months.

a. Start Excel, then save the workbook as **EX F-Rug Sales.xlsx** in the drive and folder where you store your Data Files.

b. Name the first sheet **January**, name the second sheet **February**, and name the third sheet **March**.

c. Group the worksheets.

d. With the worksheets grouped, add the title **Shore Road Rugs** centered across cells A1 and B1. Enter the label **Sales** in cell B2. Enter rug labels in column A beginning in cell A3 and ending in cell A9. Use the following rug types in the range A3:A9: **Wool**, **Custom**, **Antique**, **Commercial**, **Cotton, Indoor/Outdoor**, and **Runners**. Add the label **TOTAL** in cell A10. Enter your own sales data in the range B3:B9.

e. Enter the formula to sum the Amount column in cell B10. Ungroup the worksheets, and enter your own data for each of the sales categories in the January, February, and March sheets.

f. Display each worksheet in its own window, then arrange the three sheets vertically.

g. Hide the window displaying the March sheet. Unhide the March sheet window.

h. Split the March window into two panes: the upper pane displaying rows 1 through 5, and the lower pane displaying rows 6 through 10. Scroll through the data in each pane, then remove the split.

i. Close the windows displaying EX F-Rug Sales.xlsx:2 and EX F-Rug Sales.xlsx:3, then maximize the EX F-Rug Sales.xlsx workbook.

j. Add the keywords **rugs custom** to your workbook, using the Document Properties Panel.

k. Group the worksheets again.

l. Add headers to all three worksheets that include your name in the left section and the sheet name in the center section.

m. With the worksheets still grouped, format the worksheets appropriately.

n. Ungroup the worksheets, then mark the workbook status as final. Close the workbook, reopen the workbook, and enable editing.

o. Save the workbook, submit the workbook to your instructor, then exit Excel.

# Independent Challenge 2

As the payroll manager at New Media, a Web Development firm, you decide to organize the weekly timecard data using Excel worksheets. You use a separate worksheet for each week and track the hours for employees with different job classifications. A hyperlink in the worksheet provides pay rates for each classification, and custom views limit the information that is displayed.

a. Start Excel, open the file EX F-4.xlsx from the drive and folder where you store your Data Files, then save it as **EX F-Timesheets**.

b. Compare the data in the workbook by arranging the Week 1, Week 2, and Week 3 sheets horizontally.

c. Maximize the Week 1 window. Unlock the hours data in the Week 1 sheet and protect the worksheet. Verify that the employee names, numbers, and classifications cannot be changed. Verify that the total hours data can be changed, but do not change the data.

d. Unprotect the Week 1 sheet, and create a custom view called **Complete Worksheet** that displays all the data.

e. Hide column E and create a custom view of the data in the range A1:D22. Name the view **Employee Classifications**. Display each view, then return to the Complete Worksheet view.

f. Add a page break between columns D and E so that the Total Hours data prints on a second page. Preview the worksheet, then remove the page break. (*Hint*: Use the Breaks button on the Page Layout tab.)

# Independent Challenge 2 (continued)

FIGURE F-22

g. Add a hyperlink to the Classification heading in cell D1 that links to the file EX F-Classifications.xlsx. Add a ScreenTip that reads Pay rates, then test the hyperlink. Compare your screen to Figure F-22.

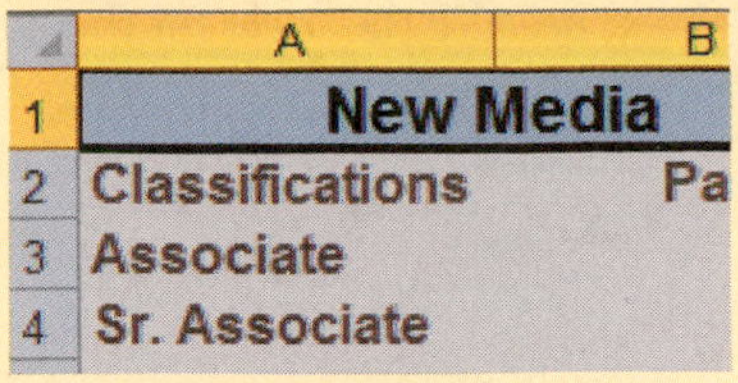

h. Save the EX F-Classifications workbook as an Excel 97-2003 workbook, reviewing the Compatibility Checker information. Close the EX F-Classifications.xls file.

i. Group the three worksheets in the EX F-Timesheets.xlsx workbook, and add your name to the center footer section.

j. Save the workbook, then preview the grouped worksheets.

k. Ungroup the worksheets, and add 2-inch top and left margins to the Week 1 worksheet.

l. Hide the Week 2 and Week 3 worksheets, inspect the file and remove all document properties, personal information, and hidden worksheets. Do not remove header and footer information.

m. Add the keyword **hours** to the workbook, save the workbook, then mark it as final.

### Advanced Challenge Exercise

- Remove the final status from the workbook.
- If you have access to an Information Rights Management server, restrict the permissions to the workbook by granting only yourself permission to change the workbook.
- If you have a valid certificate authority, add a digital signature to the workbook.
- Delete the hours data in the worksheet, and save the workbook as an Excel template.

n. Submit the workbook to your instructor, close the workbook, and exit Excel.

# Independent Challenge 3

One of your responsibilities as the office manager at Chicago Management Consultants is to track supplies for the home office. You decide to create a spreadsheet to track these orders, placing each month's orders on its own sheet. You create custom views that will focus on the categories of supplies. A hyperlink will provide the supplier's contact information.

a. Start Excel, open the file EX F-5.xlsx from the drive and folder where you store your Data Files, then save it as **EX F-Supplies**.

b. Arrange the sheets for the 3 months horizontally to compare expenses, then close the extra workbook windows and maximize the remaining window.

c. Create a custom view of the entire January worksheet named **All Supplies**. Hide the paper, pens, and miscellaneous supply data, and create a custom view displaying only the hardware supplies. Call the view **Hardware**.

d. Display the All Supplies view, group the worksheets, and create a total for the total costs in cell D32 on each month's sheet. Use the Format Painter to copy the format from cell D31 to cell D32.

e. With the sheets grouped, add the sheet name to the center section of each sheet's header and your name to the center section of each sheet's footer.

f. Ungroup the sheets and use the Compatibility Checker to view the features that are unsupported in earlier Excel formats.

g. Add a hyperlink in cell A1 of the January sheet that opens the file EX F-Hardware.xlsx. Add a ScreenTip of **Hardware Supplier**. Test the link, viewing the ScreenTip, then return to the EX F-Supplies.xlsx workbook without closing the EX F-Hardware.xlsx workbook. Save the EX F-Supplies.xlsx workbook.

h. Create a workspace that includes the workbooks EX F-Supplies.xlsx and EX F-Hardware.xlsx in the tiled layout. Name the workspace **EX F-Office Supplies**. (*Hint*: Save Workspace is a button on the View tab in the Window group.)

i. Hide the EX F-Hardware.xlsx workbook, then unhide it.

j. Close the EX F-Hardware.xlsx file, and maximize the EX F-Supplies.xlsx worksheet.

k. Save the EX F-Supplies workbook as a macro-enabled workbook. Close the workbook, submit the workbook to your instructor, then exit Excel.

# Real Life Independent Challenge

Excel can be a useful tool in tracking expenses for volunteering or service learning activities. Whether you are volunteering at an organization now or will be in the future, you can use Excel to enter and organize your volunteer expenses. After your data is entered, you create custom views of the data, add a hyperlink and keywords, and save the file in an earlier version of Excel.

a. Start Excel, save the new workbook as **EX F-Volunteer Expenses** in the drive and folder where you store your Data Files.

b. Enter the label Volunteer Activity in cell A1 and Expenses in cell A2. Center each label across columns A and B. Enter the labels **Category** in cell A4 and **Amount** in cell B4. Enter your expenses in column A. Examples of expenses might be **Supplies**, **Printing**, **Postage**, **Workshops**, **Reference Materials**, **Transportation**, **Mileage**, and **Meals**. Add the corresponding expense amounts in column B.

c. Add a hyperlink to cell A1 that links to a Web page with information about your volunteer activity. If you don't have a volunteer activity, link to a volunteer organization that interests you. If necessary, adjust the formatting for cell A1 so the label is visible in the cell. (*Hint*: In the Insert Hyperlink dialog box, click the Existing File or Web Page button, and enter the address of the Web page in the Address text box.)

d. Create a custom view called **All Expenses** that displays all of the budget information. Create a custom view named **Transportation** that displays only the transportation data. Check each view, then display the All Expenses view.

e. Using the Document Panel, add your name in the Author text box, add **volunteer** in the Subject text box, and add the keywords **expenses** and **volunteer**.

f. Add a footer that includes your name on the left side of the printout. Preview the worksheet.

g. Unlock the expense amounts in the worksheet. Protect the worksheet without using a password.

h. Remove the worksheet protection, then save the workbook.

i. Save the workbook in Excel 97-2003 format, then close the EX F-Volunteer Expenses.xls file.

## Advanced Challenge Exercise

- Open the EX F-Volunteer Expenses.xlsx file and verify the worksheet is not protected.
- Enable the workbook to be changed by multiple people simultaneously.
- Set up the shared workbook so that all future changes will be tracked, then change the data for two of your dollar amounts.
- Review the tracked changes, and accept the first change and reject the second change.
- Save and close the workbook.

j. Submit the workbook to your instructor. Exit Excel.

# Visual Workshop

Start Excel, open the file EX F-6.xlsx from the drive and folder where you store your Data Files, then save it as **EX F-Ocean View**. Make your worksheet look like the one shown in Figure F-23. The text in cell A4 is a hyperlink to the EX F-Price Information workbook, and it has been formatted in the standard color of green. The worksheet background is the Data File EX F-7.gif. Enter your name in the footer, preview the worksheet, then submit the worksheet to your instructor.

FIGURE F-23

| | A | B | C | D | E | F | G | H | I | J |
|---|---|---|---|---|---|---|---|---|---|---|
| 1 | Ocean View Realty | | | | | | | | | |
| 2 | Seasonal Rentals | | | | | | | | | |
| 3 | Listing Number | Location | Type | Bed | Bath | Pets | | | | |
| 4 | 1025 | Waterfront | Condominium | 2 | 1 | No | | | | |
| 5 | 1564 | Village | House | 4 | 2 | No | | | | |
| 6 | 1999 | 1 block from water | House | 4 | 2 | Yes | | | | |
| 7 | 1485 | 1 mile from water | Condominium | 2 | 2 | No | | | | |
| 8 | 1324 | Waterfront | Condominium | 4 | 2 | No | | | | |
| 9 | 1524 | Village | House | 2 | 1 | No | | | | |
| 10 | 1332 | Waterfront | House | 3 | 1 | Yes | | | | |
| 11 | 1563 | Village | Condominium | 3 | 2 | No | | | | |
| 12 | 1966 | 1 block from water | House | 4 | 2 | Yes | | | | |
| 13 | 1458 | 1 mile from water | Condominium | 2 | 2 | No | | | | |
| 14 | 1221 | Waterfront | House | 4 | 2 | No | | | | |
| 15 | 1469 | Village | House | 2 | 1 | No | | | | |

# Managing Data Using Tables

**Files You Will Need:**

EX G-1.xlsx
EX G-2.xlsx
EX G-3.xlsx
EX G-4.xlsx
EX G-5.xlsx

In addition to using Excel spreadsheet features, you can analyze and manipulate data in a table structure. An Excel **table** is an organized collection of rows and columns of similarly structured worksheet data. For example, a table might contain customer information, with a different customer in each row, with columns holding address, phone, and sales data for each customer. You can use a table to work with data independently of other data on your worksheet. When you designate a particular range of worksheet data as a table and format it, Excel automatically extends its formatting to adjacent cells when you add data. In addition, all table formulas are updated to include the new data. Without a table, you would have to manually adjust formatting and formulas every time you add data to a range. A table lets you easily change the order of information while keeping all row information together. You can also use a table to show and perform calculations on only the type of data you need, making it easier to understand large lists of data. In this unit, you'll learn how to plan and create a table; add, change, find, and delete table information; and then sort table data, perform table calculations, and print a table. Quest uses tables to analyze tour data. The vice president of sales, Kate Morgan, asks you to help her build and manage a table of 2013 tour information.

**OBJECTIVES**

Plan a table

Create and format a table

Add table data

Find and replace table data

Delete table data

Sort table data

Use formulas in a table

Print a table

# Planning a Table

Tables are a convenient way to understand and manage large amounts of information. When planning a table, consider what information you want your table to contain and how you want to work with the data, now and in the future. As you plan a table, you should understand its most important components. A table is organized into rows called records. A **record** is a table row that contains data about an object, person, or other item. Records are composed of fields. **Fields** are columns in the table; each field describes a characteristic of the record, such as a customer's last name or street address. Each field has a **field name**, which is a column label, such as "Address," that describes its contents. Tables usually have a **header row** as the first row that contains the field names. To plan your table, use the steps below.  Kate asks you to compile a table of the 2013 tours. Before entering the tour data into an Excel worksheet, you plan the table contents.

**DETAILS**

## As you plan your table, use the following guidelines:

- ### Identify the purpose of the table
  The purpose of the table determines the kind of information the table should contain. You want to use the tours table to find all departure dates for a particular tour and to display the tours in order of departure date. You also want to quickly calculate the number of available seats for a tour.

- ### Plan the structure of the table
  In designing your table's structure, determine the fields (the table columns) you need to achieve the table's purpose. You have worked with the sales department to learn the type of information they need for each tour. Figure G-1 shows a layout sketch for the table. Each row will contain one tour record. The columns represent fields that contain pieces of descriptive information you will enter for each tour, such as the name, departure date, and duration.

- ### Plan your row and column structure
  You can create a table from any contiguous range of cells on your worksheet. Plan and design your table so that all rows have similar types of information in the same column. A table should not have any blank rows or columns. Instead of using blank rows to separate table headings from data, use a table style, which will use formatting to make column labels stand out from your table data. Figure G-2 shows a table, populated with data, that has been formatted using a table style.

- ### Document the table design
  In addition to your table sketch, you should make a list of the field names to document the type of data and any special number formatting required for each field. Field names should be as short as possible while still accurately describing the column information. When naming fields it is important to use text rather than numbers because Excel could interpret numbers as parts of formulas. Your field names should be unique and not easily confused with cell addresses, such as the name D2. You want your tours table to contain eight field names, each one corresponding to the major characteristics of the 2013 tours. Table G-1 shows the documentation of the field names in your table.

**FIGURE G-1:** Table layout sketch

2013 Quest Tours

| Tour | Depart Date | Number of Days | Seat Capacity | Seats Reserved | Price | Air Included | Insurance Included |

- Header row will contain field names
- Each tour will be placed in a table row

**FIGURE G-2:** Formatted table with data

| | A | B | C | D | E | F | G | H |
|---|---|---|---|---|---|---|---|---|
| 1 | Tour | Depart Date | Number of Days | Seat Capacity | Seats Reserved | Price | Air Included | Insurance Included |
| 2 | Pacific Odyssey | 1/12/2013 | 14 | 50 | 50 | $ 2,105 | Yes | No |
| 3 | Old Japan | 1/13/2013 | 21 | 46 | 41 | $ 1,964 | Yes | No |
| 4 | Costa Rica | 1/19/2013 | 10 | 31 | 28 | $ 1,833 | Yes | Yes |
| 5 | Yellowstone | 1/21/2013 | 18 | 50 | 40 | $ 1,700 | Yes | Yes |
| 6 | Yellowstone | 1/31/2013 | 18 | 20 | 0 | $ 1,005 | Yes | Yes |
| 7 | Amazing Amazon | 2/22/2013 | 14 | 44 | 38 | $ 2,154 | No | No |
| 8 | Hiking Patagonia | 2/28/2013 | 7 | 20 | 15 | $ 2,822 | Yes | No |
| 9 | Pearls of the Orient | 3/13/2013 | 14 | 45 | 15 | $ 2,400 | Yes | No |
| 10 | Silk Road Travels | 3/19/2013 | 18 | 23 | 19 | $ 2,031 | Yes | Yes |
| 11 | Photographing France | 3/20/2013 | 7 | 20 | 20 | $ 1,541 | Yes | Yes |
| 12 | Green Adventures in Ecuador | 3/23/2013 | 18 | 25 | 22 | $ 2,450 | No | No |
| 13 | African National Parks | 4/8/2013 | 30 | 12 | 10 | $ 3,115 | Yes | Yes |
| 14 | Experience Cambodia | 4/11/2013 | 12 | 35 | 21 | $ 2,441 | Yes | No |
| 15 | Old Japan | 4/15/2013 | 21 | 47 | 30 | $ 1,900 | Yes | No |
| 16 | Costa Rica | 4/18/2013 | 10 | 30 | 20 | $ 2,800 | Yes | Yes |
| 17 | Yellowstone | 4/20/2013 | 18 | 51 | 31 | $ 1,652 | Yes | Yes |
| 18 | Amazing Amazon | 4/23/2013 | 14 | 43 | 30 | $ 2,133 | No | No |
| 19 | Catalonia Adventure | 5/9/2013 | 14 | 51 | 30 | $ 2,587 | Yes | No |
| 20 | Treasures of Ethiopia | 5/18/2013 | 10 | 41 | 15 | $ 1,638 | Yes | Yes |

Excel 2010

**TABLE G-1:** Table documentation

| field name | type of data | description of data |
|---|---|---|
| Tour | Text | Name of tour |
| Depart Date | Date | Date tour departs |
| Number of Days | Number with 0 decimal places | Duration of the tour |
| Seat Capacity | Number with 0 decimal places | Maximum number of people the tour can accommodate |
| Seats Reserved | Number with 0 decimal places | Number of reservations for the tour |
| Price | Accounting with 0 decimal places and $ symbol | Tour price (This price is not guaranteed until a 30% deposit is received) |
| Air Included | Text | Yes: Airfare is included in the price<br>No: Airfare is not included in the price |
| Insurance Included | Text | Yes: Insurance is included in the price<br>No: Insurance is not included in the price |

# Creating and Formatting a Table

Once you have planned the table structure, the sequence of fields, and appropriate data types, you are ready to create the table in Excel. After you create a table, a Table Tools Design tab appears, containing a gallery of table styles. **Table styles** allow you to easily add formatting to your table by using preset formatting combinations of fill color, borders, type style, and type color.  Kate asks you to build a table with the 2013 tour data. You begin by entering the field names. Then you enter the tour data that corresponds to each field name, create the table, and format the data using a table style.

## STEPS

**TROUBLE**
Don't worry if your field names are wider than the cells; you will fix this later.

1. **Start Excel, open the file EX G-1.xlsx from the drive and folder where you store your Data Files, then save it as EX G-2013 Tours**

2. **Beginning in cell A1 of the Practice sheet, enter each field name in a separate column, as shown in Figure G-3**

   Field names are usually in the first row of the table.

**QUICK TIP**
Do not insert extra spaces at the beginning of a cell because it can affect sorting and finding data in a table.

3. **Enter the information from Figure G-4 in the rows immediately below the field names, leaving no blank rows**

   The data appears in columns organized by field name.

4. **Select the range A1:H4, click the Format button in the Cells group, click AutoFit Column Width, then click cell A1**

   Resizing the column widths this way is faster than double-clicking the column divider lines.

**QUICK TIP**
You can also create a table using the shortcut key combination [Ctrl] + T.

5. **With cell A1 selected, click the Insert tab, click the Table button in the Tables group, in the Create Table dialog box verify that your table data is in the range $A$1:$H$4, and make sure My table has headers is checked as shown in Figure G-5, then click OK**

   The data range is now defined as a table. **Filter list arrows**, which let you display portions of your data, now appear next to each column header. When you create a table, Excel automatically applies a table style. The default table style has a dark blue header row and alternating gray and white data rows. The Table Tools Design tab appears, and the Table Styles group displays a gallery of table formatting options. You decide to choose a different table style from the gallery.

6. **Click the Table Styles More button ⊞, scroll to view all of the table styles, then move the mouse pointer over several styles without clicking**

   The Table Styles gallery on the Table Tools Design tab has three style categories: Light, Medium, and Dark. Each category has numerous design types; for example, in some of the designs, the header row and total row are darker and the rows alternate colors. The available table designs use the current workbook theme colors so the table coordinates with your existing workbook content. If you select a different workbook theme and color scheme in the Themes group on the Page Layout tab, the Table Styles gallery uses those colors. As you point to each table style, Live Preview shows you what your table will look like with the style applied. However, you only see a preview of each style; you need to click a style to apply it.

7. **Click the Table Style Medium 21 to apply it to your table, then click cell A1**

   Compare your table to Figure G-6.

**FIGURE G-3:** Field names entered in row 1

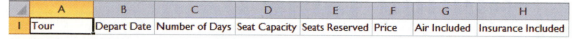

| | A | B | C | D | E | F | G | H |
|---|---|---|---|---|---|---|---|---|
| 1 | Tour | Depart Date | Number of Days | Seat Capacity | Seats Reserved | Price | Air Included | Insurance Included |

**FIGURE G-4:** Three records entered in the worksheet

| | A | B | C | D | E | F | G | H |
|---|---|---|---|---|---|---|---|---|
| 1 | Tour | Depart Date | Number of Days | Seat Capacity | Seats Reserved | Price | Air Included | Insurance Included |
| 2 | Pacific Odyssey | 1/12/2013 | 14 | 50 | 50 | 2105 | Yes | No |
| 3 | Old Japan | 1/13/2013 | 21 | 46 | 41 | 1964 | Yes | No |
| 4 | Costa Rica | 1/19/2013 | 10 | 31 | 28 | 1833 | Yes | Yes |
| 5 | | | | | | | | |

**FIGURE G-5:** Insert Table dialog box

Table range

Verify that this box is checked

**FIGURE G-6:** Formatted table with three records

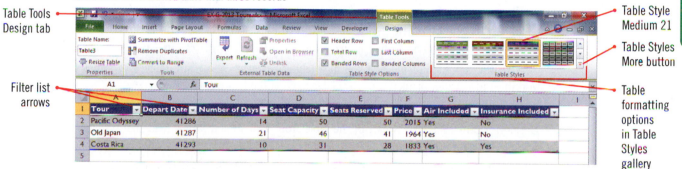

Table Tools Design tab

Filter list arrows

Table Style Medium 21

Table Styles More button

Table formatting options in Table Styles gallery

## Changing table style options

You can change a table's appearance by using the check boxes in the Table Styles Options group on the Table Tools Design tab. For example, you can turn on or turn off the following options: **banding**, which creates different formatting for adjacent rows and columns; special formatting for first and last columns; Total Row, which calculates totals for each column; and Header Row, which displays or hides the header row. Use these options to modify a table's appearance either before or after applying a table style. For example, if your table has banded rows, you can select the Banded Columns check box to change the table to be displayed with banded columns. Also, you may want to deselect the Header Row check box to hide a table's header row if a table will be included in a presentation. Figure G-7 shows the available table style options.

You can also create your own table style by clicking the Table Styles More button, then at the bottom of the Table Styles Gallery, clicking New Table Style. In the New Table Quick Style dialog box, name the style in the Name text box, click a table element, then format selected table elements by clicking Format. You can also set a custom style as the default style for your tables by checking the Set as default table quick style for this document check box. You can click Clear at the bottom of the Table Styles gallery if you want to clear a table style.

**FIGURE G-7:** Table Styles Options

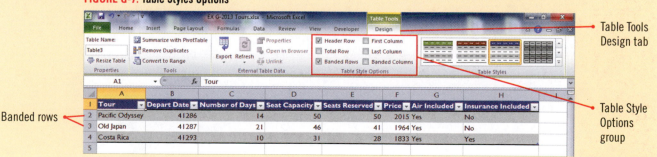

Banded rows

Table Tools Design tab

Table Style Options group

# Adding Table Data

You can add records to a table by typing data directly below the last row of the table. After you press [Enter], the new row becomes part of the table and the table formatting extends to the new data. When the active cell is the last cell of a table, you can add a new row by pressing [Tab]. You can also insert rows in any table location. If you decide you need additional data fields, you can add new columns to a table. You can also expand a table by dragging the sizing handle in a table's lower-right corner; drag down to add rows and drag to the right to add columns.  After entering all of the 2013 tour data, Kate decides to offer two additional tours. She also wants the table to display the number of available seats for each tour and whether visas are required for the destination.

## STEPS

1. **Click the 2013 Tours sheet tab**

   The 2013 sheet containing the 2013 tour data becomes active.

2. **Scroll down to the last table row, click cell A65 in the table, enter the data for the new Costa Rica tour, as shown in Figure G-8, then press [Enter]**

   As you scroll down, the table headers are visible at the top of the table as long as the active cell is inside the table. The new Costa Rica tour is part of the table. You want to enter a record about a new January tour above row 6.

3. **Scroll up to and click the inside left edge of cell A6 to select the table row data, click the Insert list arrow in the Cells group, then click Insert Table Rows Above**

   Clicking the left edge of the first cell in a table row selects the entire table row, rather than the entire worksheet row. A new blank row 6 is available to enter the new record.

4. **Click cell A6, then enter the Yellowstone record, as shown in Figure G-9**

   The new Yellowstone tour is part of the table. You want to add a new field that displays the number of available seats for each tour.

5. **Click cell I1, enter the field name Seats Available, then press [Enter]**

   The new field becomes part of the table, and the header formatting extends to the new field. The AutoCorrect menu allows you to undo or stop the automatic table expansion, but in this case you decide to leave this feature on. You want to add another new field to the table to display tours that require visas, but this time you will add the new field by resizing the table.

**QUICK TIP**
You can also resize a table by clicking the Table Tools Design tab, clicking the Resize Table button in the Properties group, selecting the new data range for the table, then clicking OK.

6. **Scroll down until cell I66 is visible, drag the sizing handle in the table's lower-right corner one column to the right to add column J to the table, as shown in Figure G-10**

   The table range is now A1:J66, and the new field name is Column1.

7. **Scroll up to and click cell J1, enter Visa Required, then press [Enter]**

8. **Click the Insert tab, click the Header & Footer button in the Text group, enter your name in the center header text box, click cell A1, click the Normal button ⊞ in the status bar, then save the workbook**

**FIGURE G-8:** New record in row 65

| | | | | | | | | |
|---|---|---|---|---|---|---|---|---|
| 62 | Pacific Odyssey | 12/21/2013 | 14 | 50 | 10 | $ 2,105 | Yes | No |
| 63 | Yellowstone | 12/30/2013 | 18 | 51 | 15 | $ 2,922 | Yes | Yes |
| 64 | Old Japan | 12/31/2013 | 21 | 47 | 4 | $ 2,100 | Yes | No |
| 65 | Costa Rica | 1/30/2013 | 7 | 20 | 0 | $ 1,927 | Yes | Yes |
| 66 | | | | | | | | |
| 67 | | | | | | | | |
| 68 | | | | | | | | |

New record in row 65

**FIGURE G-9:** New record in row 6

| | A | B | C | D | E | F | G | H |
|---|---|---|---|---|---|---|---|---|
| 1 | Tour | Depart Date | Number of Days | Seat Capacity | Seats Reserved | Price | Air Included | Insurance Included |
| 2 | Pacific Odyssey | 1/12/2013 | 14 | 50 | 50 | $ 2,105 | Yes | No |
| 3 | Old Japan | 1/13/2013 | 21 | 46 | 41 | $ 1,964 | Yes | No |
| 4 | Costa Rica | 1/19/2013 | 10 | 31 | 28 | $ 1,833 | Yes | Yes |
| 5 | Yellowstone | 1/21/2013 | 18 | 50 | 40 | $ 1,700 | Yes | Yes |
| 6 | Yellowstone | 1/31/2013 | 18 | 20 | 0 | $ 1,005 | Yes | Yes |
| 7 | Amazing Amazon | 2/22/2013 | 14 | 44 | 38 | $ 2,154 | No | No |
| 8 | Hiking Patagonia | 2/28/2013 | 7 | 20 | 15 | $ 2,822 | Yes | No |
| 9 | Pearls of the Orient | 3/13/2013 | 14 | 45 | 15 | $ 2,400 | Yes | No |
| 10 | Silk Road Travels | 3/19/2013 | 18 | 23 | 19 | $ 2,031 | Yes | Yes |

New record in row 6

Excel 2010

**FIGURE G-10:** Resizing a table using the resizing handles

| | | | | | | | | | |
|---|---|---|---|---|---|---|---|---|---|
| 56 | Exotic Morocco | 10/31/2013 | 7 | 38 | 15 | $ 1,900 | Yes | No | |
| 57 | Experience Cambodia | 10/31/2013 | 12 | 40 | 2 | $ 2,908 | Yes | No | |
| 58 | Treasures of Ethiopia | 11/18/2013 | 10 | 41 | 12 | $ 2,200 | Yes | Yes | |
| 59 | Panama Adventure | 12/18/2013 | 10 | 50 | 21 | $ 2,204 | Yes | Yes | |
| 60 | Panama Adventure | 12/18/2013 | 10 | 50 | 21 | $ 2,204 | Yes | Yes | |
| 61 | Galapagos Adventure | 12/20/2013 | 14 | 15 | 1 | $ 2,100 | Yes | Yes | |
| 62 | Galapagos Adventure | 12/20/2013 | 14 | 15 | 1 | $ 2,100 | Yes | Yes | |
| 63 | Pacific Odyssey | 12/21/2013 | 14 | 50 | 10 | $ 2,105 | Yes | No | |
| 64 | Yellowstone | 12/30/2013 | 18 | 51 | 15 | $ 2,922 | Yes | Yes | |
| 65 | Old Japan | 12/31/2013 | 21 | 47 | 4 | $ 2,100 | Yes | No | |
| 66 | Costa Rica | 1/30/2013 | 7 | 20 | 0 | $ 1,927 | Yes | Yes | |
| 67 | | | | | | | | | |

Drag sizing handle to add column J

## Selecting table elements

When working with tables you often need to select rows, columns, and even the entire table. Clicking to the right of a row number, inside column A, selects the entire table row. You can select a table column by clicking the top edge of the header. Be careful not to click a column letter or row number, however, because this selects the entire worksheet row or column. You can select the table data by clicking the upper-left corner of the first table cell. When selecting a column or a table, the first click selects only the data in the column or table. If you click a second time, you add the headers to the selection.

# Finding and Replacing Table Data

From time to time, you need to locate specific records in your table. You can use the Excel Find feature to search your table for the information you need. You can also use the Replace feature to locate and replace existing entries or portions of entries with information you specify. If you don't know the exact spelling of the text you are searching for, you can use wildcards to help locate the records. **Wildcards** are special symbols that substitute for unknown characters.  In response to a change in the bike trip from Ireland to Scotland, Kate needs to replace "Ireland" with "Scotland" in all of the tour names. She also wants to know how many Pacific Odyssey tours are scheduled for the year. You begin by searching for records with the text "Pacific Odyssey".

## STEPS

1. **Click cell A1 if necessary, click the Home tab, click the Find & Select button in the Editing group, then click Find**

   The Find and Replace dialog box opens, as shown in Figure G-11. In this dialog box, you enter criteria that specify the records you want to find in the Find what text box. You want to search for records whose Tour field contains the label "Pacific Odyssey".

2. **Type Pacific Odyssey in the Find what text box, then click Find Next**

   A2 is the active cell because it is the first instance of Pacific Odyssey in the table.

3. **Click Find Next and examine the record for each Pacific Odyssey tour found until no more matching cells are found in the table and the active cell is A2 again, then click Close**

   There are four Pacific Odyssey tours.

4. **Return to cell A1, click the Find & Select button in the Editing group, then click Replace**

   The Find and Replace dialog box opens with the Replace tab selected and "Pacific Odyssey" in the Find what text box, as shown in Figure G-12. You will search for entries containing "Ireland" and replace them with "Scotland". To save time, you will use the ( * ) wildcard to help you locate the records containing Ireland.

   **QUICK TIP**
   You can also use the question mark ( ? ) wildcard to represent any single character. For example, using "to?" as your search text would only find 3-letter words beginning with "to", such as "top" and "tot"; it would not find "tone" or "topography".

5. **Delete the text in the Find what text box, type Ir\* in the Find what text box, click the Replace with text box, then type Scotland**

   The asterisk ( * ) wildcard stands for one or more characters, meaning that the search text "Ir*" will find words such as "iron", "hair", and "bird". Because you notice that there are other table entries containing the text "ir" with a lowercase "i" (in the Air Included column heading), you need to make sure that only capitalized instances of the letter "I" are replaced.

6. **Click Options >>, click the Match case check box to select it, click Options <<, then click Find Next**

   Excel moves the cell pointer to the cell containing the first occurrence of "Ireland".

7. **Click Replace All, click OK, then click Close**

   The dialog box closes. Excel made three replacements, in cells A27, A36, and A40. The Air Included field heading remains unchanged because the "ir" in "Air" is lowercase.

8. **Save the workbook**

**FIGURE G-11:** Find and Replace dialog box

Type Pacific
Odyssey here

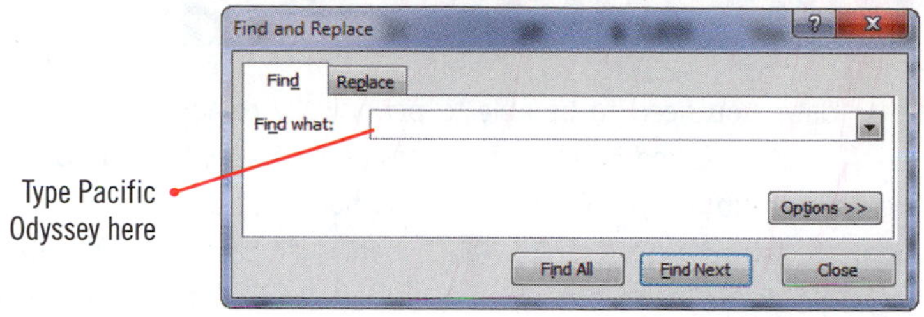

**FIGURE G-12:** The Replace tab in the Find and Replace dialog box

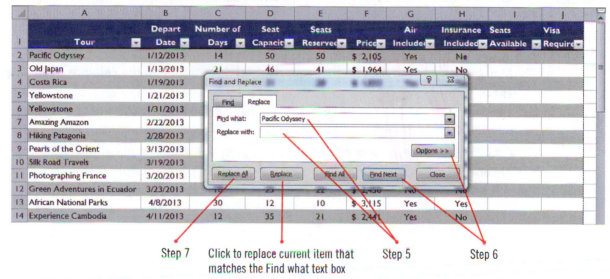

Step 7   Click to replace current item that   Step 5   Step 6
         matches the Find what text box

## Using Find and Select features

You can also use the Find feature to navigate to a specific place in a workbook by clicking the Find & Select button in the Editing group, clicking Go To, typing a cell address, then clicking OK. Clicking the Find & Select button also allows you to find comments and conditional formatting in a worksheet. You can use the Go to Special dialog box to select cells that contain different types of formulas or objects. Some Go to Special commands also appear on the Find & Select menu. Using this menu, you can also change the mouse pointer shape to the Select Objects pointer so you can quickly select drawing objects when necessary. To return to the standard Excel pointer, press [Esc].

# Deleting Table Data

To keep a table up to date, you need to be able to periodically remove records. You may even need to remove fields if the information stored in a field becomes unnecessary. You can delete table data using the Delete button in the Cells group or by dragging the sizing handle at the table's lower-right corner. You can also easily delete duplicate records from a table.  Kate is canceling the Old Japan tour that departs on 1/13/2013 and asks you to delete the record from the table. You will also remove any duplicate records from the table. Because the visa requirements are difficult to keep up with, Kate asks you to delete the field with visa information.

## STEPS

1. **Click the left edge of cell A3 to select the table row data, click the Delete button list arrow in the Cells group, then click Delete Table Rows**

   The Old Japan tour is deleted, and the Costa Rica tour moves up to row 3, as shown in Figure G-13. You can also delete a table row or a column using the Resize Table button in the Properties group of the Table Tools Design tab, or by right-clicking the row or column, pointing to Delete on the shortcut menu, then clicking Table Columns or Table Rows. You decide to check the table for duplicate records.

> ### QUICK TIP
   > You can also remove duplicates from worksheet data by clicking the Data tab, then clicking the Remove Duplicates button in the Data Tools group.

2. **Click the Table Tools Design tab, then click the Remove Duplicates button in the Tools group**

   The Remove Duplicates dialog box opens, as shown in Figure G-14. You need to select the columns that will be used to evaluate duplicates. Because you don't want to delete tours with the same destination but different departure dates, you will look for duplicate data in all of the columns.

3. **Make sure that "My data has headers" is checked and that all the columns headers are checked, then click OK**

   Two duplicate records are found and removed, leaving 62 records of data and a total of 63 rows in the table, including the header row. You want to remove the last column, which contains space for visa information.

4. **Click OK, scroll down until cell J63 is visible, drag the sizing handle of the table's lower-right corner one column to the left to remove column J from the table**

   The table range is now A1:I63, and the Visa Required field no longer appears in the table.

5. **Delete the contents of cell J1, return to cell A1, then save the workbook**

| | Tour | Depart Date | Number of Days | Seat Capacity | Seats Reserved | Price | Air Included | Insurance Included | Seats Available |
|---|---|---|---|---|---|---|---|---|---|
| 2 | Pacific Odyssey | 1/12/2013 | 14 | 50 | 50 | $ 2,105 | Yes | No | |
| 3 | Costa Rica | 1/19/2013 | 10 | 31 | 28 | $ 1,833 | Yes | Yes | |
| 4 | Yellowstone | 1/21/2013 | 18 | 50 | 40 | $ 1,700 | Yes | Yes | |
| 5 | Yellowstone | 1/31/2013 | 18 | 20 | 0 | $ 1,005 | Yes | Yes | |
| 6 | Amazing Amazon | 2/22/2013 | 14 | 44 | 38 | $ 2,154 | No | No | |
| 7 | Hiking Patagonia | 2/28/2013 | 7 | 20 | 15 | $ 2,822 | Yes | No | |
| 8 | Pearls of the Orient | 3/13/2013 | 14 | 45 | 15 | $ 2,400 | Yes | No | |
| 9 | Silk Road Travels | 3/19/2013 | 18 | 23 | 19 | $ 2,031 | Yes | Yes | |
| 10 | Photographing France | 3/20/2013 | 7 | 20 | 20 | $ 1,541 | Yes | Yes | |
| 11 | Green Adventures in Ecuador | 3/23/2013 | 18 | 25 | 22 | $ 2,450 | No | No | |
| 12 | African National Parks | 4/8/2013 | 30 | 12 | 10 | $ 3,115 | Yes | Yes | |
| 13 | Experience Cambodia | 4/11/2013 | 12 | 35 | 21 | $ 2,441 | Yes | No | |
| 14 | Old Japan | 4/15/2013 | 21 | 47 | 30 | $ 1,900 | Yes | No | |
| 15 | Costa Rica | 4/18/2013 | 10 | 30 | 20 | $ 2,800 | Yes | Yes | |
| 16 | Yellowstone | 4/20/2013 | 18 | 51 | 31 | $ 1,652 | Yes | Yes | |
| 17 | Amazing Amazon | 4/23/2013 | 14 | 43 | 30 | $ 2,133 | No | No | |
| 18 | Catalonia Adventure | 5/9/2013 | 14 | 51 | 30 | $ 2,587 | Yes | No | |
| 19 | Treasures of Ethiopia | 5/18/2013 | 10 | 41 | 15 | $ 1,638 | Yes | Yes | |
| 20 | Monasteries of Bulgaria | 5/20/2013 | 7 | 19 | 11 | $ 1,663 | Yes | Yes | |
| 21 | Biking in France | 5/23/2013 | 7 | 12 | 10 | $ 1,635 | No | No | |

Row is deleted and tours move up one row

Practice | 2013 Tours | Sheet2

FIGURE G-14: Remove Duplicates dialog box

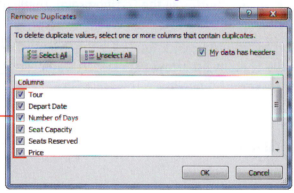

Selected columns will be checked for duplicate data

Excel 2010

# Sorting Table Data

Usually, you enter table records in the order in which you receive information, rather than in alphabetical or numerical order. When you add records to a table, you usually enter them at the end of the table. You can change the order of the records any time using the Excel **sort** feature. Because the data is structured as a table, Excel changes the order of the records while keeping each record, or row of information, together. You can sort a table in ascending or descending order on one field using the filter list arrows next to the field name. In **ascending order**, the lowest value (the beginning of the alphabet or the earliest date) appears at the top of the table. In a field containing labels and numbers, numbers appear first in the sorted list. In **descending order**, the highest value (the end of the alphabet or the latest date) appears at the top of the table. In a field containing labels and numbers, labels appear first. Table G-2 provides examples of ascending and descending sorts. Kate wants the tour data sorted by departure date, displaying tours that depart the soonest at the top of the table.

## STEPS

**QUICK TIP**

Before you sort records, consider making a backup copy of your table or create a field that numbers the records so you can return them to their original order, if necessary.

1. **Click the Depart Date filter list arrow, then click Sort Oldest to Newest**

   Excel rearranges the records in ascending order by departure date, as shown in Figure G-15. The Depart Date filter list arrow has an upward pointing arrow indicating the ascending sort in the field. You can also sort the table on one field using the Sort & Filter button.

2. **Click the Home tab, click any cell in the Price column, click the Sort & Filter button in the Editing group, then click Sort Largest to Smallest**

   Excel sorts the table, placing those records with the higher price at the top. The Price filter list arrow now has a downward pointing arrow next to the filter list arrow, indicating the descending sort order. You can also rearrange the table data using a **multilevel sort**. This type of sort rearranges the table data using more than one field, where each field is a different level, based on its importance in the sort. If you use two sort levels, the data is sorted by the first field, and the second field is sorted within each grouping of the first field. Since you have many groups of tours with different departure dates, you want to use a multilevel sort to arrange the table data by tours and then by departure dates within each tour.

**QUICK TIP**

You can also add a multilevel sort by clicking the Data tab and then clicking the Sort button in the Sort & Filter group.

3. **Click the Sort & Filter button in the Editing group, then click Custom Sort**

   The Sort dialog box opens, as shown in Figure G-16.

**QUICK TIP**

You can include capitalization as a sort criterion by clicking Options in the Sort dialog box, then selecting the Case sensitive box. When you choose this option, lowercase entries precede uppercase entries in an ascending order.

4. **Click the Sort by list arrow, click Tour, click the Order list arrow, click A to Z, click Add Level, click the Then by list arrow, click Depart Date, click the second Order list arrow, click Oldest to Newest if necessary, then click OK**

   Figure G-17 shows the table sorted alphabetically in ascending order (A–Z) by Tour and, within each tour grouping, in ascending order by the Depart Date.

5. **Save the workbook**

---

### Sorting a table using conditional formatting

If conditional formats have been applied to a table, you can sort the table using conditional formatting to arrange the rows. For example, if cells are conditionally formatted with color, you can sort a field on Cell Color, using the color with the order of On Top or On Bottom in the Sort dialog box.

**FIGURE G-15:** Table sorted by departure date

Up arrow indicates ascending sort in the field

| | A | B | C | D | E | F | G | H | I |
|---|---|---|---|---|---|---|---|---|---|
| 1 | Tour | Depart Date | Number of Days | Seat Capacity | Seats Reserved | Price | Air Included | Insurance Included | Seats Available |
| 2 | Pacific Odyssey | 1/12/2013 | 14 | 50 | 50 | $ 2,105 | Yes | No | |
| 3 | Costa Rica | 1/19/2013 | 10 | 31 | 28 | $ 1,833 | Yes | Yes | |
| 4 | Yellowstone | 1/21/2013 | 18 | 50 | 40 | $ 1,700 | Yes | Yes | |
| 5 | Costa Rica | 1/30/2013 | 7 | 20 | 0 | $ 1,927 | Yes | Yes | |
| 6 | Yellowstone | 1/31/2013 | 18 | 20 | 0 | $ 1,005 | Yes | Yes | |
| 7 | Amazing Amazon | 2/22/2013 | 14 | 44 | 38 | $ 2,154 | No | No | |
| 8 | Hiking Patagonia | 2/28/2013 | 7 | 20 | 15 | $ 2,822 | Yes | No | |
| 9 | Pearls of the Orient | 3/13/2013 | 14 | 45 | 15 | $ 2,400 | Yes | No | |
| 10 | Silk Road Travels | 3/19/2013 | 18 | 23 | 19 | $ 2,031 | Yes | Yes | |
| 11 | Photographing France | 3/20/2013 | 7 | 20 | 20 | $ 1,541 | Yes | Yes | |
| 12 | Green Adventures in Ecuador | 3/23/2013 | 18 | 25 | 22 | $ 2,450 | No | No | |
| 13 | African National Parks | 4/8/2013 | 30 | 12 | 10 | $ 3,115 | Yes | Yes | |
| 14 | Experience Cambodia | 4/11/2013 | 12 | 35 | 21 | $ 2,441 | Yes | No | |
| 15 | Old Japan | 4/15/2013 | 21 | 47 | 30 | $ 1,900 | Yes | No | |
| 16 | Costa Rica | 4/18/2013 | 10 | 30 | 20 | $ 2,800 | Yes | Yes | |
| 17 | Yellowstone | 4/20/2013 | 18 | 51 | 31 | $ 1,652 | Yes | Yes | |
| 18 | Amazing Amazon | 4/23/2013 | 14 | 43 | 30 | $ 2,133 | No | No | |
| 19 | Catalonia Adventure | 5/9/2013 | 14 | 51 | 30 | $ 2,587 | Yes | No | |
| 20 | Treasures of Ethiopia | 5/18/2013 | 10 | 41 | 15 | $ 1,638 | Yes | Yes | |
| 21 | Monasteries of Bulgaria | 5/20/2013 | 7 | 19 | 11 | $ 1,663 | Yes | Yes | |

Practice | **2013 Tours** | Sheet2

**FIGURE G-16:** Sort dialog box

Click to add additional sort levels

Click to delete sort levels

Click to display fields

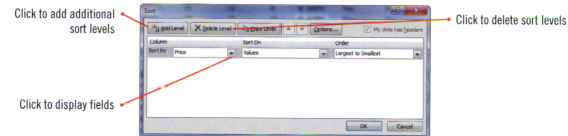

**FIGURE G-17:** Table sorted using two levels

Top-level sort on Tour arranges records by tour name

Second-level sort arranges records by departure date within each tour grouping

| | A | B | C | D | E | F | G | H |
|---|---|---|---|---|---|---|---|---|
| 1 | Tour | Depart Date | Number of Days | Seat Capacity | Seats Reserved | Price | Air Included | Insurance Included |
| 2 | African National Parks | 4/8/2013 | 30 | 12 | 10 | $ 3,115 | Yes | Yes |
| 3 | African National Parks | 10/27/2013 | 30 | 12 | 8 | $ 4,870 | Yes | Yes |
| 4 | Amazing Amazon | 2/22/2013 | 14 | 44 | 38 | $ 2,154 | No | No |
| 5 | Amazing Amazon | 4/23/2013 | 14 | 43 | 30 | $ 2,133 | No | No |
| 6 | Amazing Amazon | 8/23/2013 | 14 | 43 | 18 | $ 2,877 | No | No |
| 7 | Biking in France | 5/23/2013 | 7 | 12 | 10 | $ 1,635 | No | No |
| 8 | Biking in France | 9/23/2013 | 7 | 12 | 7 | $ 2,110 | No | No |
| 9 | Biking in Scotland | 6/11/2013 | 10 | 15 | 10 | $ 2,600 | Yes | No |
| 10 | Biking in Scotland | 7/11/2013 | 10 | 15 | 9 | $ 2,600 | Yes | No |
| 11 | Biking in Scotland | 8/11/2013 | 10 | 15 | 6 | $ 2,600 | Yes | No |
| 12 | Catalonia Adventure | 5/9/2013 | 14 | 51 | 30 | $ 2,587 | Yes | No |
| 13 | Catalonia Adventure | 6/9/2013 | 14 | 51 | 15 | $ 2,100 | Yes | No |
| 14 | Catalonia Adventure | 10/9/2013 | 14 | 51 | 11 | $ 2,100 | Yes | No |
| 15 | Corfu Sailing Voyage | 6/10/2013 | 21 | 12 | 10 | $ 2,190 | Yes | No |
| 16 | Corfu Sailing Voyage | 7/9/2013 | 21 | 12 | 1 | $ 2,190 | Yes | No |
| 17 | Costa Rica | 1/19/2013 | 10 | 31 | 28 | $ 1,833 | Yes | Yes |
| 18 | Costa Rica | 1/30/2013 | 7 | 20 | 0 | $ 1,927 | Yes | Yes |
| 19 | Costa Rica | 4/18/2013 | 10 | 30 | 20 | $ 2,800 | Yes | Yes |
| 20 | Exotic Morocco | 6/12/2013 | 7 | 38 | 25 | $ 1,900 | Yes | No |
| 21 | Exotic Morocco | 10/31/2013 | 7 | 38 | 15 | $ 1,900 | Yes | No |

Practice | **2013 Tours** | Sheet2

**TABLE G-2:** Sort order options and examples

| option | alphabetic | numeric | date | alphanumeric |
|---|---|---|---|---|
| Ascending | A, B, C | 7, 8, 9 | 1/1, 2/1, 3/1 | 12A, 99B, DX8, QT7 |
| Descending | C, B, A | 9, 8, 7 | 3/1, 2/1, 1/1 | QT7, DX8, 99B, 12A |

### Specifying a custom sort order

You can identify a custom sort order for the field selected in the Sort by box. Click the Order list arrow in the Sort dialog box, click Custom List, then click the desired custom order. Commonly used custom sort orders are days of the week (Sun, Mon, Tues, Wed, etc.) and months (Jan, Feb, Mar, etc.); alphabetic sorts do not sort these items properly.

Managing Data Using Tables

# Using Formulas in a Table

Many tables are large, making it difficult to know from viewing them the "story" the table tells. The Excel table calculation features help you summarize table data so you can see important trends. After you enter a single formula into a table cell, the **calculated columns** feature fills in the remaining cells with the formula's results. The column continues to fill with the formula results as you enter rows in the table. This makes it easy to update your formulas because you only need to edit the formula once, and the change will fill in to the other column cells. The **structured reference** feature allows your formulas to refer to table columns by names that are automatically generated when you create the table. These names automatically adjust as you add or delete table fields. An example of a table reference is =[Sales]–[Costs], where Sales and Costs are field names in the table. Tables also have a specific area at the bottom called the **table total row** for calculations using the data in the table columns. The cells in this row contain a dropdown list of functions that can be used for the column calculation. The table total row adapts to any changes in the table size. Kate wants you to use a formula to calculate the number of available seats for each tour. You will also add summary information to the end of the table.

## STEPS

1. **Click cell I2, then type =[**

    A list of the table field names appears, as shown in Figure G-18. Structured referencing allows you to use the names that Excel created when you defined your table to reference fields in a formula. You can choose a field by clicking it and pressing [TAB] or by double-clicking the field name.

2. **Click [Seat Capacity], press [Tab], then type ]**

    Excel begins the formula, placing [Seat Capacity] in the cell in blue and framing the Seat Capacity data in a blue border.

3. **Type -[, double-click [Seats Reserved], then type ]**

    Excel places [Seats Reserved] in the cell in green and outlines the Seats Reserved data in a green border.

4. **Press [Enter]**

    The formula result, 2, is displayed in cell I2. The table column also fills with the formula displaying the number of available seats for each tour.

> **QUICK TIP**
>
> You can undo the calculated column results by clicking Undo Calculated Column in the AutoCorrect Options list. You can turn off the Calculated Columns feature by clicking Stop Automatically Creating Calculated Columns in the AutoCorrect Options list.

5. **Click the AutoCorrect Options list arrow** ⚡▾

    Because the calculated columns option saves time, you decide to leave the feature on. You want to display the total number of available seats on all of the tours.

6. **Click any cell inside the table if necessary, click the Table Tools Design tab, then click the Total Row check box in the Table Style Options group to select it**

    A total row appears at the bottom of the table, and the sum of the available seats, 1028, is displayed in cell I64. You can select other formulas in the total row.

7. **Click cell C64, then click the cell list arrow on the right side of the cell**

    The list of available functions appears, as shown in Figure G-19. You want to find the average tour length.

8. **Click Average, then save your workbook**

    The average tour length, 13 days, appears in cell C64.

**FIGURE G-18:** Table field names

| | A | B | C | D | E | F | G | H | I | J |
|---|---|---|---|---|---|---|---|---|---|---|
| 1 | Tour | Depart Date | Number of Days | Seat Capacity | Seats Reserved | Price | Air Included | Insurance Included | Seats Available | |
| 2 | African National Parks | 4/8/2013 | 30 | 12 | 10 | $ 3,115 | Yes | Yes | =[ | |
| 3 | African National Parks | 10/27/2013 | 30 | 12 | 8 | $ 4,870 | Yes | Yes | | |
| 4 | Amazing Amazon | 2/22/2013 | 14 | 44 | 38 | $ 2,154 | No | No | | |
| 5 | Amazing Amazon | 4/23/2013 | 14 | 43 | 30 | $ 2,133 | No | No | | |
| 6 | Amazing Amazon | 8/23/2013 | 14 | 43 | 18 | $ 2,877 | No | No | | |
| 7 | Biking in France | 5/23/2013 | 7 | 12 | 10 | $ 1,635 | No | No | | |
| 8 | Biking in France | 9/23/2013 | 7 | 12 | 7 | $ 2,110 | No | No | | |
| 9 | Biking in Scotland | 6/11/2013 | 10 | 15 | 10 | $ 2,600 | Yes | No | | |
| 10 | Biking in Scotland | 7/11/2013 | 10 | 15 | 9 | $ 2,600 | Yes | No | | |
| 11 | Biking in Scotland | 8/11/2013 | 10 | 15 | 6 | $ 2,600 | Yes | No | | |
| 12 | Catalonia Adventure | 5/9/2013 | 14 | 51 | 30 | $ 2,587 | Yes | No | | |
| 13 | Catalonia Adventure | 6/9/2013 | 14 | 51 | 15 | $ 2,100 | Yes | No | | |
| 14 | Catalonia Adventure | 10/9/2013 | 14 | 51 | 11 | $ 2,100 | Yes | No | | |
| 15 | Corfu Sailing Voyage | 6/10/2013 | 21 | 12 | 10 | $ 2,190 | Yes | No | | |
| 16 | Corfu Sailing Voyage | 7/9/2013 | 21 | 12 | 1 | $ 2,190 | Yes | No | | |

Dropdown list: Tour, Depart Date, Number of Days, Seat Capacity, Seats Reserved, Price, Air Included, Insurance Included, Seats Available

Table field names

**FIGURE G-19:** Functions in the Total Row

| | Tour | Depart Date | Number of | Seat Capac | Seats Reser | Price | Air Includ | Insurance I | Seats |
|---|---|---|---|---|---|---|---|---|---|
| 54 | Treasures of Ethiopia | 5/18/2013 | 10 | 41 | 15 | $ 1,638 | Yes | Yes | |
| 55 | Treasures of Ethiopia | 11/18/2013 | 10 | 41 | 12 | $ 2,200 | Yes | Yes | |
| 56 | Wild River Escape | 6/27/2013 | 10 | 21 | 21 | $ 1,944 | No | No | |
| 57 | Wild River Escape | 8/27/2013 | 10 | 21 | 11 | $ 1,944 | No | No | |
| 58 | Yellowstone | 1/21/2013 | 18 | 50 | 40 | $ 1,700 | Yes | Yes | |
| 59 | Yellowstone | 1/31/2013 | 18 | 20 | 0 | $ 1,005 | Yes | Yes | |
| 60 | Yellowstone | 4/20/2013 | 18 | 51 | 31 | $ 1,652 | Yes | Yes | |
| 61 | Yellowstone | 8/20/2013 | 18 | 51 | 20 | $ 2,922 | Yes | Yes | |
| 62 | Yellowstone | 9/11/2013 | 18 | 51 | 20 | $ 2,922 | Yes | Yes | |
| 63 | Yellowstone | 12/30/2013 | 18 | 51 | 15 | $ 2,922 | Yes | Yes | |
| 64 | Total | | | | | | | | |
| 65 | | | | | | | | | |
| 66 | | | | | | | | | |
| 67 | | | | | | | | | |
| 68 | | | | | | | | | |
| 69 | | | | | | | | | |
| 70 | | | | | | | | | |
| 71 | | | | | | | | | |

Dropdown list: None, Average, Count, Count Numbers, Max, Min, Sum, StdDev, Var, More Functions...

Functions available in the Total Row

## Using structured references

When you create a table from worksheet data, Excel creates a default table name such as Table1. This table name appears in structured references. Structured references make it easier to work with formulas that use table data. You can reference the entire table, columns in the table, or specific data. Structured references are especially helpful to use in formulas because they automatically adjust as data ranges change in a table, so you don't need to edit formulas.

Managing Data Using Tables

# Printing a Table

You can determine the way a table will print using the Page Layout tab. Because tables often have more rows than can fit on a page, you can define the first row of the table (containing the field names) as the **print title**, which prints at the top of every page. Most tables do not have any descriptive information above the field names on the worksheet, so to augment the field name information, you can use headers and footers to add identifying text, such as the table title or the report date. Kate asks you for a printout of the tour information. You begin by previewing the table.

**STEPS**

1.  **Click the File tab, click Print, then view the table preview**
    Below the table you see 1 of 3.

2.  **In the Preview window, click the Next Page button ▶ in the Preview area to view the second page, then click ▶ again to view the third page**
    All of the field names in the table fit across the width of the page. Because the records on pages 2 and 3 appear without column headings, you want to set up the first row of the table, which contains the field names, as a repeating print title.

**QUICK TIP**

You can hide or print headings and gridlines using the check boxes in the Sheet Options group on the Page Layout tab. You might want to hide a work-sheet's headings if it will be displayed in a presentation.

3.  **Click the Page Layout tab, click the Print Titles button in the Page Setup group, click inside the Rows to repeat at top text box under Print titles, scroll up to row 1 if necessary, click any cell in row 1 on the table, then compare your Page Setup dialog box to Figure G-20**
    When you select row 1 as a print title, Excel automatically inserts an absolute reference to the row that will repeat at the top of each page.

4.  **Click the Print Preview button in the Page Setup dialog box, click ▶ in the preview window to view the second page, then click ▶ again to view the third page**
    Setting up a print title to repeat row 1 causes the field names to appear at the top of each printed page. The printout would be more informative with a header to identify the table information.

**QUICK TIP**

You can also add a header or a footer by clicking the Page Layout View in the status bar and click-ing in the header or footer area.

5.  **Click the Insert tab, click the Header & Footer button in the Text group, click the left header section text box, then type 2013 Tours**

6.  **Select the left header section information, click the Home tab, click the Increase Font Size button A⁺ in the Font group twice to change the font size to 14, click the Bold button B in the Font group, click any cell in the table, then click the Normal button ⊞ in the status bar**

7.  **Save the table, preview it, close the workbook, exit Excel, then submit the workbook to your instructor**
    Compare your printed table with Figure G-21.

**FIGURE G-20:** Page Setup dialog box

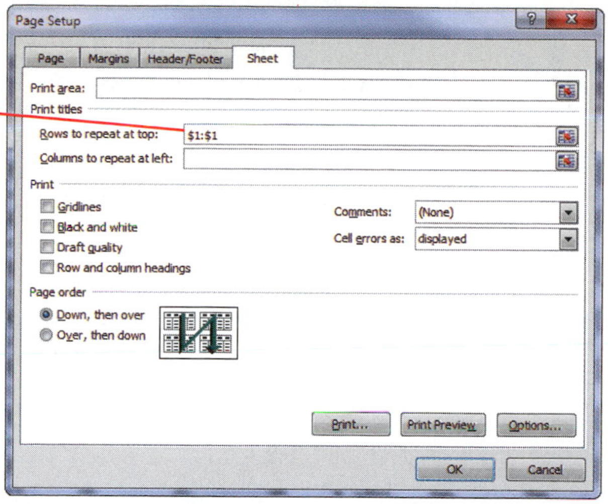

Print title is set to row 1

Rows to repeat at top: $1:$1

**FIGURE G-21:** Printed table

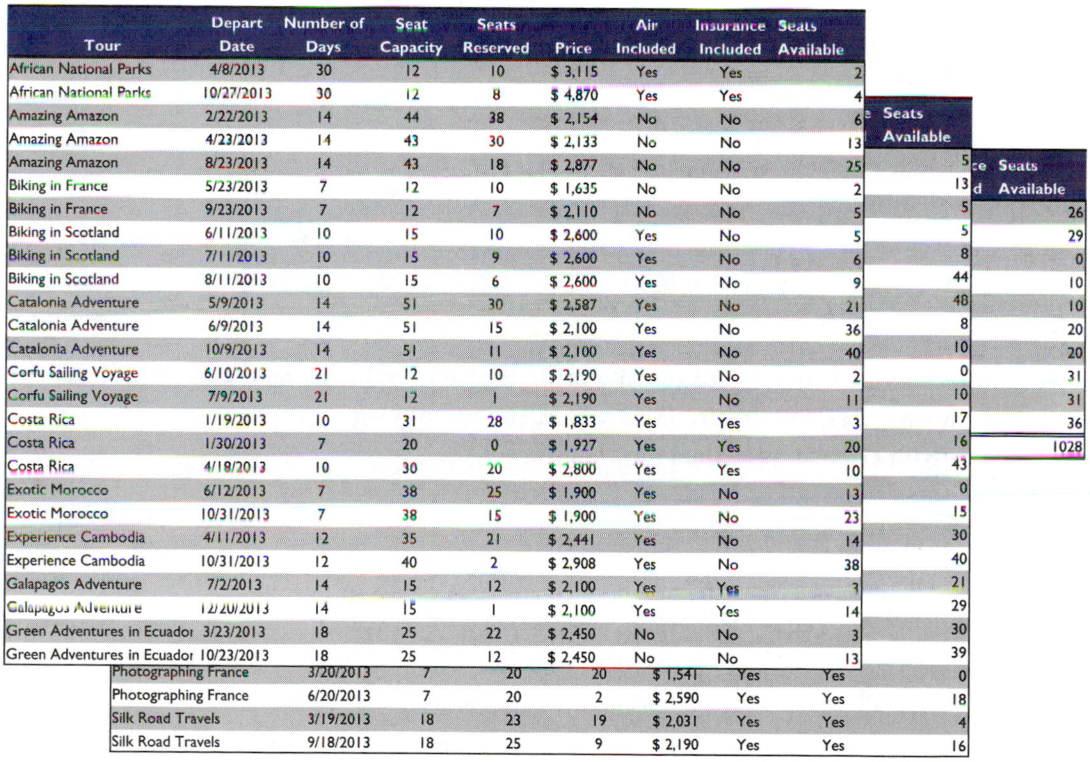

| Tour | Depart Date | Number of Days | Seat Capacity | Seats Reserved | Price | Air Included | Insurance Included | Seats Available |
|------|-------------|----------------|---------------|----------------|-------|--------------|--------------------|-----------------|
| African National Parks | 4/8/2013 | 30 | 12 | 10 | $ 3,115 | Yes | Yes | 2 |
| African National Parks | 10/27/2013 | 30 | 12 | 8 | $ 4,870 | Yes | Yes | 4 |
| Amazing Amazon | 2/22/2013 | 14 | 44 | 38 | $ 2,154 | No | No | 6 |
| Amazing Amazon | 4/23/2013 | 14 | 43 | 30 | $ 2,133 | No | No | 13 |
| Amazing Amazon | 8/23/2013 | 14 | 43 | 18 | $ 2,877 | No | No | 25 |
| Biking in France | 5/23/2013 | 7 | 12 | 10 | $ 1,635 | No | No | 2 |
| Biking in France | 9/23/2013 | 7 | 12 | 7 | $ 2,110 | No | No | 5 |
| Biking in Scotland | 6/11/2013 | 10 | 15 | 10 | $ 2,600 | Yes | No | 5 |
| Biking in Scotland | 7/11/2013 | 10 | 15 | 9 | $ 2,600 | Yes | No | 6 |
| Biking in Scotland | 8/11/2013 | 10 | 15 | 6 | $ 2,600 | Yes | No | 9 |
| Catalonia Adventure | 5/9/2013 | 14 | 51 | 30 | $ 2,587 | Yes | No | 21 |
| Catalonia Adventure | 6/9/2013 | 14 | 51 | 15 | $ 2,100 | Yes | No | 36 |
| Catalonia Adventure | 10/9/2013 | 14 | 51 | 11 | $ 2,100 | Yes | No | 40 |
| Corfu Sailing Voyage | 6/10/2013 | 21 | 12 | 10 | $ 2,190 | Yes | No | 2 |
| Corfu Sailing Voyage | 7/9/2013 | 21 | 12 | 1 | $ 2,190 | Yes | No | 11 |
| Costa Rica | 1/19/2013 | 10 | 31 | 28 | $ 1,833 | Yes | Yes | 3 |
| Costa Rica | 1/30/2013 | 7 | 20 | 0 | $ 1,927 | Yes | Yes | 20 |
| Costa Rica | 4/18/2013 | 10 | 30 | 20 | $ 2,800 | Yes | Yes | 10 |
| Exotic Morocco | 6/12/2013 | 7 | 38 | 25 | $ 1,900 | Yes | No | 13 |
| Exotic Morocco | 10/31/2013 | 7 | 38 | 15 | $ 1,900 | Yes | No | 23 |
| Experience Cambodia | 4/11/2013 | 12 | 35 | 21 | $ 2,441 | Yes | No | 14 |
| Experience Cambodia | 10/31/2013 | 12 | 40 | 2 | $ 2,908 | Yes | No | 38 |
| Galapagos Adventure | 7/2/2013 | 14 | 15 | 12 | $ 2,100 | Yes | Yes | 3 |
| Galapagos Adventure | 12/20/2013 | 14 | 15 | 1 | $ 2,100 | Yes | Yes | 14 |
| Green Adventures in Ecuador | 3/23/2013 | 18 | 25 | 22 | $ 2,450 | No | No | 3 |
| Green Adventures in Ecuador | 10/23/2013 | 18 | 25 | 12 | $ 2,450 | No | No | 13 |
| Photographing France | 3/20/2013 | 7 | 20 | 20 | $ 1,541 | Yes | Yes | 0 |
| Photographing France | 6/20/2013 | 7 | 20 | 2 | $ 2,590 | Yes | Yes | 18 |
| Silk Road Travels | 3/19/2013 | 18 | 23 | 19 | $ 2,031 | Yes | Yes | 4 |
| Silk Road Travels | 9/18/2013 | 18 | 25 | 9 | $ 2,190 | Yes | Yes | 16 |

Overlapping table fragments (Seats Available column):

| ce Seats Available |
|--------------------|
| 13 |
| 5 |
| 5 |
| 8 |
| 44 |
| 48 |
| 8 |
| 10 |
| 0 |
| 10 |
| 17 |
| 16 |
| 43 |
| 0 |
| 15 |
| 30 |
| 40 |
| 21 |
| 29 |
| 30 |
| 39 |

| Seats Available |
|-----------------|
| 26 |
| 29 |
| 0 |
| 10 |
| 10 |
| 20 |
| 20 |
| 31 |
| 31 |
| 36 |
| 1028 |

## Setting a print area

Sometimes you will want to print only part of a worksheet. To do this, select any worksheet range, click the File tab, click Print, click the Print Active Sheets list arrow, then click Print Selection. If you want to print a selected area repeatedly, it's best to define a **print area**, the area of the worksheet that previews and prints when you use the Print command in Backstage view. To set a print area, select the range of data on the worksheet that you want to print, click the Page Layout tab, click the Print Area button in the Page Setup group, then click Set Print Area. You can add to the print area by selecting a range, clicking the Print Area button, then clicking Add to Print Area. A print area can consist of one contiguous range of cells, or multiple areas in different parts of a worksheet.

# Practice

For current SAM information, including versions and content details, visit SAM Central (http://www.cengage.com/samcentral). If you have a SAM user profile, you may have access to hands-on instruction, practice, and assessment of the skills covered in this unit. Since various versions of SAM are supported throughout the life of this text, check with your instructor for the correct instructions and URL/Web site for accessing assignments.

## Concepts Review

**FIGURE G-22**

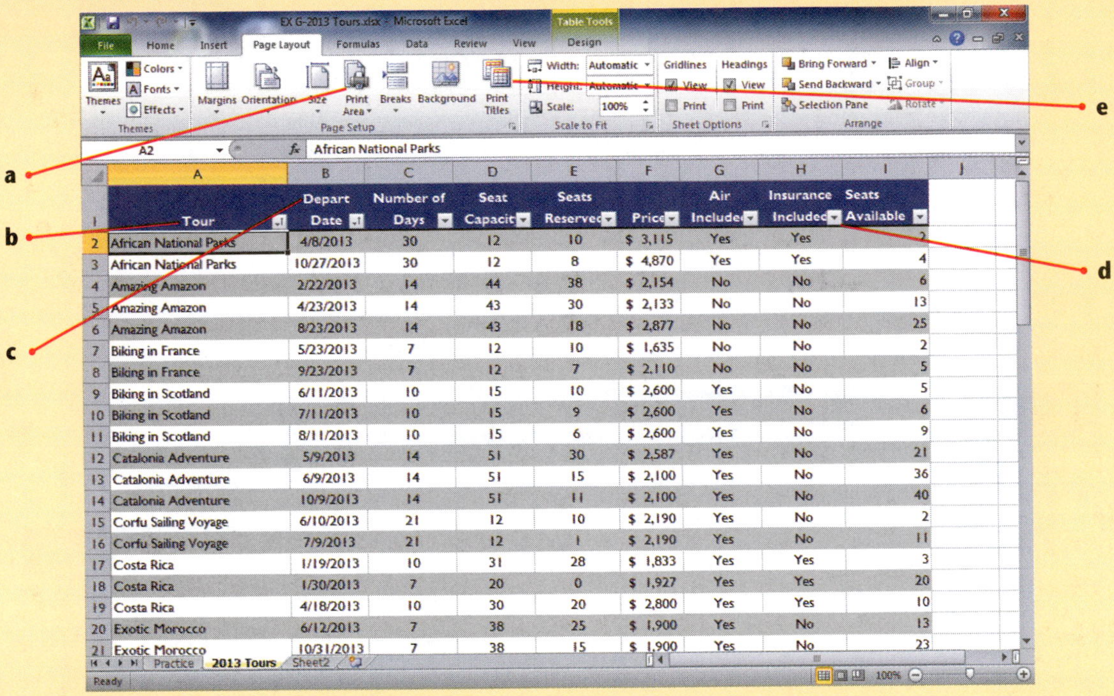

1. Which element do you click to set a range in a table that will print using Quick Print?
2. Which element do you click to print field names at the top of every page?
3. Which element do you click to sort field data on a worksheet?
4. Which element points to a second-level sort field?
5. Which element points to a top-level sort field?

## Match each term with the statement that best describes it.

6. Sort
7. Field
8. Table
9. Record
10. Header row

a. Organized collection of related information in Excel
b. Arrange records in a particular sequence
c. Column in an Excel table
d. First row of a table containing field names
e. Row in an Excel table

**Select the best answer from the list of choices.**

11. **Which of the following Excel sorting options do you use to sort a table of employee names in order from Z to A?**
    - **a.** Ascending
    - **b.** Absolute
    - **c.** Descending
    - **d.** Alphabetic

12. **Which of the following series appears in descending order?**
    - **a.** 8, 6, 4, C, B, A
    - **b.** 4, 5, 6, A, B, C
    - **c.** C, B, A, 6, 5, 4
    - **d.** 8, 7, 6, 5, 6, 7

13. **You can easily add formatting to a table by using:**
    - **a.** Print titles.
    - **b.** Table styles.
    - **c.** Print areas.
    - **d.** Calculated columns.

14. **When printing a table on multiple pages, you can define a print title to:**
    - **a.** Include the sheet name in table reports.
    - **b.** Include appropriate fields in the printout.
    - **c.** Exclude from the printout all rows under the first row.
    - **d.** Include field names at the top of each printed page.

## Skills Review

1. **Create and format a table.**
    - **a.** Start Excel, open the file EX G-2.xlsx from the drive and folder where you store your data files, then save it as **EX G-Employees**.
    - **b.** Using the Practice sheet, enter the field names in the first row and the first two records in rows two and three, as shown in Table G-3. Create a table using the data you entered.

**TABLE G-3**

| Last Name | First Name | Years Employed | Department | Full/Part Time | Training Completed |
|-----------|-----------|----------------|------------|----------------|--------------------|
| Lane | Sarah | 4 | Print Books | F | Y |
| Magnum | Darrin | 3 | E-Books | P | N |

   - **c.** On the Staff sheet, create a table with a header row. Adjust the column widths, if necessary, to display the field names.
   - **d.** Apply a table style of Light 12 to the table, and adjust the column widths if necessary.
   - **e.** Enter your name in the center section of the worksheet footer, then save the workbook.

2. **Add table data.**
    - **a.** Add a new record in row seven for **Hank Worthen**, a 5-year employee in print book sales. Hank works full time and has completed training. Adjust the height of the new row to match the other table rows.
    - **b.** Insert a table row above Jill Krosby's record, and add a new record for **Stacy Atkins**. Stacy works full time, has worked at the company for 2 years in E-Books, and has not completed training.
    - **c.** Insert a new data field in cell G1 with a label **Weeks Vacation**. Adjust the column width, and wrap the label in the cell to display the field name with **Weeks** above **Vacation**. (*Hint*: Use the Wrap Text button in the Alignment group on the Home tab.)
    - **d.** Add a new column to the table by dragging the table's sizing handle, and give the new field a label of **Employee #**. Widen the column to fit the label.
    - **e.** Save the file.

3. **Find and replace table data.**
    - **a.** Return to cell A1.
    - **b.** Open the Find and Replace dialog box and if necessary uncheck the Match Case option. Find the first record that contains the text **Print Books**.
    - **c.** Find the second and third records that contain the text **Print Books**.
    - **d.** Replace all **Print Books** text in the table with **Books**, then save the file.

# Skills Review (continued)

**4. Delete table data.**

  **a.** Go to cell A1.

  **b.** Delete the record for Sarah Lane.

  **c.** Use the Remove Duplicates button to confirm that the table does not have any duplicate records.

  **d.** Delete the Employee # table column, then delete its column header, if necessary.

  **e.** Save the file.

**5. Sort table data.**

  **a.** Sort the table by years employed in largest to smallest order.

  **b.** Sort the table by last name in A to Z order.

  **c.** Perform a multilevel sort: Sort the table first by Full/Part Time in A to Z order and then by last name in A to Z order.

  **d.** Check the table to make sure the records appear in the correct order.

  **e.** Save the file.

**6. Use formulas in a table.**

  **a.** In cell G2, enter the formula that calculates an employee's vacation time; base the formula on the company policy that employees working at the company less than 3 years have 2 weeks of vacation. At 3 years of employment and longer, an employee has 3 weeks of vacation time. Use the table's field names where appropriate. (*Hint*: The formula is: =IF([Years Employed]<3,2,3.)

  **b.** Check the table to make sure the formula filled into the cells in column G and that the correct vacation time is calculated for all cells in the column.

  **c.** Add a Total Row to display the total number of vacation weeks.

  **d.** Change the function in the Total Row to display the average number of vacation weeks.

  **e.** Compare your table to Figure G-23, then save the workbook.

**FIGURE G-23**

| | A | B | C | D | E | F | G |
|---|---|---|---|---|---|---|---|
| 1 | Last Name | First Name | Years Employed | Department | Full/Part Time | Training Complete | Weeks Vacation |
| 2 | Atkins | Stacy | 2 | E-Books | F | N | 2 |
| 3 | Gray | Jen | 1 | Books | F | N | 2 |
| 4 | Krosby | Jill | 2 | E-Books | F | Y | 2 |
| 5 | Worthen | Hank | 5 | Books | F | Y | 3 |
| 6 | Magnum | Darrin | 3 | E-Books | P | N | 3 |
| 7 | Rogers | Mary | 1 | E-Books | P | Y | 2 |
| 8 | Total | | | | | | 2.333333333 |
| 9 | | | | | | | |

**7. Print a table.**

  **a.** Add a header that reads **Employees** in the center section, then format the header in bold with a font size of 16.

  **b.** Add column A as a print title that repeats at the left of each printed page.

  **c.** Preview your table to check that the last names appear on both pages.

  **d.** Change the page orientation to landscape, save the workbook.

  **e.** Submit your worksheet to your instructor. Close the workbook, then exit Excel.

# Independent Challenge 1

You are the marketing director for a national pharmaceutical firm. Your administrative assistant created an Excel worksheet with customer data including the results of an advertising survey. You will create a table using the customer data, and analyze the survey results to help focus the company's advertising expenses in the most successful areas.

**a.** Start Excel, open the file EX G-3.xlsx from the drive and folder where you store your Data Files, then save it as **EX G-Customers**.

**b.** Create a table from the worksheet data, and apply Table Style Light 16. Widen the columns as necessary to display the table data.

**c.** Add the two records shown in Table G-4 to the table:

**TABLE G-4**

| Last Name | First Name | Street Address | City | State | Zip | Area Code | Ad Source |
|-----------|-----------|----------------|------|-------|------|-----------|-----------|
| Ross | Cathy | 92 Arrow St. | Seattle | WA | 98101 | 206 | TV |
| Jones | Sarah | 402 9th St. | Seattle | WA | 98001 | 206 | Newspaper |

**d.** Find the record for Mary Riley, then delete it.

**e.** Click cell A1 and replace all instances of **TV** with **Cable TV**. Compare your table to Figure G-24.

**FIGURE G-24**

| | A | B | C | D | E | F | G | H |
|---|---|---|---|---|---|---|---|---|
| 1 | Last Name | First Name | Street Address | City | State | Zip | Area Code | Ad Source |
| 2 | Kelly | Karen | 19 North St. | San Francisco | CA | 94177 | 415 | Newspaper |
| 3 | Johnson | Mel | Hamilton Park St. | San Francisco | CA | 94107 | 415 | Newspaper |
| 4 | Markette | Kathy | 1 Spring St | San Luis | CA | 94018 | 510 | Radio |
| 5 | Worthen | Sally | 2120 Central St. | San Francisco | CA | 93772 | 415 | Retail Website |
| 6 | Herbert | Greg | 1192 Dome St. | San Diego | CA | 93303 | 619 | Newspaper |
| 7 | Chavez | Jane | 11 Northern St | San Diego | CA | 92208 | 619 | Cable TV |
| 8 | Chelly | Yvonne | 900 Sola St. | San Diego | CA | 92106 | 619 | Retail Website |
| 9 | Smith | Carolyn | 921 Lopez St. | San Diego | CA | 92104 | 619 | Newspaper |
| 10 | Oren | Scott | 72 Yankee St. | Brookfield | CT | 06830 | 203 | Health Website |
| 11 | Warner | Salvatore | 100 Westside St. | Chicago | IL | 60620 | 312 | Newspaper |
| 12 | Roberts | Bob | 56 Water St. | Chicago | IL | 60618 | 771 | Retail Website |
| 13 | Miller | Hope | 111 Stratton St | Chicago | IL | 60614 | 773 | Newspaper |
| 14 | Duran | Maria | Galvin St. | Chicago | IL | 60614 | 773 | Health Website |
| 15 | Roberts | Bob | 56 Water St. | Chicago | IL | 60614 | 312 | Newspaper |
| 16 | Graham | Shelley | 989 26th St. | Chicago | IL | 60611 | 773 | Education Website |
| 17 | Kelly | Janie | 9 First St. | San Francisco | CA | 94177 | 415 | Newspaper |
| 18 | Kim | Janie | 9 First St. | San Francisco | CA | 94177 | 415 | Health Website |
| 19 | Williams | Tasha | 1 Spring St. | Reading | MA | 03882 | 413 | Newspaper |
| 20 | Juarez | Manuel | 544 Cameo St. | Belmont | MA | 02483 | 617 | Newspaper |
| 21 | Masters | Latrice | 88 Las Puntas Rd. | Boston | MA | 02205 | 617 | Education Website |
| 22 | Kooper | Peter | 671 Main St. | Cambridge | MA | 02138 | 617 | Cable TV |
| 23 | Kelly | Shawn | 22 Kendall St. | Cambridge | MA | 02138 | 617 | Education Website |
| 24 | Rodriguez | Virginia | 123 Main St. | Boston | MA | 02007 | 617 | Radio |
| 25 | Frei | Carol | 123 Elm St. | Salem | MA | 01970 | 978 | Newspaper |
| 26 | Stevens | Crystal | 14 Waterford St. | Salem | MA | 01970 | 508 | Radio |
| 27 | Ichikawa | Pam | 232 Shore Rd. | Boston | MA | 01801 | 617 | Newspaper |
| 28 | Paxton | Gail | 100 Main St. | Woburn | MA | 01801 | 508 | Newspaper |
| 29 | Spencer | Robin | 293 Serenity Dr. | Concord | MA | 01742 | 508 | Radio |
| 30 | López | Luis | 1212 City St | Kansas City | MO | 64105 | 816 | Cable TV |

**f.** Remove duplicate records where all fields are identical.

**g.** Sort the list by Last Name in A to Z order.

**h.** Sort the list again by Area Code in Smallest to Largest order.

**i.** Sort the table first by State in A to Z order, then within the state, by Zip in Smallest to Largest order.

**j.** Enter your name in the center section of the worksheet footer.

**k.** Add a centered header that reads **Customer Survey Data** in bold with a font size of 16.

**l.** Add print titles to repeat the first row at the top of printed pages.

**m.** Save the workbook, then preview it.

## Advanced Challenge Exercise

- Create a print area that prints only the first six columns of the table.
- Print the print area.
- Clear the print area.

**n.** Save the workbook, close the workbook, submit the workbook to your instructor, then exit Excel.

# Independent Challenge 2

You own Green Place, a paint store that sells environmentally friendly paint by the gallon. Your customers are primarily contractors who purchase items in quantities of 10 or more for their customers. You decide to plan and build a table of sales information with eight records using the items sold.

a. Prepare a plan for a table that states your goal, outlines the data you need, and identifies the table elements.

b. Sketch a sample table on a piece of paper, indicating how the table should be built. Create a table documenting the table design including the field names, type of data, and description of the data. Some examples of items are clay paint, lime wash, low VOC paint, milk paint, and zero VOC paint.

c. Start Excel, create a new workbook, then save it as **EX G-Store Items** in the drive and folder where you store your Data Files. Enter the field names from Table G-6 in the designated cells.

d. Enter eight data records using your own data.

e. Create a table using the data in the range A1:E9. Adjust the column widths as necessary.

f. Apply the Table Style Light 18 to the table.

g. Add a field named **Total** in cell F1.

h. Enter a formula to calculate the total (Quantity*Cost) in cell F2. Check that the formula was filled down in the column.

i. Format the Cost and Total columns using the Accounting number format with two decimal places and the dollar symbol ( $ ). Adjust the column widths as necessary.

j. Add a new record to your table in row 10. Add another record above row 4.

k. Sort the table in ascending order by Item.

l. Enter your name in the worksheet footer, then save the workbook.

m. Preview the worksheet, then submit your worksheet to your instructor.

n. Close the workbook, then exit Excel.

**TABLE G-6**

| cell | field name |
|------|------------|
| A1 | Customer Last |
| B1 | Customer First |
| C1 | Item |
| D1 | Quantity |
| E1 | Cost |

# Independent Challenge 3

You are the project manager at a construction firm. You are managing your accounts using an Excel worksheet and have decided that a table will provide additional features to help you keep track of the accounts. You will use the table sorting features and table formulas to analyze your account data.

a. Start Excel, open the file EX G-4.xlsx from the drive and folder where you store your Data Files, then save it as **EX G-Accounts**.

b. Create a table with the worksheet data, and apply Table Style Light 10. Adjust the column widths as necessary.

c. Sort the table on the Budget field using the Smallest to Largest order.

d. Sort the table using two fields, by Contact in A to Z order, then by Budget in Smallest to Largest order. Compare your table to Figure G-25.

**FIGURE G-25**

| | A | B | C | D | E | F |
|---|---|---|---|---|---|---|
| 1 | Project | Deadline | Code | Budget | Expenses | Contact |
| 2 | Town of Northfield Dam | 6/1/2013 | AA1 | $ 200,000 | $ 30,000 | Cathy Brown |
| 3 | South Apartments | 4/30/2013 | C43 | $ 200,000 | $ 170,000 | Cathy Brown |
| 4 | Warren Condominium | 10/10/2013 | C21 | $ 450,000 | $ 400,000 | Cathy Brown |
| 5 | Langley Parking Lot | 7/10/2013 | V13 | $ 690,000 | $ 700,000 | Cathy Brown |
| 6 | Route 100 | 1/15/2013 | C43 | $ 100,000 | $ 150,000 | Jill Saunders |
| 7 | 1st Street Bridge | 11/15/2013 | V53 | $ 200,000 | $ 210,000 | Jill Saunders |
| 8 | Green Ridge Condominium | 5/1/2013 | AA5 | $ 400,000 | $ 230,210 | Jill Saunders |
| 9 | Rangely Industrial Park | 9/30/2013 | V51 | $ 400,000 | $ 320,000 | Jill Saunders |
| 10 | Northridge School | 3/15/2013 | A3A | $ 600,000 | $ 610,000 | Kim Jess |
| 11 | West Mall | 11/15/2013 | B12 | $ 710,000 | $ 600,000 | Kim Jess |
| 12 | | | | | | |

Managing Data Using Tables

## Independent Challenge 3 (continued)

e. Add the new field label **Balance** in cell G1, and adjust the column width as necessary. Format the Budget, Expenses, and Balance columns using the Accounting format with no decimal places and the dollar symbol ( $ ).

f. Enter a formula in cell G2 that uses structured references to table fields to calculate the balance on an account as the Budget minus the Expenses.

g. Add a new record for a project named **North Mall** with a deadline of **2/15/2013**, a code of **AB2**, a budget of **$300,000**, expenses of **$150,000**, and a contact of **Cathy Brown**.

h. Verify that the formula accurately calculated the balance for the new record.

i. Replace all of the Jill Saunders data with **Jill Jones**.

j. Enter your name in the center section of the worksheet footer, add a center section header of **Accounts** using formatting of your choice, change the page orientation to landscape, then save the workbook.

### Advanced Challenge Exercise

- Sort the table on the Balance field using the Smallest to Largest order.
- Use conditional formatting to format the cells of the table containing negative balances with a light red fill with dark red text.
- Sort the table using the Balance field with the order of no cell color on top.
- Format the table to emphasize the Balance column, and turn off the banded rows. (*Hint*: Use the Table Style Options on the Table Tools Design tab.)
- Compare your table with Figure G-26. Save the workbook.

**FIGURE G-26**

| | A | B | C | D | E | F | G |
|---|---|---|---|---|---|---|---|
| 1 | Project | Deadline | Code | Budget | Expenses | Contact | Balance |
| 2 | South Apartments | 4/30/2013 | C43 | $ 200,000 | $ 170,000 | Cathy Brown | $ 30,000 |
| 3 | Warren Condominium | 10/10/2013 | C21 | $ 450,000 | $ 400,000 | Cathy Brown | $ 50,000 |
| 4 | Rangely Industrial Park | 9/30/2013 | V51 | $ 400,000 | $ 320,000 | Jill Jones | $ 80,000 |
| 5 | West Mall | 11/15/2013 | B12 | $ 710,000 | $ 600,000 | Kim Jess | $ 110,000 |
| 6 | North Mall | 2/15/2013 | AB2 | $ 300,000 | $ 150,000 | Cathy Brown | $ 150,000 |
| 7 | Green Ridge Condominium | 5/1/2013 | AA5 | $ 400,000 | $ 230,210 | Jill Jones | $ 169,790 |
| 8 | Town of Northfield Dam | 6/1/2013 | AA1 | $ 200,000 | $ 30,000 | Cathy Brown | $ 170,000 |
| 9 | Route 100 | 1/15/2013 | C43 | $ 100,000 | $ 150,000 | Jill Jones | $ (50,000) |
| 10 | Langley Parking Lot | 7/10/2013 | V13 | $ 690,000 | $ 700,000 | Cathy Brown | $ (10,000) |
| 11 | 1st Street Bridge | 11/15/2013 | V53 | $ 200,000 | $ 210,000 | Jill Jones | $ (10,000) |
| 12 | Northridge School | 3/15/2013 | A3A | $ 600,000 | $ 610,000 | Kim Jess | $ (10,000) |
| 13 | | | | | | | |
| 14 | | | | | | | |

k. Submit the worksheet to your instructor, close the workbook, then exit Excel.

# Real Life Independent Challenge

You have decided to organize your recording collection using a table in Excel. This will enable you to easily find songs in your music library. You will add records as you purchase new music and delete records if you discard a recording.

a. Using the fields Title, Artist, Genre, and Format, prepare a diagram of your table structure.

b. Document the table design by detailing the type of data that will be in each field and a description of the data. For example, in the Format field you may have .mp3, .aac, .wma, or other formats.

c. Start Excel, create a new workbook, then save it as **EX G-Music** in the drive and folder where you store your Data Files.

d. Enter the field names into the worksheet, enter the records for seven of your music recordings, then save the workbook.

e. Create a table that contains your music information. Resize the columns as necessary.

f. Choose a Table Style, and apply it to your table.

g. Add a new field with a label of **Media/Player**. Enter information in the new table column describing the media or player where your music is stored, such as iPod, iPhone, CD, or Computer.

h. Add a record to the table for the next recording you will purchase.

i. Sort the records by the Format field using A to Z order.

j. Add a Total row to your table, and verify that the Count function accurately calculated the number of your recordings.

k. Enter your name in the worksheet footer, then save the workbook.

l. Submit the worksheet to your instructor, close the workbook, then exit Excel.

# Visual Workshop

Start Excel, open the file EX G-5.xlsx from the drive and folder where you store your Data Files, then save it as **EX G-Products**. Create the table and sort the data as shown in Figure G-27. (*Hint*: The table is formatted using Table Style Medium 7.) Add a worksheet header with the sheet name in the center section that is formatted in bold with a size of 14. Enter your name in the center section of the worksheet footer. Save the workbook, preview the table, close the workbook, submit the worksheet to your instructor, then exit Excel.

**FIGURE G-27**

| Order Number | Order date | Amount | Shipping | Sales Rep |
|---|---|---|---|---|
| 1533 | 10/14/2013 | $ 10,057 | Air | Ellie Cranson |
| 7897 | 3/15/2013 | $ 22,587 | Ground | Ellie Cranson |
| 1123 | 5/30/2013 | $ 125,879 | Air | Ellie Cranson |
| 2199 | 2/15/2013 | $ 236,014 | Air | Ellie Cranson |
| 1154 | 10/15/2013 | $ 312,845 | Air | Ellie Cranson |
| 5423 | 2/1/2013 | $ 1,369 | Air | Gene Coburn |
| 2186 | 6/1/2013 | $ 132,558 | Ground | Gene Coburn |
| 9021 | 1/15/2013 | $ 198,257 | Ground | Gene Coburn |
| 1115 | 8/30/2013 | $ 200,521 | Ground | Gene Coburn |
| 2100 | 2/10/2013 | $ 32,987 | Ground | Neil Boxer |
| 2130 | 11/15/2013 | $ 82,496 | Air | Neil Boxer |

Managing Data Using Tables

# Analyzing Table Data

**Files You Will Need:**

EX H-1.xlsx
EX H-2.xlsx
EX H-3.xlsx
EX H-4.xlsx
EX H-5.xlsx
EX H-6.xlsx

Excel tables let you manipulate and analyze data in many ways. One way is to filter a table so that it displays only the rows that meet certain criteria. In this unit, you will display selected records using the AutoFilter feature, create a custom filter, and filter a table using an Advanced Filter. In addition, you will learn to insert automatic subtotals, use lookup functions to locate table entries, and apply database functions to summarize table data that meet specific criteria. You'll also learn how to restrict entries in a column by using data validation.  The vice president of sales, Kate Morgan, asks you to display information from a table of the 2013 scheduled tours to help the sales representatives with customer inquiries. She also asks you to prepare summaries of the tour sales for a presentation at the international sales meeting.

**OBJECTIVES**

Filter a table

Create a custom filter

Filter a table with the Advanced Filter

Extract table data

Look up values in a table

Summarize table data

Validate table data

Create subtotals

# Filtering a Table

An Excel table lets you easily manipulate large amounts of data to view only the data you want, using a feature called **AutoFilter**. When you create a table, arrows automatically appear next to each column header. These arrows are called **filter list arrows**, **AutoFilter list arrows**, or **list arrows**, and you can use them to **filter** a table to display only the records that meet criteria you specify, temporarily hiding records that do not meet those criteria. For example, you can use the filter list arrow next to the Tour field header to display only records that contain Nepal Trekking in the Tour field. Once you filter data, you can copy, chart, and print the displayed records. You can easily clear a filter to redisplay all the records.  Kate asks you to display only the records for the Yellowstone tours. She also asks for information about the tours that sell the most seats and the tours that depart in March.

**STEPS**

1. **Start Excel, open the file EX H-1.xlsx from the drive and folder where you save your Data Files, then save it as EX H-Tours**

2. **Click the Tour list arrow**

   Sort options appear at the top of the menu, advanced filtering options appear in the middle, and at the bottom is a list of the tour data from column A, as shown in Figure H-1. Because you want to display data for only the Yellowstone tours, your **search criterion** (the text you are searching for) is Yellowstone. You can select one of the Tour data options in the menu, which acts as your search criterion.

   **QUICK TIP**
   You can also filter the table to display only the Yellowstone tour information by clicking the Tour list arrow, entering "Yellowstone" in the Search text box on the menu options below Text Filters, then clicking OK.

3. **In the list of tours for the Tour field, click Select All to clear the checks from the tours, scroll down the list of tours, click Yellowstone, then click OK**

   Only those records containing "Yellowstone" in the Tour field appear, as shown in Figure H-2. The row numbers for the matching records change to blue, and the list arrow for the filtered field has a filter icon. Both indicate that there is a filter in effect and that some of the records are temporarily hidden.

4. **Move the pointer over the Tour list arrow**

   The ScreenTip Tour: Equals "Yellowstone" describes the filter for the field, meaning that only the Yellowstone records appear. You decide to remove the filter to redisplay all of the table data.

5. **Click the Tour list arrow, then click Clear Filter From "Tour"**

   You have cleared the Yellowstone filter, and all the records reappear. You want to display the most popular tours, those that are in the top five percent of seats reserved.

   **QUICK TIP**
   You can also filter or sort a table by the color of the cells if conditional formatting has been applied.

6. **Click the Seats Reserved list arrow, point to Number Filters, click Top 10, select 10 in the middle box, type 5, click the Items list arrow, click Percent, then click OK**

   Excel displays the records for the top five percent in the number of Seats Reserved field, as shown in Figure H-3. You decide to clear the filter to redisplay all the records.

7. **On the Home tab, click the Sort & Filter button in the Editing group, then click Clear**

   You can clear a filter using either the AutoFilter menu command or the Sort and Filter menu on the Home tab. You have cleared the filter and all the records reappear. The Sort and Filter button is convenient for clearing multiple filters at once. You want to find all of the tours that depart in March.

8. **Click the Depart Date list arrow, point to Date Filters, point to All Dates in the Period, then click March**

   Excel displays the records for only the tours that leave in March. You decide to clear the filter and display all of the records.

   **QUICK TIP**
   You can also clear a filter by clicking the Clear button in the Sort & Filter group on the Data tab.

9. **Click the Sort & Filter button in the Editing group, click Clear, then save the workbook**

**FIGURE H-1:** Worksheet showing filter options

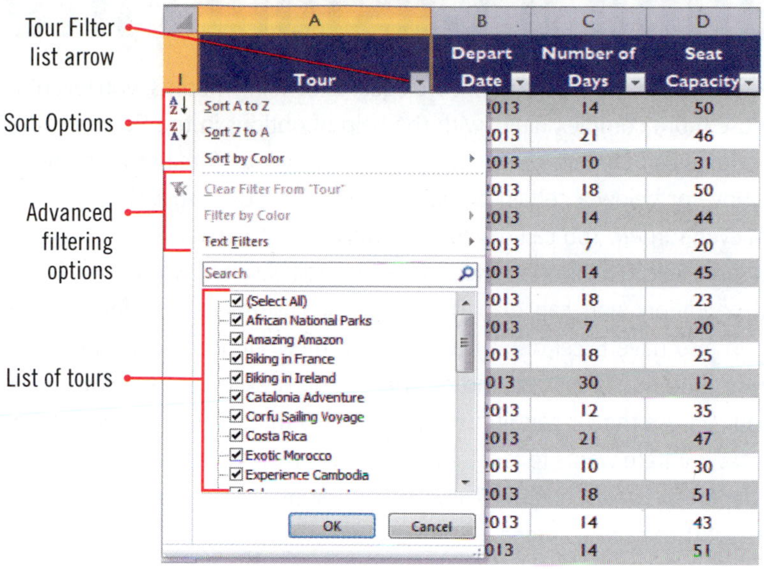

Tour Filter list arrow

Sort Options

Advanced filtering options

List of tours

| | A | B | C | D |
|---|---|---|---|---|
| | Tour | Depart Date | Number of Days | Seat Capacity |

Sort A to Z
Sort Z to A
Sort by Color

Clear Filter From "Tour"
Filter by Color
Text Filters

Search

☑ (Select All)
☑ African National Parks
☑ Amazing Amazon
☑ Biking in France
☑ Biking in Ireland
☑ Catalonia Adventure
☑ Corfu Sailing Voyage
☑ Costa Rica
☑ Exotic Morocco
☑ Experience Cambodia

OK     Cancel

| Date | Days | Capacity |
|---|---|---|
| 2013 | 14 | 50 |
| 2013 | 21 | 46 |
| 2013 | 10 | 31 |
| 2013 | 18 | 50 |
| 2013 | 14 | 44 |
| 2013 | 7 | 20 |
| 2013 | 14 | 45 |
| 2013 | 18 | 23 |
| 2013 | 7 | 20 |
| 2013 | 18 | 25 |
| 2013 | 30 | 12 |
| 2013 | 12 | 35 |
| 2013 | 21 | 47 |
| 2013 | 10 | 30 |
| 2013 | 18 | 51 |
| 2013 | 14 | 43 |
| 2013 | 14 | 51 |

**FIGURE H-2:** Table filtered to show Yellowstone tours

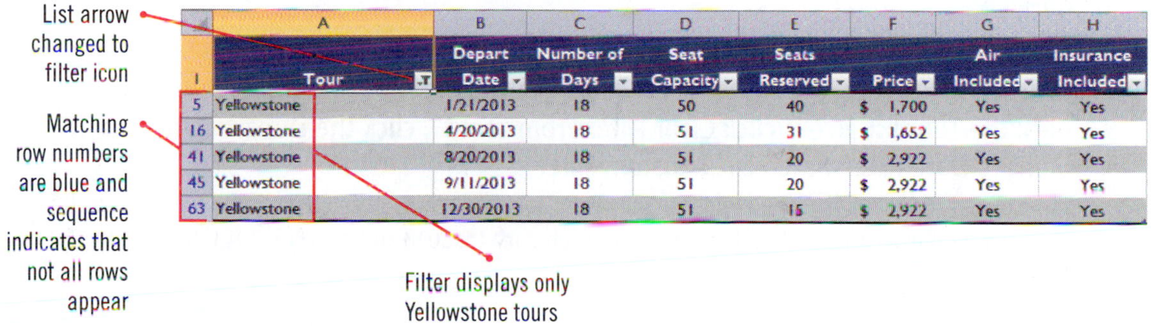

List arrow changed to filter icon

Matching row numbers are blue and sequence indicates that not all rows appear

| | A | B | C | D | E | F | G | H |
|---|---|---|---|---|---|---|---|---|
| | Tour | Depart Date | Number of Days | Seat Capacity | Seats Reserved | Price | Air Included | Insurance Included |
| 5 | Yellowstone | 1/21/2013 | 18 | 50 | 40 | $ 1,700 | Yes | Yes |
| 16 | Yellowstone | 4/20/2013 | 18 | 51 | 31 | $ 1,652 | Yes | Yes |
| 41 | Yellowstone | 8/20/2013 | 18 | 51 | 20 | $ 2,922 | Yes | Yes |
| 45 | Yellowstone | 9/11/2013 | 18 | 51 | 20 | $ 2,922 | Yes | Yes |
| 63 | Yellowstone | 12/30/2013 | 18 | 51 | 15 | $ 2,922 | Yes | Yes |

Filter displays only Yellowstone tours

**FIGURE H-3:** Table filtered with top 5% of Seats Reserved

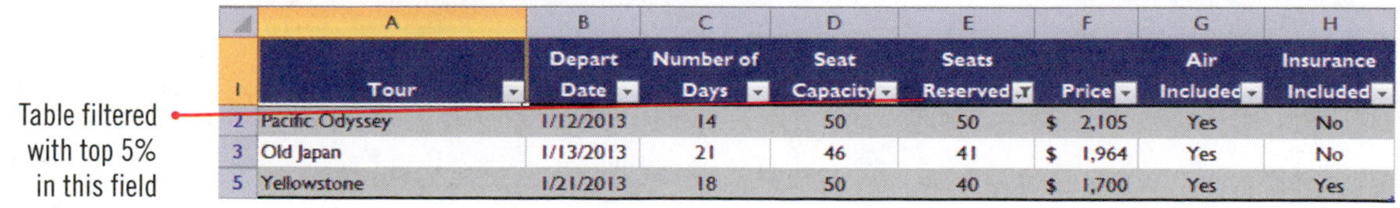

Table filtered with top 5% in this field

| | A | B | C | D | E | F | G | H |
|---|---|---|---|---|---|---|---|---|
| | Tour | Depart Date | Number of Days | Seat Capacity | Seats Reserved | Price | Air Included | Insurance Included |
| 2 | Pacific Odyssey | 1/12/2013 | 14 | 50 | 50 | $ 2,105 | Yes | No |
| 3 | Old Japan | 1/13/2013 | 21 | 46 | 41 | $ 1,964 | Yes | No |
| 5 | Yellowstone | 1/21/2013 | 18 | 50 | 40 | $ 1,700 | Yes | Yes |

Analyzing Table Data

# Creating a Custom Filter

While AutoFilter lists can display records that are equal to certain amounts, you will often need more detailed filters. You can use more complex filters with the help of options in the Custom AutoFilter dialog box. For example, your criteria can contain comparison operators such as "greater than" or "less than" that let you display values above or below a certain amount. You can also use **logical conditions** like And and Or to narrow a search even further. You can have Excel display records that meet a criterion in a field *and* another criterion in that same field. This is often used to find records between two values. For example, by specifying an And logical condition, you can display records for customers with incomes between $40,000 *and* $70,000. You can also have Excel display records that meet either criterion in a field by specifying an Or condition. The Or condition is used to find records that satisfy either of two values. For example, in a table of book data you can use the Or condition to find records that contain either Beginning *or* Introduction in the title name.  Kate wants to locate tours for customers who like active vacations. She also wants to find tours that depart between February 15, 2013, and April 15, 2013. She asks you to create custom filters to find the tours satisfying these criteria.

## STEPS

1.  **Click the Tour list arrow, point to Text Filters, then click Contains**

    The Custom AutoFilter dialog box opens. You enter your criteria in the text boxes. The left text box on the first line currently displays "contains." You want to display tours that contain the word "sailing" in their names.

2.  **Type sailing in the right text box on the first line**

    You want to see entries that contain either sailing or biking.

**QUICK TIP**

When specifying criteria in the Custom Filter dialog box, you can use the ( ? ) wildcard to represent any single character and the ( * ) wildcard to represent any series of characters.

3.  **Click the Or option button to select it, click the left text box list arrow on the second line, scroll to and select contains, then type biking in the right text box on the second line**

    Your completed Custom AutoFilter dialog box should match Figure H-4.

4.  **Click OK**

    The dialog box closes, and only those records having "sailing" or "biking" in the Tour field appear in the worksheet. You want to find all tours that depart between February 15, 2013 and April 15, 2013.

5.  **Click the Tour list arrow, click Clear Filter From "Tour", click the Depart Date list arrow, point to Date Filters, then click Custom Filter**

    The Custom AutoFilter dialog box opens. The word "equals" appears in the left text box on the first line. You want to find the departure dates that are between February 15, 2013 and April 15, 2013 (that is, after February 15 *and* before April 15).

6.  **Click the left text box list arrow on the first line, click is after, then type 2/15/2013 in the right text box on the first line**

    The And condition is selected, which is correct.

7.  **Click the left text box list arrow on the second line, select is before, type 4/15/2013 in the right text box on the second line, then click OK**

    The records displayed have departing dates between February 15, 2013, and April 15, 2013. Compare your records to those shown in Figure H-5.

8.  **Click the Depart Date list arrow, click Clear Filter From "Depart Date", then add your name to the center section of the footer**

    You have cleared the filter, and all the tour records reappear.

**FIGURE H-4: Custom AutoFilter dialog box**

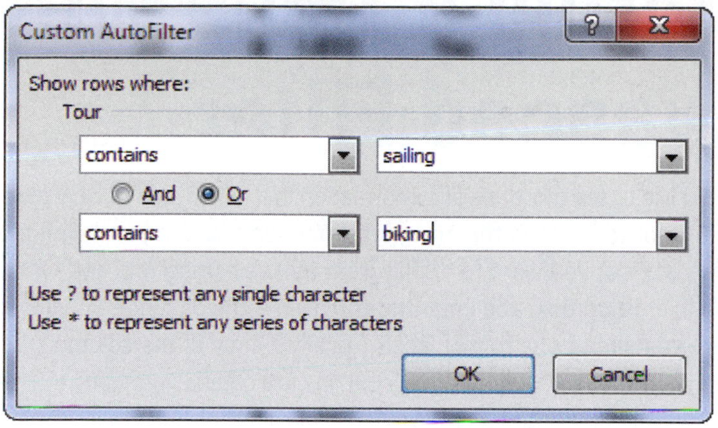


Excel 2010

**FIGURE H-5: Results of custom filter**

| | A Tour | B Depart Date | C Number of Days | D Seat Capacity | E Seats Reserved | F Price | G Air Included | H Insurance Included |
|---|---|---|---|---|---|---|---|---|
| 6 | Amazing Amazon | 2/22/2013 | 14 | 44 | 38 | $ 2,154 | No | No |
| 7 | Hiking Patagonia | 2/28/2013 | 7 | 20 | 15 | $ 2,822 | Yes | No |
| 8 | Pearls of the Orient | 3/13/2013 | 14 | 45 | 15 | $ 2,400 | Yes | No |
| 9 | Silk Road Travels | 3/19/2013 | 18 | 23 | 19 | $ 2,031 | Yes | Yes |
| 10 | Photographing France | 3/20/2013 | 7 | 20 | 20 | $ 1,541 | Yes | Yes |
| 11 | Green Adventures in Ecuador | 3/23/2013 | 18 | 25 | 22 | $ 2,450 | No | No |
| 12 | African National Parks | 4/8/2013 | 30 | 12 | 10 | $ 3,115 | Yes | Yes |
| 13 | Experience Cambodia | 4/11/2013 | 12 | 35 | 21 | $ 2,441 | Yes | No |

Departing dates are between 2/15 and 4/15

## Using more than one rule when conditionally formatting data

You can apply conditional formatting to table cells in the same way that you can format a range of worksheet data. You can add multiple rules by clicking the Home tab, clicking the Conditional Formatting button in the Styles group, then clicking New Rule for each additional rule that you want to apply. You can also add rules using the Conditional Formatting Rules Manager, which displays all of the rules for a data range. To use the Rules Manager, click the Home tab, click the Conditional Formatting button in the Styles group, click Manage Rules, then click New Rule for each rule that you want to apply to the data range. After you have applied conditional formatting such as color fills, icon sets, or color scales to a numeric table range, you can use AutoFilter to sort or filter based on the colors or symbols.

# Filtering a Table with the Advanced Filter

If you would like to see more specific information in a table, such as view date and insurance information for a specific tour or tours, then the Advanced Filter command is very helpful. Using the Advanced Filter, you can specify data that you want to display from the table using And and Or conditions. Rather than entering the criteria in a dialog box, you enter the criteria in a criteria range on your worksheet. A **criteria range** is a cell range containing one row of labels (usually a copy of the column labels) and at least one additional row underneath the row of labels that contains the criteria you want to match. Placing the criteria in the same row indicates that the records you are searching for must match both criteria; that is, it specifies an **And condition**. Placing the criteria in the different rows indicates that the records you are searching for must match only one of the criterion; that is, it specifies an **Or condition**. With the criteria range on the worksheet, you can easily see the criteria by which your table is sorted. You can also use the criteria range to create a macro using the Advanced Filter feature to automate the filtering process for data that you filter frequently. Another advantage of the Advanced Filter is that you can move filtered table data to a different area of the worksheet or to a new worksheet, as you will see in the next lesson. Kate wants to identify tours that depart after 6/1/2013 and that cost less than $2,000. She asks you to use the Advanced Filter to retrieve these records. You begin by defining the criteria range.

STEPS

1. **Select table rows 1 through 6, click the Insert list arrow in the Cells group, click Insert Sheet Rows; click cell A1, type Criteria Range, then click the Enter button ☑ on the Formula bar**

   Six blank rows are added above the table. Excel does not require the label "Criteria Range", but it is useful to see the column labels as you organize the worksheet and use filters.

2. **Select the range A7:H7, click the Copy button 🗐 in the Clipboard group, click cell A2, click the Paste button in the Clipboard group, then press [Esc]**

   Next, you want to insert criteria that will display records for only those tours that depart after June 1, 2013 and that cost under $2,000.

3. **Click cell B3, type >6/1/2013, click cell F3, type <2000, then click ☑**

   You have entered the criteria in the cells directly beneath the Criteria Range labels, as shown in Figure H-6.

4. **Click any cell in the table, click the Data tab, then click the Advanced button in the Sort & Filter group**

   The Advanced Filter dialog box opens, with the table (list) range already entered. The default setting under Action is to filter the table in its current location ("in-place") rather than copy it to another location.

5. **Click the Criteria range text box, select the range A2:H3 in the worksheet, then click OK**

   You have specified the criteria range and used the filter. The filtered table contains eight records that match both criteria—the departure date is after 6/1/2013 and the price is less than $2,000, as shown in Figure H-7. You'll filter this table even further in the next lesson.

---

**QUICK TIP**

You can apply multiple criteria by using AutoFilter a second time on the results of the previously filtered data. Each additional filter builds on the results of the filtered data and filters the data further.

---

**TROUBLE**

If your filtered records don't match Figure H-7, make sure there are no spaces between the > symbol and the 6 in cell B3 and the < symbol and the 2 in cell F3.

**FIGURE H-6:** Criteria in the same row

| | A | B | C | D | E | F | G | H |
|---|---|---|---|---|---|---|---|---|
| 1 | Criteria Range | | | | | | | |
| 2 | Tour | Depart Date | Number of Days | Seat Capacity | Seats Reserved | Price | Air Included | Insurance Included |
| 3 | | >6/1/2013 | | | | <2000 | | |
| 4 | | | | | | | | |
| 5 | | | | | | | | |
| 6 | | | | | | | | |
| 7 | Tour | Depart Date | Number of Days | Seat Capacity | Seats Reserved | Price | Air Included | Insurance Included |
| 8 | Pacific Odyssey | 1/12/2013 | 14 | 50 | 50 | $ 2,105 | Yes | No |

Filtered records will
match these criteria

**FIGURE H-7:** Filtered table

| | A | B | C | D | E | F | G | H |
|---|---|---|---|---|---|---|---|---|
| 1 | Criteria Range | | | | | | | |
| 2 | Tour | Depart Date | Number of Days | Seat Capacity | Seats Reserved | Price | Air Included | Insurance Included |
| 3 | | >6/1/2013 | | | | <2000 | | |
| 4 | | | | | | | | |
| 5 | | | | | | | | |
| 6 | | | | | | | | |
| 7 | Tour | Depart Date | Number of Days | Seat Capacity | Seats Reserved | Price | Air Included | Insurance Included |
| 33 | Exotic Morocco | 6/12/2013 | 7 | 38 | 25 | $ 1,900 | Yes | No |
| 34 | Kayak Newfoundland | 6/12/2013 | 7 | 20 | 15 | $ 1,970 | Yes | Yes |
| 37 | Wild River Escape | 6/27/2013 | 10 | 21 | 21 | $ 1,944 | No | No |
| 42 | Kayak Newfoundland | 7/12/2013 | 7 | 20 | 15 | $ 1,970 | Yes | Yes |
| 44 | Magnificent Montenegro | 7/27/2013 | 10 | 48 | 0 | $ 1,890 | No | No |
| 46 | Kayak Newfoundland | 8/12/2013 | 7 | 20 | 12 | $ 1,970 | Yes | Yes |
| 49 | Wild River Escape | 8/27/2013 | 10 | 21 | 11 | $ 1,944 | No | No |
| 61 | Exotic Morocco | 10/31/2013 | 7 | 38 | 15 | $ 1,900 | Yes | No |

Depart dates are after 6/1/2013          Prices are less than $2,000

## Using advanced conditional formatting options

You can emphasize top- or bottom-ranked values in a field using conditional formatting. To highlight the top or bottom values in a field, select the field data, click the Conditional Formatting button in the Styles group on the Home tab, point to Top/Bottom Rules, select a Top or Bottom rule, if necessary enter the percentage or number of cells in the selected range that you want to format, select the format for the cells that meet the top or bottom criteria, then click OK. You can also format your worksheet or table data using icon sets and color scales based on the cell values. A **color scale** uses a set of two, three, or four fill colors to convey relative values. For example, red could fill cells to indicate they have higher values and green could signify lower values. To add a color scale, select a data range, click the Home tab, click the Conditional

Formatting button in the Styles group, then point to Color Scales. On the submenu, you can select preformatted color sets or click More Rules to create your own color sets. **Icon sets** let you visually communicate relative cell values by adding icons to cells based on the values they contain. An upward-pointing green arrow might represent the highest values, and downward-pointing red arrows could represent lower values. To add an icon set to a data range, select a data range, click the Conditional Formatting button in the Styles group, then point to Icon Sets. You can customize the values that are used as thresholds for color scales and icon sets by clicking the Conditional Formatting button in the Styles group, clicking Manage Rules, clicking the rule in the Conditional Formatting Rules Manager dialog box, then clicking Edit Rule.

Analyzing Table Data

# Extracting Table Data

Whenever you take the time to specify a complicated set of search criteria, it's a good idea to extract the matching records, rather than filtering it in place. When you **extract** data, you place a copy of a filtered table in a range that you specify in the Advanced Filter dialog box. This way, you won't accidentally clear the filter or lose track of the records you spent time compiling. To extract data, you use an Advanced Filter and enter the criteria beneath the copied field names, as you did in the previous lesson. You then specify the location where you want the extracted data to appear.  Kate needs to filter the table one step further to reflect only the Wild River Escape or Kayak Newfoundland tours in the current filtered table. She asks you to complete this filter by specifying an Or condition, which you will do by entering two sets of criteria in two separate rows. You decide to save the filtered records by extracting them to a different location in the worksheet.

## STEPS

1. **In cell A3, enter Wild River Escape, then in cell A4, enter Kayak Newfoundland**

   The new sets of criteria need to appear in two separate rows, so you need to copy the previous filter criteria to the second row.

2. **Copy the criteria in B3:F3 to B4:F4**

   The criteria are shown in Figure H-8. When you use the Advanced Filter this time, you indicate that you want to copy the filtered table to a range beginning in cell A75, so that Kate can easily refer to the data, even if you use more filters later.

3. **If necessary, click the Data tab, then click Advanced in the Sort & Filter group**

4. **Under Action, click the Copy to another location option button to select it, click the Copy to text box, then type A75**

   The last time you filtered the table, the criteria range included only rows 2 and 3, and now you have criteria in row 4.

> **QUICK TIP**
> Make sure the criteria range in the Advanced Filter dialog box includes the field names and the number of rows underneath the names that contain criteria. If you leave a blank row in the criteria range, Excel filters nothing and shows all records.

5. **Edit the contents of the Criteria range text box to show the range $A$2:$H$4, click OK, then if necessary scroll down until row 75 is visible**

   The matching records appear in the range beginning in cell A75, as shown in Figure H-9. The original table, starting in cell A7, contains the records filtered in the previous lesson.

6. **Press [Ctrl][Home], then click the Clear button in the Sort & Filter group**

   The original table is displayed starting in cell A7, and the extracted table remains in A75:H80.

7. **Save the workbook**

**FIGURE H-8:** Criteria in separate rows

| | A | B | C | D | E | F | G | H |
|---|---|---|---|---|---|---|---|---|
| 1 | Criteria Range | | | | | | | |
| 2 | Tour | Depart Date | Number of Days | Seat Capacity | Seats Reserved | Price | Air Included | Insurance Included |
| 3 | Wild River Escape | >6/1/2013 | | | | <2000 | | |
| 4 | Kayak Newfoundland | >6/1/2013 | | | | <2000 | | |
| 5 | | | | | | | | |

Criteria on two lines indicates an OR condition

**FIGURE H-9:** Extracted data records

| | Tour | Depart Date | Number of Days | Seat Capacity | Seats Reserved | Price | Air Included | Insurance Included |
|---|---|---|---|---|---|---|---|---|
| 75 | Tour | Depart Date | Days | Seat Capacity | Seats Reserved | Price | Air Included | Insurance Included |
| 76 | Kayak Newfoundland | 6/12/2013 | 7 | 20 | 15 | $ 1,970 | Yes | Yes |
| 77 | Wild River Escape | 6/27/2013 | 10 | 21 | 21 | $ 1,944 | No | No |
| 78 | Kayak Newfoundland | 7/12/2013 | 7 | 20 | 15 | $ 1,970 | Yes | Yes |
| 79 | Kayak Newfoundland | 8/12/2013 | 7 | 20 | 12 | $ 1,970 | Yes | Yes |
| 80 | Wild River Escape | 8/27/2013 | 10 | 21 | 11 | $ 1,944 | No | No |
| 81 | | | | | | | | |

Only Wild River Escape and Kayak Newfoundland tours

Depart date after 6/1/2013

Price is less than $2,000

## Understanding the criteria range and the copy-to location

When you define the criteria range and the copy-to location in the Advanced Filter dialog box, Excel automatically creates the range names Criteria and Extract for these ranges in the worksheet. The Criteria range includes the field names and any criteria rows underneath them. The Extract range includes just the field names above the extracted table. You can select these ranges by clicking the Name box list arrow, then clicking the range name. If you click the Name Manager button in the Defined Names group on the Formulas tab, you will see these new names and the ranges associated with each one.

# Looking Up Values in a Table

The Excel VLOOKUP function helps you locate specific values in a table. VLOOKUP searches vertically (V) down the far left column of a table, then reads across the row to find the value in the column you specify, much as you might look up a number in a phone book: You locate a person's name, then read across the row to find the phone number you want.  Kate wants to be able to find a tour destination by entering the tour code. You will use the VLOOKUP function to accomplish this task. You begin by viewing the table name so you can refer to it in a lookup function.

## STEPS

**QUICK TIP**

You can change table names to better represent their content so they are easier to use in formulas. Click the table in the list of names in the Name Manager text box, click Edit, type the new table name in the Name text box, then click OK.

1. **Click the Lookup sheet tab, click the Formulas tab in the Ribbon, then click the Name Manager button in the Defined Names group**

   The named ranges for the workbook appear in the Name Manager dialog box, as shown in Figure H-10. The Criteria and Extract ranges appear at the top of the range name list. At the bottom of the list is information about the three tables in the workbook. Table1 refers to the table on the Tours sheet, Table2 refers to the table on the Lookup sheet, and Table3 refers to the table on the Subtotals worksheet. The Excel structured reference feature automatically created these table names when the tables were created.

2. **Click Close**

   You want to find the tour represented by the code 653S. The VLOOKUP function lets you find the tour name for any trip code. You will enter a trip code in cell L2 and a VLOOKUP function in cell M2.

3. **Click cell L2, enter 653S, click cell M2, click the Lookup & Reference button in the Function Library group, then click VLOOKUP**

   The Function Arguments dialog box opens, with boxes for each of the VLOOKUP arguments. Because the value you want to find is in cell L2, L2 is the Lookup_value. The table you want to search is the table on the Lookup sheet, so its assigned name, Table2, is the Table_array.

**QUICK TIP**

If you want to find only the closest match for a value, enter TRUE in the Range_lookup text box. However, this can give misleading results if you are looking for an exact match. If you use FALSE and Excel can't find the value, you see an error message.

4. **With the insertion point in the Lookup_value text box, click cell L2, click the Table_array text box, then type Table2**

   The column containing the information that you want to find and display in cell M2 is the second column from the left in the table range, so the Col_index_num is 2. Because you want to find an exact match for the value in cell L1, the Range_lookup argument is FALSE.

5. **Click the Col_index_num text box, type 2, click the Range_lookup text box, then enter FALSE**

   Your completed Function Arguments dialog box should match Figure H-11.

6. **Click OK**

   Excel searches down the far-left column of the table until it finds a trip code that matches the one in cell L2. It then looks in column 2 of the table range and finds the tour for that record, Green Adventures in Ecuador, and displays it in cell M2. You use this function to determine the tour for one other trip code.

7. **Click cell L2, type 325B, then click the Enter button ☑ on the formula bar**

   The VLOOKUP function returns the value of Costa Rica in cell M2.

8. **Press [Ctrl][Home], then save the workbook**

---

### Finding records using the DGET function

You can also use the DGET function to find a record in a table that matches specified criteria. For example, you could use the criteria of L1:L2 in the DGET function. When using DGET, you need to include [#All] after your table name in the formula to include the column labels that are used for the criteria range.

**FIGURE H-10:** Named ranges in the workbook

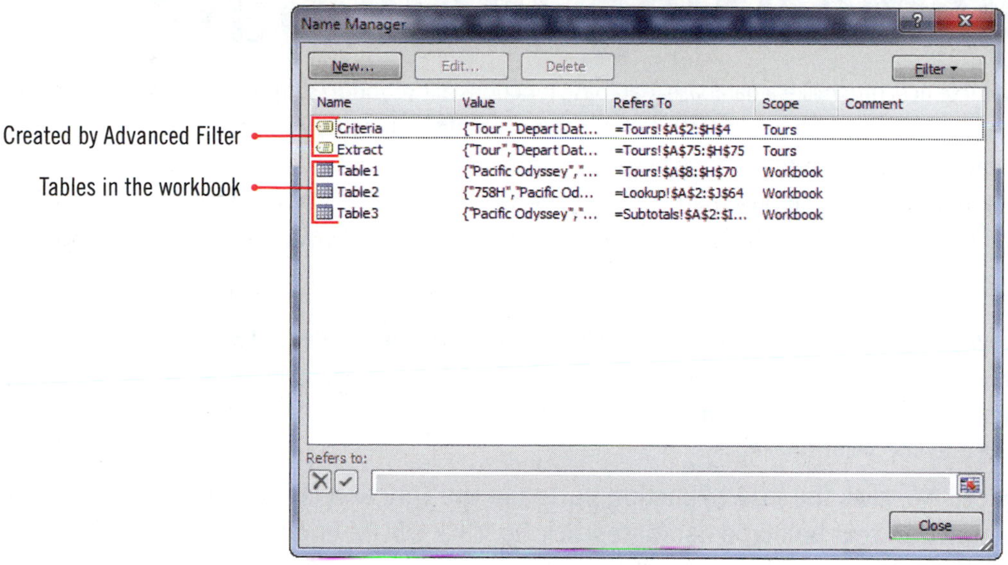

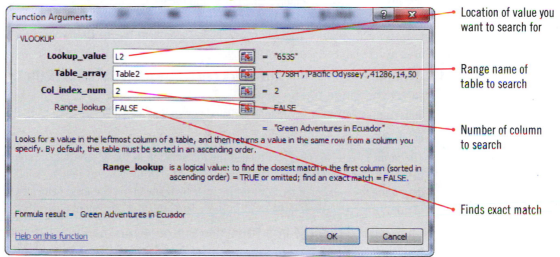

Created by Advanced Filter

Tables in the workbook

**FIGURE H-11:** Completed Function Arguments dialog box for VLOOKUP

Location of value you want to search for

Range name of table to search

Number of column to search

Finds exact match

## Using the HLOOKUP and MATCH functions

The VLOOKUP (Vertical Lookup) function is useful when your data is arranged vertically, in columns. When your data is arranged horizontally in rows, use the HLOOKUP (Horizontal Lookup) function. HLOOKUP searches horizontally across the upper row of a table until it finds the matching value, then looks down the number of rows you specify. The arguments for this function are identical to those for the VLOOKUP function, with one exception. Instead of a Col_index_number, HLOOKUP uses a Row_index_number, which indicates the location of the row you want to search. For example, if you want to search the fourth row from the top of the table range, the Row_index_number should be 4. You can use the MATCH function when you want the position of an item in a range. The MATCH function uses the syntax: MATCH (lookup_value,lookup_array,match_ type) where the lookup_value is the value you want to match in the lookup_array range. The match_type can be 0 for an exact match, 1 for matching the largest value that is less than or equal to lookup_value, or –1 for matching the smallest value that is greater than or equal to the lookup_value.

# Summarizing Table Data

Because a table acts much like a database, database functions allow you to summarize table data in a variety of ways. When working with a sales activity table, for example, you can use Excel to count the number of client contacts by sales representative or to total the amount sold to specific accounts by month. Table H-1 lists database functions commonly used to summarize table data.  Kate is considering adding tours for the 2013 schedule. She needs your help in evaluating the number of seats available for scheduled tours.

**STEPS**

1. **Review the criteria range for the Yellowstone tour in the range L4:L5**

   The criteria range in L4:L5 tells Excel to summarize records with the entry "Yellowstone" in the Tour column. The functions will be in cells N6 and N7. You use this criteria range in a DSUM function to sum the seats available for only the Yellowstone tours.

2. **Click cell N6, click the Insert Function button in the Function Library group, in the Search for a function text box type database, click Go, click DSUM under Select a function, then click OK**

   The first argument of the DSUM function is the table, or database.

**QUICK TIP**

Because the DSUM formula uses the column headings to locate and sum the table data, the header row needs to be included in the database range.

3. **In the Function Arguments dialog box, with the insertion point in the Database text box, move the pointer over the upper-left corner of cell A1 until the pointer becomes ↘, click once, then click again**

   The first click selects the table's data range, and the second click selects the entire table, including the header row. The second argument of the DSUM function is the label for the column that you want to sum. You want to total the number of available seats. The last argument for the DSUM function is the criteria that will be used to determine which values to total.

**QUICK TIP**

You can move the Function Arguments dialog box if it overlaps a cell or range that you need to click. You can also click the Collapse Dialog Box button ▦, select the cell or range, then click the Expand Dialog box button ▦ to return to the Function Arguments dialog box.

4. **Click the Field text box, then click cell G1, Seats Available; click the Criteria text box and select the range L4:L5**

   Your completed Function Arguments dialog box should match Figure H-12.

5. **Click OK**

   The result in cell N6 is 8. Excel totaled the information in the Seats Available column for those records that meet the criterion of Tour equals Yellowstone. The DCOUNT and the DCOUNTA functions can help you determine the number of records meeting specified criteria in a database field. DCOUNTA counts the number of nonblank cells. You will use DCOUNTA to determine the number of tours scheduled.

6. **Click cell N7, click the Insert Function button 𝑓ₓ on the formula bar, in the Search for a function text box type database, click Go, select DCOUNTA from the Select a function list, then click OK**

7. **With the insertion point in the Database text box, move the pointer over the upper-left corner of cell A1 until the pointer becomes ↘, click once, click again to include the header row, click the Field text box and click cell B1, click the Criteria text box and select the range L4:L5, then click OK**

   The result in cell N7 is 5, and it indicates that there are five Yellowstone tours scheduled for the year. You also want to display the number of seats available for the Hiking Patagonia tours.

8. **Click cell L5, type Hiking Patagonia, then click the Enter button ☑ on the formula bar**

   Figure H-13 shows that 18 seats are available in the two Hiking Patagonia tours.

**FIGURE H-12:** Completed Function Arguments dialog box for DSUM

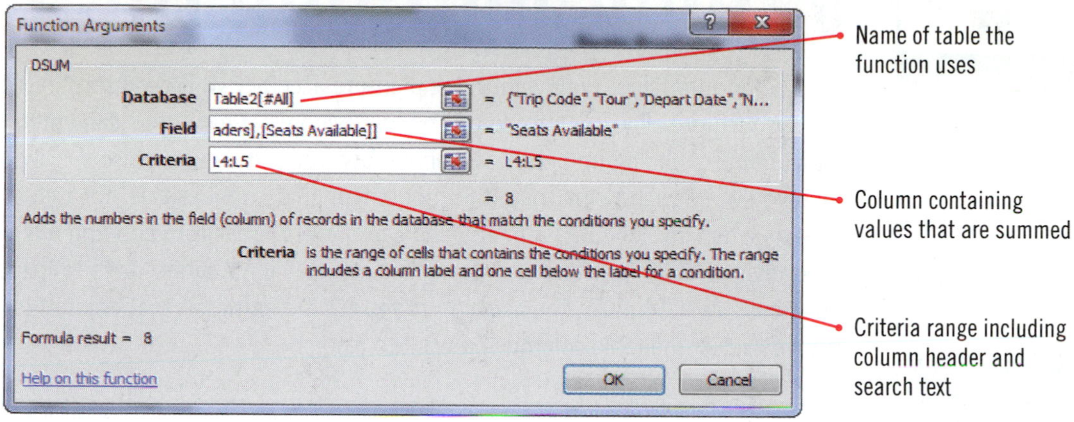

Name of table the function uses

Column containing values that are summed

Criteria range including column header and search text

**FIGURE H-13:** Result generated by database functions

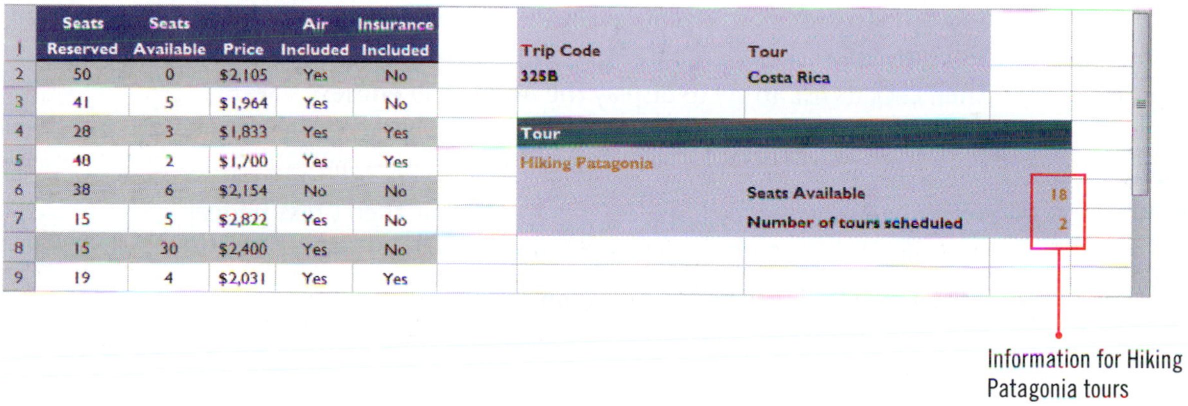

Information for Hiking Patagonia tours

**TABLE H-1:** Common database functions

| function | result |
|----------|--------|
| DGET | Extracts a single record from a table that matches criteria you specify |
| DSUM | Totals numbers in a given table column that match criteria you specify |
| DAVERAGE | Averages numbers in a given table column that match criteria you specify |
| DCOUNT | Counts the cells that contain numbers in a given table column that match criteria you specify |
| DCOUNTA | Counts the cells that contain nonblank data in a given table column that match criteria you specify |

Analyzing Table Data

# Validating Table Data

When setting up tables, you want to help ensure accuracy when you or others enter data. The Excel data validation feature allows you to do this by specifying what data users can enter in a range of cells. You can restrict data to whole numbers, decimal numbers, or text. You can also specify a list of acceptable entries. Once you've specified what data the program should consider valid for that cell, Excel displays an error message when invalid data is entered and can prevent users from entering any other data that it considers to be invalid.  Kate wants to make sure that information in the Air Included column is entered consistently in the future. She asks you to restrict the entries in that column to two options: Yes and No. First, you select the table column you want to restrict.

**STEPS**

1. **Click the top edge of the Air Included column header**

   The column data is selected.

**QUICK TIP**

To specify a long list of valid entries, type the list in a column or row elsewhere in the worksheet, then type the list range in the Source text box.

2. **Click the Data tab, click the Data Validation button in the Data Tools group, click the Settings tab if necessary, click the Allow list arrow, then click List**

   Selecting the List option lets you type a list of specific options.

3. **Click the Source text box, then type Yes, No**

   You have entered the list of acceptable entries, separated by commas, as shown in Figure H-14. You want the data entry person to be able to select a valid entry from a drop-down list.

**TROUBLE**

If you get an invalid data error, make sure that cell I1 is not included in the selection. If I1 is included, open the Data Validation dialog box, click Clear All, click OK, then begin with Step 1 again.

4. **Click the In-cell dropdown check box to select it if necessary, then click OK**

   The dialog box closes, and you return to the worksheet.

5. **Click the Home tab, click any cell in the last table row, click the Insert list arrow in the Cells group, click Insert Table Row Below, click the last cell in the Air Included column, then click its list arrow to display the list of valid entries**

   The drop-down list is shown in Figure H-15. You could click an item in the list to have it entered in the cell, but you want to test the data restriction by entering an invalid entry.

6. **Click the list arrow to close the list, type Maybe, then press [Enter]**

   A warning dialog box appears and prevents you from entering the invalid data, as shown in Figure H-16.

7. **Click Cancel, click the list arrow, then click Yes**

   The cell accepts the valid entry. The data restriction ensures that records contain only one of the two correct entries in the Air Included column. The table is ready for future data entry.

8. **Delete the last table row, add your name to the center section of the footer, then save the workbook**

---

### Restricting cell values and data length

In addition to providing an in-cell drop-down list for data entry, you can use data validation to restrict the values that are entered into cells. For example, if you want to restrict cells to values less than a certain number, date, or time, click the Data tab, click the Data Validation button in the Data Tools group, and on the Settings tab, click the Allow list arrow, select Whole number, Decimal, Date, or Time, click the Data list arrow, select less than, then in the bottom text box, enter the maximum value. You can also limit the length of data entered into cells by choosing Text length in the Allow list, clicking the Data list arrow and selecting less than, then entering the maximum length in the Maximum text box.

**FIGURE H-14:** Creating data restrictions

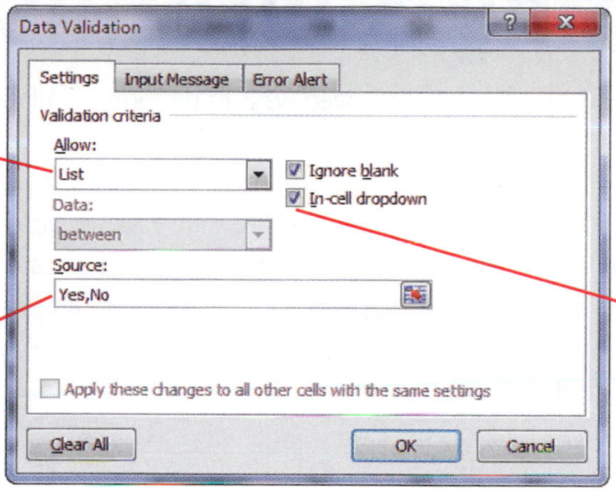

Restricts entries to a list of valid options →

List of valid options →

→ Displays a list of valid options during data entry

**FIGURE H-15:** Entering data in restricted cells

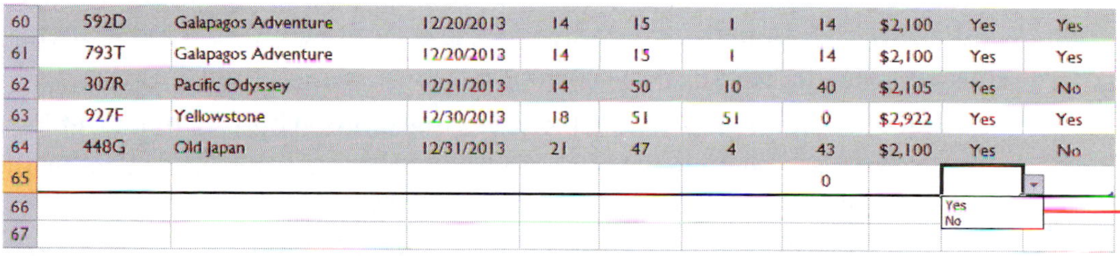

| 60 | 592D | Galapagos Adventure | 12/20/2013 | 14 | 15 | 1 | 14 | $2,100 | Yes | Yes |
| 61 | 793T | Galapagos Adventure | 12/20/2013 | 14 | 15 | 1 | 14 | $2,100 | Yes | Yes |
| 62 | 307R | Pacific Odyssey | 12/21/2013 | 14 | 50 | 10 | 40 | $2,105 | Yes | No |
| 63 | 927F | Yellowstone | 12/30/2013 | 18 | 51 | 51 | 0 | $2,922 | Yes | Yes |
| 64 | 448G | Old Japan | 12/31/2013 | 21 | 47 | 4 | 43 | $2,100 | Yes | No |
| 65 | | | | | | | 0 | | | |
| 66 | | | | | | | | | Yes | |
| 67 | | | | | | | | | No | |

→ Dropdown list

**FIGURE H-16:** Invalid data warning

Microsoft Excel

The value you entered is not valid.

A user has restricted values that can be entered into this cell.

Retry    Cancel    Help

Was this information helpful?

## Adding input messages and error alerts

You can customize the way data validation works by using the two other tabs in the Data Validation dialog box: Input Message and Error Alert. The Input Message tab lets you set a message that appears when the user selects that cell. For example, the message might contain instructions about what type of data to enter. On the Input Message tab, enter a message title and message, then click OK. The Error Alert tab lets you set one of three alert levels if a user enters invalid data. The Information level displays your message with the information icon but allows the user to proceed with data entry. The Warning level displays your information with the warning icon and gives the user the option to proceed with data entry or not. The Stop level, which you used in this lesson, displays your message and only lets the user retry or cancel data entry for that cell.

# Creating Subtotals

In a large range of data, you will often need ways to perform calculations that summarize groups within the data. For example, you might need to subtotal the sales for several sales reps listed in a table. The Excel Subtotals feature provides a quick, easy way to group and summarize a range of data. It lets you create not only subtotals using the SUM function, but other statistics as well, including COUNT, AVERAGE, MAX, and MIN. However, subtotals cannot be used in an Excel table, nor can it rearrange data. Before you can add subtotals to table data, you must first convert the data to a range and sort it.  Kate wants you to group data by tours, with subtotals for the number of seats available and the number of seats reserved. You begin by converting the table to a range.

**STEPS**

1. Click the **Subtotals sheet tab**, click any cell inside the table, click the **Table Tools Design tab**, click the **Convert to Range button** in the Tools group, then click **Yes**

   Before you can add the subtotals, you must first sort the data. You decide to sort it in ascending order, first by tour and then by departure date.

2. Click the **Data tab**, click the **Sort button** in the Sort & Filter group, in the Sort dialog box click the **Sort by list arrow**, click **Tour**, then click the **Add Level button**, click the **Then by list arrow**, click **Depart Date**, verify that the order is **Oldest to Newest**, then click **OK**

   You have sorted the range in ascending order, first by tour, then by departure date.

3. Click any cell in the data range, then click the **Subtotal button** in the Outline group

   The Subtotal dialog box opens. Here you specify the items you want subtotaled, the function you want to apply to the values, and the fields you want to summarize.

4. Click the **At each change in list arrow**, click **Tour**, click the **Use function list arrow**, click **Sum**; in the "Add subtotal to" list, click the **Seats Reserved** and **Seats Available check boxes** to select them, if necessary, then click the **Insurance Included check box** to deselect it

5. If necessary, click the **Replace current subtotals** and **Summary below data check boxes** to select them

   Your completed Subtotal dialog box should match Figure H-17.

**QUICK TIP**

You can click the **−** button to hide or the **+** button to show a group of records in the subtotaled structure.

6. Click **OK**, then scroll down so you can see row 90

   The subtotaled data appears, showing the calculated subtotals and grand total in columns E and F, as shown in Figure H-18. Excel displays an outline to the left of the worksheet, with outline buttons to control the level of detail that appears. The button number corresponds to the detail level that is displayed. You want to show the second level of detail, the subtotals and the grand total.

7. Click the **outline symbol** 2

   Only the subtotals and the grand total appear.

**QUICK TIP**

You can remove subtotals in a worksheet by clicking the Subtotal button and clicking Remove All. The subtotals no longer appear, and the Outline feature is turned off automatically.

8. Add your name to the center section of the footer, preview the worksheet, click the **No Scaling list arrow**, click **Fit Sheet on One Page** to scale the worksheet to print on one page, then save the workbook

9. Close the workbook, exit Excel, then submit the workbook to your instructor

**FIGURE H-17:** Completed Subtotal dialog box

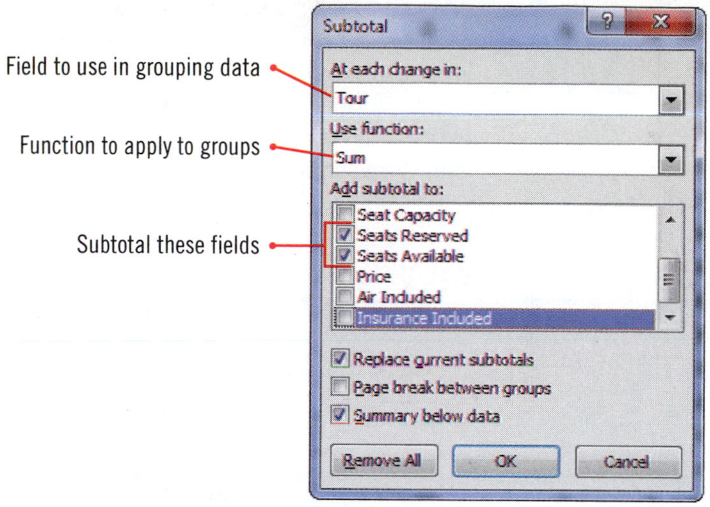

Field to use in grouping data → 

Function to apply to groups → 

Subtotal these fields → 

**FIGURE H-18:** Portion of subtotaled table

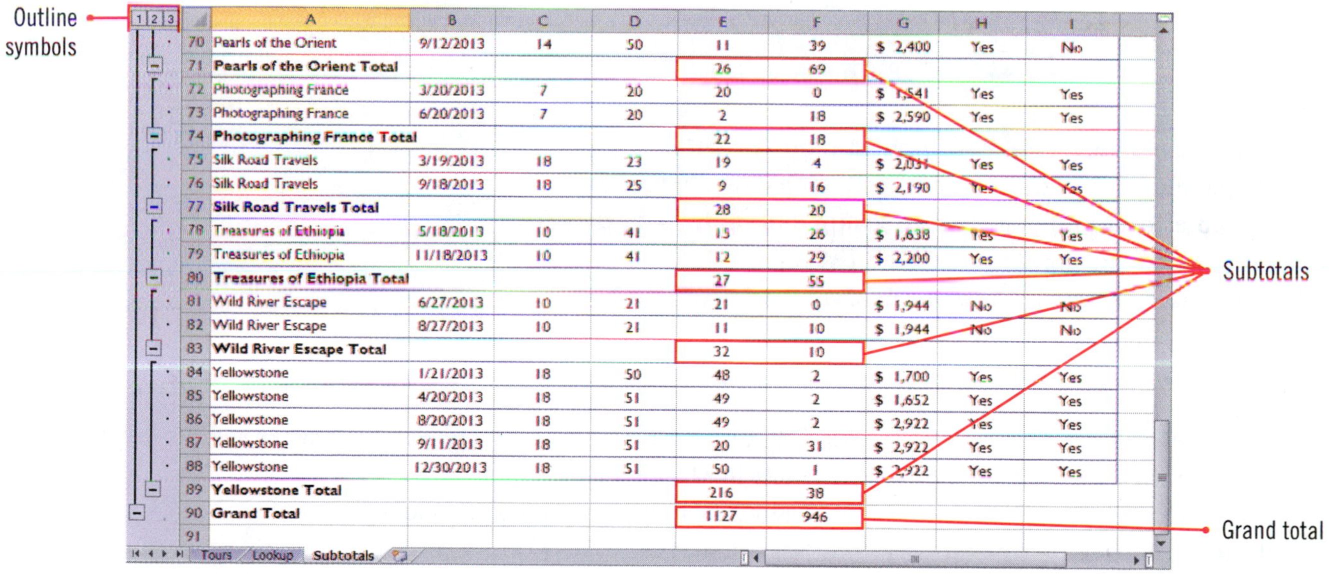

Outline symbols →

| | | A | B | C | D | E | F | G | H | I |
|---|---|---|---|---|---|---|---|---|---|---|
| · | 70 | Pearls of the Orient | 9/12/2013 | 14 | 50 | 11 | 39 | $ 2,400 | Yes | No |
| − | 71 | **Pearls of the Orient Total** | | | | 26 | 69 | | | |
| · | 72 | Photographing France | 3/20/2013 | 7 | 20 | 20 | 0 | $ 1,541 | Yes | Yes |
| · | 73 | Photographing France | 6/20/2013 | 7 | 20 | 2 | 18 | $ 2,590 | Yes | Yes |
| − | 74 | **Photographing France Total** | | | | 22 | 18 | | | |
| · | 75 | Silk Road Travels | 3/19/2013 | 18 | 23 | 19 | 4 | $ 2,031 | Yes | Yes |
| · | 76 | Silk Road Travels | 9/18/2013 | 18 | 25 | 9 | 16 | $ 2,190 | Yes | Yes |
| − | 77 | **Silk Road Travels Total** | | | | 28 | 20 | | | |
| · | 78 | Treasures of Ethiopia | 5/18/2013 | 10 | 41 | 15 | 26 | $ 1,838 | Yes | Yes |
| · | 79 | Treasures of Ethiopia | 11/18/2013 | 10 | 41 | 12 | 29 | $ 2,200 | Yes | Yes |
| − | 80 | **Treasures of Ethiopia Total** | | | | 27 | 55 | | | |
| · | 81 | Wild River Escape | 6/27/2013 | 10 | 21 | 21 | 0 | $ 1,944 | No | No |
| · | 82 | Wild River Escape | 8/27/2013 | 10 | 21 | 11 | 10 | $ 1,944 | No | No |
| − | 83 | **Wild River Escape Total** | | | | 32 | 10 | | | |
| · | 84 | Yellowstone | 1/21/2013 | 18 | 50 | 48 | 2 | $ 1,700 | Yes | Yes |
| · | 85 | Yellowstone | 4/20/2013 | 18 | 51 | 49 | 2 | $ 1,652 | Yes | Yes |
| · | 86 | Yellowstone | 8/20/2013 | 18 | 51 | 49 | 2 | $ 2,922 | Yes | Yes |
| · | 87 | Yellowstone | 9/11/2013 | 18 | 51 | 20 | 31 | $ 2,922 | Yes | Yes |
| · | 88 | Yellowstone | 12/30/2013 | 18 | 51 | 50 | 1 | $ 2,922 | Yes | Yes |
| − | 89 | **Yellowstone Total** | | | | 216 | 38 | | | |
| − | 90 | **Grand Total** | | | | 1127 | 946 | | | |
| | 91 | | | | | | | | | |

→ Subtotals

→ Grand total

Tours  Lookup  Subtotals

# Practice

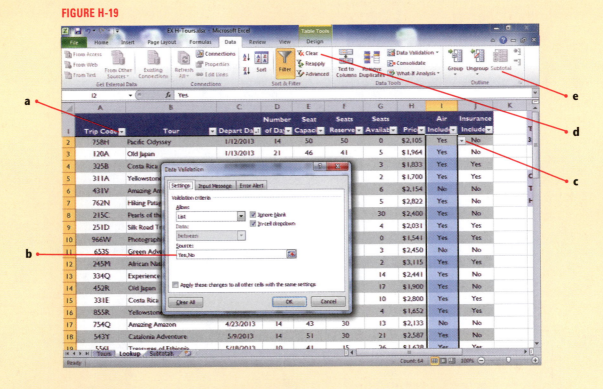

For current SAM information, including versions and content details, visit SAM Central (http://www.cengage.com/samcentral). If you have a SAM user profile, you may have access to hands-on instruction, practice, and assessment of the skills covered in this unit. Since various versions of SAM are supported throughout the life of this text, check with your instructor for the correct instructions and URL/Web site for accessing assignments.

## Concepts Review

FIGURE H-19

1. Which element would you click to remove a filter?
2. Which element points to an in-cell drop-down list arrow?
3. Which element do you click to group and summarize data?
4. Which element points to a field's list arrow?
5. Where do you specify acceptable data entries for a table?

**Match each term with the statement that best describes it.**

6. Extracted table
7. Table_array
8. Criteria range
9. Data validation
10. DSUM

a. Cell range when Advanced Filter results are copied to another location
b. Range in which search conditions are set
c. Restricts table entries to specified options
d. Name of the table searched in a VLOOKUP function
e. Function used to total table values that meet specified criteria

**Select the best answer from the list of choices.**

11. The _____ logical condition finds records matching both listed criteria.
   a. And
   b. Or
   c. True
   d. False

12. What does it mean when you select the Or option when creating a custom filter?
   a. Either criterion can be true to find a match.
   b. Neither criterion has to be 100% true.
   c. Both criteria must be true to find a match.
   d. A custom filter requires a criteria range.

# Skills Review

## 1. Filter a table.

**a.** Start Excel, open the file EX H-2.xlsx from the drive and folder where you store your Data Files, then save it as **EX H-NE Compensation**.

**b.** With the Compensation sheet active, filter the table to list only records for employees in the Boston branch.

**c.** Clear the filter, then add a filter that displays the records for employees in the Boston and Philadelphia branches.

**d.** Redisplay all employees, then use a filter to show the three employees with the highest annual salary.

**e.** Redisplay all the records.

## 2. Create a custom filter.

**a.** Create a custom filter showing employees hired before 1/1/2010 or after 12/31/2010.

**b.** Create a custom filter showing employees hired between 1/1/2010 and 12/31/2010.

**c.** Enter your name in the worksheet footer, then preview the filtered worksheet.

**d.** Redisplay all records.

**e.** Save the workbook.

## 3. Filter and extract a table with the Advanced Filter.

**a.** You want to retrieve a list of employees who were hired before 1/1/2011 and who have an annual salary of more than $70,000 a year. Define a criteria range by inserting six new rows above the table on the worksheet and copying the field names into the first row.

**b.** In cell D2, enter the criterion **<1/1/2011**, then in cell G2 enter **>70000**.

**c.** Click any cell in the table.

**d.** Open the Advanced Filter dialog box.

**e.** Indicate that you want to copy to another location, enter the criteria range **A1:J2**, verify that the List range is $A$7:$J$17, then indicate that you want to place the extracted list in the range starting at cell **A20**.

**f.** Confirm that the retrieved list meets the criteria as shown in Figure H-20.

**g.** Save the workbook, then preview the worksheet.

**FIGURE H-20**

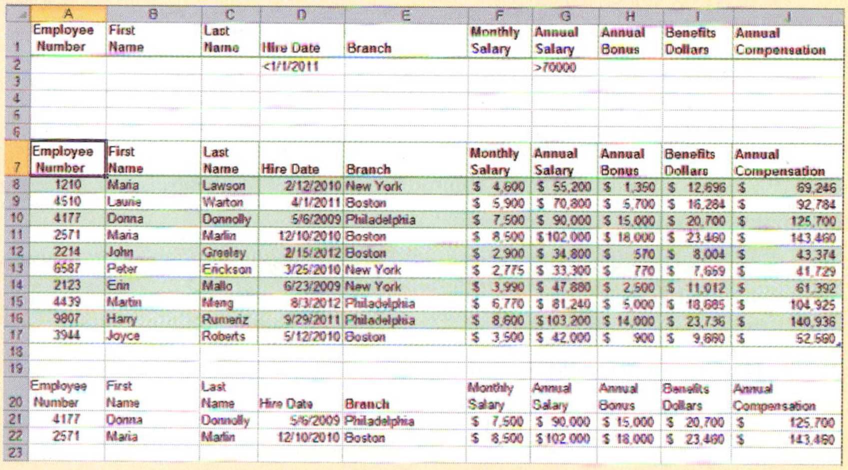

## 4. Look up values in a table.

**a.** Click the Summary sheet tab. Use the Name Manager to view the table names in the workbook, then close the dialog box.

**b.** You will use a lookup function to locate an employee's annual compensation; enter the Employee Number **2214** in cell A17.

**c.** In cell B17, use the VLOOKUP function and enter **A17** as the Lookup_value, **Table2** as the Table_array, **10** as the Col_index_num, and **FALSE** as the Range_lookup; observe the compensation displayed for that employee number, then check it against the table to make sure it is correct.

**d.** Enter another Employee Number, **4177**, in cell A17, and view the annual compensation for that employee.

**e.** Format cell B17 with the Accounting format with the $ symbol and no decimal places.

**f.** Save the workbook.

## 5. Summarize table data.

**a.** You want to enter a database function to average the annual salaries by branch, using the New York branch as the initial criterion. In cell E17, use the DAVERAGE function, and click the upper-left corner of cell A1 twice to select the table and its header row as the Database, select cell G1 for the Field, and select the range D16:D17 for the Criteria. Verify that the average New York salary is 45460.

**b.** Test the function further by entering the text **Philadelphia** in cell D17. When the criterion is entered, cell E17 should display 91480.

## Skills Review (continued)

**c.** Format cell E17 in Accounting Table format with the $ symbol and no decimal places.

**d.** Save the workbook.

**6. Validate table data.**

**a.** Select the data in column E of the table, and set a validation criterion specifying that you want to allow a list of valid options.

**b.** Enter a list of valid options that restricts the entries to **New York**, **Boston**, and **Philadelphia**. Remember to use a comma between each item in the list.

**c.** Indicate that you want the options to appear in an in-cell drop-down list, then close the dialog box.

**d.** Add a row to the table. Go to cell E12, then select Boston in the drop-down list.

**e.** Select the data in column F in the table, and indicate that you want to restrict the data entered to only whole numbers. In the Minimum text box, enter **1000**; in the Maximum text box, enter **10000**. Close the dialog box.

**f.** Click cell F12, enter **15000**, then press [Enter]. You should get an error message.

**g.** Click Cancel, then enter **7000**.

**h.** Complete the new record by adding an Employee Number of **1112**, a First Name of **Caroline**, a Last Name of **Schissel**, a Hire Date of **2/1/2013**, and an Annual Bonus of **$1000**. Format the range F12:J12 as Accounting with no decimal places and using the $ symbol. Compare your screen to Figure H-21.

**FIGURE H-21**

| | A | B | C | D | E | F | G | H | I | J |
|---|---|---|---|---|---|---|---|---|---|---|
| 1 | Employee Number | First Name | Last Name | Hire Date | Branch | Monthly Salary | Annual Salary | Annual Bonus | Benefits Dollars | Annual Compensation |
| 2 | 1210 | Maria | Lawson | 2/12/2010 | New York | $ 4,600 | $ 55,200 | $ 1,350 | $ 12,696 | $ 69,246 |
| 3 | 4510 | Laurie | Warton | 4/1/2011 | Boston | $ 5,900 | $ 70,800 | $ 5,700 | $ 16,284 | $ 92,784 |
| 4 | 4177 | Donna | Donnolly | 5/6/2009 | Philadelphia | $ 7,500 | $ 90,000 | $ 15,000 | $ 20,700 | $ 125,700 |
| 5 | 2571 | Maria | Martin | 12/10/2010 | Boston | $ 8,500 | $ 102,000 | $ 18,000 | $ 23,460 | $ 143,460 |
| 6 | 2214 | John | Greeley | 2/15/2012 | Boston | $ 2,900 | $ 34,800 | $ 570 | $ 8,004 | $ 43,374 |
| 7 | 6587 | Peter | Erickson | 3/25/2010 | New York | $ 2,775 | $ 33,300 | $ 770 | $ 7,659 | $ 41,729 |
| 8 | 2123 | Erin | Mallo | 6/23/2009 | New York | $ 3,990 | $ 47,880 | $ 2,500 | $ 11,012 | $ 61,392 |
| 9 | 4439 | Martin | Meng | 8/3/2012 | Philadelphia | $ 6,770 | $ 81,240 | $ 5,000 | $ 18,685 | $ 104,925 |
| 10 | 9807 | Harry | Rumeriz | 9/29/2011 | Philadelphia | $ 8,600 | $ 103,200 | $ 14,000 | $ 23,736 | $ 140,936 |
| 11 | 3944 | Joyce | Roberts | 5/12/2010 | Boston | $ 3,500 | $ 42,000 | $ 900 | $ 9,660 | $ 52,560 |
| 12 | 1112 | Caroline | Schissel | 2/1/2013 | Boston | $ 7,000 | $ 84,000 | $ 1,000 | $ 19,320 | $ 104,320 |
| 13 | | | | | | | | | | |
| 14 | | | | | | | | | | |
| 15 | | | | | | | | | | |
| 16 | Employee Number | Annual Compensation | | | Branch | Average Annual Salary | | | | |
| 17 | 4177 | $ 125,700 | | | Philadelphia | $ 91,480 | | | | |

**i.** Add your name to the center section of the footer, save the worksheet, then preview the worksheet.

**7. Create subtotals.**

**a.** Click the Subtotals sheet tab.

**b.** Use the Branch field list arrow to sort the table in ascending order by branch.

**c.** Convert the table to a range.

**d.** Group and create subtotals of the Annual Compensation data by branch, using the SUM function.

**e.** Click the 2 outline button on the outline to display only the subtotals and the grand total. Compare your screen to Figure H-22.

**FIGURE H-22**

| 1 2 3 | | A | B | C | D | E | F | G | H | I | J |
|---|---|---|---|---|---|---|---|---|---|---|---|
| | 1 | Employee Number | First Name | Last Name | Hire Date | Branch | Monthly Salary | Annual Salary | Annual Bonus | Benefits Dollars | Annual Compensation |
| + | 6 | | | | | Boston Total | | | | | $ 332,178 |
| + | 10 | | | | | New York Total | | | | | $ 172,367 |
| + | 14 | | | | | Philadelphia Total | | | | | $ 371,561 |
| − | 15 | | | | | Grand Total | | | | | $ 876,107 |
| | 16 | | | | | | | | | | |

**f.** Enter your name in the worksheet footer, save the workbook, then preview the worksheet.

**g.** Save the workbook, close the workbook, exit Excel, then submit your workbook to your instructor.

# Independent Challenge 1

As the manager of Miami Dental, a dental supply company, you spend a lot of time managing your inventory. To help with this task, you have created an Excel table that you can extract information from using filters. You also need to add data validation and summary information to the table.

**a.** Start Excel, open the file EX H-3.xlsx from the drive and folder where you store your Data Files, then save it as **EX H-Dental**.

**b.** Using the table data on the Inventory sheet, create a filter to display information about only the product bond refill. Clear the filter.

# Independent Challenge 1 (continued)

c. Use a Custom Filter to generate a list of products with a quantity greater than 20. Clear the filter.

d. Copy the labels in cells A1:F1 into A16:F16. Type **Bond Refill** in cell A17, and type **Small** in cell C17. Use the Advanced Filter with a criteria range of A16:F17 to extract a table of small bond refills to the range of cells beginning in cell A20. Enter your name in the worksheet footer, save the workbook, then preview the worksheet.

e. Click the Summary sheet tab, select the table data in column B. Open the Data Validation dialog box, then indicate you want to use a validation list with the acceptable entries of **Berkley**, **Bromen**, **Lincoln**, **Mallory**. Make sure the In-cell dropdown check box is selected.

f. Test the data validation by trying to change a cell in column B of the table to **Loring**.

g. Using Figure H-23 as a guide, enter a function in cell E18 that calculates the total quantity of bond refill available in your inventory. Enter your name in the worksheet footer, preview the worksheet, then save the workbook.

h. On the Subtotals sheet, sort the table in ascending order by product. Convert the table to a range. Insert subtotals by product using the Subtotal function, then select Quantity in the "Add Subtotal to" box. Remove the check box for the Total field, if necessary. Use the appropriate button on the outline to display only the subtotals and grand total. Save the workbook, then preview the worksheet.

FIGURE H-23

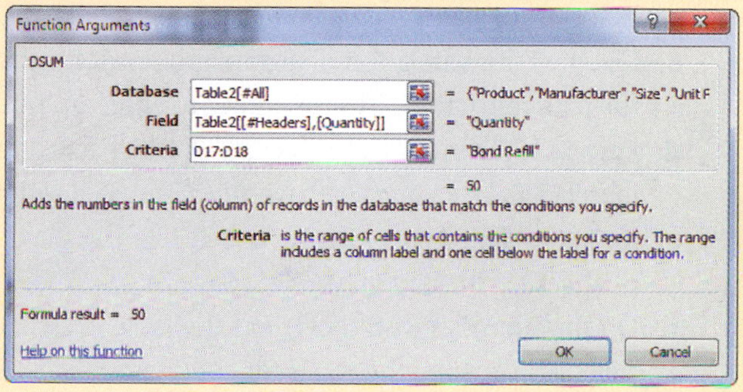


### Advanced Challenge Exercise

- Clear the subtotals from the worksheet.
- Use conditional formatting to add icons to the quantity field using the following criteria: quantities greater than or equal to 20 are formatted with a green check mark, quantities greater than or equal to 10 but less than 20 are formatted with a yellow exclamation point, and quantities less than 10 are formatted with a red x. Use Figure H-24 as a guide to adding the formatting rule, then compare your Quantity values to Figure H-25. (*Hint*: You may need to click in the top Value text box for the correct value to display for the red x.)
- Save the workbook then preview the worksheet.

i. Submit the workbook to your instructor. Close the workbook, then exit Excel.

FIGURE H-24

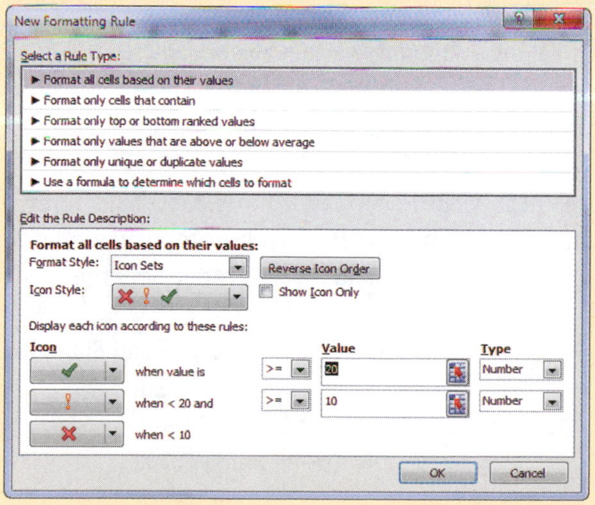


FIGURE H-25

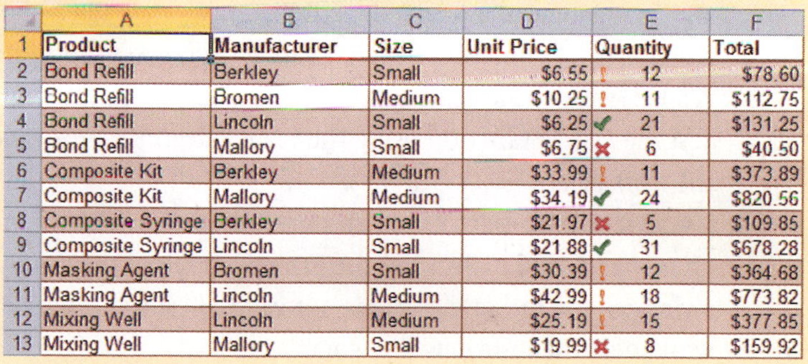

| | A | B | C | D | E | F |
|---|---|---|---|---|---|---|
| 1 | Product | Manufacturer | Size | Unit Price | Quantity | Total |
| 2 | Bond Refill | Berkley | Small | $6.55 | 12 | $78.60 |
| 3 | Bond Refill | Bromen | Medium | $10.25 | 11 | $112.75 |
| 4 | Bond Refill | Lincoln | Small | $6.25 | 21 | $131.25 |
| 5 | Bond Refill | Mallory | Small | $6.75 | 6 | $40.50 |
| 6 | Composite Kit | Berkley | Medium | $33.99 | 11 | $373.89 |
| 7 | Composite Kit | Mallory | Medium | $34.19 | 24 | $820.56 |
| 8 | Composite Syringe | Berkley | Small | $21.97 | 5 | $109.85 |
| 9 | Composite Syringe | Lincoln | Small | $21.88 | 31 | $678.28 |
| 10 | Masking Agent | Bromen | Small | $30.39 | 12 | $364.68 |
| 11 | Masking Agent | Lincoln | Medium | $42.99 | 18 | $773.82 |
| 12 | Mixing Well | Lincoln | Medium | $25.19 | 15 | $377.85 |
| 13 | Mixing Well | Mallory | Small | $19.99 | 8 | $159.92 |

# Independent Challenge 2

You are an accountant for an electrical supply company where you track the accounts receivables. The business supplies both residential and commercial electricians. You have put together an invoice table to track sales for the month of October. Now that you have this table, you would like to manipulate it in several ways. First, you want to filter the table to show only invoices over a certain amount with certain order dates. You also want to subtotal the total column by residential and commercial supplies. To prevent data entry errors you will restrict entries in the Order Date column. Finally, you would like to add database and lookup functions to your worksheet to efficiently retrieve data from the table.

    **a.** Start Excel, open the file EX H-4.xlsx from the drive and folder where you store your Data Files, then save it as **EX H-Invoices**.

    **b.** Use the Advanced Filter to show invoices with amounts more than $100.00 ordered before 10/15/2013, using cells A27:B28 to enter your criteria and extracting the results to cell A33. (*Hint*: You don't need to specify an entire row as the criteria range.) Enter your name in the worksheet footer.

    **c.** Use the Data Validation dialog box to restrict entries to those with order dates between 10/1/2013 and 10/31/2013. Test the data restrictions by attempting to enter an invalid date in cell B25.

    **d.** Enter **23721** in cell G28. Enter a VLOOKUP function in cell H28 to retrieve the total based on the invoice number entered in cell G28. Make sure you have an exact match with the invoice number. Test the function with the invoice number 23718.

    **e.** Enter the date **10/1/2013** in cell J28. Use the database function, DCOUNT, in cell K28 to count the number of invoices for the date in cell J28. Save the workbook, then preview the worksheet.

    **f.** On the Subtotals worksheet, sort the table in ascending order by Type, then convert the table to a range. Create subtotals showing the totals for commercial and residential invoices. (*Hint*: Sum the Total field.) Display only the subtotals for the commercial and residential accounts along with the grand total.

    **g.** Save the workbook, preview the worksheet, close the workbook, then exit Excel. Submit the workbook to your instructor.

# Independent Challenge 3

You are the manager of Home Design, a paint and decorating store. You have created an Excel table that contains your order data, along with the amounts for each item ordered and the date the order was placed. You would like to manipulate this table to display product categories and ordered items meeting specific criteria. You would also like to add subtotals to the table and add database functions to total orders. Finally, you want to restrict entries in the Category column.

    **a.** Start Excel, open the file EX H-5.xlsx from the drive and folder where you store your Data Files, then save it as **EX H-Home**.

    **b.** Create an advanced filter that extracts records with the following criteria to cell A42: orders greater than $1000 having dates either before 9/10/2013 or after 9/24/2013. (*Hint*: Recall that when you want records to meet one criterion or another, you need to place the criteria on separate lines.) Enter your name in the worksheet footer.

    **c.** Use the DSUM function in cell H2 to let worksheet users find the total order amounts for the category entered in cell G2. Format the cell containing the total order using the Accounting format with the $ symbol and no decimals. Test the DSUM function using the Paint category name. (The sum for the Paint category should be $10,668.) Preview the worksheet.

    **d.** Use data validation to create an in-cell drop-down list that restricts category entries to "Paint", "Wallpaper", "Hardware", and "Tile". Use the Error Alert tab of the Data Validation dialog box to set the alert level to the Warning style with the message "Data is not valid." Test the validation in the table with valid and invalid entries. Save the workbook, then preview the worksheet.

    **e.** Using the Subtotals sheet, sort the table by category in ascending order. Convert the table to a range, and add Subtotals to the order amounts by category.

    **f.** Use the outline to display only category names with subtotals and the grand total.

# Independent Challenge 3 (continued)

### Advanced Challenge Exercise

- Clear the subtotals from the worksheet.
- Conditionally format the Order data using Top/Bottom Rules to emphasize the cells containing the top 10 percent with yellow fill and dark yellow text.
- Add another rule to format the bottom 10 percent in the Order column with a light red fill.

g. Save the workbook, then preview the worksheet.

h. Close the workbook, exit Excel, then submit the workbook to your instructor.

# Real Life Independent Challenge

You decide to organize your business and personal contacts using the Excel table format to allow you to easily look up contact information. You want to include addresses and a field documenting whether the contact relationship is personal or business. You enter your contact information in an Excel worksheet that you will convert to a table so you can easily filter the data. You also use lookup functions to locate phone numbers when you provide a last name in your table. Finally, you restrict the entries in the Relationship field to values in drop-down lists to simplify future data entry and reduce errors.

a. Start Excel, open a new workbook, then save it as **EX H-Contacts** in the drive and folder where you store your Data Files.

b. Use the structure of Table H-2 to enter at least six of your personal and business contacts into a worksheet. (*Hint:* You will need to format the Zip column using the Zip Code type of the Special category.) In the Relationship field, enter either Business or Personal. If you don't have phone numbers for all the phone fields, leave them blank.

**TABLE H-2**

| Last name | First name | Cell phone | Home phone | Work phone | Street address | City | State | Zip | Relationship |
|-----------|------------|------------|------------|------------|----------------|------|-------|-----|--------------|

c. Use the worksheet information to create a table. Use the Name Manager dialog box to edit the table name to **Contacts**.

d. Create a filter that retrieves records of personal contacts. Clear the filter.

e. Create a filter that retrieves records of business contacts. Clear the filter.

f. Restrict the Relationship field entries to Business or Personal. Provide an in-cell drop-down list allowing the selection of these two options. Add an input message of **Select from the dropdown list**. Add an Information-level error message of **Choose Business or Personal**. Test the validation by adding a new record to your table.

g. Below your table, create a phone lookup area with the following labels in adjacent cells: **Last name**, **Cell phone**, **Home phone**, **Work phone**.

h. Enter one of the last names from your table under the label Last Name in your phone lookup area.

i. In the phone lookup area, enter lookup functions to locate the cell phone, home phone, and work phone numbers for the contact last name that you entered in the previous step. Make sure you match the last name exactly.

j. Enter your name in the center section of the worksheet footer, save the workbook, then preview the worksheet.

k. Close the workbook, exit Excel, then submit the workbook to your instructor.

# Visual Workshop

Open the file EX H-6.xlsx from the drive and folder where you save your Data Files, then save it as **EX H-Schedule**. Complete the worksheet as shown in Figure H-26. An in-cell drop-down list has been added to the data entered in the Room field. The range A18:G21 is extracted from the table using the criteria in cells A15:A16. Add your name to the worksheet footer, save the workbook, preview the worksheet, then submit the workbook to your instructor.

**FIGURE H-26**

| | A | B | C | D | E | F | G | H |
|---|---|---|---|---|---|---|---|---|
| 1 | Spring 2013 Schedule of Yoga Classes | | | | | | | |
| 2 | | | | | | | | |
| 3 | Class Code | Class | Time | Day | Room | Fee | Instructor | |
| 4 | Y100 | Basics | 8:00 | Monday | Mat Room | $10 | Martin | |
| 5 | Y101 | Power | 9:00 | Tuesday | Equipment Room | $15 | Grey | |
| 6 | Y102 | Hatha | 10:00 | Wednesday | Mat Room | $10 | Marshall | |
| 7 | Y103 | Kripalu | 11:00 | Monday | Mat Room | $10 | Bradley | |
| 8 | Y104 | Basics | 1:00 | Friday | Mat Room | $10 | Pauley | |
| 9 | Y105 | Power | 2:00 | Saturday | Equipment Room | $15 | Dash | |
| 10 | Y106 | Hatha | 3:00 | Tuesday | Mat Room | $10 | Robinson | |
| 11 | Y107 | Power | 4:00 | Monday | Equipment Room | $15 | Walsh | |
| 12 | Y108 | Basics | 5:00 | Tuesday | Mat Room | 10 | Matthews | |
| 13 | | | | | Please select Mat Room or Equipment Room | | | |
| 14 | | | | | | | | |
| 15 | Class | | | | | | | |
| 16 | Power | | | | | | | |
| 17 | | | | | | | | |
| 18 | Class Code | Class | Time | Day | Room | Fee | Instructor | |
| 19 | Y101 | Power | 9:00 | Tuesday | Equipment Room | $15 | Grey | |
| 20 | Y105 | Power | 2:00 | Saturday | Equipment Room | $15 | Dash | |
| 21 | Y107 | Power | 4:00 | Monday | Equipment Room | $15 | Walsh | |
| 22 | | | | | | | | |
| 23 | | | | | | | | |

# Automating Worksheet Tasks

**Files You Will Need:**

EX I-1.xlsx
EX I-2.xlsx

A **macro** is a named set of instructions you can create that performs tasks automatically, in an order you specify. You create macros to automate Excel tasks that you perform frequently. Because they perform tasks rapidly, macros can save you a great deal of time. For example, if you usually enter your name and date in a worksheet footer, you can record the keystrokes in an Excel macro that enters the text and inserts the current date automatically when you run the macro. In this unit, you will plan and design a simple macro, then record and run it. You will then edit the macro and explore ways to make it more easily available as you work. Kate Morgan, the North America regional vice president of sales at Quest, wants you to create a macro for the sales division. The macro needs to automatically insert text that identifies the worksheet as a sales division document.

**OBJECTIVES**

Plan a macro

Enable a macro

Record a macro

Run a macro

Edit a macro

Assign keyboard shortcuts to macros

Use the Personal Macro Workbook

Assign a macro to a button

# Planning a Macro

You create macros for Excel tasks that you perform frequently. For example, you can create a macro to enter and format text or to save and print a worksheet. To create a macro, you record the series of actions using the macro recorder built into Excel, or you write the instructions in a special programming language. Because the sequence of actions in a macro is important, you need to plan the macro carefully before you record it.  Kate wants you to create a macro for the sales division that inserts the text "Quest Sales" in the upper-left corner of any worksheet. You work with her to plan the macro.

### To plan a macro, use the following guidelines:

- **Assign the macro a descriptive name**

  The first character of a macro name must be a letter; the remaining characters can be letters, numbers, or underscores. Letters can be uppercase or lowercase. Spaces are not allowed in macro names; use underscores in place of spaces. Press [Shift][-] to enter an underscore character. Kate wants you to name the macro "DivStamp". See Table I-1 for a list of macros that could be created to automate other tasks at Quest.

- **Write out the steps the macro will perform**

  This planning helps eliminate careless errors. Kate writes a description of the macro she wants, as shown in Figure I-1.

- **Decide how you will perform the actions you want to record**

  You can use the mouse, the keyboard, or a combination of the two. Kate wants you to use both the mouse and the keyboard.

- **Practice the steps you want Excel to record, and write them down**

  Kate has written down the sequence of actions she wants you to include in the macro.

- **Decide where to store the description of the macro and the macro itself**

  Macros can be stored in an active workbook, in a new workbook, or in the **Personal Macro Workbook**, a special workbook used only for macro storage. Kate asks you to store the macro in a new workbook.

**FIGURE I-1:** Paper description of planned macro

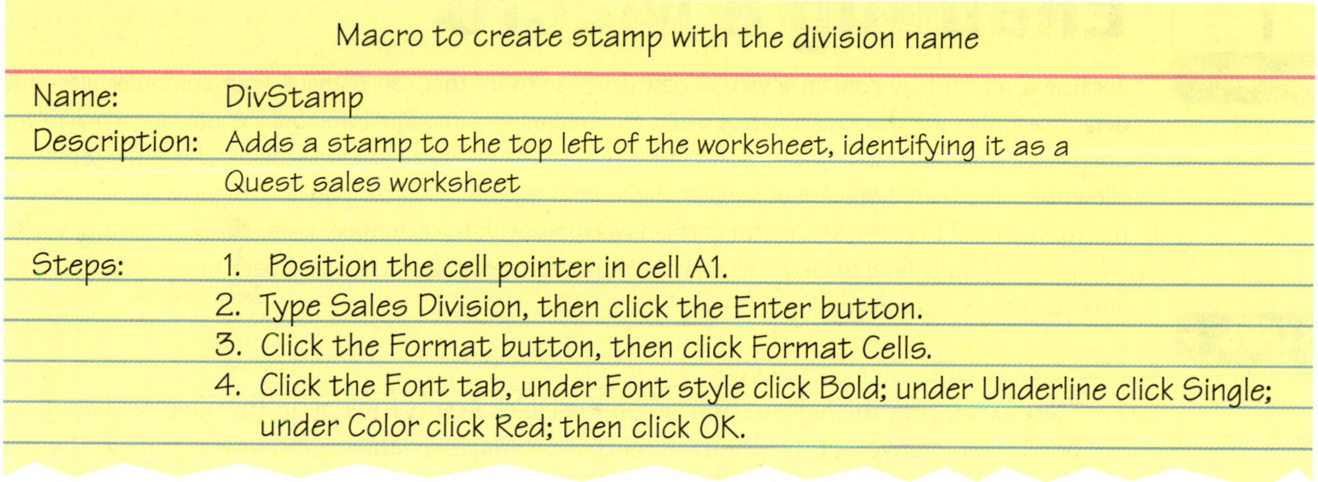

### Macro to create stamp with the division name

Name:      DivStamp

Description:  Adds a stamp to the top left of the worksheet, identifying it as a
Quest sales worksheet

Steps:
1. Position the cell pointer in cell A1.
2. Type Sales Division, then click the Enter button.
3. Click the Format button, then click Format Cells.
4. Click the Font tab, under Font style click Bold; under Underline click Single; under Color click Red; then click OK.

**Excel 2010**

**TABLE I-1:** Possible macros and their descriptive names

| description of macro | descriptive name for macro |
| --- | --- |
| Enter a frequently used proper name, such as "Kate Morgan" | KateMorgan |
| Enter a frequently used company name, such as Quest | Company_Name |
| Print the active worksheet on a single page, in landscape orientation | FitToLand |
| Add a footer to a worksheet | FooterStamp |
| Add totals to a worksheet | AddTotals |

# Enabling a Macro

Because a macro may contain a **virus**—destructive software that can damage your computer files—the default security setting in Excel disables macros from running. Although a workbook containing a macro will open, if macros are disabled, they will not function. You can manually change the Excel security setting to allow macros to run if you know a macro came from a trusted source. When saving a workbook with a macro, you need to save it as a macro-enabled workbook with the extension .xlsm. Kate asks you to change the security level to enable all macros. You will change the security level back to the default setting after you create and run your macros.

## STEPS

1. **Start Excel, click the Save button 💾 on the Quick Access toolbar, in the Save As dialog box click the Save as type list arrow, click Excel Macro-Enabled Workbook (*.xlsm), then in the File name text box type EX I-Macro Workbook**

2. **Navigate to the drive and folder where you store your Data Files, then click Save**

   The security settings that enable macros are available on the Developer tab. The Developer tab does not appear by default, but you can display it by customizing the Ribbon.

   > **QUICK TIP**
   > If the Developer tab is displayed on your Ribbon, skip steps three and four.

3. **Click the File tab, click Options, then click Customize Ribbon in the category list**

   The Customize the Ribbon options open in the Excel Options dialog box, as shown in Figure I-2.

4. **Click the Developer check box in the Main Tabs area on the right side of the screen to select it, then click OK**

   The Developer tab appears on the Ribbon. You are ready to change the security settings.

5. **Click the Developer tab, then click the Macro Security button in the Code group**

   The Trust Center dialog box opens, as shown in Figure I-3.

6. **Click Macro Settings if necessary, click the Enable all macros (not recommended; potentially dangerous code can run) option button to select it, then click OK**

   The dialog box closes. Macros remain enabled until you disable them by deselecting the Enable all macros option. As you work with Excel, you should disable macros when you are not working with them.

**FIGURE I-2:** Excel Options dialog box

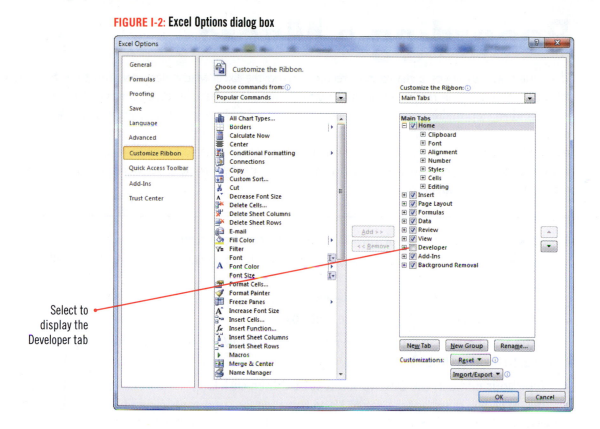

Select to display the Developer tab

**FIGURE I-3:** Trust Center dialog box

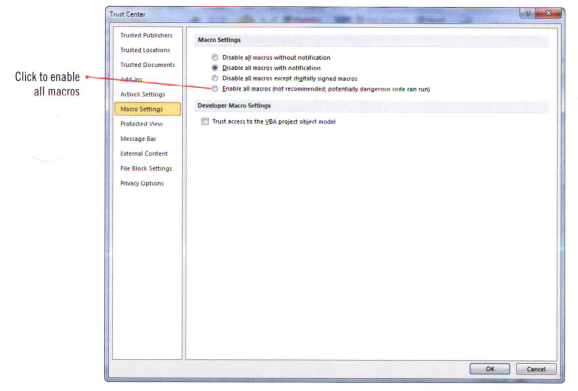

Click to enable all macros

## Disabling macros

To prevent viruses from running on your computer, you should disable all macros when you are not working with them. To disable macros, click the Developer tab, then click the Macro Security button in the Code group. Clicking any of the first three options disables macros. The first option disables all macros without notifying you. The second option notifies you when macros are disabled, and the third option allows only digitally signed macros to run.

# Recording a Macro

The easiest way to create a macro is to record it using the Excel Macro Recorder. You turn the Macro Recorder on, name the macro, enter the keystrokes and select the commands you want the macro to perform, then stop the recorder. As you record the macro, Excel automatically translates each action into program code that you can later view and modify. You can take as long as you want to record the macro; a recorded macro contains only your actions, not the amount of time you took to record it. Kate wants you to create a macro that enters a division "stamp" in cell A1 of the active worksheet. You create this macro by recording your actions.

## STEPS

> **QUICK TIP**
>
> You can also click the Record Macro button in the Code group on the Developer tab, or the Macros button in the Macros group of the View tab to record a new macro.

1. **Click the Record Macro button on the left side of the status bar**

   The Record Macro dialog box opens, as shown in Figure I-4. The default name Macro1 is selected. You can either assign this name or enter a new name. This dialog box also lets you assign a shortcut key for running the macro and assign a storage location for the macro.

2. **Type DivStamp in the Macro name text box**

3. **If the Store macro in list box does not display "This Workbook", click the list arrow and select This Workbook**

4. **Type your name in the Description text box, then click OK**

   The dialog box closes, and the Record Macro button on the status bar is replaced with a Stop Recording button. Take your time performing the steps below. Excel records every keystroke, menu selection, and mouse action that you make.

5. **Press [Ctrl][Home]**

   When you begin an Excel session, macros record absolute cell references. By beginning the recording with a command to move to cell A1, you ensure that the macro includes the instruction to select cell A1 as the first step, in cases where A1 is not already selected.

> **QUICK TIP**
>
> You can press [Ctrl][Enter] instead of clicking the Enter button.

6. **Type Quest Sales in cell A1, then click the Enter button ✓ on the Formula Bar**

7. **Click the Home tab, click the Format button in the Cells group, then click Format Cells**

8. **Click the Font tab, in the Font style list box click Bold, click the Underline list arrow and click Single, click the Color list arrow and click the Red, Accent 2 Theme color (first row, sixth color from the left), then compare your dialog box to Figure I-5**

> **QUICK TIP**
>
> You can also click the Stop Recording button in the Code group on the Developer tab to stop recording a macro.

9. **Click OK, click the Stop Recording button on the left side of the status bar, click cell D1 to deselect cell A1, then save the workbook**

   Figure I-6 shows the result of recording the macro.

**FIGURE I-4:** Record Macro dialog box

Type macro name here →

Type your name and description of macro here →

*[Record Macro dialog box showing:]*
Record Macro

Macro name:
Macro1

Shortcut key:
Ctrl+ [ ]

Store macro in:
This Workbook

Description:
[ ]

OK    Cancel

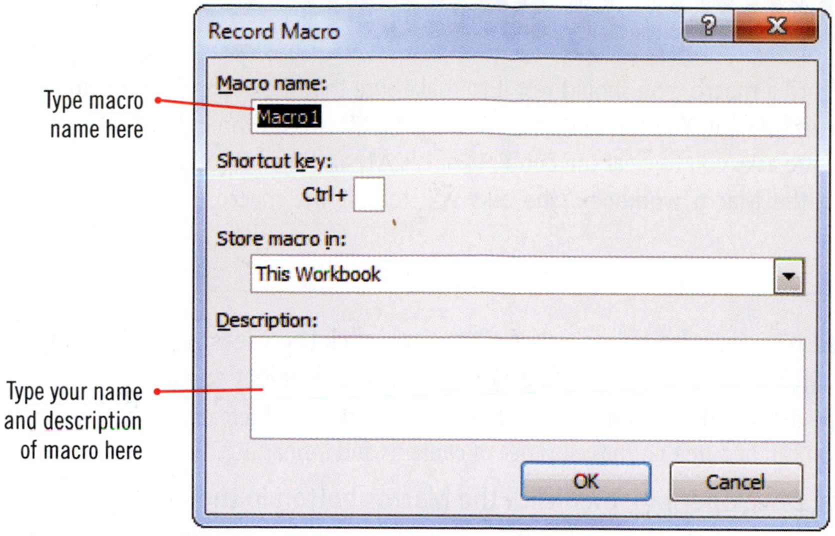

**FIGURE I-5:** Font tab of the Format Cells dialog box

*[Format Cells dialog box showing:]*
Format Cells

Number | Alignment | Font | Border | Fill | Protection

Font:
Calibri

Cambria (Headings)
Calibri (Body)
Adobe Caslon Pro
Adobe Caslon Pro Bold
Adobe Fangsong Std R
Adobe Garamond Pro

Font style:
Bold

Regular
Italic
Bold
Bold Italic

Size:
11

8
9
10
11
12
14

Underline:
Single

Color:

Normal font

Effects
☐ Strikethrough
☐ Superscript
☐ Subscript

Preview

AaBbCcYyZz

This is a TrueType font.  The same font will be used on both your printer and your screen.

OK    Cancel

Macro will apply these formatting attributes to the text

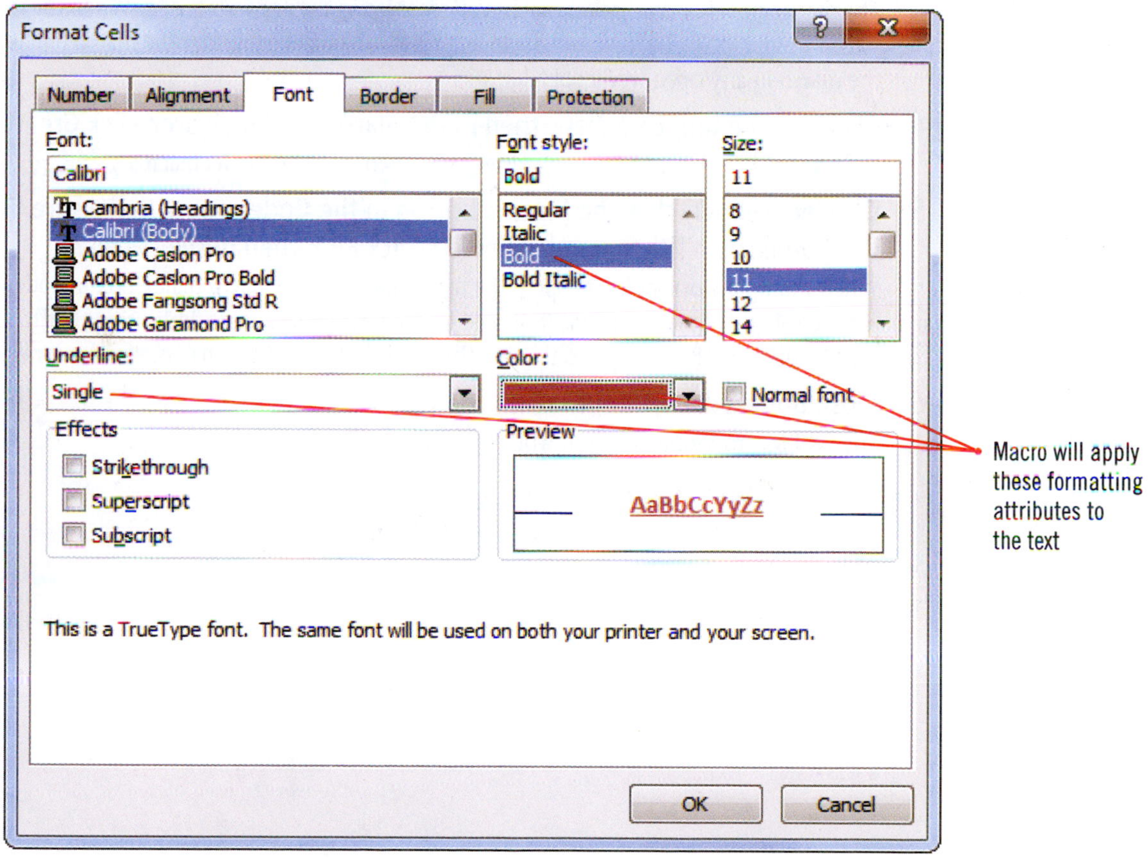

**FIGURE I-6:** Sales Division stamp

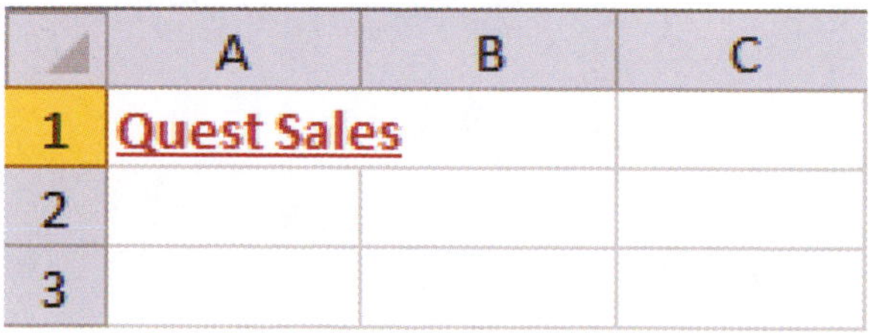

| ◢ | A | B | C |
|---|---|---|---|
| 1 | Quest Sales | | |
| 2 | | | |
| 3 | | | |

Automating Worksheet Tasks

# Running a Macro

Once you record a macro, you should test it to make sure that the actions it performs are correct. To test a macro, you **run** (play) it. You can run a macro using the Macros button in the Code group of the Developer tab.  Kate asks you to clear the contents of cell A1, and then test the DivStamp macro. After you run the macro in the Macro workbook, she asks you to test the macro once more from a newly opened workbook.

**STEPS**

1. **Click cell A1, click the Home tab if necessary, click the Clear button ✏ in the Editing group, click Clear All, then click any other cell to deselect cell A1**

   When you delete only the contents of a cell, any formatting still remains in the cell. By using the Clear All option you can be sure that the cell is free of contents and formatting.

2. **Click the Developer tab, then click the Macros button in the Code group**

   The Macro dialog box, shown in Figure I-7, lists all the macros contained in the open workbooks. If other people have used your computer, other macros may be listed.

3. **Make sure DivStamp is selected, as you watch cell A1 click Run, then deselect cell A1**

   The macro quickly plays back the steps you recorded in the previous lesson. When the macro is finished, your screen should look like Figure I-8. As long as the workbook containing the macro remains open, you can run the macro in any open workbook.

4. **Click the File tab, click New, then in the Blank Workbook area click Create**

   Because the EX I-Macro Workbook.xlsm is still open, you can use its macros.

5. **Deselect cell A1, click the Macros button in the Code group, make sure 'EX I-Macro Workbook.xlsm'!DivStamp is selected, click Run, then deselect cell A1**

   When multiple workbooks are open, the macro name in the Macro dialog box includes the workbook name between single quotation marks, followed by an exclamation point, indicating that the macro is outside the active workbook. Because you only used this workbook to test the macro, you don't need to save it.

6. **Close Book2.xlsx without saving changes**

   The EX I-Macro Workbook.xlsm workbook remains open.

**FIGURE I-7:** Macro dialog box

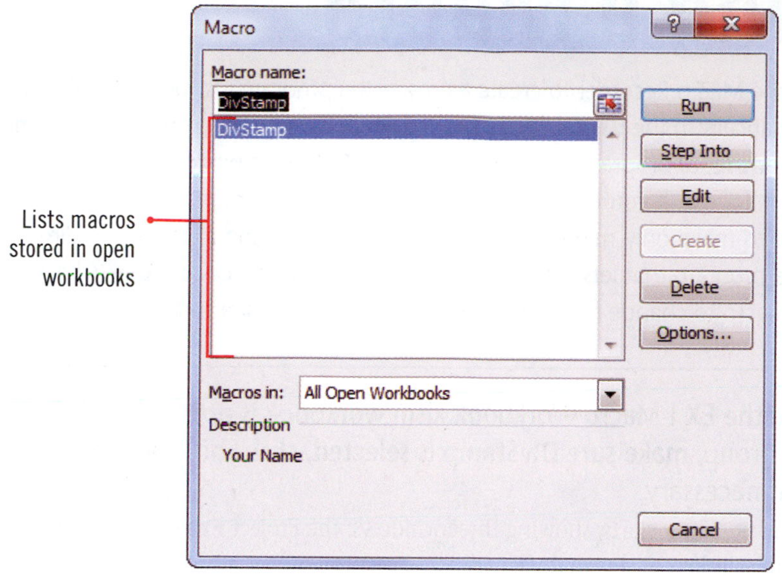

Lists macros stored in open workbooks →

Macro

Macro name:

DivStamp

DivStamp

Macros in: All Open Workbooks

Description

Your Name

Run

Step Into

Edit

Create

Delete

Options...

Cancel

**FIGURE I-8:** Result of running DivStamp macro

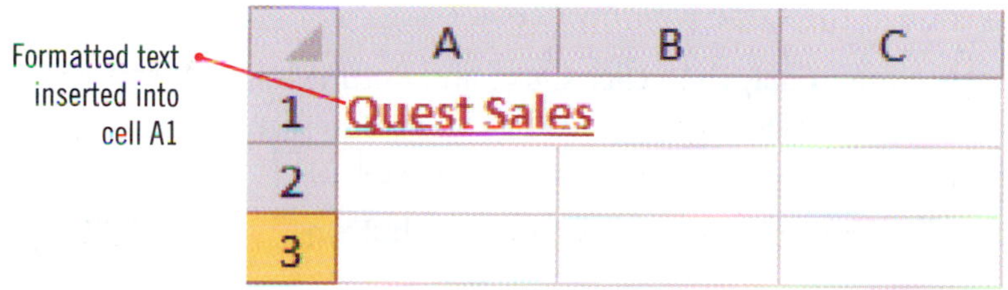

Formatted text inserted into cell A1 →

|   | A | B | C |
|---|---|---|---|
| 1 | Quest Sales | | |
| 2 | | | |
| 3 | | | |

## Running a macro automatically

You can create a macro that automatically performs certain tasks when the workbook in which it is saved is opened. This is useful for actions you want to do every time you open a workbook. For example, you may import data from an external data source into the workbook or format the worksheet data in a certain way. To create a macro that will automatically run when the workbook is opened, you need to name the macro Auto_Open and save it in the workbook.

# Editing a Macro

When you use the Macro Recorder to create a macro, the program instructions, called **program code**, are recorded automatically in the **Visual Basic for Applications (VBA)** programming language. Each macro is stored as a **module**, or program code container, attached to the workbook. After you record a macro, you might need to change it. If you have a lot of changes to make, it might be best to record the macro again. But if you need to make only minor adjustments, you can edit the macro code directly using the **Visual Basic Editor**, a program that lets you display and edit your macro code.  Kate wants you to modify the DivStamp macro to change the point size of the department stamp to 14.

## STEPS

1. **Make sure the EX I-Macro Workbook.xlsm workbook is open, click the Macros button in the Code group, make sure DivStamp is selected, click Edit, then maximize the Code window, if necessary**

   The Visual Basic Editor starts, showing three windows: the Project Explorer window, the Properties window, and the Code window, as shown in Figure I-9.

**TROUBLE**

If the Properties window does not appear in the lower-left portion of your screen, click the Properties Window button in the Visual Basic Standard toolbar, then resize it as shown in the figure if necessary.

2. **Click Module 1 in the Project Explorer window if it's not already selected, then examine the steps in the macro, comparing your screen to Figure I-9**

   The name of the macro and your name appear at the top of the module window. Below this area, Excel has translated your keystrokes and commands into macro code. When you open and make selections in a dialog box during macro recording, Excel automatically stores all the dialog box settings in the macro code. For example, the line .FontStyle = "Bold" was generated when you clicked Bold in the Format Cells dialog box. You also see lines of code that you didn't generate directly while recording the DivStamp macro, for example, .Name = "Calibri".

3. **In the line .Size = 11, double-click 11 to select it, then type 14**

   Because Module1 is attached to the workbook and not stored as a separate file, any changes to the module are saved automatically when you save the workbook.

4. **Review the code in the Code window**

**QUICK TIP**

You can return to Excel without closing the module by clicking the View Microsoft Excel button on the Visual Basic Editor toolbar.

5. **Click File on the menu bar, then click Close and Return to Microsoft Excel**

   You want to rerun the DivStamp macro to make sure the macro reflects the change you made using the Visual Basic Editor. You begin by clearing the division name from cell A1.

6. **Click cell A1, click the Home tab, click the Clear button in the Editing group, then click Clear All**

**QUICK TIP**

Another way to start the Visual Basic Editor is to click the Developer tab, then click the Visual Basic button in the Code group.

7. **Click any other cell to deselect cell A1, click the Developer tab, click the Macros button in the Code group, make sure DivStamp is selected, click Run, then deselect cell A1**

   The department stamp is now in 14-point type, as shown in Figure I-10.

8. **Save the workbook**

Automating Worksheet Tasks

**FIGURE I-9:** Visual Basic Editor showing Module1

Properties
window
button

Project
Explorer
window
with Module1
selected

Properties
window
showing
properties
for Module1

Comments
appear in
green

Code
window

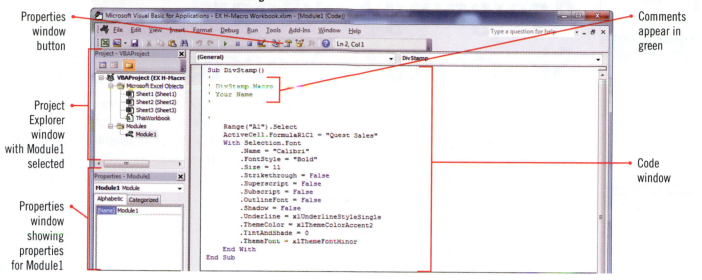

**FIGURE I-10:** Result of running edited DivStamp macro

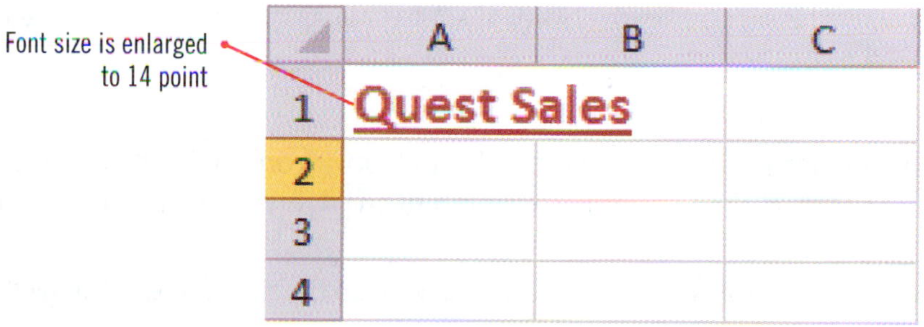

Font size is enlarged
to 14 point

|   | A | B | C |
|---|---|---|---|
| 1 | Quest Sales | | |
| 2 | | | |
| 3 | | | |
| 4 | | | |

## Adding comments to Visual Basic code

With practice, you will be able to interpret the lines of macro code. Others who use your macro, however, might want to review the code to, for example, learn the function of a particular line. You can explain the code by adding comments to the macro. **Comments** are explanatory text added to the lines of code. When you enter a comment, you must type an apostrophe ( ' ) before the comment text.

Otherwise, the program tries to interpret it as a command. On the screen, comments appear in green after you press [Enter], as shown in Figure I-9. You can also insert blank lines as comments in the macro code to make the code more readable. To do this, type an apostrophe, then press [Enter].

Excel 2010

# Assigning Keyboard Shortcuts to Macros

For macros that you run frequently, you can run them by using shortcut key combinations instead of the Macro dialog box. You can assign a shortcut key combination to any macro. Using shortcut keys saves you time by reducing the number of actions you need to take to run a macro. You assign shortcut key combinations in the Record Macro dialog box.  Kate also wants you to create a macro called Region to enter the company region into a worksheet. You assign a shortcut key combination to run the macro.

**STEPS**

1. **Click cell B2**

   You want to record the macro in cell B2, but you want the macro to enter the region of North America anywhere in a worksheet. Therefore, you do not begin the macro with an instruction to position the cell pointer, as you did in the DivStamp macro.

2. **Click the Record Macro button 📊 on the status bar**

   The Record Macro dialog box opens. Notice the option Shortcut key: Ctrl+ followed by a blank box. You can type a letter (A–Z) in the Shortcut key text box to assign the key combination of [Ctrl] plus that letter to run the macro. Because some common Excel shortcuts use the [Ctrl][letter] combination, such as [Ctrl][C] for Copy, you decide to use the key combination [Ctrl][Shift] plus a letter to avoid overriding any of these shortcut key combinations.

   **QUICK TIP**
   Be careful when choosing letters for a keyboard shortcut. The letters entered in the shortcut key text box are case sensitive.

3. **With the default macro name selected, type Region, click the Shortcut key text box, press and hold [Shift], type C, then in the Description box type your name**

   You have assigned the shortcut key combination [Ctrl][Shift][C] to the Region macro. After you create the macro, you will use this shortcut key combination to run it. Compare your screen with Figure I-11. You are ready to record the Region macro.

4. **Click OK to close the dialog box**

5. **Type North America in cell B2, click the Enter button ✔ on the formula bar, press [Ctrl][I] to italicize the text, click the Stop Recording button ⬛ on the status bar, then deselect cell B2**

   North America appears in italics in cell B2. You are ready to run the macro in cell A5 using the shortcut key combination.

6. **Click cell A5, press and hold [Ctrl][Shift], type C, then deselect the cell**

   The region appears in cell A5, as shown in Figure I-12. The macro played back in the selected cell (A5) instead of the cell where it was recorded (B2) because you did not begin recording the macro by clicking cell B2.

**FIGURE I-11:** Record Macro dialog box with shortcut key assigned

Record Macro

Macro name:

Region

Shortcut key:

Ctrl+Shift+ C ← Shortcut to run macro

Store macro in:

This Workbook

Description:

Your Name|

OK    Cancel

**FIGURE I-12:** Result of running the CompanyName macro

|  | A | B | C |
|---|---|---|---|
| 1 | **Quest Sales** | | |
| 2 | | *North America* | |
| 3 | | | |
| 4 | | | |
| 5 | *North America* | | |
| 6 | | | |
| 7 | | | |
| 8 | | | |

Result of recording macro in cell B2

Result of running macro in cell A5

## Using relative referencing when creating a macro

By default, Excel records absolute cell references in macros. You can record a macro's actions based on the relative position of the active cell by clicking the Use Relative References button in the Code group prior to recording the action. For example, when you create a macro using the default setting of absolute referencing, bolding the range A1:D1 will always bold that range when the macro is run. However, if you click the Use Relative References button when recording the macro before bolding the range, then running the macro will not necessarily result in bolding the range A1:D1. The range that will be bolded will depend on the location of the active cell when the macro is run. If the active cell is A4, then the range A4:D4 will be bolded. Selecting the Use Relative References button highlights the button name, indicating it is active, as shown in Figure I-13. The button remains active until you click it again to deselect it. This is called a **toggle**, meaning that it acts like an off/on switch: it retains the relative reference setting until you click it again to turn it off or you exit Excel.

**FIGURE I-13:** Relative Reference button selected

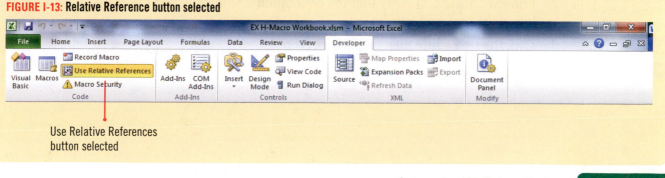

Use Relative References button selected

Excel 2010

# Using the Personal Macro Workbook

When you create a macro, it is automatically stored in the workbook in which you created it. But if you wanted to use that macro in another workbook, you would have to copy the macro to that workbook. Instead, it's easier to store commonly used macros in the Personal Macro Workbook. The **Personal Macro Workbook** is an Excel file that is always available, unless you specify otherwise, and gives you access to all the macros it contains, regardless of which workbooks are open. The Personal Macro Workbook file is automatically created the first time you choose to store a macro in it, and is named PERSONAL.XLSB. You can add additional macros to the Personal Macro Workbook by saving them in the workbook. By default, the PERSONAL.XLSB workbook opens each time you start Excel, but you don't see it because Excel designates it as a hidden file.  Kate often likes to print her worksheets in landscape orientation with 1" left, right, top, and bottom margins. She wants you to create a macro that automatically formats a worksheet for printing this way. Because she wants to use this macro in future workbooks, she asks you to store the macro in the Personal Macro Workbook.

## STEPS

1. **Click the Record Macro button** 🖼 **on the status bar**
   The Record Macro dialog box opens.

2. **Type FormatPrint in the Macro name text box, click the Shortcut key text box, press and hold [Shift], type F, then click the Store macro in list arrow**
   You have named the macro FormatPrint and assigned it the shortcut combination [Ctrl][Shift][F]. This Workbook storage option is selected by default, indicating that Excel automatically stores macros in the active workbook, as shown in Figure I-14. You can also choose to store the macro in a new workbook or in the Personal Macro Workbook.

**TROUBLE**
If a dialog box appears saying that a macro is already assigned to this shortcut combination, choose another letter for a keyboard shortcut. If a dialog box appears with the message that a macro named FormatPrint already exists, click Yes to replace it.

3. **Click Personal Macro Workbook, in the Description text box enter your name, then click OK**
   The recorder is on, and you are ready to record the macro keystrokes.

4. **Click the Page Layout tab, click the Orientation button in the Page Setup group, click Landscape, click the Margins button in the Page Setup group, click Custom Margins, then enter 1 in the Top, Left, Bottom, and Right text boxes**
   Compare your margin settings to Figure I-15.

5. **Click OK, then click the Stop Recording button** 🔲 **on the status bar**
   You want to test the macro.

**TROUBLE**
You may have to wait a few moments for the macro to finish. If you are using a different letter for the shortcut key combination, type that letter instead of the letter F.

6. **Activate Sheet2, in cell A1 type Macro Test, press [Enter], press and hold [Ctrl][Shift], then type F**
   The FormatPrint macro plays back the sequence of commands.

7. **Preview Sheet2 and verify that the orientation is landscape and the margins are 1" on the left, right, top, and bottom**

8. **Click the Home tab, then save the workbook**

FIGURE I-14: Record Macro dialog box showing macro storage options

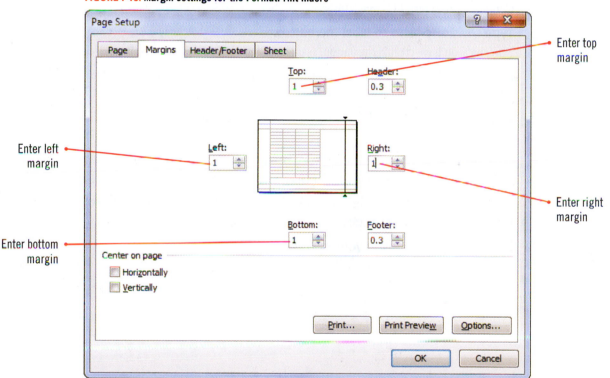

FIGURE I-15: Margin settings for the FormatPrint macro

## Working with the Personal Macro Workbook

Once you use the Personal Macro Workbook, it opens automatically each time you start Excel so you can add macros to it. By default, the Personal Macro Workbook is hidden in Excel as a precautionary measure so you don't accidentally delete anything from it. If you need to delete a macro from the Personal Macro Workbook, click the View tab, click Unhide in the Window group, click PERSONAL.XLSB, then click OK. To hide the Personal Macro Workbook, make it the active workbook, click the View tab, then click Hide in the Window group. If you should see a message that Excel is unable to record to your Personal Macro Workbook, check to make sure it is enabled: Click the File tab, click Options, click Add-ins, click Disabled Items, then click Go. If your Personal Macro Workbook is listed in the Disabled items dialog box, click its name, then click Enable.

# Assigning a Macro to a Button

When you create macros for others who will use your workbook, you might want to make the macros more visible so they're easier to use. In addition to using shortcut keys, you can run a macro by assigning it to a button on your worksheet. Then when you click the button the macro will run.  To make it easier for people in the sales division to run the DivStamp macro, Kate asks you to assign it to a button on the workbook. You begin by creating the button.

## STEPS

1. **Click Sheet3, click the Insert tab, click the Shapes button in the Illustrations group, then click the first rectangle in the Rectangles group**

   The mouse pointer changes to a + symbol.

2. **Click at the top-left corner of cell A8, and drag the pointer to the lower-right corner of cell B9**

   Compare your screen to Figure I-16.

3. **Type Division Macro to label the button**

   Now that you have created the button, you are ready to assign the macro to it.

4. **Right-click the new button, then on the shortcut menu click Assign Macro**

   The Assign Macro dialog box opens.

5. **Click DivStamp under "Macro name", then click OK**

   You have assigned the DivStamp macro to the button.

6. **Click any cell to deselect the button, then click the button**

   The DivStamp macro plays, and the text Quest Sales appears in cell A1, as shown in Figure I-17.

7. **Save the workbook, preview Sheet3, close the workbook, then exit Excel, clicking No when asked to save changes to the Personal Macro Workbook**

8. **Submit the workbook to your instructor**

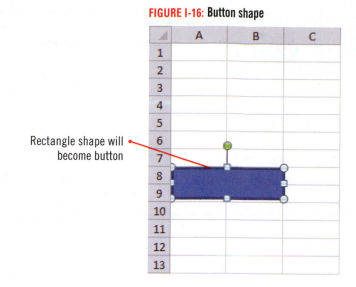

**FIGURE I-16:** Button shape

Rectangle shape will become button

**FIGURE I-17:** Sheet3 with the Sales Division text

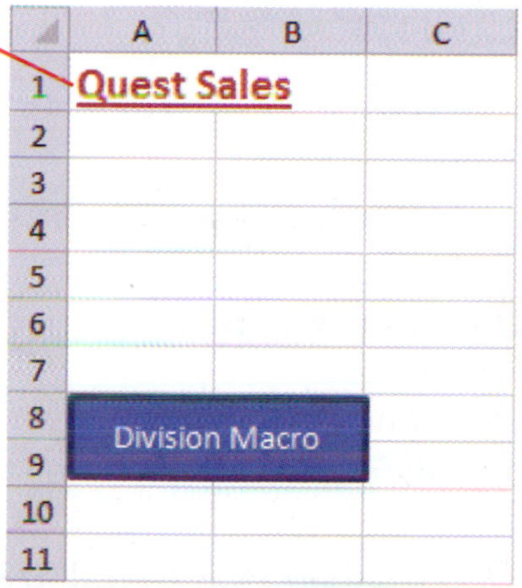

Result of running macro using the button

Quest Sales

Division Macro

### Formatting a macro button

You can format macro buttons using 3-D effects, clip art, photographs, fills, and shadows. To format a button, right-click it and select Format Shape from the shortcut menu. In the Format Shape dialog box you can select from many features such as Fill, Line Color, Line Style, Shadow, Reflection, Glow and Soft Edges, 3-D Format, 3-D Rotation, Picture Color, and Text Box. To add an image to the button, click Fill, then click the Picture or texture fill option button. To insert a picture from a file, click File, select a picture, then click Insert. To insert a clip art picture, click Clip Art, select a picture, then click OK. You may need to resize your button to fully display a picture. You may also want to move the text on the button if it overlaps the image. Figure I-18 shows a button formatted with clip art.

**FIGURE I-18:** Button formatted with clip art

Format

# Practice

**SAM**

For current SAM information, including versions and content details, visit SAM Central (http://www.cengage.com/samcentral). If you have a SAM user profile, you may have access to hands-on instruction, practice, and assessment of the skills covered in this unit. Since various versions of SAM are supported throughout the life of this text, check with your instructor for the correct instructions and URL/Web site for accessing assignments.

## Concepts Review

**FIGURE I-19**

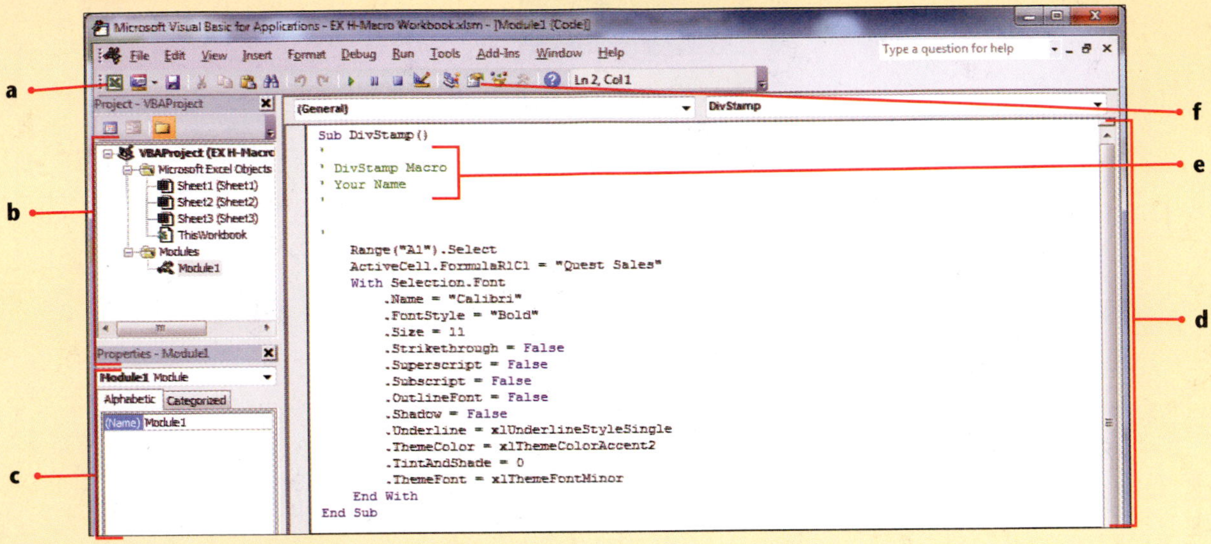

1. Which element do you click to return to Excel without closing the module?
2. Which element points to comments?
3. Which element points to the Properties Window button?
4. Which element points to the Code window?
5. Which element points to the Properties window?
6. Which element points to the Project Explorer window?

## Match each term or button with the statement that best describes it.

7. Virus
8. Macro
9. Personal Macro Workbook
10. Comments
11. Visual Basic Editor

a. Set of instructions that performs a task in a specified order
b. Statements that appear in green explaining the macro
c. Destructive software that can damage computer files
d. Used to make changes to macro code
e. Used to store frequently used macros

## Select the best answer from the list of choices.

12. Which of the following is the best candidate for a macro?
    a. Nonsequential tasks
    b. Often-used sequences of commands or actions
    c. Seldom-used commands or tasks
    d. One-button or one-keystroke commands

13. You can open the Visual Basic Editor by clicking the _____ button in the Macro dialog box.
    a. Programs
    b. Edit
    c. Modules
    d. Visual Basic Editor

14. A Macro named _____ will automatically run when the workbook it is saved in opens.
    a. Auto_Open
    b. Default
    c. Macro1
    d. Open_Macro

**15.** Which of the following is *not* true about editing a macro?

   **a.** You edit macros using the Visual Basic Editor.

   **b.** You can type changes directly in the existing program code.

   **c.** A macro cannot be edited and must be recorded again.

   **d.** You can make more than one editing change in a macro.

**16.** Why is it important to plan a macro?

   **a.** Planning helps prevent careless errors from being introduced into the macro.

   **b.** Macros can't be deleted.

   **c.** It is impossible to edit a macro.

   **d.** Macros won't be stored if they contain errors.

**17.** Macros are recorded with relative references:

   **a.** In all cases.

   **b.** Only if the Use Relative References button is selected.

   **c.** By default.

   **d.** Only if the Use Absolute References button is not selected.

**18.** You can run macros:

   **a.** From the Macro dialog box.

   **b.** From shortcut key combinations.

   **c.** From a button on the worksheet.

   **d.** Using all of the above.

**19.** Macro security settings can be changed using the _____ tab.

   **a.** Developer

   **b.** Home

   **c.** Security

   **d.** Review

# Skills Review

**1. Plan and enable a macro.**

   **a.** You need to plan a macro that enters and formats your name and e-mail address in a worksheet.

   **b.** Write out the steps the macro will perform.

   **c.** Write out how the macro could be used in a workbook.

   **d.** Start Excel, open a new workbook, then save it as a Macro-Enabled workbook named **EX I-Macros** in the drive and folder where you store your Data Files. (*Hint*: The file will have the file extension .xlsm.)

   **e.** Use the Excel Options feature to display the Developer tab if it is not showing in the Ribbon.

   **f.** Using the Trust Center dialog box, enable all macros.

**2. Record a macro.**

   **a.** You want to record a macro that enters and formats your name and e-mail address in the range A1:A2 in a worksheet using the steps below.

   **b.** Name the macro **MyEmail**, store it in the current workbook, and make sure your name appears as the person who recorded the macro.

   **c.** Record the macro, entering your name in cell A1 and your e-mail address in cell A2. (*Hint*: You need to press [Ctrl][Home] first to ensure cell A1 will be selected when the macro runs.)

   **d.** Resize column A to fit the information entirely in that column.

   **e.** Add an outside border around the range A1:A2 and format the font using red from the Standard Colors.

   **f.** Add bold formatting to the text in the range A1:A2.

   **g.** Stop the recorder and save the workbook.

**3. Run a macro.**

   **a.** Clear cell entries and formats in the range affected by the macro, then resize the width of column A to 8.43.

   **b.** Run the MyEmail macro to place your name and e-mail information in the range A1:A2.

   **c.** On the worksheet, clear all the cell entries and formats generated by running the MyEmail macro. Resize the width of column A to 8.43.

   **d.** Save the workbook.

## Skills Review (continued)

**4. Edit a macro.**

   **a.** Open the MyEmail macro in the Visual Basic Editor.

   **b.** Change the line of code above the last line from Selection.Font.
      Bold = True to Selection.Font.Bold = False.

   **c.** Use the Close and Return to Microsoft Excel option on the File
      menu to return to Excel.

   **d.** Test the macro on Sheet1, and compare your worksheet to Figure I-20
      verifying that the text is not bold.

   **e.** Save the workbook.

**FIGURE I-20**

|   | A | B |
|---|---|---|
| 1 | Your Name | |
| 2 | yourname@yourschool.edu | |
| 3 | | |
| 4 | | |
| 5 | | |

**5. Assign keyboard shortcuts to macros.**

   **a.** You want to record a macro that enters your e-mail address in italics with a font color of green, without underlining, in
      the selected cell of a worksheet, using the steps below.

   **b.** Record the macro called **EmailStamp** in the current workbook, assigning your macro the shortcut key combination
      [Ctrl][Shift][E], storing it in the current workbook, with your name in the description.

   **c.** After you record the macro, clear the contents and formats from the cell
      containing your e-mail address that you used to record the macro.

**FIGURE I-21**

   **d.** Use the shortcut key combination to run the EmailStamp macro in a cell other
      than the one in which it was recorded. Compare your macro result to
      Figure I-21. Your e-mail address may appear in a different cell.

   **e.** Save the workbook.

|   | E | F | G |
|---|---|---|---|
| | | | |
| | | | |
| | *yourname@yourschool.edu* | | |

**6. Use the Personal Macro Workbook.**

   **a.** Using Sheet1, record a new macro called **FitToLand** and store it in the
      Personal Macro Workbook with your name in the Description text box. If you already have a macro named FitToLand
      replace that macro. The macro should set the print orientation to landscape.

   **b.** After you record the macro, display Sheet2, and enter **Test data for FitToLand macro** in cell A1.

   **c.** Preview Sheet2 to verify that the orientation is set to portrait.

   **d.** Run the FitToLand macro. (You may have to wait a few moments.)

   **e.** Add your name to the Sheet2 footer, then preview Sheet2 and verify that it is now in Landscape orientation.

   **f.** Save the workbook.

**7. Assign a macro to a button.**

   **a.** Enter **Button Test** in cell A1 of Sheet3.

   **b.** Using the rectangle shape, draw a rectangle in the range A7:B8. Compare your
      worksheet to Figure I-22.

**FIGURE I-22**

   **c.** Label the button with the text **Landscape**.

   **d.** Assign the macro PERSONAL.XLSB!FitToLand to the button.

   **e.** Verify that the orientation of Sheet3 is set to portrait.

   **f.** Run the FitToLand macro using the button.

   **g.** Preview the worksheet, and verify that it is in landscape view.

   **h.** Add your name to the Sheet3 footer, then save the workbook.

   **i.** Close the workbook, exit Excel without saving the FitToLand macro in the
      Personal Macro Workbook, then submit your workbook to your instructor.

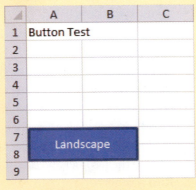

|   | A | B | C |
|---|---|---|---|
| 1 | Button Test | | |
| 2 | | | |
| 3 | | | |
| 4 | | | |
| 5 | | | |
| 6 | | | |
| 7 | | Landscape | |
| 8 | | | |
| 9 | | | |

# Independent Challenge 1

As a computer-support employee of Smith and Jones Consulting Group, you need to develop ways to help your fellow
employees work more efficiently. Employees have asked for Excel macros that can do the following:

- Adjust the column widths to display all column data in a worksheet.
- Place the company name of Smith and Jones Consulting Group in the header of a worksheet.

# Independent Challenge 1 (continued)

a. Plan and write the steps necessary for each macro.

b. Start Excel, open the Data File EX I-1.xlsx from the drive and folder where you store your Data Files, then save it as a macro-enabled workbook called **EX I-Consulting**.

c. Check your macro security on the Developer tab to be sure that macros are enabled.

d. Create a macro named **ColumnFit**, save it in the EX I-Consulting.xlsm workbook, assign the ColumnFit macro a shortcut key combination of [Ctrl][Shift][C], and add your name in the description area for the macro. Record the macro using the following instructions:

- Record the ColumnFit macro to adjust a worksheet's column widths to display all data. (*Hint*: Select the entire sheet, click the Home tab, click the Format button in the Cells group, select AutoFit Column Width, then click cell A1 to deselect the worksheet.)
- End the macro recording.

e. Format the widths of columns A through G to 8.43, then test the ColumnFit macro with the shortcut key combination [Ctrl][Shift][C].

f. Create a macro named **CompanyName**, and save it in the EX I-Consulting.xlsm workbook. Assign the macro a shortcut key combination of [Ctrl][Shift][D], and add your name in the description area for the macro.

g. Record the CompanyName macro. The macro should place the company name of Smith and Jones Consulting Group in the center section of the worksheet header.

h. Enter **CompanyName test data** in cell A1 of Sheet2, and test the CompanyName macro using the shortcut key combination [Ctrl][Shift][D]. Preview Sheet2 to view the header.

i. Edit the CompanyName macro in the Visual Basic Editor to change the company name from Smith and Jones Consulting Group to **Smith Consulting Group**. Close the Visual Basic Editor and return to Excel.

j. Add a rectangle button to the Sheet3 in the range A6:B7. Label the button with the text **Company Name**.

k. Assign the CompanyName macro to the button.

Excel 2010

**FIGURE I-23**

l. Enter **New CompanyName Test** in cell A1. Use the button to run the CompanyName macro. Preview the worksheet checking the header to be sure it is displaying the new company name. Compare your screen to Figure I-23.

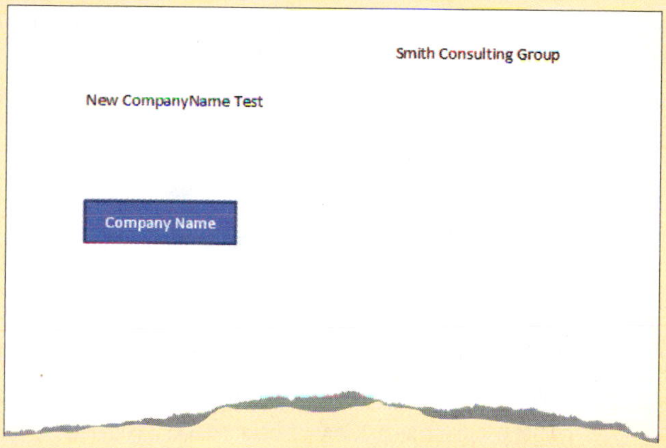

## Advanced Challenge Exercise

- Format the button using the fill color of your choice. (*Hint*: Right-click the button and select Format Shape from the shortcut menu.)
- Format the button to add the 3-D effect of your choice.
- Add a shadow in the color of your choice to the button.

m. Enter your name in the footers of all three worksheets. Save the workbook, close the workbook, then submit the workbook to your instructor and exit Excel.

# Independent Challenge 2

You are an assistant to the VP of Sales at American Beverage Company, a distributor of juices, water, and soda to supermarkets. As part of your work, you create spreadsheets with sales projections for different regions of the company. You frequently have to change the print settings so that workbooks print in landscape orientation with custom margins of 1" on the top and bottom. You also add a header with the company name on every worksheet. You have decided that it's time to create a macro to streamline this process.

a. Plan and write the steps necessary to create the macro.

b. Check your macro security settings to confirm that macros are enabled.

# Independent Challenge 2 (continued)

c. Start Excel, create a new workbook, then save it as a macro-enabled file named **EX I-Sales Macro** in the drive and folder where you store your Data Files.

d. Create a macro that changes the page orientation to landscape, adds custom margins of 1" on the top and bottom of the page, adds a header of **American Beverage Company** in the center section formatted as Bold with a font size of 14 points. Name the macro **Format**, add your name in the description, assign it the shortcut key combination [Ctrl][Shift][W], and store it in the current workbook.

e. Go to Sheet2 and enter the text **Format Test** in cell A1. Test the macro using the shortcut key combination of [Ctrl][Shift][W]. Preview Sheet2 to check the page orientation, margins, and the header.

f. Enter the text **Format Test** in cell A1 of Sheet3, add a rectangular button with the text Format Worksheet to run the Format macro, then test the macro using the button.

g. Preview the Visual Basic code for the macro.

h. Save the workbook, close the workbook, exit Excel, then submit the workbook to your instructor.

# Independent Challenge 3

You are the eastern region sales manager of Bio Pharma, a biotech consulting firm. You manage the California operations and frequently create workbooks with data from the office locations. It's tedious to change the tab names and colors every time you open a new workbook, so you decide to create a macro that will add the office locations and colors to your three default worksheet tabs, as shown in Figure I-24.

**FIGURE I-24**

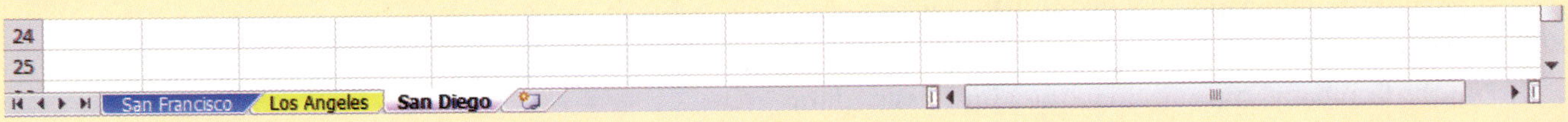

a. Plan and write the steps to create the macro described above.

b. Start Excel and open a new workbook.

c. Create the macro using the plan you created in Step a, name it **SheetFormat**, assign it the shortcut key combination [Ctrl][Shift][Z], store it in the Personal Macro Workbook, and add your name in the description area.

d. After recording the macro, close the workbook without saving it.

e. Open a new workbook, then save it as a macro-enabled workbook named **EX I-Office Test** in the drive and folder where you store your Data Files. Use the shortcut key combination of [Ctrl][Shift][Z] to test the macro in the new workbook.

f. Unhide the PERSONAL.XLSB workbook. (*Hint*: Click the View tab, click the Unhide button in the Window group, then click PERSONAL.XLSB.)

g. Edit the SheetFormat macro using Figure I-25 as a guide, changing the San Diego sheet name to Berkeley. (*Hint*: There are three instances of San Diego that need to be changed.)

**FIGURE I-25**

```
Sub SheetFormat()
'
' SheetFormat Macro
' Your Name '
'
' Keyboard Shortcut: Ctrl+Shift+Z
'
    Sheets("Sheet1").Select
    Sheets("Sheet1").Name = "San Francisco"
    Sheets("San Francisco").Select
    With ActiveWorkbook.Sheets("San Francisco").Tab
        .Color = 12611584
        .TintAndShade = 0
    End With
    Sheets("Sheet2").Select
    Sheets("Sheet2").Name = "Los Angeles"
    Sheets("Los Angeles").Select
    With ActiveWorkbook.Sheets("Los Angeles").Tab
        .Color = 65535
        .TintAndShade = 0
    End With
    Sheets("Sheet3").Select
    Sheets("Sheet3").Name = "Berkeley"
    Sheets("Berkeley").Select
    With ActiveWorkbook.Sheets("Berkeley").Tab
        .Color = 10498160
        .TintAndShade = 0
    End With
End Sub
```

# Independent Challenge 3 (continued)

**h.** Open a new workbook, then save it as a macro-enabled workbook named **EX I-Office Test New** in the drive and folder where you store your Data Files. Test the edited macro using the shortcut key combination of [Ctrl][Shift][Z].

**i.** Add a new sheet in the workbook, and name it **Code**. Copy the SheetFormat macro code from the Personal Macro Workbook, and paste it in the Code sheet beginning in cell A1. Save the workbook, close the workbook, then submit the EX I-Office Test New workbook to your instructor.

**j.** Hide the PERSONAL.XLSB workbook. (*Hint*: With the PERSONAL.XLSB workbook active, click the View tab, then click the Hide button in the Window group.)

**k.** Close the workbook, click No to save the PERSONAL.XLSB changes, then exit Excel.

## Real Life Independent Challenge

Excel can be a helpful tool in keeping track of hours worked at a job or on a project. A macro can speed up the repetitive process of entering a formula to total your hours each week.

**a.** Start Excel, create a new workbook, then save it as **EX I-Hours** in the drive and folder where you store your Data Files. Be sure to save it as a macro-enabled file.

**b.** If necessary, change your security settings to enable macros.

**c.** Use Table I-2 as a guide in entering labels and hours into a worksheet tracking your work or project effort.

**d.** Create a macro named **TotalHours** in the cell adjacent to the Total label that can be activated by the [Ctrl][Shift][T] key combination. Save the macro in the EX I-Hours workbook, and add your name in the description area.

**e.** The TotalHours macro should do the following:
- Total the hours for the week.
- Boldface the Total amount and the Total label to its left.

**f.** Test the macro using the key combination [Ctrl][Shift][T].

**g.** Add a button to the range A11:B12 with the label **Total**.

**h.** Assign the TotalHours macro to the Total button.

**i.** Test the macro using the button.

**j.** Enter your name in the footer, then save your workbook.

**k.** Open the macro in the Visual Basic Editor, and preview the macro code.

**TABLE I-2**

| | |
|---|---|
| Monday | 5 |
| Tuesday | 8 |
| Wednesday | 5 |
| Thursday | 8 |
| Friday | 9 |
| Saturday | 5 |
| Sunday | 0 |
| Total | |

### Advanced Challenge Exercise

- Edit the macro code to add a comment with a description of your work or project.
- Add another comment with your e-mail address.
- Above the keyboard comment enter the comment **Macro can be run using the Total button**.

**l.** Return to Excel, save and close the workbook, exit Excel, then submit the workbook to your instructor.

# Visual Workshop

Start Excel, open the Data File EX I-2.xlsx from the drive and folder where you store your Data Files, then save it as a macro-enabled workbook called **EX I-Payroll**. Create a macro with the name **TotalHours** in the EX I-Payroll workbook that does the following:

- Totals the weekly hours for each employee by totaling the hours for the first employee and copying that formula for the other employees
- Adds a row at the top of the worksheet and inserts a label of **Hours** in a font size of 14 point, centered across all columns
- Adds your name in the worksheet footer

Compare your macro results to Figure I-26. Test the macro, edit the macro code as necessary, then save the workbook. Submit the workbook to your instructor.

**FIGURE I-26**

| | A | B | C | D | E | F | G | H | I | J |
|---|---|---|---|---|---|---|---|---|---|---|
| 1 | Hours | | | | | | | | | |
| 2 | | Monday | Tuesday | Wednesday | Thursday | Friday | Saturday | Sunday | Total | |
| 3 | Mary Jones | 8 | 2 | 8 | 8 | 2 | 2 | 0 | 30 | |
| 4 | Jack McKay | 4 | 8 | 7 | 8 | 8 | 5 | 1 | 41 | |
| 5 | Keith Drudge | 5 | 4 | 6 | 5 | 4 | 4 | 0 | 28 | |
| 6 | Sean Lavin | 7 | 6 | 5 | 6 | 6 | 2 | 2 | 34 | |
| 7 | Kerry Baker | 9 | 6 | 8 | 7 | 6 | 6 | 0 | 42 | |
| 8 | Justin Regan | 6 | 3 | 6 | 3 | 3 | 7 | 0 | 28 | |
| 9 | Carol Hodge | 7 | 5 | 2 | 6 | 8 | 5 | 3 | 36 | |
| 10 | Rick Thomas | 2 | 7 | 8 | 6 | 7 | 2 | 0 | 32 | |
| 11 | Kris Young | 0 | 4 | 4 | 4 | 4 | 4 | 1 | 21 | |
| 12 | Lisa Russell | 7 | 8 | 2 | 8 | 8 | 1 | 0 | 34 | |
| 13 | | | | | | | | | | |

# Enhancing Charts

**Files You Will Need:**

EX J-1.xlsx

EX J-2.xlsx

EX J-3.xlsx

EX J-4.xlsx

EX J-5.xlsx

EX J-6.xlsx

chartlogo.gif

cookie.gif

golfball.gif

Although Excel offers a variety of eye-catching chart types, you can customize your charts for even greater impact. In this unit, you learn to enhance your charts by manipulating chart data, formatting axes, and rotating the chart. You clarify your data display by adding a data table, special text effects, and a picture. You also show trends in data using sparklines and trendlines. As you enhance your charts, keep in mind that too much customization can be distracting. Your goal in enhancing charts should be to communicate your data more clearly and accurately. Quest's vice president of sales, Kate Morgan, has requested charts comparing sales in the Quest regions over the first two quarters. You will produce these charts and enhance them to improve their appearance and make the worksheet data more accessible.

**OBJECTIVES**

Customize a data series

Change a data source and add data labels

Format the axes of a chart

Add a data table to a chart

Rotate a chart

Enhance a chart with WordArt and pictures

Add sparklines to a worksheet

Identify data trends

# Customizing a Data Series

A **data series** is the sequence of values that Excel uses to **plot**, or create, a chart. You can format the data series in a chart to make the chart more attractive and easier to read. As with other Excel elements, you can change the data series borders, patterns, or colors. Kate wants you to create a chart showing the sales for each region in January and February. You begin by creating a column chart, which you will customize to make it easier to compare the sales for each region.

**STEPS**

1. **Start Excel, open the file EX J-1.xlsx from the drive and folder where you store your Data Files, then save it as EX J-Region Sales**

   To begin, Kate wants to see how each region performed over January and February. The first step is to select the data you want to appear in the chart. In this case, you want the row labels in cells A3:A6 and the data for January and February in cells B2:C6, including the column labels.

2. **Select the range A2:C6**

TROUBLE

If your chart over-
laps the worksheet
data, you can drag
its edge to move it
below row 6.

3. **Click the Insert tab, click the Column button in the Charts group, then click the 3-D Clustered Column chart (the first chart in the 3-D Column group)**

   The column chart compares the January and February sales for each branch, as shown in Figure J-1. You decide to display the data so that it is easier to compare the monthly sales for each branch.

4. **Click the Switch Row/Column button in the Data group**

   The legend now contains the region data, and the horizontal axis groups the bars by month. Kate can now easily compare the branch sales for each month. The graph will be easier to read if the U.S. data series is plotted in a color that is easier to distinguish.

QUICK TIP

You can also format
a data series by click-
ing the data series
on the chart, clicking
the Chart Tools
Layout tab, then
clicking the Format
Selection button in
the Current Selec-
tion group.

5. **Right-click the Jan U.S. data series bar (the far-left bar on the graph), click Format Data Series from the shortcut menu, click Fill in the left pane of the Format Data Series dialog box, click the Solid fill option button, click the Color list arrow, select Purple, Accent 6 in the Theme Colors group, then click Close**

6. **Point to the edge of the chart, then drag the chart to place its upper-left corner in cell A8**

   You can resize a chart by dragging its corner sizing handles. When a chart is resized this way, all of the elements are resized to maintain its appearance.

7. **Drag the chart's lower-right sizing handle to fit the chart in the range A8:H23, then compare your chart to Figure J-2**

8. **Save the workbook**

**FIGURE J-1:** Chart comparing Jan and Feb sales for each region

Chart data

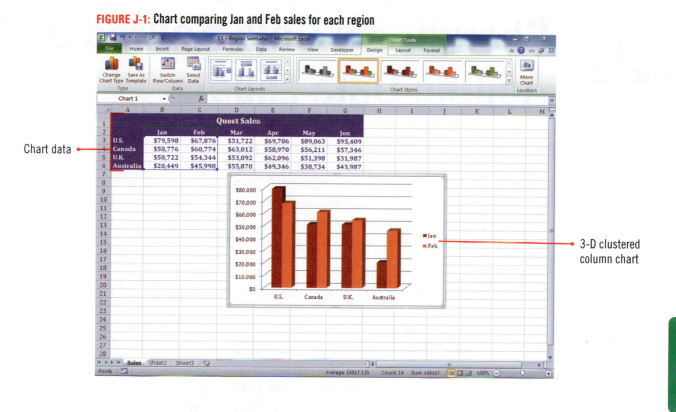

3-D clustered column chart

**FIGURE J-2:** Chart comparing region sales in Jan and Feb

Customized U.S. data series

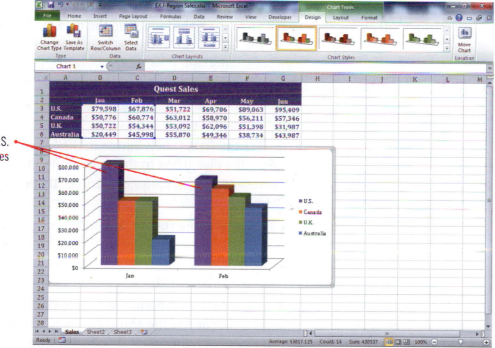

## Adding width and depth to data series

You can change the gap depth and the gap width in 3-D bar or column charts by right-clicking one of the data series of the chart then clicking Format Data Series from the shortcut menu. With Series Options selected in the left pane of the Format Data Series dialog box, you can move the Gap Depth and Gap Width sliders from No Gap (or 0%) to Large Gap (or 500%). Increasing the gap width adds space between each set of data on the chart by increasing the width of the chart's data series. Increasing the gap depth adds depth to all categories of data.

# Changing a Data Source and Adding Data Labels

As you update your workbooks with new data, you may also need to add data series to (or delete them from) a chart. Excel makes it easy to revise a chart's data source and to rearrange chart data. To communicate chart data more clearly, you can add descriptive text, called a **data label**, which appears above a data marker in a chart.  Kate wants you to create a chart showing the branch sales for the first quarter. You need to add the March data to your chart so that it reflects the first-quarter sales. Kate asks you to add data labels to clarify the charted data and to make the chart more attractive. It will be easier to compare the branch sales in a 3-D column chart that is not clustered.

## STEPS

1. **Click the Chart Tools Design tab if necessary, click the Change Chart Type button in the Type group, in the Change Chart Type dialog box click 3-D Column (the last chart in the first row), then click OK**

   The chart bars are no longer clustered. You want to change the data view to compare branch sales for each month in the new chart type.

2. **Click the Switch Row/Column button in the Data group**

   The labels that were in the legend are now on the horizontal axis. You want to add the March data to the chart.

**QUICK TIP**

You can also add data to a chart by clicking the Select Data button in the Data group of the Chart Tools Design tab, selecting the new range of cells in the Select Data Source dialog box, then click OK.

3. ▶ **Click the edge of the chart to select it if necessary, then drag the lower-right corner of the data border in worksheet cell C6 to the right to include the data in column D**

   The March data series appears on the chart, as shown in Figure J-3. You want to make the columns more attractive and decide to use one of the preformatted chart styles.

4. **Click the More button ⬇ in the Chart Styles group, then click Style 26**

   The January data bars are now a maroon color, and all of the data bars have shadows. You want to add data labels to your chart indicating the exact amount of sales each bar represents.

**QUICK TIP**

You can also add data labels by clicking the Chart Tools Design tab, clicking the More button in the Chart Layouts group, and selecting a chart layout with data labels.

5. ▶ **Click the Chart Tools Layout tab, click the Data Labels button in the Labels group, click More Data Label Options, then drag the dialog box to the right of the chart**

   Data labels on the chart show the exact value of each data point above each bar. The data labels are hard to read against the dark shadows of the columns. You decide to add a white background fill to the labels.

6. **With the Jan data labels selected, click Fill in the Format Data Labels dialog box, click the Solid fill option button to select it, click the Color list arrow, then click White, Background1 (the first theme color)**

   The January data labels now have a white background.

7. **Click one of the Feb data labels on the chart, click Fill in the Format Data labels dialog box, click the Solid fill option button, click one of the Mar data labels on the chart, click Fill in the Format Data labels dialog box, click the Solid fill option button, then click Close**

   The data labels are still difficult to read because they are crowded together. You decide to resize the chart to add space between the columns.

8. **Drag the chart's lower-right sizing handle to fit the chart in the range A8:L30, then compare your chart to Figure J-4**

**FIGURE J-3:** Chart with March data series added

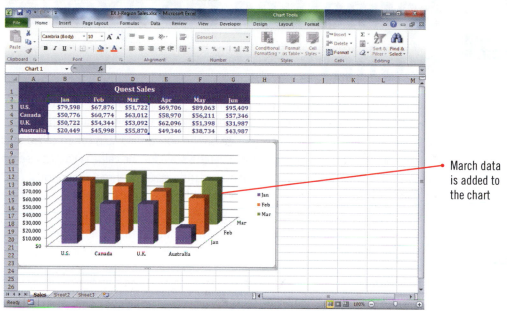

March data is added to the chart

**FIGURE J-4:** Chart with data labels

U.S. data labels

## Moving, removing, and formatting legends

To change the position of a legend or to remove it, click the Chart Tools Layout tab, click the Legend button in the Labels group, then select the desired legend position or select None to remove the legend. To format a legend's position, fill, border color and style, or shadows, click More Legend Options at the bottom of the Legend menu. You can add textured fills or pictures and customize the border and shadow characteristics. If you position the Format Legend dialog box next to the legend, you can use the Excel Live Preview feature to try out different effects, such as those shown in Figure J-5. To change a legend's font size, right-click the legend text, click Font on the shortcut menu, then adjust the font size in the Font dialog box. You can also drag a legend to any location.

**FIGURE J-5:** Formatted legend

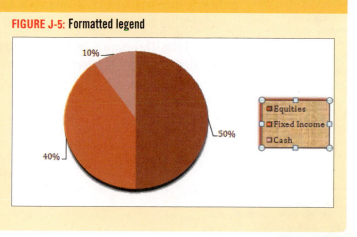

Excel 2010

Enhancing Charts

Excel 229

# Formatting the Axes of a Chart

Excel plots and formats chart data and places the chart axes within the chart's **plot area**. Data values in two-dimensional charts are plotted on the vertical y-axis (often called the **value axis** because it usually shows value levels). Categories are plotted on the horizontal x-axis (often called the **category axis** because it usually shows data categories). Excel creates a scale for the value (y) axis based on the highest and lowest values in the series and places intervals along the scale. A three-dimensional (3-D) chart, like the one in Figure J-6, has a third axis displaying the chart's depth. You can override the Excel default formats for chart axes at any time by using the Format Axis dialog box.  Kate asks you to increase the maximum number on the value axis and change the axis number format. She would also like you to add axes titles to explain the plotted data.

## STEPS

1. **Click the chart to select it if necessary, click the** Chart Tools Layout tab, **click the** Axes button **in the Axes group, point to** Primary Vertical Axis, **then click** More Primary Vertical Axis Options

   The Format Axis dialog box opens. The minimum, maximum, and unit Axis Options are set to Auto, and the default scale settings appear in the text boxes on the right. You can override any of these settings by clicking the Fixed option buttons and entering new values.

**QUICK TIP**

You can change the scale of the axis: Click the Chart Tools Layout tab, click the Axes button in the Axes group, point to Primary Vertical Axis, click More Primary Vertical Axes Options, click the Fixed option button in the Major unit group, then type the new scale interval value in the Fixed text box.

2. **With Axis Options selected in the list on the left, click the** Fixed option button **in the Maximum line, press [Tab], in the Fixed text box type** 90000, **then click** Close

   Now 90,000 appears as the maximum value on the value axis, and the chart bar heights adjust to reflect the new value. Next, you want the vertical axis values to appear without additional zeroes to make the chart data easier to read.

3. **Click the** Axes button **in the Axes group, point to** Primary Vertical Axis, **then click** Show Axis in Thousands

   The values are reduced to two digits and the word "Thousands" appears in a text box to the left of the values. You decide that vertical and horizontal axis titles would improve the clarity of the chart information.

4. **Click the** Axis Titles button **in the Labels group, point to** Primary Vertical Axis Title, **then click** Rotated Title

   A text box containing the text "Axis Title" appears on the vertical axis, next to "Thousands".

**QUICK TIP**

You can press [Enter] after typing a chart or legend title to complete the process.

5. **Type** Sales, **then click outside the text box to deselect it**

   The word "Sales" appears in the Vertical axis label. You decide to label the horizontal axis.

6. **Click the** Axis Titles button **in the Labels group, point to** Primary Horizontal Axis Title, **click** Title Below Axis, **type** Regions, **then click outside the text box to deselect it**

7. **Drag the** Thousands text box **on the vertical axis lower in the Chart Area to match Figure J-7, then deselect it**

**FIGURE J-6:** Chart elements in a 3-D chart

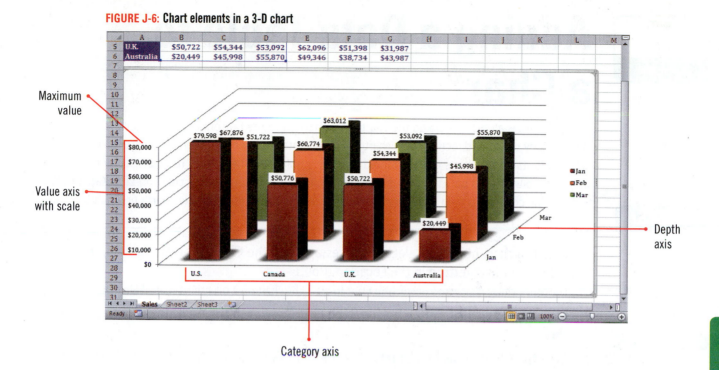

Maximum value

Value axis with scale

Depth axis

Category axis

**FIGURE J-7:** Chart with formatted axes

New maximum

Axis scale in thousands

Vertical axis title

Horizontal axis title

# Adding a Data Table to a Chart

A **data table** is a grid containing the chart data, attached to the bottom of a chart. Data tables are useful because they display—directly on the chart itself—the data you used to generate a chart. It's good practice to add data tables to charts that are stored separately from worksheet data. You can display data tables in line, area, column, and bar charts, and print them automatically along with a chart.  Kate wants you to move the chart to its own worksheet and add a data table to emphasize the chart's first-quarter data.

**STEPS**

1. **Click the chart object to select it if necessary, click the Chart Tools Design tab, then click the Move Chart button in the Location group**

   The Move Chart dialog box opens. You want to place the chart on a new sheet named First Quarter.

2. **Click the New sheet option button, type First Quarter in the New sheet text box, then click OK**

   **QUICK TIP**

   You can also add a data table by clicking the Chart Tools Design tab, and selecting a chart with a data table from the Chart Layouts gallery.

3. **Click the Chart Tools Layout tab, click the Data Table button in the Labels group, then click Show Data Table with Legend Keys**

   A data table with the first-quarter data and a key to the legend appears at the bottom of the chart, as shown in Figure J-8. The data table would stand out more if it were formatted.

4. **Click the Data Table button in the Labels group, then click More Data Table Options**

   The Format Data Table dialog box opens.

   **QUICK TIP**

   To hide a data table, click the Data Table button in the Labels group, then click None.

5. **Click Border Color in the left pane, click the Solid line option button to select it, click the Color list arrow, click the Orange, Accent2 color in the Theme Colors section, click Close, then click the chart area to deselect the data table**

   The data table now has orange borders. The left side of the data table contains legend keys, showing which series each color represents, so you don't need the legend that appears on the right of the chart.

   **QUICK TIP**

   You can also remove a legend by clicking the Legend button in the Labels group of the Chart Tools Layout tab and clicking None.

6. **Click the legend to select it, then press [Delete]**

   Now the only legend for the chart is part of the data table, as shown in Figure J-9.

7. **Save the workbook**

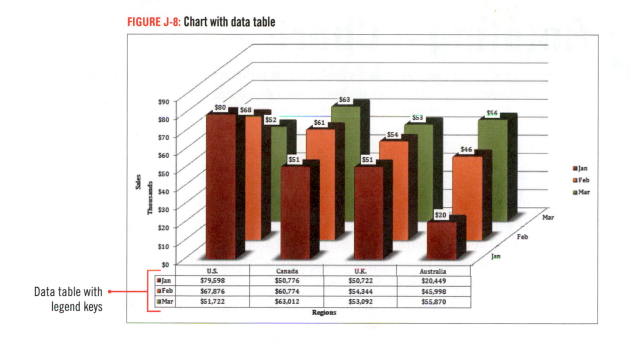

Data table with
legend keys

| | U.S. | Canada | U.K. | Australia |
|---|---|---|---|---|
| ■Jan | $79,598 | $50,776 | $50,722 | $20,449 |
| ■Feb | $67,876 | $60,774 | $54,344 | $45,998 |
| ■Mar | $51,722 | $63,012 | $53,092 | $55,870 |

Regions

**FIGURE J-9:** Chart with formatted data table

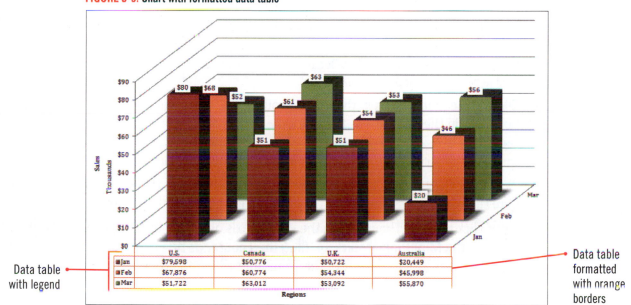

Data table
with legend

Data table
formatted
with orange
borders

| | U.S. | Canada | U.K. | Australia |
|---|---|---|---|---|
| ■Jan | $79,598 | $50,776 | $50,722 | $20,449 |
| ■Feb | $67,876 | $60,774 | $54,344 | $45,998 |
| ■Mar | $51,722 | $63,012 | $53,092 | $55,870 |

Regions

## Using the Modeless Format dialog box

Many of the buttons on the Chart Tools Layout tab have a More
...Options command at the bottom of the menu that appears when
you click them. For example, clicking the Data Table button allows
you to click More Data Table Options. The Format dialog box that
opens when you click it allows you to format the selected data table.
But while the dialog box is open, you can also click and format other
elements. The Format dialog boxes are **modeless,** which means that
when they are open, you can click on other chart elements and then
change their formatting in the same dialog box, whose options
adjust to reflect the selected element. You are not restricted to
changing only one object—you are not in a single **mode** or limited
set of possible choices. For example if the Format Data Table dialog
box is open and you click a data label, the dialog box changes to
Format Data Labels. If you click the legend, the dialog box becomes
the Format Legend dialog box, allowing you to modify the legend
characteristics.

# Rotating a Chart

Three-dimensional (3-D) charts do not always display data in the most effective way. In many cases, one or more of a chart's data points can obscure the view of other data points, making the chart difficult to read. By rotating and/or changing the chart's depth, you can make the data easier to understand.  Kate wants you to rotate the chart and increase the depth. You will begin by hiding the data table so it doesn't overlap the view of the data.

## STEPS

1. **Click the chart to select it if necessary, click the Chart Tools Layout tab, click the Data Table button in the Labels group, then click None**

2. **Click the 3-D Rotation button in the Background group, then if necessary click 3-D Rotation in the list on the left pane of the Format Chart Area dialog box**
   The 3-D rotation options are shown in Figure J-10.

3. **In the Chart Scale section, click the Right Angle Axes check box to deselect it, double-click the X: text box in the Rotation section, then enter 50**
   The X: Rotation setting rotates the chart to the left and right. You can also click the Left and Right buttons or the up and down arrows to rotate the chart.

> **QUICK TIP**
> You can also click the Up and Down buttons in the Rotation area of the dialog box to rotate the chart up and down.

4. **Double-click the Y: text box, then enter 30**
   The Y: Rotation setting rotates the chart up and down. You decide to change the depth of the columns.

5. **Double-click the Depth (% of base) text box in the Chart Scale section, then enter 200, then click Close**
   Deleting the data table removed the legend so you decide to add a legend to the chart. Also, the axes titles need to be adjusted for the new chart layout.

6. **Click the Legend button in the Labels group, click Show Legend at Bottom, right-click the text Sales in the vertical axis title, click the Font Size list arrow in the Mini toolbar, then click 18**
   The vertical axis label is now easier to read. You will format the horizontal axis similarly.

7. **Right-click the text Regions in the horizontal axis title, click the Font Size list arrow in the Mini toolbar, click 18, then drag the Regions title closer to the horizontal axis**

8. **Right-click the text Thousands in the vertical axis display units label, click the Font Size list arrow in the Mini toolbar, click 14, drag the Thousands title closer to the vertical axis, drag the Sales title to the left of the Thousands title, then compare your chart to Figure J-11.**
   The chart columns now appear deeper and less crowded, with labels positioned in the correct place, making the chart easier to read.

9. **Save the workbook**

---

### Making 3-D charts easier to read

In addition to rotating a chart, there are other ways to view smaller data points that may be obscured by larger data markers in the front of a 3-D chart. To reverse the order in which the data series are charted, you can click the Axes button in the Axes group of the Chart Tools Layout tab, point to Depth Axis, click More Depth Axis Options, click the Series in reverse order check box in the Format Axis dialog box to select it, then click Close. Another way to see smaller data series in the back of a 3-D chart is to add transparency to the large data markers in the front of the chart. To do this, right-click the data series that you want to make transparent, click Format Data Series on the shortcut menu, click Fill in the Format Data Series dialog box, click either the Solid fill or Gradient fill option buttons, move the slider on the Transparency bar to a percentage that allows you to see the other data series on the chart, then click Close. If you have a picture on the chart's back wall, adding transparency to the series in front of it makes more of the picture visible.

**FIGURE J-10:** 3-D Rotation options

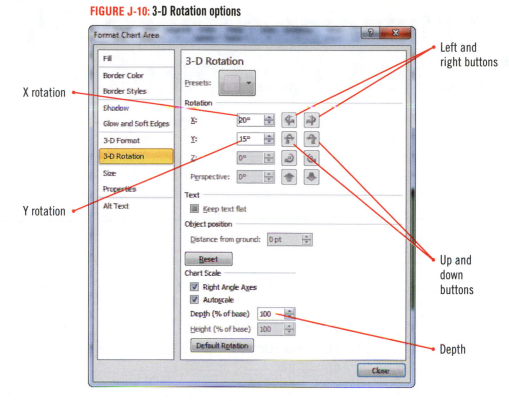

X rotation

Y rotation

Left and right buttons

Up and down buttons

Depth

**FIGURE J-11:** Chart with increased depth and rotation

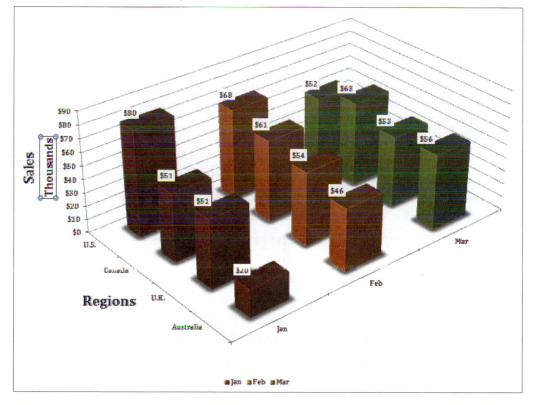

## Charting data accurately

The purpose of a chart is to help viewers to interpret the worksheet data. When creating charts, you need to make sure that your chart accurately portrays your data. Charts can sometimes misrepresent data and thus mislead people. For example, you can change the y-axis units or its starting value to make charted sales values appear larger than they are. Even though you may have correctly labeled the sales values on the chart, the height of the data points will lead people viewing the chart to think the sales are higher than the labeled values. So use caution when you modify charts to make sure you accurately represent your data.

# Enhancing a Chart with WordArt and Pictures

You can enhance your chart or worksheet titles using **WordArt**, which is preformatted text. Once you've added WordArt text, you can edit or format it by adding 3-D effects and shadows. WordArt text is a shape rather than text. This means that you cannot treat WordArt objects as if they were labels entered in a cell; that is, you cannot sort, use the spell checker, or use their cell references in formulas. You can further enhance your chart by adding a picture to one of the chart elements.  Kate wants you to add a WordArt title to the first-quarter chart. She also wants you to add the Quest logo to the chart. You will begin by adding a title to the chart.

## STEPS

**QUICK TIP**

To delete a chart title, right-click it, then select Delete from the shortcut menu. You can also select the chart title and press [Delete].

1. **Click the chart to select it if necessary, click the Chart Tools Layout tab, click the Chart Title button in the Labels group, then click Above Chart**

   A chart title text box appears above the chart.

2. **With the Chart Title text box selected, type First Quarter Sales, then click the Enter button ☑ on the Formula Bar**

3. **Click the Chart Tools Format tab, then click the More button ▾ in the WordArt Styles group**

   The WordArt Gallery opens, as shown in Figure J-12. This is where you select the style for your text.

4. **Click Fill – White, Outline – Accent 1 (the fourth style in the first row), then click outside the chart title to deselect it**

   The title text becomes formatted with outlined letters. You decide the chart would look better if the gridlines were not visible.

5. **Click the Chart Tools Layout tab, click the Gridlines button in the Axes group, click Primary Horizontal Gridlines, then click None**

   Kate wants you to add the Quest logo to the back wall of the chart to identify the company data.

**QUICK TIP**

You can also enhance a chart by adding a picture to the data markers, chart area, plot area, legend, or chart floor.

6. **Click the chart to select it if necessary, click the Chart Tools Format tab, click the Chart Elements list arrow in the Current Selection group, then click Back Wall**

   The back wall of the chart is selected, as shown by the four small circles on its corners.

7. **Click the Format Selection button in the Current Selection group, click the Picture or texture fill option button to select it in the Format Wall dialog box, click File, navigate to the location where you store your Data Files, click the chartlogo.gif file, click Insert, then click Close**

8. **Click the Insert tab, click the Header & Footer button in the Text group, click the Custom Footer button, enter your name in the Center section, click OK, then click OK again**

   The Quest logo appears on the back wall of the chart. Compare your chart to Figure J-13.

---

### Adding WordArt to a worksheet

You can use WordArt to add interest to the text on a worksheet. To insert WordArt, click the Insert tab, click the WordArt button in the Text group, choose a WordArt Style from the gallery, then replace the WordArt text "Your Text Here" with your text. You can use the Text Fill list arrow in the WordArt Styles group to add a solid, picture, gradient, or texture fill to your text. The Text Outline list arrow in the WordArt Styles group allows you to add color, weight, and dashes to the text outline. You can use the Text Effects button in the WordArt Styles group to add shadows, reflections, glows, bevels, 3-D rotations, and transformations to the WordArt text.

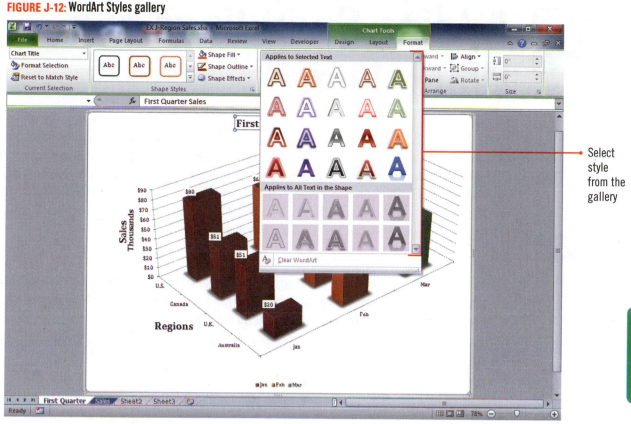

Select style from the gallery

Title formatted with WordArt

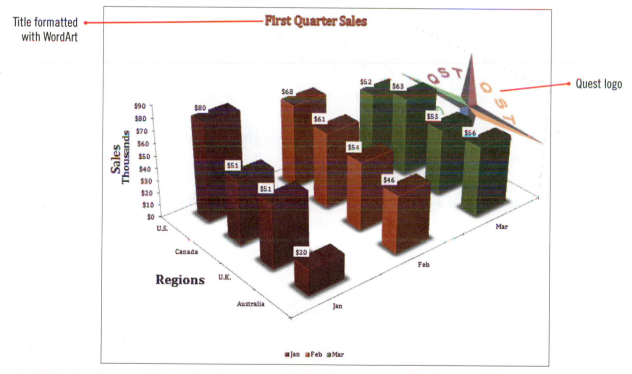

Quest logo

## Rotating chart labels

You can rotate the category labels on a chart so that longer labels won't appear crowded. Select the Category Axis on the chart, click the Chart Tools Format tab, click the Format Selection button in the Current Selection group, click Alignment in the left pane of the dialog box, click the Text direction list arrow, then select the rotation option for the labels. Rotating labels works best in two-dimensional charts because labels on three-dimensional charts often overlap as they are moved. You can also select a custom angle for horizontally aligned axis labels on two-dimensional charts.

Excel 2010

# Adding Sparklines to a Worksheet

You can enhance your worksheets by adding sparklines to the worksheet cells. **Sparklines** are miniature charts that show data trends in a worksheet range such as sales increases or decreases. Sparklines are also used to highlight maximum and minimum values in a range of data. Sparklines usually appear close to the data they represent. Any changes that you make to a worksheet are reflected in the sparklines that represent the data. After you add sparklines to a worksheet, you can change the sparkline and color. You can also format high and low data points in special colors. Kate wants you to add sparklines to the Sales worksheet to illustrate the sales trends for the first half of the year.

## STEPS

1. **Click the Sales sheet, click cell H3 to select it, click the Insert tab if necessary, click Line in the Sparklines group, verify that the insertion point is in the Data Range text box, select the range B3:G3 on the worksheet, then click OK**

   A sparkline showing the sales trend for the U.S. appears in cell H3. You can copy the sparkline to cells representing other regions.

2. **With cell H3 selected, drag the fill handle to fill the range H4:H6**

   The sparklines for all four regions are shown in Figure J-14. You decide to change the sparklines to columns.

3. **Click cell H3, then click the Column button in the Type group of the Sparkline Tools Design tab**

   All of the sparklines in column H appear as columns. The column heights represent the values of the data in the adjacent rows. You want the sparklines to appear in a theme color.

**QUICK TIP**

You can also change the color scheme of your sparklines by choosing a format from the Style gallery on the Sparkline Tools Design tab.

4. **Click the Sparkline Color list arrow in the Style group, then click Indigo Accent 5 from the Theme colors**

   The sparklines match the worksheet format. You want to highlight the high and low months using theme colors.

5. **Click the Marker Color list arrow in the Style group, point to High Point, then select Orange Accent 2 from the Theme Colors**

6. **Click the Marker Color list arrow in the Style group, point to Low Point, select Olive Green Accent 3 from the Theme Colors, then compare your worksheet to Figure J-15**

### Creating a chart template

After you create a custom chart with specific formatting, you can save it as a chart template. You can create future charts based on your saved chart templates, and they will reflect your custom formatting. Chart templates have .crtx as their file extension. If you use a custom chart frequently, you can save the template as the default chart type. To save a chart as a chart template, click the Chart Tools Design tab, click Save As Template in the Type group, enter a file-name in the Save Chart Template dialog box, then click Save. Your chart template will be saved in the Microsoft\Templates\Charts folder. When you want to format a chart like your chart template, you need to apply the template. Select your chart, click the Insert tab, click a chart type in the Charts group, click All Chart Types, click the Templates folder in the Change Chart Type dialog box, select a template in the My Templates area, then click OK.

**FIGURE J-14: Sales trend sparklines**

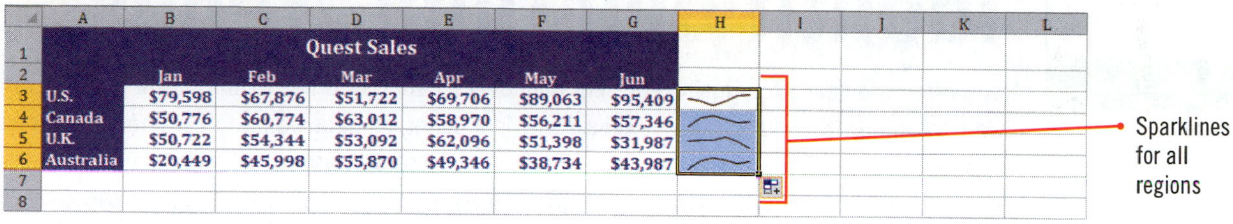

| | A | B | C | D | E | F | G | H | I | J | K | L |
|---|---|---|---|---|---|---|---|---|---|---|---|---|
| 1 | | | | Quest Sales | | | | | | | | |
| 2 | | Jan | Feb | Mar | Apr | May | Jun | | | | | |
| 3 | U.S. | $79,598 | $67,876 | $51,722 | $69,706 | $89,063 | $95,409 | | | | | |
| 4 | Canada | $50,776 | $60,774 | $63,012 | $58,970 | $56,211 | $57,346 | | | | | |
| 5 | U.K. | $50,722 | $54,344 | $53,092 | $62,096 | $51,398 | $31,987 | | | | | |
| 6 | Australia | $20,449 | $45,998 | $55,870 | $49,346 | $38,734 | $43,987 | | | | | |
| 7 | | | | | | | | | | | | |
| 8 | | | | | | | | | | | | |

Sparklines for all regions

**FIGURE J-15: Formatted sparklines**

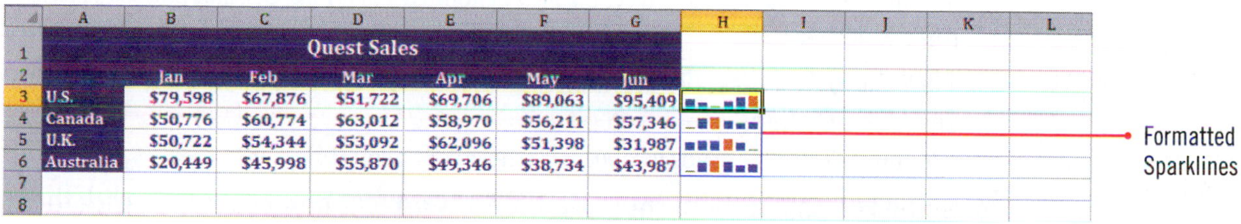

| | A | B | C | D | E | F | G | H | I | J | K | L |
|---|---|---|---|---|---|---|---|---|---|---|---|---|
| 1 | | | | Quest Sales | | | | | | | | |
| 2 | | Jan | Feb | Mar | Apr | May | Jun | | | | | |
| 3 | U.S. | $79,598 | $67,876 | $51,722 | $69,706 | $89,063 | $95,409 | | | | | |
| 4 | Canada | $50,776 | $60,774 | $63,012 | $58,970 | $56,211 | $57,346 | | | | | |
| 5 | U.K. | $50,722 | $54,344 | $53,092 | $62,096 | $51,398 | $31,987 | | | | | |
| 6 | Australia | $20,449 | $45,998 | $55,870 | $49,346 | $38,734 | $43,987 | | | | | |
| 7 | | | | | | | | | | | | |
| 8 | | | | | | | | | | | | |

Formatted Sparklines

Enhancing Charts

# Identifying Data Trends

You often use charts to visually represent data over a period of time. To emphasize patterns in data, you can add trendlines to your charts. A **trendline** is a series of data points on a line that shows data values representing the general direction in a data series. In some business situations, you can use trendlines to predict future data based on past trends.  Kate wants you to compare the U.S. and U.K. sales performance over the first two quarters and to project sales for each region in the following 3 months, assuming past trends. You begin by charting the 6-months sales data in a 2-D Column chart.

**STEPS**

1. On the Sales sheet select the range **A2:G6**, click the **Insert tab**, click the **Column button** in the Charts group, then click the **Clustered Column button** (the first chart in the 2-D Column group)

2. Drag the chart left until its upper-left corner is at the upper-left corner of cell **A8**, then drag the **middle-right sizing handle** right to the border between column G and column H
   You are ready to add a trendline for the U.S. data series.

3. Click the **U.S. January data point** (the far-left column in the chart) to select the U.S. data series, click the **Chart Tools Layout tab**, click the **Trendline button** in the Analysis group, then click **Linear Trendline**
   A linear trendline identifying U.S. sales trends in the first 6 months is added to the chart, along with an entry in the legend identifying the line. You need to compare the U.S. sales trend with the U.K. sales trend.

4. Click the **U.K. January data point** (the third column in the chart) to select the U.K. data series, click the **Trendline button**, then click **Linear Trendline**
   The chart now has two trendlines, making it easy to compare the sales trends of the U.S. and the U.K. branches. Now you want to project the next 3-months sales for the U.S. and U.K. sales branches based on the past 6-month trends.

**TROUBLE**

If you have trouble selecting the trendline, you can click the Chart Tools Layout tab, click the Chart Elements list arrow in the Current Selection group, then select Series "U.S." Trendline 1.

5. Click the **U.S. data series trendline**, click the **Trendline button**, then click **More Trendline Options**
   The Format Trendline dialog box opens, as shown in Figure J-16.

6. In the Forecast section, enter **3** in the Forward text box, click **Close**, click the **U.K. data series trendline**, click the **Trendline button**, click **More Trendline Options**, enter **3** in the Forward text box, then click **Close**
   The trendlines project an additional 3 months, predicting the future sales trends for the U.S. and U.K. regions, assuming that past trends continue. The two trendlines look identical, so you decide to format them.

7. Click the **U.S. data series trendline**, click the **Trendline button**, click **More Trendline Options**, click the **Custom option button** in the Trendline Name section, then type **U.S. Trends** in the Custom text box

8. Click **Line Color** in the left pane of the dialog box, click the **Solid line option button**, click the **Color list arrow**, select **Red** in the Standard colors section, click **Line Style** in the left pane, click the **Dash type list arrow**, select the **Dash option**, then click **Close**
   The U.S. data series trendline is now a red dashed line and is clearly identified in the legend.

9. Select the **U.K. data series trendline**, repeat Steps 7 and 8 but use the name **U.K. Trends** and a **Purple** dashed line, then click outside the chart and go to cell **A1**

10. Enter your name in the center section of the Sales sheet footer, save the workbook, preview the Sales sheet, close the workbook, submit the workbook to your instructor, then exit Excel
    The completed worksheet is shown in Figure J-17.

Enhancing Charts

**FIGURE J-16:** Format Trendline dialog box

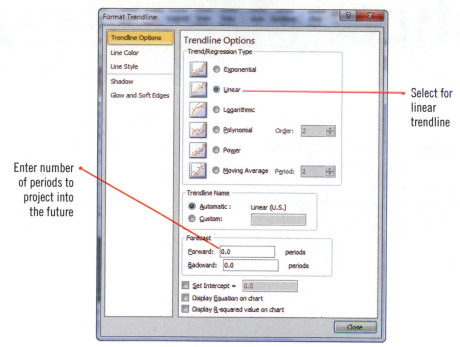

Select for linear trendline

Enter number of periods to project into the future

**FIGURE J-17:** Sales chart with trendlines for U.S. and U.K. data

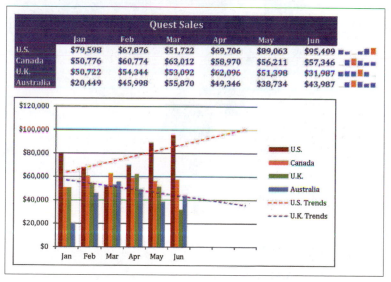

## Choosing the right trendline for your chart

Trendlines can help you forecast where your data is headed and understand its past values. This type of data analysis is called **regression analysis** in mathematics. You can choose from four types of trendlines: Linear, Exponential, Linear Forecast, and Two-Period Moving Average. A **linear trendline** is used for data series with data points that have the pattern of a line. An exponential trendline is a curved line that is used when data values increase or decrease quickly. You cannot use an exponential trendline if your data contains negative values. A linear forecast trendline is a linear trendline with a two-period forecast. A two-period moving average smooths out fluctuations in data by averaging the data points.

# Practice

For current SAM information, including versions and content details, visit SAM Central (http://www.cengage.com/samcentral). If you have a SAM user profile, you may have access to hands-on instruction, practice, and assessment of the skills covered in this unit. Since various versions of SAM are supported throughout the life of this text, check with your instructor for the correct instructions and URL/Web site for accessing assignments.

## Concepts Review

1. Which element points to the vertical axis title?
2. Which element points to the vertical axis?
3. Which element points to the chart title?
4. Which element points to the chart legend?
5. Which element points to a data label?
6. Which element points to the horizontal category axis?

**FIGURE J-18**

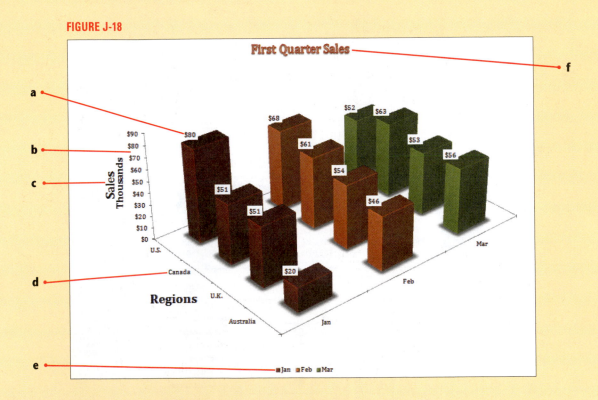

## Match each term with the statement that best describes it.

7. Plot area
8. Data series
9. X-axis
10. Sparklines
11. Trendlines

a. Category axis
b. Miniature charts that show data trends
c. Line charts that can be used to predict future data
d. Sequence of values plotted on a chart
e. Location holding data charted on the axes

**Select the best answer from the list of choices.**

12. **Which of the following is true regarding WordArt?**
    a. WordArt is a shape.
    b. Cell references to WordArt can be used in formulas.
    c. Spelling errors in WordArt can be detected by the spell checker.
    d. Cells containing WordArt can be sorted.

13. **Descriptive text that appears above a data marker is called a:**
    a. Data label.
    b. Data series.
    c. High point.
    d. Period.

14. **A chart's scale:**
    a. Always has a maximum of 80000.
    b. Can be adjusted.
    c. Always has a minimum of 0.
    d. Always appears in units of 10.

15. **Which Chart Tools tab is used to format the axes of a chart?**
    a. Layout
    b. Design
    c. Insert
    d. Format

16. **What is a data table?**
    a. The data used to create a chart, displayed in a grid
    b. A customized data series
    c. A grid with chart data displayed above a chart
    d. A three-dimensional arrangement of data on the y-axis

# Skills Review

1. **Customize a data series.**
    a. Start Excel, open the file EX J-2.xlsx from the drive and folder where you save your Data Files, then save it as **EX J-Pastry Sales**.
    b. With the Sales sheet active, select the range A2:D6.
    c. Create a 3-D column chart using the selected data. (*Hint*: Do not choose the 3-D clustered column chart.)
    d. Move and resize the chart to fit in the range A8:G20.
    e. Change the color of the January data series to a light blue color in the Standard Colors group.
    f. Save the workbook.

2. **Change a data source and add data labels.**
    a. Add the April, May, and June data to the chart.
    b. Change the chart view by exchanging the row and column data.
    c. Resize the chart to fill the range A8:J28 to display the new data.
    d. Change the chart view back to show the months in the legend by exchanging the row and column data. Add data labels to your chart. Delete the data labels for all but the June series. (*Hint*: Click one of the data labels in the series, then press [Delete].) Move any June data labels that are difficult to view.
    e. Save the workbook.

3. **Format the axes of a chart.**
    a. Change the vertical axis major unit to 1000. (*Hint*: Use the Format Axis dialog box to set the Major unit to a fixed value of 1000.)
    b. Change the display of the vertical axis values to Thousands, then move the Thousands label lower along the axis so it appears centered between $2 and $4.
    c. Set the value axis maximum to 5000.
    d. Add a horizontal axis title below the chart. Label the axis **Products**.
    e. Move the horizontal axis title so it appears between the Cookies and Brownies axis labels.
    f. Save the workbook.

# Skills Review (continued)

**4. Add a data table to a chart.**

  **a.** Move the chart to its own sheet named **Sales Chart**.

  **b.** Add a data table with legend keys.

  **c.** Move the horizontal axis title up to a location above the data table between the Cookies and Brownies axis labels.

  **d.** Format the data table to change the border color to the standard color purple.

  **e.** Save the workbook, then compare your screen to Figure J-19.

**5. Rotate a chart.**

  **a.** Remove the data table and adjust the axes titles as necessary.

  **b.** Set the X: rotation to 70 degrees.

  **c.** Set the Y: rotation to 20 degrees.

  **d.** Change the depth to 180% of the base.

  **e.** Adjust the axes titles. Add a white fill to the June data labels to make them visible. Save the workbook.

**6. Enhance a chart with WordArt and pictures.**

  **a.** Add a chart title of **Pastry Sales** to the top of the chart. Format the chart title with WordArt Fill – None, Outline - Accent 2 (the second style on the first line).

  **b.** Position the new title approximately half way across the top of the chart and closer to the chart.

  **c.** Select the legend. Format the legend with the picture cookie.gif from the drive and folder where you store your Data Files.

  **d.** Increase the size of the legend to show the picture of the cookie. Compare your chart to Figure J-20.

  **e.** Add your name to the chart footer, then save the workbook.

**7. Add Sparklines to a worksheet.**

  **a.** On the Sales worksheet, add a Line sparkline to cell H3 that represents the data in the range B3:G3.

  **b.** Copy the sparkline in cell H3 into the range H4:H6.

  **c.** Change the sparklines to columns.

  **d.** Change the Sparkline color to Blue-Gray, Accent 6 (the last color in the top row of Theme colors).

  **e.** Save the workbook.

**8. Identify data trends.**

  **a.** Create a 2-D line chart using the data in the range A2:G6, then move and resize the chart to fit in the range A8:G20.

  **b.** Add a linear trendline to the Muffins data series.

  **c.** Change the trendline color to red and the line style to Square Dot.

  **d.** Set the forward option to six periods to view the future trend, increase the width of the chart to the border between columns J and K, deselect the chart, then compare your screen to Figure J-21.

**FIGURE J-19**

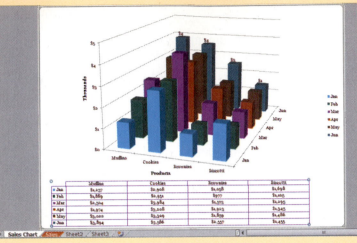

**FIGURE J-20**

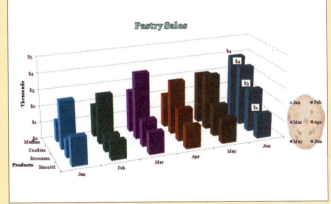

**FIGURE J-21**

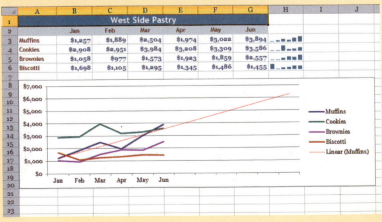

    Enhancing Charts

## Skills Review (continued)

**e.** Add your name to the center footer section, save the workbook, preview the worksheet, close the workbook, then submit the workbook to your instructor.

**f.** Exit Excel.

## Independent Challenge 1

You are the assistant to the vice president of marketing at the Metro-West Philharmonic located outside of Boston. The vice president has asked you to chart some information from a recent survey of the Philharmonic's customers. Your administrative assistant has entered the survey data in an Excel worksheet, which you will use to create two charts.

**a.** Start Excel, open the file titled EX J-3.xlsx from the drive and folder where you store your Data Files, then save it as **EX J-Customer Demographics**.

**b.** Using the data in A2:B7 of the Education Data worksheet, create a 3-D pie chart (the first chart in the 3-D Pie group) on the worksheet.

**c.** Move the chart to a separate sheet named **Education Chart**. Format the chart using chart Style 34.

**d.** Add a title of **Education Data** above the chart. Format the title using WordArt Gradient Fill – Dark Red, Accent 1 (fourth style in the third row). Change the chart title font to a size of 28, and center it over the chart.

**e.** Add data labels to the outside end of the data points. Format the legend text in a 14-point font. (*Hint:* Use the font options on the Home tab or the Mini toolbar.)

**f.** Select the Bachelor's degree pie slice by clicking the chart, then clicking the Bachelor's degree slice. Change the slice color to the standard color of Olive Green, Accent 3 from the Theme colors. (*Hint:* On the Chart Tools Format tab, click the Format Selection button in the Current Selection group and use the Format Data Point dialog box.) Compare your chart to Figure J-22.

**g.** On the Income Data worksheet, use the data in A2:B6 to create a standard clustered column (the first chart in the 2-D Column group) chart.

**h.** Delete the legend. (*Hint:* Select the legend and press [Delete].)

**i.** Place the chart on a new sheet named **Income Chart**. Format the chart using chart Style 7.

**j.** Add a chart title of **Income Data** above the chart, and format the title using WordArt Style Gradient Fill - Blue, Accent 4, Reflection.

**k.** Title the category axis **Income**. Format the category axis title in 18-point bold. (*Hint:* Use the font options on the Home tab or use the Mini toolbar.)

**FIGURE J-22**

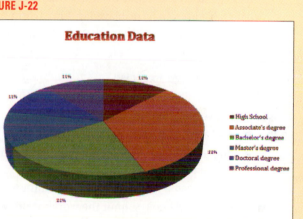

**l.** Enter your name in the center sections of the footers of the Income Chart and Education Chart sheets.

**m.** Save the workbook, preview the Income Chart and the Education Chart sheets.

**n.** Close the workbook, submit the workbook to your instructor, and exit Excel.

## Independent Challenge 2

You manage the Chicago Athletic Club, which offers memberships for swimming, tennis, and fitness. You also offer a full membership that includes all of the activities at the club. The club owner has asked you to assemble a brief presentation on the membership data over the past 4 years while it has been under your management. You decide to include a chart showing the memberships in each category as well as an analysis of trends in memberships.

**a.** Start Excel, open the file titled EX J-4.xlsx from the drive and folder where you store your Data Files, then save it as **EX J-Memberships**.

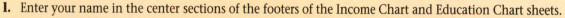

# Independent Challenge 2 (continued)

b. Create a clustered bar chart (the first chart in the 2-D Bar group) on the worksheet, comparing the membership enrollments in the four types of memberships. Format the chart using chart Style 7.

c. Change the row and column data so the years are shown in the legend.

d. Add a chart title of **Membership Data** above the chart, and format it using WordArt Style Gradient Fill – Green, Accent 4, Reflection.

e. Add Line sparklines to cells F4:F7 showing the membership trend from 2010 to 2013, moving the chart as necessary.

f. Format the sparklines using Sparkline Style Accent 5 (no dark or light).

g. Add a new membership type of **Family** in row 8 of the worksheet with the following data:

| Year | Membership |
|------|-----------|
| 2010 | 1445 |
| 2011 | 1877 |
| 2012 | 1925 |
| 2013 | 2557 |

h. Add the new data to the bar chart. Copy the sparklines into cell F8.

i. Move the chart to a sheet named **Membership Chart**.

j. Add a horizontal axis title of **Number of Memberships**, and format the title in 18-point bold font.

k. Add a data table with legend keys to the chart. Delete the legend on the right side of the chart. Format the data table lines to be displayed in Tan, Accent 6 (the last Theme color in the top row). Compare your chart to Figure J-23.

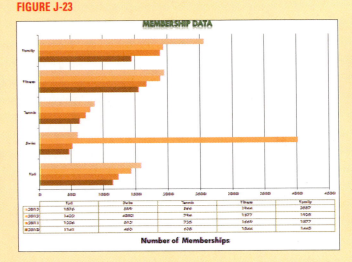

**FIGURE J-23**

### Advanced Challenge Exercise

■ Use the Format Data Series dialog box to add a border color of Tan Accent 6, Darker 50% to the bars that represent the year 2010 in the chart.

■ Add a top circle bevel of width 10 pt. to the bars that represent the year 2013 in the chart.

■ Add a border to the plot area of the chart with the color of Gold, Accent 5.

l. Enter your name in the center section of the Membership Chart sheet footer, save the workbook, then preview the sheet.

m. Close the workbook, submit the workbook to your instructor, then exit Excel.

# Independent Challenge 3

You manage the Pine Hills Pro Shop. You meet twice a year with the store owner to discuss store sales trends. You decide to use a chart to represent the sales trends for the department's product categories. You begin by charting the sales for the first 5 months of the year. Then you add data to the chart and analyze the sales trend using a trendline. Lastly, you enhance the chart by adding a data table, titles, and a picture.

a. Start Excel, open the file EX J-5.xlsx from the drive and folder where you store your Data Files, then save the workbook as **EX J-Golf Sales**.

b. Create a 3-D column chart on the worksheet showing the May through July sales information. Move the upper-left corner of the chart to cell A8 on the worksheet.

c. Format the May data series using the color yellow on the standard colors.

d. Add the Aug, Sep, and Oct data to the chart.

e. Move the chart to its own sheet named **May - Oct**.

Enhancing Charts

# Independent Challenge 3 (continued)

f. Rotate the chart with an X:Rotation of 40 degrees, a Y Rotation of 50 degrees, a perspective of 15 and the Depth (% of base) of 200.

**FIGURE J-24**

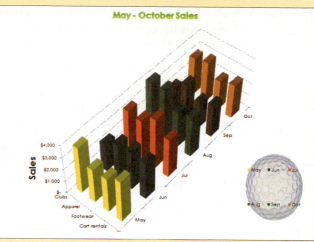

g. Add a chart title of **May - October Sales** above the chart. Format the chart title using the WordArt Style Gradient Fill – Green, Accent1.

h. Add a rotated title of **Sales** in 20-point bold to the vertical axis.

i. Change the value axis scale to a maximum of **4000**.

j. Insert the golfball.gif picture from the drive and folder where your Data Files are stored into the legend area of the chart. Move the legend lower in the chart area and increase its width. Compare your chart to Figure J-24.

### Advanced Challenge Exercise

- Move the legend to the upper-left side of the chart.
- Change the value axis scale to increment by 500.
- Remove the primary horizontal gridlines. Add a gradient fill of your choice to the plot area.

k. Enter your name in the center footer section of the chart sheet, save the workbook, then preview the chart.

l. Close the workbook, submit the workbook to your instructor, then exit Excel.

## Real Life Independent Challenge

**This Independent Challenge requires an Internet connection.**

Stock charts are used to graph a stock's high, low, and closing prices. You will create a stock chart using 4 weeks of high, low, and close prices for a stock that you are interested in tracking.

a. Start Excel, save a new workbook as **EX J-Stock Chart** in the drive and folder where you store your Data Files.

b. Use your Web browser to research the weekly high, low, and close prices for a stock over the past 4 weeks. (*Hint*: You may need to search for historical prices.)

c. Create a worksheet with the data from your chart. Enter the column labels **Date**, **High**, **Low**, and **Close** in columns A, B, C, and D. In the Date column, enter the Friday dates for the past 4 weeks starting with the oldest date. In columns B, C, and D, enter the high, low, and closing prices for your stock. Apply a document theme and formatting of your choice.

d. Create a High-Low-Close stock chart using your worksheet data. (*Hint*: To find the stock charts, click the Other Charts button.)

e. Format the horizontal axis to change the major unit to 7 days.

f. Change the color of the high-low lines to the standard color of red.

g. Add a rotated vertical axis title of **Stock Price**. Format the title in 14-point bold.

h. Format the Close data series in a color of purple from the standard colors and a size of 5. (*Hint*: You can change the size using the Marker Options in the Format Data Series dialog box.)

i. Add a chart title with your stock name above the chart. Format the title with a WordArt style of your choice from the WordArt Styles gallery. Change the vertical axis minimum and maximum values as necessary to view the chart lines.

j. Format the chart area using a gradient fill and transparency of your choice. Move the chart so it is below the worksheet data, leaving a couple of empty worksheet rows between the data and the chart.

k. Add Line sparklines to the cell below the Closing prices in the worksheet to show the trend of the stock over the past month. Format the sparklines in a color of your choice.

l. Enter your name in the center footer section of the worksheet, save the workbook, then preview the worksheet.

m. Close the workbook, submit the workbook to your instructor, then exit Excel.

# Visual Workshop

Open the file EX J-6.xlsx from the drive and folder where you store your Data Files, and create the custom chart shown in Figure J-25. Save the workbook as **EX J-Organic Sales**. Study the chart and worksheet carefully to make sure you select the displayed chart type with all the enhancements shown. Enter your name in the center section of the worksheet footer, then preview the worksheet in landscape orientation on one page. Submit the workbook to your instructor.

**FIGURE J-25**

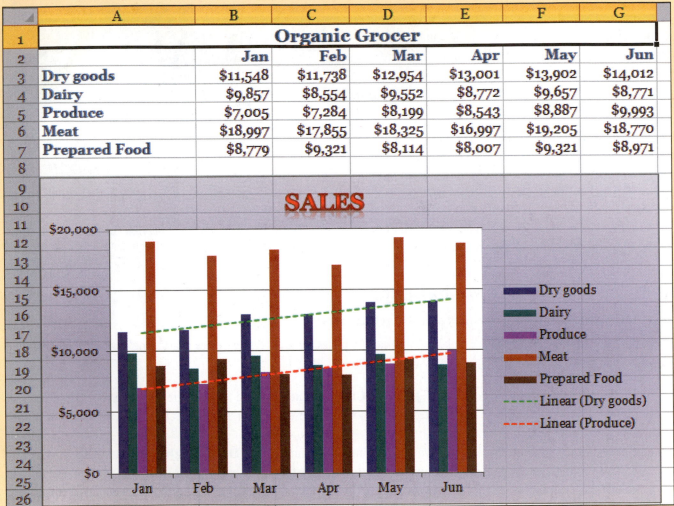

# Using What-if Analysis

## Files You Will Need:

EX K-1.xlsx

EX K-2.xlsx

EX K-3.xlsx

EX K-4.xlsx

EX K-5.xlsx

EX K-6.xlsx

EX K-7.xlsx

Each time you use a worksheet to explore different outcomes for Excel formulas, you are performing a **what-if analysis**. For example, what would happen to a firm's overall expense budget if company travel expenses decreased by 30 percent? Using Excel, you can perform a what-if analysis in many ways. In this unit, you learn to track what-if scenarios and generate summary reports using the Excel Scenario Manager. You design and manipulate data tables to project outcomes. Also, you use the Goal Seek feature to solve a what-if analysis. Finally, you use Solver to perform a complex what-if analysis involving multiple variables and use the Analysis ToolPak to generate descriptive statistics about your data.  Kate Morgan, the vice president of sales at Quest, is meeting with the U.S. region manager to discuss sales projections for the first half of the year. Kate asks you to help analyze the U.S. sales data in preparation for her meeting.

**OBJECTIVES**

Define a what-if analysis

Track a what-if analysis with Scenario Manager

Generate a scenario summary

Project figures using a data table

Use Goal Seek

Set up a complex what-if analysis with Solver

Run Solver and summarize results

Analyze data using the Analysis ToolPak

# Defining a What-if Analysis

By performing a what-if analysis in a worksheet, you can get immediate answers to questions such as "What happens to profits if we sell 25 percent more of a certain product?" or "What happens to monthly payments if interest rates rise or fall?". A worksheet you use to produce a what-if analysis is often called a **model** because it acts as the basis for multiple outcomes or sets of results. To perform a what-if analysis in a worksheet, you change the value in one or more **input cells** (cells that contain data rather than formulas), then observe the effects on dependent cells. A **dependent cell** usually contains a formula whose resulting value changes depending on the values in the input cells. A dependent cell can be located either in the same worksheet as the changing input value or in another worksheet. Kate Morgan has received projected sales data from regional managers. She has created a worksheet model to perform an initial what-if analysis, as shown in Figure K-1. She thinks the U.S. sales projections for the months of February, March, and April should be higher. You first review the guidelines for performing a what-if analysis.

## DETAILS

### When performing a what-if analysis, use the following guidelines:

- **Understand and state the purpose of the worksheet model**

  Identify what you want to accomplish with the model. What problem are you trying to solve? What questions do you want the model to answer for you? Kate's Quest worksheet model is designed to total Quest sales projections for the first half of the year and to calculate the percentage of total sales for each Quest region. It also calculates the totals and percentages of total sales for each month.

- **Determine the data input value(s) that, if changed, affect the dependent cell results**

  In a what-if analysis, changes in the content of the data input cells produces varying results in the output cells. You will use the model to work with three data input values: the February, March, and April values for the U.S. region, in cells C3, D3, and E3, respectively.

- **Identify the dependent cell(s) that will contain results**

  The dependent cells usually contain formulas, and the formula results adjust as you enter different values in the input cells. The results of two dependent cell formulas (labeled Total and Percent of Total Sales) appear in cells H3 and I3, respectively. The totals for the months of February, March, and April in cells C7, D7, and E7 are also dependent cells, as are the percentages for these months in cells C8, D8, and E8.

- **Formulate questions you want the what-if analysis to answer**

  It is important that you know the questions you want your model to answer. In the Quest model, you want to answer the following questions: (1) What happens to the U.S. regional percentage if the sales for the months of February, March, and April are each increased by $5000? (2) What happens to the U.S. regional percentage if the sales for the months of February, March, and April are each increased by $10,000?

- **Perform the what-if analysis**

  When you perform the what-if analysis, you explore the relationships between the input values and the dependent cell formulas. In the Quest worksheet model, you want to see what effect a $5000 increase in sales for February, March, and April has on the dependent cell formulas containing totals and percentages. Because the sales amounts for these months are located in cells C3, D3, and E3, any formula that references the cells is directly affected by a change in these sales amounts—in this case, the total formulas in cells H3, C7, D7, and E7. Because the formula in cell I3 references cell H3, a change in the sales amounts affects this cell as well. The percentage formulas in cells C8, D8, and E8 will also change because they reference the total formulas in cells C7, D7, and E7. Figure K-2 shows the result of the what-if analysis described in this example.

# Independent Challenge 3 (continued)

f. Rotate the chart with an X:Rotation of 40 degrees, a Y Rotation of 50 degrees, a perspective of 15 and the Depth (% of base) of 200.

g. Add a chart title of **May - October Sales** above the chart. Format the chart title using the WordArt Style Gradient Fill – Green, Accent1.

h. Add a rotated title of **Sales** in 20-point bold to the vertical axis.

i. Change the value axis scale to a maximum of **4000**.

j. Insert the golfball.gif picture from the drive and folder where your Data Files are stored into the legend area of the chart. Move the legend lower in the chart area and increase its width. Compare your chart to Figure J-24.

FIGURE J-24

## Advanced Challenge Exercise

- Move the legend to the upper-left side of the chart.
- Change the value axis scale to increment by 500.
- Remove the primary horizontal gridlines. Add a gradient fill of your choice to the plot area.

k. Enter your name in the center footer section of the chart sheet, save the workbook, then preview the chart.

l. Close the workbook, submit the workbook to your instructor, then exit Excel.

# Real Life Independent Challenge

**This Independent Challenge requires an Internet connection.**

Stock charts are used to graph a stock's high, low, and closing prices. You will create a stock chart using 4 weeks of high, low, and close prices for a stock that you are interested in tracking.

a. Start Excel, save a new workbook as **EX J-Stock Chart** in the drive and folder where you store your Data Files.

b. Use your Web browser to research the weekly high, low, and close prices for a stock over the past 4 weeks. (*Hint*: You may need to search for historical prices.)

c. Create a worksheet with the data from your chart. Enter the column labels **Date**, **High**, **Low**, and **Close** in columns A, B, C, and D. In the Date column, enter the Friday dates for the past 4 weeks starting with the oldest date. In columns B, C, and D, enter the high, low, and closing prices for your stock. Apply a document theme and formatting of your choice.

d. Create a High-Low-Close stock chart using your worksheet data. (*Hint*: To find the stock charts, click the Other Charts button.)

e. Format the horizontal axis to change the major unit to 7 days.

f. Change the color of the high-low lines to the standard color of red.

g. Add a rotated vertical axis title of **Stock Price**. Format the title in 14-point bold.

h. Format the Close data series in a color of purple from the standard colors and a size of 5. (*Hint*: You can change the size using the Marker Options in the Format Data Series dialog box.)

i. Add a chart title with your stock name above the chart. Format the title with a WordArt style of your choice from the WordArt Styles gallery. Change the vertical axis minimum and maximum values as necessary to view the chart lines.

j. Format the chart area using a gradient fill and transparency of your choice. Move the chart so it is below the worksheet data, leaving a couple of empty worksheet rows between the data and the chart.

k. Add Line sparklines to the cell below the Closing prices in the worksheet to show the trend of the stock over the past month. Format the sparklines in a color of your choice.

l. Enter your name in the center footer section of the worksheet, save the workbook, then preview the worksheet.

m. Close the workbook, submit the workbook to your instructor, then exit Excel.

# Visual Workshop

Open the file EX J-6.xlsx from the drive and folder where you store your Data Files, and create the custom chart shown in Figure J-25. Save the workbook as **EX J-Organic Sales**. Study the chart and worksheet carefully to make sure you select the displayed chart type with all the enhancements shown. Enter your name in the center section of the worksheet footer, then preview the worksheet in landscape orientation on one page. Submit the workbook to your instructor.

**FIGURE J-25**

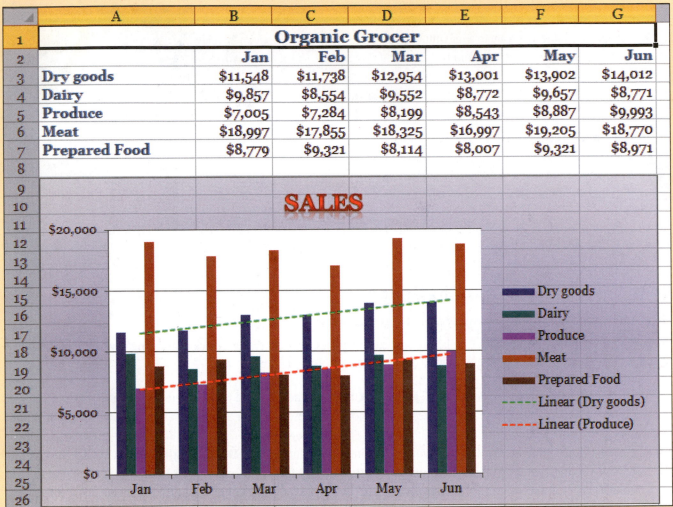

# Using What-if Analysis

**Files You Will Need:**

EX K-1.xlsx
EX K-2.xlsx
EX K-3.xlsx
EX K-4.xlsx
EX K-5.xlsx
EX K-6.xlsx
EX K-7.xlsx

Each time you use a worksheet to explore different outcomes for Excel formulas, you are performing a **what-if analysis**. For example, what would happen to a firm's overall expense budget if company travel expenses decreased by 30 percent? Using Excel, you can perform a what-if analysis in many ways. In this unit, you learn to track what-if scenarios and generate summary reports using the Excel Scenario Manager. You design and manipulate data tables to project outcomes. Also, you use the Goal Seek feature to solve a what-if analysis. Finally, you use Solver to perform a complex what-if analysis involving multiple variables and use the Analysis ToolPak to generate descriptive statistics about your data.  Kate Morgan, the vice president of sales at Quest, is meeting with the U.S. region manager to discuss sales projections for the first half of the year. Kate asks you to help analyze the U.S. sales data in preparation for her meeting.

**OBJECTIVES**

Define a what-if analysis

Track a what-if analysis with Scenario Manager

Generate a scenario summary

Project figures using a data table

Use Goal Seek

Set up a complex what-if analysis with Solver

Run Solver and summarize results

Analyze data using the Analysis ToolPak

# Defining a What-if Analysis

By performing a what-if analysis in a worksheet, you can get immediate answers to questions such as "What happens to profits if we sell 25 percent more of a certain product?" or "What happens to monthly payments if interest rates rise or fall?". A worksheet you use to produce a what-if analysis is often called a **model** because it acts as the basis for multiple outcomes or sets of results. To perform a what-if analysis in a worksheet, you change the value in one or more **input cells** (cells that contain data rather than formulas), then observe the effects on dependent cells. A **dependent cell** usually contains a formula whose resulting value changes depending on the values in the input cells. A dependent cell can be located either in the same worksheet as the changing input value or in another worksheet. Kate Morgan has received projected sales data from regional managers. She has created a worksheet model to perform an initial what-if analysis, as shown in Figure K-1. She thinks the U.S. sales projections for the months of February, March, and April should be higher. You first review the guidelines for performing a what-if analysis.

## DETAILS

### When performing a what-if analysis, use the following guidelines:

- #### Understand and state the purpose of the worksheet model
  Identify what you want to accomplish with the model. What problem are you trying to solve? What questions do you want the model to answer for you? Kate's Quest worksheet model is designed to total Quest sales projections for the first half of the year and to calculate the percentage of total sales for each Quest region. It also calculates the totals and percentages of total sales for each month.

- #### Determine the data input value(s) that, if changed, affect the dependent cell results
  In a what-if analysis, changes in the content of the data input cells produces varying results in the output cells. You will use the model to work with three data input values: the February, March, and April values for the U.S. region, in cells C3, D3, and E3, respectively.

- #### Identify the dependent cell(s) that will contain results
  The dependent cells usually contain formulas, and the formula results adjust as you enter different values in the input cells. The results of two dependent cell formulas (labeled Total and Percent of Total Sales) appear in cells H3 and I3, respectively. The totals for the months of February, March, and April in cells C7, D7, and E7 are also dependent cells, as are the percentages for these months in cells C8, D8, and E8.

- #### Formulate questions you want the what-if analysis to answer
  It is important that you know the questions you want your model to answer. In the Quest model, you want to answer the following questions: (1) What happens to the U.S. regional percentage if the sales for the months of February, March, and April are each increased by $5000? (2) What happens to the U.S. regional percentage if the sales for the months of February, March, and April are each increased by $10,000?

- #### Perform the what-if analysis
  When you perform the what-if analysis, you explore the relationships between the input values and the dependent cell formulas. In the Quest worksheet model, you want to see what effect a $5000 increase in sales for February, March, and April has on the dependent cell formulas containing totals and percentages. Because the sales amounts for these months are located in cells C3, D3, and E3, any formula that references the cells is directly affected by a change in these sales amounts—in this case, the total formulas in cells H3, C7, D7, and E7. Because the formula in cell I3 references cell H3, a change in the sales amounts affects this cell as well. The percentage formulas in cells C8, D8, and E8 will also change because they reference the total formulas in cells C7, D7, and E7. Figure K-2 shows the result of the what-if analysis described in this example.

**FIGURE K-1:** Worksheet model for a what-if analysis

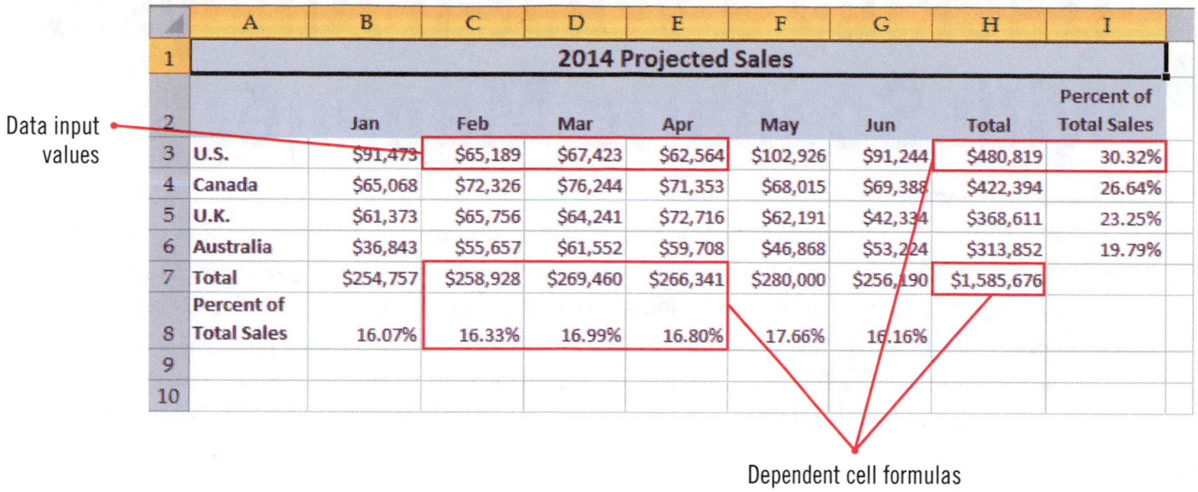

Data input values →

| | A | B | C | D | E | F | G | H | I |
|---|---|---|---|---|---|---|---|---|---|
| 1 | | | | 2014 Projected Sales | | | | | |
| 2 | | Jan | Feb | Mar | Apr | May | Jun | Total | Percent of Total Sales |
| 3 | U.S. | $91,473 | $65,189 | $67,423 | $62,564 | $102,926 | $91,244 | $480,819 | 30.32% |
| 4 | Canada | $65,068 | $72,326 | $76,244 | $71,353 | $68,015 | $69,388 | $422,394 | 26.64% |
| 5 | U.K. | $61,373 | $65,756 | $64,241 | $72,716 | $62,191 | $42,334 | $368,611 | 23.25% |
| 6 | Australia | $36,843 | $55,657 | $61,552 | $59,708 | $46,868 | $53,224 | $313,852 | 19.79% |
| 7 | Total | $254,757 | $258,928 | $269,460 | $266,341 | $280,000 | $256,190 | $1,585,676 | |
| 8 | Percent of Total Sales | 16.07% | 16.33% | 16.99% | 16.80% | 17.66% | 16.16% | | |
| 9 | | | | | | | | | |
| 10 | | | | | | | | | |

Dependent cell formulas

**FIGURE K-2:** Changed input values and dependent formula results

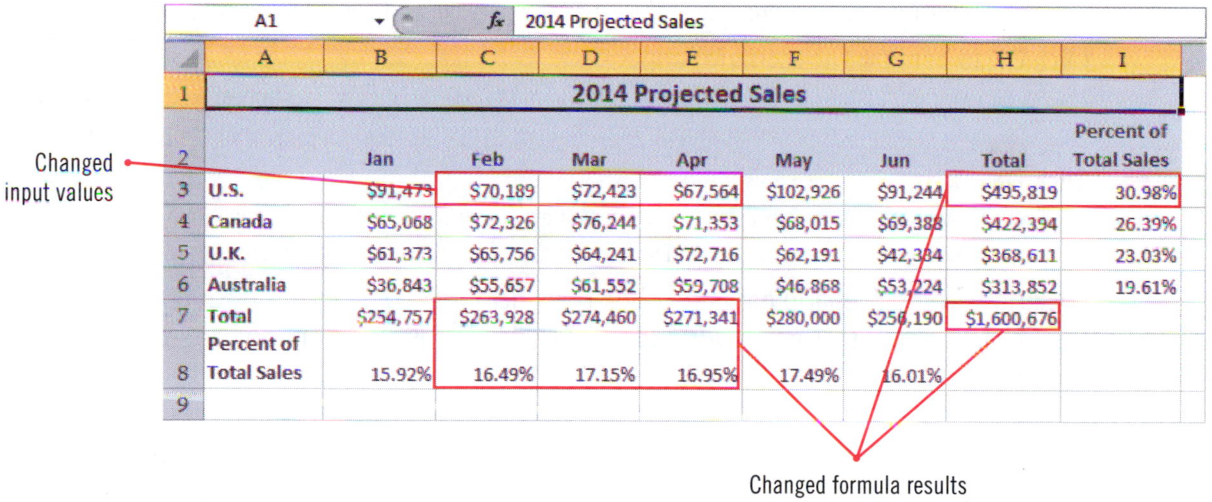

A1     $fx$   2014 Projected Sales

Changed input values →

| | A | B | C | D | E | F | G | H | I |
|---|---|---|---|---|---|---|---|---|---|
| 1 | | | | 2014 Projected Sales | | | | | |
| 2 | | Jan | Feb | Mar | Apr | May | Jun | Total | Percent of Total Sales |
| 3 | U.S. | $91,473 | $70,189 | $72,423 | $67,564 | $102,926 | $91,244 | $495,819 | 30.98% |
| 4 | Canada | $65,068 | $72,326 | $76,244 | $71,353 | $68,015 | $69,388 | $422,394 | 26.39% |
| 5 | U.K. | $61,373 | $65,756 | $64,241 | $72,716 | $62,191 | $42,334 | $368,611 | 23.03% |
| 6 | Australia | $36,843 | $55,657 | $61,552 | $59,708 | $46,868 | $53,224 | $313,852 | 19.61% |
| 7 | Total | $254,757 | $263,928 | $274,460 | $271,341 | $280,000 | $256,190 | $1,600,676 | |
| 8 | Percent of Total Sales | 15.92% | 16.49% | 17.15% | 16.95% | 17.49% | 16.01% | | |
| 9 | | | | | | | | | |

Changed formula results

# Tracking a What-if Analysis with Scenario Manager

A **scenario** is a set of values you use to observe different worksheet results. For example, you might plan to sell 100 of a particular item, at a price of $5 per item, producing sales results of $500. But what if you reduced the price to $4 or increased it to $6? Each of these price scenarios would produce different sales results. A changing value, such as the price in this example, is called a **variable**. The Excel Scenario Manager simplifies the process of what-if analysis by allowing you to name and save multiple scenarios with variable values in a worksheet.  Kate asks you to use Scenario Manager to create scenarios showing how a U.S. sales increase can affect total Quest sales over the 3-month period of February through April.

## STEPS

1. **Start Excel, open the file EX K-1.xlsx from the drive and folder where you store your Data Files, then save it as EX K-Sales**

   The first step in defining a scenario is choosing the changing cells. **Changing cells** are those that will vary in the different scenarios.

2. **With the Projected Sales sheet active, select range C3:E3, click the Data tab, click the What-If Analysis button in the Data Tools group, then click Scenario Manager**

   The Scenario Manager dialog box opens with the following message: No Scenarios defined. Choose Add to add scenarios. You decide to create three scenarios. You want to be able to easily return to your original work-sheets values, so your first scenario contains those figures.

3. **Click Add, drag the Add Scenario dialog box to the right if necessary until columns A and B are visible, then type Original Sales Figures in the Scenario name text box**

   The range in the Changing cells box shows the range you selected, as shown in Figure K-3.

4. **Click OK to confirm the scenario range**

   The Scenario Values dialog box opens, as shown in Figure K-4. The existing values appear in the changing cell boxes. Because you want this scenario to reflect the current worksheet values, you leave these unchanged.

**QUICK TIP**
You can delete a scenario by selecting it in the Scenario Manager dialog box and clicking Delete.

5. **Click OK**

   The Scenario Manager dialog box reappears with the new scenario, named Original Sales Figures, listed in the Scenarios box. You want to create a second scenario that will show the effects of increasing sales by $5,000.

6. **Click Add; in the Scenario name text box type Increase Feb, Mar, Apr by 5000; verify that the Changing cells text box reads C3:E3, then click OK; in the Scenario Values dialog box, change the value in the $C$3 text box to 70189, change the value in the $D$3 text box to 72423, change the value in the $E$3 text box to 67564, then click Add**

   You are ready to create a third scenario. It will show the effects of increasing sales by $10,000.

7. **In the Scenario name text box, type Increase Feb, Mar, Apr by 10000 and click OK; in the Scenario Values dialog box, change the value in the $C$3 text box to 75189, change the value in the $D$3 text box to 77423, change the value in the $E$3 text box to 72564, then click OK**

   The Scenario Manager dialog box reappears, as shown in Figure K-5. You are ready to display the results of your scenarios in the worksheet.

**QUICK TIP**
To edit a scenario, select it in the Scenario Manager dialog box, click the Edit button, then edit the Scenario.

8. **Make sure the Increase Feb, Mar, Apr by 10000 scenario is still selected, click Show, notice that the percent of U.S. sales in cell I3 changes from 30.32% to 31.62%; click Increase Feb, Mar, Apr by 5000, click Show, notice that the U.S. sales percent is now 30.98%; click Original Sales Figures, click Show to return to the original values, then click Close**

9. **Save the workbook**

Cell range containing value that you will change

Your user name and date will be different

FIGURE K-4: Scenario Values dialog box

| | A | B | C | D | E | F | G | H | I | J | K | L |
|---|---|---|---|---|---|---|---|---|---|---|---|---|
| 1 | | | | **2014 Projected Sales** | | | | | | | | |
| 2 | | Jan | Feb | Mar | Apr | May | Jun | Total | Percent of Total Sales | | | |
| 3 | U.S. | $91,473 | $65,189 | $67,423 | $62,564 | $102,926 | $91,244 | $480,819 | 30.32% | | | |
| 4 | Canada | $65,068 | $72,326 | $76,244 | $71,353 | $68,015 | $69,388 | $422,394 | 26.64% | | | |
| 5 | U.K. | $61,373 | $65,756 | $64,241 | $72,716 | $62,191 | $42,334 | $368,611 | 23.25% | | | |
| 6 | Australia | $36,843 | $55,657 | $61,552 | $59,708 | $46,868 | $53,224 | $313,852 | 19.79% | | | |
| 7 | Total | $254,757 | $258,928 | $269,460 | $266,341 | $280,000 | $256,190 | $1,585,676 | | | | |
| 8 | Percent of Total Sales | 16.07% | 16.33% | 16.99% | 16.80% | 17.66% | 16.16% | | | | | |
| 9 | | | | | | | | | | | | |
| 10 | | | | | | | | | | | | |
| 11 | | | | | | | | | | | | |
| 12 | | | | | | | | | | | | |
| 13 | | | | | | | | | | | | |
| 14 | | | | | | | | | | | | |
| 15 | | | | | | | | | | | | |
| 16 | | | | | | | | | | | | |

Scenario Values

Enter values for each of the changing cells.
1: $C$3  65189
2: $D$3  67423
3: $E$3  62564

Changing cell boxes with original values

FIGURE K-5: Scenario Manager dialog box with three scenarios listed

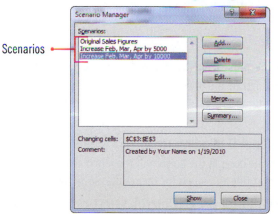

Scenarios

Scenario Manager

Scenarios:
Original Sales Figures
Increase Feb, Mar, Apr by 5000
Increase Feb, Mar, Apr by 10000

Changing cells: $C$3:$E$3
Comment: Created by Your Name on 1/19/2010

## Merging scenarios

Excel stores scenarios in the workbook and on the worksheet in which you created them. To apply scenarios from another worksheet or workbook into the current worksheet, click the Merge button in the Scenario Manager dialog box. The Merge Scenarios dialog box opens, letting you select scenarios from other locations. When you click a sheet name in the sheet list, the text under the sheet list tells you how many scenarios exist on that sheet. To merge scenarios from another workbook, such as those sent to you in a workbook by a coworker, open the other workbook file, click the Book list arrow in the Merge Scenarios dialog box, then click the workbook name. When you merge workbook scenarios, it's best if the workbooks have the same structure, so that there is no confusion of cell values.

# Generating a Scenario Summary

Although it may be useful to display the different scenario outcomes when analyzing data, it can be difficult to keep track of them. In most cases, you will want to refer to a single report that summarizes the results of all the scenarios in a worksheet. A **scenario summary** is an Excel table that compiles data from the changing cells and corresponding result cells for each scenario. For example, you might use a scenario summary to illustrate the best, worst, and most likely scenarios for a particular set of circumstances. Using cell naming makes the summary easier to read because the names, not the cell references, appear in the report.  Now that you have defined Kate's scenarios, she needs you to generate and print a scenario summary report. You begin by creating names for the cells in row 2 based on the labels in row 1, so that the report will be easier to read.

## STEPS

1. **Select the range B2:I3, click the Formulas tab, click the Create from Selection button in the Defined Names group, click the Top row check box to select it if necessary, then click OK**

   Excel creates the names for the data in row 3 based on the labels in row 2. You decide to review them.

   **QUICK TIP**
   You can also click the Name box list arrow on the formula bar to view cell names.

2. **Click the Name Manager button in the Defined Names group**

   The eight labels appear, along with other workbook names, in the Name Manager dialog box, confirming that they were created, as shown in Figure K-6. Now you are ready to generate the scenario summary report.

3. **Click Close to close the Name Manager dialog box, click the Data tab, click the What-If Analysis button in the Data Tools group, click Scenario Manager, then click Summary in the Scenario Manager dialog box**

   Excel needs to know the location of the cells that contain the formula results that you want to see in the report. You want to see the results for U.S. total and percentage of sales, and on overall Quest sales.

4. **With the Result cells text box selected, click cell H3 on the worksheet, type , (a comma), click cell I3, type , (a comma), then click cell H7**

   With the report type and result cells specified, as shown in Figure K-7, you are now ready to generate the report.

   **QUICK TIP**
   To see the Comments for each scenario, which by default contain the creator name and creation date, click the plus sign to the left of row 3.

5. **Click OK**

   A summary of the worksheet's scenarios appears on a new sheet titled Scenario Summary. The report shows outline buttons to the left of and above the worksheet so that you can hide or show report details. Because the Current Values column shows the same values as the Original Sales Figures column, you decide to delete column D.

6. **Right-click the column D heading, then click Delete in the shortcut menu**

   Next, you notice that the notes at the bottom of the report refer to the column that no longer exists. You also want to make the report title and labels for the result cells more descriptive.

7. **Select the range B13:B15, press [Delete], select cell B2, edit its contents to read Scenario Summary for U.S. Sales, click cell C10, then edit its contents to read Total U.S. Sales**

   **QUICK TIP**
   The scenario summary is not linked to the worksheet. If you change the values in the worksheet, you must generate a new scenario summary.

8. **Click cell C11, edit its contents to read Percent U.S. Sales, click cell C12, edit its contents to read Total Quest Sales, then click cell A1**

   The completed scenario summary is shown in Figure K-8.

9. **Add your name to the center section of the Scenario Summary sheet footer, change the page orientation to landscape, then save the workbook and preview the worksheet**

**FIGURE K-6:** Name Manager dialog box displaying new names

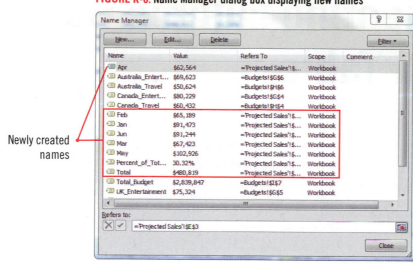

Newly created names

**FIGURE K-7:** Scenario Summary dialog box

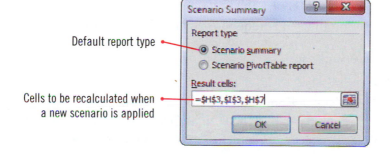

Default report type

Cells to be recalculated when a new scenario is applied

**FIGURE K-8:** Completed Scenario Summary report

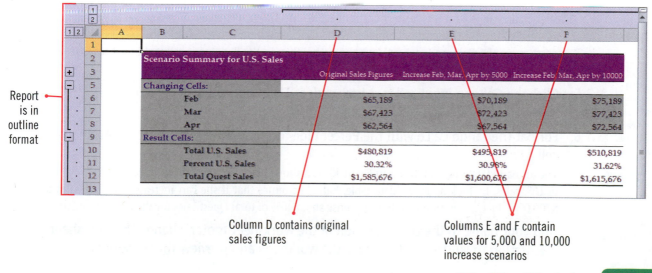

Report is in outline format

Column D contains original sales figures

Columns E and F contain values for 5,000 and 10,000 increase scenarios

Using What-if Analysis

# Projecting Figures Using a Data Table

Another way to answer what-if questions in a worksheet is by using a data table. A **data table** is a range of cells that simultaneously shows the varying resulting values when one or more input values is changed in a formula. For example, you could use a data table to display your monthly mortgage payment based on several different interest rates. A **one-input data table** is a table that shows the result of varying one input value, such as the interest rate.  Now that you have completed Kate's analysis, she wants you to find out how the U.S. sales percentage would change as U.S. total sales increased.

**STEPS**

1. **Click the Projected Sales sheet tab, enter Total U.S. Sales in cell K1, widen column K to fit the label, in cell K2 enter 480819, in cell K3 enter 530819, select the range K2:K3, drag the fill handle to select the range K4:K6, then format the values using the Accounting number format with zero decimal places**

   You begin setting up your data table by entering the total U.S. sales from cell H3 and then increasing the amount by increments of $50,000. These are the **input values** in the data table. With the varying input values listed in column K, you enter a formula reference to cell I3 that you want Excel to use in calculating the resulting percentages (the **output values**) in column L, based on the possible sales levels in column K.

2. **Click cell L1, type =, click cell I3, click the Enter button ✔ on the formula bar, then format the value in cell L1 using the Percentage format with two decimal places**

   The value in cell I3, 30.32%, appears in cell L1, and the cell name =Percent_of_Total_Sales appears in the formula bar, as shown in Figure K-9. Because it isn't necessary for users of the data table to see the value in cell L1, you want to hide the cell's contents from view.

3. **With cell L1 selected, click the Home tab, click the Format button in the Cells group, click Format Cells, click the Number tab in the Format Cells dialog box if necessary, click Custom under Category, select any characters in the Type box, type ;;; (three semicolons), then click OK**

   The three semicolons hide the values in a cell. With the table structure in place, you can now generate the data table showing percentages for the varying sales amounts.

4. **Select the range K1:L6, click the Data tab, click the What-If Analysis button in the Data Tools group, then click Data Table**

   You have highlighted the range that makes up the table structure. The Data Table dialog box opens, as shown in Figure K-10. This is where you indicate in which worksheet cell you want the varying input values (the sales figures in column K) to be substituted. Because the percentage formula in cell I3 (which you just referenced in cell L1) uses the total sales in cell H3 as input, you enter a reference to cell H3. You place this reference in the Column input cell text box, rather than in the Row input cell text box, because the varying input values are arranged in a column in your data table structure.

**TROUBLE**

If you receive the message "Selection not valid", repeat Step 4, taking care to select the entire range K1:L6.

5. **Click the Column input cell text box, click cell H3, then click OK**

   Excel completes the data table by calculating percentages for each sales amount.

6. **Format the range L2:L6 with the Percentage format with two decimal places, then click cell A1**

   The formatted data table is shown in Figure K-11. It shows the sales percentages for each of the possible levels of U.S. sales. By looking at the data table, Kate determines that if she can increase total U.S. sales to over $700,000, the U.S. division will then comprise about 40% of total Quest sales for the first half of 2014.

**QUICK TIP**

You cannot delete individual output values in a data table; you must delete all output values.

7. **Add your name to the center section of the worksheet footer, change the worksheet orientation to landscape, then save the workbook and preview the worksheet**

Using What-if Analysis

**FIGURE K-9:** One-input data table structure

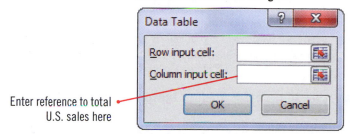

L1  =Percent_of_Total_Sales

| | Jan | Feb | Mar | Apr | May | Jun | Total | Percent of Total Sales | | | |
|---|---|---|---|---|---|---|---|---|---|---|---|
| | | | | | | | | | | Total U.S. Sales | 30.32% |
| U.S. | $91,473 | $65,189 | $67,423 | $62,564 | $102,926 | $91,244 | $480,819 | 30.32% | $ | 480,819 | |
| Canada | $65,068 | $72,326 | $76,244 | $71,353 | $68,015 | $69,388 | $422,394 | 26.64% | $ | 530,819 | |
| U.K. | $61,373 | $65,756 | $64,241 | $72,716 | $62,191 | $42,334 | $368,611 | 23.25% | $ | 580,819 | |
| Australia | $36,843 | $55,657 | $61,552 | $59,708 | $46,868 | $53,224 | $313,852 | 19.79% | $ | 630,819 | |
| Total | $254,757 | $258,928 | $269,460 | $266,341 | $280,000 | $256,190 | $1,585,676 | | $ | 680,819 | |
| Percent of Total Sales | 16.07% | 16.33% | 16.99% | 16.80% | 17.66% | 16.16% | | | | | |

Value displayed in cell I3

Varying sales totals

**FIGURE K-10:** Data Table dialog box

Data Table

Row input cell:

Column input cell:

Enter reference to total U.S. sales here

OK     Cancel

**FIGURE K-11:** Completed data table with resulting values

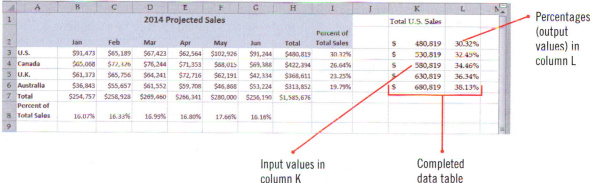

Input values in column K

Completed data table

Percentages (output values) in column L

Excel 2010

---

## Creating a two-input data table

A **two-input data table** shows the resulting values when two different input values are varied in a formula. You could, for example, use a two-input data table to calculate your monthly car payment based on varying interest rates and varying loan terms, as shown in Figure K-12. In a two-input data table, different values of one input cell appear across the top row of the table, while different values of the second input cell are listed down the left column. You create a two-input data table the same way that you created a one-input data table, except you enter both a row and a column input cell. In the example shown in Figure K-12, the two-input data table structure was created by first entering the number of payments in the range B6:D6 and rates in the range A7:A19. Then the data table values were created by first selecting the range A6:D19, clicking the Data tab, clicking the What-If Analysis button in the Data Tools group, then clicking Data Table. In the Data Table dialog box, the row input value is the term in cell C2. The column input value is the

interest rate in cell B2. You can check the accuracy of these values by cross-referencing the values in the data table with those in row 2 where you can see that an interest rate of 7% for 36 months has a monthly payment of $617.54.

**FIGURE K-12:** Two-input data table

| Loan Amount | Interest Rate | # Payments | Monthly Payment |
|---|---|---|---|
| $ 20,000.00 | 7.00% | 36 | $617.54 |
| | | | |
| | **Car Payment for $20,000 Loan** | | |
| | | **Term** | |
| | 36 | 48 | 60 |
| 6.48% | $612.80 | $474.11 | $391.14 |
| 6.61% | $613.98 | $475.31 | $392.35 |
| 6.74% | $615.17 | $476.52 | $393.58 |
| 6.87% | $616.35 | $477.72 | $394.80 |
| 7.00% | $617.54 | $478.92 | $396.02 |
| 7.13% | $618.73 | $480.13 | $397.25 |
| 7.26% | $619.92 | $481.34 | $398.48 |
| 7.39% | $621.11 | $482.55 | $399.71 |
| 7.52% | $622.31 | $483.76 | $400.95 |
| 7.65% | $623.50 | $484.98 | $402.19 |
| 7.78% | $624.70 | $486.20 | $403.43 |
| 7.91% | $625.90 | $487.41 | $404.67 |
| 8.04% | $627.10 | $488.63 | $405.91 |

# Using Goal Seek

You can think of goal seeking as a what-if analysis in reverse. In a what-if analysis, you might try many sets of values to achieve a certain solution. To **goal seek**, you specify a solution, then ask Excel to find the input value that produces the answer you want. "Backing into" a solution in this way, sometimes referred to as **backsolving**, can save a significant amount of time. For example, you can use Goal Seek to determine how many units must be sold to reach a particular sales goal or to determine what expense levels are necessary to meet a budget target.  After reviewing her data table, Kate has a follow-up question: What January U.S. sales target is required to bring the January Quest sales percentage to 17%, assuming the sales for the other regions don't change? You use Goal Seek to answer her question.

## STEPS

1. **Click cell B8**

   The first step in using Goal Seek is to select a goal cell. A **goal cell** contains a formula in which you can substitute values to find a specific value, or goal. You use cell B8 as the goal cell because it contains the percent formula.

2. **Click the Data tab, click the What-If Analysis button in the Data Tools group, then click Goal Seek**

   The Goal Seek dialog box opens. The Set cell text box contains a reference to cell B8, the percent formula cell you selected in Step 1. You need to indicate that the figure in cell B8 should equal 17%.

3. **Click the To value text box, then type 17%**

   The value 17% represents the desired solution you want to reach by substituting different values in the By changing cell.

4. **Click the By changing cell text box, then click cell B3**

   You have specified that you want cell B3, the U.S. January amount, to change to reach the 17% solution, as shown in Figure K-13.

5. **Click OK**

   The Goal Seek Status dialog box opens with the following message: "Goal Seeking with Cell B8 found a solution." By changing the sales amount in cell B3 to $109,232, Goal Seek achieves a January percentage of 17.

   **QUICK TIP**
   Before you select another command, you can return the worksheet to its status prior to the Goal Seek by pressing [Ctrl][Z].

6. **Click OK, then click cell A1**

   Changing the sales amount in cell B3 changes the other dependent values in the worksheet (B7, H3, I3, and H7) as shown in Figure K-14.

7. **Save the workbook, then preview the worksheet**

**FIGURE K-13:** Completed Goal Seek dialog box

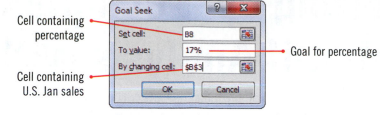

Cell containing percentage

Cell containing U.S. Jan sales

Goal for percentage

**FIGURE K-14:** Worksheet with new dependent values

| | A | B | C | D | E | F | G | H | I | J |
|---|---|---|---|---|---|---|---|---|---|---|
| 1 | | | | **2014 Projected Sales** | | | | | | |
| 2 | | Jan | Feb | Mar | Apr | May | Jun | Total | **Percent of Total Sales** | |
| 3 | U.S. | $109,232 | $65,189 | $67,423 | $62,564 | $102,926 | $91,244 | $498,578 | 31.09% | |
| 4 | Canada | $65,068 | $72,326 | $76,244 | $71,353 | $68,015 | $69,388 | $422,394 | 26.34% | |
| 5 | U.K. | $61,373 | $65,756 | $64,241 | $72,716 | $62,191 | $42,334 | $368,611 | 22.99% | |
| 6 | Australia | $36,843 | $55,657 | $61,552 | $59,708 | $46,868 | $53,224 | $313,852 | 19.57% | |
| 7 | Total | $272,516 | $258,928 | $269,460 | $266,341 | $280,000 | $256,190 | $1,603,435 | | |
| 8 | Percent of Total Sales | 17.00% | 16.15% | 16.81% | 16.61% | 17.46% | 15.98% | | | |
| 9 | | | | | | | | | | |
| 10 | | | | | | | | | | |
| 11 | | | | | | | | | | |

New target values calculated by Goal Seek

New dependent values

Using What-if Analysis

# Setting up a Complex What-if Analysis with Solver

The Excel Solver is an **add-in** program that provides optional features. It must be installed before you can use it. Solver finds the best solution to a problem that has several inputs. The cell containing the formula is called the **target cell**, or **objective**. As you learned earlier, cells containing the values that vary are called "changing cells." Solver is helpful when you need to perform a complex what-if analysis involving multiple input values or when the input values must conform to specific limitations or restrictions called **constraints**. Kate decides to fund each region with the same amount, $757,500, to cover expenses. She adjusts the travel and entertainment allocations to keep expenditures to the allocated amount of $757,500. You use Solver to help Kate find the best possible allocation.

## STEPS

**TROUBLE**

If Solver is not on your Data tab, click the File tab, click Options, click Add-Ins, in the list of Add-ins click Solver Add-in, click Go, in the Add-Ins dialog box click the Solver Add-in check box to select it, then click OK.

1. **Click the Budgets sheet tab**

   This worksheet is designed to calculate the travel, entertainment, and other budgets for each region. It assumes fixed costs for communications, equipment, advertising, salaries, and rent. You use Solver to change the entertainment and travel amounts in cells G3:H6 (the changing cells) to achieve your target of a total budget of $3,030,000 in cell I7 (the target cell). You want your solution to include a constraint on cells G3:H6 specifying that each region is funded $757,500. Based on past budgets, you know there are two other constraints: the travel budgets must include at least $80,000, and the entertainment budgets must include at least $93,000. It is a good idea to enter constraints on the worksheet for documentation purposes, as shown in Figure K-15.

2. **Click the Data tab, then click the Solver button in the Analysis group**

   In the Solver Parameters dialog box opens, you indicate the target cell with its objective, the changing cells, and the constraints under which you want Solver to work. You begin by entering your total budget objective.

**TROUBLE**

If your Solver Parameters dialog box has entries in the By Changing Cells box or in the Subject to the Constraints box, click Reset All, click OK, then continue with Step 3.

3. **With the insertion point in the Set Objective text box, click cell I7 in the worksheet, click the Value Of option button, double-click the Value Of text box, then type 3,030,000**

   You have specified an objective of $3,030,000 for the total budget. In typing the total budget figure, be sure to type the commas.

4. **Click the By Changing Variable Cells text box, then select the range G3:H6 on the worksheet**

   You have told Excel which cells to vary to reach the goal of $3,030,000 total budget. You need to specify the constraints on the worksheet values to restrict the Solver's answer to realistic values.

5. **Click Add, with the insertion point in the Cell Reference text box in the Add Constraint dialog box, select the range I3:I6 in the worksheet, click the list arrow in the dialog box, click =, then with the insertion point in the Constraint text box click cell C9**

   As shown in Figure K-16, the Add Constraint dialog box specifies that cells in the range I3:I6, the total region budget amounts, should be equal to the value in cell C9. Next, you need to add the constraint that the budgeted entertainment amounts should be at least $93,000.

**QUICK TIP**

If your solution needs to be an integer, you can select it in the Add Constraint dialog box.

6. **Click Add, with the insertion point in the Cell Reference text box select the range G3:G6 in the worksheet, click the list arrow, select >=, with the insertion point in the Constraint text box click cell C11**

   Next, you need to specify that the budgeted travel amounts should be greater than or equal to $80,000.

7. **Click Add, with the insertion point in the Cell Reference text box select the range H3:H6, select >=, with the insertion point in the Constraint text box click cell C10, then click OK**

   The Solver Parameters dialog box opens with the constraints listed, as shown in Figure K-17. In the next lesson, you run Solver and generate solutions to the budget constraints.

**FIGURE K-15:** Worksheet set up for a complex what-if analysis

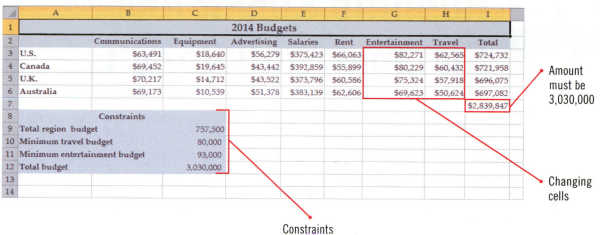

Amount must be 3,030,000

Changing cells

Constraints

**FIGURE K-16:** Adding constraints

Cells containing region budget amounts

Value in cell C9 should be 757,500

**FIGURE K-17:** Completed Solver Parameters dialog box

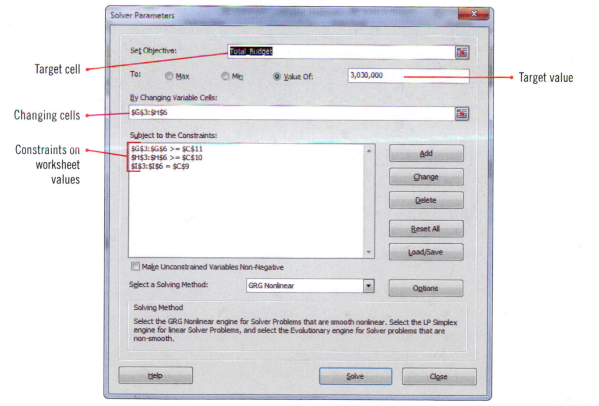

Target cell

Target value

Changing cells

Constraints on worksheet values

Using What-if Analysis

# Running Solver and Summarizing Results

After entering all the parameters in the Solver Parameters dialog box, you can run Solver to find a solution. In some cases, Solver may not be able to find a solution that meets all of your constraints. Then you would need to enter new constraints and try again. Once Solver finds a solution, you can choose to create a summary of the solution or a special report displaying the solution. You have finished entering the parameters in the Solver Parameters dialog box.  Kate wants you to run Solver and create a summary of the solution on a separate worksheet.

## STEPS

1. **Make sure your Solver Parameters dialog box matches Figure K-17 in the previous lesson**

2. **Click Solve**

   The Solver Results dialog box opens, indicating that Solver has found a solution, as shown in Figure K-18. The solution values appear in the worksheet, but you decide to save the solution values in a summary worksheet and display the original values in the worksheet.

3. **Click Save Scenario, enter Adjusted Budgets in the Scenario Name text box, click OK, in the Solver Results dialog box click the Restore Original Values option button, then click OK to close the Solver Results dialog box**

   The Solver Results dialog box closes, and the original values appear in the worksheet. You will display the Solver solution values on a separate sheet.

4. **Click the What-If Analysis button in the Data Tools group, click Scenario Manager, with the Adjusted Budgets scenario selected in the Scenario Manager dialog box click Summary, then click OK**

   The Solver results appear on the Scenario Summary 2 worksheet, as shown in Figure K-19. To keep the budget at $3,030,000 and equally fund each region, the travel and entertainment budget allocations are calculated in column E labeled Adjusted Budgets. You want to format the solution values on the worksheet.

5. **Select Column A, click the Home tab if necessary, click the Delete button in the Cells group, right-click the Scenario Summary 2 sheet tab, click Rename on the shortcut menu, type Adjusted Budgets, then press [Enter]**

6. **Select the range A16:A18, press [Delete], select the range A2:D3, click the Fill Color list arrow, then click Blue, Accent 2**

7. **Select the range A5:D15, click the Fill Color list arrow, click Blue, Accent 2, Lighter 80%, right-click the row 1 header to select the row, click Delete, select cell A1, then enter Solver Solution**

   The formatted Solver solution is shown in Figure K-20.

8. **Enter your name in the center section of the worksheet footer, save the workbook, then preview the worksheet**

   You have successfully found the best budget allocations using Solver.

**FIGURE K-18:** Solver Results dialog box

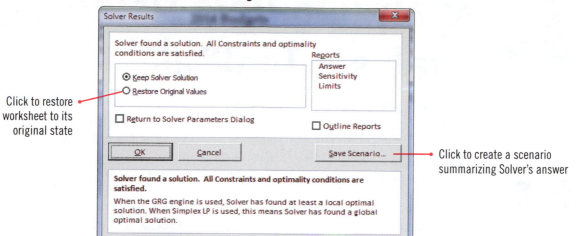

Click to restore worksheet to its original state

Click to create a scenario summarizing Solver's answer

**FIGURE K-19:** Solver Summary

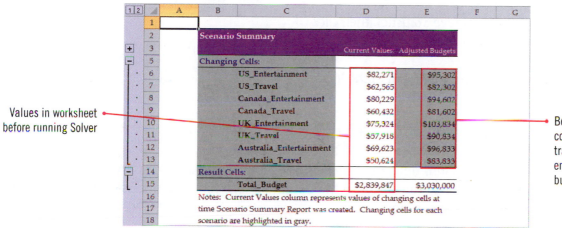

Values in worksheet before running Solver

Best possible combination of travel and entertainment budget allocations

**FIGURE K-20:** Formatted Solver Summary

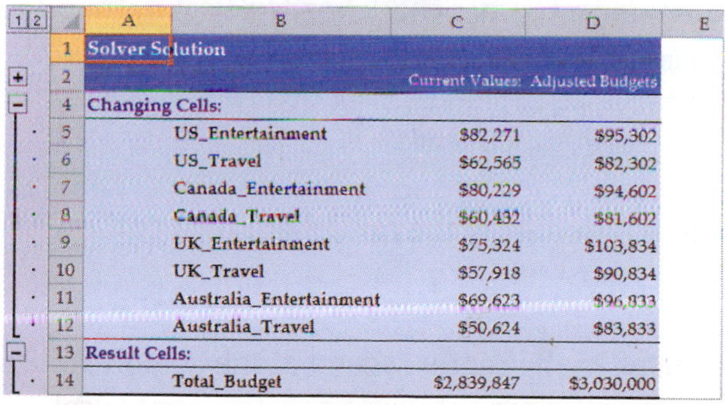

## Understanding Answer Reports

Instead of saving Solver results as a scenario, you can select from three types of answer reports in the Solver Results window. One of the most useful is the Answer Report, which compares the original values with the Solver's final values. The report has three sections. The top section has the target cell information; it compares the original value of the target cell with the final value. The middle section of the report contains information about the adjustable cells. It lists the original and final values for all cells that were changed to reach the target value. The last report section has information about the constraints. Each constraint that was added into Solver is listed in the Formula column along with the cell address and a description of the cell data. The Cell Value column contains the Solver solution values for the cells. These values will be different from your worksheet values if you restored the original values to your worksheet rather than keeping Solver's solution. The Status column contains information on whether the constraints were binding or not binding in reaching the solution. If a solution is not binding, the slack—or how far the result is from the constraint value—is provided. Frequently, the answer report shows equality constraints as nonbinding with a slack of zero.

# Analyzing Data Using the Analysis ToolPak

The Analysis ToolPak is an Excel add-in that contains many statistical analysis tools. The Descriptive Analysis tool in the Data Analysis dialog box generates a statistical report including mean, median, mode, minimum, maximum, and sum for an input range you specify on your worksheet.  After reviewing the projected sales figures for the Quest regions, Kate decides to statistically analyze the projected regional sales totals submitted by the managers. You use the Analysis ToolPak to help her generate the sales statistics.

**STEPS**

**TROUBLE**

If Data Analysis is not on your Data tab, click the File tab, click Options, click Add-Ins, in the list of Add-ins click Analysis ToolPak, click Go, in the Add-Ins dialog box click the Analysis ToolPak check box to select it, then click OK.

1. **Click the Projected Sales sheet tab, click the Data tab, then click the Data Analysis button in the Analysis group**

   The Data Analysis dialog box opens, listing the available analysis tools.

2. **Click Descriptive Statistics, then click OK**

   The Descriptive Statistics dialog box opens, as shown in Figure K-21.

3. **With the insertion point in the Input Range text box, select the range H3:H6 on the worksheet**

   You have told Excel to use the total projected sales cells in the statistical analysis. You need to specify that the data is grouped in a column and the results should be placed on a new worksheet named Region Statistics.

**QUICK TIP**

Selecting the New Worksheet Ply option places the statistical output on a new worksheet in the workbook.

4. **Click the Columns option button in the Grouped By: area if necessary, click the New Worksheet Ply option button in the Output options section if necessary, then type Region Statistics in the text box**

   You want to add the summary statistics to the new worksheet.

**QUICK TIP**

If there are fewer than four data values, the Kurtosis will display the DIV/0! error value.

5. **Click the Summary statistics check box to select it, then click OK**

   The statistics are generated and placed on the new worksheet named Region Statistics. Table K-1 describes some of the statistical values provided in the worksheet. Column A is not wide enough to view the labels, and the worksheet needs a descriptive title.

6. **Widen column A to display the row labels, then edit the contents of cell A1 to read Total Projected Sales Jan – Jun**

7. **Enter your name in the center section of the Region Statistics footer, preview the report, save the workbook, close the workbook, then exit Excel**

8. **Submit the workbook to your instructor**

   The completed report is shown in Figure K-22.

---

### Choosing the right tool for your data analysis

The Analysis ToolPak offers 19 options for data analysis. ANOVA, or the analysis of variance, can be applied to one or more samples of data. The regression option creates a table of statistics from a least-squares regression. The correlation choice measures how strong of a linear relationship exists between two random variables. A moving average is often calculated for stock prices or any other data that is time sensitive. Moving averages display long-term trends by smoothing out short-term changes. The Random Number Generation creates a set of random numbers between values that you specify. The Rank and Percentile option creates a report of the ranking and percentile distribution.

**FIGURE K-21:** Descriptive Statistics dialog box

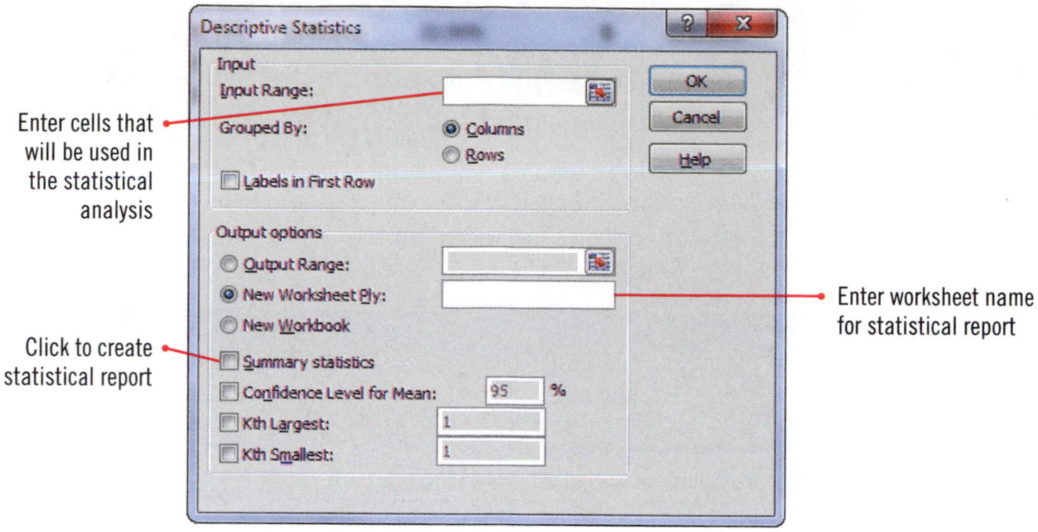

Enter cells that will be used in the statistical analysis

Click to create statistical report

Enter worksheet name for statistical report

**Descriptive Statistics**

Input
Input Range:
Grouped By:
- ● Columns
- ○ Rows
☐ Labels in First Row

Output options
- ○ Output Range:
- ● New Worksheet Ply:
- ○ New Workbook
- ☐ Summary statistics
- ☐ Confidence Level for Mean: 95 %
- ☐ Kth Largest: 1
- ☐ Kth Smallest: 1

OK
Cancel
Help

**FIGURE K-22:** Completed Report

*Total Projected Sales Jan - Jun*

| | |
|---|---|
| Mean | 400858.7 |
| Standard Error | 39394.23 |
| Median | 395502.5 |
| Mode | #N/A |
| Standard Deviation | 78788.46 |
| Sample Variance | 6.21E+09 |
| Kurtosis | -0.54301 |
| Skewness | 0.342022 |
| Range | 184725.8 |
| Minimum | 313852 |
| Maximum | 498577.8 |
| Sum | 1603435 |
| Count | 4 |

**TABLE K-1:** Descriptive statistics

| statistic | definition |
|---|---|
| Mean | The average of a set of numbers |
| Median | The middle value of a set of numbers |
| Mode | The most common value in a set of numbers |
| Standard Deviation | The measure of how widely spread the values in a set of numbers are; if the values are all close to the mean, the standard deviation is close to zero |
| Range | The difference between the largest and smallest values in a set of numbers |
| Minimum | The smallest value in a set of numbers |
| Maximum | The largest value in a set of numbers |
| Sum | The total of the values in a set of numbers |
| Count | The number of values in a set of numbers |
| Skewness | The measure of the asymmetry of the values in a set of numbers |
| Sample Variance | The measure of how scattered the values in a set of numbers are from an expected value |
| Kurtosis | The measure of the peakedness or flatness of a distribution of data |

# Practice

For current SAM information, including versions and content details, visit SAM Central (http://www.cengage.com/samcentral). If you have a SAM user profile, you may have access to hands-on instruction, practice, and assessment of the skills covered in this unit. Since various versions of SAM are supported throughout the life of this text, check with your instructor for the correct instructions and URL/Web site for accessing assignments.

## Concepts Review

**FIGURE K-23**

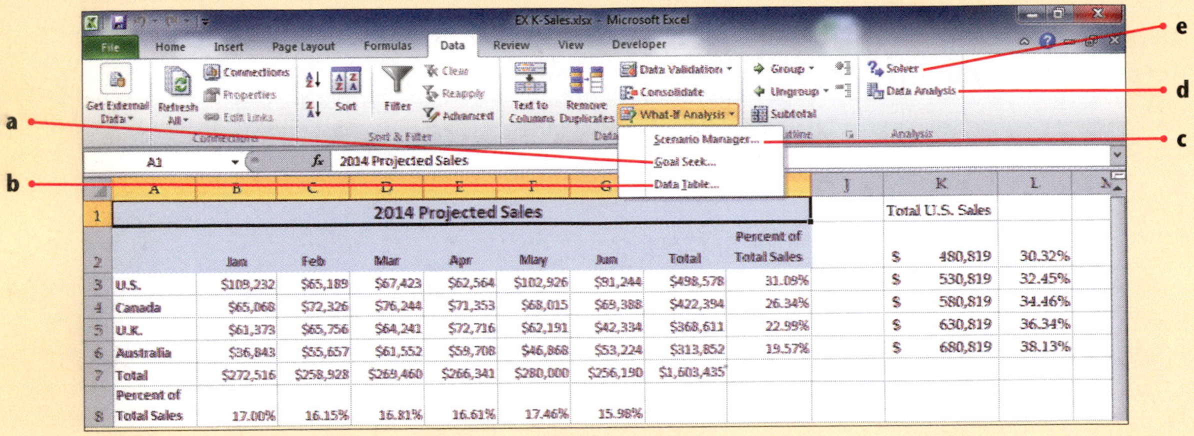

1. Which element do you click to perform a statistical analysis on worksheet data?
2. Which element do you click to create a range of cells showing the resulting values with varied formula input?
3. Which element do you click to perform a what-if analysis involving multiple input values with constraints?
4. Which element do you click to name and save different sets of values to forecast worksheet results?
5. Which element do you click to find the input values that produce a specified result?

## Match each term with the statement that best describes it.

6. One-input data table
7. Solver
8. Goal Seek
9. Scenario summary
10. Two-input data table

a. Add-in that helps you solve complex what-if scenarios with multiple input values

b. Separate sheet with results from the worksheet's scenarios

c. Generates values resulting from varying two sets of changing values in a formula

d. Helps you backsolve what-if scenarios

e. Generates values resulting from varying one set of changing values in a formula

## Select the best answer from the list of choices.

11. To hide the contents of a cell from view, you can use the custom number format:
   a. ;;;
   b. —
   c. Blank
   d. " "

12. The _____ button in the Scenario Manager dialog box allows you to bring scenarios from another workbook into the current workbook.
   a. Combine
   b. Add
   c. Import
   d. Merge

**13.** When you use Goal Seek, you specify a _____, then find the values that produce it.

    **a.** Row input cell                                 **c.** Solution

    **b.** Column input cell                               **d.** Changing value

**14.** In Solver, the cell containing the formula is called the:

    **a.** Changing cell.                                 **c.** Input cell.

    **b.** Target cell.                                   **d.** Output cell.

**15.** Which of the following Excel add-ins can be used to generate a statistical summary of worksheet data?

    **a.** Solver                                        **c.** Analysis ToolPak

    **b.** Lookup Wizard                               **d.** Conditional Sum

# Skills Review

**1. Define a what-if analysis.**

    **a.** Start Excel, open the file EX K-2.xlsx from the drive and folder where you store your Data Files, then save it as **EX K-Repair**.

    **b.** Examine the Auto Repair worksheet to determine the purpose of the worksheet model.

    **c.** Locate the data input cells.

    **d.** Locate any dependent cells.

    **e.** Examine the worksheet to determine problems the worksheet model can solve.

**2. Track a what-if analysis with Scenario Manager.**

    **a.** On the Auto Repair worksheet, select the range B3:B5, then use the Scenario Manager to set up a scenario called **Most Likely** with the current data input values.

    **b.** Add a scenario called **Best Case** using the same changing cells, but change the Labor cost per hour in the $B$3 text box to **80**, change the Parts cost per job in the $B$4 text box to **65**, then change the Hours per job value in cell $B$5 to **1.5**.

    **c.** Add a scenario called **Worst Case**. For this scenario, change the Labor cost per hour in the $B$3 text box to **95**, change the Parts cost per job in the $B$4 text box to **80**, then change the Hours per job in the $B$5 text box to **3**.

    **d.** If necessary, drag the Scenario Manager dialog box to the right until columns A and B are visible.

    **e.** Show the Worst Case scenario results, and view the total job cost.

    **f.** Show the Best Case scenario results, and observe the job cost. Finally, display the Most Likely scenario results.

    **g.** Close the Scenario Manager dialog box.

    **h.** Save the workbook.

**3. Generate a scenario summary.**

    **a.** Create names for the input value cells and the dependent cell using the range A3:B7.

    **b.** Verify that the names were created.

    **c.** Create a scenario summary report, using the Cost to complete job value in cell B7 as the result cell.

    **d.** Edit the title of the Summary report in cell B2 to read **Scenario Summary for Auto Repair**.

    **e.** Delete the Current Values column.

    **f.** Delete the notes beginning in cell B11. Compare your worksheet to Figure K-24.

    **g.** Return to cell A1, enter your name in the center section of the Scenario Summary sheet footer, save the workbook, then preview the Scenario Summary sheet.

**FIGURE K-24**

| | A | B | C | D | E | F |
|---|---|---|---|---|---|---|
| 1 | | | | | | |
| 2 | | Scenario Summary for Auto Repair | | | | |
| 3 | | | | Most Likely | Best Case | Worst Case |
| 5 | | **Changing Cells:** | | | | |
| 6 | | | Labor_cost_per_hour | $90.00 | $80.00 | $95.00 |
| 7 | | | Parts_cost_per_job | $70.00 | $65.00 | $80.00 |
| 8 | | | Hours_per_job | 2.00 | 1.50 | 3.00 |
| 9 | | **Result Cells:** | | | | |
| 10 | | | Cost_to_complete_job | $250.00 | $185.00 | $365.00 |

# Skills Review (continued)

**4. Project figures using a data table.**

  **a.** Click the Auto Repair sheet tab.

  **b.** Enter the label **Labor $** in cell D3.

  **c.** Format the label so that it is boldfaced and right-aligned.

  **d.** In cell D4, enter **75**; then in cell D5, enter **80**.

  **e.** Select the range D4:D5, then use the fill handle to extend the series to cell D8.

  **f.** In cell E3, reference the job cost formula by entering **=B7**.

  **g.** Format the contents of cell E3 as hidden, using the ;;; Custom formatting type on the Number tab of the Format Cells dialog box.

  **h.** Generate the new job costs based on the varying labor costs. Select the range D3:E8 and create a data table. In the Data Table dialog box, make cell B3 (the labor cost) the column input cell.

  **i.** Format the range E4:E8 as currency with two decimal places. Compare your worksheet to Figure K-25.

  **j.** Enter your name in the center section of the worksheet footer, save the workbook, then preview the worksheet.

**FIGURE K-25**

| | A | B | C | D | E |
|---|---|---|---|---|---|
| 1 | Auto Repair Model | | | | |
| 2 | | | | | |
| 3 | Labor cost per hour | $90.00 | | Labor $ | |
| 4 | Parts cost per job | $70.00 | | 75 | $220.00 |
| 5 | Hours per job | 2.00 | | 80 | $230.00 |
| 6 | | | | 85 | $240.00 |
| 7 | Cost to complete job: | $250.00 | | 90 | $250.00 |
| 8 | | | | 95 | $260.00 |
| 9 | | | | | |

**5. Use Goal Seek.**

  **a.** Click cell B7, and open the Goal Seek dialog box.

  **b.** Assuming the labor rate and the hours remain the same, determine what the parts would have to cost so that the cost to complete the job is $220. (*Hint*: Enter a job cost of **220** as the To value, and enter **B4** (the Parts cost) as the By changing cell. Write down the parts cost that Goal Seek finds.

  **c.** Click OK, then use [Ctrl][Z] to reset the parts cost to its original value.

  **d.** Enter the cost of the parts in cell A14.

  **e.** Assuming the parts cost and hours remain the same, determine the fee for the labor so that the cost to complete the job is $175. Use [Ctrl][Z] to reset the labor cost to its original value. Enter the labor cost in cell A15.

  **f.** Save the workbook, then preview the worksheet.

**6. Set up a complex what-if analysis with Solver.**

  **a.** With the Brake Repair sheet active, open the Solver Parameters dialog box.

  **b.** Make B14 (the total repair costs) the objective cell, with a target value of 15,000.

  **c.** Use cells B6:D6 (the number of scheduled repairs) as the changing cells.

  **d.** Specify that cells B6:D6 must be integers. (*Hint*: Select int in the Add Constraint dialog box.)

  **e.** Specify a constraint that cells B6:D6 must be greater than or equal to 10.

**7. Run Solver and summarize results.**

  **a.** Use Solver to find a solution.

  **b.** Save the solution as a scenario named **Repair Solution**, and restore the original values to the worksheet.

  **c.** Create a scenario summary using the Repair Solution scenario, delete the notes at the bottom of the solution, and rename the worksheet Repair Solution. Compare your worksheet to Figure K-26.

  **d.** Enter your name in the center section of the worksheet footer, save the workbook, then preview the worksheet.

**FIGURE K-26**

| | A | B | C | D | E |
|---|---|---|---|---|---|
| 1 | | | | | |
| 2 | | Scenario Summary | | | |
| 3 | | | | Current Values: | Repair Solution |
| 5 | | Changing Cells: | | | |
| 6 | | | $B$6 | 25 | 20 |
| 7 | | | $C$6 | 35 | 31 |
| 8 | | | $D$6 | 15 | 12 |
| 9 | | Result Cells: | | | |
| 10 | | | $B$14 | $17,950.00 | $15,000.00 |

# Skills Review (continued)

**8. Analyze data using the Analysis ToolPak.**

a. With the Brake Repair sheet active, generate summary descriptive statistics for the repair cost per model, using cells B10:D10 as the input range. (*Hint*: The input is grouped in a row.) Place the new statistics on a worksheet named **Repair Cost Statistics**.

b. Widen columns as necessary to view the statistics.

c. Change the contents of cell A1 to **Repair Cost Per Model**. Delete row 9 containing the kurtosis error information. (This was generated because you only have three data values.) Compare your worksheet to Figure K-27.

d. Add your name to the center section of the worksheet footer, then preview the worksheet.

e. Save and close the workbook, submit the workbook to your instructor, then exit Excel.

**FIGURE K-27**

| | A | B |
|---|---|---|
| 1 | *Repair Cost Per Model* | |
| 2 | | |
| 3 | Mean | 5983.333333 |
| 4 | Standard Error | 1626.238844 |
| 5 | Median | 7125 |
| 6 | Mode | #N/A |
| 7 | Standard Deviation | 2816.728303 |
| 8 | Sample Variance | 7933958.333 |
| 9 | Skewness | -1.524287472 |
| 10 | Range | 5275 |
| 11 | Minimum | 2775 |
| 12 | Maximum | 8050 |
| 13 | Sum | 17950 |
| 14 | Count | 3 |
| 15 | | |

# Independent Challenge 1

You are the manager for Smith & Weston, an environmental consulting firm based in Chicago. You are planning a computer hardware upgrade for the engineers in the company. The vice president of finance at the company has asked you to research the monthly cost for a $100,000 equipment loan to purchase the new computers. You will create a worksheet model to determine the monthly payments based on several different interest rates and loan terms, using data from the company's bank. Using Scenario Manager, you will create the following three scenarios: a 4-year loan at 7.5 percent; a 3-year loan at 6.75 percent; and a 2-year loan at 6.5 percent. You will also prepare a scenario summary report outlining the payment details.

a. Start Excel, open the file EX K-3.xlsx from the drive and folder where you store your Data Files, then save it as **EX K-Equipment Loan**.

b. Create cell names for the cells B4:B11 based on the labels in cells A4:A11, using the Create Names from Selection dialog box.

c. Use Scenario Manager to create scenarios that calculate the monthly payment on a $100,000 loan under the three sets of loan possibilities listed below. (*Hint*: Create three scenarios using cells B5:B6 as the changing cells.)

| Scenario Name | Interest Rate | Term |
|---|---|---|
| 7.5%  4 Yr | .075 | 48 |
| 6.75%  3 Yr | .0675 | 36 |
| 6.5%  2 Yr | .065 | 24 |

d. Show each scenario to make sure it performs as intended, then display the 7.5% 4 Yr scenario.

e. Generate a scenario summary titled **Scenario Summary for $100,000 Hardware Purchase**. Use cells B9:B11 as the Result cells.

f. Delete the Current Values column in the report, and delete the notes at the bottom of the report.

g. Enter your name in the center section of the Scenario Summary sheet footer. Save the workbook, then preview the scenario summary.

## Advanced Challenge Exercise

- Copy the range A1:B11 from the Loan sheet, and paste it on Sheet2. Widen the columns as necessary. Rename Sheet2 to **My Loan**.
- Create a new scenario in the copied sheet called **Local**, using an interest rate and term available at a local lending institution. Test the new scenario by displaying the local values in the worksheet.
- Return to the Loan sheet and merge the scenario from the My Loan sheet into the Loan sheet. (*Hint*: Use the Merge option in the Scenario Manager dialog box.)
- Verify that the Local scenario appears in the Scenario Manager dialog box of the Loan sheet, then generate a scenario summary titled **Advanced Scenario Summary**, using cells B9:B11 as the Result cells. Delete the Current Values column in the report and the notes at the bottom.

Excel 2010

# Independent Challenge 1 (continued)

- Enter your name in the center section of the Scenario Summary 2 sheet footer, save the workbook, then preview the Advanced Scenario Summary.

**h.** Close the workbook, exit Excel, then submit the workbook to your instructor.

# Independent Challenge 2

You are a CFO at Northern Interactive, an interactive media consulting company based in Minneapolis. The company president has asked you to prepare a loan summary report for a business expansion. You need to develop a model to show what the monthly payments would be for a $500,000 loan with a range of interest rates. You will create a one-input data table that shows the results of varying interest rates in 0.2% increments, then you will use Goal Seek to specify a total payment amount for this loan application.

**a.** Start Excel, open the file EX K-4.xlsx from the drive and folder where you store your Data Files, then save it as **EX K-Capital Loan Payment Model**.

**b.** Reference the monthly payment amount from cell B9 in cell E4, and format the contents of cell E4 as hidden.

**c.** Using cells D4:E13, create a one-input data table structure with varying interest rates for a 5-year loan. Use cells D5:D13 for the interest rates, with 9% as the lowest possible rate and 10.6% as the highest. Vary the rates in between by 0.2%. Use Figure K-28 as a guide.

**d.** Generate the data table that shows the effect of varying interest rates on the monthly payments. Use cell B5, the Annual Interest Rate, as the column input cell. Format the range E5:E13 as currency with two decimal places.

**FIGURE K-28**

| | A | B | C | D |
|---|---|---|---|---|
| 1 | Northern Interactive | | | |
| 2 | | | | |
| 3 | | | | |
| 4 | Loan Amount | $500,000.00 | | Interest Rate |
| 5 | Annual Interest Rate | 9.80% | | 9.00% |
| 6 | Term in Months | 60 | | 9.20% |
| 7 | | | | 9.40% |
| 8 | | | | 9.60% |
| 9 | Monthly Payment: | $10,574.39 | | 9.80% |
| 10 | Total Payments: | $634,463.11 | | 10.00% |
| 11 | Total Interest: | $134,463.11 | | 10.20% |
| 12 | | | | 10.40% |
| 13 | | | | 10.60% |
| 14 | | | | |

**e.** Select cell B10 and use Goal Seek to find the interest rate necessary for a total payment amount of $600,000. Use cell B5, the Annual Interest Rate, as the By changing cell. Accept the solution found by Goal Seek.

## Advanced Challenge Exercise

- Reference the monthly payment amount from cell B9 in cell A13, and format the contents of cell A13 as hidden.
- Using cells A13:C22, create a two-input data table structure with varying interest rates for 10- and 15-year terms. Use Figure K-29 as a guide.
- Generate the data table that shows the effect of varying interest rates and loan terms on the monthly payments. (*Hint*: Use cell B6, Term in Months, as the row input cell, and cell B5, the Annual Interest Rate, as the column input cell.)
- Format the range B14:C22 as currency with two decimal places.

**f.** Enter your name in the center section of the worksheet footer, save the workbook, then preview the worksheet.

**g.** Close the workbook, exit Excel, then submit the workbook to your instructor.

**FIGURE K-29**

| | A | B | C | D | E | F |
|---|---|---|---|---|---|---|
| 1 | Northern Interactive | | | | | |
| 2 | | | | | | |
| 3 | | | | | | |
| 4 | Loan Amount | $500,000.00 | | Interest Rate | | |
| 5 | Annual Interest Rate | 7.42% | | 9.00% | $10,379.18 | |
| 6 | Term in Months | 60 | | 9.20% | $10,427.78 | |
| 7 | | | | 9.40% | $10,476.51 | |
| 8 | | | | 9.60% | $10,525.38 | |
| 9 | Monthly Payment: | $10,000.00 | | 9.80% | $10,574.39 | |
| 10 | Total Payments: | $600,000.00 | | 10.00% | $10,623.52 | |
| 11 | Total Interest: | $100,000.00 | | 10.20% | $10,672.79 | |
| 12 | | | | 10.40% | $10,722.20 | |
| 13 | | | 120 | 180 | 10.60% | $10,771.74 |
| 14 | | 7.00% | | | | |
| 15 | | 7.25% | | | | |
| 16 | | 7.50% | | | | |
| 17 | | 7.75% | | | | |
| 18 | | 8.00% | | | | |
| 19 | | 8.25% | | | | |
| 20 | | 8.50% | | | | |
| 21 | | 8.75% | | | | |
| 22 | | 9.00% | | | | |
| 23 | | | | | | |

# Independent Challenge 3

You are the owner of Home Health, a home medical products company based in Boston. You are considering adding local delivery service to your business. You decide on a plan to purchase a combination of vans, sedans, and compact cars that can deliver a total of 1500 cubic feet of products. You want to first look at how the interest rate affects the monthly payments for each vehicle type you are considering purchasing. To do this, you use Goal Seek. You need to keep the total monthly payments for all of the vehicles at or below $6,000. You use Solver to help find the best possible combination of vehicles.

a. Start Excel, open the file EX K-5.xlsx from the drive and folder where you store your Data Files, then save it as **EX K-Vehicle Purchase**.

b. Use Goal Seek to find the interest rate that produces a monthly payment for the van purchase of $1,650, and write down the interest rate that Goal Seek finds. Record the interest rate in cell A19, enter **Interest rate for $1650 van payment** in cell B19, then reset the interest rate to its original value.

c. Use Goal Seek to find the interest rate that produces a monthly payment for the sedan purchase of $950. Record the interest rate in cell A20, enter **Interest rate for $950 sedan payment** in cell B20, then reset the interest rate to its original value of 6.75%.

d. Use Goal Seek to find the interest rate that produces a monthly payment for the compact purchase of $790. Record the interest rate in cell A21, enter **Interest rate for $790 compact payment** in cell B21, then reset the interest rate to its original value.

e. Assign cell B8 the name **Quantity_Van**, name cell C8 **Quantity_Sedan**, name cell D8 **Quantity_Compact**, and name cell B15 **Total_Monthly_Payments**. Use Solver to set the total delivery capacity of all vehicles to 1500. Use the quantity to purchase, cells B8:D8, as the changing cells. Specify that cells B8:D8 must be integers. Make sure that the total monthly payments amount in cell B15 is less than or equal to $6,000.

f. Generate a scenario named **Delivery Solution** with the Solver values, and restore the original values in the worksheet. Create a scenario summary using the Delivery Solution scenario, delete the notes at the bottom of the solution, and edit cell B2 to contain **Solver Solution**.

g. Enter your name in the center footer section of both worksheets. Preview both worksheets, then save the workbook.

h. Close the workbook, then submit the workbook to your instructor.

# Real Life Independent Challenge

You decide to take out a loan for a new car. You haven't decided whether to finance the car for 3, 4, or 5 years. You will create scenarios for car loans with the different terms, using interest rates at your local lending institution. You will summarize the scenarios to make them easy to compare.

a. Start Excel, open the file EX K-6.xlsx from the drive and folder where you store your Data Files, then save it as **EX K-Car Payment**.

b. Research the interest rates for 3-year, 4-year, and 5-year auto loans at your local lending institution. Record your 48-month interest rate in cell B3 of the worksheet. Change the data in cell B2 to the price of a car you would like to purchase, then widen columns as necessary.

c. Create cell names for the cells B2:B9 based on the labels in cells A2:A9.

d. Create a scenario named **48 months** to calculate the monthly payment for your loan amount, using the 48-month term and the corresponding interest rate at your lending institution.

e. Create a scenario named **36 months** to calculate the monthly payment for your loan amount, using the 36-month term and the corresponding interest rate at your lending institution.

f. Create a scenario named **60 months** to calculate the monthly payment for your loan amount, using the 60-month term and the corresponding interest rate at your lending institution.

g. Generate a scenario summary titled **Scenario Summary for Car Purchase** that summarizes the payment information in cells B7:B9 for the varying interest rates and terms. Delete the Current Values column in the report and the notes at the bottom of the report.

h. Enter your name in the center section of the scenario summary footer, then preview the scenario summary.

i. Enter your name in the center section of the Loan sheet footer, then preview the Loan sheet.

j. Save the workbook, close the workbook, then exit Excel and submit the workbook to your instructor.

# Visual Workshop

Open the file EX K-7.xlsx from the drive and folder where you save your Data Files, then save it as **EX K-Atlanta Manufacturing**. Create the worksheet shown in Figure K-30. (*Hint:* Use Goal Seek to find the Hourly labor cost to reach the total profit in cell H11 in the figure and accept the solution.) Then generate descriptive statistics for the products' total profits on a worksheet named **Manufacturing Profits**, as shown in Figure K-31. Add your name to the center footer section of each sheet, change the orientation of the Profit sheet to landscape, then preview and print both worksheets.

**FIGURE K-30**

| | A | B | C | D | E | F | G | H |
|---|---|---|---|---|---|---|---|---|
| 1 | | | | Atlanta Manufacturing | | | | |
| 2 | | | | January Production | | | | |
| 3 | Hourly Labor Cost | $61.18 | | | | | | |
| 4 | | | | | | | | |
| 5 | | | | | | | | |
| 6 | Product Number | Hours | Parts Cost | Cost to Produce | Retail Price | Unit Profit | Units Produced | Total Profit |
| 7 | NA1547 | 8 | $452 | $ 941.43 | $1,695.00 | $ 753.57 | 327 | $ 246,417.12 |
| 8 | CB5877 | 10 | $214 | $ 825.79 | $1,588.00 | $ 762.21 | 407 | $ 310,220.07 |
| 9 | QW5287 | 15 | $384 | $1,301.68 | $1,995.00 | $ 693.32 | 321 | $ 222,554.82 |
| 10 | TY8894 | 17 | $610 | $1,650.04 | $2,544.00 | $ 893.96 | 247 | $ 220,807.99 |
| 11 | Total Profit | | | | | | | $ 1,000,000.00 |
| 12 | | | | | | | | |

**FIGURE K-31**

| | A | B |
|---|---|---|
| 1 | Profit Statistics | |
| 2 | | |
| 3 | Mean | 250000 |
| 4 | Standard Error | 20905.95 |
| 5 | Median | 234486 |
| 6 | Mode | #N/A |
| 7 | Standard Deviation | 41811.9 |
| 8 | Sample Variance | 1.75E+09 |
| 9 | Kurtosis | 2.254124 |
| 10 | Skewness | 1.575897 |
| 11 | Range | 89412.07 |
| 12 | Minimum | 220808 |
| 13 | Maximum | 310220.1 |
| 14 | Sum | 1000000 |
| 15 | Count | 4 |
| 16 | | |

## UNIT
# L
Excel 2010

# Analyzing Data with PivotTables

**Files You Will Need:**

EX L-1.xlsx
EX L-2.xlsx
EX L-3.xlsx
EX L-4.xlsx
EX L-5.xlsx
EX L-6.xlsx
EX L-7.xlsx

Excel PivotTables and PivotCharts let you summarize large quantities of data in a compact layout. You can interact with the PivotTable or PivotChart to explore the relationships within your data and display your findings in an easy-to-understand format. Excel includes two PivotTable features: PivotTable reports and PivotChart reports. In this unit, you plan, design, create, update, and change the layout and format of a PivotTable report and a PivotChart report.  Kate Morgan, the vice president of sales at Quest, is preparing for the annual meeting for the United States region. She decides to analyze product sales in Quest's Chicago, New York, and Miami branches over the past year. Kate asks you to create a PivotTable to summarize the 2013 sales data by quarter, product, and branch. She then has you illustrate the information using a PivotChart.

**OBJECTIVES**

Plan and design a PivotTable report

Create a PivotTable report

Change a PivotTable's summary function and design

Filter and sort PivotTable data

Update a PivotTable report

Change a PivotTable's structure and format

Create a PivotChart report

Use the GETPIVOTDATA function

# Planning and Designing a PivotTable Report

The Excel **PivotTable Report** feature lets you summarize large amounts of columnar worksheet data in an interactive table format. You can freely rearrange, or "pivot," parts of the table structure around the data to summarize any data values within the table by category. Creating a PivotTable report (often called a PivotTable) involves only a few steps. Before you begin, however, you need to review the data and consider how a PivotTable can best summarize it.  Kate asks you to design a PivotTable to display Quest's sales information for its branches in the United States. You begin by reviewing guidelines for creating PivotTables.

## DETAILS

### Before you create a PivotTable, think about the following guidelines:

- **Review the source data**

  Before you can effectively summarize data in a PivotTable, you need to understand the source data's scope and structure. The source data does not have to be defined as a table, but should be in a table-like format. That is, it should have column headings, should not have any blank rows or columns, and should have the same type of data in each column. To create a meaningful PivotTable, make sure that one or more of the fields has repeated information so that the PivotTable can effectively group it. Also be sure to include numeric data that the PivotTable can total for each group. The data columns represent categories of data, which are called **fields**, just as in a table. You are working with sales information that Kate received from Quest's U.S. branch managers, shown in Figure L-1. Information is repeated in the Product ID, Category, Branch, and Quarter columns, and numeric information is displayed in the Sales column, so you will be able to summarize this data effectively in a PivotTable.

- **Determine the purpose of the PivotTable and write the names of the fields you want to include**

  The purpose of your PivotTable is to summarize sales information by quarter across various branches. You want your PivotTable to summarize the data in the Product ID, Category, Branch, Quarter, and Sales columns, so you include those fields in your PivotTable.

- **Determine which field contains the data you want to summarize and which summary function you want to use**

  You want to summarize sales information by summing the Sales field for each product in a branch by quarter. You'll do this by using the Excel SUM function.

- **Decide how you want to arrange the data**

  The PivotTable layout you choose is crucial to delivering the message you intend. Product ID will appear in the PivotTable columns, Branch and Quarter will appear in rows, and the PivotTable will summarize Sales figures, as shown in Figure L-2.

- **Determine the location of the PivotTable**

  You can place a PivotTable in any worksheet of any workbook. Placing a PivotTable on a separate worksheet makes it easier to locate and prevents you from accidentally overwriting parts of an existing sheet. You decide to create the PivotTable as a new worksheet in the current workbook.

Analyzing Data with PivotTables

**FIGURE L-1:** Sales worksheet

| | A | B | C | D | E | F |
|---|---|---|---|---|---|---|
| 1 | United States Sales | | | | | |
| 2 | Product ID | Category | Branch | Quarter | Sales | |
| 3 | 240 | Travel Accessory | Chicago | 1 | $ 2,300.56 | |
| 4 | 240 | Travel Accessory | Chicago | 2 | $ 5,767.76 | |
| 5 | 240 | Travel Accessory | Chicago | 3 | $ 4,883.65 | |
| 6 | 240 | Travel Accessory | Chicago | 4 | $ 5,697.45 | |
| 7 | 110 | Travel Insurance | Chicago | 1 | $ 980.65 | |
| 8 | 110 | Travel Insurance | Chicago | 2 | $ 2,634.69 | |
| 9 | 110 | Travel Insurance | Chicago | 3 | $ 2,400.74 | |
| 10 | 110 | Travel Insurance | Chicago | 4 | $ 3,612.93 | |
| 11 | 340 | Tour | Chicago | 1 | $ 8,995.43 | |
| 12 | 340 | Tour | Chicago | 2 | $ 7,976.43 | |
| 13 | 340 | Tour | Chicago | 3 | $ 8,232.65 | |
| 14 | 340 | Tour | Chicago | 4 | $ 8,631.98 | |
| 15 | 780 | Travel Accessory | Chicago | 1 | $ 999.65 | |
| 16 | 780 | Travel Accessory | Chicago | 2 | $ 2,334.56 | |
| 17 | 780 | Travel Accessory | Chicago | 3 | $ 2,210.32 | |
| 18 | 780 | Travel Accessory | Chicago | 4 | $ 1,245.67 | |
| 19 | 640 | Travel Insurance | Chicago | 1 | $ 1,289.65 | |
| 20 | 640 | Travel Insurance | Chicago | 2 | $ 6,434.56 | |
| 21 | 640 | Travel Insurance | Chicago | 3 | $ 6,110.32 | |
| 22 | 640 | Travel Insurance | Chicago | 4 | $ 6,345.67 | |
| 23 | 510 | Tour | Chicago | 1 | $ 999.43 | |
| 24 | 510 | Tour | Chicago | 2 | $ 1,954.43 | |
| 25 | 510 | Tour | Chicago | 3 | $ 2,412.65 | |
| 26 | 510 | Tour | Chicago | 4 | $ 2,661.98 | |
| 27 | 240 | Travel Accessory | Miami | 1 | $ 1,394.32 | |
| 28 | 240 | Travel Accessory | Miami | 2 | $ 3,231.80 | |
| 29 | 240 | Travel Accessory | Miami | 3 | $ 3,511.65 | |

Data with repeated information

Numeric data

**FIGURE L-2:** Example of a PivotTable report

| | A | B | C | D | E | F | G | H | I |
|---|---|---|---|---|---|---|---|---|---|
| 3 | Sum of Sales | Column Labels | | | | | | | |
| 4 | Row Labels | 110 | 240 | 340 | 510 | 640 | 780 | Grand Total | |
| 5 | ⊟ Chicago | 9629.01 | 18649.42 | 33836.49 | 8028.49 | 20180.2 | 6790.2 | 97113.81 | |
| 6 | 1 | 980.65 | 2300.56 | 8995.43 | 999.43 | 1289.65 | 999.65 | 15565.37 | |
| 7 | 2 | 2634.69 | 5767.76 | 7976.43 | 1954.43 | 6434.56 | 2334.56 | 27102.43 | |
| 8 | 3 | 2400.74 | 4883.65 | 8232.65 | 2412.65 | 6110.32 | 2210.32 | 26250.33 | |
| 9 | 4 | 3612.93 | 5697.45 | 8631.98 | 2661.98 | 6345.67 | 1245.67 | 28195.68 | |
| 10 | ⊟ Miami | 32108.38 | 10825.72 | 32465.18 | 9567.18 | 10281.51 | 10001.51 | 105249.48 | |
| 11 | 1 | 6634.43 | 1394.32 | 7790.34 | 2310.34 | 1376.34 | 1766.34 | 21272.11 | |
| 12 | 2 | 8324.65 | 3231.8 | 6814.87 | 2524.87 | 3394.21 | 3524.21 | 27814.61 | |
| 13 | 3 | 8324.65 | 3511.65 | 8883.54 | 2183.54 | 2587.53 | 2307.53 | 27798.44 | |
| 14 | 4 | 8824.65 | 2687.95 | 8976.43 | 2548.43 | 2923.43 | 2403.43 | 28364.32 | |
| 15 | ⊟ New York | 15057.69 | 10266.97 | 29929.87 | 19171.87 | 8969.93 | 16919.93 | 100316.26 | |
| 16 | 1 | 4921.45 | 1940.57 | 6369.43 | 2119.43 | 1418.43 | 1758.43 | 18527.74 | |
| 17 | 2 | 3319.92 | 2374.32 | 7628.78 | 3880.78 | 2183.98 | 5413.98 | 24801.76 | |
| 18 | 3 | 4176.89 | 3216.65 | 8198.9 | 6728.9 | 2577.98 | 4317.98 | 29217.3 | |
| 19 | 4 | 2639.43 | 2735.43 | 7732.76 | 6442.76 | 2789.54 | 5429.54 | 27769.46 | |
| 20 | Grand Total | 56795.08 | 39742.11 | 96231.54 | 36767.54 | 39431.64 | 33711.64 | 302679.55 | |

Product ID values are column labels

Branches and quarters are row labels

PivotTable summarizes sales figures by product number, branch, and quarter

# Creating a PivotTable Report

Once you've planned and designed your PivotTable report, you can create it. After you create the PivotTable, you **populate** it by adding fields to areas in the PivotTable. A PivotTable has four areas: the Report Filter, which is the field by which you want to filter, or show selected data in, the PivotTable; the Row Labels, which contain the fields whose labels will describe the values in the rows; the Column Labels, which appear above the PivotTable values and describe the columns; and the Values, which summarize the numeric data.  With the planning and design stage complete, you are ready to create a PivotTable that summarizes sales information. Kate will use the information in her presentation to the branch managers in the Chicago, New York, and Miami offices.

**STEPS**

1. **Start Excel if necessary, open the file EX L-1.xlsx from the drive and folder where you store your Data Files, then save it as EX L-US Sales**

   This worksheet contains the year's sales information for Quest's U.S. branches, including Product ID, Category, Branch, Quarter, and Sales. The records are sorted by branch.

2. **Click the Insert tab, then click the PivotTable button in the Tables group**

   The Create PivotTable dialog box opens, as shown in Figure L-3. This is where you specify the type of data source you want to use for your PivotTable: an Excel Table/Range or an external data source such as a database file. You also specify where you want to place the PivotTable.

3. **Make sure the Select a table or range option button is selected and the range Sales!$A$2:$E$74 appears in the Table/Range text box, make sure the New Worksheet option button is selected, then click OK**

   The PivotTable appears on the left side of the worksheet and the PivotTable Field List pane appears on the right, as shown in Figure L-4. You populate the PivotTable by clicking field check boxes in the Field List pane. The diagram area at the bottom of the PivotTable Field List task pane represents the main PivotTable areas and helps you track field locations as you populate the PivotTable. You can also drag fields among the diagram areas to change the PivotTable layout.

   > **QUICK TIP**
   > To remove a field from a PivotTable, click the field's check box to uncheck it.

4. **Click the Branch field check box in the PivotTable Field List**

   Because the Branch field is nonnumeric, Excel adds it to the Row Labels area.

5. **Click the Product ID check box in the PivotTable Field List pane**

   The Product ID field name appears in the Values area in the diagram area, and the Product ID information is automatically added to the PivotTable. But because the data type of the Product ID field is numeric, the field is added to the Values area of the PivotTable and the Product ID values are summed. Instead, you want the Product IDs as column headers in the PivotTable.

6. **Click the Sum of Product ID list arrow in the Values area at the bottom of the PivotTable Field List, then choose Move to Column Labels**

   The Product ID field becomes a column label, causing the Product ID values to appear in the PivotTable as column headers. You can also drag fields to place them directly in the area you choose.

   > **QUICK TIP**
   > You can click the Collapse Outline button [ − ] next to the branch names to collapse the outline and hide the quarter details. You can display hidden quarter values by clicking the Expand Outline button [ + ] next to any field name on a PivotTable to expand an outline.

7. **Drag the Quarter field from the top of the PivotTable Field List and drop it below the Branch field in the Row Labels area at the bottom, then select the Sales field check box in the PivotTable Field List**

   You have created a PivotTable that totals U.S. sales, with the Product IDs as column headers and Branches and Quarters as row labels. Adding the Quarter field as a row label below the Branches field displays the quarters below each branch in the Row Labels area of the PivotTable. Because the data in the Sales field is numeric, the Sales field is added to the Values area. SUM is the Excel default function for data fields containing numbers, so Excel automatically calculates the sum of the sales in the PivotTable. The PivotTable tells you that Miami sales of Product #110 were twice the New York sales level and more than three times the Chicago sales level. Product #340 was the best selling product overall, as shown in the Grand Total row. See Figure L-5.

8. **Save the workbook**

Analyzing Data with PivotTables

**FIGURE L-3:** Create PivotTable dialog box

Data source you want to use for the PivotTable

Location where you want to place PivotTable

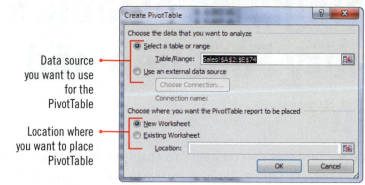

**FIGURE L-4:** New PivotTable ready to receive field data

PivotTable

PivotTable Field List pane

Click check boxes to add field to the PivotTable

Diagram of the PivotTable areas

Excel 2010

**FIGURE L-5:** New PivotTable with fields in place

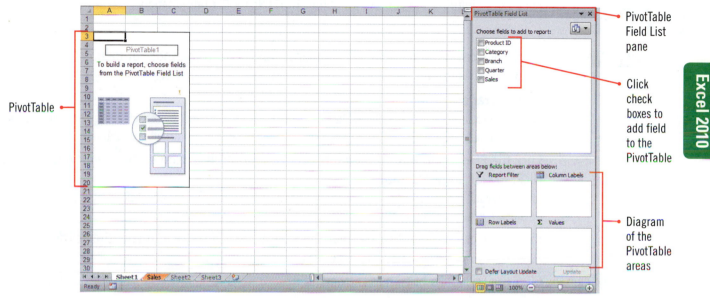

Miami sales for this product are twice as high as New York and three times Chicago's sales

Product 340 shows highest sales overall

| | Column Labels | | | | | | |
|---|---|---|---|---|---|---|---|
| Sum of Sales | | | | | | | |
| Row Labels | 110 | 240 | 340 | 510 | 640 | 780 | Grand Total |
| ⊟Chicago | 9629.01 | 18649.42 | 33836.49 | 8028.49 | 20180.2 | 6790.2 | 97113.81 |
| 1 | 980.65 | 2300.56 | 8995.43 | 999.43 | 1289.65 | 999.65 | 15565.37 |
| 2 | 2634.69 | 5767.76 | 7976.43 | 1954.43 | 6434.56 | 2334.56 | 27102.43 |
| 3 | 2400.74 | 4883.65 | 8232.65 | 2412.65 | 6110.32 | 2210.32 | 26250.33 |
| 4 | 3612.93 | 5697.45 | 8631.98 | 2661.98 | 6345.67 | 1245.67 | 28195.68 |
| ⊟Miami | 32108.38 | 10825.72 | 32465.18 | 9567.18 | 10281.51 | 10001.51 | 105249.48 |
| 1 | 6634.43 | 1394.32 | 7790.34 | 2310.34 | 1376.34 | 1766.34 | 21272.11 |
| 2 | 8324.65 | 3231.8 | 6814.87 | 2524.87 | 3394.21 | 3524.21 | 27814.61 |
| 3 | 8324.65 | 3511.65 | 8883.54 | 2183.54 | 2587.53 | 2307.53 | 27798.44 |
| 4 | 8824.65 | 2687.95 | 8976.43 | 2548.43 | 2923.43 | 2403.43 | 28364.32 |
| ⊟New York | 15057.69 | 10266.97 | 29929.87 | 19171.87 | 8969.93 | 16919.93 | 100316.26 |
| 1 | 4921.45 | 1940.57 | 6369.43 | 2119.43 | 1418.43 | 1758.43 | 18527.74 |
| 2 | 3319.92 | 2374.32 | 7628.78 | 3880.78 | 2183.98 | 5413.98 | 24801.76 |
| 3 | 4176.89 | 3216.65 | 8198.9 | 6728.9 | 2577.98 | 4317.98 | 29217.3 |
| 4 | 2639.43 | 2735.43 | 7732.76 | 6442.76 | 2789.54 | 5429.54 | 27769.46 |
| Grand Total | 56795.08 | 39742.11 | 96231.54 | 36767.54 | 39431.64 | 33711.64 | 302679.55 |

## Changing the PivotTable layout

The default layout for PivotTables is the compact form; the row labels are displayed in a single column, and the second-level field items (such as the quarters in the U.S. Sales example) are indented for readability. You can change the layout of your PivotTable by clicking the PivotTable Tools Design tab, clicking the Report Layout button in the Layout group, then clicking either Show in Outline Form or Show in Tabular Form. The tabular form and the outline form show each row label in its own column. The outline form places subtotals at the top of every column. The tabular and outline layouts take up more space on a worksheet than the compact layout.

# Changing a PivotTable's Summary Function and Design

A PivotTable's **summary function** controls what calculation Excel uses to summarize the table data. Unless you specify otherwise, Excel applies the SUM function to numeric data and the COUNT function to data fields containing text. However, you can easily change the SUM function to a different summary function.  Kate wants you to calculate the average sales for the U.S. branches using the AVERAGE function, and to improve the appearance of the PivotTable for her presentation.

## STEPS

**QUICK TIP**

You can also change the summary function by clicking the Field Settings button in the Active Field group on the PivotTable Tools Options tab.

1. **Right-click cell A3, then point to Summarize Values By in the shortcut menu**

   The menu shows that the Sum function is selected by default, as shown in Figure L-6.

2. **Click Average**

   The data area of the PivotTable shows the average sales for each product by branch and quarter, and cell A3 now contains "Average of Sales". You want to view the PivotTable data without the subtotals.

3. **Click the PivotTable Tools Design tab, click the Subtotals button in the Layout group, then click Do Not Show Subtotals**

   After reviewing the data, you decide that it would be more useful to sum the sales information than to average it. You also want to redisplay the subtotals.

4. **Right-click cell A3, point to Summarize Values By in the shortcut menu, then click Sum**

   Excel recalculates the PivotTable—in this case, summing the sales data instead of averaging it.

**QUICK TIP**

You can control the display of grand totals by clicking the PivotTable Tools Design tab, and clicking the Grand Totals button in the Layout group.

5. **Click the Subtotals button in the Layout group, then click Show all Subtotals at Top of Group**

   In the same way that tables have styles available to quickly format them, PivotTables have a gallery of styles to choose from. You decide to add a PivotTable style to the PivotTable to improve its appearance.

6. **Click the More button ⊡ in the PivotTable Styles gallery, then click Pivot Style Light 13**

   To further improve the appearance of the PivotTable, you will remove the unnecessary headers of "Column Labels" and "Row Labels".

7. **Click the PivotTable Tools Options tab, then click the Field Headers button in the Show group**

   The data would be more readable if it were in currency format.

**TROUBLE**

If you don't see the Active Field group, click the Active Field button to display the Field Settings button.

8. **Click any sales value in the PivotTable, click the Field Settings button in the Active Field group, click Number Format in the Value Field Settings dialog box, select Currency in the Category list, make sure Decimal places is 2 and Symbol is $, click OK, then click OK again**

   You decide to give the PivotTable sheet a more descriptive name. When you name a PivotTable sheet, it is best to avoid using spaces in the name. If a PivotTable name contains a space, you must put single quotes around the name if you refer to it in a function.

9. **Rename Sheet1 PivotTable, add your name to the worksheet footer, save the workbook, then preview the worksheet**

   The PivotTable is easier to read now that it is formatted as shown in Figure L-7.

**FIGURE L-6:** Shortcut menu showing Sum function selected

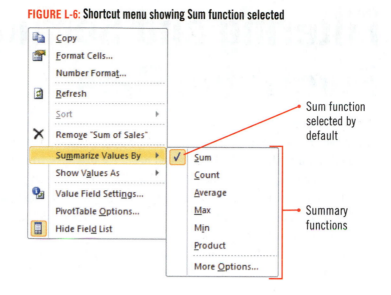

Sum function selected by default

Summary functions

**FIGURE L-7:** Formatted PivotTable

| | A | B | C | D | E | F | G | H | I |
|---|---|---|---|---|---|---|---|---|---|
| 1 | | | | | | | | | |
| 2 | | | | | | | | | |
| 3 | Sum of Sales | | | | | | | | |
| 4 | | 110 | 240 | 340 | 510 | 640 | 780 | Grand Total | |
| 5 | ⊟Chicago | $9,629.01 | $18,649.42 | $33,836.49 | $8,028.49 | $20,180.20 | $6,790.20 | $97,113.81 | |
| 6 | 1 | $980.65 | $2,300.56 | $8,995.43 | $999.43 | $1,289.65 | $999.65 | $15,565.37 | |
| 7 | 2 | $2,634.69 | $5,767.76 | $7,976.43 | $1,954.43 | $6,434.56 | $2,334.56 | $27,102.43 | |
| 8 | 3 | $2,400.74 | $4,883.65 | $8,232.65 | $2,412.65 | $6,110.32 | $2,210.32 | $26,250.33 | |
| 9 | 4 | $3,612.93 | $5,697.45 | $8,631.98 | $2,661.98 | $6,345.67 | $1,245.67 | $28,195.68 | |
| 10 | ⊟Miami | $32,108.38 | $10,825.72 | $32,465.18 | $9,567.18 | $10,281.51 | $10,001.51 | $105,249.48 | |
| 11 | 1 | $6,634.43 | $1,394.32 | $7,790.34 | $2,310.34 | $1,376.34 | $1,766.34 | $21,272.11 | |
| 12 | 2 | $8,324.65 | $3,231.80 | $6,814.87 | $2,524.87 | $3,394.21 | $3,524.21 | $27,814.61 | |
| 13 | 3 | $8,324.65 | $3,511.65 | $8,883.54 | $2,183.54 | $2,587.53 | $2,307.53 | $27,798.44 | |
| 14 | 4 | $8,824.65 | $2,687.95 | $8,976.43 | $2,548.43 | $2,923.43 | $2,403.43 | $28,364.32 | |
| 15 | ⊟New York | $15,057.69 | $10,266.97 | $29,929.87 | $19,171.87 | $8,969.93 | $16,919.93 | $100,316.26 | |
| 16 | 1 | $4,921.45 | $1,940.57 | $6,369.43 | $2,119.43 | $1,418.43 | $1,758.43 | $18,527.74 | |
| 17 | 2 | $3,319.92 | $2,374.32 | $7,628.78 | $3,880.78 | $2,183.98 | $5,413.98 | $24,801.76 | |
| 18 | 3 | $4,176.89 | $3,216.65 | $8,198.90 | $6,728.90 | $2,577.98 | $4,317.98 | $29,217.30 | |
| 19 | 4 | $2,639.43 | $2,735.43 | $7,732.76 | $6,442.76 | $2,789.54 | $5,429.54 | $27,769.46 | |
| 20 | Grand Total | $56,795.08 | $39,742.11 | $96,231.54 | $36,767.54 | $39,431.64 | $33,711.64 | $302,679.55 | |
| 21 | | | | | | | | | |
| 22 | | | | | | | | | |

## Using the Show buttons

To display and hide PivotTable elements, you can use the buttons in the Show group on the PivotTable Tools Options tab. For example, the Field List button will hide or display the PivotTable Field List pane. The +/– Buttons button will hide or display the Expand and Collapse Outline buttons, and the Field Headers button will hide or display the Row and Column Label headers on the PivotTable.

# Filtering and Sorting PivotTable Data

When you worked with Excel tables, you used filters to hide and display table data. You can restrict the display of PivotTable data using a **Slicer**, graphic object with a set of buttons that allow you to easily filter your PivotTable data to show only the data you need. For example, you can use the buttons in a slicer to show only data about a specific product in your PivotTable. You can also filter a PivotTable using a **report filter**, which lets you filter PivotTable data using a list arrow to show data based on one or more field values. For example, if you add a field with monthly data to the Report Filter area, you can filter a PivotTable so that only data representing the January sales appears in the PivotTable. In addition to filtering PivotTable data, you can also sort PivotTable data to organize it in ascending or descending order. Kate wants you to sort the PivotTable so she can see sales data about specific products for specific quarters.

**STEPS**

1.  **Click cell H5, click the PivotTable Tools Options tab if necessary, then click the Sort button in the Sort & Filter group**
    The Sort By Value dialog box opens. As you select options in the dialog box, the Summary information at the bottom of the dialog box changes to describe the sort results using your field names.

2.  **Click the Largest to Smallest option button to select it in the Sort options section, make sure the Top to Bottom option button is selected in the Sort direction section, review the sort description in the Summary section of the dialog box, then click OK**
    The branches are arranged in the PivotTable in decreasing order of total sales from top to bottom. You want to easily display the sales for specific product IDs.

    > **QUICK TIP**
    > You can select multiple values on a slicer by pressing [Ctrl] while clicking buttons on a Slicer.

3.  **Click any cell in the PivotTable, click the Insert Slicer button in the Sort & Filter group, click the Product ID check box in the Insert Slicers dialog box to select it, then click OK**
    A slicer appears containing a column of buttons representing the Product ID numbers as shown in Figure L-8. Slicers can be formatted using different styles and formatting options. See Table L-1 for a summary of slicer formatting options. You decide to filter the data so it displays the data for only the Product ID 510.

4.  **Click the 510 button in the Slicer shape**
    The PivotTable filters the sales data to display the Product ID 510 data only, as shown in Figure L-9. In the Slicer shape, the Clear Filter symbol changes, indicating the PivotTable is filtered to display the selected field. You decide to clear the filter and remove the Slicer shape from the PivotTable worksheet.

    > **QUICK TIP**
    > You can also click the Hide All button in the Selection and Visibility pane to remove Slicer shapes.

5.  **Click the Clear Filter button in the Slicer shape, click the Selection Pane button in the Arrange group of the Slicer Tools Options tab, click the Visibility button in the Selection and Visibility pane, then close the Selection and Visibility pane**
    You want to display the PivotTable data by quarter using a Report Filter.

    > **TROUBLE**
    > If the PivotTable Field List is not visible, click the PivotTable Tools Options tab, and click the Field List button in the Show group.

6.  **In the PivotTable Field List, click the Quarter field list arrow in the Row Labels area, then select Move to Report Filter**
    The Quarter field moves up to cell A1, and a list arrow and the word "(All)" appear in cell B1. The list arrow allows you to filter the data in the PivotTable by Quarter. "(All)" indicates that the PivotTable currently shows data for all quarters. You decide to filter the data so it displays the data for only the fourth quarter.

7.  **In the PivotTable cell B1, click the Quarter list arrow, click 4, then click OK**
    The PivotTable filters the sales data to display the fourth quarter only, as shown in Figure L-10. The Quarter field list arrow changes to a filter symbol. A filter symbol also appears to the right of the Quarter field in the PivotTable Field List pane, indicating that the PivotTable is filtered and summarizes only a portion of the PivotTable data.

8.  **Save the workbook**

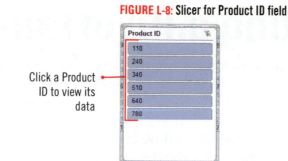

**FIGURE L-8:** Slicer for Product ID field

Click a Product ID to view its data

**FIGURE L-9:** PivotTable filtered by Product ID

Only data for Product ID 510 appears in PivotTable

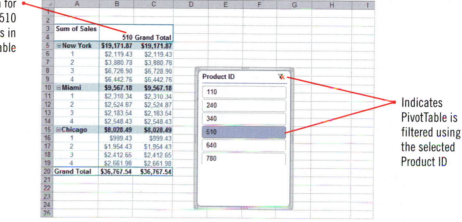

Indicates PivotTable is filtered using the selected Product ID

**FIGURE L-10:** PivotTable filtered by fourth quarter

Fourth quarter sales data

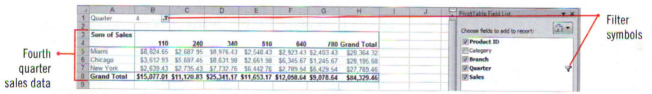

Filter symbols

**TABLE L-1:** Options for formatting slicers

| to | action | group/command/key |
|---|---|---|
| Apply a slicer style | Click Slicer Tools Options tab | Slicer Styles group |
| Change button order | Click Slicer Tools Options tab | Slicer group/Slicer Settings button |
| Change caption name | Click Slicer Tools Options tab | Slicer group/Slicer Caption text box |
| Change slicer size, or columns | Click Slicer Tools Options tab | Buttons group |
| Change slicer position | Right-click slicer | Size and Properties command |
| Delete slicer | Click slicer's edge | [Delete] key |

## Filtering PivotTables using multiple values

You can select multiple values when filtering a PivotTable report using a report filter. After clicking a field's report filter list arrow in the top section of the PivotTable Field List or in cell B1 on the PivotTable itself, click the Select Multiple Items check box at the bottom of the filter selections. This allows you to select multiple values for the filter. For example, selecting 1 and 2 as the report filter in a PivotTable with quarters would display all of the data for the first two quarters. You can also select multiple values for the row and column labels by clicking the Row Label list arrow or the Column Label list arrow in cells A4 and B3 on the PivotTable and selecting the data items that you want to display.

# Updating a PivotTable Report

The data in a PivotTable report looks like typical worksheet data. Because the PivotTable data is linked to a **data source** (the data you used to create the PivotTable), however, the values and results in the PivotTable are read-only values. That means you cannot move or modify a part of a PivotTable by inserting or deleting rows, editing results, or moving cells. To change PivotTable data, you must edit the items directly in the data source, then update, or **refresh**, the PivotTable to reflect the changes.  Kate just learned that sales information for a custom group tour sold in New York during the fourth quarter was never entered into the Sales worksheet. Kate asks you to add information about this tour to the data source and PivotTable. You start by inserting a row for the new information in the Sales worksheet.

## STEPS

1. **Click the Sales sheet tab**

   By inserting the new row in the correct position by branch, you will not need to sort the data again.

**QUICK TIP**

If you want to change the source data range for your PivotTable, click the PivotTable Tools Options tab, then click the Change Data Source button in the Data group.

2. **Right-click the row 51 heading, then click Insert on the shortcut menu**

   A blank row appears as the new row 51, and the data in the old row 51, moves down to row 52. You now have room for the tour data.

3. **Enter the data for the new tour in row 51 using the following information**

   | | |
   |---|---|
   | Product ID | 450 |
   | Category | Tour |
   | Branch | New York |
   | Quarter | 4 |
   | Sales | 3010.04 |

   The PivotTable does not yet reflect the additional data.

4. **Click the PivotTable sheet tab, then verify that the Quarter 4 data appears**

   The fourth quarter list does not currently include the new tour information, and the grand total is $84,329.46. Before you refresh the PivotTable data, you need to make sure that the cell pointer is located within the PivotTable range.

**QUICK TIP**

If you want Excel to refresh your PivotTable report automatically when you open the workbook in which it is contained, click the Options button in the PivotTable group, click the Data tab in the PivotTable Options dialog box, click the Refresh data when opening the file check box, then click OK.

5. **Click anywhere within the PivotTable if necessary, click the PivotTable Tools Options tab, then click the Refresh button in the Data group**

   The PivotTable now contains a column for the new product ID, which includes the new tour information, in column H, and the grand total has increased by the amount of the tour's sales ($3,010.04) to $87,339.50, as shown in Figure L-11.

6. **Save the workbook**

### Grouping PivotTable data

You can group PivotTable data to analyze specific values in a field as a unit. For example, you may want to group sales data for quarters one and two to analyze sales for the first half of the year. To group PivotTable data, you need to first select the rows and columns that you want to group, click the PivotTable Tools Options tab, then click the Group Selection button in the Group group. After you group data you can summarize it by clicking the Field Settings button in the Active Field group, clicking the Custom button in the Field

Settings dialog box, selecting the function that you want to use to summarize the data, then clicking OK. You can click the Collapse Outline button ▬ next to the group name to collapse the group and show the function results. You can click the Expand Outline button ➕ next to the group name to display the rows or columns in the group. To ungroup data, select the Group name in the PivotTable, then click the Ungroup button in the Group group.

FIGURE L-11: Updated PivotTable report

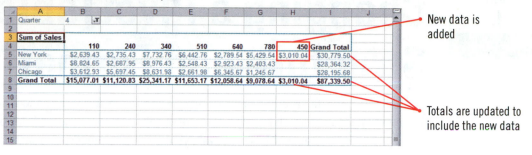

New data is added

Totals are updated to include the new data

FIGURE L-12: Insert Calculated Field dialog box

New field name

Formula to increase sales by 10%

Fields you can use in the formula

**Insert Calculated Field**

Name: Increase Sales

Formula: = Sales*1.1

Fields:
Product ID
Category
Branch
Quarter
Sales

Insert Field

Add
Delete
OK
Close

FIGURE L-13: PivotTable with Calculated Field

New calculated field

| | A | B | C | D | E | F |
|---|---|---|---|---|---|---|
| 1 | Quarter | 4 | | | | |
| 2 | | | | | | |
| 3 | | 110 | | 240 | | 340 |
| 4 | | Sum of Sales | Sum of Increase Sales | Sum of Sales | Sum of Increase Sales | Sum of Sales | Sum of Incr |
| 5 | New York | $2,639.43 | $ 2,903.37 | $2,735.43 | $ 3,008.97 | $7,732.76 | $ |
| 6 | Miami | $8,824.65 | $ 9,707.12 | $2,687.95 | $ 2,956.75 | $8,976.43 | $ |
| 7 | Chicago | $3,612.93 | $ 3,974.22 | $5,697.45 | $ 6,267.20 | $8,631.98 | $ |
| 8 | Grand Total | $15,077.01 | $ 16,584.71 | $11,120.83 | $ 12,232.91 | $25,341.17 | $ |

PivotTable Field List

Choose fields to add to report:
☑ **Product ID**
☐ Category
☑ **Branch**
☑ **Quarter**
☑ Sales
☑ Increase Sales

## Adding a calculated field to a PivotTable

You can use formulas to analyze PivotTable data in a field by adding a calculated field. A calculated field appears in the PivotTable Field List pane and can be manipulated like other PivotTable fields. To add a calculated field, click any cell in the PivotTable, click the PivotTable Tools Options tab, click the Fields, Items, & Sets button in the Calculations group, then click Calculated Field. The Insert Calculated Field dialog box opens. Enter the field name in the Name text box, click in the Formula text box, click a field name in the Fields list that you want to use in the formula, and click Insert Field. Use standard arithmetic operators to enter the formula you want to use. For example Figure L-12 shows a formula to increase Sales data by 10 percent. After entering the formula in the Insert Calculated Field dialog box, click Add, then click OK. The new field with the formula results appears in the PivotTable, and the field is added to the PivotTable Field List as shown in Figure L-13.

Excel 2010

# Changing a PivotTable's Structure and Format

What makes a PivotTable such a powerful analysis tool is the ability to change the way data is organized in the report. You can easily change the structure of a PivotTable by adding fields or by moving fields to new positions in the PivotTable. Kate asks you to include category information in the sales report. She is also interested in viewing the PivotTable in different arrangements to find the best organization of data for her presentation.

## STEPS

1. **Make sure that the PivotTable sheet is active, that the active cell is located anywhere inside the PivotTable, and that the PivotTable Field List is visible**

**QUICK TIP**

You can change the amount an inner row is indented by clicking the Options button in the PivotTable group on the PivotTable Tools Options tab, clicking the Layout & Format tab, then changing the number for the character(s) in the Layout section.

2. **Click the Category check box in the PivotTable Field List**

   Because the category data is nonnumeric, it is added to the Row Labels area. The PivotTable displays the category sales information for each branch. When you have two row labels, the data is organized by the values in the outer field and then by the data in the inner field. The inner field values are indented to make them easy to distinguish from the outer field. You can move fields within an area of a PivotTable by dragging and dropping them to the desired location. When you drag a field, the pointer appears with a PivotTable outline attached to its lower-right corner.

3. **In the diagram section of the PivotTable Field List, locate the Row Labels area, then drag the Category field up and drop it above the Branch field**

   The category field is now the outer or upper field, and the branch field is the inner or lower field. The PivotTable is restructured to display the sales data by the category values and then the branch values within the category field. The subtotals now reflect the sum of the categories, as shown in Figure L-14. You can also move fields to new areas in the PivotTable.

4. **In the diagram area of the PivotTable Field List, drag the Category field from the Row Labels area to the Column Labels area, then drag the Product ID field from the Column Labels area to the Row Labels area below the Branch field**

   The PivotTable now displays the sales data with the category values in the columns and then the product IDs grouped by branches. The product ID values are indented below the branches because the Product ID field is the inner row label.

**QUICK TIP**

As you move fields around in a PivotTable, you can control when the PivotTable structure is updated to reflect your changes. Click the Defer Layout Update check box at the bottom of the PivotTable Field List window. When you are ready to update the PivotTable, click the Update button.

5. **In the diagram area of the PivotTable Field List, drag the Category field from the Column Labels area to the Report Filter area above the Quarter field, then drag the Product ID field from the Row Labels area to the Column Labels area**

   The PivotTable now has two filters. The upper filter, Category, summarizes data using all of the categories. Kate asks you to display the tour sales information for all quarters.

6. **Click the Category list arrow in cell B1 of the PivotTable, click Tour, click OK, click the Quarter filter list arrow, click All, then click OK**

   The PivotTable displays sales totals for the Tour category for all quarters. Kate asks you to provide the sales information for all categories.

7. **Click the Category filter arrow, click All, then click OK**

   The completed PivotTable appears as shown in Figure L-15.

8. **Save the workbook, change the page orientation of the PivotTable sheet to landscape, then preview the PivotTable**

**FIGURE L-14:** PivotTable structured by branches within categories

Category is
outer field

Branch is inner
field and
values are
indented

| | A | B | C | D | E | F | G | H | I | J |
|---|---|---|---|---|---|---|---|---|---|---|
| 1 | Quarter | 4 | | | | | | | | |
| 2 | | | | | | | | | | |
| 3 | **Sum of Sales** | | | | | | | | | |
| 4 | | | 110 | 240 | 340 | 510 | 640 | 780 | 450 | Grand Total |
| 5 | ⊟ **Tour** | | | $25,341.17 | $11,653.17 | | | $3,010.04 | $40,004.38 | |
| 6 | New York | | | $7,732.76 | $6,442.76 | | | $3,010.04 | $17,185.56 | |
| 7 | Miami | | | $8,976.43 | $2,548.43 | | | | $11,524.86 | |
| 8 | Chicago | | | $8,631.98 | $2,661.98 | | | | $11,293.96 | |
| 9 | ⊟ **Travel Accessory** | | $11,120.83 | | | | $9,078.64 | | $20,199.47 | |
| 10 | New York | | $2,735.43 | | | | $5,429.54 | | $8,164.97 | |
| 11 | Chicago | | $5,697.45 | | | | $1,245.67 | | $6,943.12 | |
| 12 | Miami | | $2,687.95 | | | | $2,403.43 | | $5,091.38 | |
| 13 | ⊟ **Travel Insurance** | $15,077.01 | | | | $12,058.64 | | | $27,135.65 | |
| 14 | Miami | $8,824.65 | | | | $2,923.43 | | | $11,748.08 | |
| 15 | Chicago | $3,612.93 | | | | $6,345.67 | | | $9,958.60 | |
| 16 | New York | $2,639.43 | | | | $2,789.54 | | | $5,428.97 | |
| 17 | **Grand Total** | $15,077.01 | $11,120.83 | $25,341.17 | $11,653.17 | $12,058.64 | $9,078.64 | $3,010.04 | $87,339.50 | |
| 18 | | | | | | | | | | |
| 19 | | | | | | | | | | |
| 20 | | | | | | | | | | |

**FIGURE L-15:** Completed PivotTable report

| | A | B | C | D | E | F | G | H | I |
|---|---|---|---|---|---|---|---|---|---|
| 1 | Category | (All) | | | | | | | |
| 2 | Quarter | (All) | | | | | | | |
| 3 | | | | | | | | | |
| 4 | **Sum of Sales** | | | | | | | | |
| 5 | | 110 | 240 | 340 | 510 | 640 | 780 | 450 | Grand Total |
| 6 | Miami | $32,108.38 | $10,825.72 | $32,465.18 | $9,567.18 | $10,281.51 | $10,001.51 | | $105,249.48 |
| 7 | New York | $15,057.69 | $10,266.97 | $29,929.87 | $19,171.87 | $8,969.93 | $16,919.93 | $3,010.04 | $103,326.30 |
| 8 | Chicago | $9,629.01 | $18,649.42 | $33,836.49 | $8,028.49 | $20,180.20 | $6,790.20 | | $97,113.81 |
| 9 | **Grand Total** | $56,795.08 | $39,742.11 | $96,231.54 | $36,767.54 | $39,431.64 | $33,711.64 | $3,010.04 | $305,689.59 |
| 10 | | | | | | | | | |

## Adding conditional formatting to a PivotTable

You can add conditional formatting to a PivotTable to make it easier to compare the data values. The conditional formatting is applied to cells in a PivotTable the same way as it is to non-PivotTable data. The conditional formatting rules follow the PivotTable cells when you move fields to different areas of the PivotTable. Figure L-16 shows a PivotTable that uses data bars to visually display the sales data.

**FIGURE L-16:** PivotTable with Conditional Formatting

| 5 | | 110 | 240 | 340 | 510 | 640 | 780 | 450 |
|---|---|---|---|---|---|---|---|---|
| 6 | **Miami** | $32,108.38 | $10,825.72 | $32,465.18 | $9,567.18 | $10,281.51 | $10,001.51 | |
| 7 | **New York** | $15,057.69 | $10,266.97 | $29,929.87 | $19,171.87 | $8,969.93 | $16,919.93 | $3,010.04 |
| 8 | **Chicago** | $9,629.01 | $18,649.42 | $33,836.49 | $8,028.49 | $20,180.20 | $6,790.20 | |
| 9 | **Grand Total** | $56,795.08 | $39,742.11 | $96,231.54 | $36,767.54 | $39,431.64 | $33,711.64 | $3,010.04 |
| 10 | | | | | | | | |

Excel 2010

# Creating a PivotChart Report

A **PivotChart report** is a chart that you create from data or from a PivotTable report. Table L-2 describes how the elements in a PivotTable report correspond to the elements in a PivotChart report. When you create a PivotChart directly from data, Excel automatically creates a corresponding PivotTable report. If you change a PivotChart report by filtering or sorting the charted elements, Excel updates the corresponding PivotTable report to show the new data values. You can move the fields of a PivotChart using the PivotTable Field List window; the new layout will be reflected in the PivotTable.  Kate wants you to chart the fourth quarter tour sales and the yearly tour sales average for her presentation. You create the PivotChart report from the PivotTable data.

## STEPS

1. **Click the Category list arrow in cell B1, click Tour, click OK, click the Quarter list arrow, click 4, then click OK**

   The fourth quarter tour sales information appears in the PivotTable. You want to create the PivotChart from the PivotTable information you have displayed.

2. **Click any cell in the PivotTable, click the PivotTable Tools Options tab, then click the PivotChart button in the Tools group**

   The Insert Chart dialog box opens and shows a gallery of chart types.

3. **Click the Clustered Column chart if necessary, then click OK**

   The PivotChart appears on the worksheet as shown in Figure L-17. The chart has Field buttons that enable you to filter and sort a PivotChart in the same way that you do a PivotTable. It will be easier to view the PivotChart if it is on its own sheet.

   > **QUICK TIP**
   > You can sort and filter the axis and legend fields by clicking their field button list arrows on the PivotChart and selecting a sort or filter option.

4. **Click the Move Chart button in the Location group, click the New sheet option button, type PivotChart in the text box, click OK**

   The chart represents the fourth quarter tour sales. Kate asks you to change the chart to show the average sales for all quarters.

5. **Click the Quarter field button at the top of the PivotChart, click All, then click OK**

   The chart now represents the sum of tour sales for the year as shown in Figure L-18. You can change a PivotChart's summary function to display averages instead of totals.

   > **TROUBLE**
   > If the PivotTable Field List is not visible, click the PivotChart Tools Analyze tab, then click the Field List button to display it.

6. **Click the Sum of Sales list arrow in the Values area of the PivotTable Field List, click Value Field Settings, click Average on the Summarize Values by tab, then click OK**

   The PivotChart report recalculates to display averages. The chart would be easier to understand if it had a title.

7. **Click the PivotChart Tools Layout tab, click the Chart Title button in the Labels group, click Above Chart, type Average Tour Sales, press [Enter], then drag the chart title border to center the title over the columns if necessary**

   You are finished filtering the chart data and decide to remove the field buttons.

   > **TROUBLE**
   > If you click the Field Buttons list arrow then you need to click Hide All to remove the filter buttons.

8. **Click the PivotChart Tools Analyze tab, then click the Field Buttons button in the Show/Hide group**

9. **Enter your name in the PivotChart sheet footer, save the workbook, then preview the PivotChart report**

   The final PivotChart report displaying the average tour sales for the year is shown in Figure L-19.

**FIGURE L-17:** PivotChart with fourth quarter tour sales

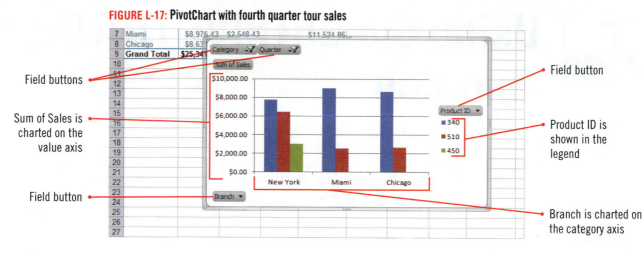

Field buttons

Sum of Sales is charted on the value axis

Field button

Field button

Product ID is shown in the legend

Branch is charted on the category axis

**FIGURE L-18:** PivotChart displaying tour sales for the year

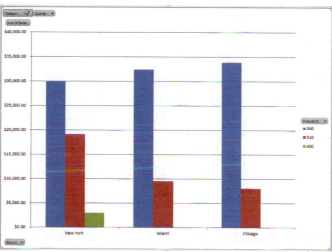

**FIGURE L-19:** Completed PivotChart report

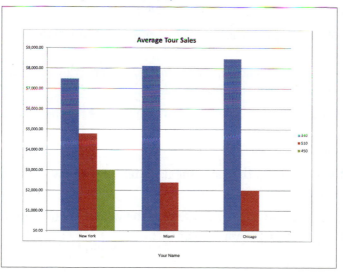

**TABLE L-2:** PivotTable and PivotChart elements

| PivotTable items | PivotChart items |
| --- | --- |
| Row labels | Axis fields (categories) |
| Column labels | Legend fields (series) |
| Report filters | Report filters |

# Using the GETPIVOTDATA Function

Because you can rearrange a PivotTable so easily, you can't use an ordinary cell reference when you want to reference a PivotTable cell in another worksheet. The reason is that if you change the way data is displayed in a PivotTable, the data moves, rendering an ordinary cell reference incorrect. Instead, to retrieve summary data from a PivotTable, you need to use the Excel GETPIVOTDATA function. See Figure L-20 for the GETPIVOTDATA function format.  Kate wants to include the yearly sales total for the Chicago branch in the Sales sheet. She asks you to retrieve this information from the PivotTable and place it in the Sales sheet. You use the GETPIVOTDATA function to retrieve this information.

## STEPS

1. **Click the PivotTable sheet tab**

   The sales figures in the PivotTable are average values for tours. You decide to show sales information for all categories and change the summary information back to Sum.

2. **Click the Category filter arrow in cell B1, click All, then click OK**

   The PivotChart report displays sales information for all categories.

3. **Right-click cell A4 on the PivotTable, point to Summarize Values By on the shortcut menu, then click Sum**

   The PivotChart report recalculates to display sales totals. Next, you want to include the total for sales for the Chicago branch in the Sales sheet by retrieving it from the PivotTable.

4. **Click the Sales sheet tab, click cell G1, type Total Chicago Sales:, click the Enter button ✓ on the formula bar, click the Home tab, click the Align Text Right button ≡ in the Alignment group, click the Bold button B in the Font group, then adjust the width of column G to display the label in cell G1**

   You want the GETPIVOTDATA function to retrieve the total Chicago sales from the PivotTable. Cell I8 on the PivotTable contains the data you want to return to the Sales sheet.

5. **Click cell G2, type =, click the PivotTable sheet tab, click cell I8 on the PivotTable, then click ✓**

   The GETPIVOTDATA function, along with its arguments, is inserted into cell G2 of the Sales sheet, as shown in Figure L-21. You want to format the sales total.

6. **Click the Accounting Number Format button $ in the Number group**

   The current sales total for the Chicago branch is $97,113.81. This is the same value displayed in cell I8 of the PivotTable.

7. **Enter your name in the Sales sheet footer, save the workbook, then preview the first page of the Sales worksheet**

8. **Close the file, exit Excel, then submit the workbook to your instructor**

   The Sales worksheet is shown in Figure L-22.

**FIGURE L-20:** Format of GETPIVOTDATA function

=GETPIVOTDATA("Sales",PivotTable!$A$4,"Branch","Chicago")

Field from where data is extracted

PivotTable name and cell in the report that contains the data you want to retrieve

Field and value pair that describe the data you want to retrieve

**FIGURE L-21:** GETPIVOTDATA function in the Sales sheet

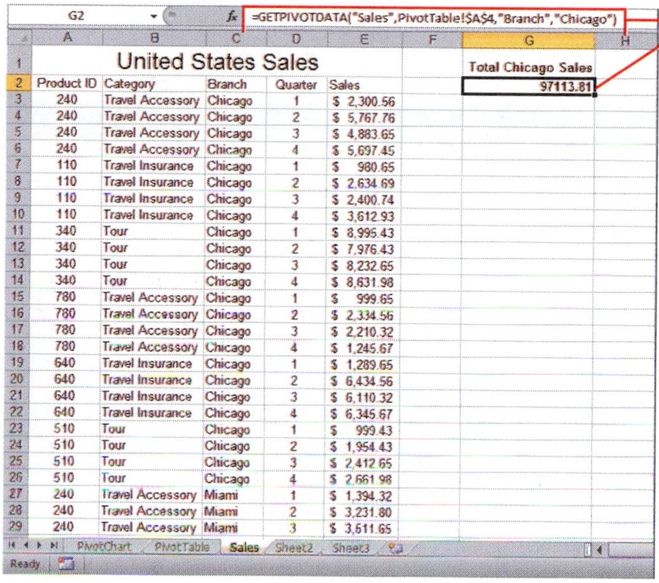

Function is entered into the formula bar, and the result is placed in the cell

**FIGURE L-22:** Completed Sales worksheet showing total Chicago sales

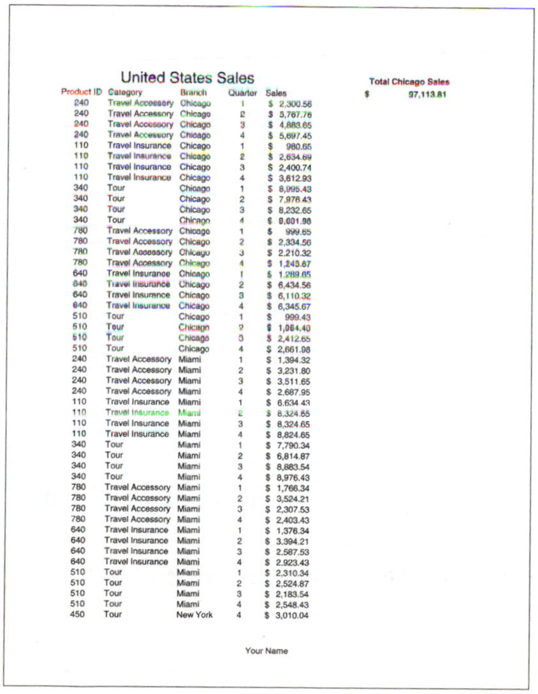

Excel 2010

## Working with PivotTable versions

PivotTables created using Excel 2010 have a version of 12, which is the same version used in Excel 2007 PivotTables. PivotTables created using Excel 2002 and Excel 2003 have a version of 10 which has fewer PivotTable features. If you are working in Compatibility Mode in Excel 2010 by saving a workbook in an earlier Excel format, any PivotTable that you create will have a version of 10, but if you save the PivotTable file as an .xlsx file and reopen it, the PivotTable will be upgraded to version 12 when it is refreshed.

# Practice

For current SAM information, including versions and content details, visit SAM Central (http://www.cengage.com/samcentral). If you have a SAM user profile, you may have access to hands-on instruction, practice, and assessment of the skills covered in this unit. Since various versions of SAM are supported throughout the life of this text, check with your instructor for the correct instructions and URL/Web site for accessing assignments.

## Concepts Review

**FIGURE L-23**

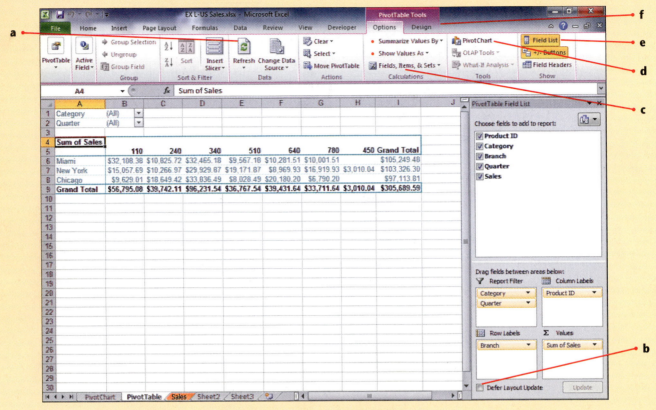

1. Which element do you click to create a chart based on the data in a PivotTable?
2. Which element do you click to create a calculated field in a PivotTable?
3. Which element do you click to control when PivotTable changes will occur?
4. Which element do you click to display a gallery of PivotTable Styles?
5. Which element do you click to update a PivotTable?
6. Which element do you click to display or hide the PivotTable Field List pane?

## Match each term with the statement that best describes it.

7. Slicer
8. PivotTable Row Label
9. Summary function
10. Compact form
11. GETPIVOTDATA function

a. Retrieves information from a PivotTable
b. Default layout for a PivotTable
c. PivotTable filtering tool
d. PivotChart axis field
e. Determines if data is summed or averaged

**Select the best answer from the list of choices.**

12. When a numeric field is added to a PivotTable, it is placed in the _____ area.
    a. Row Labels
    b. Values
    c. Column Labels
    d. Report Filter

13. Which PivotTable report area allows you to display only certain data using a list arrow?
    a. Values
    b. Column Labels
    c. Row Labels
    d. Report Filter

14. To make changes to PivotTable data, you must:
    a. Drag a column header to the column area.
    b. Create a page field.
    c. Edit cells in the source list, and then refresh the PivotTable.
    d. Edit cells in the PivotTable, then refresh the source list.

15. When a nonnumeric field is added to a PivotTable, it is placed in the _____ area.
    a. Values
    b. Report Filter
    c. Column Labels
    d. Row Labels

16. The default summary function for data fields containing numbers in an Excel PivotTable is:
    a. Count.
    b. Max.
    c. Sum.
    d. Average.

# Skills Review

1. **Plan and design a PivotTable report.**
   a. Start Excel, open the file titled EX L-2.xlsx from the drive and folder where you store your Data Files, then save it as **EX L-Product Sales**.
   b. Review the fields and data values in the worksheet.
   c. Verify that the worksheet data contains repeated values in one or more fields.
   d. Verify that there are not any blank rows or columns in the range A1:E25.
   e. Verify that the worksheet data contains a field that can be summed in a PivotTable.

2. **Create a PivotTable report.**
   a. Create a PivotTable report on a new worksheet using the Sales worksheet data in the range A1:E25.
   b. Add the Product ID field in the PivotTable Field List pane to the Column Labels area.
   c. Add the Sales field in the PivotTable Field List pane to the Values Area.
   d. Add the Store field in the PivotTable Field List pane to the Row Labels area.
   e. Add the Sales Rep field in the PivotTable Field List pane to the Row Labels area below the Store field.

3. **Change a PivotTable's summary function and design.**
   a. Change the PivotTable summary function to Average.
   b. Rename the new sheet **Sales PivotTable**.
   c. Change the PivotTable Style to Pivot Style Medium 13. Format the sales values in the PivotTable as Currency with a $ symbol and two decimal places.
   d. Enter your name in the center section of the PivotTable report footer, then save the workbook.
   e. Change the Summary function back to Sum. Remove the headers "Row Labels" and "Column Labels."

4. **Filter and sort PivotTable data.**
   a. Sort the stores in ascending order by total sales.
   b. Use a Slicer to filter the PivotTable to display sales for only the Portland store.
   c. Clear the filter and then display sales for only the DC store.
   d. Clear the filter and then display the Selection and Visibility pane. Turn off the visibility of the Store Slicer shape, and close the Selection and Visibility pane.
   e. Add the Region field to the Report Filter area in the PivotTable Field List pane. Use the Report Filter to display sales for only the East region. Display sales for all regions.
   f. Save the workbook.

## Skills Review (continued)

**5. Update a PivotTable report.**

  **a.** With the Sales PivotTable sheet active, note the NY total for Product ID 300.

  **b.** Activate the Sales sheet, and change K. Lyons's sales of Product ID 300 in cell D7 to **$9,000**.

  **c.** Refresh the PivotTable so it reflects the new sales figure.

  **d.** Verify the NY total for Product ID 300 increased by $157.

  **e.** Save the workbook.

**6. Change a PivotTable's structure and format.**

  **a.** In the PivotTable Field List, drag the Product ID field from the Column Labels area to the Row Labels area.

  **b.** Drag the Sales Rep field from the Row Labels area to the Column Labels area.

  **c.** Drag the Store field from the Row Labels area to the Report Filter area.

  **d.** Drag the Product ID field back to the Column Labels area.

  **e.** Drag the Store field back to the Row Labels area.

  **f.** Remove the Sales Rep field from the PivotTable.

  **g.** Compare your completed PivotTable to Figure L-24, save the workbook.

**7. Create a PivotChart report.**

  **a.** Use the existing PivotTable data to create a Clustered Column PivotChart report.

  **b.** Move the PivotChart to a new worksheet, and name the sheet **PivotChart**.

  **c.** Add the title **Total Sales** above the chart.

  **d.** Filter the chart to display only sales data for Product ID 300. Display the sales data for all Product IDs. Hide all of the Field Buttons.

  **e.** Add your name to the center section of the PivotChart sheet footer. Compare your PivotChart to Figure L-25, save the workbook.

**8. Use the GETPIVOTDATA function.**

  **a.** In cell D27 of the Sales sheet type = , click the Sales PivotTable sheet, click the cell that contains the grand total for LA, then press [Enter].

  **b.** Review the GETPIVOTDATA function that you entered in cell D27.

  **c.** Enter your name in the Sales sheet footer, compare your Sales sheet to Figure L-26, save the workbook, then preview the sales worksheet.

  **d.** Close the workbook and exit Excel.

  **e.** Submit the workbook to your instructor.

**FIGURE L-24**

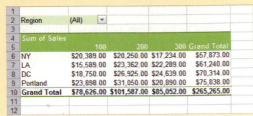

| Sum of Sales | 100 | 200 | 300 | Grand Total |
|---|---|---|---|---|
| NY | $20,389.00 | $20,250.00 | $17,234.00 | $57,873.00 |
| LA | $15,589.00 | $23,362.00 | $22,289.00 | $61,240.00 |
| DC | $18,750.00 | $26,925.00 | $24,639.00 | $70,314.00 |
| Portland | $23,898.00 | $31,050.00 | $20,890.00 | $75,838.00 |
| Grand Total | $78,626.00 | $101,587.00 | $85,052.00 | $265,265.00 |

Region (All)

**FIGURE L-25**

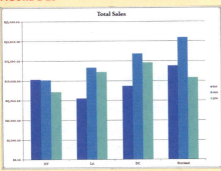

Total Sales

**FIGURE L-26**

| | Product ID | Region | Store | Sales | Sales Rep |
|---|---|---|---|---|---|
| 2 | 100 | West | LA | $10,934 | H. Jeung |
| 3 | 200 | West | LA | $16,512 | H. Jeung |
| 4 | 300 | West | LA | $18,511 | H. Jeung |
| 5 | 100 | East | NY | $11,989 | K. Lyons |
| 6 | 200 | East | NY | $9,750 | K. Lyons |
| 7 | 300 | East | NY | $9,000 | K. Lyons |
| 8 | 100 | West | Portland | $13,998 | M. Holak |
| 9 | 200 | West | Portland | $20,550 | M. Holak |
| 10 | 300 | West | Portland | $15,690 | M. Holak |
| 11 | 100 | East | DC | $10,850 | J. Forum |
| 12 | 200 | East | DC | $16,225 | J. Forum |
| 13 | 300 | East | DC | $19,331 | J. Forum |
| 14 | 100 | West | LA | $4,655 | D. Janes |
| 15 | 200 | West | LA | $6,850 | D. Janes |
| 16 | 300 | West | LA | $3,778 | D. Janes |
| 17 | 100 | East | NY | $8,400 | L. Sorrento |
| 18 | 200 | East | NY | $10,500 | L. Sorrento |
| 19 | 300 | East | NY | $8,234 | L. Sorrento |
| 20 | 100 | West | Portland | $9,900 | T. Leni |
| 21 | 200 | West | Portland | $10,500 | T. Leni |
| 22 | 300 | West | Portland | $5,200 | T. Leni |
| 23 | 100 | East | DC | $7,900 | M. Gregoire |
| 24 | 200 | East | DC | $10,700 | M. Gregoire |
| 25 | 300 | East | DC | $5,308 | M. Gregoire |
| 26 | | | | | |
| 27 | | | LA Sales for July: | $61,240 | |
| 28 | | | | | |

# Independent Challenge 1

You are the accountant for the Service Department of an automobile dealer. The Service Department employs three technicians that service cars purchased at the dealership. Until recently, the owner had been tracking the technicians' hours manually in a log. You have created an Excel worksheet to track the following basic information: service date, technician name, job #, job category, hours, and warranty information. The owner has asked you to analyze the billing data to provide information about the number of hours being spent on the various job categories. He also wants to find out how much of the technicians' work is covered by warranties. You will create a PivotTable that sums the hours by category and technician. Once the table is completed, you will create a column chart representing the billing information.

  **a.** Start Excel, open the file titled EX L-3.xlsx from the drive and folder where you store your Data Files, then save it as **EX L-Service**.

# Independent Challenge 1 (continued)

b. Create a PivotTable on a separate worksheet that sums hours by technician and category. Use Figure L-27 as a guide.

c. Name the new sheet **PivotTable**, and apply the Pivot Style Medium 14.

d. Add a Slicer to filter the PivotTable using the category data. Display only service data for the category Level 1. Remove the filter, and remove the Category Slicer visibility.

e. Add the Warranty field to the Report Filter area of the PivotTable. Display only the PivotTable data for jobs covered by warranties.

f. Remove the headers of "Column Labels" and "Row Labels" from the PivotTable.

g. Create a clustered column PivotChart that shows the warranty hours. Move the PivotChart to a new sheet named **PivotChart**.

h. Add the title **Warranty Hours** above the chart.

i. Change the PivotChart filter to display hours where the work was not covered by a warranty. Edit the chart title to read **Nonwarranty Hours**.

j. Hide the field buttons on the chart.

k. Add your name to the center section of the PivotTable and PivotChart footers, then save the workbook. Preview the PivotTable and the PivotChart.

l. Close the workbook and exit Excel. Submit the workbook to your instructor.

**FIGURE L-27**

# Independent Challenge 2

You are the owner of an office supply store called Office Solutions based in Miami. You sell products at the store as well as online. You also take orders by phone from your catalog customers. You have been using Excel to maintain a sales summary for the second quarter sales of the different types of products sold by the company. You want to create a PivotTable to analyze and graph the sales in each product category by month and type of order.

a. Start Excel, open the file titled EX L-4.xlsx from the drive and folder where you store your Data Files, then save it as **EX L-Office Solutions**.

b. Create a PivotTable on a new worksheet named **PivotTable** that sums the sales amount for each category across the rows and each type of sale down the columns. Add the month field as an inner row label. Use Figure L-28 as a guide.

c. Move the month field to the Report Filter location. Display the sum of sales data for the month of April.

d. Turn off the grand totals for the columns. (*Hint*: Use the Grand Totals button on the Design tab and choose On for Rows Only.)

e. Change the summary function in the PivotTable to Average.

f. Format the sales values using the Currency format with two decimal places and the $ symbol.

g. On the Sales worksheet, change the April online paper sales in cell D3 to $28,221. Update the PivotTable to reflect this increase in sales.

h. Sort the average sales of categories from smallest to largest using the grand total of sales.

i. Create a stacked column PivotChart report for the average April sales data for all three types of sales.

j. Change the PivotChart to display the June sales data.

k. Move the PivotChart to a new sheet, and name the chart sheet **PivotChart**.

l. Add the title **Average June Sales** above your chart.

**FIGURE L-28**

| Drag fields between areas below: | |
| --- | --- |
| ▼ Report Filter | ▦ Column Labels |
| | Type ▼ |
| ▦ Row Labels | Σ Values |
| Category ▼ | Sum of Sale ▼ |
| Month ▼ | |
| ☐ Defer Layout Update | Update |

# Independent Challenge 2 (continued)

## Advanced Challenge Exercise

- On the PivotTable, move the Month field from the Report Filter to the Row Label area of the PivotTable below the Category field. Add a Slicer to filter the PivotTable by month.
- Use the Slicer to display the April and May sales data. (*Hint*: You can select multiple fields in the Slicer shape by holding [Ctrl] and clicking the field names.)
- Format the Slicer shape using the Slicer Style Dark 1 in the Slicer Styles gallery on the Slicer Tools Options tab.
- Remove the Row Labels and Column Labels headers in cells A4 and B3.
- Check the PivotChart to be sure that the new data is displayed.
- Change the chart title to describe the charted sales.

**m.** Add your name to the center section of the PivotTable and PivotChart worksheet footers, save the workbook, then preview the PivotTable and the PivotChart.

**n.** Close the workbook and exit Excel. Submit the workbook to your instructor.

# Independent Challenge 3

You are the North American sales manager for a drug store supply company with sales offices in the United States and Canada. You use Excel to keep track of the staff in the San Francisco, Los Angeles, Chicago, St. Louis, Toronto, Montreal, Vancouver, Boston, and New York offices. Management asks you to provide a summary table showing information on your sales staff, including their locations, status, and titles. You will create a PivotTable and PivotChart summarizing this information.

**a.** Start Excel, open the file titled EX L-5.xlsx from the drive and folder where you store your Data Files, then save it as **EX L-Sales Employees**.

**b.** On a new worksheet, create a PivotTable that shows the number of employees in each city, with the names of the cities listed across the columns, the titles listed down the rows, and the status indented below the titles. (*Hint*: Remember that the default summary function for cells containing text is Count.) Use Figure L-29 as a guide. Rename the new sheet **PivotTable**.

**FIGURE L-29**

| Count of Last Name | Column Labels | | | | | | | | | |
|---|---|---|---|---|---|---|---|---|---|---|
| Row Labels | Boston | Chicago | Los Angeles | Montreal | New York | San Francisco | St. Louis | Toronto | Vancouver | Grand Total |
| ⊟ Sales Manager | 1 | 2 | 1 | 1 | 2 | 3 | 2 | 3 | 1 | 16 |
|   Full-time | | 2 | 1 | 1 | 2 | 2 | 1 | 2 | 1 | 12 |
|   Part-time | 1 | | | | | 1 | 1 | 1 | | 4 |
| ⊟ Sales Representative | 4 | 2 | 5 | 4 | 7 | 7 | 2 | 3 | 3 | 37 |
|   Full-time | 3 | 1 | 4 | 3 | 5 | 5 | 1 | 2 | 2 | 26 |
|   Part-time | 1 | 1 | 1 | 1 | 2 | 2 | 1 | 1 | 1 | 11 |
| Grand Total | 5 | 4 | 6 | 5 | 9 | 10 | 4 | 6 | 4 | 53 |

**c.** Change the structure of the PivotTable to display the data as shown in Figure L-30.

**d.** Add a report filter using the region field. Display only the U.S. employees.

**e.** Create a clustered column PivotChart from the PivotTable and move the chart to its own sheet named PivotChart. Rearrange the fields to create the PivotChart shown in Figure L-31.

**f.** Add the title **U.S. Sales Staff** above the chart.

**g.** Add the Pivot Style Light 18 style to the PivotTable.

**h.** Insert a new row in the Employees worksheet above row 7. In the new row, add information reflecting the recent hiring of Kathy Crosby, a full-time sales manager at the Boston office. Update the PivotTable to display the new employee information.

**i.** Add the label **Total Chicago Staff** in cell G1 of the Employees sheet. Widen column G to fit the label.

**FIGURE L-30**

| Count of Last Name | Column Labels | | |
|---|---|---|---|
| Row Labels | Full-time | Part-time | Grand Total |
| ⊟ Sales Manager | 12 | 4 | 16 |
|   Boston | | 1 | 1 |
|   Chicago | 2 | | 2 |
|   Los Angeles | 1 | | 1 |
|   Montreal | 1 | | 1 |
|   New York | 2 | | 2 |
|   San Francisco | 2 | 1 | 3 |
|   St. Louis | 1 | 1 | 2 |
|   Toronto | 2 | 1 | 3 |
|   Vancouver | 1 | | 1 |
| ⊟ Sales Representative | 26 | 11 | 37 |
|   Boston | 3 | 1 | 4 |
|   Chicago | 1 | 1 | 2 |
|   Los Angeles | 4 | 1 | 5 |
|   Montreal | 3 | 1 | 4 |
|   New York | 5 | 2 | 7 |
|   San Francisco | 5 | 2 | 7 |
|   St. Louis | 1 | 1 | 2 |
|   Toronto | 2 | 1 | 3 |
|   Vancouver | 2 | 1 | 3 |
| Grand Total | 38 | 15 | 53 |

# Independent Challenge 3 (continued)

**j.** Enter a function in cell H1 that retrieves the total number of employees located in Chicago from the PivotTable. Change the page orientation of the Employees sheet to landscape.

FIGURE L-31

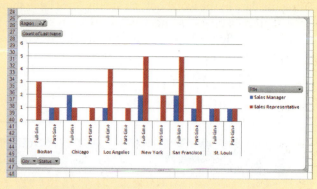

### Advanced Challenge Exercise

- Use a Slicer to filter the PivotTable to display only the data for the cities of Boston, Chicago, Los Angeles, and San Francisco.
- Change the Slicer caption from City to **Sales Office**. (*Hint*: Use the Slicer Settings button in the Slicer group of the Slicer Tools Option tab.)
- Add another Slicer for the Title field to display only the sales representatives.
- Display the Visibility pane, and use the Re-order buttons at the bottom of the pane to move the Sales Office Slicer to the top of the list of Shapes.
- Verify that the number of Chicago employees in cell H1 of the Employees sheet is now 2.

**k.** Add your name to the center section of all three worksheet footers, save the workbook, then preview the PivotTable, the first page of the Employee worksheet, and the PivotChart.

**l.** Close the workbook and exit Excel. Submit the workbook to your instructor.

# Real Life Independent Challenge

PivotTables can be effective tools for analyzing your personal investments. You will use a PivotTable and a PivotChart to represent the short-term trend for four stocks by summarizing the performance of the stocks over five business days. You will use a PivotTable function to display each stock's weekly high, and you will use a PivotChart to represent each stock's five-day performance.

**a.** Start Excel, open the file EX L-6.xlsx, then save it as **EX L-Stocks** in the drive and folder where you save your Data Files.

**b.** If you have stock information available you can replace the data in the file with your own data.

**c.** Create a PivotTable on a new worksheet that sums the stock prices for each stock across the rows and for each day down the columns. Rename the PivotTable sheet **PivotTable**.

**d.** Format the sales figures as Currency with two decimal places, and apply the Pivot Style Light 20 format.

**e.** Turn off the grand totals for both the rows and columns.

**f.** Add the Exchange field to the Report Filter area of the PivotTable. Display only the NASDAQ data, then redisplay the data from both exchanges.

**g.** Create a clustered column PivotChart report from your data. Move the PivotChart to its own sheet named **PivotChart**. Change the column chart to a clustered bar chart. (*Hint*: Use the Change Chart Type button.)

**h.** Add grand totals for the rows of the PivotTable. Change the summary function to MAX, then change the label in cell G4 from Grand Total to **Highest Price**. Widen column G to fit the label.

**i.** Enter the label **Highest Price** in cell F1 of the Stocks sheet. Widen column F to fit the label. Enter the MSFT stock symbol in cell F2. If you are using your own data, enter one of your stock symbols in cell F2.

**j.** Enter a function in cell G2 that retrieves the highest price for the stock in cell F2 over the past five days from the PivotTable.

**k.** Change the structure of the PivotTable, moving the Day field to the Row Labels area below the Stock field and Exchange to the Column Labels area. Verify that the highest price for the MSFT stock (or your own stock if you are using personal data) is still correct on the Stocks worksheet.

**l.** Change the PivotChart type to a line.

**m.** Add your name to the center section of the footer for the PivotChart, the PivotTable, and the Stocks worksheet, save the workbook, then preview the three worksheets.

**n.** Close the workbook and exit Excel. Submit the workbook to your instructor.

# Visual Workshop

Open the file EX L-7.xlsx from the drive and folder where you store your Data Files, then save it as **EX L-Real Estate**. Using the data in the workbook, create the PivotTable shown in Figure L-32 on a worksheet named PivotTable, then generate a PivotChart on a new sheet named PivotChart as shown in Figure L-33. (*Hint*: The PivotTable has been formatted using the Pivot Style Medium 12.) Add your name to the PivotTable and the PivotChart footers, then preview the PivotTable and the PivotChart. Save the workbook, close the workbook, exit Excel, then submit the workbook to your instructor.

**FIGURE L-32**

| Sum of Sales | | Jan | Feb | Mar | Grand Total |
|---|---|---|---|---|---|
| ⊟ DC | | $37,522,921.00 | $104,517,200.00 | $109,525,142.00 | $251,565,263.00 |
| | Commercial | $4,511,899.00 | $6,505,556.00 | $8,504,845.00 | $19,522,300.00 |
| | Land | $17,505,645.00 | $30,503,133.00 | $38,515,452.00 | $86,524,230.00 |
| | Residential | $15,505,377.00 | $67,508,511.00 | $62,504,845.00 | $145,518,733.00 |
| ⊟ Miami | | $48,830,890.00 | $108,522,460.00 | $68,143,450.00 | $225,496,800.00 |
| | Commercial | $2,742,221.00 | $9,030,458.00 | $9,049,554.00 | $20,822,233.00 |
| | Land | $25,043,225.00 | $80,489,557.00 | $19,045,454.00 | $124,578,236.00 |
| | Residential | $21,045,444.00 | $19,002,445.00 | $40,048,442.00 | $80,096,331.00 |
| ⊟ NY | | $117,564,007.00 | $81,054,224.00 | $128,071,884.00 | $326,690,115.00 |
| | Commercial | $8,018,009.00 | $3,015,222.00 | $11,025,664.00 | $22,058,895.00 |
| | Land | $70,518,444.00 | $50,027,452.00 | $40,025,444.00 | $160,571,340.00 |
| | Residential | $39,027,554.00 | $28,011,550.00 | $77,020,776.00 | $144,059,880.00 |
| Grand Total | | $203,917,818.00 | $294,093,884.00 | $305,740,476.00 | $803,752,178.00 |

**FIGURE L-33**

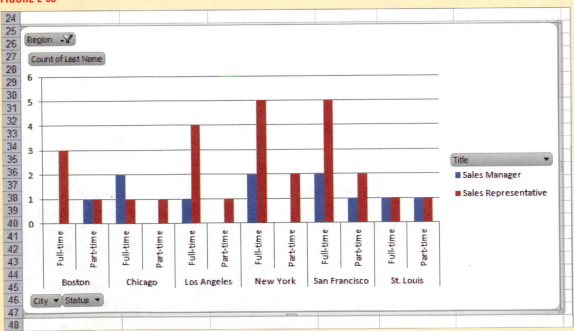

# Exchanging Data with Other Programs

**Files You Will Need:**

EX M-1.txt
EX M-2.accdb
EX M-3.jpg
EX M-4.docx
EX M-5.xlsx
EX M-6.pptx
EX M-7.xlsx
EX M-8.xlsx
EX M-9.txt
EX M-10.accdb
EX M-11.gif
EX M-12.xlsx
EX M-13.pptx
EX M-14.xlsx
EX M-15.xlsx
EX M-16.pptx
EX M-17.txt
EX M-18.docx
EX M-19.xlsx
EX M-20.xlsx
EX M-21.docx
EX M-22.gif
EX M-23.docx
EX M-24.xlsx

In a Windows environment, you can freely exchange data among Excel and most other Windows programs, a process known as integration. In this unit, you plan a data exchange between Excel and other Microsoft Office programs.  Quest's upper management has asked Kate Morgan, the vice president of sales, to research the possible purchase of Service Adventures, a small company specializing in combining travel with volunteer work for corporate employees. Kate is reviewing the organization's files and developing a presentation on the feasibility of acquiring the company. To complete this project, Kate asks you to help set up the exchange of data between Excel and other programs.

**OBJECTIVES**

Plan a data exchange

Import a text file

Import a database table

Insert a graphic file in a worksheet

Embed a workbook in a Word document

Link a workbook to a Word document

Link an Excel chart to a PowerPoint slide

Import a table into Access

# Planning a Data Exchange

Because the tools available in Microsoft Office programs are designed to be compatible, exchanging data between Excel and other programs is easy. The first step involves planning what you want to accomplish with each data exchange.  Kate asks you to use the following guidelines to plan data exchanges between Excel and other programs in order to complete the business analysis project.

**DETAILS**

### To plan an exchange of data:

**QUICK TIP**

For more information on importable file formats, see the Help topic "File formats that are supported in Excel."

- **Identify the data you want to exchange, its file type, and, if possible, the program used to create it**

  Whether the data you want to exchange is a graphics file, a database file, a worksheet, or consists only of text, it is important to identify the data's **source program** (the program used to create it) and the file type. Once you identify the source program, you can determine options for exchanging the data with Excel. Kate needs to analyze a text file containing the Service Adventures tour sales. Although she does not know the source program, Kate knows that the file contains unformatted text. A file that consists of text but no formatting is sometimes called an **ASCII** or **text** file. Because ASCII is a universally accepted file format, Kate can easily import an ASCII file into Excel. See Table M-1 for a partial list of other file formats that Excel can import. Excel can also import older file formats as well as templates, backup files, and workspace files that are easily accessible in Excel.

- **Determine the program with which you want to exchange data**

  Besides knowing which program created the data you want to exchange, you must also identify which program will receive the data, called the **destination program**. This determines the procedure you use to perform the exchange. You might want to insert a graphic object into an Excel worksheet or add a spreadsheet to a Word document. Kate received a database table of Service Adventures' corporate customers created with the Access database program. After determining that Excel can import Access tables and reviewing the import procedure, she imports the database file into Excel so she can analyze it using Excel tools.

- **Determine the goal of your data exchange**

  Windows offers two ways to transfer data within and between programs that allow you to retain some connection with the source program. These data transfer methods use a Windows feature known as **object linking and embedding**, or **OLE**. The data to be exchanged, called an **object**, may consist of text, a worksheet, or any other type of data. You use **embedding** to insert a copy of the original object in the destination document and, if necessary, to subsequently edit this data separately from the source document. This process is illustrated in Figure M-1. You use **linking** when you want the information you inserted to be updated automatically if the data in the source document changes. This process is illustrated in Figure M-2. You learn more about embedding and linking later in this unit. Kate has determined that she needs to use both object embedding and object linking for her analysis and presentation project.

- **Set up the data exchange**

  When you exchange data between two programs, it is often best to start both programs before starting the exchange. You might also want to tile the program windows on the screen either horizontally or vertically so that you can see both during the exchange. You will work with Excel, Word, Access, and PowerPoint when exchanging data for this project.

- **Execute the data exchange**

  The steps you use will vary, depending on the type of data you want to exchange. Kate is ready to have you start the data exchanges for the business analysis of Service Adventures.

**FIGURE M-1:** Embedded object

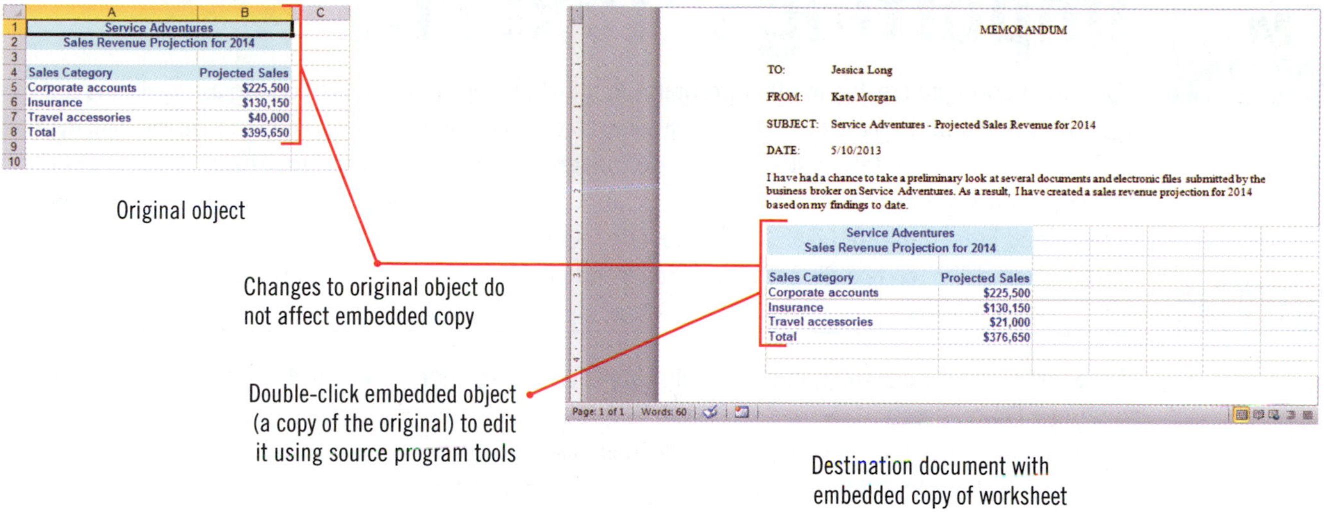

Original object

Changes to original object do
not affect embedded copy

Double-click embedded object
(a copy of the original) to edit
it using source program tools

Destination document with
embedded copy of worksheet

**FIGURE M-2:** Linked object

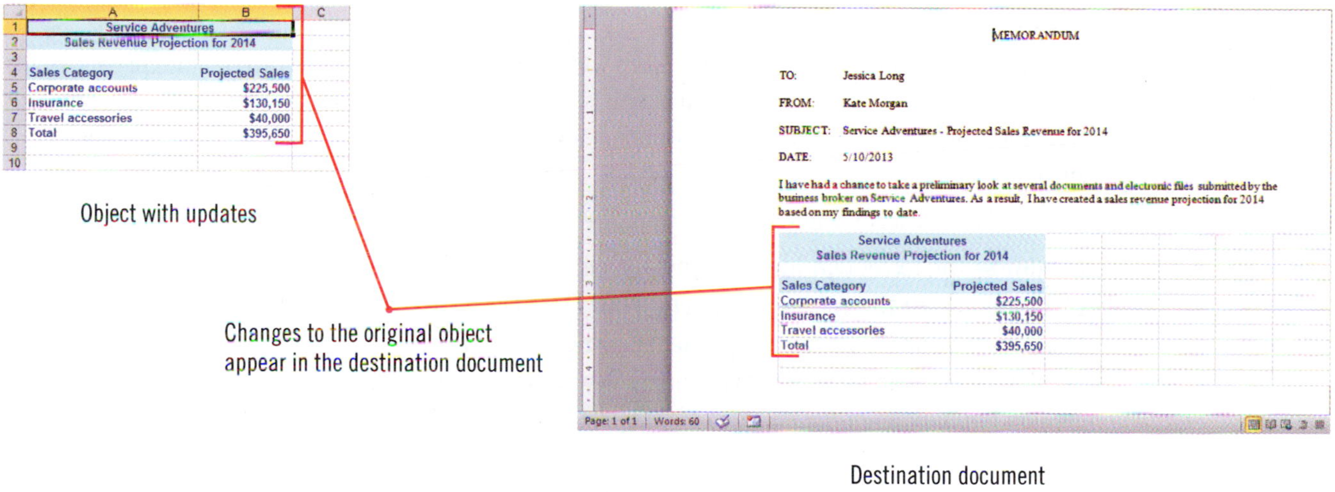

Object with updates

Changes to the original object
appear in the destination document

Destination document

**TABLE M-1:** Importable file formats and extensions

| file format | file extension(s) | file format | file extension(s) |
|-------------|-------------------|-------------|-------------------|
| Access | .mdb, .accdb | All Data Sources | .odc, .udl, .dsn |
| Text | .txt, .prn, .csv, .dif, .sylk | OpenDocument Spreadsheet | .ods |
| Query | .iqy, .dqy, .oqy, .rqy | XML | .xml |
| Web page | .htm, .html, .mht, .mhtml | dBASE | .dbf |

# Importing a Text File

You can import data created in other programs into Excel by opening the file, as long as Excel can read the file type. After importing the file, you use the Save As command on the Office menu to save the data in Excel format. Text files use a tab or space as the **delimiter**, or column separator, to separate columns of data. When you import a text file into Excel, the Text Import Wizard automatically opens and describes how text is separated in the imported file.  Now that Kate has planned the data exchange, she wants you to import a tab-delimited text file containing ranch and profit data from Service Adventures.

## STEPS

1. **Start Excel if necessary, click the File tab, click Open, then navigate to the folder containing your Data Files**

    The Open dialog box shows only those files that match the file types listed in the Files of type box—usually Microsoft Excel files. In this case, however, you're importing a text file.

2. **Click All Excel Files, click Text Files (\*.prn; \*.txt; \*.csv), click EX M-1.txt, then click Open**

    The first Text Import Wizard dialog box opens, as shown in Figure M-3. Under Original data type, the Delimited option button is selected. In the Preview of file box, line 1 indicates that the file contains two columns of data: Branch and Profit. No changes are necessary in this dialog box.

3. **Click Next**

    The second Text Import Wizard dialog box opens. Under Delimiters, Tab is selected as the delimiter, indicating that tabs separate the columns of incoming data. The Data preview box contains a line showing where the tab delimiters divide the data into columns.

4. **Click Next**

    The third Text Import Wizard dialog box opens with options for formatting the two columns of data. Under Column data format, the General option button is selected. The Data preview area shows that both columns will be formatted with the General format. This is the best formatting option for text mixed with numbers.

5. **Click Finish**

    Excel imports the text file into the blank worksheet as two columns of data: Branch and Profit.

6. **Maximize the Excel window if necessary, click the File tab, click Save As, in the Save As dialog box navigate to the folder containing your Data Files, click the Save as type list arrow, click Excel workbook (\*.xlsx), change the filename to EX M-Branch Profit, then click Save**

    The file is saved as an Excel workbook, and the new name appears in the title bar. The sheet tab automatically changes to the name of the imported file, EX M-1. The worksheet information would be easier to read if it were formatted and if it showed the total profit for all regions.

7. **Double-click the border between the headers in columns A and B, click cell A8, type Total Profit, click cell B8, on the Home tab click the Sum button Σ in the Editing group, then click the Enter button ✔ on the formula bar**

8. **Rename the sheet tab Profit, center the column labels, apply bold formatting to them, format the data in column B using the Currency style with the $ symbol and no decimal places, then click cell A1**

    Figure M-4 shows the completed worksheet, which analyzes the text file data you imported into Excel.

9. **Add your name to the center section of the worksheet footer, save the workbook, preview the worksheet, close the workbook, then submit the workbook to your instructor**

Original data is
delimited

Two column
headings

Preview of data

> **Text Import Wizard - Step 1 of 3**
>
> The Text Wizard has determined that your data is Delimited.
>
> If this is correct, choose Next, or choose the data type that best describes your data.
>
> Original data type
>
> Choose the file type that best describes your data:
>
> ◉ Delimited     - Characters such as commas or tabs separate each field.
> ○ Fixed width   - Fields are aligned in columns with spaces between each field.
>
> Start import at row:  1        File origin:    437 : OEM United States
>
> Preview of file C:\Users\Lynn\Desktop\Excel 2010\Unit M\Master Files\Data Files\EX M-1.txt.
>
> 1 BranchProfit
> 2 Miami210023
> 3 Chicago341774
> 4 New York182921
> 5 Los Angeles263910
>
> Cancel    < Back    Next >    Finish

**FIGURE M-4:** Completed worksheet with imported text file

|    | A | B | C |
|----|-----------|-------------|---|
| 1  | **Branch** | **Profit** |   |
| 2  | Miami | $210,023 |   |
| 3  | Chicago | $341,774 |   |
| 4  | New York | $182,921 |   |
| 5  | Los Angeles | $263,910 |   |
| 6  | Boston | $274,512 |   |
| 7  | Portland | $189,531 |   |
| 8  | Total Profit | $1,462,671 |   |
| 9  |           |             |   |
| 10 |           |             |   |

Total profit added
after importing data

Columns from text file

## Importing files using other methods

Another way to open the Text Import Wizard to import a text file into Excel is to click the Data tab, click the From Text button in the Get External Data group, select a data source in the Import Text File dialog box, then click Import. You can also drag the icon representing a text file on the Windows desktop into a blank worksheet window. Excel will create a worksheet from the data without using the Wizard.

Excel 2010

# Importing a Database Table

In addition to importing text files, you can also use Excel to import data from database tables. A **database table** is a set of data organized using columns and rows that is created in a database program. A **database program** is an application, such as Microsoft Access, that lets you manage large amounts of data organized in tables. Figure M-5 shows an Access table. To import data from an Access table into Excel, you can copy the table in Access and paste it into an Excel worksheet. This method places a copy of the Access data into Excel; the data will not be refreshed in Excel if you change the data in the Access file. If you need the data in Excel to be updated when changes are made to it in Access, you create a connection, or a **link**, to the database. This allows you to work with current data in Excel without recopying the data from Access whenever the Access data changes.  Kate received a database table containing Service Adventures' corporate customer information, which was created with Access. She asks you to import this table into an Excel workbook, creating a connection to the Access data. She would also like you to format, sort, and total the data.

## STEPS

1. Click the File Tab, click New, then click Create
   A new workbook opens, displaying a blank worksheet for you to use to import the Access data.

**TROUBLE**

If your screen does not show the From Access button in the Get External Data group, click the Get External Data button, click From Access, then navigate to the folder containing your Data Files. The Add-Ins you have installed and your screen resolution will affect the configuration of your Data tab.

2. Click the Data tab, click the From Access button in the Get External Data group, then navigate to the folder containing your Data Files if necessary

3. Click EX M-2.accdb, click Open, verify that the Table option button and the Existing worksheet button are selected, then click OK in the Import Data dialog box
   Excel inserts the Access data into the worksheet as a table with the table style Medium 2 format applied, as shown in Figure M-6.

4. Rename the sheet tab Customer Information, then format the data in columns F and G with the Currency format with the $ symbol and no decimal places
   You are ready to sort the data using the values in column G.

5. Click the cell G1 list arrow, then click Sort Smallest to Largest
   The records are reorganized in ascending order according to the amount of the 2013 orders.

6. Click the Table Tools Design tab if necessary, click the Total Row check box in the Table Style Options group to select it, click cell F19, click the cell F19 list arrow next to cell F19, select Sum from the drop-down function list, then click cell A1
   Your completed worksheet should match Figure M-7.

7. Add your name to the center section of the worksheet footer, change the worksheet orientation to landscape, save the workbook as EX M-Customer Information, then preview the worksheet

**FIGURE M-5:** Access Table

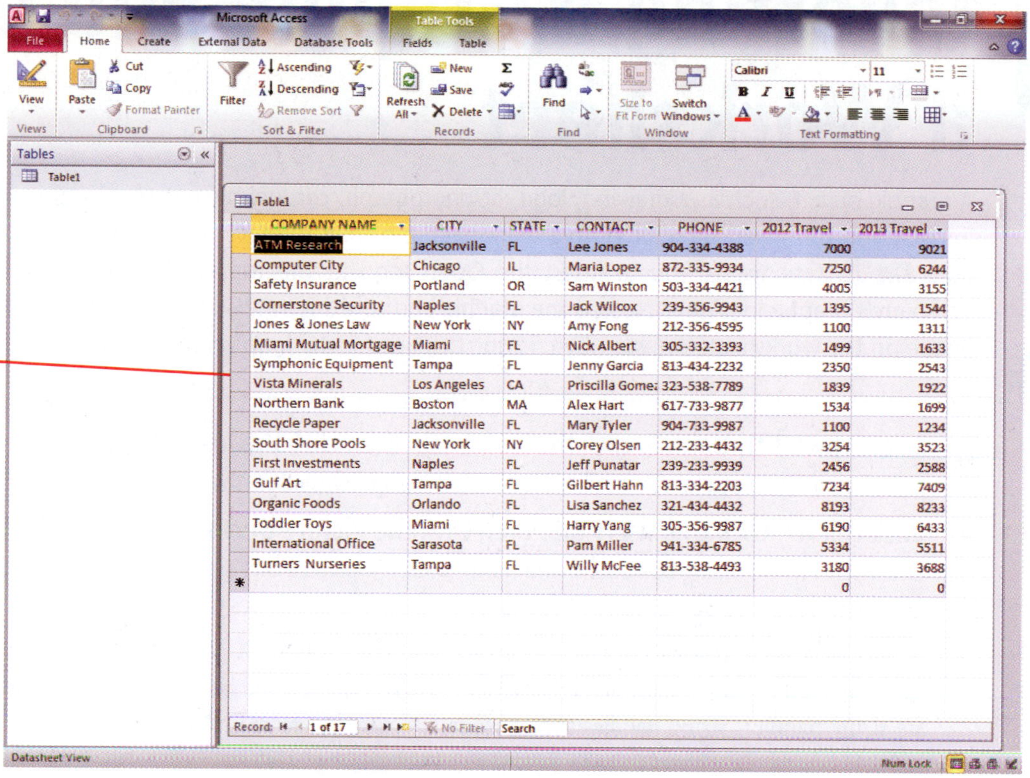

Table data →

**FIGURE M-6:** Imported Access table

**FIGURE M-7:** Completed worksheet containing imported data

Data is sorted in ascending order by 2013 values →

Totals for 2012 and 2013 orders

Exchanging Data with Other Programs

# Inserting a Graphic File in a Worksheet

A graphic object, such as a drawing, logo, or photograph, can greatly enhance your worksheet's visual impact. You can insert a picture into a worksheet and then format it using the options on the Format tab.  Kate wants you to insert the Quest logo at the top of the customer worksheet. The company's graphic designer created the graphic and saved it in JPG format. You insert and format the image on the worksheet. You start by creating a space for the logo on the worksheet.

## STEPS

1. **Select rows 1 through 5, click the Home tab, then click the Insert button in the Cells group**
   Five blank rows appear above the header row, leaving space to insert the picture.

2. **Click cell A1, click the Insert tab, then click the Picture button in the Illustrations group**
   The Insert Picture dialog box opens. You want to insert a picture that already exists in a file. The file you will insert has a .jpg file extension, so it is called a "jay-peg" file. JPEG files can be viewed in a Web browser.

3. **Navigate to the folder containing your Data Files, click EX M-3.jpg, then click Insert**
   Excel inserts the image and displays the Picture Tools Format tab. The small circles around the picture's border are sizing handles. Sizing handles appear when a picture is selected; you use them to change the size of a picture.

4. **Position the pointer over the sizing handle in the logo's lower-right corner until the pointer becomes ⬉, then click and drag the corner up and to the left so that the logo's outline fits within rows 1 through 5**
   Compare your screen to Figure M-8. You decide to remove the logo's white background.

### QUICK TIP
The Remove Background button removes the entire background of an image and doesn't allow you to select a color to make transparent.

5. **With the image selected, click the Color button in the Adjust group of the Picture Tools Format tab, click Set Transparent Color, then use ✎ to click the white background on the logo**
   The logo is now transparent, and shows the worksheet gridlines behind it. You decide that the logo will be more visually interesting with a frame and a border color.

6. **With the image selected, click the More button ▾ in the Picture Styles group, point to several styles and observe the effect on the graphic, click the Reflected Beveled, White style (the third from the right in the last row), click the Picture Border button in the Picture Styles group, then click Blue, Accent 1, Lighter 40% in the Theme Colors group**
   You decide to add a glow to the image.

7. **Click the Picture Effects button in the Picture Styles group, point to Glow, point to More Glow Colors, click Blue, Accent 1, Lighter 80% in the Theme Colors group, resize the logo as necessary to fit it in rows 1 through 5, then drag the logo above the column D data**
   You decide to add an artistic effect to the image.

8. **Click the Artistic Effects button in the Adjust group, click Light Screen (First effect in the third row), then click cell A1**
   Compare your worksheet to Figure M-9.

9. **Save the workbook, preview the worksheet, close the workbook, exit Excel, then submit the workbook to your instructor**

**FIGURE M-8:** Logo resized

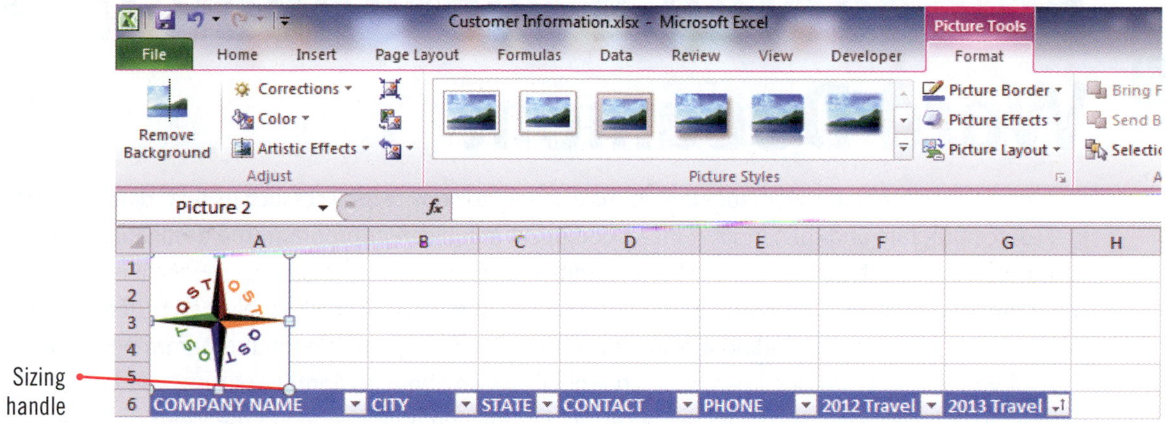

Sizing handle

**FIGURE M-9:** Worksheet with formatted picture

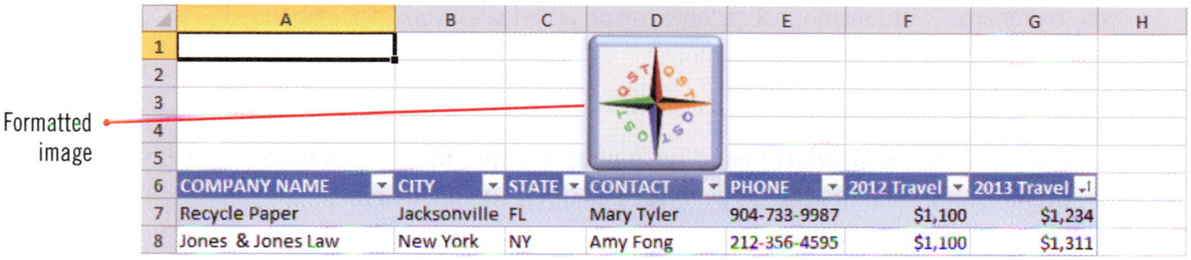

Formatted image

| COMPANY NAME | CITY | STATE | CONTACT | PHONE | 2012 Travel | 2013 Travel |
|---|---|---|---|---|---|---|
| Recycle Paper | Jacksonville | FL | Mary Tyler | 904-733-9987 | $1,100 | $1,234 |
| Jones & Jones Law | New York | NY | Amy Fong | 212-356-4595 | $1,100 | $1,311 |

## Formatting SmartArt graphics

SmartArt graphics provide another way to visually communicate information on a worksheet. A **SmartArt graphic** is a professionally designed illustration with text and graphics. Each SmartArt type communicates a kind of information or relationship, such as a list, process, or hierarchy. Each type has various layouts you can choose. For example, you can choose from 4 pyramid layouts, 16 process layouts, or 31 picture layouts, allowing you to illustrate your information in many different ways. To insert a SmartArt graphic into a worksheet, click the Insert tab, then click the SmartArt button in the Illustrations group. In the Choose a SmartArt Graphic dialog box,

choose from eight SmartArt types: List, Process, Cycle, Hierarchy, Relationship, Matrix, Pyramid, and Picture. The dialog box also describes the type of information that is appropriate for each selected layout. After you choose a layout and click OK, a SmartArt object appears on your worksheet. As you enter text in the text entry areas, the graphics automatically resize to fit the text. The SmartArt Tools Design tab lets you choose color schemes and styles for your SmartArt. You can add effects to SmartArt graphics using choices on the SmartArt Tools Format tab. Figure M-10 shows examples of SmartArt graphics.

**FIGURE M-10:** Examples of SmartArt graphics

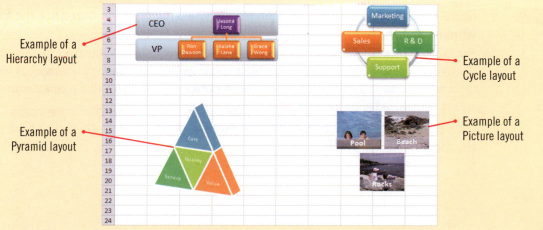

Example of a Hierarchy layout

Example of a Cycle layout

Example of a Pyramid layout

Example of a Picture layout

# Embedding a Workbook in a Word Document

Microsoft Office programs work together to make it easy to copy an object (such as text, data, or a graphic) in a source program and then insert it into a document in a different program (the destination program). If you insert the object using a simple Paste command, however, you retain no connection to the source program. That's why it is often more useful to embed objects rather than simply paste them. Embedding allows you to edit an Excel workbook from within the source program using that program's commands and tools. If you send a Word document with an embedded workbook to another person, you do not need to send a separate Excel file with it. All the necessary information is embedded in the Word document. When you embed information, you can either display the data itself or an icon representing the data; users double-click the icon to view the embedded data. An icon is often used rather than the data when the file is sent electronically. ⬛🎨 Kate decides to update Jessica Long, the CEO of Quest, on the project status. She asks you to prepare a Word memo that includes the projected sales workbook embedded as an icon. You begin by starting Word and opening the memo.

## STEPS

1. **Open a Windows Explorer window, navigate to the folder containing your Data Files, then double-click the file EX M-4.docx to open the file in Word**

   The memo opens in Word.

2. **Click the File tab, click Save As, navigate to the folder containing your Data Files, change the file name to EX M-Service Adventures Memo, then click Save**

   You want to embed the workbook below the last line of the document.

3. **Press [Ctrl][End], click the Insert tab, click the Object button in the Text group, then click the Create from File tab**

   Figure M-11 shows the Create from File tab in the Object dialog box. You need to indicate the file you want to embed.

4. **Click Browse, navigate to the drive and folder where you store your Data Files, click EX M-5.xlsx, click Insert, then select the Display as icon check box**

   You will change the icon label to a more descriptive name.

**QUICK TIP**

To display a different icon to represent the file, click the Change Icon button in the Object dialog box, scroll down the icon list in the Change Icon dialog box, and select any icon.

5. **Click Change Icon, select the text in the Caption text box, type Projected Sales, then click OK twice**

   The memo contains an embedded copy of the sales projection data, displayed as an icon, as shown in Figure M-12.

**TROUBLE**

If the Excel program window does not come to the front automatically, click the Excel icon in the taskbar.

6. **Double-click the Projected Sales icon on the Word memo, then maximize the Excel window and the worksheet window if necessary**

   The Excel program starts and displays the embedded worksheet, with its location displayed in the title bar, as shown in Figure M-13. Any changes you make to the embedded object using Excel tools are not reflected in the source document. Similarly, if you open the source document in the source program, changes you make are not reflected in the embedded copy.

7. **Click the File tab, click Close, exit Excel, click the Word File tab, then click Save to save the memo**

**FIGURE M-11:** Object dialog box

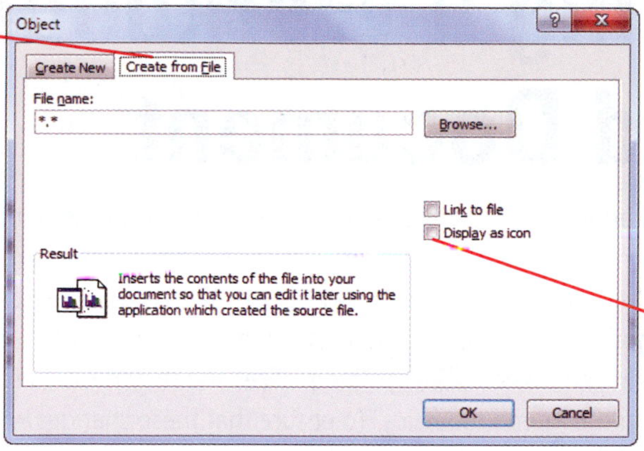

Click this tab
to embed an
existing file

Click to display
object as an icon

**FIGURE M-12:** Memo with embedded worksheet

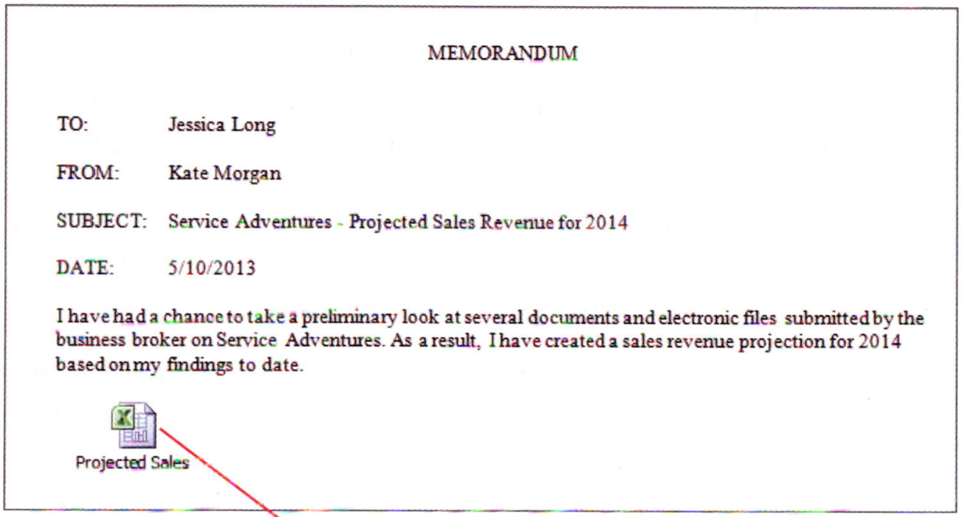

MEMORANDUM

TO:        Jessica Long

FROM:      Kate Morgan

SUBJECT:   Service Adventures - Projected Sales Revenue for 2014

DATE:      5/10/2013

I have had a chance to take a preliminary look at several documents and electronic files submitted by the
business broker on Service Adventures. As a result, I have created a sales revenue projection for 2014
based on my findings to date.

Projected Sales

Icon representing the
embedded Excel worksheet

**FIGURE M-13:** Embedded worksheet opened in Excel

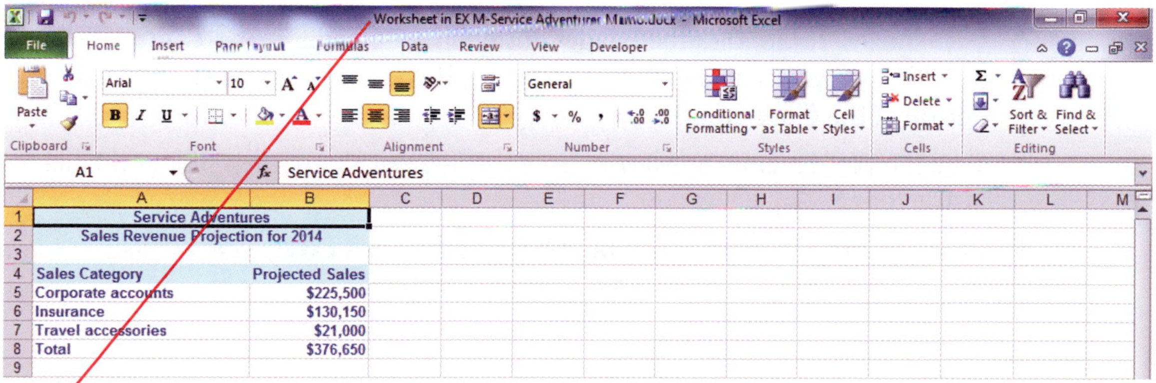

|   | A | B |
|---|---|---|
| 1 | Service Adventures | |
| 2 | Sales Revenue Projection for 2014 | |
| 3 | | |
| 4 | Sales Category | Projected Sales |
| 5 | Corporate accounts | $225,500 |
| 6 | Insurance | $130,150 |
| 7 | Travel accessories | $21,000 |
| 8 | Total | $376,650 |
| 9 | | |

Location of the
embedded worksheet

# Linking a Workbook to a Word Document

**Linking** a workbook to another file retains a connection with the original document as well as the original program. When you link a workbook to another program, the link contains a connection to the source document so that, when you double-click it, the source document opens for editing. Once you link a workbook to another program, any changes you make to the original workbook (the source document) are reflected in the linked object.  Kate realizes she may need to make some changes to the workbook she embedded in the memo to Jessica. To ensure that these changes will be reflected in the memo, she feels you should use linking instead of embedding. She asks you to delete the embedded worksheet icon and replace it with a linked version of the same workbook.

## STEPS

1. With the Word memo still open, click the Projected Sales Worksheet icon to select it if necessary, then press [Delete]

   The workbook is no longer embedded in the memo. The linking process is similar to embedding.

**QUICK TIP**

If you want to link part of an existing worksheet to another file, in the destination document paste the information as a link using one of the link options from the Paste Options list. You can also use the Paste button list arrow in the Clipboard group.

2. Make sure the insertion point is below the last line of the memo, click the Insert tab, click the Object button in the Text group, then click the Create from File tab in the Object dialog box

3. Click Browse, navigate to the drive and folder where you store your Data Files, click EX M-5.xlsx, click Insert, select the Link to file check box, then click OK

   The memo now displays a linked copy of the sales projection data, as shown in Figure M-14. In the future, any changes made to the source file, EX M-5, will also be made to the linked copy in the Word memo. You verify this by making a change to the source file and viewing its effect on the Word memo.

4. Click the File tab, click Save, then close the Word memo, exit Word, then close any open Excel windows if necessary

**TROUBLE**

If you get an error message, exit Excel and repeat the step.

5. Start Excel, open the file EX M-5.xlsx from the drive and folder where you store your Data Files, click cell B7, type 40,000, then press [Enter]

   You want to verify that the same change was made automatically to the linked copy of the workbook.

**TROUBLE**

If your link didn't update, right click the Excel data and select Update Links on the shortcut menu.

6. Start Word, open the EX M-Service Adventures Memo.docx file from the drive and folder where you store your Data Files, then click Yes if asked if you want to update the document's links

   The memo displays the new value for Travel accessories, and the total has been updated as shown in Figure M-15

7. Click the Insert tab, click the Header button in the Header & Footer group, click Edit Header, type your name in the Header area, then click the Close Header and Footer button in the Close group

8. Save the Word memo, preview it, close the file, exit Word, then submit the file to your instructor

9. Close the Excel worksheet without saving it, then exit Excel

MEMORANDUM

TO:        Jessica Long

FROM:      Kate Morgan

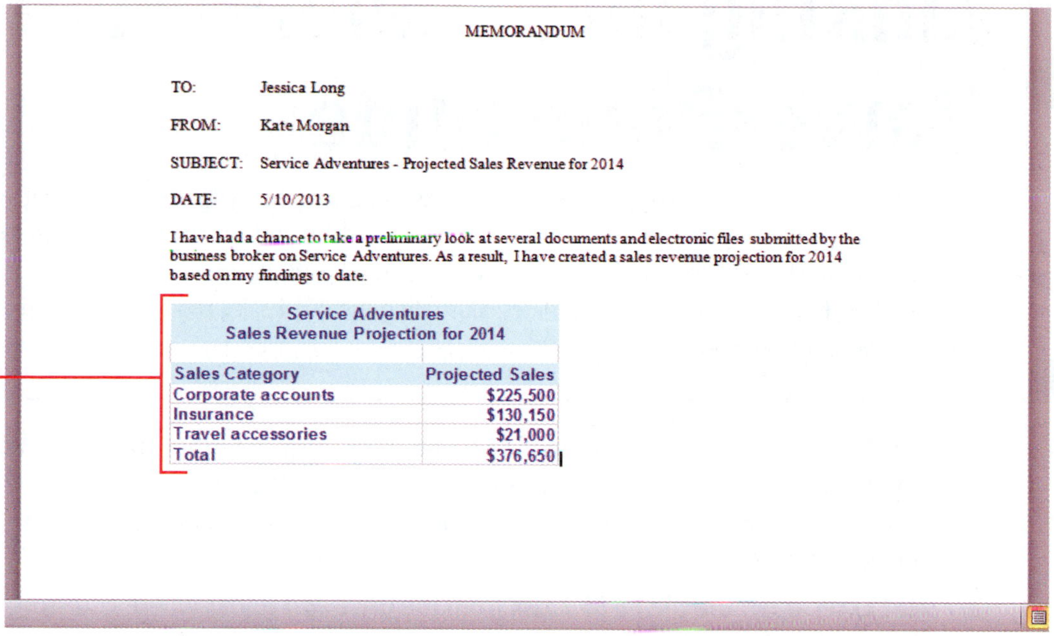

SUBJECT:   Service Adventures - Projected Sales Revenue for 2014

DATE:      5/10/2013

I have had a chance to take a preliminary look at several documents and electronic files submitted by the business broker on Service Adventures. As a result, I have created a sales revenue projection for 2014 based on my findings to date.

**Linked worksheet**

| Service Adventures Sales Revenue Projection for 2014 | |
|---|---|
| Sales Category | Projected Sales |
| Corporate accounts | $225,500 |
| Insurance | $130,150 |
| Travel accessories | $21,000 |
| Total | $376,650 |

**Excel 2010**

FIGURE M-15: Memo with link updated

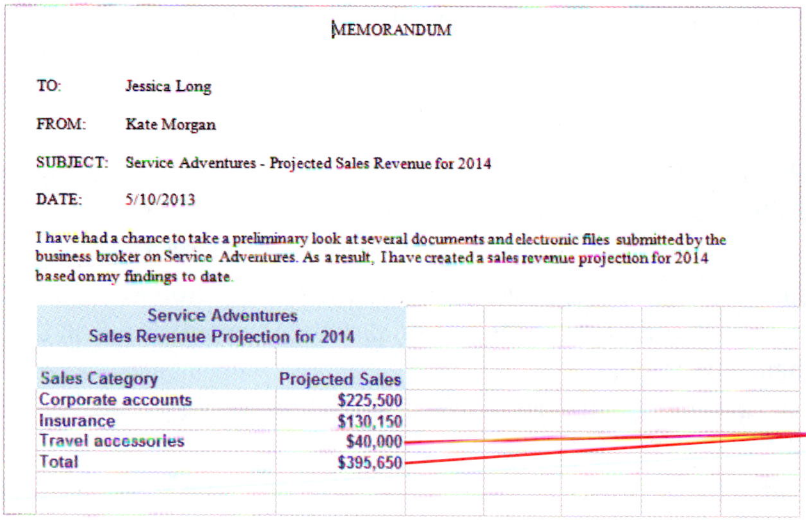

MEMORANDUM

TO:        Jessica Long

FROM:      Kate Morgan

SUBJECT:   Service Adventures - Projected Sales Revenue for 2014

DATE:      5/10/2013

I have had a chance to take a preliminary look at several documents and electronic files submitted by the business broker on Service Adventures. As a result, I have created a sales revenue projection for 2014 based on my findings to date.

| Service Adventures Sales Revenue Projection for 2014 | |
|---|---|
| Sales Category | Projected Sales |
| Corporate accounts | $225,500 |
| Insurance | $130,150 |
| Travel accessories | $40,000 |
| Total | $395,650 |

**Values update to match those in the source document**

## Managing links

When you open a document containing linked data, you are asked if you want to update the linked data. You can manage the updating of links by clicking the File tab, and clicking Edit Links to Files in the right pane. The Links dialog box opens, allowing you to change a link's update from the default setting of automatic to manual. The Links dialog box also allows you to change the link source, permanently break a link, open the source file, and manually update a link. If you send your linked files to another user, the links will be broken because the linked file path references the local machine where you inserted the links. Because the file path will not be valid on the recipient user's machine, the links will no longer be updated when the user opens the destination document. To correct this, recipients who have both the destination and source documents can use the Links dialog box to change the link's source in the destination document to their own machines. Then the links will be automatically updated when they open the destination document in the future.

# Linking an Excel Chart to a PowerPoint Slide

Microsoft PowerPoint is a **presentation graphics** program that you can use to create slide show presentations. PowerPoint slides can include a mix of text, data, and graphics. Adding an Excel chart to a slide can help to illustrate data and give your presentation more visual appeal. Kate asks you to add an Excel chart to one of the PowerPoint slides, illustrating the 2014 sales projection data. She wants you to link the chart in the PowerPoint file.

## STEPS

1. **Start PowerPoint, then open the file EX M-6.pptx from the drive and folder where you store your Data Files, then save it as EX M-Management Presentation**

   The presentation appears in Normal view and contains three panes, as shown in Figure M-16. You need to open the Excel file and copy the chart that you will paste in the PowerPoint presentation.

2. **Start Excel, open the file EX M-7.xlsx from the drive and folder where you store your Data Files, right-click the Chart Area on the Sales Categories sheet, click Copy on the shortcut menu, then click the PowerPoint program button on the taskbar to display the presentation**

   You need to add an Excel chart to Slide 2, "2014 Sales Projections." To add the chart, you first need to select the slide on which it will appear.

   > **TROUBLE**
   > If you don't see Copy on the short-cut menu, you may have clicked the Plot area rather than the Chart area. Clicking the white area sur-rounding the pie will display the Copy command on the menu.

3. **Click Slide 2 in the left pane, right-click Slide 2 in the slide pane, then click the Use Destination Theme & Link Data button (third from the right) in the Paste Options group**

   A pie chart illustrating the 2014 sales projections appears in the slide. The chart matches the colors and fonts in the presentation, which is the destination document. You decide to edit the link so it will update automatically if the data source changes.

4. **Click the File tab, click Edit Links to Files at the bottom of the right pane, in the Links dialog box click the Automatic option button, then click Close**

   You want to apply a style to the chart before saving the PowerPoint file.

   > **QUICK TIP**
   > The default setting for updating links in PowerPoint file is Manual.

5. **Click the Chart Tools Design tab, click the More button in the Chart Styles group, click Style 26 in the Chart Styles gallery, click the Save button on the Quick Access toolbar, then close the file**

   Kate has learned that the sales projections for the Travel accessories category has increased based on late sales for the current year.

6. **Switch to Excel, click the Sales sheet tab, change the Travel accessories value in cell B7 to 45,000, then press [Enter]**

   You decide to reopen the PowerPoint presentation to check the chart data.

   > **QUICK TIP**
   > To update links in an open PowerPoint file, click the File tab, click Edit Links to Files in the right pane, click the link in the Links list, click Update Now, then click Close.

7. **Switch to PowerPoint, open the file EX M-Management Presentation.pptx, click Update Links, click Slide 2 in the left pane, then point to the Travel accessories pie slice**

   The ScreenTip shows that the chart has updated to display the revised Travel accessories value, $45,000, you entered in the Excel workbook. Slide Show view displays the slide on the full screen the way the audience will see it.

8. **Click the Slide Show button on the status bar**

   The finished sales projection slide is complete, as shown in Figure M-17.

9. **Press [Esc] to return to Normal view; with Slide 2 selected click the Insert tab, click the Header & Footer button in the Text group, select the Footer check box, type your name in the Footer text box, click Apply, save and close the presentation, close the Excel file without saving it, exit PowerPoint and Excel, then submit the file to your instructor**

**FIGURE M-16:** Presentation in Normal view

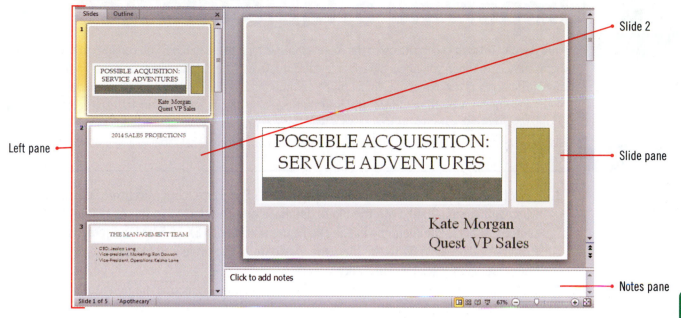

Left pane

Slide 2

Slide pane

Notes pane

**FIGURE M-17:** Completed Sales Projections slide in Slide Show view

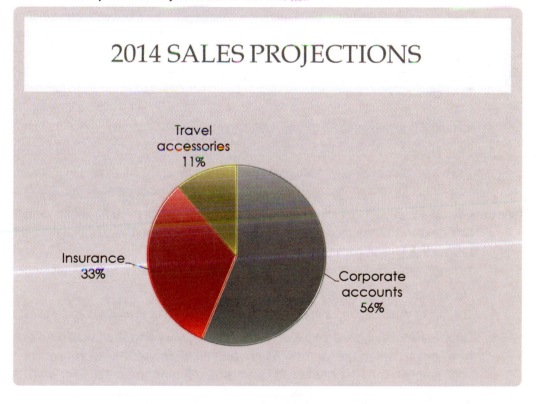

# Importing a Table into Access

If you need to analyze Excel data using the more extensive tools of a database, you can import the table into Microsoft Access. When you import Excel table data into Access, the data becomes an Access table using the same field names as the Excel table. In the process of importing an Excel table, Access specifies a primary key for the new table. A **primary key** is the field that contains unique information for each record (row) of information.  Kate has just received a workbook containing salary information for the managers at Service Adventures, organized in a table. She asks you to convert the Excel table to a Microsoft Access table.

**STEPS**

1. **Click the Start button on the taskbar, point to All Programs, click Microsoft Office, click Microsoft Access 2010; with the Blank database button selected in the Available Templates section, change the filename in the File Name text box to EX M-SA Management, click the Browse button 📁 next to the filename, navigate to the drive and folder where you store your Data Files, click OK, then click Create**

   The database window for the EX M-SA Management database opens. You are ready to import the Excel table data.

2. **Click the External Data tab, then click the Excel button in the Import & Link group**

   The Get External Data - Excel Spreadsheet dialog box opens, as shown in Figure M-18. This dialog box allows you to specify how you want the data to be stored in Access.

3. **Click the Browse button, navigate to the drive and folder where you store your Data Files, click EX M-8.xlsx, click Open, if necessary click the Import the source data into a new table in the current database option button, then click OK**

   The first Import Spreadsheet Wizard dialog box opens, with the Compensation worksheet selected, and a sample of the sheet data in the lower section. In the next dialog box, you indicate that you want to use the column headings in the Excel table as the field names in the Access database.

4. **Click Next, make sure the First Row Contains Column Headings check box is selected, then click Next**

   The Wizard allows you to review and change the field properties by clicking each column in the lower section of the window. You will not make any changes to the field properties.

5. **Click Next**

   The Wizard allows you to choose a primary key for the table. The table's primary key field contains unique information for each record; the ID Number field is unique for each person in the table.

**QUICK TIP**
Specifying a primary key allows you to retrieve data more quickly in the future.

6. **Click the Choose my own primary key option, make sure "ID Number" appears in the text box next to the selected option button, click Next, note the name assigned to the new table, click Finish, then click Close**

   The name of the new Access table ("Compensation") appears in the Navigation pane.

7. **Double-click Compensation: in the Navigation Pane**

   The data from the Excel worksheet appears in a new Access table, as shown in Figure M-19.

8. **Double-click the border between the Monthly Salary and the Click to Add column headings to widen the Monthly Salary column, then use the last row of the table to enter your name in the First Name and Last Name columns and enter 0 for an ID Number**

9. **Click the Save button 💾 on the Quick Access toolbar, close the file, then exit Access**

**FIGURE M-18:** Get External Data – Excel Spreadsheet dialog box

Data source

Specify how you want data to be stored in Access

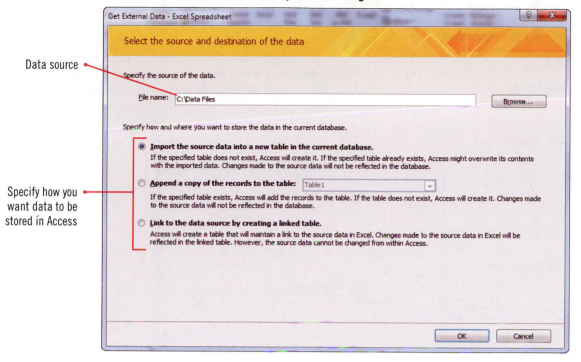

**FIGURE M-19:** Completed Access table

Access table

Primary key

Excel 2010

# Practice

## Concepts Review

For current SAM information, including versions and content details, visit SAM Central (http://www.cengage.com/samcentral). If you have a SAM user profile, you may have access to hands-on instruction, practice, and assessment of the skills covered in this unit. Since various versions of SAM are supported throughout the life of this text, check with your instructor for the correct instructions and URL/Web site for accessing assignments.

**FIGURE M-20**

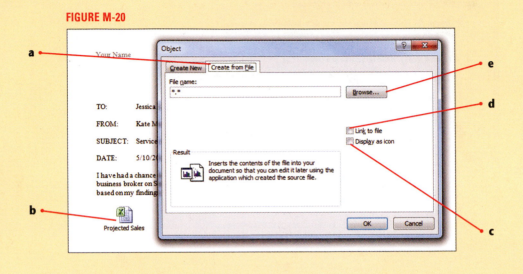

1. Which element do you click to insert an existing object into a Word document rather than creating a new file?
2. Which element do you click to embed information that can be viewed by double-clicking an icon?
3. Which element do you double-click to display an embedded Excel workbook?
4. Which element do you click to find a file to be embedded or linked?
5. Which element do you click to insert an object that maintains a connection to the source document?

## Match each term with the statement that best describes it.

6. Embedding
7. Source document
8. Destination document
9. Presentation graphics program
10. Linking
11. OLE

a. File from which the object to be embedded or linked originates
b. Copies an object and retains a connection with the source program and source document
c. Document receiving the object to be embedded or linked
d. Data transfer method used in Windows programs
e. Copies an object and retains a connection with the source program only
f. Used to create slide shows

## Select the best answer from the list of choices.

12. An ASCII file:
    a. Contains text but no formatting.
    b. Contains formatting but no text.
    c. Contains a PowerPoint presentation.
    d. Contains an unformatted worksheet.

13. An object consists of:
    a. A worksheet only.
    b. Text, a worksheet, or any other type of data.
    c. Text only.
    d. Database data only.

14. A column separator in a text file is called a(n):
    a. Object.
    b. Link.
    c. Delimiter.
    d. Primary key.

**15. To view a workbook that has been embedded as an icon in a Word document, you need to:**

   **a.** Drag the icon.

   **b.** Double-click the icon.

   **c.** Click View, then click Worksheet.

   **d.** Click File, then click Open.

**16. A field that contains unique information for each record in a database table is called a(n):**

   **a.** ID Key.

   **b.** Primary key.

   **c.** First key.

   **d.** Header key.

## Skills Review

**1. Import a text file.**

   **a.** Start Excel, open the tab-delimited text file titled EX M-9.txt from the drive and folder where you store your Data Files, then save it as a Microsoft Office Excel workbook with the name **EX M-West Street Tea**.

   **b.** Widen the columns as necessary so that all the data is visible.

   **c.** Format the data in columns B and C using the Currency style with two decimal places.

   **d.** Center the column labels and apply bold formatting, as shown in Figure M-21.

   **e.** Add your name to the center section of the worksheet footer, save the workbook, preview the worksheet, close the workbook, then submit the workbook to your instructor.

**FIGURE M-21**

| | A | B | C | D |
|---|---|---|---|---|
| 1 | **Item** | **Cost** | **Price** | |
| 2 | Pot, small | $8.55 | $17.50 | |
| 3 | Pot, large | $10.15 | $27.00 | |
| 4 | Pot, decorated | $15.55 | $27.70 | |
| 5 | Pot, china | $20.15 | $31.90 | |
| 6 | Basket, small | $14.95 | $27.80 | |
| 7 | Basket, large | $20.80 | $33.90 | |
| 8 | Kettle, small | $18.75 | $28.45 | |
| 9 | Kettle, large | $24.30 | $33.75 | |
| 10 | Mug, large | $1.95 | $5.70 | |
| 11 | | | | |

**2. Import a database table.**

   **a.** In Excel, use the From Access button in the Get External Data group on the Data tab to import the Access Data File EX M-10.accdb from the drive and folder where you store your Data Files, then save it as a Microsoft Excel workbook named **EX M-February Budget**.

   **b.** Rename the sheet with the imported data **Budget**.

   **c.** Change the column labels so they read as follows: **Budget Category**, **Budget Item**, **Month**, and **Amount Budgeted**.

   **d.** Adjust the column widths as necessary.

   **e.** Add a total row to the table to display the sum of the budgeted amounts in cell D26.

   **f.** Apply the Medium 5 Table Style. Format range D2:D26 using the Accounting style, the $ symbol, and no decimal places.

   **g.** Save the workbook, and compare your screen to Figure M-22.

**3. Insert a graphic file in a worksheet.**

   **a.** Add four rows above row 1 to create space for an image.

   **b.** In rows 1 through 4, insert the picture file EX M-11.gif from the drive and folder where you store your Data Files.

   **c.** Resize and reposition the picture as necessary to make it fit in rows 1 through 4.

   **d.** Apply the Moderate frame, White style, and change the border color to Purple, Accent 4, Lighter 60%. Resize the picture to fit the image and the border in the first four rows. Center the picture in the range A1:D4.

   **e.** Compare your worksheet to Figure M-23, add your name to the center section of the worksheet footer, preview the workbook, save and close the workbook, then submit the workbook to your instructor.

**FIGURE M-22**

| | A | B | C | D |
|---|---|---|---|---|
| 1 | **Budget Category** | **Budget Item** | **Month** | **Amount Budgeted** |
| 2 | Compensation | Benefits | Feb | $ 62,000 |
| 3 | Compensation | Bonuses | Feb | $ 29,110 |
| 4 | Compensation | Commissions | Feb | $ 21,610 |
| 5 | Compensation | Conferences | Feb | $ 77,654 |
| 6 | Compensation | Promotions | Feb | $ 65,570 |
| 7 | Compensation | Payroll Taxes | Feb | $ 14,980 |
| 8 | Compensation | Salaries | Feb | $ 43,240 |
| 9 | Compensation | Training | Feb | $ 59,600 |
| 10 | Facility | Lease | Feb | $ 48,200 |
| 11 | Facility | Maintenance | Feb | $ 61,310 |
| 12 | Facility | Other | Feb | $ 58,230 |
| 13 | Facility | Rent | Feb | $ 75,600 |
| 14 | Facility | Telephone | Feb | $ 61,030 |
| 15 | Facility | Utilities | Feb | $ 58,510 |
| 16 | Supplies | Food | Feb | $ 61,430 |
| 17 | Supplies | Computer | Feb | $ 45,290 |
| 18 | Supplies | General Office | Feb | $ 42,520 |
| 19 | Supplies | Other | Feb | $ 55,200 |
| 20 | Supplies | Outside Services | Feb | $ 47,010 |
| 21 | Equipment | Computer | Feb | $ 47,210 |
| 22 | Equipment | Other | Feb | $ 41,450 |
| 23 | Equipment | Cash Registers | Feb | $ 53,630 |
| 24 | Equipment | Software | Feb | $ 63,590 |
| 25 | Equipment | Telecommunications | Feb | $ 57,170 |
| 26 | **Total** | | | $ 1,251,144 |
| 27 | | | | |

**FIGURE M-23**

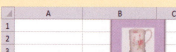

| | A | B | C | D |
|---|---|---|---|---|
| 1 | | | | |
| 2 | | | | |
| 3 | | | | |
| 4 | | | | |
| 5 | **Budget Category** | **Budget Item** | **Month** | **Amount Budgeted** |
| 6 | Compensation | Benefits | Feb | $ 62,000 |
| 7 | Compensation | Bonuses | Feb | $ 29,110 |

Excel 2010

# Skills Review (continued)

4. **Embed a workbook in a Word document.**

   a. Start Word, create a memo header addressed to your instructor, enter your name in the From line, enter **February Salaries** as the subject, and enter the current date in the Date line.

   b. In the memo body, use the Object dialog box to embed the workbook EX M-12.xlsx from the drive and folder where you store your Data Files, displaying it as an icon with the caption **Salary Details**.

   c. Save the document as **EX M-February Salaries** in the drive and folder where you store your Data Files, then double-click the icon to verify that the workbook opens. (*Hint*: If the workbook does not appear after you double-click it, click the Excel icon on the taskbar.)

   d. Close the workbook and return to Word.

   e. Compare your memo to Figure M-24.

5. **Link a workbook to a Word document.**

   a. Delete the icon in the memo body.

   b. In the memo body, link the workbook EX M-12.xlsx, displaying the data, not an icon.

   c. Save the document, then note that Mindy Guan's salary is $6,800. Close the document.

   d. Open the EX M-12.xlsx workbook in Excel, and change Mindy Guan's salary to **$8,800**.

   e. Open the **EX M-February Salaries** document in Word, update the links, and verify that Mindy Guan's salary has changed to $8,800 and that the new total salaries amount is $50,940, as shown in Figure M-25. (*Hint*: If the dialog box does not open, giving you the opportunity to update the link, then right-click the worksheet object and click Update Links.)

   f. Save the **EX M-February Salaries** document, preview the memo, close the document, exit Word, then submit the document to your instructor.

   g. Close the EX M-12 workbook without saving changes, then exit Excel.

6. **Link an Excel chart to a PowerPoint slide.**

   a. Start PowerPoint.

   b. Open the PowerPoint file EX M-13.pptx from the drive and folder where you store your Data Files, then save it as **EX M-Budget Meeting**.

   c. Display Slide 2, February Expenditures.

   d. Link the chart, using the formatting for the destination file, from the Excel file EX M-14.xlsx from the drive and folder where you store your Data Files to Slide 2. Edit the link to be updated automatically. Save and close the Ex M-Budget Meeting file.

   e. Change the Equipment amount on Sheet1 of the file EX M-14 to $200,000, open the EX M-Budget Meeting file, updating the links, and verify the Equipment percentage changed from 12% to 15% on Slide 2.

   f. Add a footer to Slide 2 with your name, then view the slide in Slide Show view. Resize the chart to fit on the slide if necessary. Compare your slide to Figure M-26.

   g. Press [Esc] to return to Normal view.

   h. Save the presentation, exit PowerPoint, close EX M-14 without saving it, then submit the presentation to your instructor.

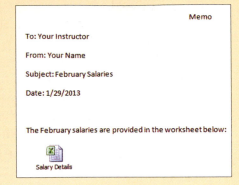

**FIGURE M-24**

Memo

To: Your Instructor

From: Your Name

Subject: February Salaries

Date: 1/29/2013

The February salaries are provided in the worksheet below:

Salary Details

**FIGURE M-25**

Memo

To: Your Instructor

From: Your Name

Subject: February Salaries

Date: 1/29/2013

The February salaries are provided in the worksheet below:

| West Street Tea Salary Summary | | | |
|---|---|---|---|
| First Name | Last Name | Position | Salary |
| Mindy | Guan | Manager | $ 8,800 |
| John | Kelley | Manager | $ 6,500 |
| Mary | O'Riley | Manager | $ 6,600 |
| Sally | Walkman | Sales Associate | $ 7,600 |
| Sarah | Jaffee | Custodian | $ 7,040 |
| Kathy | Alexander | Sales Associate | $ 6,900 |
| Greg | Holak | Sales Associate | $ 7,500 |
| | | Total | $ 50,940 |

**FIGURE M-26**

February Expenditures

Equipment 15%

Compensation 39%

Supplies 19%

Facility 27%

Your Name

Exchanging Data with Other Programs

## Skills Review (continued)

**7. Import a table into Access.**

  **a.** Start Access.

  **b.** Create a blank database named **EX M-Budget** on the drive and folder where you store your Data Files.

  **c.** Use the External Data tab to import the Excel table in the file EX M-15.xlsx from the drive and folder where you store your Data Files. Use the first row as column headings, store the data in a new table, let Access add the primary key, and use the default table name February Budget.

  **d.** Open the February Budget table in Access, and widen the columns as necessary to fully display the field names and field information.

  **e.** Enter your name in the Budget Category column of row 25 in the table, save the database file, compare your screen to Figure M-27, exit Access, then submit the database file to your instructor.

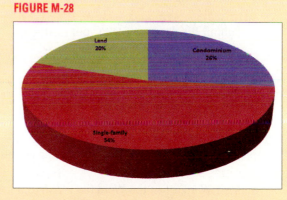

# Independent Challenge 1

You are a real estate agent for the Sarasota branch of West Coast Realty. You have been asked to give a presentation to the regional manager about your sales in the past month. To illustrate your sales data, you will add an Excel chart to one of your slides, showing the different types of property sales and the sales amounts for each type.

  **a.** Start Excel, create a new workbook, then save it as **EX M-June Sales** in the drive and folder where you store your Data Files.

  **b.** Enter the property types and the corresponding sales amounts shown in Table M-2 into the EX M-June Sales workbook. Name the sheet with the sales data **Sales**.

  **c.** Create a 3-D pie chart from the sales data on a new sheet named **Chart**. Format it using Chart Layout 1 and Style 2. Increase the font size of the data labels to 14 and apply bold formatting. (*Hint*: Click a data label on the chart and then use the Mini toolbar.) Delete the chart title. Your chart should look like Figure M-28.

  **d.** Copy the chart to the Clipboard.

  **e.** Start PowerPoint, open the PowerPoint Data File EX M-16.pptx from the drive and folder where you store your Data Files, then save it as **EX M-Sales Presentation**.

  **f.** Link the Excel chart to Slide 2 using the destination theme. Use the sizing handles to change the size if necessary, and drag the chart to position it in the center of the slide if necessary.

  **g.** View the slide in Slide Show view, then press [Esc] to end the show.

  **h.** Add a footer to Slide 2 with your name, then save the presentation.

  **i.** Close the presentation, exit PowerPoint, then submit the PowerPoint file to your instructor.

  **j.** Save the workbook, then close the workbook, and exit Excel.

**TABLE M-2**

| property type | sales |
| --- | --- |
| Condominium | $3,300,400 |
| Single-family | $6,700,200 |
| Land | $2,500,200 |

**FIGURE M-28**

# Independent Challenge 2

You are opening a new fitness center, Total Fitness, in San Francisco, California. The owner of a fitness center in the area is retiring and has agreed to sell you a text file containing his list of supplier information. You need to import this text file into Excel so that you can manipulate the data. Later, you will convert the Excel file to an Access table so that you can give it to your business partner who is building a supplier database.

# Independent Challenge 2 (continued)

a. Start Excel, open the file EX M-17.txt from the drive and folder where you store your Data Files, then save it as an Excel file named **EX M-Fitness Suppliers**. (*Hint*: This is a tab-delimited text file.)

b. Adjust the column widths as necessary. Rename the worksheet **Suppliers**.

c. Create a table using data on the Suppliers sheet, and apply the Table Style Light 18 format.

d. Sort the worksheet data in ascending order by Supplier. Your worksheet should look like Figure M-29.

e. Add your name to the center section of the worksheet footer, save and close the workbook, then exit Excel.

f. Start Access, create a new blank database on the drive and folder where you store your Data Files. Name the new database **EX M-Suppliers**.

g. Use the External Data tab to import the Excel file EX M-Fitness Suppliers from the drive and folder where you store your Data Files. Use the column labels as the field names, store the data in a new table, let Access add the primary key, and accept the default table name.

**FIGURE M-29**

| | A | B | C | D | E | F | G |
|---|---|---|---|---|---|---|---|
| 1 | Supplier | Address | City | State | Zip | Phone | Contact |
| 2 | Ace Equipment | 2 Jean St | Oakland | CA | 94611 | 510-422-9923 | R. Jurez |
| 3 | All Equipment | PO Box 9870 | Milpitas | CA | 94698 | 408-345-9343 | F. Gerry |
| 4 | Best Start | 102 Lake Dr | San Diego | CA | 93112 | 212-223-9934 | S. Werthen |
| 5 | Cool Equipment | 232 Corn Ave | Daly City | CA | 94623 | 415-465-7855 | O. Rolins |
| 6 | East Coast Equipment | 343 Upham St | Los Angeles | CA | 93111 | 213-887-4456 | P. Newhall |
| 7 | Fitness Pro | 223 Main St | Ventura | CA | 93143 | 213-332-5568 | A. Blume |
| 8 | Handley Exercise | 44 West St | Brisbane | CA | 94453 | 415-223-9912 | H. Jones |
| 9 | Jones Equipment | 394 19th Ave | San Francisco | CA | 94554 | 415-444-9932 | L. Smith |
| 10 | Sports Plus | 33 Jackson St | Fresno | CA | 96899 | 608-332-8790 | J. Jerry |
| 11 | Sports Pro | 998 Little St | San Francisco | CA | 94622 | 415-665-7342 | W. Kitter |
| 12 | Sports Unlimited | 77 Sunrise St | Malibu | CA | 93102 | 213-223-5432 | J. Walsh |
| 13 | West Coast Sports | 8 High St | San Jose | CA | 94671 | 408-332-9981 | K. McGuire |

h. Open the Suppliers table and AutoFit the columns. (Table1 will be removed when the file is closed.)

i. Enter your name in the Supplier column in row 13, save and then close the table, and exit Access.

## Advanced Challenge Exercise

- Create a copy of the EX M-Fitness Suppliers.xlsx file with the name **EX M-Fitness Suppliers_ACE** on the drive and folder where you store your Data Files.

- Using Access, create a new blank database named **EX M-Suppliers_ACE** on the drive and folder where your store your Data Files. Link the Excel data in the EX M-Fitness Suppliers _ACE file to the EX M-Suppliers_ACE database file.

- Close the database file, open the EX M-Fitness Suppliers _ACE.xlsx file, and change the contact for the Ace Equipment supplier to J. Smith. Save and close the Excel file.

- Open the EX M-Suppliers_ACE database, and verify that the contact name was updated in the Suppliers table, then close the table and exit Access.

j. Submit the database file to your instructor.

# Independent Challenge 3

You are the newly hired manager at People Alliance, a mutual funds firm specializing in consumer products. An employee, Karen Holden, has completed a two-year training period as an assistant and you would like to promote her to an associate position with a higher salary. You have examined the salaries of the other associates in the company and will present this information to the vice president of Human Resources, requesting permission to grant Karen a promotion and an increase in salary.

a. Start Word, open the Word file EX M-18.docx from the drive and folder where you store your Data Files, then save it as **EX M-Promotion**.

b. Add your name to the From line of the memo, and change the date to the current date.

c. At the end of the memo, embed the workbook EX M-19.xlsx as an icon from the drive and folder where you store your Data Files. Change the caption for the icon to **Salaries**. Double-click the icon to verify that the workbook opens.

d. Close the workbook, return to Word, delete the Salaries icon, and link the workbook EX M-19 to the memo, displaying the data, not an icon.

e. Save the EX M-Promotion memo, and close the file.

f. Open the EX M-19 workbook, and change Karen Holden's salary to $55,000.

g. Open the EX M-Promotion memo, update the links, and make sure Karen Holden's salary is updated.

# Independent Challenge 3 (continued)

### Advanced Challenge Exercise

- ■ Delete the worksheet at the bottom of the Promotion memo. Copy the range A1:C10 from Sheet1 of the EX M-19 workbook to the Clipboard. (*Tip*: You are not copying the gross salary information because you do not want it to appear in the memo.)
- ■ Return to the EX M-Promotion memo, and use the Paste Special dialog box to paste a link to the range A1:C10 from EX M-19 that is on the Clipboard. Use Figure M-30 as a guide. Save and close the memo.
- ■ Change Karen Holden's position to Associate in the EX M-19 workbook. Verify the new position information is displayed in the EX M-Promotion memo when the memo is opened with the links updated.

**h.** Save and close the memo. Exit Word and submit the memo to your instructor.

**i.** Close EX M-19 without saving the changes to Karen Holden's information, then exit Excel.

**FIGURE M-30**

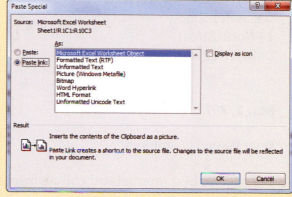

# Real Life Independent Challenge

You decide to create a daily schedule of your pet's activities to give to the person who will care for your pet when you go on vacation. As part of this schedule, you record the times and corresponding activities that your pet engages in daily. You also record when medicine should be taken. You will include the schedule in a Word document that provides your contact information. You decide to link the workbook so that schedule changes will be reflected in the information you provide to the pet sitter.

**a.** Start Excel, open the file EX M-20.xlsx from the drive and folder where you store your Data Files, then save it as **EX M-Schedule**.

**b.** Use the structure of the worksheet to record your pet's schedule. Change the data in columns A and B to reflect your pet's times and activities. If you do not have any data to enter, create your own or use the data provided on the worksheet.

**c.** Save and close the EX M-Schedule workbook, then exit Excel.

**d.** Open the Data File EX M-21.docx from the drive and folder where you store your Data Files, then save it as **EX M-Contact Information**.

**e.** Enter your name at the bottom of the document. Change the document data to reflect your destination and contact information. If you do not have any data to enter, use the provided document data.

**f.** Below the line "Here is a schedule of Junior's daily activities:", create a linked version of the worksheet to the EX M-Schedule workbook.

**g.** Save the file, then preview the EX M-Contact Information document.

**h.** Close the Word document, exit Word, then submit the Word document to your instructor.

### Advanced Challenge Exercise

- ■ Open the EX M-Schedule.xlsx workbook from the drive and folder where you store your Data Files. Add rows at the top of the worksheet to display a picture of your pet. Add as many rows as necessary. Insert a picture of your pet in the new rows. You can use the picture EX M-22.gif if you don't have a picture.
- ■ Resize the picture, and move it to the top center of the new worksheet rows. Use the rotation options of your choice to rotate the picture. (*Hint*: You can rotate a picture by clicking the Rotate button in the Arrange group on the Picture Tools Format tab.)
- ■ Use the picture effects options of your choice to change the picture.
- ■ Save the workbook and preview the sheet.
- ■ Close the workbook, exit Excel, then submit the workbook to your instructor.

# Visual Workshop

Create the document shown in Figure M-31 by opening the Word file EX M-23.docx and linking the data from the Excel file EX M-24.xlsx. Replace Management in the last line of the document with your name. Save the document as **EX M-Price Increase**, close the document, exit Word and Excel. Submit the file to your instructor.

FIGURE M-31

Dallas Pet Supply
14 North Street
Dallas, TX 75201


May 1, 2013

Dear Valued Customers,

Despite our best internal cost containment measures we have experienced cost increases in transportation and materials. To address these costs we will increase the prices for the products listed below on orders received and shipped after June 1, 2013.

| Product | Item Code | Price |
|---|---|---|
| Dog Bed Large | A324 | $152.99 |
| Dog Bed Small | A325 | $131.57 |
| Dog Brush Set | A251 | $35.94 |
| Dog Crate Large | A409 | $139.99 |
| Dog Crate Medium | A407 | $121.22 |
| Dog Crate Small | A408 | $108.57 |
| Cat Bed | B101 | $105.99 |
| Cat Play Set | B211 | $42.99 |
| Dog Collar | A135 | $25.19 |
| Cat Collar | B132 | $20.36 |
| Cat Post | B755 | $19.99 |
| Dog Toy Set | A884 | $39.54 |

Thank you for your understanding and continued business.


Regards,

Your Name

**UNIT N**

Excel 2010

**Files You Will Need:**

EX N-1.xlsx
EX N-2.xlsx
EX N-3.xsd
EX N-4.xml
EX N-5.xml
EX N-6.htm
EX N-7.xlsx
EX N-8.xsd
EX N-9.xml
EX N-10.htm
EX N-11.xlsx
EX N-12.xlsx
EX N-13.xlsx
EX N-14.htm
EX N-15.xsd
EX N-16.xml
EX N-17.xsd
EX N-18.xml
EX N-19.htm

# Sharing Excel Files and Incorporating Web Information

Increasingly, Excel users share workbooks with others, over the Web as well as on private networks. Sharing workbooks allows others to review, revise, and provide feedback on worksheet data. In addition, users frequently incorporate up-to-date information from the Web into their workbooks and prepare their own data for posting on the Web.  Kate Morgan, the vice president of sales for Quest, wants to share information with corporate office employees and branch managers using the company's intranet and the Web.

**OBJECTIVES**

Share Excel files

Set up a shared workbook for multiple users

Track revisions in a shared workbook

Apply and modify passwords

Work with XML schemas

Import and export XML data

Run Web queries to retrieve external data

Import and export HTML data

# Sharing Excel Files

Microsoft Excel provides many different ways to share spreadsheets with people in your office, in your organization, or anywhere on the Web. When you share workbooks, you have to consider how you will protect information that you don't want everyone to see and how you can control revisions others will make to your files. Also, some information you want to use might not be in Excel format. For example, there is a great deal of information published on the Web in HTML format, so Excel allows you to import HTML to your worksheets. You can also export your worksheet data in HTML format. However, many companies find the XML format to be more flexible than HTML for storing and exchanging data, so they are increasingly using XML to store and exchange data both internally and externally. Excel allows you to easily import and export XML data as well. You can also retrieve data from the Web using queries. Figure N-1 shows methods of importing to and exporting from workbooks.  Kate considers the best way to share her Excel workbooks with corporate employees and branch managers.

## DETAILS

### To share worksheet information, consider the following issues:

- **Allowing others to use a workbook**

  While many of your workbooks are for your own use, you will want to share some of them with other users. When users **share** your workbooks, they can simultaneously open them from a network server, modify them electronically, and return their revisions to you for incorporation with others' changes. You can view each user's name and the date each change was made. To share a workbook, you need to turn on the sharing feature for that workbook. Kate wants to obtain feedback on Quest sales data from the branch managers, so she sets up her workbook so others can use it.

- **Controlling access to workbooks on a server**

  When you place a workbook on a network server, you will probably want to control who can open and change it. You can do this using Excel passwords. Kate assigns a password to her workbook, then posts the workbook on the Quest server. She gives the corporate staff and branch managers the password, so only they can open the workbook and revise it.

- **HTML data**

  You can paste data from a Web page into a worksheet and then manipulate and format it using Excel. You can also save Excel workbook information in HTML format so you can publish it on an intranet or on the Web. Kate decides to publish the worksheet with the North American sales information in HTML format on the company intranet, as shown in Figure N-2

- **Working with XML data**

  Importing and storing data in XML format allows you to use it in different situations. For example, a company might store all of its sales data in an XML file and make different parts of the file available to various departments such as marketing and accounting. These departments can extract information that is relevant to their purposes from the file. A subset of the same XML file might be sent to vendors or other business associates who only require certain types of sales data stored in the XML file. Kate decides to import XML files that contain sales information from the Miami and New York branches to get a sales summary for Quest's eastern region.

- **Using an Excel query to retrieve data from the Web**

  You can use built-in Excel queries to import up-to-date stock quotes and currency rates from the MSN Money Web site. These queries import data from the Web into an Excel workbook, where you can organize and manipulate the information using Excel spreadsheet and graphics tools. Kate decides to use a query to get currency rate information for her analysis of the sales data from the Quest Canada branches, as shown in Figure N-3.

## FIGURE N-1: Importing and exporting data

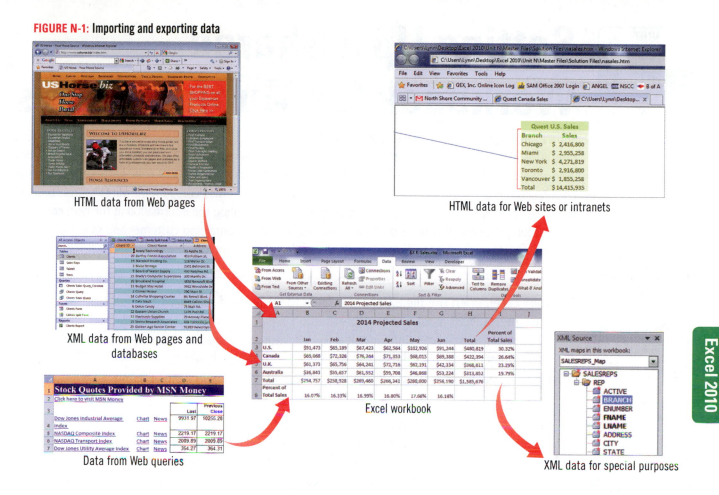

HTML data from Web pages

HTML data for Web sites or intranets

XML data from Web pages and databases

Excel workbook

Data from Web queries

XML data for special purposes

## FIGURE N-2: North America sales information displayed in a Web browser

Excel data published in a browser

## FIGURE N-3: Data retrieved from the Web using a Web query

Excel worksheet with imported currency information

| Name | In US$ | Per US$ |
|---|---|---|
| Argentine Peso to US Dollar | 0.26069 | 3.836 |
| Australian Dollar to US Dollar | 0.88168 | 1.134 |
| Bahraini Dinar to US Dollar | 2.6487 | 0.378 |
| Bolivian Boliviano to US Dollar | 0.14225 | 7.03 |
| Brazilian Real to US Dollar | 0.54127 | 1.848 |
| British Pound to US Dollar | 1.5903 | 0.629 |
| Canadian Dollar to US Dollar | 0.94197 | 1.062 |
| Chile Peso to US Dollar | 0.00186 | 538.8 |
| Chinese Yuan to US Dollar | 0.14639 | 6.831 |
| Colombian Peso to US Dollar | 0.00051 | 1971 |
| Czech Koruna to US Dollar | 0.05326 | 18.775 |
| Danish Krone to US Dollar | 0.18658 | 5.36 |
| Euro to US Dollar | 1.3885 | 0.72 |
| Egyptian Pound* to US Dollar | 0.18297 | 5.466 |
| Hong Kong Dollar to US Dollar | 0.12874 | 7.768 |
| Hungarian Forint to US Dollar | 0.00511 | 195.7 |
| Indian Rupee to US Dollar | 0.02171 | 46.06 |
| Indonesia Rupiah to US Dollar | 0.00011 | 9330 |
| Japanese Yen to US Dollar | 0.011 | 90.95 |
| Jordanian Dinar to US Dollar | 1.4094 | 0.71 |
| Kenyan Shilling to US Dollar | 0.01313 | 76.15 |
| South Korean Won to US Dollar | 0.00087 | 1153 |

# Setting Up a Shared Workbook for Multiple Users

You can make an Excel file a **shared workbook** so that several users can open and modify it at the same time. This is useful for workbooks that you want others to review on a network server, where the workbook is equally accessible to all network users. When you share a workbook, you can have Excel keep a list of all changes to the workbook, which you can view and print at any time.  Kate wants to get feedback from selected corporate staff and branch managers before presenting the information at the next corporate staff meeting. She asks you to help her put a shared workbook containing customer and sales data on the company's network. You begin by making her Excel file a shared workbook.

## STEPS

1. **Start Excel, open the file EX N-1.xlsx from the drive and folder where you store your Data Files, then save it as EX N-Sales Information**

   The workbook with the sales information opens, displaying two worksheets. The first contains tour sales data for the Quest U.S. branches; the second is a breakdown of the branch sales by sales associate.

2. **Click the Review tab, then click the Share Workbook button in the Changes group**

   The Share Workbook dialog box opens, as shown in Figure N-4.

> **QUICK TIP**
> The Advanced tab of the Share Workbook dialog box allows you to specify the length of time the change history is saved and when the file will be updated with the changes.

3. **Click the Editing tab, if necessary**

   The dialog box lists the names of people who are currently using the workbook. You are the only user, so your name, or the name of the person entered as the computer user, appears, along with the current date and time.

> **QUICK TIP**
> To return a shared workbook to unshared status, click the Review tab, click the Share Workbook button in the Changes group, then deselect the Allow changes by more than one user at the same time option on the Editing tab of the Share Workbook dialog box.

4. **Click to select the check box next to Allow changes by more than one user at the same time. This also allows workbook merging., then click OK**

   A dialog box appears, asking if you want to save the workbook. This will resave it as a shared workbook.

5. **Click OK**

   Excel saves the file as a shared workbook. The title bar now reads EX N-Sales Information.xlsx [Shared], as shown in Figure N-5. This version replaces the unshared version.

### Sharing workbooks using Excel Web App

The Excel Web App is an online program that lets you collaborate on Excel workbooks with others using a Web browser, without needing the Excel program installed on any users' computers. You need a Windows Live ID to access Windows Live SkyDrive where you store and access your Excel workbooks. To post your workbook to Windows Live SkyDrive from Excel, click the File tab, click Save & Send, click Save to Web, if necessary sign in using your Windows Live ID username and password, click the folder where you want to save the document, then click Save As. Assign a filename and online folder destination, then click Save.

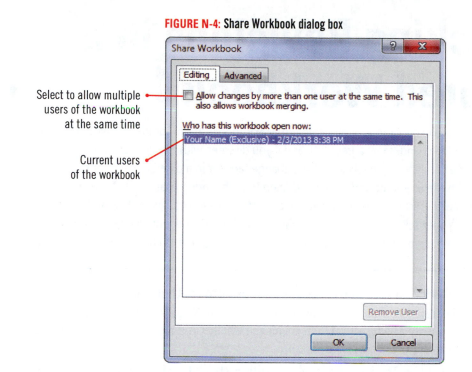

**FIGURE N-4:** Share Workbook dialog box

Select to allow multiple users of the workbook at the same time

Current users of the workbook

**FIGURE N-5:** Shared workbook

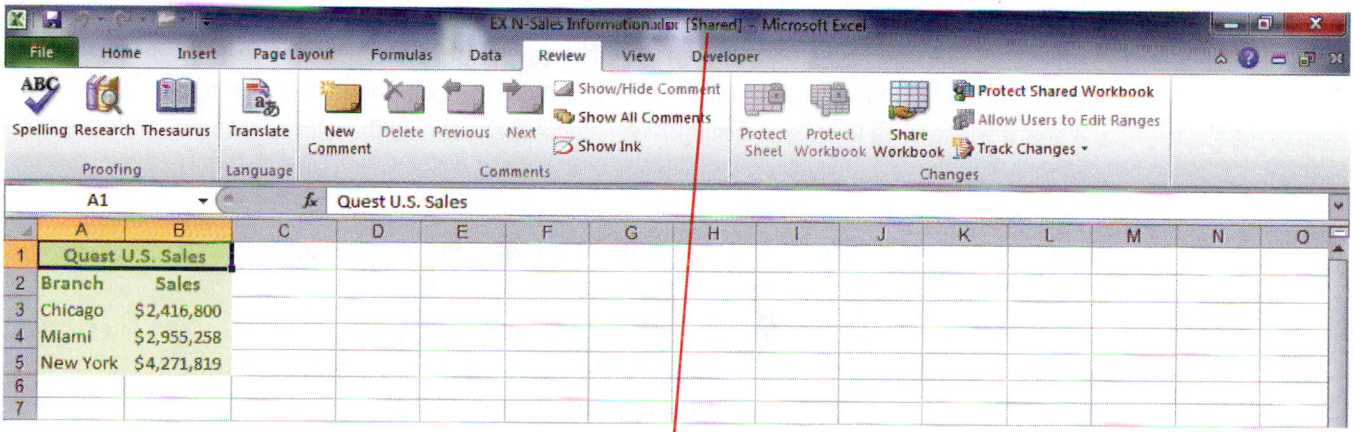

Title bar indicates the workbook is shared

## Merging workbooks

Instead of putting the shared workbook on a server to be shared simultaneously, you might want to distribute copies to your reviewers via e-mail. Once everyone has entered their changes and returned their workbook copies to you, you can merge the changed copies into one master workbook that contains everyone's changes. Each copy you distribute must be designated as shared, and the Change History feature on the Advanced tab of the Share Workbook dialog box must be activated. Occasionally a conflict occurs when two users are trying to edit the same cells in a shared workbook. In this case, the second person to save the file will see a Resolve Conflicts dialog box and need to choose Accept Mine or Accept Other. To merge workbooks, you need to add the Compare and Merge Workbooks command to the Quick Access toolbar by clicking the File tab, clicking Options, and clicking Quick Access toolbar. Click All Commands in the Choose commands from list, click Compare and Merge Workbooks, click Add, then click OK. Once you get the changed copies back, open the master copy of the workbook, then click the Compare and Merge Workbooks button on the Quick Access toolbar. The Select Files to Merge Into Current Workbook dialog box opens. Select the workbooks you want to merge (you can use the [Ctrl] key to select more than one workbook), then click OK.

# Tracking Revisions in a Shared Workbook

When you share workbooks, it is often helpful to **track** modifications, or identify who made which changes. You can accept the changes you agree with, and if you disagree with any changes you can reject them. When you activate the Excel change tracking feature, changes appear in a different color for each user. Each change is identified with the username and date. In addition to highlighting changes, Excel keeps track of changes in a **change history**, a list of all changes that you can place on a separate worksheet so you can review them all at once.  Kate asks you to set up the shared Sales Information workbook so that Excel tracks all future changes. You then open a workbook that is on the server and review its changes and the change history.

**STEPS**

1. **Click the Track Changes button in the Changes group, then click Highlight Changes**

   The Highlight Changes dialog box opens, as shown in Figure N-6, allowing you to turn on change tracking. You can also specify which changes to highlight and whether you want to display changes on the screen or save the change history in a separate worksheet.

2. **Click to select the Track changes while editing check box if necessary, remove check marks from all other boxes except for Highlight changes on screen, click OK, then click OK in the dialog box that informs you that you have yet to make changes**

   Leaving the When, Who, and Where check boxes blank allows you to track all changes.

   > **QUICK TIP**
   > Cells changed by other users appear in different colors.

3. **Click the Sales by Rep sheet tab, change the sales figure for Sanchez in cell C3 to 290,000, press [Enter], then move the mouse pointer over the cell you just changed**

   A border with a small triangle in the upper-left corner appears around the cell you changed, and a ScreenTip appears with the date, the time, and details about the change, as shown in Figure N-7.

4. **Save and close the workbook**

   Jose Silva has made changes to a version of this workbook. You want to open this workbook and view the details of these changes and accept the ones that appear to be correct.

5. **Open the file EX N-2.xlsx from the drive and folder where you store your Data Files, save it as EX N-Sales Information Edits, click the Review tab if necessary, click the Track Changes button in the Changes group, click Accept/Reject Changes, click the When check box in the Select Changes to Accept or Reject dialog box to deselect it, then click OK**

   You will accept the first four changes that Jose made to the workbook and reject his last change. You also want to see a list of all changes.

6. **Click Accept four times to approve the first four changes, click Reject to undo Jose's fifth change, click the Track Changes button in the Changes group, click Highlight Changes, click the When check box in the Highlight Changes dialog box to deselect it, click to select the List changes on a new sheet check box, then click OK**

   A new sheet named History opens, as shown in Figure N-8, with Jose's changes in a filtered list. Because saving the file closes the History sheet, you need to copy the information to a new worksheet.

7. **Copy the range A1:I6 on the History sheet, click the Insert Worksheet button ⊞ next to the History sheet tab, on the new sheet click cell A1, click the Home tab, click the Paste button in the Clipboard group, widen columns E, F, H, and I to display the information in the columns, then rename the new sheet tab Saved History**

   > **TROUBLE**
   > You can enter a footer in Page Layout view if the Header & Footer button is not available. Not all commands are available in shared workbooks.

8. **Add a footer with your name to the Saved History sheet, save and close the workbook, then submit the workbook to your instructor**

   The Saved History sheet shows all of Jose's changes to the workbook.

**FIGURE N-6:** Highlight Changes dialog box

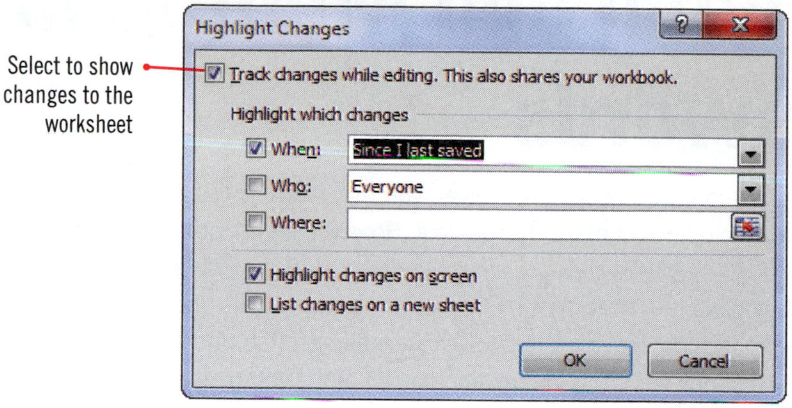

Select to show changes to the worksheet →

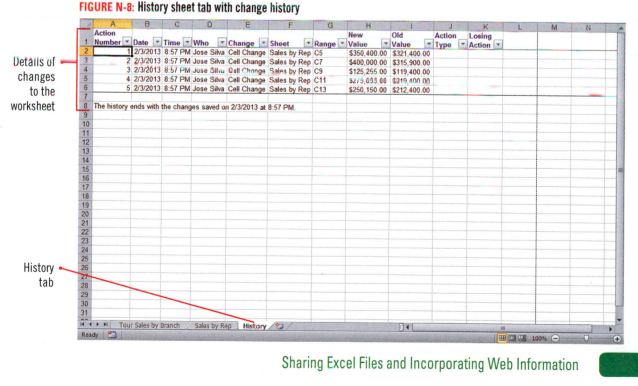

**FIGURE N-7:** Tracked change

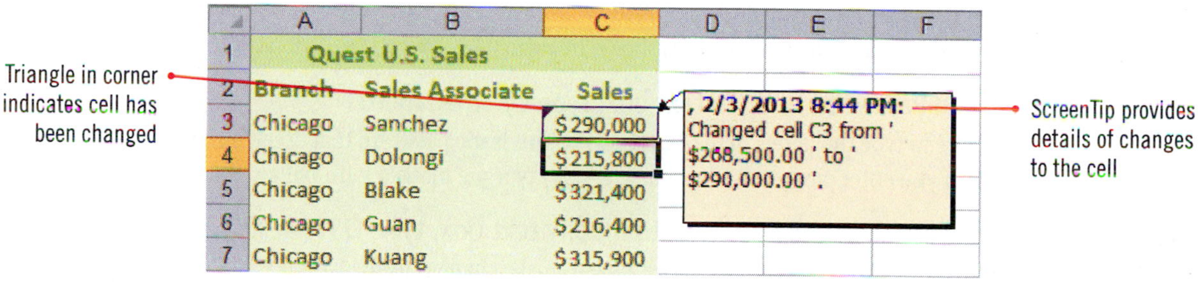

Triangle in corner indicates cell has been changed →

← ScreenTip provides details of changes to the cell

**FIGURE N-8:** History sheet tab with change history

Details of changes to the worksheet

History tab

Excel 2010

# Applying and Modifying Passwords

When you place a shared workbook on a server, you may want to use a password so that only authorized people will be able to open it or make changes to it. However, it's important to remember that *if you lose your password, you will not be able to open or change the workbook.* Passwords are case sensitive, so you must type them exactly as you want users to type them, with the same spacing and using the same case. For security, it is a good idea to include uppercase and lowercase letters and numbers in a password.  Kate wants you to put the workbook with sales information on one of the company's servers. You decide to save a copy of the workbook with two passwords: one that users will need to open it, and another that they will use to make changes to it.

## STEPS

**QUICK TIP**

You can also use a password to encrypt the contents of a workbook by clicking the File tab, clicking Protect Workbook in the middle pane, clicking Encrypt with Password, and entering a password.

1. **Open the file EX N-1.xlsx from the drive and folder where you store your Data Files, click the File Tab, click Save As, click the Tools list arrow in the bottom of the Save As dialog box, then click General Options**

   The General Options dialog box opens, with two password boxes: one to open the workbook, and one to allow changes to the workbook, as shown in Figure N-9.

2. **In the Password to open text box, type QSTmanager01**

   Be sure to type the letters in the correct cases. This is the password that users must type to open the workbook. When you enter passwords, the characters you type are masked with bullets (• • •) for security purposes.

**QUICK TIP**

You can press [Enter] rather than clicking OK after entering a password. This allows you to keep your hands on the keyboard.

3. **Press [Tab], in the Password to modify text box, type QSTsales02, then click OK**

   This is the password that users must type to make changes to the workbook. A dialog box asks you to verify the first password by reentering it.

4. **Enter QSTmanager01 in the first Confirm Password dialog box, click OK, enter QSTsales02 in the second Confirm Password dialog box, then click OK**

5. **Change the filename to EX N-Sales Information PW, if necessary navigate to the location where you store your Data Files, click Save, then close the workbook**

**QUICK TIP**

To delete a password, reopen the General Options dialog box, highlight the symbols for the existing password, press [Delete], click OK, change the filename, then click Save.

6. **Reopen the workbook EX N-Sales Information PW, enter the password QSTmanager01 when prompted for a password, click OK, then enter QSTsales02 to obtain write access**

   The Password dialog box is shown in Figure N-10. Obtaining write access for a workbook allows you to modify it.

7. **Click OK, change the sales figure for the Chicago branch in cell B3 to 2,500,000, then press [Enter]**

   You were able to make this change because you obtained write access privileges using the password "QSTsales02".

8. **Save and close the workbook**

**FIGURE N-9:** General Options dialog box

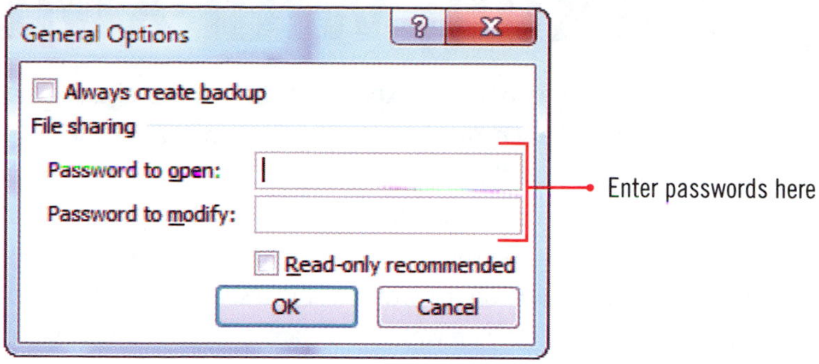

Enter passwords here

**FIGURE N-10:** Password entry prompt

Password is masked with bullets for security

### Creating strong passwords for Excel workbooks

Strong passwords will help to protect your workbooks from security threats. A **strong password** has at least 14 characters that are not commonly used. Although your password needs to be easy to remember, it should be difficult for other people to guess. Avoid using your birthday, your pet's name, or other personal information in your password. Also avoid dictionary words and repeated characters. Instead, mix the types of characters using uppercase and lowercase letters, numbers, and special characters such as @ and %. Microsoft offers an online password checker to test your passwords for security. See Table N-1 for rules and examples for creating strong passwords.

**TABLE N-1:** Rules for creating strong passwords

| rule | example |
| --- | --- |
| Include numbers | 5qRyz8O6w |
| Add symbols | lQx!u%z7q9 |
| Increase complexity | 4!%5Zq^c6# |
| Use long passwords | Z7#l%2!q9!6@i9&Wb |

# Working with XML Schemas

Using Excel you can import and export XML data and analyze it using Excel tools. To import XML data, Excel requires a file called a schema that describes the structure of the XML file. A **schema** contains the rules for the XML file by listing all of the fields in the XML document and their characteristics, such as the type of data they contain. A schema is used to **validate** XML data, making sure the data follows the rules given in the file. Once a schema is attached to a workbook, a schema is called a **map**. When you map an element to a worksheet, you place the element name on the worksheet in a specific location. Mapping XML elements allows you to choose the XML data from a file with which you want to work in the worksheet. 🎨 Kate has been given XML files containing sales information from the U.S. branches. She asks you to prepare a workbook to import the sales representatives' XML data. You begin by adding a schema to a worksheet that describes the XML data.

## STEPS

**TROUBLE**

If the Developer tab does not appear, click the File tab, click Options, click Customize Ribbon, and select the Developer check box.

1. **Create a new workbook, save it as EX N-Sales Reps in the drive and folder where you store your Data Files, click the Developer tab, then click the Source button in the XML group**
   The XML Source pane opens. This is where you specify a schema, or map, to import. A schema has the extension .xsd. Kate has provided you with a schema she received from the IT Department describing the XML file structure.

2. **Click XML Maps at the bottom of the task pane**
   The XML Maps dialog box opens, listing the XML maps or schemas in the workbook. There are no schemas in the Sales Reps workbook at this time, as shown in Figure N-11.

**QUICK TIP**

You can delete a map from a workbook by clicking the XML Maps button at the bottom of the XML Source task pane to open the XML Maps dialog box. In the dialog box select the map that you want to delete, click Delete, then click OK.

3. **Click Add in the XML Maps dialog box, navigate to the drive and folder containing your Data Files in the Select XML Source dialog box, click EX N-3.xsd, click Open, then click OK**
   The schema elements appear in the XML Source task pane. Elements in a schema describe data similarly to the way field names in an Excel table describe the data in their columns. You choose the schema elements from the XML Source pane with which you want to work on your worksheet and map them to the worksheet. Once on the worksheet, the elements are called fields.

4. **Click the BRANCH element in the XML Source task pane and drag it to cell A1 on the worksheet, then use Figure N-12 as a guide to drag the FNAME, LNAME, SALES, and ENUMBER fields to the worksheet**
   The mapped elements appear in bolded format in the XML Source pane. The fields on the worksheet have filter arrows because Excel automatically creates a table on the worksheet as you map the schema elements. You decide to remove the ENUMBER field from the table.

**QUICK TIP**

Make sure that you right-click the ENUMBER element in the XML Source task pane and not the field on the worksheet.

5. **Right-click the ENUMBER element in the XML Source task pane, then click Remove element**
   ENUMBER is no longer formatted in bold because it is no longer mapped to the worksheet. This means that when XML data is imported, the ENUMBER field will not be populated with data. However, the field name remains in the table on the worksheet.

6. **Drag the table resizing arrow to the left to remove cell E1 from the table**
   Because you plan to import XML data from different files, you want to be sure that data from one file will not overwrite data from another file when it is imported into the worksheet. You also want to be sure that Excel validates the imported data against the rules specified in the schema.

7. **Click any cell in the table, click the Developer tab, then click the Map Properties button in the XML group**
   The XML Map Properties dialog box opens, as shown in Figure N-13.

8. **Click the Validate data against schema for import and export check box to select it, if necessary click the Append new data to existing XML tables option button to select it, then click OK**
   You are ready to import XML data into your worksheet.

**FIGURE N-11:** XML Maps dialog box

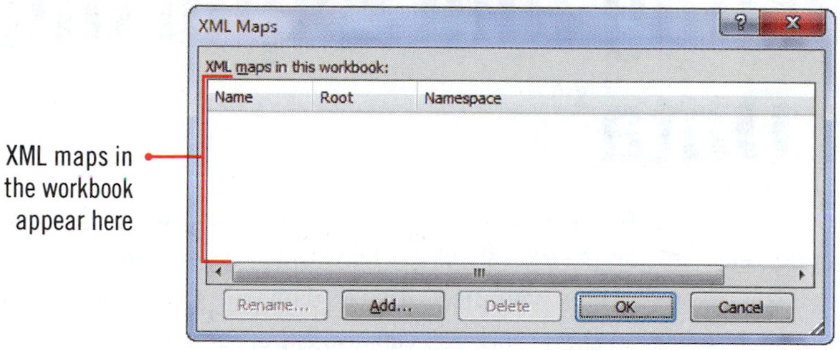

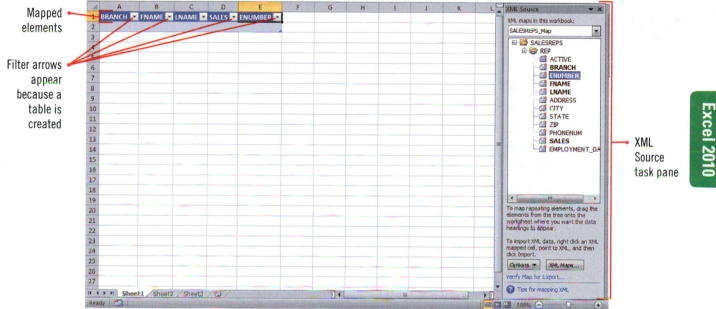

XML maps in
the workbook
appear here

**FIGURE N-12:** XML elements mapped to the worksheet

Mapped
elements

Filter arrows
appear
because a
table is
created

XML
Source
task pane

Excel 2010

**FIGURE N-13:** XML Map Properties dialog box

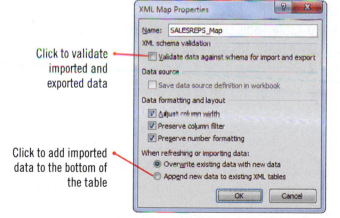

Click to validate
imported and
exported data

Click to add imported
data to the bottom of
the table

## Learning more about XML

XML is a universal data format for business and industry information sharing. Using XML, you can store structured information related to services, products, or business transactions and easily share and exchange the information with others. XML provides a way to express structure in data. Structured data is tagged, or marked up, to indicate its content. For example, an XML data marker (tag) that contains an item's cost might be named COST. Excel's ability to work with XML data allows you to access the large amount of information stored in the XML format. For example, organizations have developed many XML applications with a specific focus, such as MathML (Mathematical Markup Language) and RETML (Real Estate Transaction Markup Language).

# Importing and Exporting XML Data

After the mapping is complete, you can import any XML file with a structure that conforms to the workbook schema. The mapped elements on the worksheet will fill with (or be **populated** with) data from the XML file. If an element is not mapped on the worksheet, then its data will not be imported. Once you import the XML data, you can analyze it using Excel tools. You can also export data from an Excel workbook to an XML file.  Kate asks you to combine the sales data for the Miami and New York branches that are contained in XML files. She would like you to add a total for the combined branches and export the data from Excel to an XML file.

## STEPS

1. **Click cell A1, click the Developer tab if necessary, then click the Import button in the XML group**

   The Import XML dialog box opens.

2. **Navigate to the folder containing your Data Files if necessary, click EX N-4.xml, then click Import**

   The worksheet is populated with data from the XML file that contains the Miami sales rep information. Excel only imports data for the mapped elements. You decide to add the sales rep data for the New York branch to the worksheet.

3. **Click the Import button in the XML group, navigate to the folder containing your Data Files in the Import XML dialog box if necessary, click EX N-5.xml, then click Import**

   The New York branch sales rep data is added to the Miami branch data. You decide to total the sales figures for all sales reps.

4. **Click the Table Tools Design tab, then click the Total Row check box to select it**

   The total sales amount of 4999777 appears in cell D25. You decide to format the table.

5. **Select the range of cells D2:D25, click the Home tab, click the Accounting Number Format button $ in the Number group, click the Decrease Decimal button in the Number group twice, click the Table Tools Design tab, click the More button in the Table Styles group, select Table Style Light 18, then click cell A1**

   Compare your completed table to Figure N-14.

6. **Enter your name in the center section of the worksheet footer, then preview the table**

   You will export the combined sales rep data as an XML file. Because not all of the elements in the schema were mapped to fields in your Excel table, you do not want the data exported from the table to be validated against the schema.

7. **Click any cell in the table, click the Developer tab, click the Map Properties button in the XML group, then click the Validate data against schema for import and export check box to deselect it**

   The Map Properties dialog box with the validation turned off is shown in Figure N-15. You are ready to export the XML data.

8. **Click OK, click the Export button in the XML group, navigate to the folder containing your Data Files in the Export XML dialog box, enter the name EX N-East Reps in the File name text box, click Export, then save and close the workbook**

   The sales data is saved in your Data File location in XML format, in the file called EX N-East Reps.xml.

**FIGURE N-14:** Completed table with combined sales rep data

| | A | B | C | D | E |
|---|---|---|---|---|---|
| 1 | BRANCH ▼ | FNAME ▼ | LNAME ▼ | SALES ▼ | |
| 2 | Miami | Chris | Murray | $    223,998 | |
| 3 | Miami | Deb | Gosselin | $    125,670 | |
| 4 | Miami | Lindsey | Crosby | $    313,200 | |
| 5 | Miami | Bert | Nahab | $    219,400 | |
| 6 | Miami | Kate | Deveney | $    312,700 | |
| 7 | Miami | Mary | Lyons | $    222,345 | |
| 8 | Miami | Ed | Hansen | $    181,345 | |
| 9 | Miami | Dawn | Magnari | $    129,300 | |
| 10 | New York | Patricia | Lyons | $    213,200 | |
| 11 | New York | Brian | Brady | $    110,400 | |
| 12 | New York | Mary | Dougan | $    219,200 | |
| 13 | New York | Peg | Nastasia | $    712,200 | |
| 14 | New York | Julio | Sadler | $    128,300 | |
| 15 | New York | Ann | Lee | $    314,200 | |
| 16 | New York | John | Bloomberg | $    210,400 | |
| 17 | New York | Pat | Harrington | $    217,300 | |
| 18 | New York | William | Galvin | $    113,452 | |
| 19 | New York | Ed | McCarthy | $    239,300 | |
| 20 | New York | George | Ryan | $    112,300 | |
| 21 | New York | Rod | Stedman | $    123,567 | |
| 22 | New York | Al | Tessier | $    218,200 | |
| 23 | New York | Kathy | Vodel | $    210,400 | |
| 24 | New York | Ken | Perkins | $    129,400 | |
| 25 | Total | | | $  4,999,777 | |
| 26 | | | | | |
| 27 | | | | | |

Imported data is formatted

Total sales

Sheet1　Sheet2　Sheet3

Ready

Excel 2010

**FIGURE N-15:** XML Map Properties dialog box

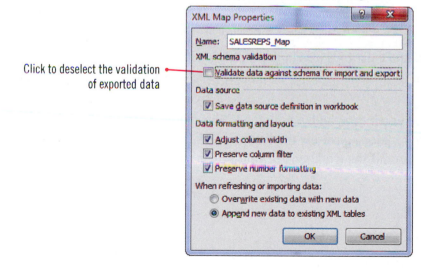

Click to deselect the validation of exported data

**Importing XML data without a schema**

You can import XML data without a schema, and Excel will create one for you. In this situation all of the XML elements are mapped to the Excel worksheet, and the data in all of the fields is populated using the XML file. When a schema is not used, you are unable to validate the data that is imported. You also need to delete all of the fields in the table that you will not use in the worksheet, which can be time consuming.

# Running Web Queries to Retrieve External Data

Often you'll want to incorporate information from the Web into an Excel worksheet for analysis. Using Excel, you can obtain data from a Web site by running a **Web query** and save that information in an existing or new Excel workbook. You must be connected to the Internet to run a Web query. You can save Web queries to use them again later; a saved query has an .iqy file extension. Several Web query files come with Excel.  As part of an effort to summarize the North American sales for Quest, Kate needs to obtain currency rate information for the Canadian dollar to adjust the data from the Toronto and Vancouver branches. She asks you to run a Web query to obtain the most current currency rate information from the Web.

## STEPS

**TROUBLE**

Depending on your screen's settings and the Add-Ins you have installed, you might not see an Existing Connections button; you may instead see a Get External Data button. If so, click the Get External Data button, then click Existing Connections.

1. **Create a new workbook, then save it as EX N-Currency Rates in the drive and folder where you store your Data Files**

2. **Close the XML Source task pane if necessary, click the Data tab, then click the Existing Connections button in the Get External Data group**

   The Existing Connections dialog box opens, with all of the connections displayed, including the queries that come with Excel.

3. **Scroll down if necessary, click MSN MoneyCentral Investor Currency Rates in the Connection files on this computer area if necessary, then click Open**

   The Import Data dialog box opens, as shown in Figure N-16. Here you specify the worksheet location where you want the imported data to appear.

**QUICK TIP**

You can also incorporate information from a Web page by inserting a screenshot into an Excel worksheet. Click the Screenshot button on the Insert tab, click Screen Clipping, then select the area on the Web page that you want to insert. The screenshot is inserted as a picture in the worksheet.

4. **Make sure the Existing worksheet option button is selected, click cell A1 if necessary to place =$A$1 in the Existing worksheet text box, then click OK**

   Currency rate information from the Web is placed in the workbook, as shown in Figure N-17. Kate wants you to obtain the previous closing exchange rate of the Canadian dollar.

5. **Click the Canadian Dollar to US Dollar link**

   A Web page opens in your browser displaying currency rate details for the Canadian dollar, as shown in Figure N-18.

6. **Close your browser window, add your name to the center footer section of the worksheet, save the workbook, preview the first page of the worksheet, close the workbook, exit Excel, then submit the workbook to your instructor**

**FIGURE N-16:** Import Data dialog box

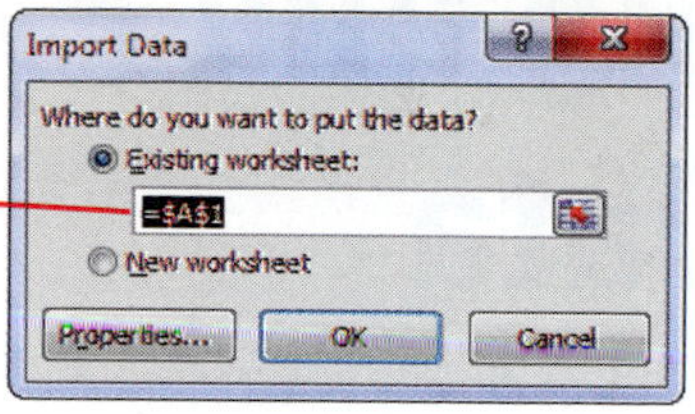

Location on worksheet where imported data will appear

**FIGURE N-17:** Currency rates quote

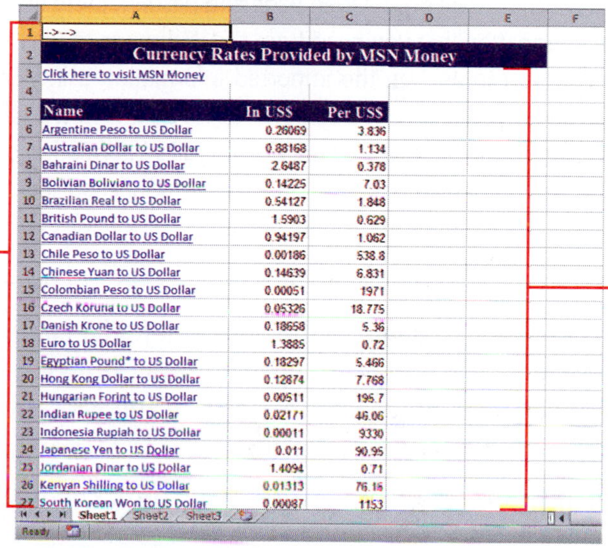

Currency rates from the Web

Your numbers will differ depending on the date you run the query

**FIGURE N-18:** Rate details for the Canadian dollar

Your values will differ depending on the date you run the query

## Creating your own Web queries

The easiest way to retrieve data from a particular Web page on a regular basis is to create a customized Web query. Click the Data tab, click the From Web button in the Get External Data group (or click the Get External Data button and click the From Web button). In the Address text box in the New Web Query dialog box, type the address of the Web page from which you want to retrieve data, then click Go. Click the yellow arrows next to the information you want to bring into a worksheet or click the upper-left arrow to import the entire page, verify that the information that you want to import has a green checkmark next to it, then click Import. The Import Data dialog box opens and allows you to specify where you want the imported data placed in the worksheet. You can save a query for future use by clicking the Save Query button 🔲 in the New Web Query dialog box before you click Import. The query is saved as a file with an .iqy file extension.

# Importing and Exporting HTML Data

Although you can open HTML files directly in Excel, most often the information that you want to include in a worksheet is published on the Web and you don't have the HTML file. In this situation you can import the HTML data by copying the data on the Web page and pasting it into an Excel worksheet. This allows you to bring in only the information that you need from the Web page to your worksheet. Once the HTML data is in your worksheet, you can analyze the imported information using Excel features. You can also export worksheet data as an HTML file that you can then share on a Web site.  The Toronto and Vancouver branch managers have published the Canada branch sales information on the company intranet. Kate asks you to import the published sales data into an Excel worksheet so she can summarize it using Excel tools. She also wants you to export the summarized data to an HTML file she can post on the company intranet.

## STEPS

**QUICK TIP**

You need to use Internet Explorer as your browser for this lesson.

1. **In Windows Explorer, navigate to the drive and folder containing your Data Files, double-click the EX N-6.htm file to open it in your browser, then copy the two table rows on the Web page containing the Toronto and Vancouver sales information**

    You are ready to paste the information from the Web page into an Excel worksheet.

2. **Start Excel, open the file EX N-1.xlsx from the drive and folder where you store your Data Files, then save it as EX N-North America Sales**

**TROUBLE**

Pasting the data doesn't match all of the destination formats. You will fix the formatting of the pasted data in Step 5.

3. **Right-click cell A6 on the Tour Sales by Branch sheet, click the Match Destination Formatting button ▦ in the Paste Options list**

    The Canada sales information is added to the U.S. sales data. You decide to total the sales and format the new data.

4. **Click cell A8, type Total, press [Tab], click the Sum button Σ in the Editing group, then press [Enter]**

5. **Select the range A5:B5, click the Format Painter button ✔ in the Clipboard group, select the range A6:B8, then click cell A1**

    Compare your worksheet to Figure N-19. Kate is finished with the analysis and formatting of the North America branches. She wants the combined information published in a Web page.

6. **Click the File tab, then click Save As**

    The Save As dialog box opens. This dialog box allows you to specify what workbook components you want to publish.

7. **Navigate to the folder containing your Data Files if necessary, click the Save as type list arrow, click Web Page (*.htm; *.html), edit the filename to read nasales.htm, click the Selection: Sheet option button, click Publish, then click Publish again**

    The HTML file is saved in your Data Files folder. To avoid problems when publishing your pages to a Web server, it is best to use lowercase characters, omit special characters and spaces, and limit your filename to eight characters with an additional three-character extension.

**QUICK TIP**

You can also open the HTM file by navigating directly to your Data Files folder and double-clicking the file name.

8. **In Windows Explorer, navigate to the drive and folder containing your Data Files, then double-click the file nasales.htm**

    The HTML version of your worksheet opens in your default browser, similar to Figure N-20.

9. **Close your browser window, click the Excel window to activate it if necessary, enter your name in the center footer section of the Tour Sales by Branch worksheet, save the workbook, preview the worksheet, close the workbook, exit Excel, then submit the workbook and the Web page file to your instructor**

**FIGURE N-19:** Worksheet with North America sales data

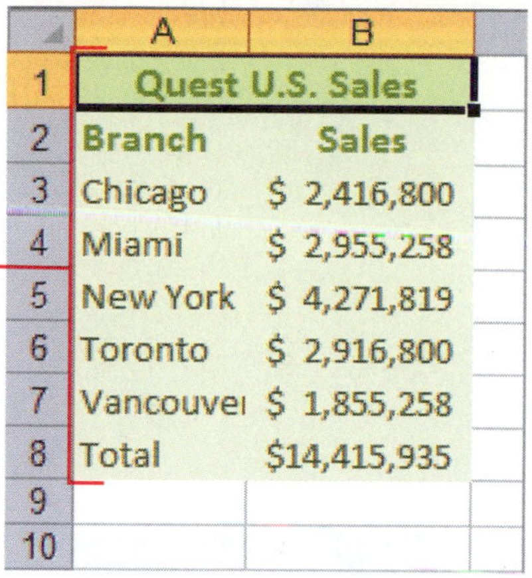

Formatted table with two rows added from HTML file

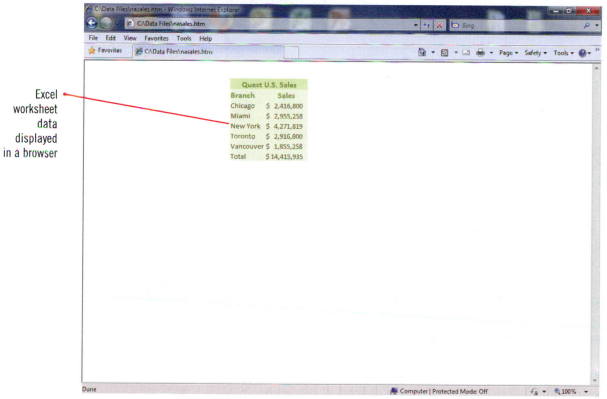

**FIGURE N-20:** North America Sales as Web page

Excel worksheet data displayed in a browser

## Adding Web hyperlinks to a worksheet

In Excel worksheets, you can create hyperlinks to information on the Web. Every Web page is identified by a unique Web address called a Uniform Resource Locator (URL). To create a hyperlink to a Web page, click the cell for which you want to create a hyperlink, click the Insert tab, click the Hyperlink button in the Links group, under Link to: make sure Existing File or Web Page is selected, specify the target for the hyperlink (the URL) in the Address text box, then click OK. If there is text in the cell, the text format changes to become a blue underlined hyperlink or the color the current workbook theme uses for hyperlinks. If there is no text in the cell, the Web site's URL appears in the cell.

# Practice

For current SAM information, including versions and content details, visit SAM Central (http://www.cengage.com/samcentral). If you have a SAM user profile, you may have access to hands-on instruction, practice, and assessment of the skills covered in this unit. Since various versions of SAM are supported throughout the life of this text, check with your instructor for the correct instructions and URL/Web site for accessing assignments.

## Concepts Review

**FIGURE N-21**

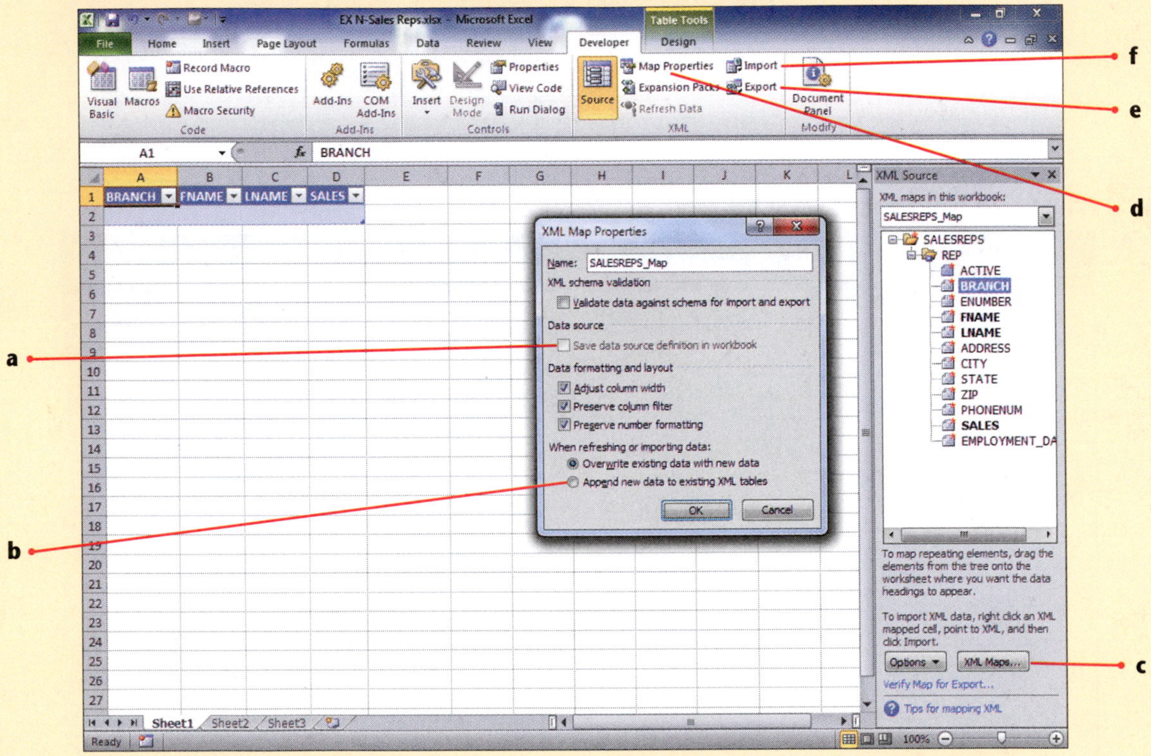

1. Which element do you click to add imported XML data below existing data in a table?
2. Which element do you click to save workbook data to an XML file?
3. Which element do you click to change the way XML data is imported and exported?
4. Which element do you click to check imported XML data using the schema rules?
5. Which element do you click to bring in XML data to a workbook table?
6. Which element do you click to add a schema to an Excel workbook?

## Match each item with the statement that best describes it.

7. Change history
8. Password
9. xsd
10. Shared workbook
11. iqy

a. The file extension for an XML schema
b. A record of edits others have made to a worksheet
c. Used to protect a workbook from unauthorized use
d. The file extension for a Web query
e. A file used by many people on a network

**Select the best answer from the list of choices.**

12. **Which of the following is the best example of a password for a workbook?**
    a. myfile
    b. MollY
    c. my%File95gz
    d. MYFILE

13. **Which of the following allows you to import data from the Web?**
    a. Web query
    b. Table query
    c. Web Wizard
    d. Data query

14. **The process of selecting XML elements to include on a worksheet is called:**
    a. Sharing.
    b. Selecting.
    c. Loading.
    d. Mapping.

15. **A file that describes the structure of XML data is called a:**
    a. Schema.
    b. Query.
    c. Layout.
    d. Detail File.

# Skills Review

1. **Set up a shared workbook for multiple users.**
   a. Start Excel, open the file EX N-7.xlsx from the drive and folder where you store your Data Files, then save it as **EX N-Sales**.
   b. Use the Share Workbook option on the Review tab to set up the workbook so that more than one person can use it at one time.
   c. Save the workbook when asked to save it.
   d. Verify the workbook is marked as Shared in the title bar.
   e. Review the regional sales data for the first two quarters of the year.

2. **Track revisions in a shared workbook.**
   a. Change the Seattle sales to **$40,000** for the first quarter and **$50,000** for the second quarter.
   b. Save the file.
   c. Display the History sheet by opening the Highlight Changes dialog box, deselecting the When check box, then selecting the option for List changes on a new sheet.
   d. Compare your History sheet to Figure N-22.
   e. Copy the range A1:I3 in the History sheet, and paste the range in Sheet2. Widen the columns to display all of the information, then rename Sheet2 to **History Sheet**.

   **FIGURE N-22**

   | Action Number | Date | Time | Who | Change | Sheet | Range | New Value | Old Value | Action Type | Losing Action |
   |---|---|---|---|---|---|---|---|---|---|---|
   | 1 | 2/4/2013 | 11:57 AM | Your Name | Cell Change | Sales | C2 | $40,000.00 | $31,988.00 | | |
   | 2 | 2/4/2013 | 11:57 AM | Your Name | Cell Change | Sales | D2 | $50,000.00 | $28,550.00 | | |

   This history ends with the changes saved on 2/4/2013 at 11:57 AM.

   f. Enter your name in the History Sheet footer, then preview the History sheet.
   g. Save the workbook, close the workbook, then submit the workbook to your instructor.

3. **Apply and modify passwords.**
   a. Open the file EX N-7.xlsx from the drive and folder where you store your Data Files, open the Save As dialog box, then open the General Options dialog box.
   b. Set the password to open the workbook as **Sales13** and the password to modify it as **FirstHalf13**.
   c. Save the password-protected file as **EX N-Sales PW** in the location where you store your Data Files.
   d. Close the workbook.
   e. Use the assigned passwords to reopen the workbook and verify that you can change it by adding your name in the center section of the Sales sheet footer, save the workbook, preview the Sales worksheet, close the workbook, then submit the workbook to your instructor.

# Skills Review (continued)

### 4. Work with XML schemas.

a. Create a new workbook, then save it as **EX N-Contact Information** in the drive and folder where you store your Data Files.

b. Open the XML Source pane, and add the XML schema EX N-8.xsd to the workbook.

c. Map the FNAME element to cell A1 on the worksheet, LNAME to cell B1, PHONENUM to cell C1, and EMPLOYMENT_DATE to cell D1.

d. Remove the EMPLOYMENT_DATE element from the map, and delete the field from the table.

e. Use the XML Map Properties dialog box to make sure imported XML data is validated using the schema.

### 5. Import and export XML data.

a. Import the XML file EX N-9.xml into the workbook.

b. Sort the worksheet list in ascending order by LNAME.

c. Add the Table Style Medium 10 to the table, and compare your screen to Figure N-23.

d. Enter your name in the center section of the worksheet footer, save the workbook, then preview the worksheet.

e. Use the XML Map Properties dialog box to turn off the validation for imported and exported worksheet data, export the worksheet data to an XML file named **EX N-Contact**, save and close the workbook.

**FIGURE N-23**

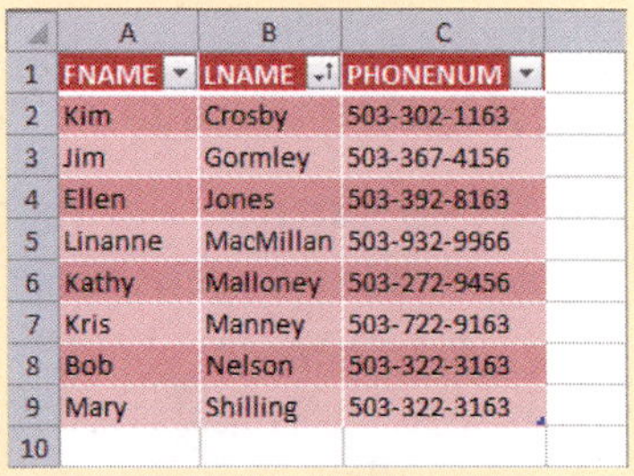

| | A | B | C |
|---|---|---|---|
| 1 | FNAME | LNAME | PHONENUM |
| 2 | Kim | Crosby | 503-302-1163 |
| 3 | Jim | Gormley | 503-367-4156 |
| 4 | Ellen | Jones | 503-392-8163 |
| 5 | Linanne | MacMillan | 503-932-9966 |
| 6 | Kathy | Malloney | 503-272-9456 |
| 7 | Kris | Manney | 503-722-9163 |
| 8 | Bob | Nelson | 503-322-3163 |
| 9 | Mary | Shilling | 503-322-3163 |
| 10 | | | |

### 6. Run Web queries to retrieve external data.

a. Create a new workbook, then save it as **EX N-Quotes** in the location where you store your Data Files.

b. Use the Existing Connections dialog box to select the MSN MoneyCentral Investor Major Indices Web query.

c. Specify that you want to place the data in cell A1 of the current worksheet. Compare your screen to Figure N-24. (You may see Invalid symbols and question mark symbols in the worksheet, but don't be concerned with these.)

d. Enter your name in the center section of the worksheet header, set the worksheet orientation to landscape, preview the worksheet, then save the workbook.

e. Close the workbook, and submit the workbook to your instructor.

**FIGURE N-24**

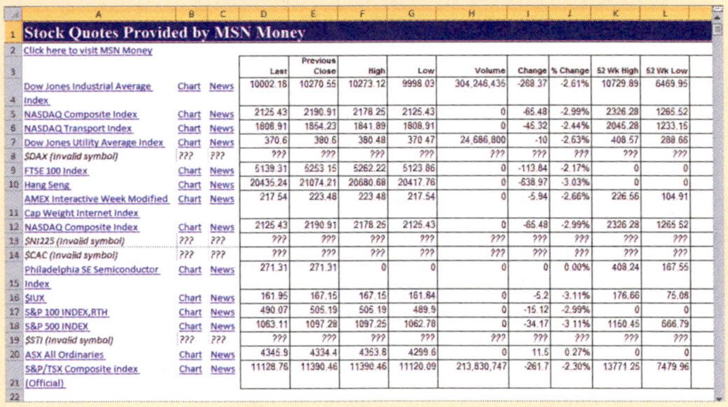

### 7. Import and export HTML data.

a. Open the file EX N-7.xlsx from the drive and folder where you store your Data Files, then save it as **EX N-Sales2**.

b. Open the file EX N-10.htm in your browser from the drive and folder where you store your Data Files. Copy the data in the four rows of the Web page (not the column headings), and paste it below the data in the Sales sheet of the EX N-Sales2 workbook.

c. On the Sales sheet, enter **Total** in cell A27, and use **AutoSum** in cell D27 to total the values in column D.

d. Adjust the formatting for the new rows to match the other rows on the Sales sheet, add your name to the center section of the worksheet footer, save the workbook, then preview the Sales sheet.

e. Save the data on the Sales sheet as an HTML file with the name **sales2.htm**.

f. Exit Excel, open the sales2.htm file in your browser, compare your screen to Figure N-25, close your browser, then submit the sales2.htm file to your instructor.

**FIGURE N-25**

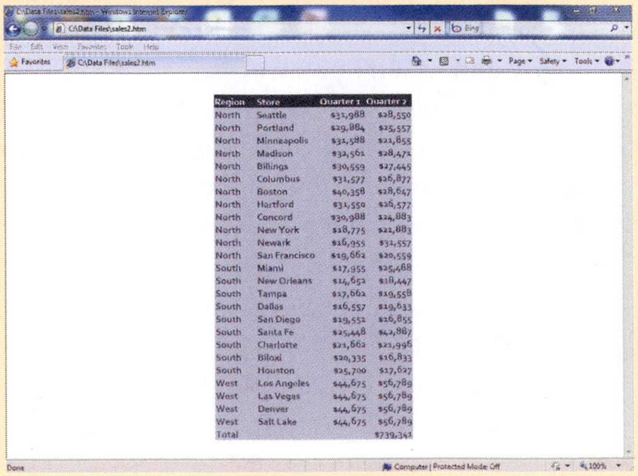

# Independent Challenge 1

New England State College has two campuses, North and South. The deans of the campuses work together on the scheduling of classes using shared Excel workbooks. As the registrar for the college, you are preparing the fall schedule as a shared workbook for the two campus deans. They will each make changes to the location data, and you will review both workbooks and accept their changes.

a. Start Excel, open the file EX N-11.xlsx from the drive and folder where you store your Data Files, then save it as **EX N-NESC**. The workbook has been shared so the other dean can modify it. Close the workbook.

b. Open the file EX N-12.xlsx from the drive and folder where you store your Data Files, then save it as **EX N-North**. This workbook is a copy of the original that has been reviewed and changed.

c. Use the Accept or Reject dialog box to accept the change made to the workbook. Save and close the workbook.

d. Open the file EX N-13.xlsx from the drive and folder where you store your Data Files, then save it as **EX N-South**. This workbook has also been reviewed and changed.

e. Use the Accept or Reject dialog box to accept the workbook change.

f. Use the Highlight Changes dialog box to highlight the change on the screen. Review the ScreenTip details.

g. Use the Highlight Changes dialog box to create a History worksheet detailing the change to the workbook. Copy the information about the change in the range A1:I2, and paste it in Sheet2. Widen the column widths as necessary, and rename Sheet2 to **History Sheet**.

h. Add your name to the center section of the History sheet footer, then preview the History worksheet. Save and close the workbook. Submit the EX N-South.xlsx workbook to your instructor.

# Independent Challenge 2

The Charleston Athletic Club is a fitness center with five fitness facilities. As the general manager you are responsible for setting and publishing the membership rate information. You decide to run a special promotion offering a 10 percent discount off the current membership prices. You will also add two new membership categories to help attract younger members. The membership rate information is published on the company Web site. You will copy the rate information from the Web page and work with it in Excel to calculate the special discounted rates. You will save the new rate information as an HTML file so it can be published on the Web.

a. Open the file EX N-14.htm from the drive and folder where you store your Data Files to display it in your browser.

b. Start Excel, create a new workbook, then save it as **EX N-Rates** in the drive and folder where you store your Data Files.

c. Copy the five rows of data, including the column headings from the table in the EX N-14 file, and paste them in the EX N-Rates workbook. Adjust the column widths and formatting as necessary. Close the EX N-14.htm file.

d. Add the new membership data from Table N-2 in rows 6 and 7 of the worksheet.

e. Enter **Special** in cell C1, and calculate each special rate in column C by discounting the prices in column B by 10%. (*Hint*: Multiply each price by .90.)

**TABLE N-2**

| Teen | 350 |
|------|-----|
| Youth | 200 |

f. Format the price information in columns B and C with the Accounting format using the $ symbol with two decimal places.

g. Add the passwords **Members11** to open the EX N-Rates workbook and **Fitness01** to modify it. Save and close the workbook, then reopen it by entering the passwords.

h. Verify that you can modify the workbook by formatting the worksheet using the Office Theme and a fill with the Theme color Olive Green, Accent 3, Lighter 80%. Compare your worksheet data to Figure N-26.

i. Add your name to the center footer section of the worksheet, save the workbook, then preview the worksheet.

j. Save the worksheet data in HTML format using the name **prices.htm**. Close the workbook and exit Excel.

k. Open the prices.htm page in your browser and print the page.

l. Close your browser. Submit the prices.htm file to your instructor.

**FIGURE N-26**

| | A | B | C | D | E | F | G |
|---|---|---|---|---|---|---|---|
| 1 | Membership | Price | Special | | | | |
| 2 | Family | $ 1,000.00 | $ 900.00 | | | | |
| 3 | Adult | $ 750.00 | $ 675.00 | | | | |
| 4 | Senior | $ 300.00 | $ 270.00 | | | | |
| 5 | College | $ 470.00 | $ 423.00 | | | | |
| 6 | Teen | $ 350.00 | $ 315.00 | | | | |
| 7 | Youth | $ 200.00 | $ 180.00 | | | | |
| 8 | | | | | | | |
| 9 | | | | | | | |

# Independent Challenge 3

You are the director of development at a local performing arts nonprofit institution. You are preparing the phone lists for your annual fundraising phone-a-thon. The donor information for the organization is in an XML file, which you will bring into Excel to organize. You will use an XML schema to map only the donors' names and phone numbers to the worksheet. This will allow you to import the donor data and limit the information that is distributed to the phone-a-thon volunteers. You will also import information about the donors from another XML file. You will export your worksheet data as XML for future use.

a. Start Excel, create a new workbook, then save it as **EX N-Donors** in the drive and folder where you store your Data Files.

b. Add the map EX N-15.xsd from the drive and folder where you store your Data Files to the workbook.

c. Map the FNAME element to cell A1, LNAME to cell B1, and PHONENUM to cell C1.

d. Import the XML data in file EX N-16.xml from the drive and folder where you store your Data Files. Make sure the data is validated using the schema as it is imported.

e. Add the Table Style Light 19 to the table. Change the field name in cell A1 to **FIRST NAME**, change the field name in cell B1 to **LAST NAME**, and change the field name in cell C1 to **PHONE NUMBER**. Widen the columns as necessary to accommodate the full field names.

f. Sort the table in ascending order by LAST NAME. Compare your sorted table to Figure N-27.

**FIGURE N-27**

| | A | B | C |
|---|---|---|---|
| 1 | FIRST NAME | LAST NAME | PHONE NUMBER |
| 2 | Peg | Alexander | 312-765-8756 |
| 3 | Ernie | Atkins | 773-167-4156 |
| 4 | Kerry | Bradley | 773-220-9456 |
| 5 | Steve | Connolly | 312-322-3163 |
| 6 | Brenda | Duran | 312-322-3163 |
| 7 | Kevin | Gonzales | 773-379-0092 |
| 8 | Amy | Land | 312-299-4298 |
| 9 | Julio | Mendez | 312-765-8756 |
| 10 | Lisa | Ng | 312-932-9966 |
| 11 | Martin | Zoll | 312-765-8756 |
| 12 | | | |

g. Open the XML Map Properties dialog box to verify the Overwrite existing data with new data option button is selected. Map the ACTIVE element to cell D1. Import the XML data in file EX N-16.xml again.

h. Map the CONTRIB_DATE element to cell E1. Import the XML data in file EX N-16.xml a third time. Change the field name in cell E1 to **LAST DONATION**, and widen the column to accommodate the full field name.

i. Filter the table to show only active donors. Compare your filtered table to Figure N-28.

j. Export the worksheet data to an XML file named **EX N-Phone List**.

**FIGURE N-28**

| | A | B | C | D | E | F |
|---|---|---|---|---|---|---|
| 1 | FIRST NAME | LAST NAME | PHONE NUMBER | ACTIVE | LAST DONATION | |
| 2 | Kerry | Bradley | 773-220-9456 | TRUE | Jan-10 | |
| 4 | Lisa | Ng | 312-932-9966 | TRUE | Jan-10 | |
| 7 | Kevin | Gonzales | 773-379-0092 | TRUE | Nov-11 | |
| 9 | Martin | Zoll | 312-765-8756 | TRUE | Dec-10 | |
| 10 | Peg | Alexander | 312-765-8756 | TRUE | Nov-09 | |
| 11 | Julio | Mendez | 312-765-8756 | TRUE | Dec-10 | |
| 12 | | | | | | |

## Advanced Challenge Exercise

- Remove the filter for the Active field.
- Add the map EX N-17.xsd from the drive and folder where you store your Data Files to the worksheet.
- Using the INFO_Map, map the DNUMBER element to cell F1 and LEVEL to cell G1.
- Import the XML data in file EX N-18.xml from the drive and folder where you store your Data Files.
- Change the field name in cell F1 to **DONOR NUMBER**.
- Add the Table Style Light 19 to the new table data.
- Filter the table to display only information for Excellent and Above Average Levels. Compare your worksheet to Figure N-29.

**FIGURE N-29**

| | A | B | C | D | E | F | G | H |
|---|---|---|---|---|---|---|---|---|
| 1 | FIRST NAME | LAST NAME | PHONE NUMBER | ACTIVE | LAST DONATION | DONOR NUMBER | LEVEL | |
| 2 | Kerry | Bradley | 773-220-9456 | TRUE | Jan-10 | 8762 | Excellent | |
| 4 | Lisa | Ng | 312-932-9966 | TRUE | Jan-10 | 1453 | Above Average | |
| 5 | Brenda | Duran | 312-322-3163 | FALSE | Jan-11 | 9087 | Excellent | |
| 6 | Steve | Connolly | 312-322-3163 | FALSE | Dec-07 | 8001 | Above Average | |
| 8 | Amy | Land | 312-299-4298 | FALSE | Feb-09 | 6002 | Above Average | |
| 10 | Peg | Alexander | 312-765-8756 | TRUE | Nov-09 | 9771 | Excellent | |
| 12 | | | | | | | | |

k. Enter your name in the center section of the worksheet footer, preview the worksheet in landscape orientation, then save the workbook.

l. Close the workbook, exit Excel, then submit the workbook to your instructor.

# Real Life Independent Challenge

You can track the history of a stock using published Web quotes that can be entered into Excel worksheets for analysis. To eliminate the data entry step, you will use the MSN MoneyCentral Investor Stock Quotes Web query in Excel. You will run the query from an Excel workbook using the symbol of a stock that you are interested in following. The stock information will be automatically inserted into your worksheet.

**a.** Start Excel, create a new workbook, then save it as **EX N-Stock Analysis** in the drive and folder where you store your Data Files.

**b.** Run the Web Query MSN MoneyCentral Investor Stock Quotes to obtain a quote for Microsoft's stock by entering the symbol for Microsoft, **MSFT**, in the Enter Parameter Value dialog box, as shown in Figure N-30.

**FIGURE N-30**

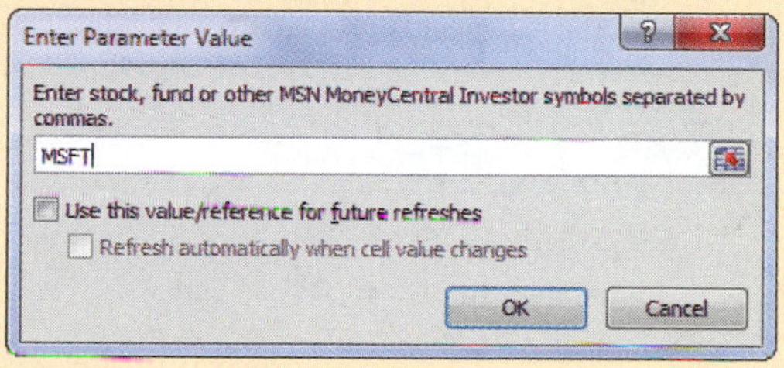

**c.** Use the Symbol Lookup hyperlink in the query results to find the symbol of a company that you are interested in researching.

**d.** Use Sheet2 of the workbook to run the Web Query MSN MoneyCentral Investor Stock Quotes to obtain a quote for the company symbol you found in the preceding step.

**e.** Place the name of the company that you are researching in cell A20. Use the name in cell A20 to add a hyperlink to the company's Web site. (*Hint*: Click the Insert tab, then click the Hyperlink button in the Links group.)

**f.** Test the link, then close the browser and return to the workbook.

**g.** Enter your name in the center section of the Sheet2 footer.

**h.** Display the chart of your stock by clicking the Chart link on Sheet2.

### Advanced Challenge Exercise

- Without closing the Browser display of your chart, return to the workbook.
- Beginning in cell A1 of Sheet3, insert a screenshot of your stock's 6m chart from the opening Web page. (*Hint*: Click the Screenshot button on the Insert tab, click Screen Clipping, then select the chart on the Web page.)
- Enter your name in the center section of the Sheet3 footer.

**i.** Preview each worksheet in the workbook in landscape orientation.

**j.** Close the workbook, close your browser, exit Excel, then submit the workbook to your instructor.

# Visual Workshop

Start Excel, create a new workbook, then save it as **EX N-Bay.xlsx** in the drive and folder where you store your Data Files. Open the file EX N-19.htm in your browser from the drive and folder where you store your Data Files. Create the Web page shown in Figure N-31 by pasting the information from the Web page into your EX N-Bay.xlsx file, formatting it, adding the fourth quarter information, adding the totals, replacing Your Name with your name, then saving it as an HTML file named **bay.htm**. Add your name to the footer of Sheet1 of the EX N-Bay.xlsx workbook, and preview the worksheet. Submit the bay.htm file and the EX N-Bay.xlsx workbook to your instructor. (*Hint*: The colors are in the Office theme.)

FIGURE N-31

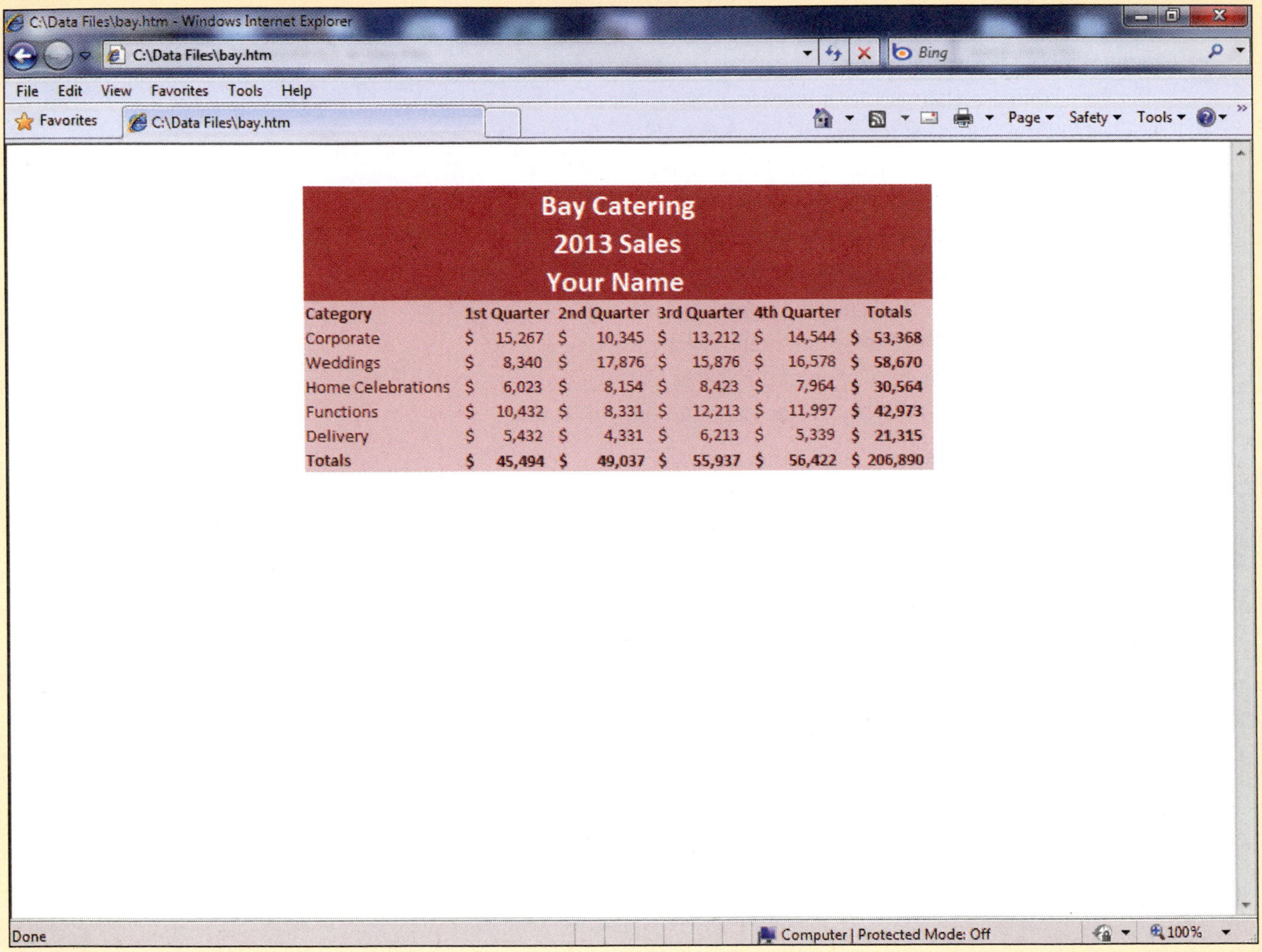


Bay Catering
2013 Sales
Your Name

| Category | 1st Quarter | 2nd Quarter | 3rd Quarter | 4th Quarter | Totals |
|---|---|---|---|---|---|
| Corporate | $ 15,267 | $ 10,345 | $ 13,212 | $ 14,544 | $ 53,368 |
| Weddings | $ 8,340 | $ 17,876 | $ 15,876 | $ 16,578 | $ 58,670 |
| Home Celebrations | $ 6,023 | $ 8,154 | $ 8,423 | $ 7,964 | $ 30,564 |
| Functions | $ 10,432 | $ 8,331 | $ 12,213 | $ 11,997 | $ 42,973 |
| Delivery | $ 5,432 | $ 4,331 | $ 6,213 | $ 5,339 | $ 21,315 |
| Totals | $ 45,494 | $ 49,037 | $ 55,937 | $ 56,422 | $ 206,890 |

# Customizing Excel and Advanced Worksheet Management

**Files You Will Need:**

EX O-1.xlsx
EX O-2.xlsx
EX O-3.xlsx
EX O-4.xlsx
EX O-5.xlsx
EX O-6.xlsx

Excel includes numerous tools and options that can help you work as efficiently as possible. In this unit, you will learn how to use some of these elements to find errors and hide the details of worksheet summaries. You'll also find out how to eliminate repetitive typing chores, save calculation time when using a large worksheet, and customize basic Excel features. Finally, you'll learn how to document your workbook and save it in a format that makes it easy to reuse. Quest's vice president of sales, Kate Morgan, asks you to help with a variety of spreadsheet-related tasks. You will use Excel tools and options to help Kate perform her work quickly and efficiently.

**OBJECTIVES**

Audit a worksheet

Control worksheet calculations

Group worksheet data

Use cell comments

Create custom AutoFill lists

Customize Excel workbooks

Customize the Excel Screen

Create and apply a template

# Auditing a Worksheet

Because errors can occur at any stage of worksheet development, it is important to include auditing as part of your workbook-building process. The Excel **auditing** feature helps you track errors and check worksheet logic. The Formula Auditing group on the Formulas tab contains several error-checking tools to help you audit a worksheet.  Kate asks you to help identify errors in the worksheet that tracks sales for the two Canadian branches to verify the accuracy of year-end totals and percentages.

## STEPS

**TROUBLE**

You will fix the formula errors that appear in cells O5 and O6.

1. **Start Excel, open the file EX O-1.xlsx from the drive and folder where you store your Data Files, then save it as EX O-Canada Sales**

2. **Click the Formulas tab, then click the Error Checking button in the Formula Auditing group**

   The Error Checking dialog box opens and alerts you to a Divide by Zero Error in cell O5, as shown in Figure O-1. The formula reads =N5/N8, indicating that the value in cell N5 will be divided by the value in cell N8. In Excel formulas, blank cells have a value of zero. This error means the value in cell N5 cannot be divided by the value in cell N8 (zero) because division by zero is not mathematically possible. To correct the error, you must edit the formula so that it references cell N7, the total of sales, not cell N8.

3. **Click Edit in Formula Bar in the Error Checking dialog box, edit the formula to read =N5/N7, click the Enter button ✓ on the formula bar, then click Resume in the Error Checking dialog box**

   The edited formula produces the correct result, .55371, in cell O5. The Error Checking dialog box indicates another error in cell N6, the total Vancouver sales. The formula reads =SUM(B6:L6) and should be =SUM(B6:M6). The top button in the Error Checking dialog box changes to "Copy Formula from Above". Since this formula in the cell N5 is correct, you will copy it.

4. **Click Copy Formula from Above**

   The Vancouver total changes to $328,430 in cell N6. The Error Checking dialog box finds another division-by-zero error in cell O6. You decide to use another tool in the Formula Auditing group to get more information about this error.

5. **Close the Error Checking dialog box, then click the Trace Precedents button in the Formula Auditing group**

   Blue arrows called **tracer arrows** point from the cells referenced by the formula to the active cell as shown in Figure O-2. The arrows help you determine if these cell references might have caused the error. The tracer arrows extend from the error to cells N6 and N8. To correct the error, you must edit the formula so that it references cell N7 in the denominator, the sales total, not cell N8.

6. **Edit the formula in the formula bar to read =N6/N7, then click ✓ on the formula bar**

   The result of the formula, .44629, appears in cell O6. The November sales for the Vancouver branch in cell L6 is unusually high compared with sales posted for the other months. You can investigate the other cells in the sheet that are affected by the value of cell L6 by tracing the cell's **dependents**—the cells that contain formulas referring to cell L6.

7. **Click cell L6, then click the Trace Dependents button in the Formula Auditing group**

   The tracer arrows run from cell L6 to cells L7 and N6, indicating that the value in cell L6 affects the total November sales and the total Vancouver sales. You decide to remove the tracer arrows and format the percentages in cells O5 and O6.

8. **Click the Remove Arrows button in the Formula Auditing group, select the range O5:O6, click the Home tab, click the Percent Style button % in the Number group, click the Increase Decimal button ⬆ twice, return to cell A1, then save the workbook**

   Now that all the errors have been identified and corrected, you are finished auditing the worksheet.

**FIGURE O-1:** Error Checking dialog box

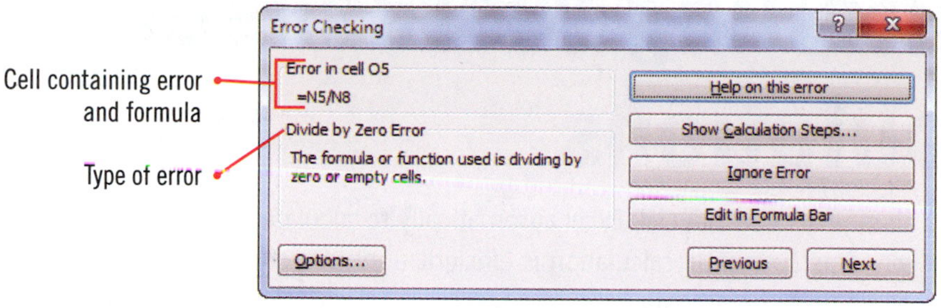

Cell containing error
and formula

Type of error

**FIGURE O-2:** Worksheet with traced error

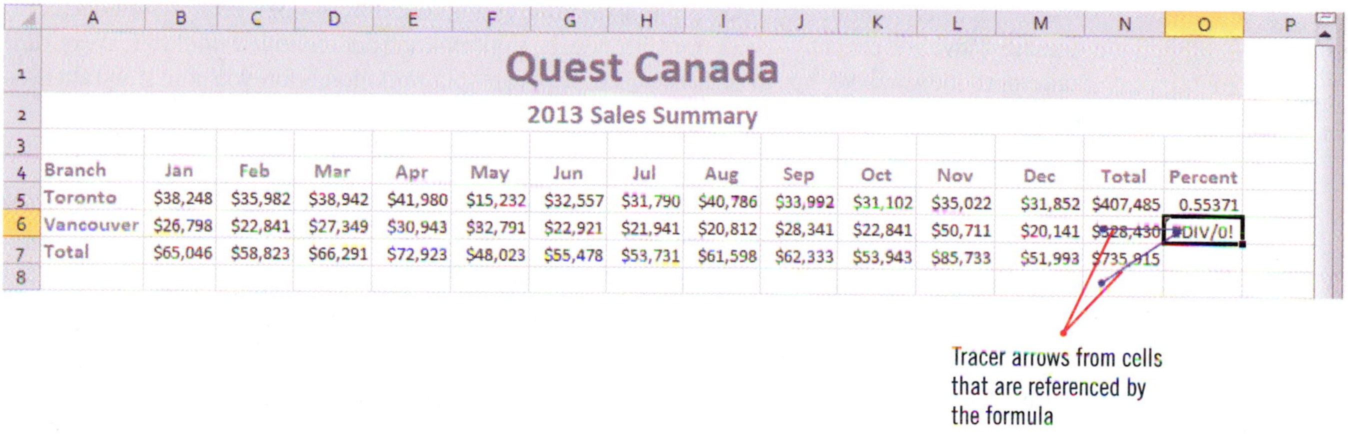

Tracer arrows from cells
that are referenced by
the formula

## Watching and evaluating formulas

As you edit your worksheet, you can watch the effect that cell changes have on selected worksheet formulas. Select the cell or cells that you want to watch, click the Formulas tab, click the Watch Window button in the Formula Auditing group, click Add Watch in the Watch Window, then click Add. The Watch Window displays the workbook name, worksheet name, the cell address you want to watch, the current cell value, and its formula. As cell values that "feed into" the formula change, the resulting formula value in the Watch Window changes. To delete a watch, you can select the cell information in the Watch Window and click Delete Watch. You can also step through the evaluation of a formula, selecting the cell that contains a formula and clicking the Evaluate Formula button in the Formula Auditing group. The formula appears in the Evaluation Window of the Evaluate Formula dialog box. As you click the Evaluate button, the cell references are replaced with their values and the formula result is calculated.

# Controlling Worksheet Calculations

Whenever you change a value in a cell, Excel automatically recalculates all the formulas in the worksheet based on that cell. This automatic calculation is efficient until you create a worksheet so large that the recalculation process slows down data entry and screen updating. Worksheets with many formulas, data tables, or functions may also recalculate slowly. In these cases, you might want to selectively determine if and when you want Excel to perform calculations. You do this by applying the **manual calculation** option. Once you change the calculation mode to manual, Excel applies manual calculation to all open worksheets.  Because Kate knows that using specific Excel calculation options can help make worksheet building more efficient, she asks you to review the formula settings in the workbook and change the formula calculations from automatic to manual calculation.

## STEPS

**QUICK TIP**

You can also change the formula calculation to manual by clicking the Calculations Options button in the Calculation group on the Formulas tab and clicking Manual.

1. **Click the File tab, click Options, then click Formulas in the list of options**

   The options related to formula calculation and error checking appear, as shown in Figure O-3.

2. **Under Calculation options, click to select the Manual option button**

   When you select the Manual option, the Recalculate workbook before saving check box automatically becomes active and contains a check mark. Because the workbook will not recalculate until you save or close and reopen the workbook, you must make sure to recalculate your worksheet before you print it and after you finish making changes.

3. **Click OK**

   Kate informs you that the December total for the Toronto branch is incorrect. You adjust the entry in cell M5 to reflect the actual sales figure.

4. **Click cell M5**

   Before making the change to cell M5, notice that in cell N5 the total for the Toronto branch is $407,485, and the Toronto percent in cell O5 is 55.37%.

**QUICK TIP**

The Calculate Now command recalculates the entire workbook. You can also manually recalculate by pressing [F9] to recalculate the workbook or [Shift][F9] to recalculate only the active sheet.

5. **Type 40,598, then click the Enter button ☑ on the formula bar**

   The total and percent formulas are *not* updated. The total in cell N5 is still $407,485 and the percentage in cell O5 is still 55.37%. The word "Calculate" appears in the status bar to indicate that a specific value in the worksheet did indeed change and that the worksheet must be recalculated.

6. **Click the Formulas tab, click the Calculate Sheet button 🖩 in the Calculation group, click cell A1, then save the workbook**

   The total in cell N5 is now $416,231 instead of $407,485, and the percentage in cell O5 is now 55.90% instead of 55.37%. The other formulas in the worksheet affected by the value in cell M5 changed as well, as shown in Figure O-4. Because this is a relatively small worksheet that recalculates quickly, you will return to automatic calculation.

**QUICK TIP**

To automatically recalculate all worksheet formulas except one- and two-input data tables, click Automatic Except for Data Tables.

7. **Click the Calculations Options button in the Calculation group, then click Automatic**

   Now any additional changes you make will automatically recalculate the worksheet formulas.

8. **Place your name in the center section of the worksheet footer, then save the workbook**

**FIGURE O-3:** Excel formula options

Click to select manual calculation of worksheet formulas

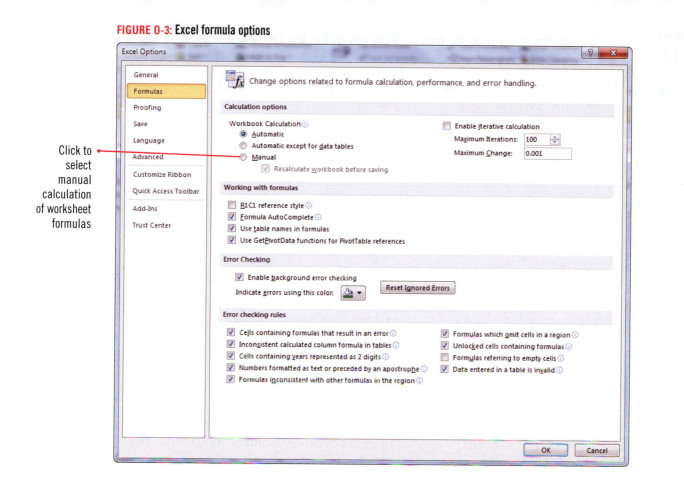

**FIGURE O-4:** Worksheet with updated values

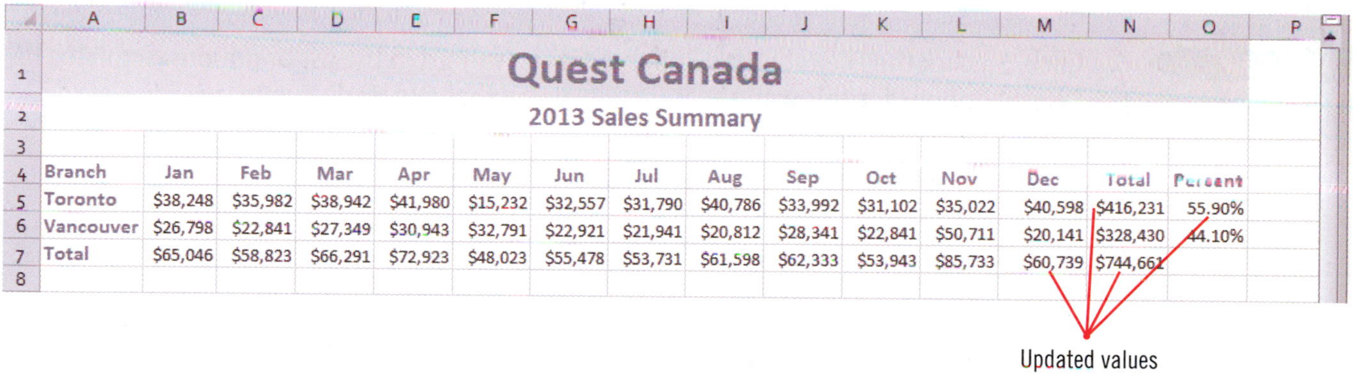

| Branch | Jan | Feb | Mar | Apr | May | Jun | Jul | Aug | Sep | Oct | Nov | Dec | Total | Percent |
|---|---|---|---|---|---|---|---|---|---|---|---|---|---|---|
| Toronto | $38,248 | $35,982 | $38,942 | $41,980 | $15,232 | $32,557 | $31,790 | $40,786 | $33,992 | $31,102 | $35,022 | $40,598 | $416,231 | 55.90% |
| Vancouver | $26,798 | $22,841 | $27,349 | $30,943 | $32,791 | $22,921 | $21,941 | $20,812 | $28,341 | $22,841 | $50,711 | $20,141 | $328,430 | 44.10% |
| Total | $65,046 | $58,823 | $66,291 | $72,923 | $48,023 | $55,478 | $53,731 | $61,598 | $62,333 | $53,943 | $85,733 | $60,739 | $744,661 | |

Quest Canada

2013 Sales Summary

Updated values

Excel 2010

# Grouping Worksheet Data

You can create groups of rows and columns on a worksheet to manage your data and make it easier to work with. The Excel grouping feature provides an outline that allows you to easily expand and collapse groups to show or hide selected worksheet data. You can turn off the outline symbols if you are using the condensed data in a report. Kate needs to give Jessica Long, the Quest CEO, the quarterly sales totals for the Canadian branches. She asks you to group the worksheet data by quarters.

## STEPS

**QUICK TIP**

You can also group worksheet data by rows to show and hide related information in rows.

1. **Click the Quarterly Summary sheet, select the range B4:D7, click the Data tab, click the Group button in the Outline group, click the Columns option button in the Group dialog box, then click OK**

   The first quarter information is grouped, and **outline symbols** that are used to hide and display details appear over the columns, as shown in Figure O-5. You continue to group the remaining quarters.

2. **Select the range F4:H7, click the Group button in the Outline group, click the Columns option button in the Group dialog box, click OK, select the range J4:L7, click the Group button in the Outline group, click the Columns option button in the Group dialog box, click OK, select the range N4:P7, click the Group button in the Outline group, click the Columns option button in the Group dialog box, click OK, then click cell A1**

   All four quarters are grouped. You decide to use the outline symbols to expand and collapse the first quarter information.

**QUICK TIP**

If you want to summarize your data using subtotals, you need to sort your data on the field that you will subtotal, click the Data tab, click the Subtotal button in the Outline group, then choose the subtotal field.

3. **Click the Collapse Outline button ☐ above the column E label, then click the Expand Outline button ☐ above the column E label**

   Clicking the ( - ) symbol temporarily hides the Q1 detail columns, and the ( - ) symbol changes to a ( + ) symbol. Clicking the ( + ) symbol expands the Q1 details and redisplays the hidden columns. The Column Level symbols in the upper-left corner of the worksheet are used to display and hide levels of detail across the entire worksheet.

4. **Click the Column Level 1 button ☐1☐**

   All of the group details collapse, and only the quarter totals are displayed.

5. **Click the Column Level 2 button ☐2☐**

   You see the quarter details again. Kate asks you to hide the quarter details and the outline symbols for her summary report.

**QUICK TIP**

You can ungroup a range of cells by clicking Ungroup in the Outline group.

6. **Click ☐1☐, click the File tab, click Options, click Advanced in the list of options, scroll to the Display options for this worksheet section, verify that Quarterly Summary is displayed as the worksheet name, click the Show outline symbols if an outline is applied check box to deselect it, then click OK**

   The quarter totals without outline symbols are shown in Figure O-6.

7. **Enter your name in the center footer section, save the workbook, then preview the worksheet**

Outline symbols

Column level buttons

Grouped data

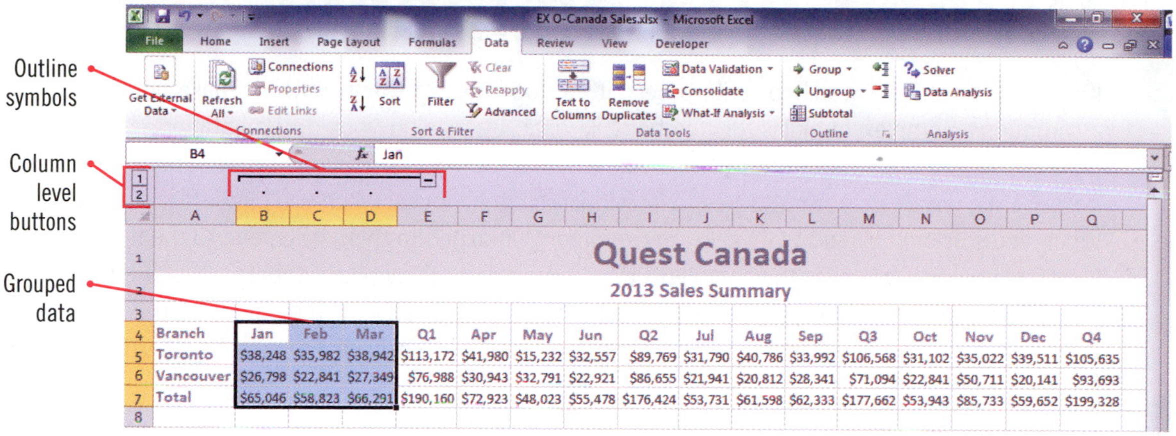

FIGURE O-6: Quarter summary

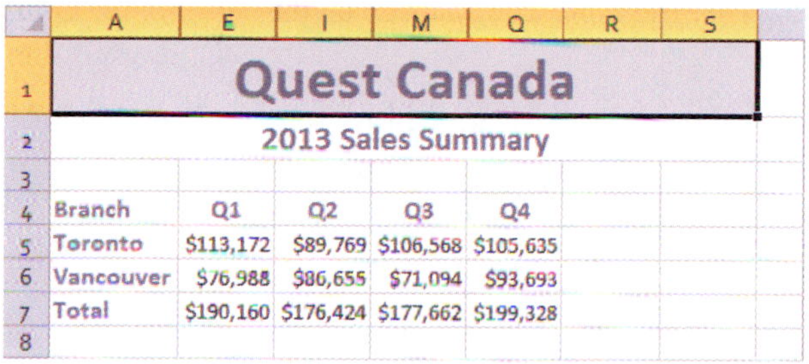

## Applying and creating custom number and date formats

When you use numbers and dates in worksheets or calculations, you can apply the Excel custom number formats, or create your own custom formats. To apply a custom cell format, click the Home tab, click the Format button in the Cells group, then click Format Cells. If necessary, click the Number tab in the Format Cells dialog box, click Custom in the Category list, then click the format you want. A number format can have four parts, each one separated by semicolons: [positive numbers];[negative numbers];[zeroes];[text]. You don't need to specify all four parts. Many of the custom formats contain codes: # represents any digit and 0 represents a digit that will always be displayed, even if the digit is 0. An underscore adds space for alignment. For example, the value –3789 appears as (3,789) if the cell is formatted as #,##0 _); (#,##0). To create your own custom format, click a format that resembles the one you want and customize it in the Type text box. For example, you could edit the #,##0_);[Red](#,##0) format to show negative numbers in blue by changing it to read #,##0_);[Blue](#,##0).

# Using Cell Comments

If you plan to share a workbook with others, it's a good idea to **document**, or make notes about, basic assumptions, complex formulas, or questionable data. By reading your documentation, a coworker can quickly become familiar with your workbook. The easiest way to document a workbook is to use **cell comments**, which are notes attached to individual cells that appear when you place the pointer over a cell. When you sort or copy and paste cells, any comments attached to them will move to the new location. In PivotTable reports, however, the comments do not move with the worksheet data.  Kate thinks one of the figures in the worksheet may be incorrect. She asks you to add a comment for Mark Ng, the Toronto branch manager, pointing out the possible error. You will start by checking the default settings for comments in a workbook.

## STEPS

1. **Click the** File tab **if necessary, click** Options, **click** Advanced **in the list of options, scroll to the Display section, click the** Indicators only, and comments on hover option button **to select it in the "For cells with comments, show:" section if necessary, then click** OK

   The other options in the "For cells with comments, show:" area allow you to display the comment and its indicator or no comments.

**QUICK TIP**

To copy only comments into a cell, copy the cell contents, right-click the destination cell, point to Paste Special, click Paste Special on the shortcut menu, click Comments in the Paste Special dialog box, then click OK.

2. **Click the** Sales sheet tab, **click cell** F5, **click the** Review tab, **then click the** New Comment button **in the Comments group**

   The Comment box opens, as shown in Figure O-7. Excel automatically includes the computer's username at the beginning of the comment. The username is the name that appears in the User name text box of the Excel Options dialog box. The white sizing handles on the border of the Comment box allow you to change the size of the box.

3. **Type** Is this figure correct? It looks low to me., **then click outside the Comment box**

   A red triangle appears in the upper-right corner of cell F5, indicating that a comment is attached to the cell. People who use your worksheet can easily display comments.

4. **Place the pointer over cell** F5

   The comment appears next to the cell. When you move the pointer outside of cell F5, the comment disappears. Kate asks you to add a comment to cell L6.

5. **Right-click cell** L6, **click** Insert Comment **on the shortcut menu, type** Is this increase due to the new marketing campaign?, **then click outside the Comment box**

   Kate asks you to delete a comment and edit a comment. You start by displaying all worksheet comments.

6. **Click cell** A1, **then click the** Show All Comments button **in the Comments group**

   The two worksheet comments are displayed on the screen, as shown in Figure O-8.

7. **Click the** Next button **in the Comments group, with the comment in cell F5 selected click the** Delete button **in the Comments group, click the** Next button **in the Comments group, click the** Edit Comment button **in the Comments group, type** Mark – **at the beginning of the comment in the Comment box, click cell** A1, **then click the** Show All Comments button **in the Comments group**

   The Show All Comments button is a toggle button: You click it once to display comments, then click it again to hide comments. You decide to preview the worksheet and the cell comment along with its associated cell reference on separate pages.

8. **Click the** File tab, **click** Print, **click** Page Setup **at the bottom of the Print pane, click the** Sheet tab, **under Print click the** Comments list arrow, **click** At end of sheet, **click** OK, **then click the** Next Page arrow **at the bottom of the preview pane to view the comments**

   Your comment appears on a separate page after the worksheet.

9. **Save the workbook**

**FIGURE O-7:** Comment box

Your user name will be different

Comment indicator

Sizing handle

Type your comment here

**FIGURE O-8:** Worksheet with comments displayed

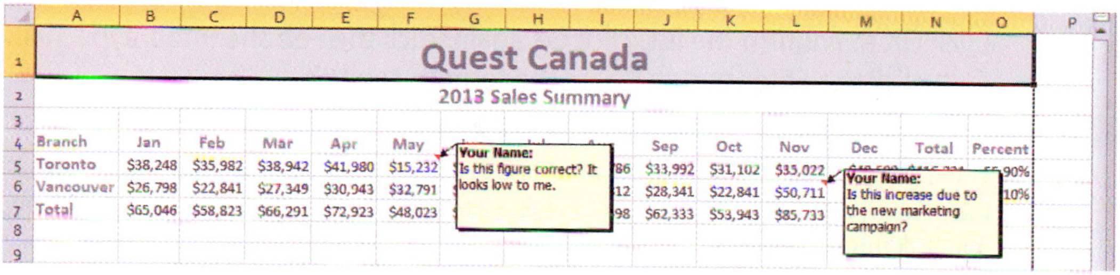

## Changing the way you work with Excel

As you work with Excel you may want to change some of the settings to suit your personal preferences. For example, you may want to change the Excel color scheme from blue to black or silver. Or you may want to turn off the Mini toolbar, which provides quick access to formatting options when you select text. Other options you may want to change are the Live Preview feature or the way the ScreenTips are displayed. You can change these settings by clicking the File tab, clicking Options, and selecting your settings in the General area of the Excel Options dialog box. Some settings have a small "i" next to them, which displays more information on the feature as you hover your mouse pointer over it.

# Creating Custom AutoFill Lists

Whenever you need to type a list of words regularly, you can save time by creating a custom list. Then you can simply enter the first value in a blank cell and drag the fill handle. Excel enters the rest of the information for you. Figure O-9 shows examples of custom lists that are built into Excel as well as a user-created custom list.  Kate often has to enter a list of Quest's sales representatives' names in her worksheets. She asks you to create a custom list to save time in performing this task. You begin by selecting the names in the worksheet.

## STEPS

**TROUBLE**

If a list of sales representatives already appears in the Custom lists box, the person using the computer before you forgot to delete it. Click the list, click Delete, click OK, then proceed with Step 3. It isn't possible to delete the four default lists for days and months.

**QUICK TIP**

You can also drag the fill handle to the right to enter a custom list.

1. Click the Jan sheet tab, then select the range A5:A24

2. Click the File tab, click Options, click Advanced, scroll down to the General section, then click Edit Custom Lists

   The Custom Lists dialog box displays the custom lists that are already built into Excel, as shown in Figure O-10. You want to define a custom list containing the sales representatives' names you selected in column A. The Import list from cells text box contains the range you selected in Step 1.

3. Click Import

   The list of names is highlighted in the Custom lists box and appears in the List entries box. You decide to test the custom list by placing it in a blank worksheet.

4. Click OK to confirm the list, click OK again, click the Feb sheet tab, type Sullivan in cell A1, then click the Enter button ✓ on the formula toolbar

5. Drag the fill handle to fill the range A2:A20

   The highlighted range now contains the custom list of sales representatives you created. Kate informs you that sales representative Bentz has been replaced by a new representative, Linden. You update the custom list to reflect this change.

6. Click the File tab, click Options, click Advanced, scroll down to the General section, click Edit Custom Lists, click the list of sales representatives names in the Custom lists box, change Bentz to Linden in the List entries box, click OK to confirm the change, then click OK again

   You decide to check the new list to be sure it is accurate.

7. Click cell C1, type Sullivan, click ✓ on the formula toolbar, drag the fill handle to fill the range C2:C20

   The highlighted range contains the updated custom list of sales representatives, as shown in Figure O-11. You've finished creating and editing your custom list, and you need to delete it from the Custom Lists dialog box in case others will be using your computer.

8. Click the File tab, click Options, click Advanced, scroll down to the General section, click Edit Custom Lists, click the list of sales representatives' names in the Custom lists box, click Delete, click OK to confirm the deletion, then click OK two more times

9. Save and close the workbook

**FIGURE O-9:** Sample custom lists

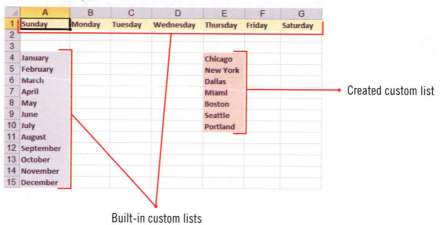

Built-in custom lists

Created custom list

**FIGURE O-10:** Custom Lists dialog box

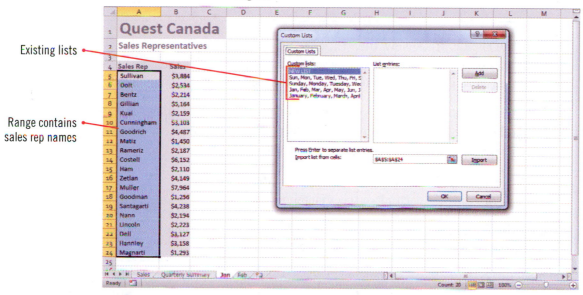

Existing lists

Range contains sales rep names

**FIGURE O-11:** Custom lists with names of sales representatives

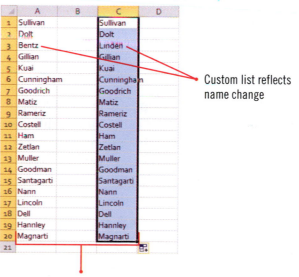

Custom list reflects name change

Names generated using the custom list

Customizing Excel and Advanced Worksheet Management

# Customizing Excel Workbooks

The Excel default settings for editing and viewing a worksheet are designed to meet the needs of the majority of Excel users. You may find, however, that a particular setting doesn't always fit your particular needs, such as the default number of worksheets in a workbook, the default worksheet view, or the default font. You have already used the Advanced category of Excel Options to create custom lists and the Formulas category to switch to manual calculation. The General category of the Excel Options dialog box contains features that are commonly used by a large number of Excel users, and you can use it to further customize Excel to suit your work habits and needs. The most commonly used categories of the Excel Options are explained in more detail in Table O-1.  Kate is interested in customizing workbooks to allow her to work more efficiently. She asks you to use a blank workbook to explore features that will help her better manage her data.

## STEPS

> **TROUBLE**
>
> If you are working on a school computer, check with your instructor or the lab administrator before changing the workbook settings in this lesson.

1. **Click the File tab, click New, then click Create**

   In the last workbook you prepared for Kate you had to add a fourth worksheet. You would like to have four worksheets displayed rather than three when a new workbook is opened.

2. **Click the File tab, click Options, in the "When creating new workbooks" area of the General options, select 3 in the Include this many sheets text box, then type 4**

   You can change the default font Excel uses in new workbooks, as shown in Figure O-12.

> **QUICK TIP**
>
> Excel's default text style is the body font, which is Calibri unless it is changed by the user.

3. **Click the Use this font list arrow, then select Arial**

   You can also change the standard workbook font size.

4. **Click the Font size list arrow, then select 12**

   Kate would rather have new workbooks open in Page Layout view.

5. **Click the Default view for new sheets list arrow, select Page Layout View, click OK to close the Excel Options dialog box, then click OK to the message about quitting and restarting Excel**

   These default settings take effect after you exit and restart Excel.

6. **Close the workbook, exit Excel, then start Excel again**

   A new workbook opens with four sheet tabs in Page Layout view and a 12-point Arial font, as shown in Figure O-13. Now that you have finished exploring the Excel workbook Options, you need to reestablish the original Excel settings.

7. **Click the File tab, click Options, in the "When creating new workbooks" area of the General options, select 4 in the Include this many sheets text box, enter 3, click the Use this font list arrow, select Body Font, select 12 in the Font size text box, type 11, click the Default view for new sheets list arrow, select Normal View, click OK twice, then close the workbook and exit Excel**

**FIGURE O-12:** General category of Excel options

Standard font defaults

Number of worksheets in a new workbook

The user name for the computer

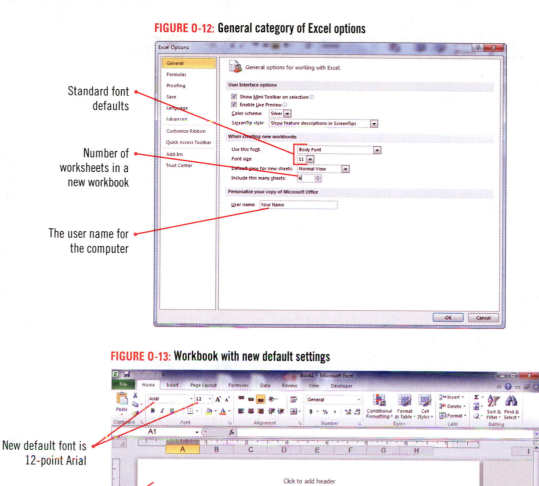

**FIGURE O-13:** Workbook with new default settings

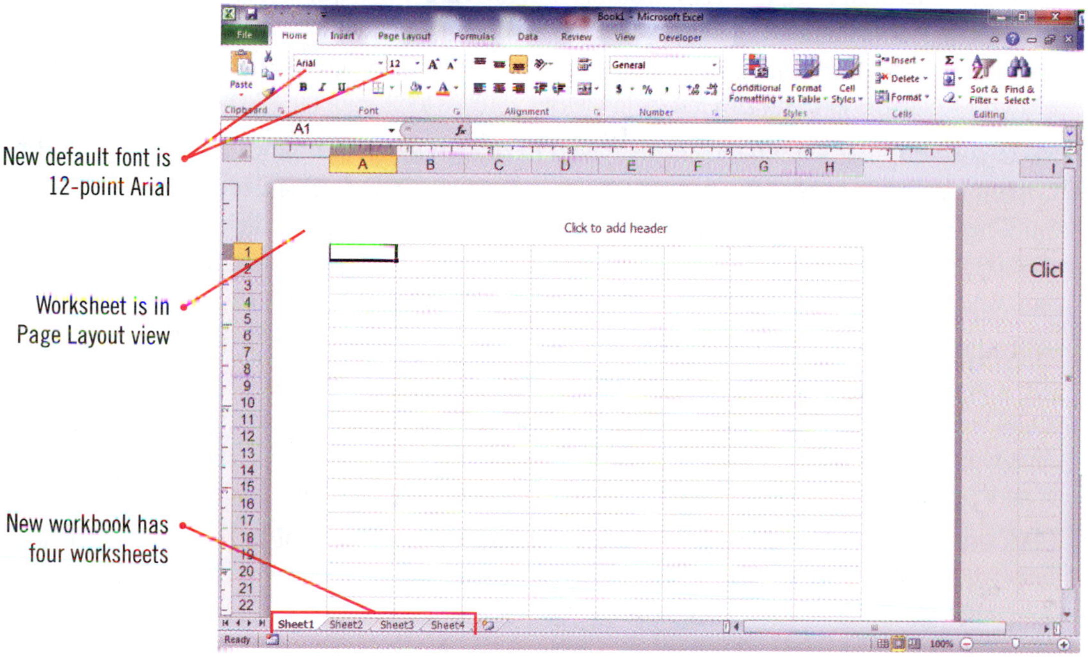

New default font is 12-point Arial

Worksheet is in Page Layout view

New workbook has four worksheets

**TABLE O-1:** Categories of Excel options

| category | allows you to |
|---|---|
| General | Change the user name and the workbook screen display |
| Formulas | Control how the worksheet is calculated, how formulas appear, and error checking settings and rules |
| Proofing | Control AutoCorrect and spell-checking options |
| Save | Select a default format and location for saving files, and customize AutoRecover settings |
| Language | Control the languages displayed and allows you to add languages |
| Advanced | Create custom lists as well as customize editing and display options |
| Customize Ribbon | Add tabs and groups to the Ribbon |
| Quick Access Toolbar | Add commands to the Quick Access toolbar |
| Add-Ins | Install Excel Add-in programs such as Solver and Analysis ToolPak |
| Trust Center | Change Trust Center settings to protect your Excel files |

# Customizing the Excel Screen

While the Quick Access toolbar and the Ribbon give you easy access to many useful Excel features, you might have other commands that you want to have readily available to speed your work. The Excel Options dialog box allows you to add commands to the Quick Access toolbar. It also lets you create your own tabs and groups on the Ribbon and customize the built-in Ribbon tabs and groups. You can use these options to quickly access commands you use frequently. For example, you might want to add the Spelling, Open, or Print Preview commands to the Quick Access toolbar, or create a tab on the Ribbon with commands you use on a particular monthly report. Kate is interested in customizing the Quick Access toolbar to include spell checking. She would also like you to add a new tab to the Ribbon with accessibility tools.

## STEPS

**QUICK TIP**

Your Quick Access toolbar might show more commands if a previous user has already customized it. You can continue with the lesson.

**QUICK TIP**

You can change the order of the buttons on the toolbar using the Move Up button ▲. You can remove buttons from the toolbar by selecting the icon and clicking the Remove button.

1. **Start Excel, then save the new file as EX O-Customized in the drive and folder where you store your Data Files**

2. **Click the Customize Quick Access Toolbar button ▼ on the Quick Access toolbar, then click More Commands**

   The Excel Options dialog box opens with the Quick Access Toolbar option selected as shown in Figure O-14. You want to add the spell checking feature to the Quick Access toolbar for the EX O-Customized workbook.

3. **Make sure Popular Commands is displayed in the Choose commands from list, click the Customize Quick Access Toolbar list arrow, select For EX O-Customized.xlsx, click the Spelling command in the Popular Commands list, click Add, then click OK**

   The Spelling button now appears on the Quick Access toolbar to the right of the Save, Undo, and Redo buttons, which appear by default. Kate wants you to add a tab to the Ribbon with a group of accessibility tools.

4. **With the Home tab selected, click the File tab, click Options, click Customize Ribbon, on the lower-right side of the Excel Options dialog box click New Tab**

   A new tab named New Tab (Custom) is displayed in the listing of Main Tabs below the Home tab. A new tab appears in the list after the currently selected tab. Under the new tab is a new group named New Group (Custom). You want to add accessibility tools to the new group.

5. **Click the Choose commands from list arrow, click Commands Not in the Ribbon, click Accessibility Checker, click Add, click Alt Text, click Add, scroll down, click Zoom In, click Add, click Zoom Out, then click Add**

   Four accessibility tools are in the custom group on the new custom tab. You decide to rename the tab and the group to identify the buttons.

6. **Click New Tab (Custom) in the Main Tabs area, click Rename, in the Rename dialog box type Accessibility, click OK, click New Group (Custom) below the Accessibility tab, click Rename, in the Rename dialog box type Accessibility Tools in the Display name text box, click OK, then click OK again**

   The new custom tab appears in the Ribbon, just to the right of the Home tab. You decide to check it to verify it contains the buttons you want.

7. **Click the Accessibility tab, compare your tab to Figure O-15, click the Zoom In button, then click the Zoom Out button**

   You will reset the Ribbon to the default settings.

8. **Click the File tab, click Options, click Customize Ribbon, on the lower-right side of the Excel Options dialog box click Reset, click Reset all customizations, click Yes, click OK, save the workbook, then close it and exit Excel**

**FIGURE O-14:** Quick Access Toolbar category of Excel options

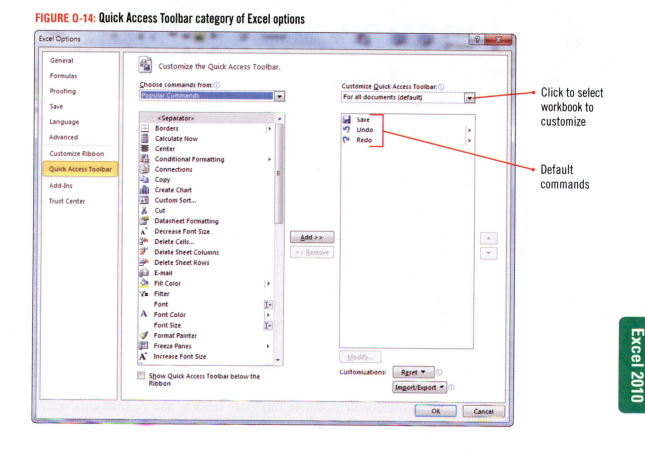

Click to select workbook to customize

Default commands

**FIGURE O-15:** Workbook with new Accessibility Tab

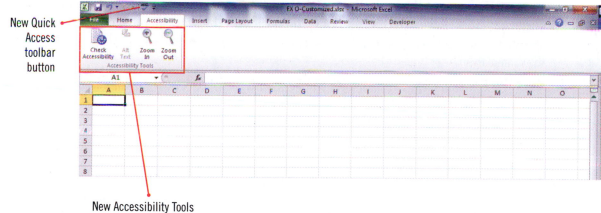

New Quick Access toolbar button

New Accessibility Tools group with four buttons

## Customizing the Quick Access toolbar

You can quickly add a button from the Ribbon to the Quick Access toolbar by right-clicking it and selecting Add to Quick Access Toolbar. Right-clicking a Ribbon button also allows you to quickly customize the Ribbon and the Quick Access toolbar. You can also move the Quick Access toolbar from its default position and minimize the Ribbon.

# Creating and Applying a Template

A template is a workbook with an .xltx file extension that contains text, formulas, macros, and formatting that you use repeatedly. Once you save a workbook as a template, it provides a model for creating a new workbook without your having to reenter standard data. You create workbooks *based on* a template. A workbook based on a template has the same content, formulas, and formatting you defined in the template, and is saved in the .xlsx format. The template file itself remains unchanged.  Kate plans to use the same formulas, titles, and row and column labels from the Sales worksheet for subsequent yearly worksheets. She asks you to create a template that will allow her to quickly prepare these worksheets.

**STEPS**

1. **Start Excel, open the file EX O-Canada Sales.xlsx from the drive and folder where you store your Data Files, then delete the Quarterly Summary, Jan, and Feb sheets.**

   The workbook now contains only the Sales sheet. You decide to use the Sales sheet structure and formulas as the basis for your new template. You want to leave the formulas in row 7 and in columns N and O so future users will not have to re-create them. But you want to delete the comment, the sales data, and the year 2013.

2. **Right-click cell L6, click Delete Comment, select the range B5:M6, press [Delete], double-click cell A2, delete 2013, delete the space before "Sales", then click cell A1**

   The divide-by-zero error messages in column O are only temporary and will disappear as soon as Kate opens a document based on the template, saves it as a workbook, and begins to enter next year's data.

**QUICK TIP**

You can save a theme for use in any Office document. Click the Page Layout tab, click the Themes button in the Themes group, then click Save Current Theme. If you save it in the Document Themes folder, it will appear as a Custom Theme in the themes palette for all your Office files.

3. **Click the Page Layout tab, click the Themes button in the Themes group, click Executive**

   You want the worksheet colors to match the new Quest colors.

4. **Click the Home tab, click the Fill Color list arrow in the Fonts group, click Ice Blue, Background 2 (third from left in the Theme Colors), click the Select All button in the upper-left corner of the worksheet, click the Font Color list arrow in the Font group, click Gray-50%, Accent 6 (last on right), then click on the worksheet to deselect the range**

   The completed template is shown in Figure O-16. You will save the template so Kate can use it for next year's sales summary.

5. **Click the File tab, click Save As, click the Save as type list arrow, then click Excel Template (*.xltx)**

   Excel adds the .xltx extension to the filename and automatically switches to the Templates folder. If you are using a computer on a network, you may not have permission to save to the Templates folder, so you save it to your Data File location.

6. **Navigate to your Data Files folder, click Save, then close the workbook and exit Excel**

   Kate asks you to test the new template. To do this, you open a workbook based on the Canada Sales template, also known as **applying** the template, and test it by entering data in the Sales worksheet.

**QUICK TIP**

If you want to edit the template, open Excel first and then open the template (the .xltx file). After making changes to the template, save it under the same name in the same location. The changes are applied only to new documents you create that are based on the template.

7. **In Windows Explorer, navigate to your Data Files folder, then double click the EX O-Canada Sales.xltx to open a workbook based on the template**

   The workbook name is EX O-Canada Sales1 as shown in Figure O-17. You want to make sure the formulas are working correctly.

8. **Click cell B5, enter 100, click cell B6, enter 200, select the range B5:B6 and use the fill handle to copy the data into the range C5:M6**

9. **Save the workbook as EX O-Template Test, close the workbook, exit Excel, then submit the workbook to your instructor**

   The completed EX O-Template Test workbook is shown in Figure O-18.

**FIGURE O-16:** Completed template

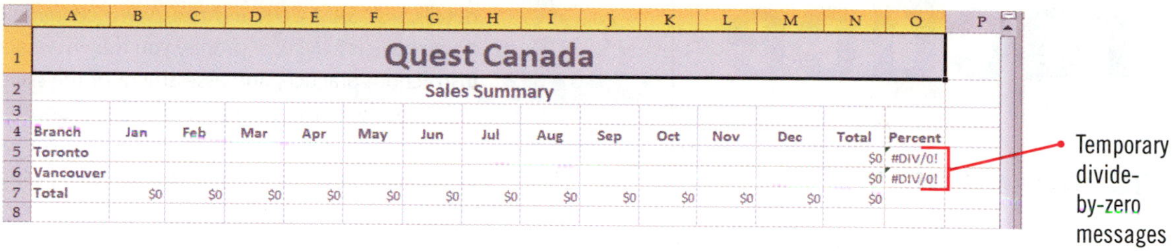

Temporary divide-by-zero messages

**FIGURE O-17:** Workbook based on template

Workbook based on template contains the template's content, formatting, and formulas

Name indicates workbook is based on template EX O-Canada Sales

**FIGURE O-18:** Completed template test

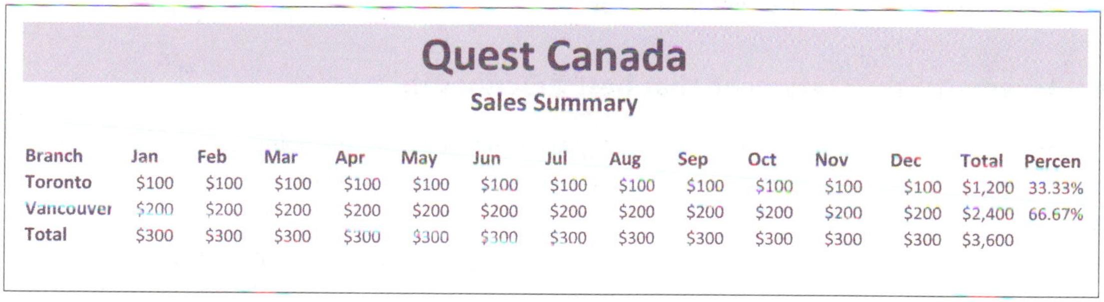

# Quest Canada

## Sales Summary

| Branch | Jan | Feb | Mar | Apr | May | Jun | Jul | Aug | Sep | Oct | Nov | Dec | Total | Percen |
|---|---|---|---|---|---|---|---|---|---|---|---|---|---|---|
| Toronto | $100 | $100 | $100 | $100 | $100 | $100 | $100 | $100 | $100 | $100 | $100 | $100 | $1,200 | 33.33% |
| Vancouver | $200 | $200 | $200 | $200 | $200 | $200 | $200 | $200 | $200 | $200 | $200 | $200 | $2,400 | 66.67% |
| Total | $300 | $300 | $300 | $300 | $300 | $300 | $300 | $300 | $300 | $300 | $300 | $300 | $3,600 | |

## Applying templates

When you save an Excel file as a template, the Template folder is the default location for the template. When you save your templates in this folder, they are available for you to use easily at a later time. To open a workbook based on the template, or **apply** the template, click the File tab, click New, then double-click the My Templates folder under Available Templates. In the New dialog box, click the template you want to use as a basis for your new workbook, then click OK. A file opens with a "1" at the end of the name's file extension. For example, selecting a template named budget.xltx will open a file called budget.xltx1. Then when you save the workbook, the Save As dialog box opens, allowing you to save the new file as an Excel file with the extension .xlsx.

# Practice

For current SAM information, including versions and content details, visit SAM Central (http://www.cengage.com/samcentral). If you have a SAM user profile, you may have access to hands-on instruction, practice, and assessment of the skills covered in this unit. Since various versions of SAM are supported throughout the life of this text, check with your instructor for the correct instructions and URL/Web site for accessing assignments.

## Concepts Review

**FIGURE O-19**

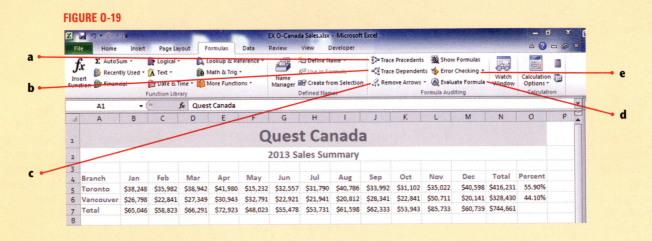

## Which element do you click to:

1. Eliminate tracers from a worksheet?
2. Locate cells that reference the active cell?
3. Locate formula errors in a worksheet?
4. Step through a formula in a selected cell?
5. Find cells that may have caused a formula error?

## Match each term with the statement that best describes it.

6. Outline symbols
7. [Shift][F9]
8. Template
9. Custom list
10. Comment

a. Note that appears when you place the pointer over a cell
b. Used to hide and display details in grouped data
c. Calculates the worksheet manually
d. A workbook with an .xltx file extension that contains text, formulas, and formatting
e. Entered in a worksheet using the fill handle

**Select the best answer from the list of choices.**

11. Which of the following categories of Excel options allows you to change the number of default worksheets in a workbook?
    - **a.** Proofing
    - **b.** General
    - **c.** Advanced
    - **d.** Formulas

12. Which of the following categories of Excel options allows you to create Custom Lists?
    - **a.** Advanced
    - **b.** Add-Ins
    - **c.** Customize
    - **d.** Formulas

13. The _____ displays the fewest details in grouped data.
    - **a.** Column Level 1 button
    - **b.** Column Level 2 button
    - **c.** Column Level 3 button
    - **d.** Column Level 4 button

14. To apply a custom list, you:
    - **a.** Type the first cell entry and drag the fill handle.
    - **b.** Click the Fill tab in the Edit dialog box.
    - **c.** Press [Shift][F9].
    - **d.** Select the list in the worksheet.

## Skills Review

1. **Audit a worksheet.**
   - **a.** Start Excel, open the file EX O-2.xlsx from the drive and folder where you store your Data Files, then save it as **EX O-Camden**.
   - **b.** Select cell B10, then use the Trace Dependents button to locate all the cells that depend on this cell.
   - **c.** Clear the arrows from the worksheet.
   - **d.** Select cell B19, use the Trace Precedents button to find the cells on which that figure is based, then correct the formula in cell B19. (*Hint*: It should be B7–B18.)
   - **e.** Use the Error Checking button to check the worksheet for any other errors. Correct any worksheet errors using the formula bar.

2. **Control worksheet calculations.**
   - **a.** Open the Formulas category of the Excel Options dialog box.
   - **b.** Change the worksheet calculations to manual.
   - **c.** Change the figure in cell B6 to **24,000**.
   - **d.** Recalculate the worksheet manually, using an appropriate key combination or button.
   - **e.** Change the worksheet calculations back to automatic using the Calculation Options button, and save the workbook.

3. **Group worksheet data.**
   - **a.** Group the income information in rows 5 and 6.
   - **b.** Group the expenses information in rows 10 through 17.
   - **c.** Hide the income details in rows 5 and 6.
   - **d.** Hide the expenses details in rows 10 through 17.
   - **e.** Enter your name in the center section of the worksheet footer, then preview the worksheet with the income and expenses detail hidden.
   - **f.** Redisplay the income and expenses details.
   - **g.** Remove the row grouping for the income and expenses details. (*Hint*: With the grouped rows selected, click the Data tab, then click the Ungroup button in the Outline group.)
   - **h.** Save the workbook.

4. **Use cell comments.**
   - **a.** Insert a comment in cell E12 that reads **Does this include newspaper advertising?**.
   - **b.** Click anywhere outside the Comment box to close it.
   - **c.** Display the comment by moving the pointer over cell E12, then check it for accuracy.
   - **d.** Edit the comment in cell E12 to read **Does this include newspaper and magazine advertising?**.

# Skills Review (continued)

   **e.** Preview the worksheet and your comment, with the comment appearing at the end of the sheet.

   **f.** Save the workbook.

**5. Create custom AutoFill lists.**

   **a.** Select the range A4:A19.

   **b.** Open the Custom Lists dialog box, and import the selected text.

   **c.** Close the dialog box.

   **d.** On Sheet2, enter **Income** in cell A1.

   **e.** Use the fill handle to enter the list through cell A15.

   **f.** Enter your name in the center section of the Sheet2 footer, then preview the worksheet.

   **g.** Open the Custom Lists dialog box again, delete the custom list you just created, then save and close the workbook.

**6. Customize Excel workbooks.**

   **a.** Open a new workbook, then open the General options of the Excel Options dialog box.

   **b.** Change the number of sheets in a new workbook to **5**.

   **c.** Change the default font of a new workbook to 14-point Times New Roman.

   **d.** Close the workbook and exit Excel.

   **e.** Start Excel and verify that the new workbook's font is 14-point Times New Roman and that it has five worksheets.

   **f.** Reset the default number of worksheets to **3** and the default workbook font to 11-point Body Font.

   **g.** Close the workbook and exit Excel.

**7. Customize the Excel screen.**

   **a.** Start Excel, open the EX O-Camden.xlsx workbook from the drive and folder where you store your Data Files, then display Sheet1.

   **b.** Use the Quick Access Toolbar category of the Excel Options dialog box to add the Print Preview and Print button to the Quick Access toolbar for the EX O-Camden.xlsx workbook.

   **c.** Use the Customize Ribbon category to add a tab named **Math** to the Ribbon with a group named **Math Tools** containing the buttons Equation and Equation Symbols. (*Hint*: These buttons are in the All Commands list.) Compare your Ribbon to Figure O-20.

   **d.** Reset the Ribbon.

   **e.** Verify that the Print Preview button has been added to the Quick Access toolbar, then save the workbook.

**FIGURE O-20**

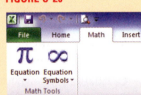

**8. Create and apply a template.**

   **a.** Delete Sheet2 and Sheet3 from the workbook.

   **b.** Delete the comment in cell E12.

   **c.** Delete the income and expense data for all four quarters. Leave the worksheet formulas intact.

   **d.** Change the fill color for cell A1 to Plum, Accent 3, in the Theme colors. Change the fill for the range B3:G3 and cells A4 and A9 to Dark Purple, Accent 4, Lighter 80%. Change the font color for the worksheet cells in the range A3:G19 to Plum, Accent 3, Darker 25%.

   **e.** Save the workbook as a template named **EX O-Camden.xltx** in the drive and folder where you store your Data Files.

   **f.** Close the template, then open a workbook based on the template by double-clicking the template in the folder where you store your Data Files.

   **g.** Test the template by entering your own data for all four quarters and in every budget category. Adjust the column widths as necessary. Your screen should be similar to Figure O-21.

**FIGURE O-21**

| | A | B | C | D | E | F | G |
|---|---|---|---|---|---|---|---|
| 1 | | Camden Chowder House | | | | | |
| 2 | | | | | | | |
| 3 | | Q1 | Q2 | Q3 | Q4 | Total | % of Total |
| 4 | Income | | | | | | |
| 5 | Beverages | $11,000 | $12,000 | $14,000 | $12,000 | $49,000 | 30% |
| 6 | Chowder | $22,000 | $23,000 | $36,000 | $33,000 | $114,000 | 70% |
| 7 | Net Sales | $33,000 | $35,000 | $50,000 | $45,000 | $163,000 | |
| 8 | | | | | | | |
| 9 | Expenses | | | | | | |
| 10 | Salaries | $13,000 | $14,000 | $17,000 | $13,000 | $57,000 | 42% |
| 11 | Rent | $4,000 | $4,000 | $4,000 | $4,000 | $16,000 | 12% |
| 12 | Advertising | $3,000 | $3,000 | $5,000 | $3,000 | $14,000 | 10% |
| 13 | Cleaning | $2,100 | $2,100 | $2,800 | $2,100 | $9,100 | 7% |
| 14 | Fish | $2,500 | $2,700 | $3,500 | $2,500 | $11,200 | 8% |
| 15 | Dairy | $1,200 | $1,300 | $1,800 | $1,200 | $5,500 | 4% |
| 16 | Beverages | $4,000 | $5,000 | $7,000 | $4,000 | $20,000 | 15% |
| 17 | Paper Products | $550 | $550 | $850 | $550 | $2,500 | 2% |
| 18 | Total Expenses | $30,350 | $32,650 | $41,950 | $30,350 | $135,300 | 100% |
| 19 | Net Profit | $2,650 | $2,350 | $8,050 | $14,650 | $27,700 | |
| 20 | | | | | | | |

## Skills Review (continued)

**h.** Save the workbook as **EX O-Camden1.xlsx** in the folder where you store your Data Files.

**i.** Preview the worksheet, close the workbook, exit Excel, then submit the workbook to your instructor.

## Independent Challenge 1

You are the VP of Human Resources at US Tel, a telecommunications contractor with offices in the east and the west regions of the United States. You are tracking the overtime hours for workers using total and percentage formulas. Before you begin your analysis, you want to check the worksheet for formula errors. Then, you group the first quarter data, add a comment to the worksheet, and create a custom list of the east and west locations and total labels.

**a.** Start Excel, open the file titled EX O-3.xlsx from the drive and folder where you store your Data Files, then save it as **EX O-Hours**.

**b.** Audit the worksheet, ignoring warnings that aren't errors and correcting the formula errors in the formula bar.

**c.** Select cell R5 and use the Trace Precedents button to show the cells used in its formula.

**d.** Select cell B10 and use the Trace Dependents button to show the cells affected by the value in the cell.

**e.** Remove all arrows from the worksheet.

**f.** Group the months Jan, Feb, and March, then use the Outline symbols to hide the first quarter details.

**g.** Add the comment **This looks low.** to cell P11. Display the comment on the worksheet so it is visible even when you are not hovering over the cell.

**h.** Create a custom list by importing the range A5:A15. Test the list in cells A1:A11 of Sheet2. Delete the custom list.

### Advanced Challenge Exercise

- Select cell S5 on the Overtime sheet, then open the Evaluate Formula dialog box.
- In the Evaluate Formula dialog box, click Evaluate three times to see the process of substituting values for cell addresses in the formula and the results of the formula calculations. Close the Evaluate Formula window.
- With cell S6 selected, open the Watch Window. Click Add Watch to add cell S6 to the Watch Window, and observe its value in the window as you change cell G6 to 35. Close the Watch Window.

**i.** Change the comment display to show only the comment indicators and the comments when hovering over the cell with the comment.

**j.** Add your name to the center section of the worksheet footer, preview the worksheet with the comment on a separate page, then save the workbook.

**k.** Close the workbook, exit Excel, then submit the workbook to your instructor.

## Independent Challenge 2

You are the property manager of the Layfayette Collection, a commercial retail property located in St. Louis. One of your responsibilities is to keep track of the property's regular monthly expenses. You have compiled a list of fixed expenses in an Excel workbook. Because the items don't change from month to month, you want to create a custom list including each expense item to save time in preparing similar worksheets in the future. You will also temporarily switch to manual formula calculation, check the total formula, and document the data.

**a.** Start Excel, open the file titled EX O-4.xlsx from the drive and folder where you store your Data Files, then save it as **EX O-Expenses**.

**b.** Select the range of cells A4:A15 on the Fixed Expenses sheet, then import the list to create a Custom List.

**c.** Use the fill handle to insert your list in cells A1:A12 in Sheet2.

**d.** Add your name to the Sheet2 footer, save the workbook, then preview Sheet2.

**e.** Delete your custom list, then return to the Fixed Expenses sheet.

**f.** Switch to manual calculation for formulas. Change the expense for Gas to $9,000.00. Calculate the worksheet formula manually. Turn on automatic calculation again.

# Independent Challenge 2 (continued)

g. Add the comment **This may increase.** to cell B4. Display the comment on the worksheet so it is visible even when the mouse pointer is not hovering over the cell.

h. Use the Error Checking dialog box for help in correcting the error in cell B16. Verify that the formula is correctly totaling the expenses in column B.

i. Trace the precedents of cell B16. Compare your worksheet to Figure O-22.

j. Remove the arrow and the comment display from the worksheet, leaving only the indicator displayed. Do not delete the comment from the worksheet cell.

k. Trace the dependents of cell B4. Remove the arrow from the worksheet.

l. Edit the comment in cell B4 to **This may increase next month.**, and add the comment **This seems low.** to cell B10.

m. Use the Next and Previous buttons in the Comments group of the Review tab to move between comments on the worksheet. Delete the comment in cell B10.

**FIGURE O-22**

| | A | B | C | D | E |
|---|---|---|---|---|---|
| 1 | **Layfayette Collection** | | | | |
| 2 | **Fixed Monthly Expenses** | | | | |
| 3 | **Item** | **Amount** | | | |
| 4 | Gas | $ 9,000.00 | | Your Name: | |
| 5 | Electricity | $ 2,877.00 | | This may increase. | |
| 6 | Water & Sewer | $ 3,098.00 | | | |
| 7 | Rubbish Removal | $ 2,009.00 | | | |
| 8 | Parking & Garage | $ 913.00 | | | |
| 9 | Fire Alarm Service | $ 200.00 | | | |
| 10 | Cleaning Service | $ 298.00 | | | |
| 11 | Building Maintenance | $ 2,160.00 | | | |
| 12 | Payroll | $ 5,011.00 | | | |
| 13 | Supplies | $ 1,509.00 | | | |
| 14 | Landscaping | $ 2,021.00 | | | |
| 15 | Legal | $ 2,695.00 | | | |
| 16 | Total | $ 31,791.00 | | | |
| 17 | | | | | |

### Advanced Challenge Exercise

- Copy the comment in cell B4 and paste it in cell B9. The Comments group on the Review tab has a button named Show Ink. Use online resources to find out how ink is used in Excel.
- Summarize your research findings in cell A20 of the worksheet.

n. Add your name to the center section of the worksheet footer, save the workbook, then preview the Fixed Expenses worksheet with the comment appearing at the end of the sheet.

o. Close the workbook, exit Excel, then submit your workbook to your instructor.

# Independent Challenge 3

As the manager of a public radio station you are responsible for the yearly budget. You use Excel to track income and expenses using formulas to total each category and to calculate the net cash flow for the organization. You want to customize your workbooks and settings in Excel so you can work more efficiently. You are also interested in grouping your data and creating a template that you can use to build next year's budget.

a. Start Excel, open the file titled EX O-5.xlsx from the drive and folder where you store your Data Files, then save it as **EX O-Budget**.

b. Add an icon to the Quick Access toolbar for the EX O-Budget.xlsx workbook to preview a worksheet.

c. Add a tab to the Ribbon named Shapes with a group named Shape Tools. Add the buttons Down Arrow, Straight Arrow Connector, and Straight Connector from the Commands Not in the Ribbon list to the new group. Compare your Ribbon and Quick Access toolbar to Figure O-23.

d. Test the new Shape Tools buttons on the Shapes tab by clicking each one and dragging an area on Sheet2 to test the shapes. Rename Sheet2 to **Shapes**, and add your name to the center footer section of the sheet.

**FIGURE O-23**

| File | Home | Shapes | Insert | Page Layout | Formulas | Data | Review | View |
|---|---|---|---|---|---|---|---|---|

Down Arrow | Straight Arrow Connector | Straight Connector
Shape Tools

EX O-Budget.xlsx - Microsoft Excel

e. Test the Print Preview button on the Quick Access toolbar by previewing the Shapes sheet.

f. On the Budget sheet, group rows 4–6 and 9–14, then use the appropriate row-level button to hide the expense and income details, as shown in Figure O-24.

g. Add your name to the center section of the worksheet footer, save the workbook, then use the Print Preview button on the Quick Access toolbar to preview the Budget worksheet.

**FIGURE O-24**

| | A | B | C | D | E | F | G |
|---|---|---|---|---|---|---|---|
| 1 | **Yearly Budget** | | | | | | |
| 2 | **Description** | **1st Qtr** | **2nd Qtr** | **3rd Qtr** | **4th Qtr** | **Total** | |
| 3 | **Income** | | | | | | |
| 7 | **Income Total** | $665,105 | $625,500 | $684,320 | $771,538 | $2,746,463 | |
| 8 | **Expenses** | | | | | | |
| 15 | **Expenses Total** | $548,578 | $609,492 | $539,249 | $602,924 | $2,300,243 | |
| 16 | **Net Cash Flow** | $116,527 | $16,008 | $145,071 | $168,614 | $446,220 | |
| 17 | | | | | | | |

# Independent Challenge 3 (continued)

**h.** Redisplay all rows, using the Outline symbols. Delete the Shapes worksheet and Sheet3. Delete all data in the Budget sheet, leaving the formulas and labels.

**i.** Save the workbook as a template named **EX O-Budget** in the drive and folder where you store your Data Files. Close the template file, and open a workbook based on the template. Save the workbook as **EX O-New Budget**.

**j.** Test the template by entering data for the four quarters. Save the workbook, then preview the worksheet using the Print Preview button on the Quick Access toolbar.

**k.** Customize Excel so that your workbooks will open with four worksheets in Page Layout view and use 12-point Trebuchet MS font.

**l.** Reset the Ribbon, close your workbook, exit Excel, and then open a new workbook to confirm the new default workbook settings. Reset the default Excel workbook to open with three sheets in Normal view and the 11-point Body Font. Close the new workbook.

## Advanced Challenge Exercise

- Open the EX O-Budget.xlsx workbook.
- Create a custom number format that displays currency with negative numbers using a blue font. (*Hint*: Edit one of the formats with a $ that displays negative numbers in a red font.)
- Apply your custom number format to cell B16. Change the first quarter membership amount in cell B4 to **$100,000**, and verify that the value in cell B16 displays using the custom number format. Save then close the workbook.

**m.** Exit Excel, then submit the EX O-Budget and EX O-New Budget workbooks and the template to your instructor.

# Real Life Independent Challenge

**This Independent Challenge requires an Internet connection.**

Excel offers predesigned templates that you can access from the Web to create your own budgets, maintain your health records, create meeting agendas, put together expense estimates, and plan projects. You can download the templates and create Excel workbooks based on the templates. Then you can add your own data, and customize the worksheet for your purposes.

**a.** Start Excel, then use the Excel help feature to search for Templates.

**b.** Review the available templates, and download a template that organizes information you commonly use at home, school, or work.

**c.** Save the template with the name **EX O-My Template.xltx** in the location where you store your Data Files. If your template was created using an earlier version of Excel, you will be working in compatibility mode. If this is the case, close the template and reopen it.

**d.** Select a theme, and format the template using the theme colors and fonts.

**e.** Add your name to the center section of the template's worksheet footer, preview the template worksheet, and change its orientation and scale if necessary to allow a worksheet based on the template to print on one page. Save the template in the drive and folder where you store your Data Files.

**f.** Close the template, open a workbook based on the template, then save the workbook as **EX O-My Template Example**.

**g.** Add a button to the workbook's Quick Access toolbar that will help you as you work in the worksheet. Enter your data in the worksheet, save the workbook, then preview the worksheet.

**h.** Close the workbook, close your browser if necessary, exit Excel, then submit both the workbook and the template to your instructor.

# Visual Workshop

Open the Data File EX O-6.xlsx from the drive and folder where you store your Data Files, then save it as **EX O-Garden Supply**. Group the data as shown after removing any errors in the worksheet. Widen columns if necessary to display the worksheet data. Your grouped results should match Figure O-25. (*Hint*: The Outline symbols have been hidden for the worksheet.) The new buttons on the Quick Access toolbar have only been added to the Garden Supply workbook. Add your name to the center section of the worksheet footer, save the workbook, then preview the worksheet. Close the workbook, exit Excel, then submit the workbook to your instructor.

**FIGURE O-25**

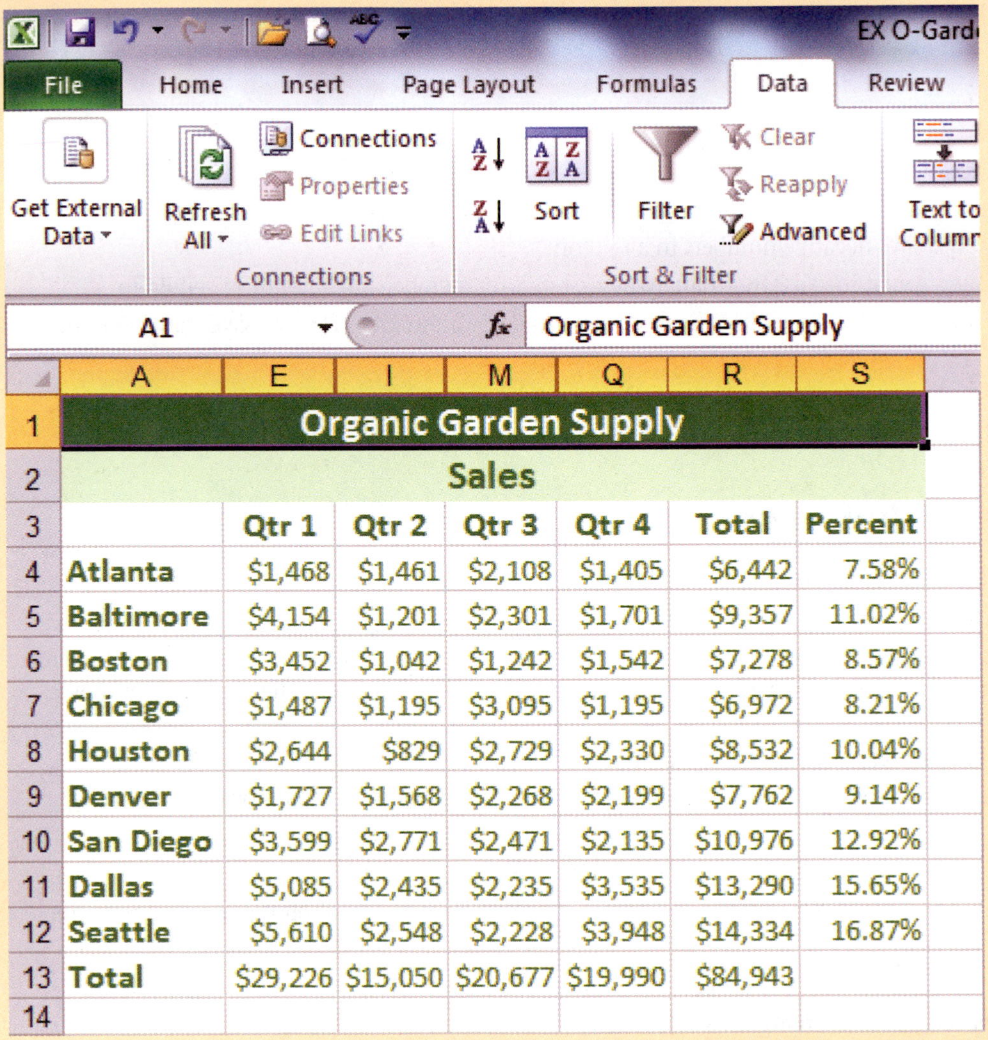

| | Qtr 1 | Qtr 2 | Qtr 3 | Qtr 4 | Total | Percent |
|---|---|---|---|---|---|---|
| | | | | | | |
| **Organic Garden Supply** | | | | | | |
| **Sales** | | | | | | |
| **Atlanta** | $1,468 | $1,461 | $2,108 | $1,405 | $6,442 | 7.58% |
| **Baltimore** | $4,154 | $1,201 | $2,301 | $1,701 | $9,357 | 11.02% |
| **Boston** | $3,452 | $1,042 | $1,242 | $1,542 | $7,278 | 8.57% |
| **Chicago** | $1,487 | $1,195 | $3,095 | $1,195 | $6,972 | 8.21% |
| **Houston** | $2,644 | $829 | $2,729 | $2,330 | $8,532 | 10.04% |
| **Denver** | $1,727 | $1,568 | $2,268 | $2,199 | $7,762 | 9.14% |
| **San Diego** | $3,599 | $2,771 | $2,471 | $2,135 | $10,976 | 12.92% |
| **Dallas** | $5,085 | $2,435 | $2,235 | $3,535 | $13,290 | 15.65% |
| **Seattle** | $5,610 | $2,548 | $2,228 | $3,948 | $14,334 | 16.87% |
| **Total** | $29,226 | $15,050 | $20,677 | $19,990 | $84,943 | |

# Programming with Excel

**Files You Will Need:**

EX P-1.xlsm
EX P-2.xlsx
EX P-3.xlsm
EX P-4.xlsm
EX P-5.xlsm
EX P-6.xlsm
EX P-7.xlsm
EX P-8.xlsm

All Excel macros are written in a programming language called Visual Basic for Applications, or simply, **VBA**. When you create a macro with the Excel macro recorder, the recorder writes the VBA instructions for you. You can also create an Excel macro by entering VBA instructions manually. The sequence of VBA statements contained in a macro is called a **procedure**. In this unit, you will view and analyze existing VBA code and write VBA code on your own. You learn how to add a conditional statement to a procedure as well as how to prompt the user for information while the macro is running. You also find out how to locate any errors, or bugs, in a macro. Finally, you will combine several macros into one main procedure.  Quest's vice president of sales, Kate Morgan, would like to automate some of the division's time-consuming tasks. You help Kate by creating five Excel macros for the sales division.

**OBJECTIVES**

View VBA code

Analyze VBA code

Write VBA code

Add a conditional statement

Prompt the user for data

Debug a macro

Create a main procedure

Run a main procedure

# Viewing VBA Code

Before you can write Excel macro procedures, you must become familiar with the VBA (Visual Basic for Applications) programming language. A common method of learning any programming language is to view existing code. To view VBA code, you open the **Visual Basic Editor**, which contains a Project window, a Properties window, and a Code window. The VBA code for macro procedures appears in the Code window. The first line of a procedure, called the **procedure header**, defines the procedure's type, name, and arguments. **Arguments** are variables used by other procedures that the main procedure might run. An empty set of parentheses after the procedure name means the procedure doesn't have any arguments. Items that appear in blue are **keywords**, which are words Excel recognizes as part of the VBA programming language. **Comments** are notes explaining the code; they are displayed in green, and the remaining code is displayed in black. You use the Visual Basic Editor to view or edit an existing macro as well as to create new ones.  Each month, Kate receives text files containing tour sales information from the Quest branches. Kate has already imported the text file for the Miami January sales into a worksheet, but it still needs to be formatted. She asks you to work on a macro to automate the process of formatting the imported information.

## STEPS

**TROUBLE**
If the Developer tab does not appear on your Ribbon, click the File tab, click Options, click Customize Ribbon on the left side of the Excel Options dialog box, click the Developer check box to select it on the right pane, then click OK.

1. **Start Excel if necessary, click the Developer tab, then click the Macro Security button in the Code group**

   The Trust Center dialog box opens, as shown in Figure P-1. You know the Quest branch files are from a trusted source, so you will allow macros to run in the workbook.

2. **Click the Enable all macros option button if necessary, then click OK**

   You are ready to open a file and view its VBA code. A macro-enabled workbook has the extension .xlsm. Although a workbook containing a macro will open if macros are disabled, they will not function.

3. **Open the file EX P-1.xlsm from the drive and folder where you store your Data Files, save it as EX P-Monthly Sales, then click the Macros button in the Code group**

   The macro dialog box opens with the FormatFile macro procedure in the list box. If you have any macros saved in your Personal Macro workbook, they are also listed in the Macro dialog box.

4. **If it is not already selected click FormatFile, click Edit, then double-click Format in the Modules area of the Project Explorer window**

   The Project Explorer window is shown in Figure P-2. Because the FormatFile procedure is contained in the Format module, clicking Format selects the Format module and displays the FormatFile procedure in the Code window. See Table P-1 to make sure your screen matches the ones shown in this unit.

**TROUBLE**
Your Project Explorer window may show additional VBA projects.

5. **Make sure both the Visual Basic window and the Code window are maximized to match Figure P-2**

6. **Examine the top three lines of code, which contain comments, and the first line of code beginning with Sub FormatFile( )**

   Notice that the different parts of the procedure appear in various colors. The first two comment lines give the procedure name and tell what the procedure does. The third comment line explains that the keyboard shortcut for this macro procedure is [Ctrl][Shift][F]. The keyword Sub in the procedure header indicates that this is a **Sub procedure**, or a series of Visual Basic statements that perform an action but do not return (create and display) a value. In the next lesson, you will analyze the procedure code to see what each line does.

**FIGURE P-1:** Macro settings in the Trust Center dialog box

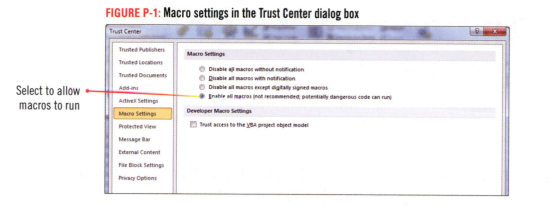

Select to allow macros to run

**FIGURE P-2:** Procedure displayed in the Visual Basic Editor

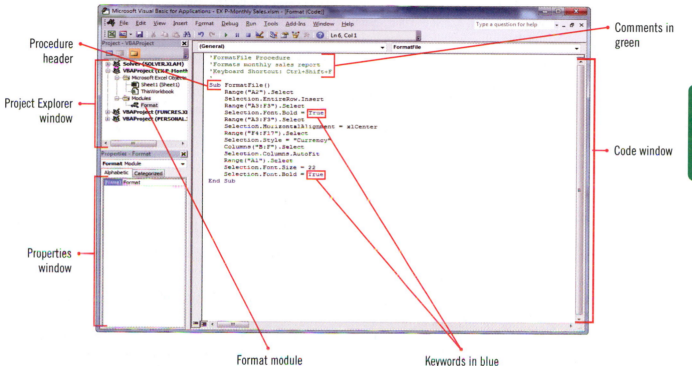

Procedure header

Project Explorer window

Properties window

Comments in green

Code window

Format module

Keywords in blue

**TABLE P-1:** Matching your screen to the unit figures

| if... | do this... |
|-------|-----------|
| The Properties window is not displayed | Click the Properties Window button 📷 on the toolbar |
| The Project Explorer window is not displayed | Click the Project Explorer button 📷 on the toolbar |
| You see only the Code window | Click Tools on the menu bar, click Options, click the Docking tab, then make sure the Project Explorer and Properties Window options are selected |
| You do not see folders in the Explorer window | Click the Toggle Folders button 📁 on the Project Explorer window Project toolbar |

## Understanding the Visual Basic Editor

A **module** is the Visual Basic equivalent of a worksheet. In it, you store macro procedures, just as you store data in worksheets. Modules, in turn, are stored in workbooks (or projects), along with worksheets. A **project** is the collection of all procedures in a workbook. You view and edit modules in the Visual Basic Editor, which is made up of three windows: Project Explorer (also called the Project window), the Code window, and the Properties window. Project Explorer displays a list of all open projects (or workbooks) and the worksheets and modules they contain. To view the procedures stored in a module, you must first select the module in Project Explorer (just as you would select a file in Windows Explorer). The Code window then displays the selected module's procedures. The Properties window displays a list of characteristics (or properties) associated with the module. A newly inserted module has only one property, its name.

Programming with Excel

Excel 371

Excel 2010

# Analyzing VBA Code

You can learn a lot about the VBA language simply by analyzing the code generated by the Excel macro recorder. The more VBA code you analyze, the easier it is for you to write your own programming code.  Before writing any new procedures, you analyze a previously written procedure that applies formatting to a worksheet. Then you open a worksheet that you want to format and run the macro.

1. **With the FormatFile procedure still displayed in the Code window, examine the next four lines of code, beginning with Range("A2").Select**

   Refer to Figure P-3 as you analyze the code in this lesson. Every Excel element, including a range, is considered an **object**. A **range object** represents a cell or a range of cells. The statement Range("A2").Select selects the range object cell A2. Notice that several times in the procedure, a line of code (or **statement**) selects a range, and then subsequent lines act on that selection. The next statement, Selection.EntireRow.Insert, inserts a row above the selection, which is currently cell A2. The next two lines of code select range A3:F3 and apply bold formatting to that selection. In VBA terminology, bold formatting is a value of an object's Bold property. A **property** is an attribute of an object that defines one of the object's characteristics (such as size) or an aspect of its behavior (such as whether it is enabled). To change the characteristics of an object, you change the values of its properties. For example, to apply bold formatting to a selected range, you assign the value True to the range's Bold property. To remove bold formatting, assign the value False.

2. **Examine the remaining lines of code, beginning with the second occurrence of the line Range("A3:F3").Select**

   The next two statements select the range object A3:F3 and center its contents, then the following two statements select the F4:F17 range object and format it as currency. Column objects B through F are then selected, and their widths set to AutoFit. Finally, the range object cell A1 is selected, its font size is changed to 22, and its Bold property is set to True. The last line, End Sub, indicates the end of the Sub procedure and is also referred to as the **procedure footer**.

3. **Click the View Microsoft Excel button**  **on the Visual Basic Editor Standard toolbar to return to Excel**

   Because the macro is stored in the EX P-Monthly Sales workbook, Kate can open this workbook and repeatedly use the macro stored there each month after she receives that month's sales data. She wants you to open the workbook containing data for Chicago's January sales and run the macro to format the data. You must leave the EX P-Monthly Sales workbook open to use the macro stored there.

4. **Open the file EX P-2.xlsx from the drive and folder where you store your Data Files, then save it as EX P-January Sales**

   This is the workbook containing the data you want to format.

5. **Press [Ctrl][Shift][F] to run the procedure**

   The FormatFile procedure formats the text, as shown in Figure P-4.

6. **Save the workbook**

   Now that you've successfully viewed and analyzed VBA code and run the macro, you will learn how to write your own code.

**FIGURE P-3:** VBA code for the FormatFile procedure

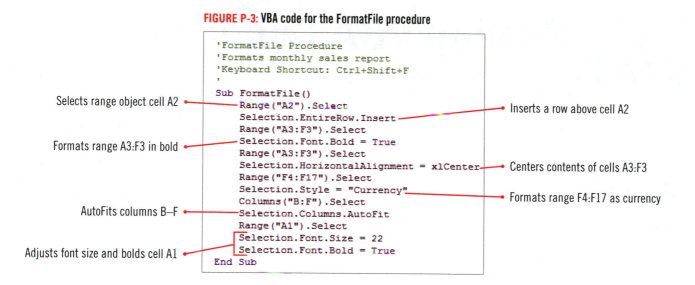

Selects range object cell A2 → `Range("A2").Select`

Inserts a row above cell A2 → `Selection.EntireRow.Insert`

Formats range A3:F3 in bold → `Selection.Font.Bold = True`

Centers contents of cells A3:F3 → `Selection.HorizontalAlignment = xlCenter`

Formats range F4:F17 as currency → `Selection.Style = "Currency"`

AutoFits columns B–F → `Selection.Columns.AutoFit`

Adjusts font size and bolds cell A1 → `Selection.Font.Size = 22` / `Selection.Font.Bold = True`

```
'FormatFile Procedure
'Formats monthly sales report
'Keyboard Shortcut: Ctrl+Shift+F
'
Sub FormatFile()
    Range("A2").Select
    Selection.EntireRow.Insert
    Range("A3:F3").Select
    Selection.Font.Bold = True
    Range("A3:F3").Select
    Selection.HorizontalAlignment = xlCenter
    Range("F4:F17").Select
    Selection.Style = "Currency"
    Columns("B:F").Select
    Selection.Columns.AutoFit
    Range("A1").Select
    Selection.Font.Size = 22
    Selection.Font.Bold = True
End Sub
```

**FIGURE P-4:** Worksheet formatted using the FormatFile procedure

Formatted title →

Row inserted →

Formatted column headings →

Range formatted as currency →

Columns widened

| | Trip Code | Depart Date | Number of Days | Seats Sold | Tour | Sales |
|---|---|---|---|---|---|---|
| 1 | **Quest Chicago January Sales** | | | | | |
| 2 | | | | | | |
| 3 | **Trip Code** | **Depart Date** | **Number of Days** | **Seats Sold** | **Tour** | **Sales** |
| 4 | 452R | 1/7/2013 | 30 | 30 | African National Parks | $125,400.00 |
| 5 | 556J | 1/13/2013 | 14 | 25 | Amazing Amazon | $ 69,875.00 |
| 6 | 675Y | 1/19/2013 | 14 | 32 | Catalonia Adventure | $100,300.00 |
| 7 | 446R | 1/20/2013 | 7 | 18 | Yellowstone | $ 46,958.00 |
| 8 | 251D | 1/21/2013 | 7 | 10 | Costa Rica | $ 28,220.00 |
| 9 | 335P | 1/22/2013 | 21 | 33 | Corfu Sailing Voyage | $105,270.00 |
| 10 | 431V | 1/25/2013 | 7 | 21 | Costa Rica Rainforests | $ 54,390.00 |
| 11 | 215C | 1/26/2013 | 14 | 19 | Silk Road Travels | $ 92,663.00 |
| 12 | 325B | 1/27/2013 | 10 | 17 | Down Under Exodus | $ 47,600.00 |
| 13 | 311A | 1/29/2013 | 18 | 20 | Essential India | $102,887.00 |
| 14 | 422R | 1/29/2013 | 7 | 24 | Exotic Morocco | $ 45,600.00 |
| 15 | 331E | 1/30/2013 | 12 | 21 | Experience Cambodia | $ 98,557.00 |
| 16 | 831P | 1/30/2013 | 14 | 15 | Galapagos Adventure | $ 52,698.00 |
| 17 | 334Q | 1/31/2013 | 18 | 10 | Green Adventures in Ecuador | $ 39,574.00 |
| 18 | | | | | | |
| 19 | | | | | | |

Excel 2010

# Writing VBA Code

To write your own code, you first need to open the Visual Basic Editor and add a module to the workbook. You can then begin entering the procedure code. In the first few lines of a procedure, you typically include comments indicating the name of the procedure, a brief description of the procedure, and shortcut keys, if applicable. When writing Visual Basic code for Excel, you must follow the formatting rules, or **syntax**, of the VBA programming language. A misspelled keyword or variable name causes a procedure to fail.  Kate would like to total the monthly sales. You help her by writing a procedure that automates this routine task.

## STEPS

**TROUBLE**

If the Code window is empty, verify that the workbook that contains your procedures (EX P-Monthly Sales) is open.

1. **With the January worksheet still displayed, click the Developer tab, then click the Visual Basic button in the Code group**

   Two projects are displayed in the Project Explorer window, EX P-Monthly Sales.xlsm (which contains the FormatFile macro) and EX P-January Sales.xlsx (which contains the monthly data). The FormatFile procedure is again displayed in the Visual Basic Editor. You may have other projects in the Project Explorer window.

2. **Click the Modules folder in the EX P-Monthly Sales.xlsm project**

   You need to store all of the procedures in the EX P-Monthly Sales.xlsm project, which is in the EX P-Monthly Sales.xlsm workbook. By clicking the Modules folder, you have activated the workbook, and the title bar changes from EX P-January Sales to EX P-Monthly Sales.

3. **Click Insert on the Visual Basic Editor menu bar, then click Module**

   A new, blank module with the default name Module1 appears in the EX P-Monthly Sales.xlsm project, under the Format module. You think the property name of the module could be more descriptive.

4. **Click (Name) in the Properties window, then type Total**

   The module name is Total. The module name should not be the same as the procedure name (which will be AddTotal). In the code shown in Figure P-5, comments begin with an apostrophe, and the lines of code under Sub AddTotal( ) have been indented using the Tab key. When you enter the code in the next step, after you type the procedure header Sub AddTotal( ) and press [Enter], the Visual Basic Editor automatically enters End Sub (the procedure footer) in the Code window.

**TROUBLE**

As you type, you may see words in drop-down lists. This optional feature is explained in the Clues to Use titled "Entering code using AutoComplete" on the next page. For now, just continue to type.

5. **Click in the Code window, then type the procedure code exactly as shown in Figure P-5, entering your name in the second line, pressing [Tab] to indent text and [Shift][Tab] to move the insertion point to the left**

   The lines that begin with ActiveCell.Formula insert the information enclosed in quotation marks into the active cell. For example, ActiveCell.Formula = "Monthly Total:" inserts the words "Monthly Total:" into cell E18, the active cell. As you type each line, Excel adjusts the spacing.

6. **Compare the procedure code you entered in the Code window with Figure P-5, make any corrections if necessary, then click the Save EX P-Monthly Sales.xlsm button 🖫 on the Visual Basic Editor Standard toolbar**

7. **Click the View Microsoft Excel button 🖾 on the toolbar, click EX P-January Sales.xlsx on the taskbar to activate the workbook if necessary, with the January worksheet displayed click the Developer tab, then click the Macros button in the Code group**

   Macro names have two parts. The first part ('EX P-Monthly Sales.xlsm'!) indicates the workbook where the macro is stored. The second part (AddTotal or FormatFile) is the name of the procedure, taken from the procedure header.

**TROUBLE**

If an error message appears, click Debug. Click the Reset button 🔲 on the toolbar, correct the error, then repeat Steps 6–8.

8. **Click 'EX P-MonthlySales.xlsm'!AddTotal to select it if necessary, then click Run**

   The AddTotal procedure inserts and formats the monthly total in cell F18, as shown in Figure P-6.

9. **Save the workbook**

**FIGURE P-5:** VBA code for the AddTotal procedure

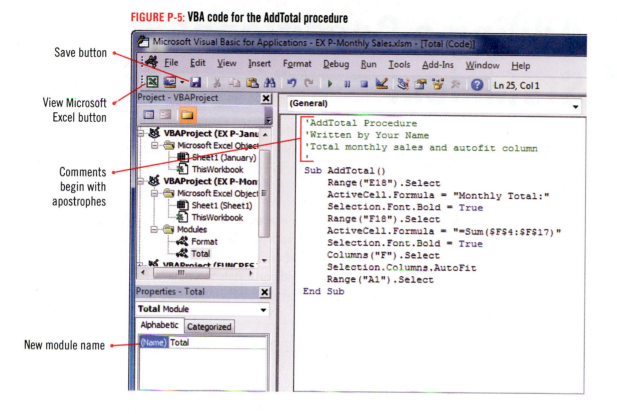

Save button

View Microsoft Excel button

Comments begin with apostrophes

New module name

```
'AddTotal Procedure
'Written by Your Name
'Total monthly sales and autofit column
'
Sub AddTotal()
    Range("E18").Select
    ActiveCell.Formula = "Monthly Total:"
    Selection.Font.Bold = True
    Range("F18").Select
    ActiveCell.Formula = "=Sum($F$4:$F$17)"
    Selection.Font.Bold = True
    Columns("F").Select
    Selection.Columns.AutoFit
    Range("A1").Select
End Sub
```

**FIGURE P-6:** Worksheet after running the AddTotal procedure

| | A | B | C | D | E | F | G |
|---|---|---|---|---|---|---|---|
| 1 | **Quest Chicago January Sales** | | | | | | |
| 2 | | | | | | | |
| 3 | **Trip Code** | **Depart Date** | **Number of Days** | **Seats Sold** | **Tour** | **Sales** | |
| 4 | 452R | 1/7/2013 | 30 | 30 | African National Parks | $ 125,400.00 | |
| 5 | 556J | 1/13/2013 | 14 | 25 | Amazing Amazon | $ 69,875.00 | |
| 6 | 675Y | 1/19/2013 | 14 | 32 | Catalonia Adventure | $ 100,300.00 | |
| 7 | 446R | 1/20/2013 | 7 | 18 | Yellowstone | $ 46,958.00 | |
| 8 | 251D | 1/21/2013 | 7 | 10 | Costa Rica | $ 28,220.00 | |
| 9 | 335P | 1/22/2013 | 21 | 33 | Corfu Sailing Voyage | $ 105,270.00 | |
| 10 | 431V | 1/25/2013 | 7 | 21 | Costa Rica Rainforests | $ 54,390.00 | |
| 11 | 215C | 1/26/2013 | 14 | 19 | Silk Road Travels | $ 92,663.00 | |
| 12 | 325B | 1/27/2013 | 10 | 17 | Down Under Exodus | $ 47,600.00 | |
| 13 | 511A | 1/29/2013 | 18 | 20 | Essential India | $ 102,887.00 | |
| 14 | 422R | 1/29/2013 | 7 | 24 | Exotic Morocco | $ 45,600.00 | |
| 15 | 331E | 1/30/2013 | 12 | 21 | Experience Cambodia | $ 98,557.00 | |
| 16 | 831P | 1/30/2013 | 14 | 15 | Galapagos Adventure | $ 52,698.00 | |
| 17 | 334Q | 1/31/2013 | 18 | 10 | Green Adventures in Ecuador | $ 39,574.00 | |
| 18 | | | | | **Monthly Total:** | **$ 1,009,992.00** | |
| 19 | | | | | | | |

Result of AddTotal procedure

## Entering code using AutoComplete

To assist you in entering the VBA code, the Editor uses **AutoComplete**, a list of words that can be used in the macro statement and match what is typed. Typically, the list appears after you press [.] (period). To include a word from the list in the macro statement, select the word in the list, then double-click it or press [Tab].

For example, to enter the Range("E12").Select instruction, type Range("E12"), then press [.] (period). Type s to bring up the words beginning with the letter "s", select the Select command in the list, then press [Tab] to enter the word "Select" in the macro statement.

# Adding a Conditional Statement

The formatting macros you entered in the previous lesson could have been created using the macro recorder. However, there are some situations where you cannot use the recorder and must type the VBA macro code. One of these situations is when you want a procedure to take an action based on a certain condition or set of conditions. For example, *if* a salesperson's performance rating is a 5 (top rating), *then* calculate a 10% bonus; otherwise (*else*), there is no bonus. One way of adding this type of conditional statement in Visual Basic is to use an **If...Then...Else statement**. The syntax for this statement is: "If *condition* Then *statements* Else [*else statements*]." The brackets indicate that the Else part of the statement is optional. Kate wants the worksheet to point out if the total sales figure meets or misses the $1,000,000 monthly quota. You use Excel to add a conditional statement that indicates this information. You start by returning to the Visual Basic Editor and inserting a new module in the Monthly Sales project.

## STEPS

1. **With the January worksheet still displayed, click the Developer tab if necessary, then click the Visual Basic button in the Code group**

2. **Verify that the Total module in the Modules folder of the EX P-Monthly Sales VBAProject is selected in the Project Explorer window, click Insert on the Visual Basic Editor menu bar, then click Module**

   A new, blank module named Module1 is inserted in the EX P-Monthly Sales workbook.

3. **In the Properties window click (Name), then type Sales**

> **QUICK TIP**
> The If...Then...Else statement is similar to the Excel IF function.

4. **Click in the Code window, then type the code exactly as shown in Figure P-7, entering your name in the second line**

   Notice the green comment lines in the middle of the code. These lines help explain the procedure.

5. **Compare the procedure you entered with Figure P-7, make any corrections if necessary, click the Save EX P-Monthly Sales.xlsm button 🖫 on the Visual Basic Editor toolbar, then click the View Microsoft Excel button 🖾 on the toolbar**

> **QUICK TIP**
> You can assign a shortcut key combination to a macro by clicking the Options button in the Macro dialog box and entering the key combination that runs the macro.

6. **If necessary, click EX P-January Sales.xlsx in the taskbar to display it, with the January worksheet displayed click the Macros button in the Code group, in the Macro dialog box click 'EX P-Monthly Sales.xlsm'!SalesStatus, then click Run**

   The SalesStatus procedure indicates the status "Met Quota", as shown in Figure P-8.

7. **Save the workbook**

**FIGURE P-7:** VBA code for the SalesStatus procedure

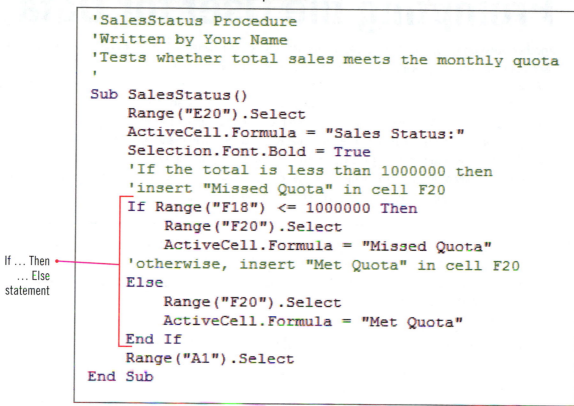

```
'SalesStatus Procedure
'Written by Your Name
'Tests whether total sales meets the monthly quota
'
Sub SalesStatus()
    Range("E20").Select
    ActiveCell.Formula = "Sales Status:"
    Selection.Font.Bold = True
    'If the total is less than 1000000 then
    'insert "Missed Quota" in cell F20
    If Range("F18") <= 1000000 Then
        Range("F20").Select
        ActiveCell.Formula = "Missed Quota"
    'otherwise, insert "Met Quota" in cell F20
    Else
        Range("F20").Select
        ActiveCell.Formula = "Met Quota"
    End If
    Range("A1").Select
End Sub
```

If ... Then ... Else statement

**FIGURE P-8:** Result of running the SalesStatus procedure

| | A | B | C | D | E | F | G |
|---|---|---|---|---|---|---|---|
| 1 | **Quest Chicago January Sales** | | | | | | |
| 2 | | | | | | | |
| 3 | Trip Code | Depart Date | Number of Days | Seats Sold | Tour | Sales | |
| 4 | 452R | 1/7/2013 | 30 | 30 | African National Parks | $ 125,400.00 | |
| 5 | 556J | 1/13/2013 | 14 | 25 | Amazing Amazon | $ 69,875.00 | |
| 6 | 675Y | 1/19/2013 | 14 | 32 | Catalonia Adventure | $ 100,300.00 | |
| 7 | 446R | 1/20/2013 | 7 | 18 | Yellowstone | $ 46,958.00 | |
| 8 | 251D | 1/21/2013 | 7 | 10 | Costa Rica | $ 28,220.00 | |
| 9 | 335P | 1/22/2013 | 21 | 33 | Corfu Sailing Voyage | $ 105,270.00 | |
| 10 | 431V | 1/25/2013 | 7 | 21 | Costa Rica Rainforests | $ 54,390.00 | |
| 11 | 215C | 1/26/2013 | 14 | 19 | Silk Road Travels | $ 92,663.00 | |
| 12 | 325B | 1/27/2013 | 10 | 17 | Down Under Exodus | $ 47,600.00 | |
| 13 | 311A | 1/29/2013 | 18 | 20 | Essential India | $ 102,887.00 | |
| 14 | 422R | 1/29/2013 | 7 | 24 | Exotic Morocco | $ 45,600.00 | |
| 15 | 331E | 1/30/2013 | 12 | 21 | Experience Cambodia | $ 98,557.00 | |
| 16 | 831P | 1/30/2013 | 14 | 15 | Galapagos Adventure | $ 52,698.00 | |
| 17 | 334Q | 1/31/2013 | 18 | 10 | Green Adventures in Ecuador | $ 39,574.00 | |
| 18 | | | | | **Monthly Total:** | $ 1,009,992.00 | |
| 19 | | | | | | | |
| 20 | | | | | Sales Status: | Met Quota | |
| 21 | | | | | | | |

Indicates status of monthly total

# Prompting the User for Data

Another situation where you must type, not record, VBA code is when you need to pause a macro to allow user input. You use the VBA InputBox function to display a dialog box that prompts the user for information. A **function** is a predefined procedure that returns (creates and displays) a value; in this case the value returned is the information the user enters. The required elements of an InputBox function are as follows: *object*.InputBox("*prompt*"), where "*prompt*" is the message that appears in the dialog box. For a detailed description of the InputBox function, use the Visual Basic Editor's Help menu. 🎨 You decide to create a procedure that will insert the user's name in the left footer area of the worksheet. You use the InputBox function to display a dialog box in which the user can enter his or her name. You also type an intentional error into the procedure code, which you will correct in the next lesson.

## STEPS

1. **With the January worksheet displayed, click the Developer tab if necessary, click the Visual Basic button in the Code group, verify that the Sales module is selected in the EX P-Monthly Sales VBAProject Modules folder, click Insert on the Visual Basic Editor menu bar, then click Module**

   A new, blank module named Module1 is inserted in the EX P-Monthly Sales workbook.

2. **In the Properties window click (Name), then type Footer**

> **QUICK TIP**
> To enlarge your Code window, place the mouse pointer on the left border of the Code window until it turns into ◄|►, then drag the border to the left until the Code window is the desired size.

3. **Click in the Code window, then type the procedure code exactly as shown in Figure P-9 entering your name in the second line**

   Like the SalesStatus procedure, this procedure also contains comments that explain the code. The first part of the code, Dim LeftFooterText As String, **declares**, or defines, LeftFooterText as a text string variable. In Visual Basic, a **variable** is a location in memory in which you can temporarily store one item of information. Dim statements are used to declare variables and must be entered in the following format: Dim *variablename* As *datatype*. The datatype here is "string." In this case, you plan to store the information received from the input box in the temporary memory location called LeftFooterText. Then you can place this text in the left footer area. The remaining statements in the procedure are explained in the comment line directly above each statement. Notice the comment pointing out the error in the procedure code. You will correct this in the next lesson.

4. **Review your code, make any necessary changes, click the Save EX P-MonthlySales.xlsm button 🖫 on the Visual Basic Editor toolbar, then click the View Microsoft Excel button 🖾 on the toolbar**

5. **With the January worksheet displayed, click the Macros button in the Code group, in the Macro dialog box click 'EX P-Monthly Sales.xlsm'!FooterInput, then click Run**

   The procedure begins, and a dialog box generated by the InputBox function opens, prompting you to enter your name, as shown in Figure P-10.

> **QUICK TIP**
> If your macro doesn't prompt you for your name, it may contain an error. Return to the Visual Basic Editor, click the Reset button 🔲, correct the error by referring to Figure P-9, then repeat Steps 4 and 5. You'll learn more about how to correct such macro errors in the next lesson.

6. **With the cursor in the text box, type your name, then click OK**

7. **Click the File tab, click Print, then view the worksheet preview**

   Although the customized footer with the date is inserted on the sheet, because of the error your name does *not* appear in the left section of the footer. In the next lesson, you will learn how to step through a procedure's code line by line. This will help you locate the error in the FooterInput procedure.

8. **Click the Home tab, then save the workbook**

   You return to the January worksheet.

**FIGURE P-9:** VBA code for the FooterInput procedure

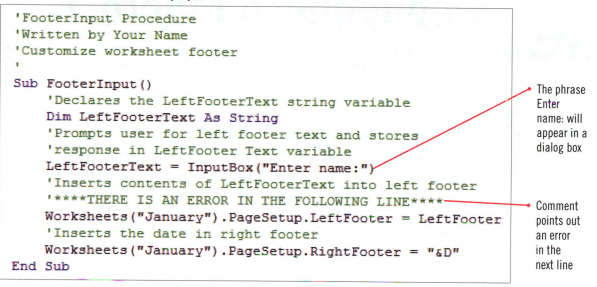

```
'FooterInput Procedure
'Written by Your Name
'Customize worksheet footer
'
Sub FooterInput()
    'Declares the LeftFooterText string variable
    Dim LeftFooterText As String
    'Prompts user for left footer text and stores
    'response in LeftFooter Text variable
    LeftFooterText = InputBox("Enter name:")
    'Inserts contents of LeftFooterText into left footer
    '****THERE IS AN ERROR IN THE FOLLOWING LINE****
    Worksheets("January").PageSetup.LeftFooter = LeftFooter
    'Inserts the date in right footer
    Worksheets("January").PageSetup.RightFooter = "&D"
End Sub
```

The phrase Enter name: will appear in a dialog box

Comment points out an error in the next line

**FIGURE P-10:** InputBox function's dialog box

User prompt

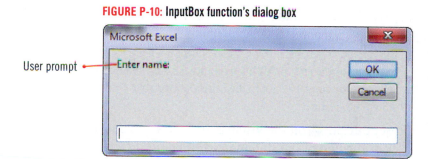

Microsoft Excel

Enter name:

OK

Cancel

Excel 2010

### Naming variables

Variable names in VBA must begin with a letter. Letters can be upper-case or lowercase. Variable names cannot include periods or spaces, and they can be up to 255 characters long. Each variable name in a procedure must be unique. Examples of valid and invalid variable names are shown in Table P-2.

**TABLE P-2:** Variable names

| valid | invalid |
|---|---|
| Sales_Department | Sales Department |
| SalesDepartment | Sales.Department |
| Quarter1 | 1stQuarter |

Programming with Excel

# Debugging a Macro

When a macro procedure does not run properly, it can be due to an error, referred to as a **bug**, in the code. To assist you in finding the bug(s) in a procedure, the Visual Basic Editor helps you step through the procedure's code, one line at a time. When you locate the error, you can then correct, or **debug**, it.  You decide to debug the macro procedure to find out why it failed to insert your name in the worksheet footer.

**STEPS**

1. **With the January worksheet displayed, click the Developer tab if necessary, click the Macros button in the Code group, in the Macro dialog box click 'EX P-Monthly Sales.xlsm'!FooterInput, then click Step Into**

   The Visual Basic Editor opens with the yellow statement selector positioned on the first statement of the procedure, as shown in Figure P-11.

2. **Press [F8] to step to the next statement**

   The statement selector skips over the comments and the line of code beginning with Dim. The Dim statement indicates that the procedure will store your name in a variable named LeftFooterText. Because Dim is a declaration of a variable and not a procedure statement, the statement selector skips it and moves to the line containing the InputBox function.

3. **Press [F8] again, with the cursor in the text box in the Microsoft Excel dialog box type your name, then click OK**

   The Visual Basic Editor opens. The statement selector is now positioned on the statement that reads Worksheets("January").PageSetup.LeftFooter = LeftFooter. This statement should insert your name (which you just typed in the text box) in the left section of the footer. This is the instruction that does not appear to be working correctly.

4. **If necessary scroll right until the end of the LeftFooter instruction is visible, then place the mouse pointer on LeftFooter**

   The value of the LeftFooter variable is displayed as shown in Figure P-12. Rather than containing your name, the variable LeftFooter at the end of this line is empty. This is because the InputBox function assigned your name to the LeftFooterText variable, not to the LeftFooter variable. Before you can correct this bug, you need to turn off the Step Into feature.

5. **Click the Reset button ⬛ on the Visual Basic Editor toolbar to turn off the Step Into feature, click at the end of the statement containing the error, then replace the variable LeftFooter with LeftFooterText**

   The revised statement now reads Worksheets("January").PageSetup.LeftFooter = LeftFooterText.

6. **Delete the comment line pointing out the error**

7. **Click the Save EX P-Monthly Sales.xlsm button 🖫 on the Visual Basic Editor toolbar, then click the View Microsoft Excel button 🗙 on the toolbar**

8. **With the January worksheet displayed click the Macros button in the Code group, in the Macro dialog box click 'EX P-Monthly Sales.xlsm'!FooterInput, click Run to rerun the procedure, when prompted type your name, then click OK**

9. **Click the File tab, click Print, then view the worksheet preview**

   Your name now appears in the left section of the footer.

10. **Click the Home tab, then save the workbook**

**FIGURE P-11:** Statement selector positioned on first procedure statement

Statement selector →

```
'FooterInput Procedure
'Written by Your Name
'Customize worksheet footer
'
Sub FooterInput()
    'Declares the LeftFooterText string variable
    Dim LeftFooterText As String
    'Prompts user for left footer text and stores
    'response in LeftFooter Text variable
    LeftFooterText = InputBox("Enter name:")
    'Inserts contents of LeftFooterText into left footer
    '****THERE IS AN ERROR IN THE FOLLOWING LINE****
    Worksheets("January").PageSetup.LeftFooter = LeftFooter
    'Inserts the date in right footer
    Worksheets("January").PageSetup.RightFooter = "&D"
End Sub
```

**FIGURE P-12:** Value contained in LeftFooter variable

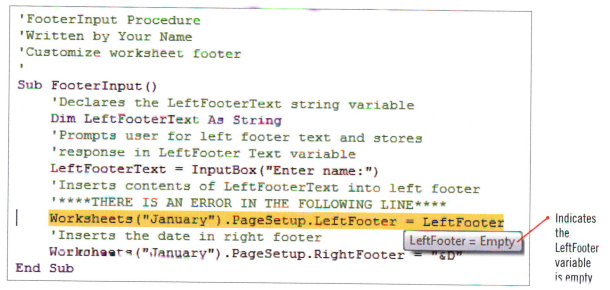

```
'FooterInput Procedure
'Written by Your Name
'Customize worksheet footer
'
Sub FooterInput()
    'Declares the LeftFooterText string variable
    Dim LeftFooterText As String
    'Prompts user for left footer text and stores
    'response in LeftFooter Text variable
    LeftFooterText = InputBox("Enter name:")
    'Inserts contents of LeftFooterText into left footer
    '****THERE IS AN ERROR IN THE FOLLOWING LINE****
    Worksheets("January").PageSetup.LeftFooter = LeftFooter
    'Inserts the date in right footer
    Worksheets("January").PageSetup.RightFooter = "&D"
End Sub
```

LeftFooter = Empty

Indicates the LeftFooter variable is empty

### Adding security to your macro projects

To add security to your projects, you can add a digital signature to the project. A digital signature guarantees the project hasn't been altered since it was signed. You should sign macros only after they are tested and ready to be distributed. If the code in a digitally signed macro project is changed in any way, its digital signature is removed. To add a digital signature to a Visual Basic project, select the project that you want to sign in the Visual Basic Project Explorer window, click the Tools menu in the Visual Basic Editor, click Digital Signature, click Choose, select the certificate, then click OK twice. When you add a digital signature to a project, the macro project is automatically re-signed whenever it is saved on your computer.

# Creating a Main Procedure

When you routinely need to run several macros one after another, you can save time by combining them into one procedure. The resulting procedure, which processes (or runs) multiple procedures in sequence, is referred to as the **main procedure**. To create a main procedure, you type a **Call statement** for each procedure you want to run. The syntax of the Call statement is Call *procedurename*, where *procedurename* is the name of the procedure you want to run. To avoid having to run her macros one after another every month, Kate asks you to create a main procedure that will run (or call) each of the procedures in the EX P-Monthly Sales workbook in sequence.

## STEPS

1. With the January worksheet displayed, click the Developer tab if necessary, then click the Visual Basic button in the Code group

2. Verify that EX P-Monthly Sales is the active project, click Insert on the menu bar, then click Module

   A new, blank module named Module1 is inserted in the EX P-Monthly Sales workbook.

3. In the Properties window click (Name), then type MainProc

4. In the Code window enter the procedure code exactly as shown in Figure P-13, entering your name in the second line

5. Compare your main procedure code with Figure P-13, correct any errors if necessary, then click the Save EX P-Monthly Sales.xlsm button 🖫 on the Visual Basic Editor Standard toolbar

   To test the new main procedure, you need an unformatted version of the EX P-January Sales worksheet.

6. Click the View Microsoft Excel button 🗷 on the toolbar, then save and close the EX P-January Sales workbook

   The EX P-Monthly Sales workbook remains open.

7. Open the file EX P-2.xlsx from the drive and folder where you store your Data Files, then save it as EX P-January Sales 2

   In the next lesson, you'll run the main procedure.

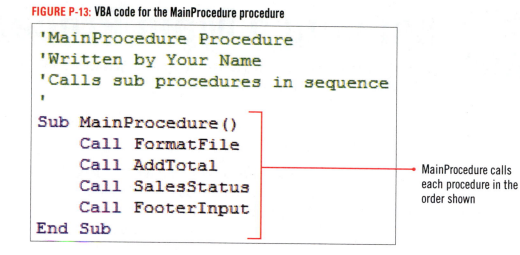

```
'MainProcedure Procedure
'Written by Your Name
'Calls sub procedures in sequence
'

Sub MainProcedure()
    Call FormatFile
    Call AddTotal
    Call SalesStatus
    Call FooterInput
End Sub
```

MainProcedure calls each procedure in the order shown

Excel 2010

## Writing and documenting VBA code

When you write VBA code in the Visual Basic Editor, you want to make it as readable as possible. This makes it easier for you or your coworkers to edit the code when changes need to be made. The procedure statements should be indented, leaving the procedure name and its End statement easy to spot in the code. This is helpful when a module contains many procedures. It is also good practice to add comments at the beginning of each procedure that describe its purpose and any assumptions made in the procedure, such as the quota amounts. You should also explain each code statement with a comment. You have seen comments inserted into VBA code by beginning the statement with an apostrophe. You can also add comments to the end of a line of VBA code by placing an apostrophe before the comment, as shown in Figure P-14.

FIGURE P-14: **VBA code with comments at the end of statements**

```
'MainProcedure Procedure
'Written by Your Name
'Calls sub procedures in sequence
'

Sub MainProcedure()
    Call FormatFile   'Run FormatFile procedure
    Call AddTotal     'Run AddTotal procedure
    Call SalesStatus  'Run SalesStatus procedure
    Call FooterInput  'Run FooterInput procedure
End Sub
```

Comments at the end of the statements are in green

# Running a Main Procedure

Running a main procedure allows you to run several macros in sequence. You can run a main procedure just as you would any other macro procedure. You have finished creating Kate's main procedure, and you are ready to run it. If the main procedure works correctly, it should format the worksheet, insert the sales total, insert a sales status message, and add your name and date to the worksheet footer.

## STEPS

**TROUBLE**

If an error message appears, click Debug, click the Reset button on the toolbar, then correct your error.

1. **With the January worksheet displayed, click the Developer tab, click the Macros button in the Code group, in the Macro dialog box click 'EX P-Monthly Sales.xlsm'!MainProcedure, click Run, when prompted type your name, then click OK**

   The MainProcedure runs the FormatFile, AddTotal, SalesStatus, and FooterInput procedures in sequence. You can see the results of the FormatFile, AddTotal, and SalesStatus procedures in the worksheet window, as shown in Figure P-16. To view the results of the FooterInput procedure, you need to switch to the Preview window.

2. **Click the File tab, click Print, view the worksheet preview and verify that your name appears in the left footer area and the date appears in the right footer area, then click the Developer tab**

3. **Click the Visual Basic button in the Code group**

   You need to add your name to the Format module.

4. **In the Project Explorer window, double-click the Format module, add a comment line after the procedure name that reads Written by [Your Name], then click the Save EX P-Monthly Sales.xlsm button**

   You want to see the options for printing VBA code.

5. **Click File on the Visual Basic Editor menu bar, then click Print**

   The Print - VBAProject dialog box opens, as shown in Figure P-17. The Current Module is selected which will print each procedure separately. It is faster to print all the procedures in the workbook at one time by clicking the Current Project option button to select it. You can also create a file of the VBA code by selecting the Print to File check box. You do not want to print the modules at this time.

**QUICK TIP**

When you complete your work with macros, you should disable macros to prevent macros containing viruses from running on your computer. To disable macros, click the Developer tab, click the Macro Security button in the Code group, click one of the Disable all macros options, then click OK.

6. **Click Cancel in the Print - VBAProject dialog box**

7. **Click the View Microsoft Excel button on the toolbar**

8. **Save the EX P-January Sales 2 workbook, then preview the worksheet**

   Compare your formatted worksheet to Figure P-18.

9. **Close the EX P-January Sales 2 workbook, close the EX P-Monthly Sales workbook, then exit Excel**

---

### Running a macro using a button

You can run a macro by assigning it to a button on your worksheet. Create a button by clicking the Insert tab, clicking the Shapes button in the Illustrations group, choosing a shape, then drawing the shape on the worksheet. After you create the button, right-click it and select Assign Macro to choose the macro the button will run. It is a good idea to label the button with descriptive text. You can also format macro buttons using clip art, photographs, fills, and shadows. You format a button using the buttons on the Drawing Tools Format tab. To add an image to the button, click Fill in the Format Shape dialog box, then click the Picture or texture fill option button. To insert a

picture from a file, click Fill in the Format Shape dialog box, click Picture or texture fill, click File, select a picture, then click Insert. To insert a clip art picture, click Clip Art, select a picture, then click OK. Figure P-15 shows a button formatted with clip art.

**FIGURE P-15: Formatted macro button**

FIGURE P-16: Result of running MainProcedure procedure

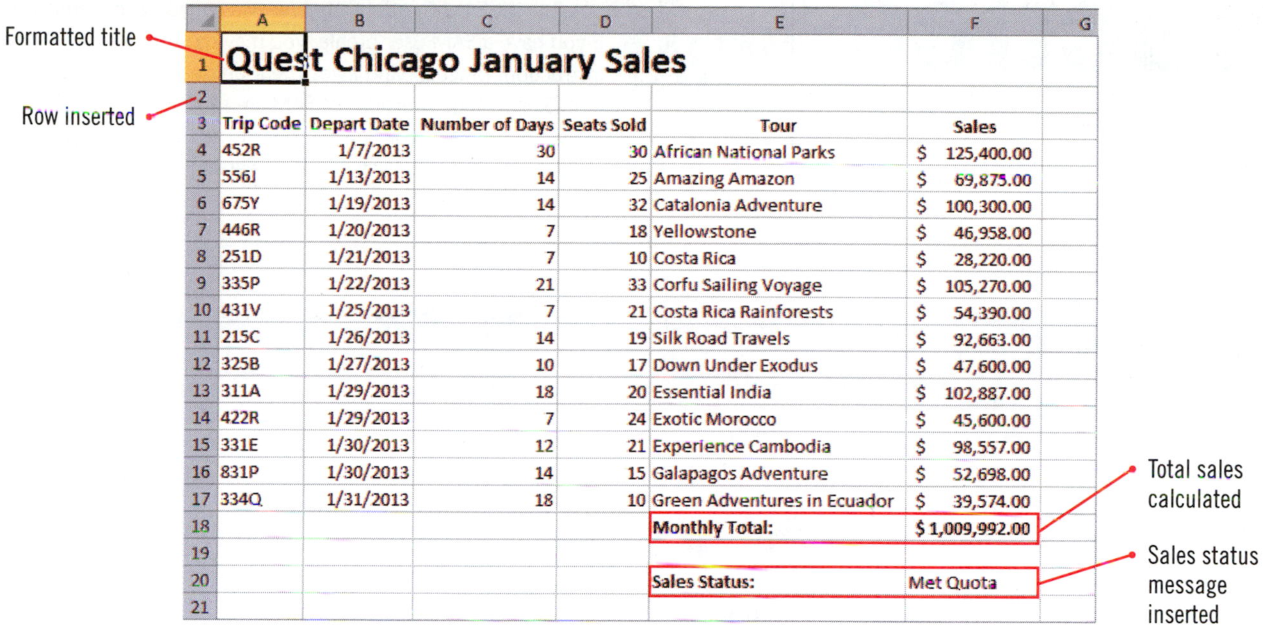

Formatted title →

Row inserted →

| | A | B | C | D | E | F | G |
|---|---|---|---|---|---|---|---|
| 1 | **Quest Chicago January Sales** | | | | | | |
| 2 | | | | | | | |
| 3 | **Trip Code** | **Depart Date** | **Number of Days** | **Seats Sold** | **Tour** | **Sales** | |
| 4 | 452R | 1/7/2013 | 30 | 30 | African National Parks | $ 125,400.00 | |
| 5 | 556J | 1/13/2013 | 14 | 25 | Amazing Amazon | $ 69,875.00 | |
| 6 | 675Y | 1/19/2013 | 14 | 32 | Catalonia Adventure | $ 100,300.00 | |
| 7 | 446R | 1/20/2013 | 7 | 18 | Yellowstone | $ 46,958.00 | |
| 8 | 251D | 1/21/2013 | 7 | 10 | Costa Rica | $ 28,220.00 | |
| 9 | 335P | 1/22/2013 | 21 | 33 | Corfu Sailing Voyage | $ 105,270.00 | |
| 10 | 431V | 1/25/2013 | 7 | 21 | Costa Rica Rainforests | $ 54,390.00 | |
| 11 | 215C | 1/26/2013 | 14 | 19 | Silk Road Travels | $ 92,663.00 | |
| 12 | 325B | 1/27/2013 | 10 | 17 | Down Under Exodus | $ 47,600.00 | |
| 13 | 311A | 1/29/2013 | 18 | 20 | Essential India | $ 102,887.00 | |
| 14 | 422R | 1/29/2013 | 7 | 24 | Exotic Morocco | $ 45,600.00 | |
| 15 | 331E | 1/30/2013 | 12 | 21 | Experience Cambodia | $ 98,557.00 | |
| 16 | 831P | 1/30/2013 | 14 | 15 | Galapagos Adventure | $ 52,698.00 | |
| 17 | 334Q | 1/31/2013 | 18 | 10 | Green Adventures in Ecuador | $ 39,574.00 | |
| 18 | | | | | **Monthly Total:** | $ 1,009,992.00 | |
| 19 | | | | | | | |
| 20 | | | | | **Sales Status:** | Met Quota | |
| 21 | | | | | | | |

Total sales calculated →

Sales status message inserted →

FIGURE P-17: Printing options for macro procedures

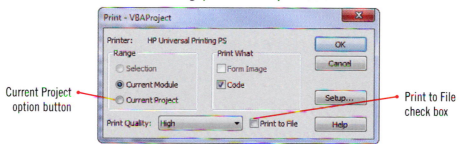

Current Project option button →

← Print to File check box

FIGURE P-18: Formatted January worksheet

# Practice

**SAM**

For current SAM information, including versions and content details, visit SAM Central (http://www.cengage.com/samcentral). If you have a SAM user profile, you may have access to hands-on instruction, practice, and assessment of the skills covered in this unit. Since various versions of SAM are supported throughout the life of this text, check with your instructor for the correct instructions and URL/Web site for accessing assignments.

## Concepts Review

FIGURE P-19

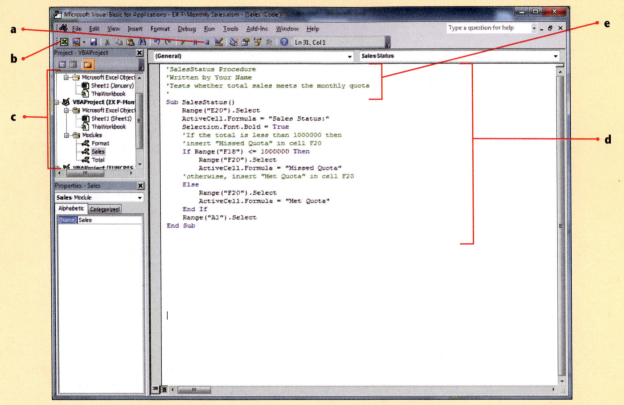

1. **Which element points to the Project Explorer window?**
2. **Which element do you click to return to Excel from the Visual Basic Editor?**
3. **Which element do you click to turn off the Step Into feature?**
4. **Which element points to the Code window?**
5. **Which element points to comments in the VBA code?**

## Match each term with the statement that best describes it.

| | |
|---|---|
| 6. **Function** | **a.** Another term for a macro in Visual Basic for Applications (VBA) |
| 7. **Sub procedure** | **b.** A procedure that returns a value |
| 8. **Procedure** | **c.** Words that are recognized as part of the programming language |
| 9. **Keywords** | **d.** A series of statements that perform an action but don't return a value |
| 10. **Comments** | **e.** Descriptive text used to explain parts of a procedure |

**Select the best answer from the list of choices.**

11. A location in memory where you can temporarily store information is a:
    - **a.** Procedure.
    - **b.** Variable.
    - **c.** Sub procedure.
    - **d.** Function.

12. You enter the statements of a macro in:
    - **a.** The Macro dialog box.
    - **b.** Any blank worksheet.
    - **c.** The Code window of the Visual Basic Editor.
    - **d.** The Properties window of the Visual Basic Editor.

13. If your macro doesn't run correctly, you should:
    - **a.** Create an If...Then...Else statement.
    - **b.** Select the macro in the Macro dialog box, click Step Into, then debug the macro.
    - **c.** Click the Project Explorer button.
    - **d.** Click the Properties button.

14. Comments are displayed in _____ in VBA code.
    - **a.** Black
    - **b.** Blue
    - **c.** Green
    - **d.** Red

15. Keywords are displayed in _____ in VBA code.
    - **a.** Blue
    - **b.** Black
    - **c.** Green
    - **d.** Red

# Skills Review

1. **View and analyze VBA code.**
    - **a.** Start Excel, open the file EX P-3.xlsm from the drive and folder where you store your Data Files, enable macros, then save it as **EX P-Home Products**.
    - **b.** Review the unformatted December worksheet.
    - **c.** Open the Visual Basic Editor.
    - **d.** Select the DataFormat module, and review the Format procedure.
    - **e.** Insert comments in the procedure code describing what action you think each line of code will perform. (*Hint*: One of the statements will sort the list by Store #.) Add comment lines to the top of the procedure to describe the purpose of the macro and to enter your name.
    - **f.** Save the macro, return to the worksheet, then run the Format macro.
    - **g.** Compare the results with the code and your comments.
    - **h.** Save the workbook.

2. **Write VBA code.**
    - **a.** Open the Visual Basic Editor, and insert a new module named **Total** in the EX P-Home Products project.
    - **b.** Enter the code for the SalesTotal procedure exactly as shown in Figure P-20. Enter your name in the second line.
    - **c.** Save the macro.
    - **d.** Return to the December worksheet, and run the SalesTotal macro. Widen column E to view the total in cell E17.
    - **e.** Save the workbook.

**FIGURE P-20**

```
'SalesTotal Procedure
'Written by Your Name
'Totals December sales
Sub SalesTotal()
    Range("E17").Select
    ActiveCell.Formula = "=SUM($E$3:$E$16)"
    Selection.Font.Bold = True
    With Selection.Borders(xlTop)
        .LineStyle = xlSingle
    End With
    Range("A1").Select
End Sub
```

## Skills Review (continued)

**3. Add a conditional statement**

a. Open the Visual Basic Editor, and insert a new module named **Goal** in the EX P-Home Products project.

b. Enter the SalesGoal procedure exactly as shown in Figure P-21. Enter your name on the second line.

c. Save the macro.

d. Return to the December worksheet, and run the SalesGoal macro. The procedure should enter the message **Missed goal** in cell E18. Save the workbook.

**FIGURE P-21**

```
'SalesGoal Procedure
'Written by Your Name
'Tests whether sales goal was met
Sub SalesGoal()
    'If the total is >=100000, then insert "Met Goal"
    'in cell E18
    If Range("E17") >= 100000 Then
        Range("E18").Select
        ActiveCell.Formula = "Met goal"
    'otherwise, insert "Missed goal" in cell E18
    Else
        Range("E18").Select
        ActiveCell.Formula = "Missed goal"
    End If
End Sub
```

**4. Prompt the user for data.**

a. Open the Visual Basic Editor, and insert a new module named **Header** in the EX P-Home Products project.

b. Enter the HeaderFooter procedure exactly as shown in Figure P-22. You are entering an error in the procedure that will be corrected in Step 5.

c. Save the macro, then return to the December worksheet, and run the HeaderFooter macro.

d. Preview the December worksheet. Your name should be missing from the left section of the footer.

e. Save the workbook.

**FIGURE P-22**

```
'HeaderFooter Procedure
'Written by Your Name
'Procedure to customize the header and footer
Sub HeaderFooter()
    'Inserts the filename in the header
    Worksheets("December").PageSetup.CenterHeader = "&F"
    'Declares the variable LeftFooterText as a string
    Dim LeftFooterText As String
    'Prompts user for left footer text
    LeftFooter = InputBox("Enter your full name:")
    'Inserts response into left footer
    Worksheets("December").PageSetup.LeftFooter = LeftFooterText
    'Inserts the date into right footer
    Worksheets("December").PageSetup.RightFooter = "&D"
End Sub
```

**5. Debug a macro.**

a. Return to the Visual Basic Editor and use the Step Into feature to locate where the error occurred in the HeaderFooter procedure. Use the Reset button to turn off the debugger.

b. Edit the procedure in the Visual Basic Editor to correct the error. (*Hint*: The error occurs on the line: LeftFooter = InputBox("Enter your full name:"). The variable that will input the response text into the worksheet footer is LeftFooterText. The line should be: LeftFooterText = InputBox("Enter your full name:").)

c. Save the macro, then return to the December worksheet, and run the HeaderFooter macro again.

d. Verify that your name now appears in the left section of the footer, then save the file.

**6. Create and run a main procedure.**

a. Return to the Visual Basic Editor, insert a new module, then name it **MainProc**.

b. Begin the main procedure by entering comments in the code window that provide the procedure's name (MainProcedure) and explain that its purpose is to run the Format, SalesTotal, SalesGoal, and HeaderFooter procedures. Enter your name in a comment.

c. Enter the procedure header **Sub MainProcedure()**.

d. Enter four Call statements that will run the Format, SalesTotal, SalesGoal, and HeaderFooter procedures in sequence.

e. Save the procedure and return to Excel.

f. Open the file EX P-3.xlsm, then save it as **EX P-Home Products 2**.

g. Run the MainProcedure macro, entering your name when prompted. (*Hint*: In the Macro dialog box, the macro procedures you created will now have EX P-Home Products.xlsm! as part of their names. This is because the macros are stored in the EX P-Home Products workbook, not in the EX P-Home Products 2 workbook.)

**FIGURE P-23**

| | A | B | C | D | E |
|---|---|---|---|---|---|
| 1 | Home Products December Sales | | | | |
| 2 | Store # | City | State | Manager | Sales |
| 3 | 11405 | Juno | FL | Clifford | $ 8,745.93 |
| 4 | 19404 | Palm Beach | FL | Cloutier | $ 8,656.83 |
| 5 | 29393 | Tampa | FL | Nelson | $ 7,654.32 |
| 6 | 29396 | Cape Coral | FL | Enos | $ 9,583.66 |
| 7 | 29399 | Daytona | FL | DiBenedetto | $ 9,228.33 |
| 8 | 29402 | Vero Beach | FL | Guapo | $ 5,534.34 |
| 9 | 29406 | Miami | FL | Monroe | $ 4,987.36 |
| 10 | 39394 | Naples | FL | Hamm | $ 6,715.68 |
| 11 | 39395 | Bonita Springs | FL | Handelmann | $ 4,225.22 |
| 12 | 39397 | Clearwater | FL | Erickson | $ 7,594.22 |
| 13 | 39398 | Delray Beach | FL | Dever | $ 8,442.90 |
| 14 | 39400 | Stuart | FL | Hahn | $ 8,001.34 |
| 15 | 39401 | Neptune | FL | Pratt | $ 5,251.22 |
| 16 | 39403 | Sanibel | FL | Lo | $ 4,643.93 |
| 17 | | | | | $99,265.28 |
| 18 | | | | | Missed goal |
| 19 | | | | | |

## Skills Review (continued)

**h.** Verify that the macro ran successfully, widen column E to display the calculated total, select cell A1, then compare your worksheet to Figure P-23.

**i.** Save the EX P-Home Products 2 workbook, preview the December worksheet to check the header and footer, then close the EX P-Home Products 2 workbook.

**j.** Save the EX P-Home Products workbook, close the workbook, exit Excel, then submit the EX P-Home Products workbook to your instructor.

# Independent Challenge 1

You have taken over the management of a small local art museum. The information systems manager asks you to document and test an Excel procedure that the previous manager wrote for the company's accountant. You will first run the macro procedure to see what it does, then add comments to the VBA code to document it. You will also enter data to verify that the formulas in the macro work correctly.

**a.** Start Excel, open the file EX P-4.xlsm from the drive and folder where you store your Data Files, enable macros, then save it as **EX P-First Quarter**.

**b.** Run the First macro, noting anything that you think should be mentioned in your documentation.

**c.** Review the First procedure in the Visual Basic Editor. It is stored in the FirstQtr module.

**d.** Document the procedure by annotating the printed code, indicating the actions the procedure performs and the objects (ranges) that are affected.

**e.** Enter your name in a comment line, then save the procedure.

**f.** Return to the Jan-Mar worksheet, and use Figure P-24 as a guide to enter data in cells B4:D6. The totals will appear as you enter the income data.

**g.** Format the range B4:D8 using the Accounting Number format with no decimals, as shown in Figure P-24.

**FIGURE P-24**

| | A | B | C | D |
|---|---|---|---|---|
| 1 | | January | February | March |
| 2 | Income | | | |
| 3 | | | | |
| 4 | Donations | $ 1,500 | $ 1,200 | $ 1,800 |
| 5 | Fundraisers | $ 2,000 | $ 2,500 | $ 2,100 |
| 6 | Grants | $ 20,000 | $ 50,000 | $ 90,000 |
| 7 | | | | |
| 8 | Total Income | $ 23,500 | $ 53,700 | $ 93,900 |
| 9 | | | | |

**h.** Check the total income calculations in row 8 to verify that the macro is working correctly.

**i.** Enter your name in the center section of the Jan-Mar sheet footer, save the workbook, then preview the worksheet.

**j.** Close the workbook, exit Excel, then submit the workbook to your instructor.

# Independent Challenge 2

You work in the Miami branch of Health Place, a nurse recruitment agency. You have three locations where you have monthly quotas for placements. Each month you are required to produce a report stating whether sales quotas were met for the following three medical facilities: Mercy Hospital, Ocean Clinic, and Assisted Home. The quotas for each month are as follows: Mercy Hospital 10, Ocean Clinic 7, and Assisted Home 4. Your sales results this month were 8, 8, and 5, respectively. You decide to create a procedure to automate your monthly task of determining the sales quota status for the placement categories. You would like your assistant to take this task over when you go on vacation next month. Because he has no previous experience with Excel, you decide to create a second procedure that prompts a user with input boxes to enter the actual placement results for the month.

**a.** Start Excel, open the file EX P-5.xlsm from the drive and folder where you store your Data Files, then save it as **EX P-Placements**.

**b.** Use the Visual Basic Editor to insert a new module named **Quotas** in the EX P-Placements workbook. Create a procedure in the new module named **PlacementQuota** that determines the quota status for each category and enters Yes or No in the Status column. The VBA code is shown in Figure P-25.

**FIGURE P-25**

```
Sub PlacementQuota()

    If Range("C4") >= 10 Then
        Range("D4").Select
        ActiveCell.Formula = "Yes"
    Else
        Range("D4").Select
        ActiveCell.Formula = "No"
    End If

    If Range("C5") >= 7 Then
        Range("D5").Select
        ActiveCell.Formula = "Yes"
    Else
        Range("D5").Select
        ActiveCell.Formula = "No"
    End If

    If Range("C6") >= 4 Then
        Range("D6").Select
        ActiveCell.Formula = "Yes"
    Else
        Range("D6").Select
        ActiveCell.Formula = "No"
    End If

End Sub
```

Excel 2010

# Independent Challenge 2 (continued)

c. Add comments to the PlacementQuota procedure, including the procedure name, your name, and the purpose of the procedure, then save it.

d. Insert a new module named **MonthlyPlacement**. Create a second procedure named **Placement** that prompts a user for placement data for each placement category, enters the input data in the appropriate cells, then calls the PlacementQuota procedure. The VBA code is shown in Figure P-26.

e. Add a comment noting the procedure name on the first line. Add a comment with your name on the second line. Add a third comment line at the top of the procedure describing its purpose. Enter comments in the code to document the macro actions. Save the procedure.

f. Run the Placement macro, and enter **8** for hospital placement, **8** for clinic placements, and **5** for assisted placements. Correct any errors in the VBA code.

**FIGURE P-26**

```
Sub Placement()

    Dim Hospital As String
    Hospital = InputBox("Enter Hospital Placements")
    Range("C4").Select
    Selection = Hospital

    Dim Clinic As String
    Clinic = InputBox("Enter Clinic Placements")
    Range("C5").Select
    Selection = Clinic

    Dim Assisted As String
    Assisted = InputBox("Enter Assisted Placements")
    Range("C6").Select
    Selection = Assisted

    Call PlacementQuota

End Sub
```

## Advanced Challenge Exercise

- Assign a shortcut of **[Ctrl][Shift][S]** to the Placement macro. Insert a line on the worksheet that tells the user to press [Ctrl][Shift][S] to enter placement data.
- Edit the Visual Basic code for the PlacementQuota procedure to reflect a change in quotas to **15** for Hospitals, **8** for Clinics, and **6** for Assisted. Change the worksheet data in the range B4:B6 to display the new quotas.
- Delete the data in cells C4:D6.
- Run the Placement macro using the shortcut key combination entering **12** for hospital placements, **10** for clinic placements, and **5** for assisted placements.

g. Add your name to the center section of the worksheet footer, save the workbook, then preview the worksheet. Close the workbook, exit Excel, then submit your workbook to your instructor.

# Independent Challenge 3

You are the marketing director at a car dealership business based in Minneapolis. You have started to advertise using a local magazine, billboards, TV, radio, and local newspapers. Every month you prepare a report with the advertising expenses detailed by source. You decide to create a macro that will format the monthly reports. You add the same footers on every report, so you will create another macro that will add a footer to a document. Finally, you will create a main procedure that calls the macros to format the report and add a footer. You begin by opening a workbook with the January data. You will save the macros you create in this workbook.

a. Start Excel, open the file EX P-6.xlsm from the drive and folder where you store your Data Files, then save it as **EX P-Auto**.

b. Insert a module named **Format**, then create a procedure named **Formatting** that:
   - Selects a cell in row 3, and inserts a row in the worksheet above it.
   - Selects the cost data in column C, and formats it as currency. (*Hint*: After the row is inserted, this range is C5:C9.)
   - Selects cell A1 before ending.

c. Save the Formatting procedure.

d. Insert a module named **Foot**, then create a procedure named **Footer** that:
   - Declares a string variable for text that will be placed in the left footer.
   - Uses an input box to prompt the user for his or her name, and places the name in the left footer.
   - Places the date in the right footer.

e. Save the Footer procedure.

f. Insert a module named **Main**, then create a procedure named MainProc that calls the Footer procedure and the Formatting procedure.

# Independent Challenge 3 (continued)

**g.** Save your work, then run the MainProc procedure. Debug each procedure as necessary. Your worksheet should look like Figure P-27.

**h.** Document each procedure by inserting a comment line with the procedure name, your name, and a description of the procedure.

**FIGURE P-27**

| | A | B | C |
|---|---|---|---|
| 1 | Twin Cities Auto | | |
| 2 | Ad Campaign | | |
| 3 | | | |
| 4 | Advertising Type | Source | Cost |
| 5 | Magazine | Twin Cities Magazine | $ 200.00 |
| 6 | Newspaper | Tribune | $ 350.00 |
| 7 | Billboard | Main Street | $ 450.00 |
| 8 | TV | Local Access Station | $  50.00 |
| 9 | Radio | WAQV | $ 500.00 |
| 10 | | | |

## Advanced Challenge Exercise

- Insert a module named **Total**, then create a procedure named **CostTotal** that does the following:
  - Totals the advertising costs in cells C5:C9, and inserts the total in cell C10.
  - Formats the total as bold, and adds a light purple fill to the total cell. (*Hint*: After a cell is selected, the VBA code Selection.Interior.ColorIndex = 39 will add a purple fill to it.)
  - Selects cell A1.
- Document the procedure with the procedure name, your name, and a description of the procedure.
- Run the CostTotal procedure. Widen column C if necessary to display the total.

**i.** Preview the January worksheet, save the workbook, close the workbook, exit Excel, then submit the workbook to your instructor.

# Real Life Independent Challenge

You decide to create a log of your discretionary expenses in an effort to track where you spend your paycheck each week. You will not track essential expenses such as auto expenses, rent/mortgage, groceries, necessary clothing, utilities, and tuition. Rather, your purpose is to identify optional items that may be targeted for reduction in an effort to meet a weekly budget. As part of this log, you record your expenses for each day of the week along with the daily amount spent in each category.

**a.** Start Excel, open the file EX P-7.xlsm from the drive and folder where you store your Data Files, then save it as **EX P-Expenses**.

**b.** Expand the modules folder to display the Expenses module. Edit the WeekExpenses procedure to record your expense categories. Record seven or fewer categories, and remember to edit the total cells and the formatting ranges in the procedure.

**c.** Run the macro and debug the procedure as necessary.

**d.** Use the worksheet to enter your expenses for each day of the past week, as best you can remember.

**e.** Save your work.

**f.** Verify that the totals are correct for each day and each category.

**g.** Enter your name as a comment in the second line of the procedure, then save the procedure.

**h.** Enter your name in the center section of the worksheet footer, then preview the worksheet.

## Advanced Challenge Exercise

- Insert a module named **Preview** with a procedure named **PreviewSheetdata** that previews a worksheet. The VBA code is shown in Figure P-28.
- Save the macro and return to the worksheet.
- Assign the macro PreviewSheetdata to a button on the worksheet. (*Hint*: Use the Rectangle tool to create the button, label the button **Print Preview**, then right-click one of the button's edges to assign the macro.)
- Test the button, then close the Print Preview.

**FIGURE P-28**

```
Sub PreviewSheetdata()


ActiveSheet.PrintPreview


End Sub
```

**i.** Save the workbook, close the workbook, exit Excel, then submit the workbook to your instructor.

# Visual Workshop

Open the file EX P-8.xlsm from the drive and folder where you store your Data Files, then save it as **EX P-Florist**. Create a macro procedure named **Formatting** in a module named **FormatFile** that will format the worksheet as shown in Figure P-29. (*Hint*: The font size is 12.) Run the macro and debug it as necessary to make the worksheet match Figure P-29. Insert your name in a comment line under the procedure name and in the worksheet footer, then preview the worksheet. Submit the workbook to your instructor.

**FIGURE P-29**

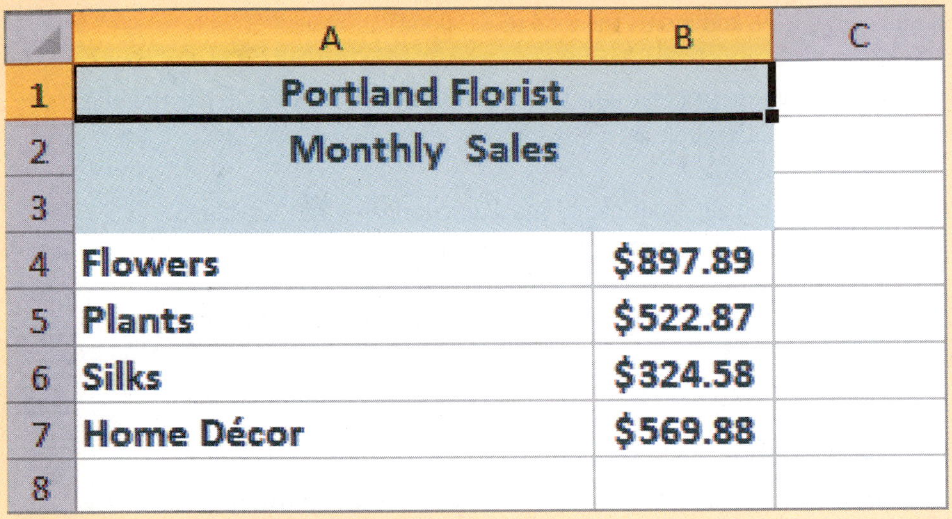

| | A | B | C |
|---|---|---|---|
| 1 | Portland Florist | | |
| 2 | Monthly Sales | | |
| 3 | | | |
| 4 | Flowers | $897.89 | |
| 5 | Plants | $522.87 | |
| 6 | Silks | $324.58 | |
| 7 | Home Décor | $569.88 | |
| 8 | | | |

**Appendix**
**Web Apps**
Office 2010

# Working with Windows Live and Office Web Apps

**Files You Will Need:**

WEB-1.pptx
WEB-2.xlsx

If the computer you are using has an active Internet connection, you can go to the Microsoft Windows Live Web site and access a wide variety of services and Web applications. For example, you can check your e-mail through Windows Live, network with your friends and coworkers, and use SkyDrive to store and share files. From SkyDrive, you can also use Office Web Apps to create and edit Word, PowerPoint, Excel, and OneNote files, even when you are using a computer that does not have Office 2010 installed. You work in the Vancouver branch of Quest Specialty Travel. Your supervisor, Mary Lou Jacobs, asks you to explore Windows Live and learn how she can use SkyDrive and Office Web Apps to work with her files online.

(*Note*: SkyDrive and Office Web Apps are dynamic Web pages, and might change over time, including the way they are organized and how commands are performed. The steps and figures in this appendix were accurate at the time this book was published.)

**OBJECTIVES**

Explore how to work online from Windows Live
Obtain a Windows Live ID and sign in to Windows Live
Upload files to Windows Live
Work with the PowerPoint Web App
Create folders and organize files on SkyDrive
Add people to your network and share files
Work with the Excel Web App

# Exploring How to Work Online from Windows Live

You can use your Web browser to upload your files to Windows Live from any computer connected to the Internet. You can work on the files right in your Web browser using Office Web Apps and share your files with people in your Windows Live network.  You review the concepts and services related to working online from Windows Live.

## DETAILS

- ### What is Windows Live?

  **Windows Live** is a collection of services and Web applications that you can use to help you be more productive both personally and professionally. For example, you can use Windows Live to send and receive e-mail, to chat with friends via instant messaging, to share photos, to create a blog, and to store and edit files using SkyDrive. Table WEB-1 describes the services available on Windows Live. Windows Live is a free service that you sign up for. When you sign up, you receive a Windows Live ID, which you use to sign in to Windows Live. When you work with files on Windows Live, you are cloud computing.

- ### What is Cloud Computing?

  The term **cloud computing** refers to the process of working with files online in a Web browser. When you save files to SkyDrive on Windows Live, you are saving your files to an online location. SkyDrive is like having a personal hard drive in the cloud.

- ### What is SkyDrive?

  **SkyDrive** is an online storage and file sharing service. With a Windows Live account, you receive access to your own SkyDrive, which is your personal storage area on the Internet. On your SkyDrive, you are given space to store up to 25 GB of data online. Each file can be a maximum size of 50 MB. You can also use SkyDrive to access Office Web Apps, which you use to create and edit files created in Word, OneNote, PowerPoint, and Excel online in your Web browser.

- ### Why use Windows Live and SkyDrive?

  On Windows Live, you use SkyDrive to access additional storage for your files. You don't have to worry about backing up your files to a memory stick or other storage device that could be lost or damaged. Another advantage of storing your files on SkyDrive is that you can access your files from any computer that has an active Internet connection. Figure WEB-1 shows the SkyDrive Web page that appears when accessed from a Windows Live account. From SkyDrive, you can also access Office Web Apps.

- ### What are Office Web Apps?

  **Office Web Apps** are versions of Microsoft Word, Excel, PowerPoint, and OneNote that you can access online from your SkyDrive. An Office Web App does not include all of the features and functions included with the full Office version of its associated application. However, you can use the Office Web App from any computer that is connected to the Internet, even if Microsoft Office 2010 is not installed on that computer.

- ### How do SkyDrive and Office Web Apps work together?

  You can create a file in Office 2010 using Word, Excel, PowerPoint, or OneNote and then upload the file to your SkyDrive. You can then open the Office file saved to SkyDrive and edit it using your Web browser and the corresponding Office Web App. Figure WEB-2 shows a PowerPoint presentation open in the PowerPoint Web App. You can also use an Office Web App to create a new file, which is saved automatically to SkyDrive while you work. In addition, you can download a file created with an Office Web App and continue to work with the file in the full version of the corresponding Office application: Word, Excel, PowerPoint, or OneNote. Finally, you can create a SkyDrive network that consists of the people you want to be able to view your folders and files on your SkyDrive. You can give people permission to view and edit your files using any computer with an active Internet connection and a Web browser.

**FIGURE WEB-1:** SkyDrive on Windows Live

Browser window

SkyDrive - Windows Live tab

By default, one folder is available on SkyDrive; you can create additional folders

The name of the person who signed into Windows Live and SkyDrive appears here

Monitors the amount of space still available on your SkyDrive

Web Apps

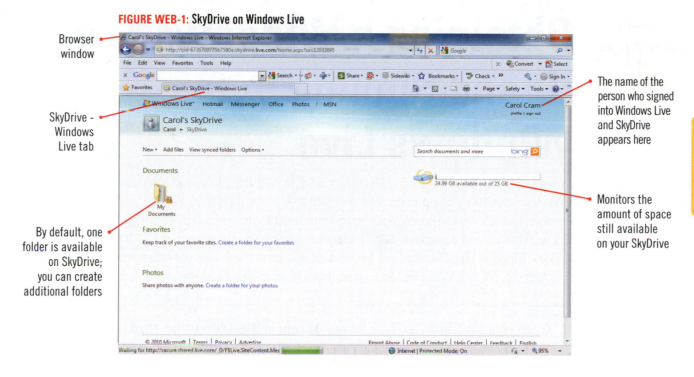

**FIGURE WEB-2:** PowerPoint presentation open in the PowerPoint Web App

Browser window

Ribbon available in PowerPoint Web App

The presentation in PowerPoint Web App maintains the same look and feel as the same procontation in the desktop version of PowerPoint

Name of PowerPoint presentation open in PowerPoint Web App

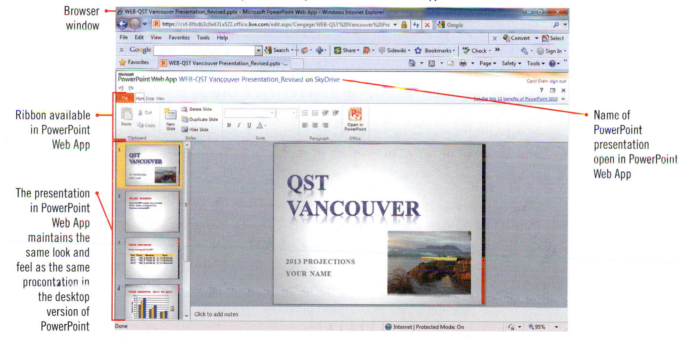

**TABLE WEB-1:** Services available via Windows Live

| service | description |
|---|---|
| E-mail | Send and receive e-mail using a Hotmail account |
| Instant Messaging | Use Messenger to chat with friends, share photos, and play games |
| SkyDrive | Store files, work on files using Office Web Apps, and share files with people in your network |
| Photos | Upload and share photos with friends |
| People | Develop a network of friends and coworkers, then use the network to distribute information and stay in touch |
| Downloads | Access a variety of free programs available for download to a PC |
| Mobile Device | Access applications for a mobile device: text messaging, using Hotmail, networking, and sharing photos |

# Obtaining a Windows Live ID and Signing In to Windows Live

To work with your files online using SkyDrive and Office Web Apps, you need a Windows Live ID. You obtain a Windows Live ID by going to the Windows Live Web site and creating a new account. Once you have a Windows Live ID, you can access SkyDrive and then use it to store your files, create new files, and share your files with friends and coworkers. 🎨 Mary Lou Jacobs, your supervisor at QST Vancouver, asks you to obtain a Windows Live ID so that you can work on documents with your coworkers. You go to the Windows Live Web site, create a Windows Live ID, and then sign in to your SkyDrive.

## STEPS

**QUICK TIP**

If you already have a Windows Live ID, go to the next lesson and sign in as directed using your account.

1. **Open your Web browser, type home.live.com in the Address bar, then press [Enter]**

   The Windows Live home page opens. From this page, you can create a Windows Live account and receive your Windows Live ID.

2. **Click the Sign up button** (Note: You may see a Sign up link instead of a button)

   The Create your Windows Live ID page opens.

3. **Click the Or use your own e-mail address link under the Check availability button or if you are already using Hotmail, Messenger, or Xbox LIVE, click the Sign in now link in the Information statement near the top of the page**

4. **Enter the information required, as shown in Figure WEB-3**

   If you wish, you can sign up for a Windows Live e-mail address such as yourname@live.com so that you can also access the Windows Live e-mail services.

**TROUBLE**

The code can be difficult to read. If you receive an error message, enter the new code that appears.

5. **Enter the code shown at the bottom of your screen, then click the I accept button**

   The Windows Live home page opens. The name you entered when you signed up for your Windows Live ID appears in the top right corner of the window to indicate that you are signed in to Windows Live. From the Windows Live home page, you can access all the services and applications offered by Windows Live. See the Verifying your Windows Live ID box for information on finalizing your account set up.

6. **Point to Windows Live, as shown in Figure WEB-4**

   A list of options appears. SkyDrive is one of the options you can access directly from Windows Live.

**TROUBLE**

Click I accept if you are asked to review and accept the Windows Live Service Agreement and Privacy Statement.

7. **Click SkyDrive**

   The SkyDrive page opens. Your name appears in the top right corner, and the amount of space available is shown on the right side of the SkyDrive page. The amount of space available is monitored, as indicated by the gauge that fills with color as space is used. Using SkyDrive, you can add files to the existing folder and you can create new folders.

8. **Click sign out in the top right corner under your name, then exit the Web browser**

   You are signed out of your Windows Live account. You can sign in again directly from the Windows Live page in your browser or from within a file created with PowerPoint, Excel, Word, or OneNote.

**FIGURE WEB-3:** Creating a Windows Live ID

Click to sign in using a Hotmail, Messenger, or Xbox Live account

Once your registration is complete, you will be asked to verify your ID

A different code will appear on your screen

Type your e-mail address

You can choose to get a Windows Live e-mail address

Enter the information required

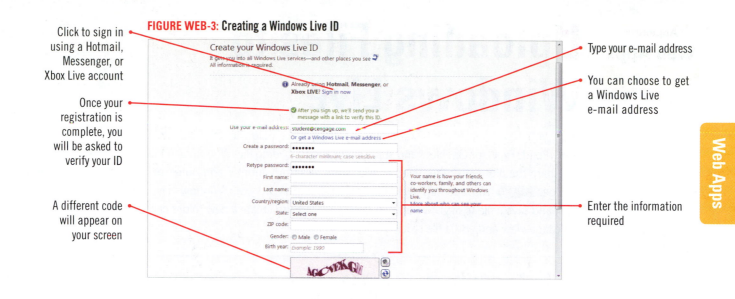

**FIGURE WEB-4:** Selecting SkyDrive

SkyDrive in the list of Windows Live options

Information about your Windows Live network

Your name appears here

Click to quickly add people to your network

An advertisement appropriate for your location appears here

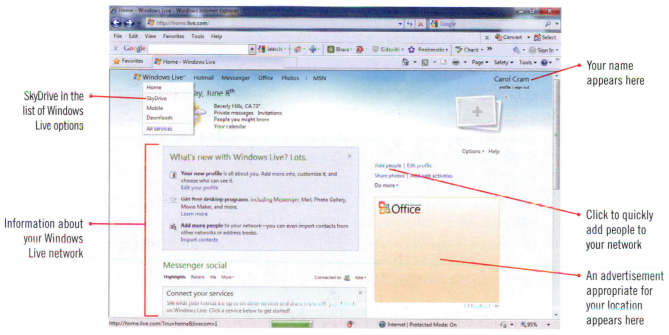

## Verifying your Windows Live ID

As soon as you accept the Windows Live terms, an e-mail is sent to the e-mail address you supplied when you created your Windows Live ID. Open your e-mail program, and then open the e-mail from Microsoft with the Subject line: Confirm your e-mail address for Windows Live. Follow the simple, step-by-step instructions in the e-mail to confirm your Windows Live ID. When the confirmation is complete, you will be asked to sign in to Windows Live, using your e-mail address and password. Once signed in, you will see your Windows Live Account page.

# Uploading Files to Windows Live

Once you have created your Windows Live ID, you can sign in to Windows Live directly from Word, PowerPoint, Excel, or OneNote and start saving and uploading files. You upload files to your SkyDrive so you can share the files with other people, access the files from another computer, or use SkyDrive's additional storage. 🎨 You open a PowerPoint presentation, access your Windows Live account from Backstage view, and save a file to SkyDrive on Windows Live. You also create a new folder called Cengage directly from Backstage view and add a file to it.

## STEPS

1. **Start PowerPoint, open the file WEB-1.pptx from the drive and folder where you store your Data Files, then save the file as WEB-QST Vancouver Presentation**

2. **Click the File tab, then click Save & Send**
   The Save & Send options available in PowerPoint are listed in Backstage view, as shown in Figure WEB-5.

3. **Click Save to Web**

> **QUICK TIP**
> Skip this step if the computer you are using signs you in automatically.

4. **Click Sign In, type your e-mail address, press [Tab], type your password, then click OK**
   The My Documents folder on your SkyDrive appears in the Save to Windows Live SkyDrive information area.

5. **Click Save As, wait a few seconds for the Save As dialog box to appear, then click Save**
   The file is saved to the My Documents folder on the SkyDrive that is associated with your Windows Live account. You can also create a new folder and upload files directly to SkyDrive from your hard drive.

6. **Click the File tab, click Save & Send, click Save to Web, then sign in if the My Documents folder does not automatically appear in Backstage view**

7. **Click the New Folder button in the Save to Windows Live SkyDrive pane, then sign in to Windows Live if directed**

8. **Type Cengage as the folder name, click Next, then click Add files**

9. **Click select documents from your computer, then navigate to the location on your computer where you saved the file WEB-QST Vancouver Presentation in Step 1**

10. **Click WEB-QST Vancouver Presentation.pptx to select it, then click Open**
    You can continue to add more files; however, you have no more files to upload at this time.

11. **Click Continue**
    In a few moments, the PowerPoint presentation is uploaded to your SkyDrive, as shown in Figure WEB-6. You can simply store the file on SkyDrive or you can choose to work on the presentation using the PowerPoint Web App.

12. **Click the PowerPoint icon 🅿️ on your taskbar to return to PowerPoint, then close the presentation and exit PowerPoint**

**FIGURE WEB-5:** Save & Send options in Backstage view

PowerPoint file

Save & Send area in Backstage view

Save to Web option

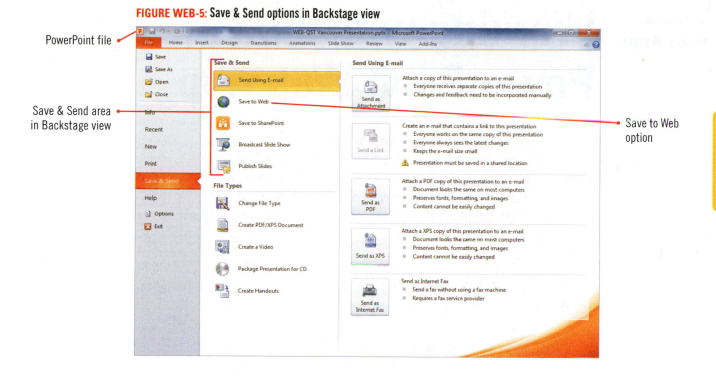

**FIGURE WEB-6:** File uploaded to the Cengage folder on Windows Live

Browser window

Path to file

Current folder menu bar

Uploaded file

# Working with the PowerPoint Web App

Once you have uploaded a file to SkyDrive on Windows Live, you can work on it using its corresponding Office Web App. **Office Web Apps** provide you with the tools you need to view documents online and to edit them right in your browser. You do not need to have Office programs installed on the computer you use to access SkyDrive and Office Web Apps. From SkyDrive, you can also open the document directly in the full Office application (for example, PowerPoint) if the application is installed on the computer you are using. 🎨 You use the PowerPoint Web App to make some edits to the PowerPoint presentation. You then open the presentation in PowerPoint and use the full version to make additional edits.

## STEPS

**TROUBLE**
Click the browser button on the taskbar, then click the Windows Live SkyDrive window to make it the active window.

1. **Click the WEB-QST Vancouver Presentation file in the Cengage folder on SkyDrive**

   The presentation opens in your browser window. A menu is available, which includes the options you have for working with the file.

2. **Click Edit in Browser, then if a message appears related to installing the Sign-in Assistant, click the Close button ✕ to the far right of the message**

   In a few moments, the PowerPoint presentation opens in the PowerPoint Web App, as shown in Figure WEB-7. Table WEB-2 lists the commands you can perform using the PowerPoint Web App.

**QUICK TIP**
The changes you make to the presentation are saved automatically on SkyDrive.

3. **Enter your name where indicated on Slide 1, click Slide 3 (New Tours) in the Slides pane, then click Delete Slide in the Slides group**

   The slide is removed from the presentation. You decide to open the file in the full version of PowerPoint on your computer so you can apply WordArt to the slide title. You work with the file in the full version of PowerPoint when you want to use functions, such as WordArt, that are not available on the PowerPoint Web App.

4. **Click Open in PowerPoint in the Office group, click OK in response to the message, then click Allow if requested**

   In a few moments, the revised version of the PowerPoint slide opens in PowerPoint on your computer.

5. **Click Enable Editing on the Protected View bar near the top of your presentation window if prompted, select QST Vancouver on the title slide, then click the Drawing Tools Format tab**

**QUICK TIP**
Use the ScreenTips to help you find the required WordArt style.

6. **Click the More button ⯆ in the WordArt Styles group to show the selection of WordArt styles, select the WordArt style Gradient Fill - Blue-Gray, Accent 4, Reflection, then click a blank area outside the slide**

   The presentation appears in PowerPoint as shown in Figure WEB-8. Next, you save the revised version of the file to SkyDrive.

7. **Click the File tab, click Save As, notice that the path in the Address bar is to the Cengage folder on your Windows Live SkyDrive, type WEB-QST Vancouver Presentation_Revised. pptx in the File name text box, then click Save**

   The file is saved to your SkyDrive.

**TROUBLE**
The browser opens to the Cengage folder but the file is not visible. Follow Step 8 to open the Cengage folder and refresh the list of files in the folder.

8. **Click the browser icon on the taskbar to open your SkyDrive page, then click Office next to your name in the SkyDrive path, view a list of recent documents, then click Cengage in the list to the left of the recent documents list to open the Cengage folder**

   Two PowerPoint files now appear in the Cengage folder.

9. **Exit the Web browser and close all tabs if prompted, then exit PowerPoint**

**FIGURE WEB-7:** Presentation opened in the PowerPoint Web App from Windows Live

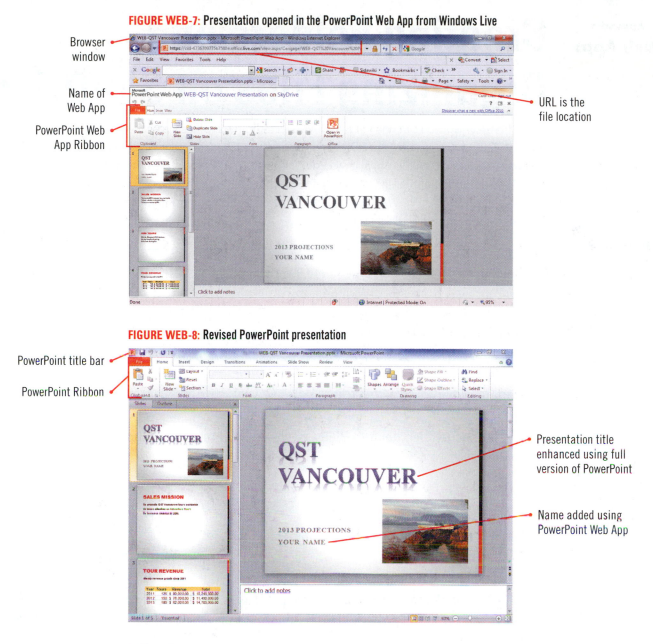

Browser window

Name of Web App

PowerPoint Web App Ribbon

URL is the file location

**FIGURE WEB-8:** Revised PowerPoint presentation

PowerPoint title bar

PowerPoint Ribbon

Presentation title enhanced using full version of PowerPoint

Name added using PowerPoint Web App

**TABLE WEB-2:** Commands on the PowerPoint Web App

| tab | commands available |
|---|---|
| File | • Open in PowerPoint: select to open the file in PowerPoint on your computer<br>• Where's the Save Button?: when you click this option, a message appears telling you that you do not need to save your presentation when you are working on it with PowerPoint Web App. The presentation is saved automatically as you work.<br>• Print • Share • Properties • Give Feedback • Privacy • Terms of Use • Close |
| Home | • Clipboard group: Cut, Copy, Paste<br>• Slides group: Add a New Slide, Delete a Slide, Duplicate a Slide, and Hide a Slide<br>• Font group: Work with text: change the font, style, color, and size of selected text<br>• Paragraph group: Work with paragraphs: add bullets and numbers, indent text, align text<br>• Office group: Open the file in PowerPoint on your computer |
| Insert | • Insert a Picture<br>• Insert a SmartArt diagram<br>• Insert a link such as a link to another file on SkyDrive or to a Web page |
| View | • Editing view (the default)<br>• Reading view<br>• Slide Show view<br>• Notes view |

# Creating Folders and Organizing Files on SkyDrive

As you have learned, you can sign in to SkyDrive directly from the Office applications PowerPoint, Excel, Word, and OneNote, or you can access SkyDrive directly through your Web browser. This option is useful when you are away from the computer on which you normally work or when you are using a computer that does not have Office applications installed. You can go to SkyDrive, create and organize folders, and then create or open files to work on with Office Web Apps.  You access SkyDrive from your Web browser, create a new folder called Illustrated, and delete one of the PowerPoint files from the My Documents folder.

## STEPS

**TROUBLE**
Go to Step 3 if you are already signed in.

1. **Open your Web browser, type home.live.com in the Address bar, then press [Enter]**
   The Windows Live home page opens. From here, you can sign in to your Windows Live account and then access SkyDrive.

**TROUBLE**
Type your Windows Live ID (your e-mail) and password, then click Sign in if prompted to do so.

2. **Sign into Windows Live as directed**
   You are signed in to your Windows Live page. From this page, you can take advantage of the many applications available on Windows Live, including SkyDrive.

3. **Point to Windows Live, then click SkyDrive**
   SkyDrive opens.

4. **Click Cengage, then point to WEB-QST Vancouver Presentation.pptx**
   A menu of options for working with the file, including a Delete button to the far right, appears to the right of the filename.

5. **Click the Delete button ⊠, then click OK**
   The file is removed from the Cengage folder on your SkyDrive. You still have a copy of the file on your computer.

6. **Point to Windows Live, then click SkyDrive**
   Your SkyDrive screen with the current selection of folders available on your SkyDrive opens, as shown in Figure WEB-9.

7. **Click New, click Folder, type Illustrated, click Next, click Office in the path under Add documents to Illustrated at the top of the window, then click View all in the list under Personal**
   You are returned to your list of folders, where you see the new Illustrated folder.

8. **Click Cengage, point to WEB-QST Vancouver Presentation_Revised.pptx, click More, click Move, then click the Illustrated folder**

9. **Click Move this file into Illustrated, as shown in Figure WEB-10**
   The file is moved to the Illustrated folder.

**FIGURE WEB-9:** Folders on your SkyDrive

Current location

Folders currently available

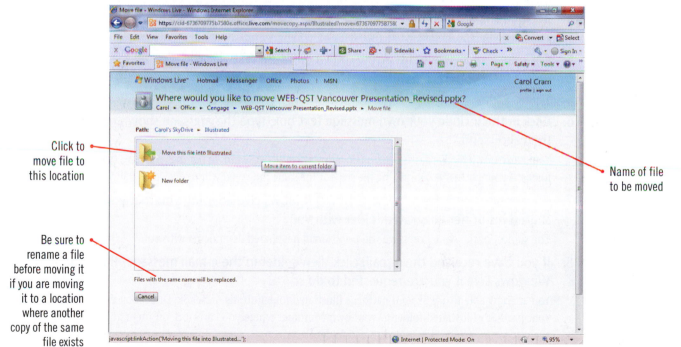

**FIGURE WEB-10:** Moving a file to the Illustrated folder

Click to move file to this location

Be sure to rename a file before moving it if you are moving it to a location where another copy of the same file exists

Name of file to be moved

# Adding People to Your Network and Sharing Files

One of the great advantages of working with SkyDrive on Windows Live is that you can share your files with others. Suppose, for example, that you want a colleague to review a presentation you created in PowerPoint and then add a new slide. You can, of course, e-mail the presentation directly to your colleague, who can then make changes and e-mail the presentation back. Alternatively, you can save time by uploading the PowerPoint file directly to SkyDrive and then giving your colleague access to the file. Your colleague can edit the file using the PowerPoint Web App, and then you can check the updated file on SkyDrive, also using the PowerPoint Web App. In this way, you and your colleague are working with just one version of the presentation that you both can update. You have decided to share files in the Illustrated folder that you created in the previous lesson with another individual. You start by working with a partner so that you can share files with your partner and your partner can share files with you.

## STEPS

**TROUBLE**
If you cannot find a partner, read the steps so you understand how the process works.

1. **Identify a partner with whom you can work, and obtain his or her e-mail address; you can choose someone in your class or someone on your e-mail list, but it should be someone who will be completing these steps when you are**

2. **From the Illustrated folder, click Share**

3. **Click Edit permissions**

   The Edit permissions page opens. On this page, you can select the individual with whom you would like to share the contents of the Illustrated folder.

4. **Click in the Enter a name or an e-mail address text box, type the e-mail address of your partner, then press [Tab]**

   You can define the level of access that you want to give your partner.

5. **Click the Can view files list arrow shown in Figure WEB-11, click Can add, edit details, and delete files, then click Save**

   You can choose to send a notification to each individual when you grant permission to access your files.

6. **Click in the Include your own message text box, type the message shown in Figure WEB-12, then click Send**

   Your partner will receive a message from Windows Live advising him or her that you have shared your Illustrated folder. If your partner is completing the steps at the same time, you will receive an e-mail from your partner.

**TROUBLE**
If you do not receive a message from Windows Live, your partner has not yet completed the steps to share the Illustrated folder.

7. **Check your e-mail for a message from Windows Live advising you that your partner has shared his or her Illustrated folder with you**

   The subject of the e-mail message will be "[Name] has shared documents with you."

**QUICK TIP**
You will know you are on your partner's SkyDrive because you will see your partner's first name at the beginning of the SkyDrive path.

8. **If you have received the e-mail, click View folder in the e-mail message, then sign in to Windows Live if you are requested to do so**

   You are now able to access your partner's Illustrated folder on his or her SkyDrive. You can download files in your partner's Illustrated folder to your own computer where you can work on them and then upload them again to your partner's Illustrated shared folder.

9. **Exit the browser**

**FIGURE WEB-11:** Editing folder permissions

Folder permissions will be changed for the Illustrated folder

Click to select network permission options

Type email address to continue to add people

Person whose permission status will change

Click to select person from list of contacts

Click to select permission option

**FIGURE WEB-12:** Entering a message to notify a person that file sharing permission has been granted

Web Apps

## Sharing files on SkyDrive

When you share a folder with other people, the people with whom you share a folder can download the file to their computers and then make changes using the full version of the corresponding Office application.

Once these changes are made, each individual can then upload the file to SkyDrive and into a folder shared with you and others. In this way, you can create a network of people with whom you share your files.

# Working with the Excel Web App

You can use the Excel Web App to work with an Excel spreadsheet on SkyDrive. Workbooks opened using the Excel Web App have the same look and feel as workbooks opened using the full version of Excel. However, just like the PowerPoint Web App, the Excel Web App has fewer features available than the full version of Excel. When you want to use a command that is not available on the Excel Web App, you need to open the file in the full version of Excel. You upload an Excel file containing a list of the tours offered by QST Vancouver to the Illustrated folder on SkyDrive. You use the Excel Web App to make some changes, and then you open the revised version in Excel 2010 on your computer.

## STEPS

1. **Start Excel, open the file WEB-2.xlsx from the drive and folder where you store your Data Files, then save the file as WEB-QST Vancouver Tours**

   The data in the Excel file is formatted using the Excel table function.

**TROUBLE**

If prompted, sign in to your Windows Live account as directed.

2. **Click the File tab, click Save & Send, then click Save to Web**

   In a few moments, you should see three folders to which you can save spreadsheets. My Documents and Cengage are personal folder that contains files that only you can access. Illustrated is a shared folder that contains files you can share with others in your network. The Illustrated folder is shared with your partner.

3. **Click the Illustrated folder, click the Save As button, wait a few seconds for the Save As dialog box to appear, then click Save**

**QUICK TIP**

Alternately, you can open your Web browser and go to Windows Live to sign in to SkyDrive.

4. **Click the File tab, click Save & Send, click Save to Web, click the Windows Live SkyDrive link above your folders, then sign in if prompted**

   Windows Live opens to your SkyDrive.

5. **Click the Excel program button [icon] on the taskbar, then exit Excel**

6. **Click your browser button on the taskbar to return to SkyDrive if SkyDrive is not the active window, click the Illustrated folder, click the Excel file, click Edit in Browser, then review the Ribbon and its tabs to familiarize yourself with the commands you can access from the Excel Web App**

   Table WEB-3 summarizes the commands that are available.

7. **Click cell A12, type Gulf Islands Sailing, press [TAB], type 3000, press [TAB], type 10, press [TAB], click cell D3, enter the formula =B3*C3, press [Enter], then click cell A1**

   The formula is copied automatically to the remaining rows as shown in Figure WEB-13 because the data in the original Excel file was created and formatted as an Excel table.

8. **Click SkyDrive in the Excel Web App path at the top of the window to return to the Illustrated folder**

   The changes you made to the Excel spreadsheet are saved automatically on SkyDrive. You can download the file directly to your computer from SkyDrive.

9. **Point to the Excel file, click More, click Download, click Save, navigate to the location where you save the files for this book, name the file WEB-QST Vancouver Tours_Updated, click Save, then click Close in the Download complete dialog box**

   The updated version of the spreadsheet is saved on your computer and on SkyDrive.

10. **Exit the Web browser**

**FIGURE WEB-13:** Updated table in the Excel Web App

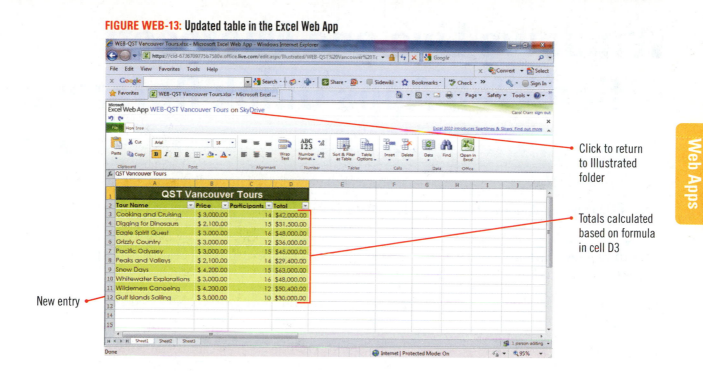

Click to return to Illustrated folder

Totals calculated based on formula in cell D3

New entry

**TABLE WEB-3:** Commands on the Excel Web App

| tab | commands available |
|-----|-------------------|
| File | • Open in Excel: select to open the file in Excel on your computer<br>• Where's the Save Button?: when you click this option, a message appears telling you that you do not need to save your spreadsheet when you are working in it with Excel Web App; the spreadsheet is saved automatically as you work<br>• Save As<br>• Share<br>• Download a Snapshot: a snapshot contains only the values and the formatting; you cannot modify a snapshot<br>• Download a Copy: the file can be opened and edited in the full version of Excel<br>• Give Feedback<br>• Privacy Statement<br>• Terms of Use<br>• Close |
| Home | • Clipboard group: Cut, Copy, Paste<br>• Font group: change the font, style, color, and size of selected labels and values, as well as border styles and fill colors<br>• Alignment group: change vertical and horizontal alignment and turn on the Wrap Text feature<br>• Number group: change the number format and increase or decrease decimal places<br>• Tables: sort and filter data in a table and modify Table Options<br>• Cells: insert and delete cells<br>• Data: refresh data and find labels or values<br>• Office: open the file in Excel on your computer |
| Insert | • Insert a Table<br>• Insert a Hyperlink to a Web page |

## Exploring other Office Web Apps

Two other Office Web Apps are Word and OneNote. You can share files on SkyDrive directly from Word or from OneNote using the same method you used to share files from PowerPoint and Excel. After you upload a Word or OneNote file to SkyDrive, you can work with it in its corresponding Office Web App. To familiarize yourself with the commands available in an Office Web App, open the file and then review the commands on each tab on the Ribbon. If you want to perform a task that is not available in the Office Web App, open the file in the full version of the application.

In addition to working with uploaded files, you can create files from new on SkyDrive. Simply sign in to SkyDrive and open a folder. With a folder open, click New and then select the Web App you want to use to create the new file.

# Windows Live and Microsoft Office Web Apps Quick Reference

| To Do This | Go Here |
|---|---|
| Access Windows Live | From the Web browser, type **home.live.com**, then click Sign In |
| Access SkyDrive on Windows Live | From the Windows Live home page, point to Windows Live, then click SkyDrive |
| Save to Windows Live from Word, PowerPoint, or Excel | File tab \| Save & Send \| Save to Web \| Select a folder \| Save As |
| Create a New Folder from Backstage view | File tab \| Save & Send \| Save to Web \| New Folder button |
| Edit a File with a Web App | From SkyDrive, click the file, then click Edit in Browser |
| Open a File in a desktop version of the application from a Web App: Word, Excel, PowerPoint | Click Open in [Application] in the Office group in each Office Web App |
| Share files on Windows Live | From SkyDrive, click the folder containing the files to share, click Share on the menu bar, click Edit permissions, enter the e-mail address of the person to share files with, click the Can view files list arrow, click Can add, edit details, and delete files, then click Save |

# Microsoft Office Specialist Skills Appendix

**Files You Will Need:**

No files needed.

Certification is an established trend in the Information Technology industry that helps match skilled people who want jobs with employers who are hiring skilled workers. Typically, a software or hardware company creates and gives exams that test competence on using specific programs or products. People who pass the exam demonstrate their ability to use the software or hardware effectively. By passing an exam, a person becomes "certified" and can prove his or her competence and knowledge of the software or hardware to prospective employers and colleagues. As a potential employee, you may have a better chance of landing a job if you are certified in the skills required for the job. As an employer, certification is another way to screen for qualified employees. This Appendix provides you with information to help you understand the Microsoft Office Specialist Certification program. It also provides a grid that lists the Microsoft Office Specialist Exam skills for Microsoft Excel 2010 and provides page references for where each skill is covered in this book. This Appendix also includes a reference section on Excel 2010 Microsoft Office Specialist Exam skills that are not covered in the lesson material in the book.

**OBJECTIVES**

Understand the Microsoft Office Specialist Certification program

Learn the Microsoft Office Specialist Certification process

Learn the Microsoft Office Specialist Certification levels

Get ready to take the exam

Take the exam

**REFERENCES**

Microsoft Office Specialist Exam skills: Excel 2010 (Core and Expert)

Additional skills for Microsoft Excel 2010

**REFERENCES**

Review these skills which are not covered in the lessons in the book to be fully prepared for the exam.

# Understanding the Microsoft Office Specialist Certification Program

The Microsoft Office Specialist program is the only comprehensive, performance-based certification program approved by Microsoft to validate desktop computer skills using the Microsoft Office 2010 programs.

## What is the Microsoft Office Specialist Program?

The Microsoft Office Specialist program provides computer program literacy by identifying important skills, measures proficiency by testing the skills, and identifies opportunities for skill enhancement through courseware. Candidates who pass an exam receive a certificate that sets them apart from their peers in the competitive job market. The certificate is a valuable credential, recognized worldwide as proof that an individual has the desktop computing skills needed to work productively and efficiently. Certification is a valuable asset to individuals who want to begin or advance their computer careers. Exams are available for: Microsoft Word, Microsoft Excel®, Microsoft Access™, Microsoft PowerPoint®, Microsoft Outlook®, and Microsoft SharePoint®.

## Who Gives the Exam?

The Microsoft Office Specialist exams are developed, marketed, and administered by Certiport, Inc., a company that has an exclusive license from Microsoft for the exams. The exams are available in a variety of languages. Exams must be taken at an authorized Certiport Center, which gives exams in a quiet room with the proper hardware and software. Trained personnel manage and proctor the exams.

## What are the Benefits of Getting Certified?

Getting certified as a Microsoft Office Specialist in one or several of the Microsoft Office 2010 programs can be beneficial to you and your current or prospective employer. Earning certification acknowledges that you have the expertise to work with Microsoft Office programs. Individuals who are Microsoft Office Specialist certified report increased competence and productivity with Microsoft Office programs. They are also more highly regarded and have increased credibility with their employers, co-workers, and clients. Certification sets you apart in today's competitive job market, bringing employment opportunities, greater earning potential and career advancement, and increased job satisfaction.

For example, if you have passed the Microsoft Excel 2010 certification exam, you have an advantage when interviewing for a job that requires knowledge and use of Excel to complete business-related tasks. Certification lets your prospective employer know that you not only have the necessary skills to perform that aspect of the job, but that you also have the initiative to prepare for, sign up for, pay for, and take an exam. Certification can help you increase your productivity within your current job and is a great way to enhance your skills without taking courses to obtain a new degree. More information about the benefits of getting certified can be found on the Certiport Web site.

> **QUICK TIP**
> Microsoft certification lets you access a member Web site, career-building tools, and training.

# Learning the Microsoft Office Specialist Certification Process

As with any process, there are steps. If you are organized, the process can be simple and you will achieve your goals. Getting a Microsoft Office Specialist certification credential is a process. After you take a course and learn the program, you can pursue certification. This book is Approved Courseware for the Microsoft Excel 2010 exam and the Microsoft Excel 2010 Expert exam, meaning that it passed a review and officially meets the skills standards set forth by Microsoft for these exams. If you complete the units and lessons including the end of unit exercises, and if you review the reference material on additional exam skills at the end of this Appendix, then you should have the necessary skills to pass the Excel 2010 Microsoft Office Specialist exams and get certified.

## Get Organized

The steps to successfully completing Microsoft Office Specialist certification are outlined in Table 1 and discussed in the remainder of this appendix. Once you have decided that you want to be certified, there are many tools, Web sites, and professionals to guide you towards to your goal.

> **QUICK TIP**
> Web addresses may change. If you cannot find what you are looking for, go to *www.microsoft.com* or *www.certiport.com* and do a search using keywords on the topic.

**Steps to getting certified**

| what to do | how to do it |
|---|---|
| 1. Choose an exam | Choose from one of the following exams, based on your skills and interests:<br>• Microsoft Office Word 2010<br>• Microsoft Office Word 2010 Expert<br>• Microsoft Office Excel 2010<br>• Microsoft Office Excel 2010 Expert<br>• Microsoft Office PowerPoint 2010<br>• Microsoft Office Outlook 2010<br>• Microsoft Office Access 2010<br>• Microsoft Office SharePoint 2010 |
| 2. Find a testing center | Find an authorized testing center near you using the Certiport Center locator at *www.certiport.com/Portal/Pages/LocatorView.aspx*. |
| 3. Prepare for the exam | Select the method that is appropriate for you, including taking a class or purchasing self-study materials. |
| 4. Take a practice test | It is recommended that candidates take a Practice Test before taking an exam.<br>• To view the practice tests available, go to *www.certiport.com/portal*.<br>• Follow the online instructions for purchasing a voucher and taking the practice test. |
| 5. Take the exam | • Contact the Certiport Center and make an appointment for the exam you want to take. Check the organization's payment and exam policies.<br>• Purchase an exam voucher at *www.certiport.com/portal*.<br>• Go to the Certiport Center to take the test, and bring a printout of the exam voucher, your Certiport username and password, and a valid picture ID. |
| 6. Receive exam results | You will find out your results immediately. If you pass, you will receive your certificate two to three weeks after the date of the exam. |

# Choose an Exam

The Microsoft Office Specialist certification program offers exams for the main applications of Microsoft Office 2010, including Word, Excel, Access, PowerPoint, Outlook, and SharePoint. You can also take a Microsoft Office Specialist exam for expert levels of Word and Excel that cover more advanced skills. You can earn the highest level of certification, Microsoft Office Specialist Master, by passing three required exams—Word 2010 Expert, Excel 2010 Expert, and PowerPoint 2010—and one elective exam—Access 2010 or Outlook 2010. Choose one or more applications that will help you in your current position or job search, or one that tests skills that match your abilities and interests.

- To learn more about the exams:

1. Go to www.microsoft.com/learning, click the link for Certification, then click the link for Microsoft Office. You can read valuable information about the different exams and the benefits of being certified. You can even find the list of skills covered in each exam on the exam Web site. Refer to Figure 1.

FIGURE 1: Microsoft Office Specialist Certification page

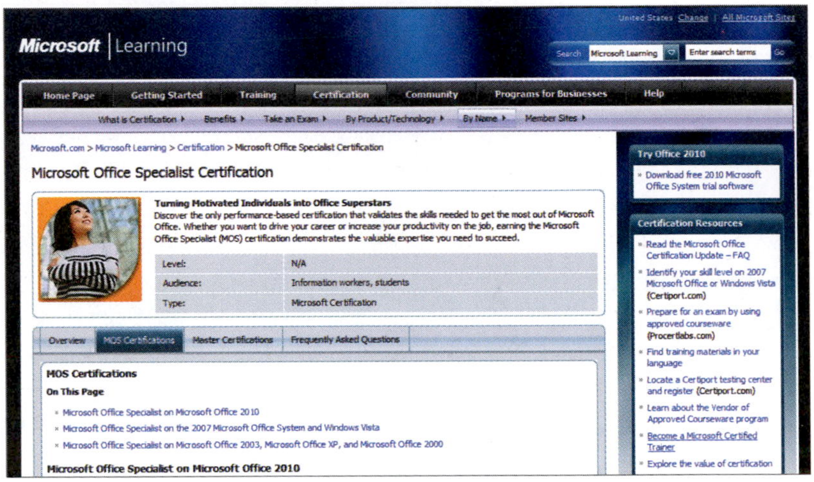

- To see the skills for a specific exam:

1. Go to http://www.microsoft.com/learning/en/us/certification/mos.aspx, click the MOS Certifications tab, search for an exam in the application you want to explore, then click the exam number link for the exam you want to take to display more detailed information, as shown in Figure 2.

FIGURE 2: Microsoft Office Specialist exam information

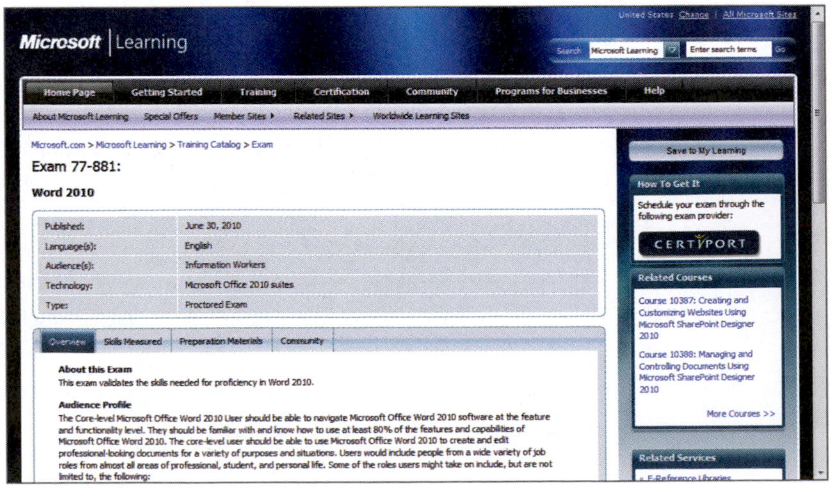

# Learning the Microsoft Office Specialist Certification Levels

The Microsoft Office Specialist certification program provides exams in two levels: Core and Expert. There is also a Master level which requires completion of more than one exam. As part of the process of deciding which exam you should take, you also need to decide the level of certification that best meets your needs.

## Microsoft Office Specialist Core Certification

The core-level user should be able to create professional-looking documents for a variety of business, school, and personal situations. The core-level user should be able to use about 80% of the features of the program. You can achieve the Microsoft Office Specialist core certification by passing any one of the following exams: Word 2010, Excel 2010, PowerPoint 2010, Access 2010, Outlook 2010, or SharePoint 2010.

## Microsoft Office Specialist Expert Certification

The expert user should be able to perform many of the advanced skills in the program at the expert level. Each test covers performance-based objectives and is designed to assess the candidates' hands-on skills using Microsoft Office. The Microsoft Office Specialist Expert Certification exams specify 75 unique performance-based tasks. You can earn the Microsoft Office Expert certification by passing one of the following exams: Word 2010 Expert and Excel 2010 Expert.

## Microsoft Office Specialist Master Certification

To achieve the Microsoft Office Master certification, you need to pass three required exams and one elective exam.

**Required**

- Microsoft Office Word 2010 Expert
- Microsoft Office Excel 2010 Expert
- Microsoft Office PowerPoint 2010

**Elective**

- Microsoft Office Access 2010

or

- Microsoft Office Outlook 2010

More information about the Microsoft Office Specialist 2010 certification series can be found at *http://www.microsoft.com/learning/en/us/certification/mos.aspx#mastercert* or on the Certiport Web site at *www.certiport.com/portal,* as shown in Figure 3.

**FIGURE 3: Certiport certification information**

# Getting Ready to Take the Exam

You have finished your studies and feel confident that you can achieve certification in one of the Microsoft Office 2010 applications. At this point you should know the program that you want to be certified in; for example, Word, Excel, PowerPoint, or Access. You also should know the level that you want to achieve, Core or Expert. Next, you need to find a test center and prepare to take the test.

## Find a Testing Center

You must take Microsoft Office Specialist certification exams at an authorized testing center, called a Certiport Center. Certiport Centers are located in educational institutions, corporate training centers, and other such locations. You can find a testing center near you using the Certiport Center locator at *www.certiport.com/portal/Pages/LocatorView.aspx*, as shown in Figure 4.

**QUICK TIP**
Certiport Centers are located in the United States and in several countries around the world.

**FIGURE 4:** Certiport Center locator

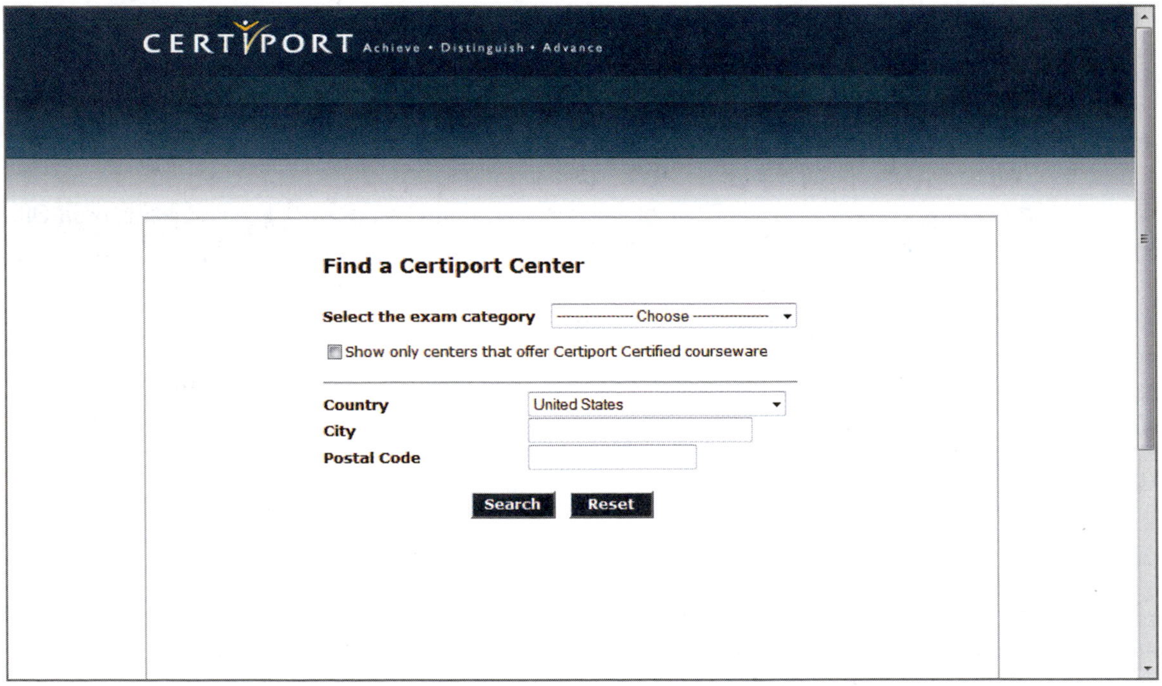

## What is the Test Like?

Completing the exercises in this book using Microsoft Excel will help you prepare for the exams. Using SAM (Skills Assessment Manager) 2010 with the book is especially helpful because SAM provides performance-based assessment on the application, similar to a Microsoft Office Specialist Exam. Learning by using both the book and SAM not only teaches you the program, but it also prepares you for the exams. The exams are primarily performance-based. Exam candidates are asked to perform a series of tasks to clearly demonstrate their skills. Each exam takes approximately 50 minutes and includes approximately 30-35 questions. As you take the test, you will be asked to complete steps in a simulated environment to show that you know the steps necessary to perform the task at hand. For example, in the Word exam you might have to balance newspaper column lengths or keep text together in columns, and it will appear as though you are actually working in the Word program as you take the test. In the Excel exam, you might have to find the sum of a column of numbers or create a pie chart, and it will appear as though you are actually working in the Excel program as you take the test.

# Prepare for the Exam: Take a Class

Reading through the exam objectives and taking a practice test can help you determine where you may need extra practice. If you are new to an Office program, you might want to take an introductory class and learn the program in its entirety. If you are already familiar with the program, you may only need to purchase study materials and learn unfamiliar skills on your own.

Taking a class—such as one that uses this book—is a good way to help you prepare for a certification exam, especially if you are a beginner. If you are an experienced user and know the basics, consider taking an advanced class. The benefits of taking a class include having an instructor as a resource, having the support of your classmates, and receiving study materials such as a lab book. Your local community college, career education center, or continuing education programs will most likely offer such courses. You can also check the Certiport Center in your area.

# Purchase Materials for Self-Study

You can prepare on your own to take an exam by purchasing materials at your local bookstore or from an online retailer. To ensure that the study materials you are purchasing are well-suited to your goal of passing the Microsoft Office Specialist certification exam, you should consider the following: favorable reviews (reviews are often available when purchasing online); a table of contents that covers the skills you want to master; and the Microsoft Office Specialist Approved Courseware logo, as shown in Figure 5. This logo indicates that Microsoft and Certiport have reviewed the book and recognize it as being an adequate tool for certification preparation.

**FIGURE 5:** Microsoft Office Specialist Approved Courseware logo

# Take a Practice Test

Consider taking an online practice test if one is available for the certification exam that you want to take. A practice test lets you determine the areas you should brush up on before taking the certification exam and helps you become familiar with the structure and format of the exam so you'll know what to expect. It is a self-assessment tool that tests you on the exam objectives and lets you know your level of proficiency. You can view the available practice tests from Certiport and register and pay for a practice test voucher at *www.certiport.com/portal*.

---

**Is Microsoft Office Specialist the same as Microsoft Certified Application Specialist?**

If you have earned a Microsoft Certified Application Specialist certification in Microsoft Office 2007, it is still valid. The name has just been changed to Microsoft Office Specialist (MOS). You can request an updated certificate from Microsoft that contains the new name.

# Taking the Exam

The Microsoft Office Specialist exams are highly regarded and therefore strictly regulated. To take an exam, you must plan ahead and follow specific rules and regulations. These policies are in place to protect you, as the test taker, as well as those that will hire you based on the results of your test. If you follow these simple steps, you will see that they are easy to do.

## Make an Appointment and Get Information

The locations of Certiport Centers are clearly available through their Web site. You should use the Certiport Center locator on their Web site at: *http://www.certiport.com/Portal/Pages/LocatorView.aspx*. Typically, the search results will offer a few choices. Once you find a center that is near you, and convenient, you should contact them. The locator also gives you a phone number so you can call them directly and ask questions. The Certiport Center staff can answer any questions you may have about scheduling, vouchers, and exam administration. Make an appointment for the exam you want to take. Be sure to ask about and verify the materials that you should bring with you when you take the exam.

## Purchase an Exam Voucher

If your Certiport Center verifies that you need a voucher to take the test, go online to their Web site and purchase a voucher from Certiport. The voucher is your proof that you registered and paid for the exam in advance.

- To pay for the exam and obtain a voucher:

1. Go to **www.certiport.com/portal**, click the **Login link**, then create a user account with a username and password of your choice.

2. At the MyCertiport screen, click the **Purchase Exam Voucher button**, then follow the onscreen instructions to purchase a voucher, as shown in Figure 6.

**FIGURE 6:** Purchase an exam voucher

# Take the Exam

You probably have been hearing this since you began your education, but it is worth repeating... if at all possible, get a good night's sleep the night before the exam! If the test is in the morning, eat a good breakfast! If the test is during the day or evening, be sure you have had something to eat so you can focus on the test. Being rested and feeling well will help you perform well on the test. You should also prepare whatever materials you need the day before the test. Running around to find your registration materials the day of the test will not help you do well. If you are late or forget any of these required items, you may not be permitted to take the exam, and may need to reschedule your test for another time.

NOTE: You must bring the following to the Certiport Center on the day of the test:

- **Your voucher, which is a printout of the electronic document you received when you paid for the test online. You will need to enter the voucher number when you log in to the test. If necessary, check with the Certiport Center to see if bringing just the voucher number, rather than a printout, is acceptable.**

- **Your Certiport username and password, which you will also have to enter at test login. You will have created a username and password when you paid for the voucher online.**

- **A valid picture ID (driver's license or valid passport).**

You may not bring any study or reference materials into the exam. You may not bring writing implements, calculators, or other materials into the test room.

# Receive Exam Results

So you have taken the test, what happens next? Exam results appear on the screen as soon as you complete the exam, so you'll know your score right away. You will receive a printout of your score to take with you. If you need additional copies, go to *www.certiport.com/portal*, and then log in and go to MyCertiport, where you can always access your exam results. If you pass the exam, you will receive an official certificate in the mail in approximately two to three weeks.

If you do not pass, refunds will not be given. But keep in mind that the exams are challenging. Do not become discouraged. If you purchased a voucher with a retake, a second chance to take the exam might be all you need to pass. Study your exam results and note areas you need to work on. Check your Certiport Center's exam retake policies for more information.

> **QUICK TIP**
> The exam results are confidential.

---

**What's it going to be like when I take the test?**

Each exam is administered within a functional copy of the Microsoft program corresponding to the exam that you are taking. The exam tests your knowledge of the program by requiring you to complete specific tasks in the program. The exam is "live in the program," which means that you will work with an actual document, spreadsheet, presentation, etc., and must perform tasks on that document. You cannot use Office Online Help during the exam. The Help feature is disabled during the exam. The overall exam is timed, although there is no time limit for each question. Most exams take up to 50 minutes, but the allotted time depends on the subject and level.

# Microsoft Office Specialist Exam Skills: Excel 2010 (Core and Expert)

## Managing the Worksheet Environment (Core)

| Skill | Page Where Covered |
|---|---|
| **Navigate through a worksheet** | |
| Use hot keys | Appendix 26 |
| Use the name box | 114 (Step 5 Tip) |
| **Print a worksheet or workbook** | |
| Print only selected worksheets | 16 (Steps 6–7, Step 7 Tip) |
| Print an entire workbook | Appendix 22 |
| Construct headers and footers | 14 (Steps 1–3, Step 3 Tip), 106 (Step 8), 136 (Steps 4–6) |
| Apply printing options | 16 (Steps 1–8, Clue) |
| Scale | 17 (Clue), 136 (Step 7, Step 7 Tip) |
| Print titles | 168 (Step 3) |
| Page setup | 136 (Steps 3–5), 168 (Steps 3–6) |
| Print area | 169 (Clue) |
| Gridlines | 16 (Step 5), 110 (Step 6 Tip) |
| **Personalize the environment by using Backstage** | |
| Manipulate the Quick Access toolbar | Office 6 (Step 2), Office 12 (Clue), 358 (Steps 2–3) |
| Customize the ribbon | 358 (Steps 4–5) |
| Tabs | 358 (Step 6) |
| Groups | 358 (Step 6) |
| Manipulate Excel default settings (Excel Options) | 356 (Steps 2–5) |
| Manipulate workbook properties (document panel) | 138 (Steps 5–6) |
| Manipulate workbook files and folders | Windows 25–43; Appendix 18 |
| Manage versions | Appendix 19 |
| AutoSave | Appendix 18 |

## Creating Cell Data (Core)

| Skill | Page Where Covered |
|---|---|
| **Construct cell data** | |
| Use paste special | 36 (Step 2 Tip) |
| Formats | Appendix 20 |
| Formulas | Appendix 20 |
| Values | Appendix 20 |
| Preview icons | Appendix 20 |
| Transpose rows | Appendix 20 |
| Transpose columns | Appendix 20 |
| Operations | Appendix 20 |
| Add | Appendix 20 |
| Divide | Appendix 20 |
| Comments | Appendix 20 |
| Validation | Appendix 20 |
| Paste as a link | Appendix 20 |

## Creating Cell Data (Continued)

| Skill | Page Where Covered |
| --- | --- |
| Cut | 32 (Step 1 Tip) |
| Move | 32 (Intro, Step 1 Tip), Appendix 36 |
| Select cell data | 4 (Steps 5–6) |
| Apply AutoFill | 36 (Step 3) |
| Copy data | 36 (Step 3) |
| Fill a series | 37 (Clue) |
| Preserve cell format | 37 (Clue) |
| Apply and manipulate hyperlinks | |
| Create a hyperlink in a cell | 140 (Step 2) |
| Modify hyperlinks | 140 (Step 4 Tip) |
| Modify hyperlinked cell attributes | 140 (Step 5) |
| Remove a hyperlink | 140 (Step 4 Tip) |

## Formatting Cells and Worksheets (Core)

| Skill | Page Where Covered |
| --- | --- |
| Apply and modify cell formats | |
| Align cell content | 56 (Steps 6–7), 57 (Clue) |
| Apply a number format | 52 (Steps 2–8) |
| Wrapping text in a cell | Appendix 21 |
| Use Format Painter | 56 (Step 5) |
| Merge or split cells | |
| Use Merge & Center | 56 (Step 6) |
| Merge across | Appendix 21 |
| Merge cells | Appendix 21 |
| Unmerge cells | Appendix 21 |
| Create row and column titles | |
| Print row and column headings | Appendix 22 |
| Print rows to repeat with titles | 168 (Step 3), Appendix 22 |
| Print columns to repeat with titles | Appendix 22 |
| Configure titles to print only on odd or even pages | Appendix 23 |
| Configure titles to skip the first worksheet page | Appendix 23 |
| Hide or unhide rows and columns | |
| Hide or unhide a column | 60 (Clue) |
| Hide or unhide a row | 60 (Clue) |
| Hide a series of columns | 134 (Step 4) |
| Hide a series of rows | 60 (Clue) |
| Manipulate Page Setup options for worksheets | |
| Configure page orientation | 16 (Steps 2–4) |
| Manage page scaling | 17 (Clue), 136 (Step 7) |
| Configure page margins | 144 (Step 6) |
| Change header and footer size | Appendix 23 |
| Create and apply cell styles | |
| Apply cell styles | 62 (Intro, Step 7), 63 (Clue) |
| Construct new cell styles | Appendix 21 |

## Managing Worksheets and Workbooks (Core)

| Skill | Page Where Covered |
|---|---|
| **Create and format worksheets** | |
| Insert worksheets | |
| Single | 4 (Step 4, bullet 5) |
| Multiple | Appendix 36 |
| Delete worksheets | |
| Single | 66 (Step 4 Tip) |
| Multiple | Appendix 36 |
| Reposition worksheets | 66 (Step 6) |
| Copy worksheets | 67 (Clue) |
| Move worksheets | Appendix 36 |
| Rename worksheets | 66 (Step 3) |
| Group worksheets | 144 (Step 2) |
| Apply color to worksheet tabs | 66 (Step 4) |
| Hide worksheet tabs | 130 (Step 7 Tip) |
| Unhide worksheet tabs | 130 (Step 7 Tip) |
| **Manipulate window views** | |
| Split window views | 131 (Clue) |
| Arrange window views | 130 (Step 4) |
| Open a new window with contents from the current worksheet | 130 (Step 2) |
| **Manipulate workbook views** | |
| Use Normal workbook view | 14 (Step 1) |
| Use Page Layout workbook view | 14 (Step 1) |
| Use Page Break workbook view | 135 (Clue) |
| Create custom views | 134 (Steps 1–3, Steps 5–7) |

## Applying Formulas and Functions (Core)

| Skill | Page Where Covered |
|---|---|
| **Create formulas** | |
| Use basic operators | 6 (All), 7 (Table), 12 (Steps 1–3) |
| Revise formulas | 12 (Steps 4–6) |
| **Enforce precedence** | |
| Order of evaluation | 26 (Clue) |
| Precedence using parentheses | 26 (Clue) |
| Precedence of operators for percent vs. exponentiation | Appendix 29 |
| **Apply cell references in formulas** | |
| Relative and absolute references | 34–35 |
| **Apply conditional logic in a formula** | |
| Create a formula with values that match conditions | 108 (Steps 1–6) |
| Edit defined conditions in a formula | 112 (Step 5) |
| Use a series of conditional logic values in a formula | Appendix 28 |
| **Apply named ranges in formulas** | |
| Define ranges in formulas | 114 (Step 3) |
| Edit ranges in formulas | 346 (Steps 3–4, 6), Appendix 29 |
| Rename a named range | 115 (Clue) |
| **Apply cell ranges in formulas** | |
| Enter a cell range definition in the formula bar | 114 (Step 5) |
| Define a cell range | 12 (Clue), 114 (Steps 2–4) |

## Presenting Data Visually (Core)

| Skill | Page Where Covered |
| --- | --- |
| Create charts based on worksheet data | 82 (Steps 2–7) |
| Apply and manipulate Illustrations | |
| Insert | 304 (Step 2) |
| Position | 304 (Step 4) |
| Size | 304 (Step 4) |
| Rotate | Appendix 24 |
| Modify clip art SmartArt | 305 (Clue) |
| Modify shape | Appendix 24 |
| Modify screenshots | Appendix 25 |
| Create and modify images by using the Image Editor | |
| Make corrections to an image | Appendix 25 |
| Sharpen or soften an image | Appendix 25 |
| Change brightness | Appendix 25 |
| Change contrast | Appendix 25 |
| Use picture color tools | 304 (Step 5) |
| Change artistic effects on an image | 304 (Steps 7–8) |
| Apply sparklines | |
| Use Line chart types | 238 (Step 1) |
| Use Column chart types | 238 (Step 3) |
| Use Win/Loss chart types | 83 (Clue) |
| Create a sparkline chart | 238 (Steps 1–2) |
| Customize a sparkline | 238 (Steps 4–6) |
| Format a sparkline | 238 (Step 4 Tip) |
| Show or hide data markers | Appendix 21 |

## Sharing Worksheet Data with Other Users (Core)

| Skill | Page Where Covered |
| --- | --- |
| Share spreadsheets by using Backstage | |
| Send a worksheet via e-mail or Skydrive | 324 (Clue), WebApps 6 |
| Change the file type to a different version of Excel | 142 (Step 1) |
| Save as PDF or XPS | 142 (Step 3 Tip), 143 (Table F-1) |
| Manage comments | |
| Insert | 352 (Steps 1–3, 5) |
| View | 352 (Steps 4, 6) |
| Edit | 352 (Step 7) |
| Delete comments | 352 (Step 7) |

## Analyzing and Organizing Data (Core)

| Skill | Page Where Covered |
| --- | --- |
| **Filter data** | |
| Define a filter | 182 (Steps 2–5), 183 (Clue) |
| Apply a filter | 178 (Steps 2–9), 184 (Steps 3–5), 185 (Clue) |
| Remove a filter | 178 (Steps 5, 9, Step 9 Tip) |
| Filter lists using AutoFilter | 178 (Steps 2–8) |
| **Sort data** | |
| Use sort options | 164 (Steps 1–4, Step 4 Tip, Clue), 165 (Table G-2, Clue) |
| Values | 164 (Steps 1–4) |
| Font color | Appendix 37 |
| Cell color | 164 (Clue) |
| **Apply conditional formatting** | |
| Apply conditional formatting to cells | 64 (Steps 1–6, Clue), 181 (Clue), 183 (Clue) |
| Use the Rule Manager to apply conditional formats | 64 (Clue), 181 (Clue), 183 (Clue) |
| Use the IF function to apply conditional formatting | Appendix 21 |
| Clear rules | Appendix 21 |
| Use icon sets | 64 (Step 2 Tip), 183 (Clue) |
| Use data bars | 64 (Steps 1–2) |

## Sharing and Maintaining Workbooks (Expert)

| Skill | Page Where Covered |
| --- | --- |
| **Apply workbook settings, properties, and data options** | |
| Set advanced properties | Appendix 36 |
| Save a workbook as a template | 360 (Step 5) |
| Import and export XML data | 332 (Steps 1–2; 7–8) |
| **Apply protection and sharing properties to workbooks and worksheets** | |
| Protect the current sheet | 132 (Steps 2–3) |
| Protect the workbook structure | 132 (Step 5) |
| Restricting permissions | 138 (Step 7) |
| Require a password to open a workbook | 328 (Steps 1–5) |
| **Maintain shared workbooks** | |
| Merge workbooks | 325 (Clue) |
| Set Track Changes options | 326 (Steps 1–2 ) |

## Applying Formulas and Functions (Expert)

| Skill | Page Where Covered |
| --- | --- |
| **Audit formulas** | |
| Trace formula precedents | 346 (Step 5) |
| Trace dependents | 346 (Step 7) |
| Trace errors | Appendix 28 |
| Locate invalid data | 346 (Step 5) |
| Locate invalid formulas | 346 (Step 2) |
| Correct errors in formulas | 346 (Step 3) and 347 (Clue), Appendix 28 |
| **Manipulate formula options** | |
| Set iterative calculation options | Appendix 29 |
| Enable or disabling automatic workbook calculation | 348 (Steps 1–3) |
| **Perform data summary tasks** | |
| Use an array formula | Appendix 28 |
| Use a SUMIFS function | 108 (Step 3) |
| **Apply functions in formulas** | |
| Find and correct errors in functions | 112 (Steps 3–5) |
| Applying arrays to functions | Appendix 31 |
| Use Statistical functions | 108 (Step 1) |
| Use Date functions | Appendix 30 |
| Use Time functions | Appendix 30 |
| Use Financial functions | 120 (Step 1) |
| Use Text functions | 106 (Step 5) |
| Cube functions | Appendix 31 |

## Presenting Data Visually (Expert)

| Skill | Page Where Covered |
| --- | --- |
| **Apply advanced chart features** | |
| Use Trend lines | 240 (Steps 1–9) |
| Use Dual axes | Appendix 37 |
| Use chart templates | 238 (Clue) |
| Use Sparklines | 238 (Steps 1–6) |
| **Apply data analysis** | |
| Use automated analysis tools | 264 (Steps 1–5 and Clue) |
| Perform What-If analysis | 250 (Steps 2–8) 254 (Steps 3–5) 256 (Steps 4–5) 257 (Clue) 258 (Steps 2–5) 260 (Steps 2–7) 262 (Steps 2–4) 263 (Clue) 264 (Steps 1–5) 265 (Table) |
| **Apply and manipulate PivotTables** | |
| Manipulate PivotTable data | 284 (Steps 1–7) |
| Use the slicer to filter and segment your PivotTable data in multiple layers | Appendix 32 |
| **Apply and manipulate PivotCharts** | |
| Create PivotChart | 286 (Steps 2–4) |
| Manipulate PivotChart data | 286 (Steps 5–8) 286 (Step 5 Tip) |
| Analyzing PivotChart data | Appendix 33 |
| **Demonstrate how to use the slicer** | |
| Choose data sets from external data connections | Appendix 32 |

# Working with Macros and Forms (Expert)

| Skill | Page Where Covered |
|---|---|
| **Create and manipulate macros** | |
| Run a macro | 208 (Steps 2–3) |
| Run a macro when a workbook is opened | 209 (Clue) |
| Run a macro when a button is clicked | 216 (Steps 1–6) |
| Record an action macro | 206 (Steps 1–9) |
| Assign a macro to a command button | Appendix 34 |
| Create a custom macro button on the Quick Access Toolbar | Appendix 34 |
| Apply modifications to a macro | 210 (Steps 1–5) |
| **Insert and manipulate form control** | |
| Insert form controls | Appendix 35 |
| Set form properties | Appendix 35 |

**Appendix**

Excel

# Additional Skills for Microsoft Excel 2010

**Files You Will Need:**

No files needed.

The units in this book cover nearly all of the skills that are specified in Microsoft's standards for the Microsoft Office Specialist Certification exams for Excel 2010. However, there are some skills that are not covered in the units. This section of the Appendix provides reference materials for the exam skills that are not covered in the units in the book. All of these skills are cross referenced in the Exam Skills Grid that precedes this page. Be sure to review this section as you prepare for the Excel 2010 Core and Expert exams.

**OBJECTIVES**

Work with files and folders

Use special cell formatting

Customize printing options

Work with graphics

Select commands with hot keys

Work with formulas

Work with functions

Work with PivotTables

Work with macros and forms

Manage workbooks

# Working with Files and Folders

To increase your productivity, you can personalize the way recently used files and folders appear in Backstage view. Also, if you accidently close a file without saving it, if an unstable program causes Excel to close abnormally, or if the power fails, you can recover your workbook, *provided the AutoRecover feature is enabled*. The AutoSave feature automatically saves your work at predetermined intervals, while the AutoRecover feature allows you to recover an AutoSaved file.

## Manipulate workbook files and folders

1. Click the **File tab** on the Ribbon to open Backstage view, then click **Recent**.
2. Right-click the file you want to keep, then click **Pin to List**. You can unpin the file by clicking the pin button.

## Add a quick access list to Backstage view

1. Click the **File tab** on the Ribbon to open Backstage view, then click **Recent**.
2. Select the **Quickly access this number of Recent Workbooks check box**, then select the number of workbooks you want to display. The number of files you requested appears beneath the Close menu command.
3. Clear this list by deselecting the check box.

## Clear the Recent Workbooks list

1. Click the **File tab** on the Ribbon to open Backstage view, then click **Recent**.
2. Right-click a file you want to remove from the list, click **Clear unpinned Workbooks**, then click **Yes**.

## Enable AutoRecover

1. Open Excel, click the **File tab** on the Ribbon, click **Options** on the Navigation bar, click **Save** in the Excel Options dialog box, then verify that the Save AutoRecover information check box is selected.

Click the up/down arrow keys to adjust the number of minutes

2. If necessary, modify the number of minutes AutoRecover saves your files, by clicking the up or down arrow to adjust the number of minutes.

3. Click OK.

## Restore an AutoRecovered version

1. Open the workbook that you want to recover, click the File tab on the Ribbon, then click Info on the Navigation bar (if it is not already selected).

2. Click the Manage Versions button to see a list of any AutoRecovered files.

# Using Special Cell Formatting

You can use special cell formatting to make worksheet text more attractive and to save time. There may be times when you want to paste only the formulas, values, or comments from a cell, or paste the cell as a link. You can perform these operations using either the buttons in the Paste palette or the Paste Special dialog box. When you point to a preview icon in the Paste palette, you see a preview of that formatting in the worksheet. Also, when cell text is too wide to fit in a cell, it will overlap into an empty cell immediately to its right. You can have text wrap within the margins of a cell. You can also merge cells together to form one cell in a variety of ways. Also, you can create cell styles to quickly apply an attractive styling to any cell or range.

Finally, you can use the Rules Manager to create, edit, delete, and reposition the order in which a conditional rule is applied, or stop a rule if a condition proves to be true. You can also create a new rule or clear rules from a worksheet, range, table, or PivotTable without using the Rules Manager.

## Use Paste Special

1. Select one or more cells, then click the **Copy button** in the Clipboard group on the Home tab on the Ribbon.

2. Click the destination cell, click the **Paste button list arrow**, then click the Paste Special option you want. The Paste Special options are described in the table below.

**QUICK TIP**

You can open the Paste Special dialog box by clicking the Paste Special command at the bottom of the Paste palette. The Paste Special dialog box lets you choose specific paste options, including those in the table below.

**Paste Special palette dialog box options**

| paste command | preview icon | used to |
| --- | --- | --- |
| Paste | | Paste cell contents and formatting |
| Formulas | | Paste formulas only |
| Formulas & Number Formatting | | Paste text and number formatting |
| Keep Source Formatting | | Paste source formatting |
| No Borders | | Paste cell contents with no cell borders |
| Keep Source Column Widths, | | Paste a column width to other column(s) |
| Transpose columns/rows | | Change columns of copied data to rows, or vice versa |
| Merge Conditional Formatting | | Paste conditional formatting rules |
| Values | | Paste displayed values only |
| Values & Number Formatting | | Paste displayed values and number formatting |
| Values & Source Formatting | | Paste displayed values and source formatting |
| Formats/Formatting | | Paste only cell formatting |
| Paste Link | | Link original data to the pasted data |
| Picture | | Paste a picture |
| Linked Picture | | Link a picture to a pasted cell |
| Add/Subtract | | Add/subtract the copied values to the values in the destination cell |
| Multiply/Divide | | Multiply/divide the copied values to the values in the destination cell |
| Comments | | Paste only comments attached to a cell |
| Validation | | Paste data validation rules |

# Wrap text in a cell

1. Select one or more cells.
2. Click the Wrap Text button 📑 in the Alignment group on the Home tab on the Ribbon.

# Merge or split cells

1. Click the Home tab on the Ribbon.
2. With the desired cells selected, in the Alignment group, click the Merge & Center list arrow 📊▾. The Merge & Center palette opens. Select an option from the table below.

**Merge and Center options**

| merge command | icon | what it does |
|---|---|---|
| Merge & Center | 📊 | Merges selected cells and centers contents |
| Merge Across | 📑 | Merges selected cell with the rightmost cell without centering the cell |
| Merge Cells | 📑 | Merges selected cell with the rightmost cell without centering the cell |
| Unmerge cells | 📑 | Restores merged cells to their original components |

# Construct new cell styles

1. Click the Home tab on the Ribbon.
2. In the Styles group, click the Cell Styles button to select it. The Cell Styles palette opens.
3. Click New Cell Style. The Style dialog box opens.
4. Type a name in the Style Name text box, then select or deselect style options from the Style Includes (By Example) list.
5. Click the Format button to choose customized formatting for your style, then click OK twice.

> **QUICK TIP**
> You can also use cell styles to modify cell hyperlinks. On the Home tab, click the Cell Styles button in the Styles group. Under Data and Model, right-click Hyperlink, then click Modify. In the Style dialog box, click Format, click the Font tab and/or the Fill tab, select the formatting options that you want, then click OK.

# Use the Rules Manager

1. Click the Home tab, click the Conditional Formatting button in the Styles group, then click Manage Rules.
2. Select the rule you want to change, then click the button that corresponds to the action you want to perform (New Rule, Edit Rule, Delete Rule, Move Up, or Move Down).
3. Click the Stop If True check box to make a rule quit executing if it is satisfied.

# Clear a rule

1. Click the Home tab on the Ribbon, click the Conditional Formatting button in the Styles group, then point to Clear Rules.
2. Select the appropriate option: Clear Rules from Selected Cells, Clear Rules from the Entire Sheet, Clear Rules from This Table, or Clear Rules from This PivotTable.

## Creating and formatting sparklines

You can create a miniature chart in a cell, called a sparkline, to show data trends in a worksheet range. To create a sparkline, click the cell, click the Insert tab, click the Line, Column, or Win/Loss button in the Sparklines group, enter the range of cells that will be represented by the Sparkline in the Data Range text box, then click OK. To display or hide data markers on a Sparkline, select or deselect the Markers check box in the Show group on the Sparkline Tools Design tab.

# Customizing Printing Options

In most cases, you'll probably want to print a specific worksheet. Occasionally, however, you may want to print an entire workbook. This is easy to do using Backstage view. Also, you can give multi-page workbooks a professional look by controlling how the column and row headings are printed. For example, multi-page data would be easier for your readers to comprehend if the column headings repeated on each page. You can also customize the printing options for a worksheet so that you control which headers or footers are printed depending on whether the printed page is odd or even. Finally, you can designate a special header or footer for the first page and change the way the header or footer is scaled.

## Print an entire workbook

1.  Click the File tab on the Ribbon to open Backstage view.
2.  Click Print, then in the Settings section of the Print tab, click the Print Active Sheets list arrow, and choose whether you want to print the active sheet, the entire workbook, or the current selection.

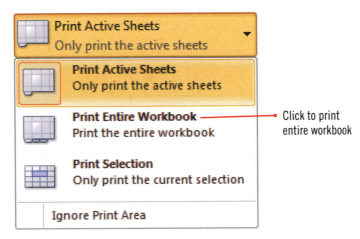

Click to print entire workbook

## Print row and column headings

1.  Click the Page Layout tab on the Ribbon.
2.  In the Page Setup group, click the Print Titles button. The Page Setup dialog box opens.

Click to collapse the dialog box

3.  If you want column headings repeated, click the Collapse button 🔲 to the right of the Rows to repeat at top text box, drag the row selection pointer ➡ over the column headings you want repeated, then click the Expand button 🔲.
4.  If you want row headings repeated, click the Collapse button 🔲 to the right of the Columns to repeat at left text box, drag the column selection pointer ⬇ over the row headings you want repeated, then click the Expand button 🔲.

## Create and configure titles

1. Click the Insert tab on the Ribbon, then click the Header & Footer button in the Text group. The worksheet automatically changes to Page Layout view.

2. Click the Header & Footer Tools Design tab on the Ribbon, then click the Different First Page check box in the Options group to select it, if you want a different header and/or footer for the first page. A text indicator (that changes to 'First Page Header' from 'Header') will appear in the header/footer area on the Page Layout view indicating that you are creating a different first page header/footer.

3. Click the Different Odd & Even Pages check box to select it, if you want a different header and/or footer for odd and even pages. A text indicator will appear in the header/footer area in Page Layout view indicating that you are creating a different odd/even page header/footer.

## Change header and footer size

1. Click the Insert tab on the Ribbon, then click the Header & Footer button in the Text group to create a header and/or footer.

2. Click the Header & Footer Tools Design tab on the Ribbon, then click the Scale with Document check box in the Options group to select it, if you want the headers/footers to use the same scale and font size that are used in the worksheet.

Select to hide header or footer from first page

Select to keep the same scale in the header/footer as in the document

**Header & Footer Tools**

Design

Go to Header  Go to Footer

Navigation

☐ Different First Page
☐ Different Odd & Even Pages

☑ Scale with Document
☑ Align with Page Margins

Options

Select to print different odd and even page headers/footers

# Working with Graphics

Shapes are wonderful additions to any worksheet, and can make your data more visually interesting. Once you create a shape, you can rotate it, or alter its shape, either to another predefined shape, or to a shape you choose. One you have created a screenshot and positioned it in your worksheet, you can modify it using tools on the Picture Tools Format tab. This tab appears when the screenshot object is selected. You can also sharpen and soften an image and make corrections for brightness and contrast.

## Rotate a shape

1. To create a shape, click the Insert tab, click the Shapes button in the Illustration group, then click any shape.

2. Drag across the worksheet to create a shape object.

3. Select the shape if necessary, then click the Drawing Tools Format tab on the Ribbon, if necessary.

4. In the Arrange group, click the Rotate button, then click one of the rotation options.

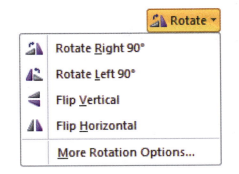

## Change a shape

1. Select an existing shape, then click the Drawing Tools Format tab on the Ribbon.

2. In the Insert Shapes group, click the Edit Shape button.

3. To change the existing shape to another shape, point to Change Shape, then click the icon for the new shape.

4. To modify the shape of the existing shape, click Edit Points. Small black squares appear on the perimeter of the shape. You can drag any of the existing points to a new location, or add a new point by clicking the perimeter with ⊹. You can then drag the new point to a new location.

Click to modify the points in a shape

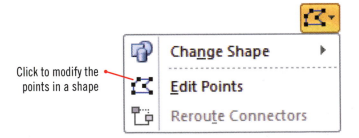

# Alter an image

1. Click a screenshot object in the worksheet, then click the Picture Tools Format tab.
2. Click the More button ⬇ in the Picture Styles group, then click any style to change the overall visual style of the image.

3. In the Picture Styles group, click the Picture Border button and click a color and line style to enhance the border surrounding the image.
4. In the Picture Styles group, click the Picture Effects button, point to an effect type, then click an effect to apply a visual effect to the image.
5. In the Picture Styles group, click the Picture Layout button, then click a Picture layout to convert the image to a SmartArt Graphic, which lets you easily arrange, caption, and resize the image.

# Correct an image

1. Click a screenshot object in the worksheet, then click the Picture Tools Format tab on the Ribbon.
2. In the Adjust group, click the Corrections button, then click a choice in the Sharpen and Soften section to change the visual acuity of the image.

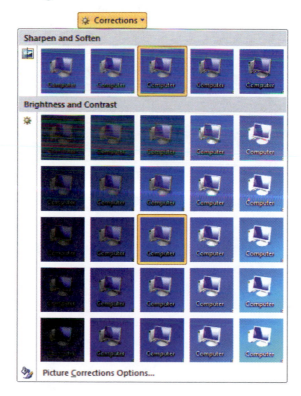

3. In the Adjust group, click the Corrections button, then click a choice in the Brightness and Contrast section to change the lighting of the image.

# Selecting Commands with Hot Keys

Although the Ribbon is designed to allow you to move quickly from command to command, you may want to navigate even more quickly. Key tips and keyboard shortcuts, often called hot keys, can help you do that. Key tips are single-character keys that you access using the [Alt] key, and that allow you to invoke a command without having to click the Ribbon. Keyboard shortcuts using the [Ctrl] key are listed in the table below. Function keys provide yet another way to speed your work. The function keys are the top row of keys on the keyboard, and provide you with single-key access to common commands. The second table below shows some common function key commands. For a complete list of keyboard shortcuts, open Help, then search on *keyboard shortcuts*.

## Navigate the Ribbon using key tips

1. Open Excel, then press [Alt]. The key tips display near each individual button.
2. Press the key indicated for the tab or command you want. For example, press N to make the Insert tab active.
3. Turn off the hot key display by pressing [Alt] or [Esc].

## Use Control key shortcuts

Press and hold [Ctrl] while pressing keys, as indicated in the table below.

Common Ctrl key shortcuts

| keyboard combination | used to | keyboard combination | used to |
|---|---|---|---|
| [CTRL][A] | Select an entire worksheet | [CTRL][O] | Display the Open dialog box |
| [CTRL][B] | Appy/remove bold formatting | [CTRL][P] | Display the Print tab in Backstage view |
| [CTRL][C] | Copy selected text to the Clipboard | [CTRL][S] | Save the active workbook |
| [CTRL][D] | Fill the selected cell(s) down | [CTRL][U] | Apply/Remove underline formatting |
| [CTRL][F] | Open the Find and Replace dialog box, with the Find tab active | [CTRL][V] | Place cut or copied text at the insertion point |
| [CTRL][G] | Open the Go To dialog box | [CTRL][W] | Close the current workbook |
| [CTRL][I] | Apply/Remove Italic formatting | [CTRL][X] | Cut the selected text to the Clipboard |

# Use function key shortcuts

Function keys give you access to several common commands with just one key press, as shown in the table below.

Common function key shortcuts

| function key | used to |
| --- | --- |
| [F1] | Open the Excel Help task pane |
| [F2] | Put the active cell in edit mode |
| [F4] | Repeat the last command or action |
| [F5] | Open the Go To dialog box |
| [F9] | Calculate all worksheets in open workbooks |
| [F12] | Open the Save As dialog box |

# Working with Formulas

If your formula results in an error, the Formula Auditing tools in Excel can help you find the sources of the error. The Trace Error tool highlights the cells used to calculate a formula. If your error is a circular reference, it is because the formula refers to the cell that contains the formula. If this reference is intentional, you can avoid this error by enabling the iteration feature. Excel then recalculates the formula for the number of times you specify. More advanced calculations can contain formulas with arrays, allowing you to calculate multiple formulas on data sets at one time. For example, to multiply the array ranges A2:A6 by B2:B6, you enter the array formula =A2:A6*B2:B6.

If you should find that a named worksheet range needs updating, you can easily modify the cells it contains or delete the range entirely using the Name Manager. Finally, in formulas with more than one mathematical operator, Excel calculates formulas based on rules of precedence, which are rules that dictate the order in which calculations in a formula will be performed. It's important to understand the rules of precedence (sometimes called the order of operations), to avoid formula errors. The table on the next page illustrates the order in which calculations are performed.

## Correct formula errors

1. Click a cell containing a formula, click the Formulas tab on the Ribbon, click the Error Checking list arrow in the Formula Auditing group, then click Trace Error to view the cells used in the formula calculations.

**QUICK TIP**

You can locate invalid data that may lead to errors in formula calculations on a worksheet by clicking the Data tab, clicking the Data Validation list arrow, then clicking Circle Invalid Data. Red circles are displayed around cells that are not consistent with data validation criteria.

| Oct | Nov | Dec | Total | Percent |
|-----|-----|-----|-------|---------|
| $31,102 | $35,022 | $31,852 | $ 35 | #DIV/0! |
| $22,841 | $50,711 | $20,141 | $308,289 | #DIV/0! |
| $53,943 | $85,733 | $51,993 | $735,915 | |

Tracer arrows to cells that are referenced by the formula

## Create an array formula

1. Select the cells where the array formula results will appear, then enter the array formula.

| PMT | | $f_x$ | =A2:A6*B2:B6 |
|-----|---|---|---|

Array formula

| | A | B | C |
|---|---|---|---|
| 1 | **Number** | **Price** | **Total** |
| 2 | 35 | $ 5.00 | =A2:A6* |
| 3 | 21 | $ 3.00 | B2:B6 |
| 4 | 100 | $ 8.00 | |
| 5 | 58 | $ 18.00 | |
| 6 | 67 | $ 22.00 | |

Array formula results will be placed here

### Nesting IF functions

You can nest IF functions to test several conditions in a formula. A nested IF function contains IF functions inside other IF functions to test these multiple conditions. The syntax for a nested IF function is:

IF(logical_test,value_if_true1,IF( logical_test 2,value_if_true2,value_if_false2 ))

The second IF statement is actually the value_if_false argument of the first IF statement.

2. Press [CTRL][SHIFT][ENTER] to display the results of the array formula.

| | A | B | C |
|---|---|---|---|
| | | | *fx* {=A2:A6*B2:B6} |
| 1 | Number | Price | Total |
| 2 | 35 | $ 5.00 | 175 |
| 3 | 21 | $ 3.00 | 63 |
| 4 | 100 | $ 8.00 | 800 |
| 5 | 58 | $ 18.00 | 1044 |
| 6 | 67 | $ 22.00 | 1474 |

Array formula results

## Enable iterative calculation

1. Click the File tab on the Ribbon, click Options, then click Formulas to view the options for calculations.

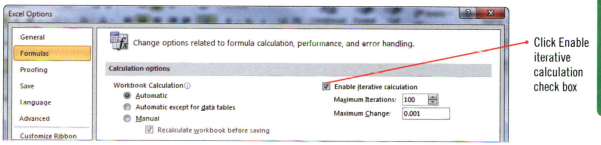

Click Enable iterative calculation check box

2. Click the Enable iterative calculation check box in the Calculation options group, enter the maximum number of iterations in the Maximum Iterations text box, enter the maximum amount of change between recalculation results in the Maximum Change text box, then click OK.

## Edit a named range

1. Click the Formulas tab on the Ribbon, then click the Name Manager button in the Defined Names group.
2. Select the name of the range you want to modify, then click Edit.
3. Click the Refers to Collapse button 📑 in the Edit Name dialog box, define the new parameters with your mouse then click the Expand button 📑, click OK, then click Close.

Ordered rules of precedence

| operator | used to |
|---|---|
| – | Subtract |
| % | Show percentage |
| ^ | Raise to a power (exponentiation) |
| * and / | Multiply and divide |
| & | Connect multiple text strings |
| = <br> < > <br> <= <br> >= <br> <> | Compare |

# Working with Functions

Your worksheet formulas may include dates and times, and Excel has functions available to help with these calculations. Excel stores dates and times in a number format that represents the number of days since the first day of the year 1900 plus the fractional part of the day. Dates represented in this way can be used in formulas and functions to calculate the time between dates or determine project deadlines.

Your functions may also include arrays. An example of an array function is the transpose function which can be used to rearrange worksheet data. You may have transposed data using a paste special option. The advantage of using an array function is that you can transpose a range of cells and if the source data is changed, that change is reflected in the transposed values. The Transpose array function is entered using the syntax =TRANSPOSE(range array). As in array formulas, you calculate an array function by pressing the key combination [Ctrl][Shift][Enter]. Pressing this key combination encloses the array function in braces, calculates the results, and displays the results in the selected range.

If you need to access data located on a data cube, Excel has built-in Cube functions to access data from a SQL Server Analysis Services.

## Enter a date and time functions

1. Click the **Formulas tab** on the Ribbon, click the **Date & Time button** in the Function Library group, then click the Date or Time function you want. Some of the available Date and Time functions are described in the table below.

Selected Date and Time functions

| function | used to |
|----------|---------|
| TODAY | Display the serial number of the date |
| NOW | Display the serial number of the date and time |
| DATE | Display the serial number for the date; the cell format must be Number or the date will be displayed |
| WEEKDAY | Display the number from 1 to 7 of the day of the week |
| TIME | Convert time from hours, minutes, and seconds to an Excel serial time |
| YEAR | Display the year for a date |
| WORKDAY | Display the serial number for a date before or after a certain number of workdays |
| HOUR | Display the hour of a time |
| MINUTE | Display the minute of a time |

# Transpose a range of data

1. Select the cells where the Transpose function results will appear, then enter the Transpose function using an array argument.

2. Press [CTRL][SHIFT][ENTER] to display the results of the array formula.

Transpose function

Transposed data

| | A | B | C | D | E | F | G | H | I | J |
|---|---|---|---|---|---|---|---|---|---|---|
| 1 | | | | | | | | | | |
| 2 | | | | | | | | | | |
| 3 | | | | | | | | | | |
| 4 | | | | | | | | | | |
| 5 | | | | | | | | | | |
| 6 | | | | | | | | | | |
| 7 | | Number | Price | | Number | 13 | 20 | 163 | 80 | |
| 8 | | 13 | 12 | | Price | 12 | 16 | 7 | 22 | |
| 9 | | 20 | 16 | | | | | | | |
| 10 | | 163 | 7 | | | | | | | |
| 11 | | 80 | 22 | | | | | | | |
| 12 | | | | | | | | | | |

E7    fx  {=TRANSPOSE(B7:C11)}

## Using data cubes

Data cubes are complex data sets with multiple dimensions. Cube functions are used to access these data cubes. They can access data from a SQL Server Analysis Services to use in a worksheet.

To find out whether a cube has a certain data item, you can use the Cube function CUBEMEMBER. The function will verify that the data is contained on the cube by returning the name of the field. For example, entering =CUBEMEMBER("Cengage" , "[Title].[Illustrated]") will return the field name Illustrated from the Title dimension of the Cengage cube.

# Working with PivotTables

You know how to use a slicer to filter PivotTables on one field. It is likely that you will create more than one filter for a PivotTable by using multiple slicers. If you want a slicer to be referenced by an Online Analytical Processing (OLAP) cube function, Access database, or SQL database you can add external data sources when creating the slicer. If you are working with an OLAP data source, your PivotTables can use What-if analysis on that data.

## Use multiple slicers to filter a PivotTable

1. Click any cell in the PivotTable, click the PivotTable Options tab on the Ribbon, then click the Insert Slicer button in the Sort & Filter group.

2. Click the check box for each field you want to filter in the Insert Slicers dialog box to select it, then click OK. A slicer is displayed for each field you selected. The figure below shows a PivotTable filtered with multiple slicers.

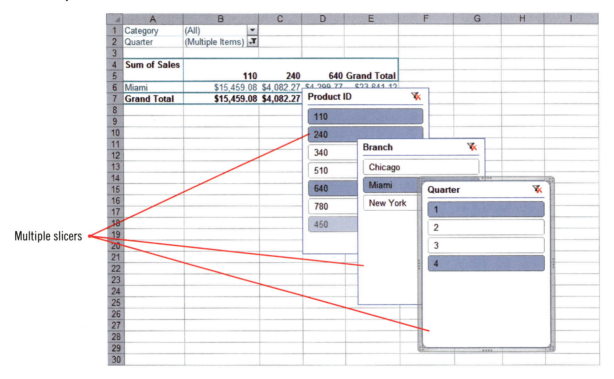

## Select an external data source for a slicer

1. Click any cell outside the PivotTable, click the Insert tab on the Ribbon, then click the Slicer button in the Filter group to open the Existing Connections dialog box.

2. Click the Show list arrow to choose a connection. You can keep the default, All Connections, or choose connection files on your computer, on the network, or in the workbook as shown in the figure below.

**QUICK TIP**

You can create a connection by clicking the Browse for More button, clicking New Source in the Select Data Source dialog box, then following the steps of the Data Connection Wizard to set up a new connection.

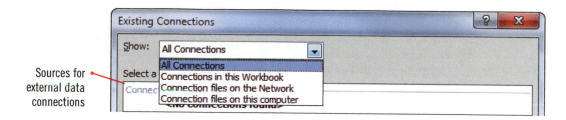

Sources for
external data
connections

3 In the Select a Connection section, click the connection you want to use, then click Open.

4. Click the check box for each field you want to filter in the Insert Slicers dialog box to select it, then click OK. A slicer is displayed for each field you selected.

5. Click one or more of the buttons to filter the PivotTable to display only data for the selected value(s).

## Using What-If Analysis for PivotTables

One of the powerful data analysis features in Excel is the ability to analyze data from an OLAP data source. What-If analysis in PivotTables allows you to modify this type of data in an Excel worksheet and then publish, or "write back," the changes to the OLAP data source. To publish this data your OLAP cube must have What-If analysis enabled.

To begin, you need to enable the What-If Analysis feature for your PivotTable by clicking the PivotTable Tools Options tab, clicking the What-If Analysis button in the Tools group, then clicking Enable What-If Analysis. You need to select the settings for calculating

changes to your PivotTable by clicking the What-If Analysis button in the Tools group, clicking Settings, selecting the Manually or Automatically option button in the What-If Analysis Settings dialog box, then clicking OK. If you select manual changes you need to recalculate the PivotTable after making changes. The Automatic setting will recalculate the PivotTable after each change automatically.

After making changes to a PivotTable, you need to publish them by clicking the What-If Analysis button in the Tools group, then clicking Publish Changes. The changes will be written back to the OLAP data source so other people can see the changes.

# Working with Macros and Forms

You can assign macros to three types of buttons: ActiveX command buttons, custom buttons on the Quick Access Toolbar, and form control buttons. These buttons can then be used to automate commands in your Excel workbooks, including things like printing, sorting, formatting, filtering, or numerical calculations. If you are using an ActiveX command button, you will need to work with the Visual Basic Editor to assign a macro to the button. Also, after creating a form control, you may want to format it to improve its appearance.

## Create a command button for a macro

1. Click the Developer tab on the Ribbon, click the Insert button in the Controls group, then click Command Button in the ActiveX Controls section as shown in the figure below.

2. Click the cell in the worksheet where you want to place the upper-left corner of the button, then click View Code in the Controls group of the Developer tab to open the Visual Basic Editor.

3. Type the name of the macro you want to assign to the button between the Private Sub and End Sub lines, then verify that Click appears in the drop-down list in the top right area of the window.

4. Click the View Microsoft Excel button ⊠ on the Visual Basic Editor Standard toolbar to return to Excel, then click the Design Mode button in the Controls group of the Developer tab. You can test your new button by clicking it to run the macro you entered in the Visual Basic Editor.

> **QUICK TIP**
>
> If the Developer tab does not appear on your Ribbon, click the File tab, click Options, click Customize Ribbon on the left side of the Excel Options dialog box, click the Developer check box to select it on the right pane, then click OK.

> **QUICK TIP**
>
> You can edit the command button by clicking the Design Mode button in the Controls group, clicking the command button, clicking the Properties button in the Controls group, then changing the properties in the Propeties window. You can format the command button by right-clicking it and selecting Format Control from the shortcut menu.

## Create a custom button for a macro

1. Right-click the Ribbon, then click Customize Quick Access Toolbar.

2. Click the Choose commands from list arrow, select Macros, then select the macro to assign to a custom button in the macro list on the left.

3. Click Add to move the macro to the list of buttons on the Quick Access Toolbar as shown in the figure below.

Click to select macros

Click to add selected macro to the Quick Access Toolbar

4. Click **OK** to close the Excel Options dialog box.

## Create a form control for a macro

1. Click the **Developer tab** on the Ribbon, click the **Insert button** in the Controls group, then click **Button (Form Control)** in the Form Controls section as shown in the figure below.

Click to add a form control button

2. Click the cell in the worksheet where you want to place the upper-left corner of the button, click the macro name in the Assign macro dialog box, then click **OK**.

> **QUICK TIP**
>
> If the Developer tab does not appear on your Ribbon, click the File tab, click Options, click Customize Ribbon on the left side of the Excel Options dialog box, click the Developer check box to select it on the right pane, then click OK.

## Format a form control

1. Right-click the form control, then select **Format Control** from the shortcut menu.
2. Edit the properties in the Format Control dialog box, then click **OK**.

> **QUICK TIP**
>
> After creating controls for a form, you may want to specify the properties for the worksheet. After inserting form controls, click the Properties button in the Controls group, then specify the desired worksheet settings in the Properties dialog box.

> **QUICK TIP**
>
> Alternative text for a button form control assists people with disabilites who cannot see the button. It is also used by search engines on the Web to catalog pages. Some browsers display alternative text while loading large images.

# Managing Workbooks

As you manage your workbooks, you may want to customize the presentation of your data. When customizing the printing options for a worksheet, you can control which headers or footers are printed depending on whether the printed page is odd or even. You can also designate a special header or footer for the first page and change the way the header or footer is scaled. Also, you can easily add or delete multiple worksheets within a workbook using the [Shift] key.

If you want to add additional summary information to your workbook, such as a subject, manager name, company name, and a category, you can use advanced properties. When analyzing your workbook data, in addition to sorting data in ascending or descending order based on alphanumeric cell contents, you can also sort by cell color, font color, or cell icon. Finally, when you chart your workbook data, you may want to compare different types of data in one chart. For example, it might be useful to see sales volume charted with revenue. You may also want to show two different scales for your chart data. By using different axes for different data series, you can see related data on one chart with different measurement scales.

## Add multiple worksheets

1. Click the Home tab on the Ribbon, press and hold [Shift], then click the number of existing worksheet tabs that correspond with the number of sheets you want to add.

2. Click the Insert list arrow in the Cells group on the Home tab, then click Insert Sheet.

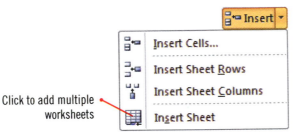

Click to add multiple worksheets

## Delete multiple worksheets

1. Click the Home tab on the Ribbon, press and hold [Shift], then click the sheet tabs of existing worksheets that you want to delete.

2. Click the Delete list arrow in the Cells group on the Home tab, then click Delete Sheet.

Click to delete multiple worksheets

> **QUICK TIP**
> To move or copy worksheets to other workbooks, right-click any sheet tab, click Move or Copy, click the To Book list arrow and select the workbook, then select the sheet before which to move the sheet and click OK.

3. Click Delete to confirm the deletion.

## Specify advanced workbook properties

1. Click the File tab on the Ribbon to open Backstage view, then click Info.

2. Click the Properties list arrow on the right side of Backstage view, then click Advanced Properties.

3. Use the Summary tab to add additional properties to the workbook.

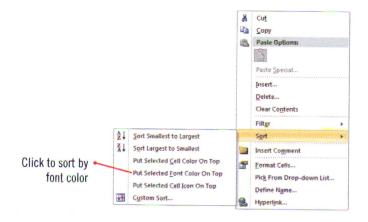

**QUICK TIP**

You can view statistical information supplied by Excel on the Statistics tab. The General tab displays file information, and the worksheet names appear on the Contents tab. Additional fields for information can be created and entered on the Custom tab.

## Organize data by font color

1.  Select a cell in the column of conditionally formatted data you want to sort by, or select the range of cells to be sorted.

2.  Right-click the selection, point to Sort, then click Put Selected Font Color on Top.

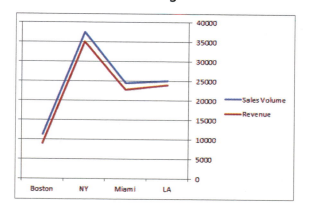

Click to sort by font color

## Chart data on two axes

1.  Select the data you want to chart, click the Insert tab on the Ribbon, then select the chart type.

2.  Click the Chart Elements list arrow and select the data series that you want to move to a secondary axis, click the Chart Tools Format tab, click Format Selection in the Current Selection group, click the Secondary Axis option button, then click Close. The data series is displayed on a secondary axis and it is scaled differently than the other data series as shown in the figure below.

# EXAM NOTES

# EXAM NOTES

# EXAM NOTES

# Glossary

**3-D reference** A worksheet reference that uses values on other sheets or workbooks, effectively creating another dimension to a workbook.

**Absolute cell reference** In a formula, a cell address that refers to a specific cell and does not change when you copy the formula; indicated by a dollar sign before the column letter and/or row number. *See also* Relative cell reference.

**Accessories** Simple Windows programs that perform specific tasks, such as the Calculator accessory for performing calculations.

**Active** The currently available document, program, or object; on the taskbar, when more than one program is open, the button for the active program appears slightly lighter.

**Active cell** The cell in which you are currently working.

**Active window** The window you are currently using; if multiple windows are open, the window with the darker title bar.

**Add-in** An extra program, such as Solver and the Analysis ToolPak, that provides optional Excel features. To activate an add-in, click the File tab, click Options, click Add-Ins, then select or deselect add-ins from the list.

**Address** A sequence of drive and folder names that describes a folder's or file's location in the file hierarchy; the highest hierarchy level is on the left, with lower hierarchy levels separated by the symbol to its right.

**Address bar** In a window, the white area just below the title bar that shows the file hierarchy, or address of the files that appear in the file list below it; the address appears as a series of links (separated by the symbol) you can click to navigate to other locations on your computer.

**Aero** A Windows 7 viewing option that shows windows as translucent objects and features subtle animations; only available on a computer that has enough memory to support Aero and on which a Windows Aero theme has been selected.

**Aero Flip 3D** A Windows 7 feature that lets you preview all open folders and documents without using the taskbar and that displays open windows in a stack if you press [Ctrl][⊞]Tab]; only available if using a Windows Aero theme.

**Aero Peek** A Windows 7 feature that lets you point to a taskbar icon representing an open program and see a thumbnail (small version) of the open fi le; only visible if the computer uses a Windows Aero theme.

**Alignment** The placement of cell contents in relation to a cell's edges; for example, left-aligned, centered, or right-aligned.

**And condition** A filtering feature that searches for records by specifying that all entered criteria must be matched.

**Application program** Any program that lets you work with files or create and edit files such as graphics, letters, financial summaries, and other useful documents, as well as view Web pages on the Internet and send and receive e-mail.

**Apply (a template)** To open a document based on an Excel template.

**Argument** Information necessary for a formula or function to calculate an answer. In the Visual Basic for Applications (VBA) programming language, variable used in procedures that a main procedure might run. *See also* Main procedure.

**Arithmetic operators** In a formula, symbols that perform mathematical calculations, such as addition (+), subraction (–), multiplication (*), division(/), or exponentiation (^).

**Ascending order** In sorting an Excel field (column), the order that begins with the letter A or the lowest number of the values in the field.

**ASCII file** A text file that contains data but no formatting; instead of being divided into columns, ASCII file data are separated, or delimited, by tabs or commas.

**Attributes** Styling characteristics such as bold, italic, and underlining that you can apply to change the way text and numbers look in a worksheet or chart. In XML, the components that provide information about the document's elements.

**Auditing** An Excel feature that helps track errors and check worksheet logic.

**AutoComplete** In the Visual Basic for Applications (VBA) programming language, a list of words that appears as you enter code; helps you automatically enter elements with the correct syntax.

**AutoFill** Feature activated by dragging the fill handle; copies a cell's contents or continues a series of entries into adjacent cells.

**AutoFill Options button** Button that appears after using the fill handle to copy cell contents; enables you to choose to fill cells with specific elements (such as formatting) of the copied cell if desired.

**AutoFilter** A table feature that lets you click a list arrow and select criteria by which to display certain types of records; *also called* filter.

**AutoFilter list arrows** *See* Filter List arrows.

**AutoFit** A feature that automatically adjusts the width of a column or the height of a row to accommodate its widest or tallest entry.

**Backsolving** A problem-solving method in which you specify a solution and then find the input value that produces the answer you want; sometimes described as a what-if analysis in reverse. In Excel, the Goal Seek feature performs backsolving.

**Backstage view** View available in all Microsoft Office programs that allows you to perform many common tasks, such as opening and saving a file, printing and previewing a document, and protecting a document before sharing it with others.

**Backup** A duplicate copy of a file that is stored in another location.

**Backward-compatible** Software feature that enables documents saved in an older version of a program to be opened in a newer version of the program.

**Banding** Worksheet formatting in which adjacent rows and columns are formatted differently.

**Border** A window's edge; drag to resize the window.

**Bug** In programming, an error that causes a procedure to run incorrectly.

**Calculated columns** In a table, a column that automatically fills in cells with formula results, using a formula entered in only one other cell in the same column.

**Calculation operators** Symbols in a formula that indicate what type of calculation to perform on the cells, ranges, or values.

**Canvas** In the Paint accessory program, the area in the center of the program window that you use to create drawings.

**Case sensitive** Describes a program's ability to differentiate between uppercase and lowercase letters; usually used to describe how an operating system evaluates passwords that users type to gain entry to user accounts.

**Category axis** Horizontal axis in a chart, usually containing the names of data categories; in a 2-dimensional chart, also known as the x-axis.

**Cell** The intersection of a column and a row in a worksheet or table.

**Cell address** The location of a cell, expressed by cell coordinates; for example, the cell address of the cell in column A, row 1 is A1.

**Cell comments** Notes you've written about a workbook that appear when you place the pointer over a cell.

**Cell pointer** Dark rectangle that outlines the active cell.

**Cell styles** Predesigned combinations of formats based on themes that can be applied to selected cells to enhance the look of a worksheet.

**Change history** A worksheet containing a list of changes made to a shared workbook.

**Changing cells** In what-if analysis, cells that contain the values that change in order to produce multiple sets of results.

**Chart sheet** A separate sheet in a workbook that contains only a chart, which is linked to the workbook data.

**Charts** Pictorial representations of worksheet data that make it easier to see patterns, trends, and relationships; *also called* graphs.

**Check box** A box that turns an option on when checked or off when unchecked.

**Click** To quickly press and release the left button on the pointing device; also called single-click.

**Clip** A media file, such as a graphic, sound, animation, or movie.

**Clip art** A graphic image, such as a corporate logo, a picture, or a photo, that can be inserted into a document.

**Clipboard** A temporary Windows storage area that holds the selections you copy or cut.

**Close button** In a Windows title bar, the rightmost button; closes the open window, program, and/or document.

**Cloud computing** When data, applications, and resources are stored on servers accessed over the Internet or a company's internal network rather than on users' computers.

**Code** *See* Program code.

**Code window** In the Visual Basic Editor, the window that displays the selected module's procedures, written in the Visual Basic programming language.

**Color scale** In conditional formatting, a formatting scheme that uses a set of two, three, or four fill colors to convey relative values of data.

**Column heading** Identifies the column letter, such as A, B, etc.; located above each column in a worksheet.

**Combination chart** Two charts in one, such as a column chart combined with a line chart, that together graph related but dissimilar data.

**Command** An instruction to perform a task, such as opening a file or emptying the Recycle Bin.

**Command button** A button you click to issue instructions to modify program objects.

**Comments** In a Visual Basic procedure, notes that explain the purpose of the macro or procedure; they are preceded by a single apostrophe and appear in green. *See also* Cell comments.

**Comparison operators** In a calculation, symbols that compare values for the purpose of true/false results.

**Compatible** The capability of different programs to work together and exchange data.

**Complex formula** A formula that uses more than one arithmetic operator.

**Conditional formatting** A type of cell formatting that changes based on the cell's value or the outcome of a formula.

**Consolidate** To combine data on multiple worksheets and display the result on another worksheet.

**Constraints** Limitations or restrictions on input data in what-if analysis.

**Contextual tab** Tab on the Ribbon that appears when needed to complete a specific task; for example, if you select a graphic, the Picture Tools Format tab appears.

**Copy** To make a duplicate copy of a file, folder, or other object that you want to store in another location.

**Criteria range** In advanced filtering, a cell range containing one row of labels (usually a copy of column labels) and at least one additional row underneath it that contains the criteria you want to match.

**Custom chart type** A specially formatted Excel chart.

**Data entry area** The unlocked portion of a worksheet where users are able to enter and change data.

**Data label** Descriptive text that appears above a data marker in a chart.

**Data marker** A graphical representation of a data point in a chart, such as a bar or column.

**Data point** Individual piece of data plotted in a chart.

**Data series** A column or row in a datasheet. Also, the selected range in a worksheet that Excel converts into a chart.

**Data source** Worksheet data used to create a chart or a PivotTable.

**Data table** A range of cells that shows the resulting values when one or more input values are varied in a formula; when one input value is changed, the table is called a one-input data table, and when two input values are changed, it is called a two-input data table. In a chart, it is a grid containing the chart data.

**Data validation** A feature that allows you to specify what data is allowable (valid) for a range of cells.

**Database** An organized collection of related information. In Excel, a database is called a table.

**Database program** An application, such as Microsoft Access, that lets you manage large amounts of data organized in tables.

**Database table** A set of data organized using columns and rows that is created in a database program.

**Debug** In programming, to find and correct an error in code.

**Declare** In the Visual Basic programming language, to assign a type, such as numeric or text, to a variable.

**Default** In a program window or dialog box, a value that is already set by the program; you can change the default to any valid value.

**Delimiter** A separator such as a space, comma, or semicolon between elements in imported data.

**Dependent cell** A cell, usually containing a formula, whose value changes depending on the values in the input cells. For example, a payment formula or function that depends on an input cell containing changing interest rates is a dependent cell.

**Descending order** In sorting an Excel field (column), the order that begins with the letter Z or the highest number of the values in the field.

**Desktop** A shaded or picture background that appears to fill the screen after a computer starts up; usually contains icons, which are small images that represent items on your computer and allow you to interact with the computer.

**Desktop background** The shaded area behind your desktop objects; can show colors, designs, or photographs, which you can customize.

**Destination program** In a data exchange, the program that will receive the data.

**Details pane** A pane located at the bottom of a window that displays information about the selected disk, drive, folder, or file.

**Device** A hardware component that is part of your computer system, such as a disk drive or a pointing device.

**Dialog box** A window with controls that lets you tell Windows how you want to complete a program command.

**Dialog box launcher** An icon available in many groups on the Ribbon that you can click to open a dialog box or task pane, offering an alternative way to choose commands. *Also called* launcher.

**Digital signature** A signature that can be added to a workbook to establish its validity and prevent it from being changed.

**Document** To make notes about basic worksheet assumptions, complex formulas, or questionable data. In a macro, to insert comments that explain the Visual Basic code.

**Document window** The portion of a program window in which you create the document; displays all or part of an open document.

**Documents folder** The folder on your hard drive used to store most of the files you create or receive from others; might contain subfolders to organize the files into smaller groups.

**Double-click** To quickly press and release or click the left button on the pointing device twice.

**Drag** To point to an object, press and hold the left button on the pointing device, move the object to a new location, and then release the left button.

**Drag and drop** To use a pointing device to move or copy a file or folder to a new location.

**Drive** A physical location on your computer where you can store files.

**Drive name** A name for a drive that consists of a letter followed by a colon, such as C: for the hard disk drive.

**Dynamic page breaks** In a larger workbook, horizontal or vertical dashed lines that represent the place where pages print separately. They also adjust automatically when you insert or delete rows or columns, or change column widths or row heights.

**Edit** To make a change to the contents of an active cell.

**Electronic spreadsheet** A computer program used to perform calculations and analyze and present numeric data.

**Element** An XML component that defines the document content.

**Embed** To insert a copy of data into a destination document; you can double-click the embedded object to modify it using the tools of the source program.

**Embedded chart** A chart displayed as an object in a worksheet.

**Exploding** Visually pulling a slice of a pie chart away from the whole pie chart in order to add emphasis to the pie slice.

**Extensible Markup Language (XML)** A system for defining languages using tags to structure data. *See also* XML.

**External reference indicator** The exclamation point (!) used in a formula to indicate that a referenced cell is outside the active sheet.

**Extract** To place a copy of a filtered table in a range you specify in the Advanced Filter dialog box.

**Field** In a table (an Excel database or a PivotTable), a column that describes a characteristic about records, such as first name or city.

**Field name** A column label that describes a field.

**File** A collection of information stored on your computer, such as a letter, video, or program.

**File extension** A three- or four-letter sequence, preceded by a period, at the end of a filename that identifies the file as a particular type of document; documents in the Rich Text Format have the file extension .rtf.

**File hierarchy** The tree-like structure of folders and files on your computer.

**File management** The ability to organize folders and files on your computer.

**Filename** A unique, descriptive name for a file that identifies the file's content.

**File properties** Details that Windows stores about a file, such as the date it was created or modified.

**Filter** To display data in an Excel table that meet specified criteria. *See also* AutoFilter.

**Filter arrows** *See* Filter list arrows.

**Filter list arrows** List arrows that appear next to field names in an Excel table; used to display portions of your data. *Also called* AutoFilter list arrows.

**Folder** An electronic container that helps you organize your computer files, like a cardboard folder on your desk; it can contain subfolders for organizing files into smaller groups.

**Folder name** A unique, descriptive name for a folder that helps identify the folder's contents.

**Font** The typeface or design of a set of characters (letters, numbers, symbols, and punctuation marks).

**Font size** The size of characters, measured in units called points.

**Font style** Format such as bold, italic, and underlining that can be applied to change the way characters look in a worksheet or chart.

**Format** The appearance of a cell and its contents, including font, font styles, font color, fill color, borders, and shading. *See also* Number format.

**Formula** A set of instructions used to perform one or more numeric calculations, such as adding, multiplying, or averaging, on values or cells.

**Formula bar** The area above the worksheet grid where you enter or edit data in the active cell.

**Formula prefix** An arithmetic symbol, such as the equal sign (=), used to start a formula.

**Freeze** To hold in place selected columns or rows when scrolling in a worksheet that is divided in panes. *See also* Panes.

**Function** A special, predefined formula that provides a shortcut for a commonly used or complex calculation, such as SUM (for calculating a sum) or FV (for calculating the future value of an investment). In the Visual Basic for Applications (VBA) programming language, a predefined procedure that returns a value, such as the InputBox function that prompts the user to enter information.

**Gadget** An optional program you can display on your desktop that presents helpful or entertaining information, such as a clock, current news headlines, a calendar, a picture album, or a weather report.

**Gallery** A visual collection of choices you can browse through to make a selection. Often available with Live Preview.

**Goal cell** In backsolving, a cell containing a formula in which you can substitute values to find a specific value, or goal.

**Goal Seek** A problem-solving method in which you specify a solution and then find the input value that produces the answer you want; sometimes described as a what-if analysis in reverse; *also called* backsolving.

**Graphs** *See* Charts.

**Gridlines** Evenly spaced horizontal and/or vertical lines used in a worksheet or chart to make it easier to read.

**Group** In a Microsoft program window's Ribbon, a section containing related command buttons.

**Hard disk** A built-in, high-capacity, high-speed storage medium for all the software, folders, and files on a computer.

**Header row** In a table, the first row that contains the field names.

**Highlighted** Describes the changed appearance of an item or other object, usually a change in its color, background color, and/or border; often used for an object on which you will perform an action, such as a desktop icon.

**Homegroup** A named group of Windows 7 computers that can share information, including libraries and printers.

**HTML (Hypertext Markup Language)** The format of pages that a Web browser can read.

**Hyperlink** An object (a filename, a word, a phrase, or a graphic) in a worksheet that, when clicked, displays another worksheet or a Web page called the target. *See also* Target.

**Icon** A small image, usually on the desktop, which represents items on your computer, such as the Recycle Bin; you can rearrange, add, and delete desktop icons.

**Icon sets** In conditional formatting, groups of images that are used to visually communicate relative cell values based on the values they contain.

**If...Then...Else statement** In the Visual Basic programming language, a conditional statement that directs Excel to perform specified actions under certain conditions; its syntax is "If *condition* Then *statements* Else [*elsestatements*]."

**Inactive window** An open window you are not currently using; if multiple windows are open, the window(s) with the dimmed title bar.

**Input cells** Spreadsheet cells that contain data instead of formulas and that act as input to a what-if analysis; input values often change to produce different results. Examples include interest rates, prices, or other data.

**Input values** In a data table, the variable values that are substituted in the table's formula to obtain varying results, such as interest rates.

**Insertion point** A blinking vertical line that appears when you click in the formula bar or in an active cell; indicates where new text will be inserted.

**Instance** A worksheet in its own workbook window.

**Integrate** To incorporate a document and parts of a document created in one program into another program; for example, to incorporate an Excel chart into a PowerPoint slide, or an Access table into a Word document.

**Integration** A process in which data is exchanged among Excel and other Windows programs; can include pasting, importing, exporting, embedding, and linking.

**Interface** The look and feel of a program; for example, the appearance of commands and the way they are organized in the program window.

**Intranet** An internal network site used by a group of people who work together.

**K**eyboard shortcut A key or a combination of keys that you press to perform a command.

**Keyword** Terms added to a workbook's Document Properties that help locate the file in a search. (Macros) In a macro procedure, a word that is recognized as part of the Visual Basic programming language.

**L**abels Descriptive text or other information that identifies data in rows, columns, or charts, but is not included in calculations.

**Landscape** Page orientation in which the contents of a page span the length of a page rather than its width, making the page wider than it is tall.

**Launch** To open or start a program on your computer.

**Legend** In a chart, information that identifies how data is represented by colors or patterns.

**Library** A window that shows files and folders stored in different storage locations; default libraries in Windows 7 include the Documents, Music, Pictures, and Videos libraries.

**Linear trendline** In an Excel chart, a straight line representing an overall trend in a data series.

**Link** The dynamic referencing of data in the same or in other workbooks, so that when data in the other location is changed, the references in the current location are automatically updated.

**List arrows** *See* Filter list arrows.

**List box** A box that displays a list of options from which you can choose (you may need to scroll and adjust your view to see additional options in the list).

**Live Preview** A feature that lets you point to a choice in a gallery or palette and see the results in the document without actually clicking the choice.

**Lock** To secure a row, column, or sheet so that data in that location cannot be changed.

**Logical conditions** Using the operators And and Or to narrow a custom filter criteria.

**Logical formula** A formula with calculations that are based on stated conditions.

**Logical test** The first part of an IF function; if the logical test is true, then the second part of the function is applied; if it is false, then the third part of the function is applied.

**Log in** To select a user account name when a computer starts up, giving access to that user's files.

**Log off** To close all windows, programs, and documents, then display the Welcome screen.

**M**acro A named set of instructions, written in the Visual Basic programming language, that performs tasks automatically in a specified order.

**Main procedure** A macro procedure containing several macros that run sequentially.

**Major gridlines** In a chart, the gridlines that represent the values at the tick marks on the value axis.

**Manual calculation** An option that turns off automatic calculation of worksheet formulas, allowing you to selectively determine if and when you want Excel to perform calculations.

**Map** An XML schema that is attached to a workbook.

**Map an XML element** A process in which XML element names are placed on an Excel worksheet in specific locations.

**Maximize button** On the right side of a window's title bar, the center button of three buttons; use to expand a window so that it fills the entire screen. In a maximized screen, this button turns into a Restore button.

**Maximized window** A window that fills the desktop.

**Menu** A list of related commands.

**Menu bar** A horizontal bar in a window that displays menu names, or categories of related commands.

**Metadata** Information that describes data and is used in Microsoft Windows document searches.

**Minimize button** On the right side of a window's title bar, the leftmost button of three buttons; use to reduce a window so that it only appears as an icon on the taskbar.

**Minimized window** A window that is visible only as an icon on the taskbar.

**Minor gridlines** In a chart, the gridlines that represent the values between the tick marks on the value axis.

**Mixed reference** Cell reference that combines both absolute and relative cell addressing.

**Mode** In dialog boxes, a state that offers a limited set of possible choices.

**Mode indicator** An area on the left end of the status bar that indicates the program's status. For example, when you are changing the contents of a cell, the word 'Edit' appears in the mode indicator.

**Model** A worksheet used to produce a what-if analysis that acts as the basis for multiple outcomes.

**Modeless** Describes dialog boxes that, when opened, allow you to select other elements on a chart or worksheet to change the dialog box options and format, or otherwise alter the selected elements.

**Module** In Visual Basic, a module is stored in a workbook and contains macro procedures.

**Mouse pointer** A small arrow or other symbol on the screen that you move by manipulating the pointing device; also called a pointer.

**Move** To change the location of a file, folder, or other object by physically placing it in another location.

**Multilevel sort** A reordering of table data using more than one column at a time.

**N**ame box Box to the left of the formula bar that shows the cell reference or name of the active cell.

**Navigate** To move around in a worksheet; for example, you can use the arrow keys on the keyboard to navigate from cell to cell, or press [Page Up] or [Page Down] to move one screen at a time. In Windows, to move around in your computer's folder and file hierarchy.

**Navigate downward** To move to a lower level in your computer's folder and file hierarchy.

**Navigate upward** To move to a higher level in your computer's folder and fi le hierarchy.

**Navigation pane** A pane on the left side of a window that contains links to folders and libraries on your computer; click an item in the Navigation pane to display its contents in the file list or click the small triangle symbols to display or hide subfolders in the Navigation pane.

**Normal view** Default worksheet view that shows the worksheet without features such as headers and footers; ideal for creating and editing a worksheet, but may not be detailed enough when formatting a document.

**Notification area** An area on the right side of the Windows 7 taskbar that displays the current time as well as icons representing programs; displays pop-up messages when a program on your computer needs your attention.

**Number format** A format applied to values to express numeric concepts, such as currency, date, and percentage.

**O**bject A chart or graphic image not located in a specific cell; contains resizing handles when selected and can be moved to any location. In object linking and embedding (OLE), the data to be exchanged between another document or program. In Visual Basic, every Excel element, including ranges.

**Object Linking and Embedding (OLE)** A Microsoft Windows technology that allows you to transfer data from one document and program to another using embedding or linking.

**Objective** *See* Target cell.

**Office Web Apps** Versions of the Microsoft Office applications with limited functionality that are available online from Windows Live SkyDrive. Users can view documents online and then edit them in the browser using a selection of functions. Office Web Apps are available for Word, PowerPoint, Excel, and One Note.

**OLE** *See* Object Linking and Embedding.

**One-input data table** A range of cells that shows resulting values when one input value in a formula is changed.

**Online collaboration** The ability to incorporate feedback or share information across the Internet or a company network or intranet.

**Operating system** A program that manages the complete operation of your computer and lets you interact with it.

**Option button** A small circle in a dialog box that you click to select only one of two or more related options.

**Or condition** The records in a search must match only one of the criterion.

**Order of precedence** Rules that determine the order in which operations are performed within a formula containing more than one arithmetic operator.

**Outline symbols** In outline view, the buttons that, when clicked, change the amount of detail in the outlined worksheet.

**Output values** In a data table, the calculated results that appear in the body of the table.

**P**age Break Preview A worksheet view that displays a reduced view of each page in your worksheet, along with page break indicators that you can drag to include more or less information on a page.

**Page Layout view** Provides an accurate view of how a worksheet will look when printed, including headers and footers.

**Panes** Sections into which you can divide a worksheet when you want to work on separate parts of the worksheet at the same time; one pane freezes, or remains in place, while you scroll in another pane until you see the desired information.

**Password** A special sequence of numbers and letters known only to selected users, that users can create to control who can access the files in their user account area; helps keep users' computer information secure.

**Paste Options button** Button that appears onscreen after pasting content; enables you to choose to paste only specific elements of the copied selection, such as the formatting or values, if desired.

**Personal macro workbook** A workbook that can contain macros that are available to any open workbook. By default, the personal macro workbook is hidden.

**PivotChart report** An Excel feature that lets you summarize worksheet data in the form of a chart in which you can rearrange, or "pivot," parts of the chart structure to explore new data relationships.

**PivotTable** Interactive table format that lets you summarize worksheet data.

**PivotTable Field List** A window containing fields that can be used to create or modify a PivotTable.

**PivotTable Report** An Excel feature that allows you to summarize worksheet data in the form of a table in which you can rearrange, or "pivot," parts of the table structure to explore new data relationships; *also called* a PivotTable.

**Plot** The Excel process that converts numerical information into data points on a chart.

**Plot area** In a chart, the area inside the horizontal and vertical axes.

**Previewing** Prior to printing, seeing onscreen exactly how the printed document will look.

**Point** A unit of measure used for font size and row height. One point is equal to 1/72nd of an inch. In Windows, to position the tip of the mouse pointer over an object, option, or item.

**Pointer** *See* Mouse pointer.

**Pointing device** A device that lets you interact with your computer by controlling the movement of the mouse pointer on your computer screen; examples include a mouse, trackball, touchpad, pointing stick, on-screen touch pointer, or a tablet.

**Pointing device action** A movement you execute with your computer's pointing device to communicate with the computer; the five pointing device actions are point, click, double-click, drag, and right-click.

**Populate** The process of importing an XML file and filling the mapped elements on the worksheet with data from the XML file. Also the process of adding data or fields to a table, PivotTable, or a worksheet.

**Portrait** Page orientation in which the contents of a page span the width of a page, so the page is taller than it is wide.

**Power button** 1) The physical button on your computer that turns your computer on. 2) The Start menu button or button on the right side of the Welcome screen that let you shut down or restart your computer. Click the button arrow to log off your user account, switch to another user, or hibernate the computer to put your computer to sleep so that your computer appears off and uses very little power.

**Presentation graphics program** A program such as Microsoft PowerPoint that you can use to create slide show presentations.

**Preview pane** A pane on the right side of a window that shows the actual contents of a selected file without opening a program; might not work for some types of files.

**Primary key** The field in a database that contains unique information for each record.

**Print area** A portion of a worksheet that you can define using the Print Area button on the Page Layout tab; after you select and define a print area, the Quick Print feature prints only that worksheet area.

**Print title** In a table that spans more than one page, the field names that print at the top of every printed page.

**Procedure** A sequence of Visual Basic statements contained in a macro that accomplishes a specific task.

**Procedure footer** In Visual Basic, the last line of a Sub procedure.

**Procedure header** The first line in a Visual Basic procedure, it defines the procedure type, name, and arguments.

**Program** A set of instructions written for a computer, such as an operating system program or an application program; *also called* an application.

**Program code** Macro instructions, written in the Visual Basic for Applications (VBA) programming language.

**Program window** The window that opens after you start a program, showing you the tools you need to use the program and any open program documents.

**Project** In the Visual Basic Editor, the equivalent of a workbook; a project contains Visual Basic modules.

**Project Explorer** In the Visual Basic Editor, a window that lists all open projects (or workbooks) and the worksheets and modules they contain.

**Properties** File characteristics, such as the author's name, keywords, or the title, that help others understand, identify, and locate the file.

**Properties window** In the Visual Basic Editor, the window that displays a list of characteristics, or properties, associated with a module.

**Property** In Visual Basic, an attribute of an object that describes its character or behavior.

**Publish** To place an Excel workbook or worksheet on a Web site or an intranet in HTML format so that others can access it using their Web browsers.

**Q**uick Access toolbar A small toolbar on the left side of a Microsoft application program window's title bar, containing icons that you click to quickly perform common actions, such as saving a file.

**R**AM (random access memory) The storage location that is part of every computer that temporarily stores open programs and documents information while a computer is on.

**Range** A selection of two or more cells, such as B5:B14.

**Range object** In Visual Basic, an object that represents a cell or a range of cells.

**Record** In a table (an Excel database), data that relates to an object or a person.

**Recycle Bin** A desktop object that stores folders and files you delete from your hard drive(s) and that enables you to restore them.

**Reference operators** In a formula, symbols which enable you to use ranges in calculations.

**Refresh** To update a PivotTable so it reflects changes to the underlying data.

**Regression analysis** A way of representing data with a mathematically-calculated trendline showing the overall trend represented by the data.

**Relative cell reference** In a formula, a cell address that refers to a cell's location in relation to the cell containing the formula and that automatically changes to reflect the new location when the formula is copied or moved; default type of referencing used in Excel worksheets. *See also* Absolute cell reference.

**Removable storage** Storage media that you can easily transfer from one computer to another, such as DVDs, CDs, or USB flash drives.

**Report filter** A feature that allows you to specify the ranges you want summarized in a PivotTable.

**Restore Down button** On the right side of a maximized window's title bar, the center of three buttons; use to reduce a window to its last non-maximized size.

**Return** In a function, to display a result.

**Ribbon** In many Microsoft application program windows, a horizontal strip near the top of the window that contains tabs (pages) of grouped command buttons that you click to interact with the program.

**Right-click** To press and release the right button on the pointing device; use to display a shortcut menu with commands you issue by left-clicking them.

**Run** To play, as a macro.

**Scenario** A set of values you use to forecast results; the Excel Scenario Manager lets you store and manage different scenarios.

**Scenario summary** An Excel table that compiles data from various scenarios so that you can view the scenario results next to each other for easy comparison.

**Schema** In an XML document, a list of the fields, called elements or attributes, and their characteristics.

**Scope** In a named cell or range, the worksheet(s) in which the name can be used.

**Screen capture** An electronic snapshot of your screen, as if you took a picture of it with a camera, which you can paste into a document.

**ScreenTip** A small box that appears when you position the mouse over an object; identifies the object when you point to it.

**Scroll** To adjust your view to see portions of the program window that are not currently in a window.

**Scroll arrow** A button at each end of a scroll bar for adjusting your view in a window in small increments in that direction.

**Scroll bars** Bars on the right edge (vertical scroll bar) and bottom edge (horizontal scroll bar) of the document window that allow you to move around in a document that is too large to fit on the screen at once.

**Search criterion** In a workbook or table search, the text you are searching for.

**Secondary axis** In a combination chart, an additional axis that supplies the scale for one of the chart types used.

**Select** To change the appearance of an item by clicking, double-clicking, or dragging across it, to indicate that you want to perform an action on it.

**Select pointer** The mouse pointer shape that looks like a white arrow oriented toward the upper-left corner of the screen.

**Share** See Shared workbook.

**Shared workbook** An Excel workbook that several users can open and modify.

**Sheet tab scrolling buttons** Allow you to navigate to additional sheet tabs when available; located to the left of the sheet tabs.

**Sheet tabs** Identify the sheets in a workbook and let you switch between sheets; located below the worksheet grid.

**Shortcut** An icon that acts as a link to a program, file, folder, or device that you use frequently.

**Shortcut menu** A menu of context-appropriate commands for an object that opens when you right-click that object.

**Shut down** To turn off your computer.

**Single-click** See Click.

**Single-file Web page** A Web page that integrates all of the worksheets and graphical elements from a workbook into a single file in the MHTML file format, making it easier to publish to the Web.

**Sizing handles** Small series of dots at the corners and edges of a chart indicating that the chart is selected; drag to resize the chart.

**SkyDrive** An online storage and file sharing service. Access to SkyDrive is through a Windows Live account. Up to 25 GB of data can be stored in a personal SkyDrive, with each file a maximum size of 50 MB.

**Slicer** A graphic object used to filter a PivotTable.

**Slider** A shape you drag to select a setting, such as the slider on the View menu that you drag to select a view.

**SmartArt graphics** Predesigned diagram types for the following types of data: List, Process, Cycle, Hierarchy, Relationship, Matrix, and Pyramid.

**Sort** To change the order of records in a table according to one or more fields, such as Last Name.

**Source program** In a data exchange, the program used to create the data you are embedding or linking.

**Sparkline** A quick, simple chart located within a cell that serves as a visual indicator of data trends.

**Spin box** A text box with up and down arrows; you can type a setting in the text box or click the arrows to increase or decrease the setting.

**Start button** The round button on the left side of the Windows 7 taskbar; click it to start programs, to find and open windows that show you the contents of your computer, to get help, and to end your Windows session, and turn off your computer.

**Stated conditions** In a logical formula, criteria you create.

**Statement** In Visual Basic, a line of code.

**Status bar** Bar at the bottom of the Excel window that provides a brief description about the active command or task in progress.

**Strong password** A password that is difficult to guess and that helps to protect your workbooks from security threats; has at least 14 characters that are a mix of upper- and lowercase letters, numbers, and special characters.

**Structured reference** Allows table formulas to refer to table columns by names that are automatically generated when the table is created.

**Subfolder** A folder within another folder for organizing sets of related files into smaller groups.

**Sub procedure** A series of Visual Basic statements that performs an action but does not return a value.

**Suite** A group of programs that are bundled together and share a similar interface, making it easy to transfer skills and program content among them.

**Summary function** In a PivotTable, a function that determines the type of calculation applied to the PivotTable data, such as SUM or COUNT.

**Switch User** To lock your user account and display the Welcome screen so another user can log on.

**Syntax** In the Visual Basic programming language, the formatting rules that must be followed so that the macro will run correctly.

**T**ab A page in an application program's Ribbon, or in a dialog box, that contains a group of related settings.

**Table** An organized collection of rows and columns of similarly structured data on a worksheet.

**Table styles** Predesigned formatting that can be applied to a range of cells or even to an entire worksheet; especially useful for those ranges with labels in the left column and top row, and totals in the bottom row or right column. *See also* Table.

**Table total row** A row you can add to the bottom of a table for calculations using the data in the table columns.

**Target** The location that a hyperlink displays after the user clicks it.

**Target cell** In what-if analysis (specifically, in Excel Solver), the cell containing the formula; *also called* objective.

**Taskbar** The horizontal bar at the bottom of the Windows 7 desktop; displays the Start button, the Notification area, and icons representing programs, folders, and/or files.

**Template** A predesigned, formatted file that serves as the basis for a new workbook; Excel template files have the file extension .xltx.

**Text annotations** Labels added to a chart to draw attention to or describe a particular area.

**Text box** A box in which you type text, such as the Search programs and files text box on the Start menu.

**Text concatenation operators** In a formula, symbols used to join strings of text in different cells.

**Text file** *See* ASCII file.

**Theme** A predefined set of colors, fonts, line and fill effects, and other formats that can be applied to an Excel worksheet and give it a consistent, professional look.

**Tick marks** Notations of a scale of measure on a chart axis.

**Title bar** The shaded top border of a window that displays the name of the window, folder, or file and the program name. Darker shading indicates the active window.

**Toggle** A button with two settings, on and off.

**Toolbar** In an application program, a set of buttons you can click to issue program commands.

**Touch pointer** A pointer on the screen for performing pointing operations with a finger if touch input is available on your computer.

**Tracer arrows** In Excel worksheet auditing, arrows that point from cells that might have caused an error to the active cell containing an error.

**Track** To identify and keep a record of who makes which changes to a workbook.

**Translucency** The transparency feature of Windows Aero that enables you to locate content by seeing through one window to the next window.

**Trendline** A series of data points on a line that shows data values that represent the general direction of the data.

**Two-input data table** A range of cells that shows resulting values when two input values in a formula are changed.

**U**SB flash drive (*Also called* a pen drive, flash drive, jump drive, keychain drive, or thumb drive.) A removable storage device for folders and files that you plug into a USB port on your computer; makes it easy to transport folders and files to other computers.

**User account** A special area in a computer's operating system where users can store their own files.

**User interface** A collective term for all the ways you interact with a software program.

**V**alidate A process in which an XML schema makes sure the XML data follows the rules outlined in the schema.

**Validation** *See* Data Validation.

**Value axis** In a chart, the axis that contains numerical values; in a 2-dimensional chart, also known as the y-axis.

**Values** Numbers, formulas, and functions used in calculations.

**Variable** In the Visual Basic programming language, an area in memory in which you can temporarily store an item of information; variables are often declared in Dim statements such as *DimNameAsString*. In an Excel scenario or what-if analysis, a changing input value, such as price or interest rate, that affects a calculated result.

**VBA** *See* Visual Basic for Applications.

**View** In Excel, a set of display or print settings that you can name and save for access at another time. You can save multiple views of a worksheet. In Windows, appearance choices for your folder contents, such as Large Icons view or Details view.

**Virus** Destructive software that can damage your computer files.

**Visual Basic Editor** A program that lets you display and edit macro code.

**Visual Basic for Applications (VBA)** A programming language used to create macros in Excel.

**Watermark** A translucent background design on a worksheet that is displayed when the worksheet is printed. Watermarks are graphic files that are inserted into the document header.

**Web query** An Excel feature that lets you obtain data from a Web, Internet, or intranet site and places it in an Excel workbook for analysis.

**Welcome screen** An initial startup screen that displays icons for each user account on the computer.

**What-if analysis** A decision-making tool in which data is changed and formulas are recalculated in order to predict various possible outcomes.

**Wildcard** A special symbol that substitutes for unknown characters in defining search criteria in the Find and Replace dialog box. The most common types of wildcards are the question mark (?), which stands for any single character, and the asterisk (*), which represents any group of characters.

**Window** A rectangular-shaped work area that displays a program or a collection of files, folders, and Windows tools.

**Windows Aero** *See* Aero.

**Windows Explorer** An accessory program that displays windows, allowing you to navigate your computer's file hierarchy and interact with your computer's contents.

**Windows Live** A collection of services and Web applications that people can access through a login. Windows Live services include access to e-mail and instant messaging, storage of files on SkyDrive, sharing and storage of photos, networking with people, downloading software, and interfacing with a mobile device.

**Windows Search** The Windows feature that lets you look for files and folders on your computer storage devices; to search, type text in the Search text box in the title bar of any open window, or click the Office button and type text in the Search programs and files text box.

**WordArt** Specially formatted text, created using the WordArt button on the Drawing toolbar.

**Workbook** A collection of related worksheets contained within a single file.

**Worksheet** A single sheet within a workbook file; also, the entire area within an electronic spreadsheet that contains a grid of columns and rows.

**Worksheet window** Area of the program window that displays part of the current worksheet; the worksheet window displays only a small fraction of the worksheet, which can contain a total of 1,048,576 rows and 16,384 columns.

**Workspace** An Excel file with an .xlw extension containing information about the identity, view, and placement of a set of open workbooks. Rather than opening each workbook individually, you can open the workspace file instead.

**X-axis** The horizontal axis in a chart; because it often shows data categories, such as months or locations, *also called* category axis.

**XML** Acronym that stands for eXtensible Markup Language, which is a language used to structure, store, and exchange information.

**Y-axis** The vertical axis in a chart; because it often shows numerical values, *also called* value axis.

**Z-axis** The third axis in a true 3-D chart, lets you compare data points across both categories and values.

**Zooming in** A feature that makes a document appear larger but shows less of it on screen at once; does not affect actual document size.

**Zooming out** A feature that shows more of a document on screen at once but at a reduced size; does not affect actual document size.

# Index

# F